Corrections

Third Edition

Mary K. Stohr: To my dad and mom, the late Robert (Stanley) Stohr and Elizabeth (Betty) Stohr. They were so skilled and loving when "correcting" and guiding their own eight children (I was third) that much of what I know about love, forgiveness, and life comes from them. I will be forever grateful for the gift they were as parents. I would also like to dedicate this to my husband, Craig Hemmens, and our daughter, Emily Rose Stohr-Gillmore, for their love and support; I could do nothing well without them.

Anthony Walsh: To my drop-dead gorgeous wife, Grace; my sons, Robert and Michael; my stepdaughters, Heidi and Kasey; my grandchildren, Robbie, Ryan, Mikey, Randy, Christopher, Ashlyn, Morgan, Stevie, Vivien, and Frankie; and my great grandchildren, Kaelyn, Logan, Keagan, Caleb, and Luke. I also want to dedicate this to Mary and her husband, Craig. We have been colleagues, friends, and coauthors for so many years that I don't know what I'll do without them now that they have moved to Washington and to greener pastures.

Sara Miller McCune founded SAGE Publishing in 1965 to support the dissemination of usable knowledge and educate a global community. SAGE publishes more than 1000 journals and over 800 new books each year, spanning a wide range of subject areas. Our growing selection of library products includes archives, data, case studies and video. SAGE remains majority owned by our founder and after her lifetime will become owned by a charitable trust that secures the company's continued independence.

Los Angeles | London | New Delhi | Singapore | Washington DC | Melbourne

Corrections

The Essentials

Third Edition

MARY K. STOHR

Washington State University

ANTHONY WALSH

Boise State University

Los Angeles | London | New Delhi
Singapore | Washington DC | Melbourne

$SAGE

FOR INFORMATION:

SAGE Publications, Inc.
2455 Teller Road
Thousand Oaks, California 91320
E-mail: order@sagepub.com

SAGE Publications Ltd.
1 Oliver's Yard
55 City Road
London EC1Y 1SP
United Kingdom

SAGE Publications India Pvt. Ltd.
B 1/I 1 Mohan Cooperative Industrial Area
Mathura Road, New Delhi 110 044
India

SAGE Publications Asia-Pacific Pte. Ltd.
3 Church Street
#10-04 Samsung Hub
Singapore 049483

Acquisitions Editor: Jessica Miller
Content Development Editor: Laura Kirkhuff
Editorial Assistant: Rebecca Lee
Production Editor: Jane Haenel
Copy Editor: D. J. Peck
Typesetter: C&M Digitals (P) Ltd.
Proofreader: Liann Lech
Indexer: Nancy Fulton
Cover Designer: Scott Van Atta
Marketing Manager: Jillian Oelsen

Printed in the United States of America

Library of Congress Cataloging-in-Publication Data

Names: Stohr, Mary K., author. | Walsh, Anthony, 1941– author.

Title: Corrections : the essentials / Mary K. Stohr, Washington State University, Anthony Walsh, Boise State University.

Description: Third Edition. | Thousand Oaks : SAGE Publications, Inc., [2018] | Revised edition of the authors' Corrections, [2016] | Includes bibliographical references and index.

Identifiers: LCCN 2017040349 | ISBN 9781506365268 (pbk. : alk. paper)

Subjects: LCSH: Corrections—United States. | Criminal justice, Administration of—United States. | Punishment—United States.

Classification: LCC HV9275 .C633 2018 | DDC 365/.973—dc23
LC record available at https://lccn.loc.gov/2017040349

This book is printed on acid-free paper.

18 19 20 21 22 10 9 8 7 6 5 4 3 2 1

BRIEF CONTENTS

DETAILED CONTENTS

PREFACE

There are plenty of excellent corrections books available for use, but we think that this particular book fills a niche for professors and students in that it is comprehensive and relatively inexpensive. These twin ideas became our goals and guided our development and writing of this textbook. We wanted to cover the most interesting and compelling information currently available on all aspects of corrections while also keeping the page limit within reason and the book published as a paperback. We hope that readers will find this work both informative and accessible.

The information in this textbook is what you might expect from major texts. However, beyond the facts, figures, and concepts commonly contained in textbooks, this book also showcases the history and research on a number of aspects of corrections. We chose, despite the relative brevity of the book, to include two chapters on history, rather than one chapter, because a historical perspective provides the framework for all that follows in corrections as in so many other social, political, and cultural initiatives and enterprises. We also believe that the presentation of research findings from academic, government, and journalistic sources will provide the context for understanding policy decisions and their consequences, both past and present.

Other special features of the book, which are designed to develop perspective, include brief comparative corrections sections that highlight what other countries are doing in terms of correctional operation. This glimpse of corrections internationally is meant to provide readers with another way of viewing correctional practice in the United States while also giving them some insight into how alternative practices might work. In many of the chapters, we also include practitioner perspective sections on the topics in those chapters; doing so allows us to learn how policy and theory get translated into practice in the field. There are also ethical dilemmas presented in each chapter that challenge students to think critically about the material and to acknowledge the complexities of the correction system.

This book can serve as a primary text for an undergraduate course in corrections or as a supplemental text for a graduate course. The areas covered are comparable to those in other major texts, with the exceptions noted above regarding the inclusion of enhanced history, research, and the comparative perspectives. Undergraduates, we hope, will find this book informative and enlivening. Graduate students might use it as an introduction, overview, and backdrop for other, more specialized books or articles. Discussion questions appear at the end of each chapter and might be used by both types of students to spur thought about, and critique of, corrections.

••• STRUCTURE OF THE BOOK

The structure of the book is much like that found in other textbooks on corrections. We begin with an overview of corrections and some key concepts. We include two chapters on history, although many textbooks have only one chapter. We then follow the flow of the corrections system, from sentencing, to jails, to probation, to prisons. We include a chapter on ethics in corrections, as the fourth chapter, to prepare students to review operations and institutional and individual actions through that kind of lens. We then stop and examine the correctional experience for staff after examining the experience for inmates and probationers in the preceding chapters. We finish the system description with a discussion of parole and reentry. In the three chapters that follow, we address the reality for women, minorities, and juveniles in corrections. We then focus attention on legal issues, capital punishment, and correctional programming and treatment. We end with a look to the future of corrections and what developments we might expect during the coming years.

••• NEW TO THIS EDITION

In this third edition of *Corrections: The Essentials,* we updated the coverage of ethical considerations, special populations, and the history of corrections to provide students with the context for understanding policy decisions and their consequences, both past and present. We also provided more coverage of disparities in sentencing and drug courts as a means of encouraging students to think critically about U.S. drug policies and the effectiveness of those policies. In fact, all chapters have been thoroughly updated to reflect the most current data, facts, figures, and research available, thus helping students understand the world of corrections today.

••• DIGITAL RESOURCES

Take a look at the interactive eBook for premium videos and SAGE journal articles.

Learn more at **edge.sagepub.com/stohressentials3e.**

 Career videos: Available only in the Interactive eBook, interviews with criminal justice professionals discussing their day-to-day work and current issues related to technology, diversity, and cutting-edge developments in their field are available.

 Feature videos: Available only in the Interactive eBook, these videos feature interviews with former inmates discussing their experiences in prison.

 SAGE news clips: Available only in the Interactive eBook, these curated Associated Press news clips showcase real-life examples to reinforce concepts.

 Journal articles: Articles from highly ranked SAGE journals such as *Crime & Delinquency, Theoretical Criminology, Criminal Justice Review,* and more can be accessed.

⑤SAGE edge™

http://edge.sagepub.com/stohressentials3e

SAGE edge offers a robust online environment featuring an impressive array of tools and resources for review, study, and further exploration, keeping both instructors and students on the cutting edge of teaching and learning. SAGE edge content is open access and available on demand. Learning and teaching have never been easier!

SAGE edge for Students provides a personalized approach to help students accomplish their coursework goals in an easy-to-use learning environment.

- Mobile-friendly **eFlashcards** strengthen understanding of key terms and concepts.

- Mobile-friendly practice **quizzes** allow for independent assessment by students of their mastery of course material.

- **Learning objectives** reinforce the most important material.

- Carefully selected chapter-by-chapter **video and multimedia content** that enhances classroom-based explorations of key topics.

- EXCLUSIVE! Access to certain full-text **SAGE journal articles** has been carefully selected for each chapter. Each article supports and expands on the concepts presented in the chapter. This feature also provides questions to focus and guide your interpretation.

SAGE edge for Instructors supports teaching by making it easy to integrate quality content and create a rich learning environment for students.

- **Test banks** that provide a diverse range of pre-written options as well as the opportunity to edit any question and/or insert personalized questions to effectively assess the students' progress and understanding.

- Editable, chapter-specific **PowerPoint® slides** offer complete flexibility for creating a multimedia presentation for the course.

- **Lecture Notes** summarize key concepts on a chapter-by-chapter basis to help with preparation for lectures and class discussions.

- **Class Activities** for individual or group projects provide lively and stimulating ideas for use in and out of class to reinforce active learning.

- A set of all the **graphics from the text,** including all of the maps, tables, and figures, in PowerPoint, .pdf, and .jpg formats for class presentations.

- Carefully selected chapter-by-chapter **video and multimedia content** that enhances classroom-based explorations of key topics.

••• ACKNOWLEDGMENTS

We would like to thank executive editor Jessica Miller. We have worked with her on this edition and other corrections texts after Jerry Westby's retirement and have appreciated her support and patience with us as we updated the book for this third edition. We also would like to thank our development editor, Laura Kirkhuff, who helped to shepherd the book through the revision process. Our copy editor, D. J. Peck, ensured that the sentences were clean, the spelling correct, and every missing reference was found.

We would also like to acknowledge each other. We were colleagues at Boise State University for many years, the last several (before Mary moved to Missouri State in 2011 and then to Washington State in 2013) with offices right next door to each other. We each have come to appreciate the work and perspectives of the other. This work was a true collaboration between us and reflects our shared belief in the possibilities for decency and justice as that is elaborated on by social institutions and their workers and by individuals willing to change.

We are also grateful to the reviewers who took the time to review early drafts of our work and who provided us with helpful suggestions for improving the chapters and the book as a whole. There is no doubt that their comments made the book much better than it would have otherwise been. Heartfelt thanks go to the following experts consulted on the first, second, and third editions:

REVIEWERS OF THE THIRD EDITION

Samantha L. Carlo, Miami Dade College; Michael S. Caudy, University of Texas at San Antonio; Erin Graybill Ellis, Texas Woman's University; Barbara Peat, University of Texas at El Paso; Jo Ann M. Short, Northern Virginia Community College; and Karin J. Storm, Brandman University.

REVIEWERS OF THE SECOND EDITION

Andy Bain, University of Mount Union (Ohio); Nikki Banks, Grand Rapids Community College; Lisa M. Carter, Florida Southern College; Meghan E. Hollis, Michigan State University; Jennifer L. Lanterman, University of Nevada, Reno; Joe Marinello, James Kane Record, California University of Pennsylvania; Joel L. Carr, Texas A&M University–Kingsville; and Caryn E. Saxon, Missouri State University.

REVIEWERS OF THE FIRST EDITION

Deborah Baskin, California State University, Los Angeles; Laura Hansen, University of Massachusetts, Boston; George Costanza, University of South Alabama; Jessie Krienert, Illinois State University; Sheree Morgan, St. Cloud State University; Mario Paparozzi, University of North Carolina, Pembroke; Marie Griffin, Arizona State University; and Robert Homant, University of Detroit.

1

The Philosophical and Ideological Underpinnings of Corrections

TEST YOUR KNOWLEDGE

Test your current knowledge of corrections by answering the following questions as true or false. Check your answers on page 389 after reading the chapter.

1. Whatever we choose to call it, corrections is about punishment, and punishment is considered to require philosophical justification.

2. The strongest deterrent against crime is the severity of punishment.

3. The fundamental principle of American justice is that punishment should fit the crime; all other factors are irrelevant.

4. As bad as it may sound, people feel pleasure when wrongdoers are punished.

5. The law assumes that people are rational and possess freedom of choice.

6. Philosophies of punishment depend quite a bit on concepts of human nature. (Are we naturally good, bad, or just selfish?)

7. Studies find that when criminals are punished they tend to be deterred from crime.

8. The United States incarcerates people at a higher rate than any other country in the world.

LEARNING OBJECTIVES

- Describe the function of corrections and its philosophical underpinnings

- Explain the function and justification of punishment

- Differentiate between the classical and positivist schools in terms of their respective stances on punishment

- Define and describe retribution, deterrence, incapacitation, rehabilitation, and reintegration

- Explain the distinction between the crime control and due process models

- Understand the usefulness of a comparative perspective

WHAT IS PUNISHMENT?

Nathaniel Hawthorne's book *The Scarlet Letter*, first published in 1850 and read in high school by generations of Americans thereafter, opened with the following words: "The founders of a new colony, whatever Utopia of human virtue and happiness they might originally project, have invariably recognized it among their earliest practical necessities to allot a portion of the virgin soil as a cemetery, and another portion as the site of a prison" (Hawthorne, 1850/2003, p. 1). Hawthorne was reminding us of two things we cannot avoid—death and human moral fallibility—and that we must make provisions for both. Of course, punishment is not all about prisons given that other forms are available. In Hawthorne's novel, Hester Prynne had been found guilty of adultery and of bearing a child out of wedlock. While all too common today, in the 17th-century Massachusetts Bay Colony it

was a major crime against "God and man." The colony was a very close-knit and homogeneous community, meaning that there was strong and widespread agreement about the norms of acceptable behavior. Hester's behavior was viewed as so outrageous that among the various penalties discussed by women viewing her trial were branding with hot irons and death "for the shame she has brought on us all." However, she was sentenced to what we might call community corrections today. She was to forever endure the scorn of her community and to forever wear the badge of shame on her dress—an elaborately embroidered letter A, branding her as an adulteress.

Such a reaction to Hester's behavior was aimed just as much at onlookers as at Hester herself—"This could happen to me too!" That is, the authorities not only wished to deter Hester from such behavior in the future but also wished to dissuade all others from similar behavior. Few people give much serious thought to why we need correctional systems, what state punishment is, why we do it, and why the urge to punish wrongdoers is universal and strong. How did such an urge get into us? What are the origins of punishment? What would society be like without it? How do we justify imposing harm on others, and what do our justifications assume about human nature? These are the issues we explore in this chapter.

••• INTRODUCTION: WHAT IS CORRECTIONS?

As Hawthorne intimated in the opening vignette, the primary responsibility of any government is to protect its citizens from those who would harm them. The military protects us from foreign threats, and the criminal justice system protects us from domestic threats posed by criminals. The criminal justice system is divided into three major subsystems—the police, the courts, and corrections—which we may call the catch 'em, convict 'em, and correct 'em trinity. Thus, corrections is a system embedded in a broader collection of protection agencies, one that comes into play after the accused has been caught by law enforcement and prosecuted and convicted by the courts.

Corrections is a generic term covering a variety of functions carried out by government (and increasingly private) agencies having to do with the punishment, treatment, supervision, and management of individuals who have been convicted or accused of criminal offenses. These functions are implemented in prisons, jails, and other secure institutions as well as in community-based correctional agencies such as probation and parole departments. Corrections is also the name we give to the field of academic study of the theories, missions, policies, systems, programs, and personnel that implement those functions as well as the behaviors and experiences of offenders. As the term implies, the correctional enterprise exists to "correct," "amend," or "put right" the attitudes and behavior of its "clientele." This is a difficult task because many offenders have a psychological, emotional, or financial investment in their current lifestyles and have no intention of being "corrected" (Andrews & Bonta, 2007; Walsh & Stohr, 2010).

Cynics think that the correctional process should be called the "punishment process" (Logan & Gaes, 1993) because the correctional enterprise is primarily about punishment—which, as Hawthorne reminded us, is an unfortunate but necessary part of life. Earlier scholars were more accurate in calling what we now call corrections **penology**, which means the study of the processes adopted for the punishment and prevention of crime. No matter what we call our prisons, jails, and other systems of formal social control, we are compelling people to do what they do not want to do, and such arm twisting is experienced by them as punitive regardless of what name we use.

When the grandparents of today's college students were in their youth, few thought of corrections as an issue of much importance. They certainly knew about prisons and jails, but few had any inkling of what probation or parole was. This blissful ignorance was a function of many things. The crime rate was much lower during the 1950s and early 1960s; thus, the correctional budget was a minor burden on their taxes, and fewer people probably knew anyone who had been in "the joint." Today the story is much different. For instance, in 1963 the violent crime rate was 168 per 100,000, and in 2012 it was 387, an increase of more than 130% (Federal Bureau of Investigation [FBI], 2013). In 1963 there were just under 300,000 people in prison in the United States, and in 2012 there were just under 1,700,000, an increase of 466% ("Trends in U.S. Corrections," 2013). Much of this increase has been driven by the war on drugs.

Corrections: Functions carried out by government and private agencies having to do with the punishment, treatment, supervision, and management of individuals who have been accused or convicted of criminal offenses.

Penology: Study of the processes and institutions involved in the punishment and prevention of crime.

Because illicit drug use was extremely rare prior to the late 1960s, there was no war on drugs. Indeed, the only drugs familiar to folks in their prime during the 1950s and 1960s were those obtained at the drugstore by prescription.

Because of the increase in crime and imprisonment, most people in the United States probably know someone who is or has been in prison or jail. In 2012 about 1 in every 35 adults in the United States was incarcerated or on probation or parole, and many more have been in the past (Glaze & Herberman, 2013). In some neighborhoods, it is not uncommon for nearly everyone to know many people under correctional supervision. For instance, nearly one in three African American men in their 20s is under some form of correctional control, and one in six has been to prison (Western, 2006). The expenditures for corrections in 2011 for all 50 states were approximately $52 billion, with 88% going for prisons and 12% going for probation and parole (Laudano, 2013).

PHOTO 1.1: A multilevel cellblock of a large American prison.

●●● FROM ARREST TO PUNISHMENT

Not everyone who commits a crime is punished, of course. Many crimes are not reported, and even if they are, relatively few are solved. Figure 1.1 is based on data from the nation's 75 largest counties and indicates the typical outcomes of 100 felony

FIGURE 1.1 Typical Outcome of 100 Felony Defendants in the 75 Largest Counties in the United States

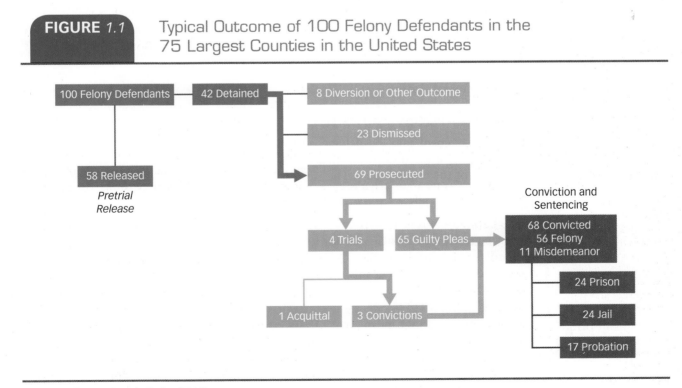

Source: Cohen and Kyckelhahn (2010).

arrestees (Cohen & Kyckelhahn, 2010). Only about two-thirds of arrestees are prosecuted (sometimes because of lack of evidence). Of those prosecuted, some are found not guilty and some are convicted of lesser (misdemeanor) offenses due to plea bargaining. This trip through the crime funnel typically results in less than 50% of arrests resulting in a jail or prison term. The impact of the war on drugs is evident in that just over 37% of these arrests were for drug-related crimes (Cohen & Kyckelhahn, 2010). Note that only 4 of the 69 arrests resulted in an actual trial, meaning that 94% of all felony prosecutions in the nation's 75 most populous counties resulted in a plea bargain in which a lighter sentence was imposed in exchange for a guilty plea.

THE THEORETICAL UNDERPINNINGS OF CORRECTIONS

Just as all theories of crime contain a view of human nature, so do all models of corrections. Some thinkers (mostly influenced by sociology) assume that human nature is socially constructed; that is, the human mind is basically a "blank slate" at birth and subsequently formed by cultural experiences. These individuals tend to see human nature as essentially good and believe that people learn to be antisocial. If people are essentially good, then the blame for criminal behavior must be located in the bad influences surrounding them.

Others (mostly influenced by evolutionary biology and the brain sciences) argue that there is an innate human nature that evolved driven by the overwhelming concerns of all living things—to survive and reproduce. These theorists do not deny that specific behaviors are learned, but they maintain that certain traits evolved in response to survival and reproductive challenges faced by our species that bias our learning in certain directions. Some of these traits, such as aggressiveness and low empathy, are useful in pursuing criminal goals (Quinsey, 2002; Walsh, 2006). This viewpoint also sees human nature as essentially selfish (not "bad," just self-centered) and maintains that people must learn to be prosocial rather than antisocial via a socialization process that teaches us to value and respect the rights and property of others as well as to develop an orientation toward wanting to do good. Criminologist Gwynn Nettler said it most colorfully on behalf of this position: "If we grow up 'naturally,' without cultivation, like weeds, we grow up like weeds—rank" (Nettler, 1984, p. 313). In other words, we learn to be bad or good. The point we are making is that the assumptions about human nature we hold influence our ideas about how we should treat the accused or convicted once they enter the correctional system.

A SHORT HISTORY OF CORRECTIONAL PUNISHMENT

Legal **punishment** may be defined as the state-authorized imposition of some form of deprivation—of liberty, resources, or even life—on a person justly convicted of a violation of the criminal law. The earliest known written code of punishment was the ancient Babylonian Code of Hammurabi, created circa 1780 B.C. (the origin of "an eye for an eye, a tooth for a tooth"). These laws codified the natural inclination of individuals harmed by others to seek revenge, but they also recognized that personal revenge must be restrained if society is not to be fractured by a cycle of tit-for-tat blood feuds. Blood feuds (revenge killings) perpetuate the injustice that "righteous" revenge was supposed to diminish. The law seeks to contain uncontrolled vengeance by substituting controlled vengeance in the form of third-party (state) punishment.

Punishment: The act of imposing some unwanted burden, such as a fine, probation, imprisonment, or death, on convicted persons in response to their crimes.

Controlled vengeance means that the state takes away the responsibility for punishing wrongdoers from the individuals who were wronged and assumes it for itself. Early state-controlled punishment, however, was typically as uncontrolled and vengeful as any grieving parent might inflict on the murderer of his or her child. In many parts of the world, prior to the 18th century, humans were considered born sinners because of the Christian legacy of Original Sin. Cruel tortures used on criminals to literally "beat the devil out of them" were justified by the need to save sinners' souls. Earthly pain was temporary and certainly preferable to an eternity of torment if sinners died unrepentant. Punishment was often barbaric regardless of whether those ordering it bothered to justify it with such arguments or even believed those arguments themselves.

The practice of brutal punishment and arbitrary legal codes began to wane with the beginning of a period historians call the Enlightenment, or the Age of Reason. The **Enlightenment** encompassed the period roughly between the late 17th century and the late 18th century and was essentially a major shift in the way people began to view the world and their place in it. It was also marked by the narrowing of the mental distance between people and the expanding of circles of individuals considered to be "just like us."

THE EMERGENCE OF THE CLASSICAL SCHOOL

Enlightenment ideas eventually led to a school of penology that has come to be known as the **Classical School**. The leader of this school, Italian nobleman and professor of law *Cesare Bonesana, Marchese di Beccaria* (1738–1794), published what was to become the manifesto for the reform of judicial and penal systems throughout Europe, *Dei Delitti e delle Pene* (*On Crimes and Punishments*) (Beccaria, 1764/1963). The book was a passionate plea to humanize and rationalize the law and to make punishment just and reasonable. Beccaria (as he is usually referred to) did not question the need for punishment, but he believed that laws should be designed to preserve public safety and order, not to avenge crime. He also took issue with the common practice of secret accusations, arguing that such practices led to general deceit and alienation in society. He argued that accused persons should be able to confront their accusers, to know the charges brought against them, and to be granted a public trial before an impartial judge as soon as possible after arrest and indictment.

Beccaria argued that punishments should be proportionate to the harm done, should be identical for identical crimes, and should be applied without reference to the social status of either offender or victim. Beccaria (1764/1963) made no effort to plumb the depths of criminal character or motivation, arguing that crime is simply the result of "the despotic spirit which is in every man" (p. 12). He also argued that the tendency of "man" to give in to the "despotic spirit" needed to be countered by the threat of punishment, which needed to be certain, swift, and severe enough to outweigh any benefits offenders get from crime if they are to be deterred from future crime. He elaborated on these three elements of punishment as follows:

> *Certainty:* "The certainty of punishment, even if it be moderate, will always make a stronger impression than the fear of another which is more terrible but combined with the hope of impunity" (p. 58).

> *Swiftness:* "The more promptly and the more closely punishment follows upon the commission of a crime, the more just and useful will it be" (p. 55).

> *Severity:* "For a punishment to attain its end, the evil which it inflicts has only to exceed the advantage derivable from the crime; in this excess of evil one should include the . . . loss of the good which the crime might have produced. All beyond this is superfluous and for that reason tyrannical" (p. 43).

Beccaria made clear that punishments must outweigh any benefits offenders get from crime if they are to be deterred from future crime.

Enlightenment: Period in history when a major shift in the way people viewed the world and their place in it occurred, moving from a supernaturalistic worldview to a naturalistic and rational worldview.

Classical School: School of penology/criminology that was a nonempirical mode of inquiry similar to the philosophy practiced by the classical Greek philosophers—one based on logic and reason.

PHOTO 1.2: Italian nobleman and professor of law Cesare Bonesana, Marchese of Beccaria (1738–1794) published what was to become the manifesto for the reform of judicial and penal systems throughout Europe, *Dei Delitti e delle Pene* (*On Crimes and Punishments*) (Beccaria, 1764/1963).

Wikimedia Commons, Public Domain

But such punishment should be as certain and swift as possible if it is to have a lasting impression on the criminal and to deter others.

Beccaria also asserted that to ensure a rational and fair penal structure, punishments for specific crimes must be decreed by written criminal codes, and the discretionary powers of judges must be severely limited. The judge's task was to determine guilt or innocence and then to impose the legislatively prescribed punishment if the accused is found guilty. Many of Beccaria's recommended reforms were implemented in a number of European countries within his lifetime (Durant & Durant, 1967). Such radical change over such a short period of time, across many different cultures, suggests that Beccaria's rational reform ideas tapped into and broadened the scope of emotions such as sympathy and empathy among the political and intellectual elite of Enlightenment Europe. We tend to feel empathy for those whom we view as "like us," and this leads to sympathy, which may lead to an active concern for their welfare. Thus, with cognition and emotion gelled into the Enlightenment ideal of the basic unity and worth of humanity, justice became both more refined and more diffuse (Walsh & Hemmens, 2014).

Another prominent figure was British lawyer and philosopher *Jeremy Bentham* (1748–1832). His major work, *Principles of Morals and Legislation* (Bentham, 1789/1948), is essentially a philosophy of social control based on the **principle of utility**, which posits that human actions should be judged as moral or immoral by their effect on the happiness of the community. The proper function of the legislature is thus to make laws aimed at maximizing the pleasure and minimizing the pain of the largest number in society—"the greatest good for the greatest number" (Bentham, 1789/1948, p. 151).

If legislators are to legislate according to the principle of utility, they must understand human motivation, which for Bentham (1789/1948) was easily summed up: "Nature has placed mankind under the governance of two sovereign masters, pain and pleasure. It is for them alone to point out what we ought to do, as well as to determine what we shall do" (p. 125). This was essentially the Enlightenment concept of human nature, which was seen as hedonistic, rational, and endowed with free will. The classical explanation of criminal behavior and how to prevent it can be derived from these three assumptions.

THE EMERGENCE OF POSITIVISM: SHOULD PUNISHMENT FIT THE OFFENDER OR THE OFFENSE?

Principle of utility: Positing that human action should be judged as moral or immoral by its effects on the happiness of the community and that the proper function of the legislature is to make laws aimed at maximizing the pleasure and minimizing the pain of the population.

Positivists: Those who believe that human actions have causes and that these causes are to be found in the thoughts and experiences that typically precede those actions.

Just as classicism arose from the 18th-century humanism of the Enlightenment, positivism arose from the 19th-century spirit of science. Classical thinkers were philosophers in the manner of the thinkers of classical Greece (hence the term *classical*), while **positivists** took on themselves the methods of empirical science from which more "positive" conclusions could be drawn (hence the term *positivism*). They were radical empiricists who insisted that only things that can be observed and measured should concern us. This being the case, they believed that concepts underlying classical thought such as rationality, free will, motivation, conscience, and human nature should be ignored as pure speculation about the unseen and immeasurable. An essential assumption of positivism is that human actions have causes and that these causes are to be found in the uniformities that typically precede those actions. The search for causes of human behavior led positivists to dismiss the classical notion that humans are free agents who are alone responsible for their actions.

Early positivism went to extremes to espouse a hard form of determinism such as that implied in the assertion that there are "born criminals." Nevertheless, positivism slowly moved the criminal justice system away from a concentration on the criminal act as the sole determinant of the type of punishment to be meted out and toward an appraisal of the characteristics and circumstances of the offender as an additional determinant. Because human actions have causes that may be out of the actor's control, the concept of legal responsibility was called into question. For instance, Italian lawyer *Raffaele Garofalo* (1852–1934) believed that because human action is often evoked by circumstances beyond human control (e.g., temperament, extreme poverty, intelligence, certain situations), the only thing to be considered at sentencing was the offender's "peculiarities," or risk factors for crime.

Garofalo's (1885/1968) only concern for individualizing sentencing was the danger offenders posed to society, and his proposed sentences ranged from execution for what he called the *extreme criminal* (whom we might call psychopaths today), to transportation to penal colonies for *impulsive criminals,* to simply changing the law to deal with what he called *endemic criminals* (those who commit what we might call victimless crimes today). German criminal lawyer Franz von Liszt, on the other hand, campaigned for customized sentencing according to the rehabilitative potential of offenders, which was to be based on what scientists find out about the causes of crime (Sherman, 2005). Customized sentencing based on both the seriousness of the crime and the history and characteristics of the criminal (thereby satisfying both classicists and positivists) is routine in the United States today.

PHOTO 1.3: Jeremy Bentham's (1748–1832) major work, *Principles of Morals and Legislation* (Bentham, 1789/1948), is essentially a philosophy of social control based on the principle of utility, which posits that human actions should be judged as moral or immoral by their effect on the happiness of the community.

THE FUNCTION OF PUNISHMENT

Although most corrections scholars agree that punishment functions as a form of social control, some view it as a barbaric throwback to pre-civilized times (Menninger, 1968). But can you imagine a society where punishment did not exist? What would such a society be like? Could it survive? If you cannot realistically imagine such a society, you are not alone given that the desire to punish those who have harmed us or otherwise cheated on the social contract is as old as the species itself. Punishment aimed at discouraging cheats is observed in every social species of animals, leading evolutionary biologists to conclude that punishment of cheats is a strategy designed by natural selection for the emergence and maintenance of cooperative behavior (Alcock, 1998; Walsh, 2014). Cooperative behavior is important for all social species and is built on mutual trust, which is why violating that trust evokes moral outrage and results in punitive sanctions. Brain imaging studies show that when subjects punish cheats, they have significantly increased blood flow to areas of the brain that respond to reward, suggesting that punishing those who have wronged us provides both emotional relief and reward (de Quervain et al., 2004; Fehr & Gachter, 2002). These studies imply that we are hardwired to "get even," as suggested by the popular saying "Vengeance is sweet."

Sociologist *Émile Durkheim* (1858–1917) contended that punishment is functional for society in that the rituals of punishment reaffirm the justness of the social norms and allow citizens to express their moral outrage when others transgress those moral norms. Durkheim also recognized that we can temper punishment with sympathy. He observed that over the course of social evolution, humankind has moved from *retributive* justice (characterized by cruel and vengeful punishments) to *restitutive* justice (characterized by reparation—"making amends"). **Retributive justice** is driven by the natural passion for punitive revenge that "ceases only when exhausted . . . only after it has destroyed" (Durkheim, 1893/1964, p. 86). **Restitutive justice** is driven by simple deterrence and is more humanistic and tolerant, although it is still "at least in part, a work of vengeance" (pp. 88–89). For Durkheim, restitutive responses to wrongdoers offer a balance between calming moral outrage, on the one hand, and exciting the emotions of empathy and sympathy, on the other.

Retributive justice:
A philosophy of punishment driven by a passion for revenge.

Restitutive justice:
A philosophy of punishment driven by simple deterrence and a need to repair the wrongs done.

PERSPECTIVE FROM A PRACTITIONER

Robert Bayer, Prison Warden

Position: Former director of corrections and prison warden; currently an adjunct professor and prison consultant

Location: Reno, Nevada

Education: BA and MA, English literature, State University of New York at Oswego; Master of Public Administration and PhD in English/Public Administration, University of Nevada, Reno

The primary duties and responsibilities of a prison warden are:

First, being responsible for one facility in a much larger network of facilities. To some degree, a warden can be considered as the mayor of a city and the director/commissioner is the governor of the state in which the city resides, ensuring that facility policies, procedures, and general orders are fine-tuned for that specific facility within the guidelines of the department. Additionally, the warden is usually responsible for the human resources, safety and security operations, budget development and implementation, and the institution's physical plant. He or she must manage critical incidents that arise and has the overall responsibility to ensure a positive work and living culture exists within that facility. To accomplish all of these tasks, the warden typically will bring extensive experience to the job. A warden is one of the highest-level management positions in a prison system and represents the "boots on the ground" administrator for the entire system.

The qualities/characteristics that are most helpful for one in this career include:

The ability to be both an administrator and a leader, with a very thorough knowledge of how a prison functions and the laws, policies, and procedures promulgated by the system; the ability to see the overall big picture of corrections and how the facility functions within that picture; a comprehension of the budget process and calendar; and the ability to be politically sensitive, personable, approachable, intelligent, hard-working, and decisive yet thoughtful. As a leader, the warden's actions must reflect the best

traditions of the agency and be completely ethical in his or her decisions and actions. The warden should reflect all of the attributes prized in the frontline employee—loyalty, dedication, honesty, and reliability—and should instill confidence in all levels of staff and inmates. Staff members want a warden who is steady under pressure and not prone to swings in mood or behavior. Ultimately, though staff members may perform an infinite variety of jobs in the facility itself, they look to the warden to ensure they have the proper orders and resources needed to keep them safe day in and day out. Finally, the warden must be a skilled communicator at all levels, with good writing and verbal skills as well as effective listening skills.

In general, a typical day for a practitioner in this career would include:

Various functions, but the day should cover all three shifts to foster good communication. One should be at the facility during each shift change to ensure access to staff members as they leave and enter the next shift, personally greeting or chatting with the support staff before the workday begins. An early morning staff meeting with the associate wardens and the maintenance supervisor is essential to review the last 24 hours of shift activities and develop a priority list of operational issues that need resolution. Next, items on the in-basket are reviewed, delegated, or responded to, and it is important to physically "walk the yard" (for about 2 hours) on a daily basis to make upper management accessible to staff and inmates and to provide the opportunity for personal observation of any issues. This is also a time to obtain firsthand feedback as to the morale, conditions, and security of the yard. Next are formally scheduled meetings with inmate families, employee group representatives, other agency representatives, and so on. Time is also spent reviewing new policies, reading inmate appeals and requests, responding to correspondence, and conducting any necessary interviews of staff. Work continues after 5:00 p.m. to complete paperwork, prepare court testimony, work on difficult personnel issues, and work on budget execution and construction. Once a week, do a facility inspection, looking at sanitation and security compliance, while focusing on a different aspect of facility operations each week (such as fire suppression readiness).

My advice to someone either wishing to study or now studying criminal justice to become a practitioner in this career field would be:

Become a "triple threat" in the field, which includes a solid understanding of operations, programs, and budget; know where you are going; study leadership and become a leader. Try to find a competent mentor in the field who will take an interest in your career and guide you on a path of experience and education that will facilitate achieving your goals. The best administrators become leaders in our field, and to succeed one needs experience, training, and education.

THE PHILOSOPHICAL ASSUMPTIONS BEHIND JUSTIFICATIONS FOR PUNISHMENT

A philosophy of punishment involves defining the concept of punishment and the values, attitudes, and beliefs contained in that definition as well as justifying the imposition of a painful burden on someone. When we speak of justifying something, we typically mean that we provide reasons for doing it both in terms of morality ("It's the right thing to do") and in terms of the goals we wish to achieve ("Do this and we'll get that"). In other words, we expect that punishment will have favorable consequences that justify its application.

Legal scholars have traditionally identified four major objectives or justifications for the practice of punishing criminals: retribution, deterrence, rehabilitation, and incapacitation. Criminal justice scholars have recently added a fifth purpose to the list: reintegration. All theories and systems of punishment are based on conceptions of basic human nature and, thus, to a great extent on ideology. The view of human nature on which the law in every country relies today is the same view enunciated by classical thinkers Beccaria and Bentham, namely, that humans are hedonistic, rational, and possessors of free will.

Hedonism is a doctrine maintaining that all life goals are desirable only as means to the end of achieving pleasure or avoiding pain. It goes without saying that pleasure is intrinsically desirable and pain is intrinsically undesirable and that we all seek to maximize the former and minimize the latter. We are assumed to pursue these goals in rational ways. **Rationality** is the state of having good sense and sound judgment. Rational sense and judgment are based (ideally) on the evidence before us at any given time, and the rational person revises his or her reasoning as new evidence arises. Rationality should not be confused with morality because its goal is self-interest, and self-interest is said to govern behavior whether in conforming or deviant directions. Crime is rational (at least in the short run) if criminals employ reason and act purposely to gain desired ends. Thus, rationality is the quality of thinking and behaving in accordance with logic and reason such that one's reality is an ordered and intelligible system for achieving goals and solving problems. For the classical scholar, the ultimate goal of any human activity is self-interest, and self-interest is assumed to govern our behavior whether it takes us in prosocial or antisocial directions.

Hedonism and rationality are combined in the concept of the **hedonistic calculus**, a method by which individuals are assumed to logically weigh the anticipated benefits of a given course of action against its possible costs. If the balance of consequences of a contemplated action is thought to enhance pleasure and/or minimize pain, then individuals will pursue it; if it is not, then they will not. If people miscalculate, as they frequently do, it is because they are ignorant of the full range of consequences of a given course of action, not because they are irrational or stupid.

Hedonism: A doctrine maintaining that all goals in life are means to the end of achieving pleasure and/or avoiding pain.

Rationality: The state of having good sense and sound judgment based on the evidence before us.

Hedonistic calculus: A method by which individuals are assumed to logically weigh the anticipated benefits of a given course of action against its possible costs.

The final assumption about human nature is that humans have free will that enables them to purposely and deliberately choose to follow a calculated course of action. This is not a radical free will position that views human will as unfettered by restraints but rather a free will in line with the concept of human agency. The concept of **human agency** maintains that humans have the capacity to make choices and the responsibility to make moral ones regardless of internal or external constraints on their ability to do so. This is a form of free will that is compatible with determinism because it recognizes both the internal and external constraints that limit our ability to do as we please. If we grant criminals the dignity of possessing agency so that they purposely weigh options before deciding on a course of action, then they "can be held responsible for that choice and can be legitimately punished" (Clarke & Cornish, 2001, p. 25). It is only with the concept of agency that we can justifiably assign praise and blame to individual actions.

●●● THE MAJOR PUNISHMENT JUSTIFICATIONS

Even though we assume that most people agree society has a right and duty to punish those who harm it, because punishment involves the state depriving individuals of life or liberty, it has always been assumed that it is in need of ethical justification. Punishment justifications rise and fall in popularity with the ideology of the times, but there are five that have been dominant in the United States over the last century: retribution, deterrence, incapacitation, rehabilitation, and reintegration. We start with the most ancient—retribution.

RETRIBUTION

Retribution is a "just deserts" model demanding that punishment match as closely as possible the degree of harm criminals have inflicted on their victims—what they justly deserve. Those who commit minor crimes deserve minor punishments, and those who commit more serious crimes deserve more severe punishments. This is the most honestly stated justification for punishment because it both taps into our most primitive punitive urges and posits no secondary purpose for it such as rehabilitation or deterrence. In other words, it does not require any favorable consequence to justify it except to maintain that justice has been served. Logan and Gaes (1993) went so far as to claim that only retributive punishment "is an affirmation of the autonomy, responsibility, and dignity of the individual" (p. 252). By holding offenders responsible and blameworthy for their actions, we are treating them as free moral agents, not as mindless rag dolls pushed here and there by negative environmental forces. California is among the states that have explicitly embraced this justification in their criminal code (California Penal Code Sec. 1170a): "The Legislature finds and declares that the purpose of imprisonment for a crime is punishment" (as cited in Barker, 2006, p. 12).

In his dissenting opinion in a famous death penalty case (*Furman v. Georgia*, 1972) in which the U.S. Supreme Court invalidated Georgia's death penalty statute, Justice Potter Stewart noted the "naturalness" of retribution and why the state, rather than individuals, must assume the retributive role:

> I cannot agree that retribution is a constitutionally impermissible ingredient in the imposition of punishment. The instinct for retribution is part of the nature of man, and channeling that instinct in the administration of criminal justice serves an important purpose in promoting the stability of a society governed by law. When people begin to believe that organized society is unwilling or unable to impose upon criminal offenders the punishment they "deserve," then there are sown the seeds of anarchy—of self-help, vigilante justice, and lynch law.

Human agency: The capacity of humans to make choices and their responsibility to make moral ones regardless of internal or external constraints on their ability to do so.

Retribution: A philosophy of punishment demanding that criminals' punishments match the degree of harm the criminals have inflicted on their victims—that is, what they justly deserve.

DETERRENCE

The principle behind **deterrence** is that people are deterred from crime by the threat of punishment. Deterrence may be either specific or general. **Specific deterrence** refers to the effect of punishment on the future behavior of persons who experience it. For specific deterrence to work, it is necessary that a previously punished person make a conscious connection between an intended criminal act and the punishment suffered as a result of similar acts committed in the past. Unfortunately, it is not always clear that such connections are made or, if they are, have the desired effect. This is either because memories of the previous consequences were insufficiently potent or because they were discounted. The trouble is that short-term rewards (such as the fruits of a crime) are easier to appreciate than long-term consequences (punishment that may never come), and there is a tendency to abandon consideration of the latter when confronted with temptation unless a person has a well-developed conscience and is future oriented. The weak of conscience and the present oriented tend to consistently discount long-term consequences in favor of short-term rewards.

Committing further crimes after being punished is called **recidivism**, which is a lot more common than rehabilitation among ex-inmates. Recidivism refers only to crimes committed after release from prison and does not apply to crimes committed while incarcerated. Nationwide in the United States, about 33% of released prisoners recidivate within the first 6 months after release, 44% within the first year, 54% by the second year, and 67.5% by the third year (M. Robinson, 2005, p. 222), and these are just the ones who are caught. Among those who do desist, a number of them cite the fear of additional punishment as a big factor (R. Wright, 1999).

Deterrence: A philosophy of punishment aimed at the prevention of crime by the threat of punishment.

Specific deterrence: The supposed effect of punishment on the future behavior of persons who experience the punishment.

Recidivism: When an ex-offender commits further crimes.

As Beccaria insisted, for punishment to positively affect future behavior, there must be a relatively high degree of certainty that punishment will follow a criminal act, the punishment must be administered very soon after the act, and it must be painful. The most important of these is certainty, but as we see from Figure 1.2 showing clearance rates for major crimes in 2015, the probability of being arrested is very low, especially for property crimes—so much for certainty. Factoring out the immorality of the enterprise, burglary appears to be a rational career option for a capable criminal.

If a person is caught, the wheels of justice grind very slowly. Typically, many months pass between the act and the imposition of punishment—so much for swiftness. This leaves the law with severity as the only element it can realistically manipulate (it can increase or decrease statutory penalties almost at will), but it is unfortunately the least effective element (M. Reynolds, 1998). Studies from the United States and the United Kingdom find substantial negative correlations (as one factor goes up, the other goes down) between the

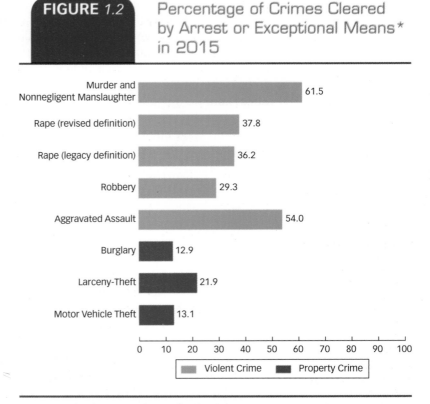

FIGURE 1.2 Percentage of Crimes Cleared by Arrest or Exceptional Means* in 2015

Crime	Percentage
Murder and Nonnegligent Manslaughter	61.5
Rape (revised definition)	37.8
Rape (legacy definition)	36.2
Robbery	29.3
Aggravated Assault	54.0
Burglary	12.9
Larceny-Theft	21.9
Motor Vehicle Theft	13.1

Violent Crime   Property Crime

Source: Federal Bureau of Investigation (2016).

*A crime cleared by "exceptional means" occurs when the police have a strong suspect but something beyond their control precludes a physical arrest (e.g., death of suspect).

likelihood of conviction (a measure of certainty) and crime rates, but they find much weaker correlations in the same direction for the severity of punishment; that is, increased severity leads to lower offending rates (Langan & Farrington, 1998).

The effect of punishment on future behavior also depends on the **contrast effect**, defined as the contrast or comparison between the possible punishment for a given crime and the usual life experience of the person who may be punished. For people with little to lose, arrest and punishment may be perceived as merely an inconvenient occupational hazard. But for those who enjoy a loving family and the security of a valued career, the prospect of incarceration is a nightmarish contrast. Like so many other things in life, deterrence works least for those who need it the most (Austin & Irwin, 2001).

General deterrence refers to the preventive effect of the threat of punishment on the general population; thus, it is aimed at *potential* offenders. Punishing offenders serves as an example to the rest of us of what may happen if we violate the law, as we noted in the opening vignette. As Radzinowicz and King (1979) put it, "People are not sent to prison primarily for their own good, or even in the hope that they will be cured of crime. . . . It is used as a warning and deterrent to others" (p. 296). The threat of punishment for law violators deters a large but unknown number of individuals who might commit crimes if no such system existed.

Are we putting too much faith in the ability of criminals and would-be criminals to calculate the costs and benefits of engaging in crime? Although many violent crimes are committed in the heat of passion or under the influence of mind-altering substances, there is evidence underscoring the classical idea that individuals do (subconsciously at least) calculate the ratio of expected pleasures to possible pains when contemplating their actions. Becker (1997) dismissed the idea that criminals lack the knowledge and foresight to take punitive probabilities into consideration when deciding whether or not to continue committing crimes. He stated, "Interviews of young people in high crime areas who do engage in crime show an amazing understanding of what punishments are, what young people can get away with, how to behave when going before a judge" (p. 20). Of course, incentives and disincentives to law-abiding or criminal behavior are perceived differently because of the contrast effect and ingrained habits: "Law abiding people habitually ignore criminal opportunities. Law breakers habitually discount the risk of punishment. Neither calculates" (van den Haag, 2003). This does not mean that criminals are impervious to realistic threats of punishment.

Deterrence theorists do not view people as calculating machines doing their mental math before engaging in any activity. They are simply saying that behavior is governed by its consequences. Our rational calculations are both subjective and bounded; we do not all make the same calculations or arrive at the same game plan when pursuing the same goals. Think how the contrast effect would influence the calculations of a zero-income, 19-year-old high school dropout with a drug problem as opposed to a 45-year-old married man with two children and a $90,000 annual income. We all make calculations with less than perfect knowledge and with different mind-sets, different temperaments, and different cognitive abilities, but to say that criminals do not make such calculations is to strip them of their humanity and to make them pawns of fate.

More general reviews of deterrence research indicate that legal sanctions do have "substantial deterrent effect" (Nagin, 1998, p. 16; see also R. Wright, 1999), and some researchers have claimed that increased incarceration rates account for about 25% of the variance in the decline in violent crime over the last decade or so (Rosenfeld, 2000; Spelman, 2000). Paternoster (2010) cited other studies demonstrating that 20%

Contrast effect: The effect of punishment on future behavior depending on how much the punishment and the usual life experience of the person being punished differ or contrast.

General deterrence: The presumed preventive effect of the threat of punishment on the general population.

to 30% of the crime drop from its peak during the early 1990s is attributable to the approximately 52% increase in the imprisonment rate. He stated, "There is a general consensus that the decline in crime is, at least in part, due to more and longer prison sentences, with much of the controversy being over how much of an effect" (p. 801). Of course, this leaves 70% to 75% of the crime drop to be explained by other factors. Unfortunately, even for the 30% figure, we cannot determine whether we are witnessing a *deterrent* effect (i.e., has crime declined because more would-be criminals have perceived a greater punitive threat?) or an *incapacitation* effect (i.e., has crime declined because more violent people are behind bars and, thus, not at liberty to commit violent crimes on the outside?). Of course, it does not need to be one or the other given that both effects may be operating. Society benefits from crime reduction regardless of why it occurs.

INCAPACITATION

Incapacitation refers to the inability of criminals to victimize people outside prison walls while they are locked up. Its rationale is summarized in J. Wilson's (1975) remark, "Wicked people exist. Nothing avails except to set them apart from innocent people" (p. 391). The incapacitation justification probably originated with *Enrico Ferri*'s concept of social defense. For Ferri (1897/1917), to determine punishment, notions of culpability, moral responsibility, and intent were secondary to an assessment of offenders' strength of resistance to criminal impulses, with the express purpose of averting future danger to society. He believed that moral insensibility and lack of foresight, underscored by low intelligence, were criminals' most marked characteristics. For Ferri, the purpose of punishment is not to deter or rehabilitate but rather to defend society from criminal predation. The characteristics of criminals prevented them from basing their behavior on rational calculus principles, so how could their behavior be deterred?

Incapacitation:
A philosophy of punishment that refers to the inability of criminals to victimize people outside prison walls while they are locked up.

Incapacitation obviously "works" while criminals are incarcerated. Currie (1999) stated that in 1995 there were 135,000 inmates in prison whose most serious crime was robbery and that each robber on average commits five robberies per year. Had these robbers been left on the streets, they would have been responsible for an additional 135,000 × 5, or 675,000, robberies on top of the 580,000 actual robberies reported to the police in 1995. Further evidence was provided by a "natural experiment" when the Italian government released one-third (about 22,000) of Italy's prison inmates with 3 years or less left to serve on their sentences in 2006. This pardon resulted from budgetary concerns and prison overcrowding concerns. Buonanno and Raphael's (2013) analysis of released convicts found that the incapacitation effect was between 14 and 18 crimes committed per year (only theft and robbery arrests were included in the analysis) after release. The estimated saving of the collective pardon was 245 million euros (about $316 million), and the estimated crime cost was between 466 million and 2.2 billion euros (between about $606 million and $2.9 billion).

The incapacitation issue has produced some lively debates about the relative costs and benefits to society of incarceration. Attempts to estimate these have proved to be difficult and controversial. In 1987, economist Edwin Zedlewski used national crime data to calculate that the typical offender commits 187 crimes a year and that the typical crime exacts $2,300 in property losses or in physical injuries and human suffering. Multiplying these figures, Zedlewski (1987) estimated that the typical imprisoned felon is

PHOTO 1.4: An inmate waits in his cell.

responsible for $430,000 in monetary costs to society each year he remains free. He then divided that figure by the cost of incarceration in 1977 ($25,000) and concluded that the social benefits of imprisonment outweigh the costs by 17 to 1.

Zedlewski's (1987) findings were severely criticized, including a critical article by supporters of incarceration who argued that the typical offender commits 15 crimes in a year rather than 187 (DiIulio & Piehl, 1991), which reduces the benefit/cost ratio to 1.38 to 1 from 17 to 1. The different estimates of criminal activity are the result of Zedlewski using the mean number (arithmetic average) of crimes per year and DiIulio and Piehl using the median number (a measure of the "typical" in which half of criminals commit fewer than 15 crimes and half commit more). Using the mean inflates the typical by averaging in the crimes committed by the most highly criminally involved offenders. Using only the dollar costs to estimate the social costs of crime, of course, ignores the tremendous physical and emotional cost to victims as well as other important considerations (S. Walker, 2001).

SELECTIVE INCAPACITATION

This brings up the idea of **selective incapacitation**, which is a punishment strategy that largely reserves prison for a select group of offenders composed primarily of violent repeat offenders but may also include other types of incorrigible offenders. Birth cohort studies (a *cohort* is a group composed of subjects having something in common such as being born within a given time frame or in a particular place) from a number of different locations find that about 6% to 10% of offenders commit the majority of all crimes. For instance, in the 1945 birth cohort studies by Wolfgang, Figlio, and Sellin (1972), 6.3% of the 9,945 cohort members committed 71% of the murders, 73% of the rapes, and 82% of the robberies attributed to members of the cohort.

Saving prison space mostly for high-rate violent offenders better protects the community and saves it money. The problem with this strategy, however, involves identifying high-rate violent offenders *before* they become high-rate violent offenders; identifying them after the fact is easy. Generally speaking, individuals who begin committing predatory delinquent acts before they reach puberty are the ones who will continue to commit crimes across the life course (DeLisi, 2005; Moffitt & Walsh, 2003). The incapacitation effect is more starkly driven home by a study of the offenses of 39 convicted murderers committed *after* they had served their time for murder and were released from prison. Between 1996 and 2000, they had 122 arrests for serious violent crimes (including 7 additional murders), 218 arrests for serious property crimes, and 863 other arrests among them (DeLisi, 2005, p. 165).

What would be the dollar costs saved had these 39 murderers not been released? The total social cost of a single murder has been estimated at $8,982,907, and the average cost of other "serious violent crimes" (rape, aggravated assault, and robbery) has been estimated as $130,035 (McCollister, French, & Fang, 2010). The 7 murders ($62,880,349) and 115 other serious violent crimes ($14,954,063) yield a total of $77,834,412, or $15,566,882 per year over the 5-year period, and that is without adding in the 218 arrests for serious property crimes and the 863 other arrests. Of course, the biggest loss of all is the grief suffered by the survivors of murder victims.

None of these authors was arguing for an increase in gross incarceration of low-rate/low-seriousness offenders. As we increase incarceration more and more, we quickly skim off the 5% to 10% of serious offenders and begin to incarcerate offenders who would best be dealt with within the community. In monetary (and other social cost) terms, we have a situation that economists call "the law of diminishing returns." In essence, this means that while we may get a big bang for our buck at first (incarcerating the most

Selective incapacitation:
A punishment strategy that largely reserves prison for a distinct group of offenders composed primarily of violent repeat offenders.

serious criminals), the bang quickly diminishes to a whimper and even turns to a net loss as we continue to reel in minor offenders.

The problem is predicting which offenders should be selectively incapacitated. Although there are a number of excellent prediction scales in use today to assist us in estimating who will and who will not become a high-rate offender, the risk of too many false positives (predicting someone will become a high-rate offender when in fact he or she will not) is always present (Piquero & Blumstein, 2007). However, incarceration decisions are not made on predictions about the future; rather, they are made on knowledge of past behavior—the past is prologue, as Shakespeare said.

REHABILITATION

The term **rehabilitation** means to restore or return to constructive or healthy activity. Whereas deterrence and incapacitation are mainly justified on classical grounds, rehabilitation is primarily a positivist concept. The rehabilitative goal is based on a medical model that used to view criminal behavior as a moral sickness requiring treatment. Today this model views criminality in terms of "faulty thinking" and views criminals as in need of "programming" rather than "treatment." The goal of rehabilitation is to change offenders' attitudes so that they come to accept that their behavior was wrong, not to deter them by the threat of further punishment. We defer further discussion of rehabilitation until Chapter 5, devoted to correctional treatment and rehabilitation.

REINTEGRATION

The goal of **reintegration** is to use the time criminals are under correctional supervision to prepare them to reenter (or reintegrate with) the free community as well equipped to do so as possible. In effect, reintegration is not much different from rehabilitation, but it is more pragmatic, focusing on concrete programs such as job training rather than attitude change. There are many challenges associated with this process, so much so that, like rehabilitation, it warrants a chapter to itself and will be discussed in detail in the context of parole.

Table 1.1 is a summary of the key elements (justification, strategy, focus of perspective, and image of offenders) of the five punishment philosophies or perspectives discussed. The commonality that they all share to various extents is, of course, the prevention of crime.

Rehabilitation:
A philosophy of punishment aimed at "curing" criminals of their antisocial behavior.

Reintegration:
A philosophy of punishment that aims to use the time criminals are under correctional supervision to prepare them to reenter the free community as well equipped to do so as possible.

| **TABLE 1.1** | Summary of Key Elements of Different Correctional Perspectives |

	Retribution	Deterrence	Incapacitation	Rehabilitation	Reintegration
Justification	Moral Just deserts	Prevention of further crime	Risk control Community protection	Offenders have correctable deficiencies	Offenders have correctable deficiencies
Strategy	None: Offenders simply deserve to be punished	Make punishment more certain, swift, and severe	Offenders cannot offend while in prison	Treatment to reduce offenders' inclination to reoffend	Concrete programming to make for successful reentry into society
Focus of perspective	The offense and just deserts	Actual and potential offenders	Actual offenders	Needs of offenders	Needs of offenders
Image of offenders	Free agents whose humanity we affirm by holding them accountable	Rational beings who engage in cost/ benefit calculations	Not to be trusted but to be constrained	Good people who have gone astray and will respond to treatment	Ordinary folks who require and will respond to concrete help

COMPARATIVE CORRECTIONS

The Four Legal Traditions and Why They Are Useful to Know

All chapters in this book have a box providing a comparative perspective on topics discussed from correctional systems in other countries. There are many advantages to studying a familiar subject from a different vantage point. The great philosopher Aristotle once said that if you only know your own culture, you don't know your own culture. How true that is—we always need something different to compare with something familiar in order to really understand the familiar. After all, we cannot know what "up," "tall," "no," and "true" mean without knowing what "down," "short," "yes," and "false" mean. Of course, other countries' correctional systems have many things in common with ours—they all have jails and prisons—but their goals and practices may depart significantly from ours. Knowledge of systems other than our own provides us with a new understanding and appreciation of our own and will better equip us to identify both the strengths and weaknesses of the American system. Our aim is to examine a representative country of each of the four main families of law in the world today: common, civil or code, Islamic, and socialist.

The countries we primarily (but not exclusively) focus on are the United Kingdom (England and Wales; the other two countries of the United Kingdom—Scotland and Northern Ireland—have separate correctional systems), France, China, and Saudi Arabia. These countries were chosen because each one best illustrates its respective family of law. The common law originated many centuries ago in England—the country with which the United States shares the heritage of law, language, and culture—and has slowly evolved over the centuries. We focus on France to examine the civil law tradition because modern civil (or code) law began under Napoleon in 1804. China was chosen because it is the largest socialist legal system in the world. Finally, Saudi Arabia was chosen to illustrate the Islamic legal tradition because the Koran (Islam's holy book) functions as the Saudi Arabian constitution (Walsh & Hemmens, 2014). The civil, socialist, and Islamic legal traditions are all code systems, which are systems that come "ready made" rather than systems that evolved slowly as did the common law. Judges in code countries cannot "make law" by precedent as they can in common law countries. Rather, they are supposed to act uniformly in accordance with the criminal code, and consequently there is less judicial oversight of the correctional system in those countries.

● ● ● THE DUE PROCESS AND CRIME CONTROL MODELS AND CULTURAL COMPARISONS

A useful way of grounding our discussion of the different correctional systems in different countries is to see how they stack up in terms of Packer's (1964/1997) crime control versus due process models of criminal justice. Packer proposed two "ideal-type" models (pure types that exaggerate differences), reflecting different value choices undergirding the operation of the criminal justice system.

The major tension between these two models is the emphasis on justice for an offended community and justice for those who offend against it. Equally moral individuals and cultures can hold very different conceptions of justice, with some placing an emphasis on justice for the offended community and others placing an emphasis on justice for those who offend against it.

Crime control model:
A model of law that emphasizes community protection from criminals and stresses that civil liberties can have real meaning only in a safe, well-ordered society.

The first model is the **crime control model**. This model emphasizes community protection from criminals and stresses that civil liberties can have real meaning only in a safe, well-ordered society. To achieve such a society, it is necessary to suppress criminal activity swiftly, efficiently, and with finality, and this demands a well-oiled criminal justice system where cases are handled informally and uniformly in "assembly line" fashion. Police officers must arrest suspects, prosecutors must prosecute them, and judges must sentence them "uncluttered with ceremonious rituals that do not advance the progress of the case" (Packer, 1964/1997, p. 4). To achieve finality, the occasions for challenging the process (appeals) must be kept to a minimum. The assumption is that such a process will more efficiently screen out the innocent and that those who are not screened out may be considered "probably guilty." Packer (1964/1997) did not want us to think of a presumption of guilt as the conceptual opposite of the presumption of innocence; rather, "reduced to its barest essentials and when operating at its most successful pitch," the crime control model consists of two elements: "(a) an administrative fact-finding process leading to the exoneration of the suspect, or to (b) the entry of a plea of guilty" (p. 5).

The **due process model** is the second model. Rather than a system run like an assembly line, the due process model is more like an obstacle course in which impediments to carrying the accused's case further are encountered at every stage of processing. Police officers must obtain warrants when possible and must not interrogate a suspect without the suspect's consent, evidence may be suppressed, and various motions may be filed that may free a factually guilty person. These and other obstacles are placed in the way to ensure that evidence is obtained in a legal manner. If the person is convicted, he or she may file numerous appeals, and it may take years to gain closure of the case. The due process model is more concerned with the integrity of the legal process than with its efficiency and with legal guilt rather than whether the accused is factually guilty. Factual guilt translates into legal guilt only if the evidence used to determine it was obtained in a procedurally correct fashion.

Which model do you prefer, and which model do you think best exemplifies the ideals of justice? It may be correct to say that under a crime control model more innocent people may be convicted, but that depends on which country we are talking about and how far along the continuum it goes in its practices. It is also true that under a due process model more (factually) guilty people will be set free, but again that depends on the country and the extent to which the model is "pure." In the first instance the individual has been unjustly victimized, and in the second instance the community has been unjustly victimized. It is clear that both models have their faults as well as their strengths. The danger of a runaway crime control model is a return to the days when due process was nonexistent, and the danger of a runaway due process model is that truth and justice may get lost in a maze of legal ritualism. But remember that these are ideal-type models that do not exist in their "pure" form anywhere in the world; rather, all criminal justice systems lie on a continuum between the crime control and due process extremes.

Packer's models are more about the processes followed in the police and prosecution legs of criminal justice (the catch 'em and convict 'em legs), but they also apply to the third leg (the correct 'em leg) of the criminal justice system. While it may be true that there is less public concern for the rights of convicted criminals than for the rights of accused criminals, and while it is also true that convicted criminals have fewer rights than law-abiding folks, the criminal justice model followed by the police and the courts in a given nation is also the model followed by its correctional system.

Figure 1.3 places the countries to be primarily discussed on a due process–crime control continuum according to the degree to which they emphasize one model or the other. Terrill (2013) noted that the United States, the United Kingdom, and France "vacillate between the two models, but they are more sensitive to due process issues, [while China and Saudi Arabia] favor the crime control model and often show little regard for the

Due process model: A model of law that stresses the accused's rights more than the rights of the community.

IN FOCUS 1.1

Is the United States Hard or Soft on Crime?

A frequently heard criticism of the criminal justice system in the United States to which we can apply the comparative perspective is that the United States is soft on crime. If we define hardness or softness on crime in terms of incarceration rates, the accompanying figure indicating incarceration rates per 100,000 for our comparison countries and certain other countries in 2015 conveys the opposite message. The retention of the death penalty by the United States, which has been eschewed by other "civilized" nations, also belies the contention that we are soft on crime. Only Russia, with a rate of 445 per 100,000, comes close to the American incarceration rate, and the closest any Western nations come to the U.S. rate are England and Wales, with a rate nearly five times lower. Comparisons among nations on this question are typically made using only Western democratic nations, leading to the conclusion that the United States is hard on crime. But if we are to make valid comparisons, we cannot cherry-pick our countries to arrive at a conclusion that fits our ideology.

If we define hardness/softness in terms of alternative punishments or the conditions of confinement, then the United States is soft on crime relative to many countries—although a better term would be *more humane.* For instance, although China is shown as having an incarceration rate more than six times lower than the U.S. rate, it is the world's leader in the proportion of its criminals it executes each year. Furthermore, punishment in some fundamentalist Islamic countries, such as Saudi Arabia and Afghanistan under the Taliban, has often included barbaric corporal punishments for offenses considered relatively minor in the West. Drinkers of alcohol may get 60 lashes, robbers may have an alternate side hand and foot amputated, and women accused of "wifely disobedience" may be subjected to corporal punishment (Walsh & Hemmens, 2014).

Another problem is that crime rates are calculated per 100,000 *citizens,* which is not the same as the rate per 100,000 *criminals.* If the United States has more criminals than these other countries, then perhaps the greater incarceration rate is justified. No one knows how many criminals any country has, but we can get a rough estimate from a country's crime rates—that is, the incarceration rate per 1,000 recorded crimes. For instance, the U.S. homicide rate is about five times that of England and Wales, which roughly matches the five times greater incarceration rate in the United States. However, when it comes to property crimes, Americans are about in the middle of the pack of nations in terms of the probability of being victimized, yet burglars serve an average of 16.2 months in prison in the United States, compared with 6.8 months in Britain and 5.3 months in Canada (Mauer, 2005). On this measure, the United States is more on the crime control end of the due process–crime control continuum than France or England and Wales. Does this mean that the United States is too hard, or Britain and Canada are too soft, on crime? From a crime control perspective, these nations can be seen as excessively soft on crime at the expense of rising crime rates, although crime has fallen in those countries since the 1990s just as it has in the United States (Baumer & Wolff, 2014).

So is the United States softer or harder on crime than other

2015 Incarceration Rates per 100,000 Population for Comparative Countries and Selected Other Countries

Country	Rate
Japan	48
France	95
Canada	106
China	119
England and Wales	148
Saudi Arabia	161
Chile	247
Russia	445
United States	698

Source: Adapted from figures provided by Walmsley (2016).

countries? The answer obviously depends on how we conceptualize and measure the concepts of hardness and softness and with which countries we compare ourselves. Compared with countries that share our democratic ideals, we are tough on crime (and because of our retention of the death penalty, some would even say barbaric); compared with countries most distant from Anglo-American ideals, we are soft on crime, and for that we should be grateful.

All societies develop rules for ensuring peace, order, predictability, and cultural survival and provide sanctions for those who do not follow them. These rules and the sanctions suffered by those accused and convicted of breaking them may differ significantly from society to society because they reflect a particular culture's history and its current social, political, and economic practices, philosophies, and ideals. This chapter briefly introduces you to correctional practices used in four societies other than the United States.

FIGURE *1.3*   Situating Comparative Countries on the Due Process–Crime Control Continuum and on Their Democracy Scores (numbers under flags)

Source: Based on data from the Economist Intelligence Unit (2014).

due process model" (p. 15). Overall, the United States is closer to a pure due process model than our comparative nations, and Saudi Arabia is the closest to a pure crime control model.

What are the criteria we used for placing our four countries on this continuum? One way of attempting to measure the degree to which a society has a due process versus crime control model is the degree to which it respects the ideals of democracy. The numbers beneath the respective flags represent each country's "democracy score" on a scale of 1 to 10 according to the Economist Intelligence Unit (2014). This score is based on 63 different factors, such as public political participation and respect for civil rights, and their scores support our ordering of countries in the figure. We should note that on a world scale, neither the United States nor Saudi Arabia occupies the top or bottom place. Norway had the highest democracy score (9.80), and North Korea had the lowest (1.08), in 2012. The French system probably represents the "right" balance between the rights of the accused (due process) and the protection of society (crime control); others may disagree with this assessment.

SUMMARY

- Corrections is a social function designed to hold, punish, supervise, deter, and possibly rehabilitate the accused or convicted. Corrections is also the study of these functions.

- Although it is natural to want to exact revenge ourselves when people do us wrong, the state has taken over this responsibility for punishment to prevent endless tit-for-tat feuds. Over social evolution, the state has moved to more restitutive forms of punishment that, while serving to tone down the community's moral outrage, tempers it with sympathy.

- Much of the credit for the shift away from retributive punishment must go to the Classical School of criminology, which was imbued with the humanistic spirit of the Enlightenment. The view of human nature (hedonistic, rational, and possessing free will) held by thinkers of the time was that punishment should primarily be used for deterrent purposes, that it should only just exceed the gains of crime, and that it should apply equally to all who have committed the same crime regardless of any individual differences.

- Opposing classical notions of punishment are those of the positivists, who rose to prominence during the 19th century and who were influenced by the spirit of science. Positivists rejected the philosophical underpinnings regarding human nature of the classicists and declared that punishment should fit the offender rather than the crime.

- The objectives of punishment are retribution, deterrence, incapacitation, rehabilitation, and reintegration, all of which have come in and out of favor over the years.

- Retribution is simply just deserts—getting the punishment one deserves with no other justification needed.

- Deterrence is the assumption that the threat of punishment causes people not to commit crimes. We identified two kinds of deterrence: specific and general. The effects of deterrence on potential offenders depend to a great extent on the contrast between the conditions of punishment and the conditions of everyday life.

- Incapacitation means that the accused and convicted cannot commit further crimes (if they did so in the first place) against the innocent while incarcerated. Incapacitation works only while offenders are behind bars, but we should be more selective about who we incarcerate.

- Rehabilitation centers around efforts to socialize offenders in prosocial directions while they are under correctional supervision so that they will not commit further crimes.

- Reintegration refers to efforts to provide offenders with concrete skills they can use that will give them a stake in conformity.

- Throughout this book, we will offer comparative perspectives on corrections from other countries, focusing primarily on the United Kingdom, France, China, and Saudi Arabia. These countries best exemplify their respective legal traditions and are situated quite far apart on Packer's crime control–due process model of criminal justice.

- The United States leads the world in the proportion of its citizens that it has in prison. Whether this is indicative of hardness on crime (more prison time for more people) or softness on crime (imprisonment as an alternative to execution or mutilation) depends on how we view hardness versus softness and with which countries we compare the United States.

KEY TERMS

Classical School, 5

Contrast effect, 12

Corrections, 2

Crime control model, 16

Deterrence, 11

Due process model, 17

Enlightenment, 5

General deterrence, 12

Hedonism, 9

Hedonistic calculus, 9

Human agency, 10

Incapacitation, 13

Penology, 2

Positivists, 6

Principle of utility, 6

Punishment, 4

Rationality, 9

Recidivism, 11

Rehabilitation, 15

Reintegration, 15

Restitutive justice, 7

Retribution, 10

Retributive justice, 7

Selective incapacitation, 14

Specific deterrence, 11

DISCUSSION QUESTIONS

1. Discuss the implications for a society that decides to eliminate all sorts of punishment in favor of forgiveness.

2. Why do we take pleasure in the punishment of wrongdoers? Is it a good or bad thing that we take pleasure in punishment? What evolutionary purpose does punishment serve?

3. Discuss the assumptions about human nature held by the classical thinkers. Are we rational, seekers of pleasure, and free moral agents? If so, does it make sense to try to rehabilitate criminals?

4. Discuss the assumptions underlying positivism in terms of the treatment of offenders. Do they support Garofalo's idea of individualized justice based on the danger the offender poses to society or von Liszt's idea of individualized justice based on the rehabilitative potential of the offender?

5. Which justification for punishment do you favor? Is it the one that you think "works" best in terms of preventing crime, or do you favor it because it fits your ideology?

6. What is your position on the hardness/softness issue relating to the U.S. stance on crime? We are tougher than other democracies. Is that acceptable to you? We are also softer than more authoritarian countries. Is that acceptable to you also? Why or why not?

$SAGE edge™

Review → Practice → Improve

Sharpen your skills with SAGE edge at **edge.sagepub.com/stohressentials3e**.

SAGE edge offers a robust online environment featuring an impressive array of free tools and resources for review, study, and further exploration, keeping both instructors and students on the cutting edge of teaching and learning.

FOR FURTHER EXPLORATION AND APPLICATION, TAKE A LOOK AT THE INTERACTIVE EBOOK FOR THESE PREMIUM RESOURCES:

▶ **Career Video 1.1** Jail Administrator

▶ **Feature Video 1.1** Offense

▶ **Feature Video 1.2** Deterrence Theory

▣ **SAGE News Clip 1.1** U.S. Prison Acting

▣ **SAGE News Clip 1.2** U.S. WH Snowden

▣ **Journal Article 1.1** From Incapacitation to Criminal Careers

▣ **Journal Article 1.2** Do More Police Lead to More Crime Deterrence?

2 Correctional History

Ancient Times to Colonial Jails

TEST YOUR KNOWLEDGE

Test your current knowledge of correctional history by answering the following questions (some as true or false). Check your answers on page 389 after reading the chapter.

1. Certain themes appear over and over in the history of corrections. (True or false?)

2. The kind of punishment one received for wronging others in ancient civilizations often depended on the wealth and status of the offended party and of the offender. (True or false?)

3. Which of the following was the first type of correctional facility: prisons, bridewells, debtors' prisons, or jails?

4. Galley slavery ended when the technological innovation of sails was employed to propel ships. (True or false?)

5. Transportation was a means of filling the colonies of Great Britain with wealthy merchants and businesspeople. (True or false?)

6. What was John Howard of 18th-century England best known for?

7. The concept of the "panopticon," devised by Jeremy Bentham, included the ingenious combination of labor and money to improve conditions of prisons. (True or false?)

8. William Penn's Great Law was based on Quaker principles and deemphasized the use of corporal and capital punishment. (True or false?)

LEARNING OBJECTIVES

- Understand the origins of corrections

- Appreciate that what we do now in corrections is often grounded in historical experience (or a repeat of it)

- Know the different types of corrections used historically

- Identify some of the key Enlightenment thinkers, their ideas, and how they changed corrections

- Describe colonial jails and early prisons in America and how they operated

- Understand historical innovations in corrections (e.g., the panopticon) and how they worked out

THREE MEN WERE FIRST PLACED IN THE MISSOURI STATE PRISON FOR HELPING SLAVES ESCAPE VIA THE **UNDERGROUND RAILROAD (1847)**

George Thompson

A multitude attended us to the prison; and the office was crowded while we were loosed from our chain, stripped, examined, recorded, one side of our hair cut close—arrayed in shining colors, and another chain put upon each of us. . . . We were treated very ungentlemanly (by the Warden and Overseer)—charged with lying when we told the simple truth, in the honesty of our souls; and then threatened with punishment—denounced as worse than highway robbers, cut-throats, or wholesale murderers, and as meaner than chicken thieves—threatened with having our tongues wired—and other things too vile and wicked to repeat.

THE RULES

1. You must not speak to any prisoner, out of your cell, nor to each other in your cell.

2. You must not look at any visitor—if it is your own brother, if you do, I'll flog you.

3. You must always take off your cap, when speaking to an officer, or when an officer speaks to you.

4. You must call no convict "Mr."

Frequently afterwards, we were checked for applying Mr. to a convict. [This is the real-world narrative of what happened when three men were first placed in the Missouri State Prison for helping slaves escape via the Underground Railroad. This account of how they were treated that first night is by G. Thompson (1847, pp. 132–133), from his book *Prison Life and Reflections*.]

••• INTRODUCTION: THE EVOLVING PRACTICE OF CORRECTIONS

The history of corrections is riddled with the best of intentions and the worst of abuses. Correctional practices and facilities (e.g., galley slavery, transportation, jails and prisons, community corrections) were created, in part, to remove the "riffraff"—both poor and criminal—from urban streets or at least to control and shape them. Prisons and community corrections were also created to avoid the use of more violent or coercive responses to such folks. In this chapter and the next, the focus is on exploring the history of the Western world's correctional operations and then American corrections, specifically, and the recurring themes that run through this history and define it.

It is somewhat ironic that one of the best early analyses of themes and practices in American prisons and jails was completed by two French visitors to the United States—*Gustave de Beaumont* and *Alexis de Tocqueville*—who experienced the virtual birthing of prisons themselves while the country was in its relative infancy in 1831 (Beaumont & Tocqueville, 1833/1964). Tocqueville, as a 26-year-old French magistrate, brought along his friend Beaumont supposedly to study America's newly minted prisons for 9 months. They ended up also observing the workings of its law, its government and political system, and its race relations, among other things (Damrosch, 2010; Tocqueville & Goldhammer, 1835/2004). The irony is that, as outsiders and social critics, Beaumont and Tocqueville could so clearly see what others, namely Americans who were thought to have "invented prisons" and who worked in them, were blind to. In this chapter, we try to "see" what those early French visitors observed about Western, and specifically American, correctional operations.

Few visitors to the United States, or residents for that matter, explored or commented on the early correctional experience for women (*Dorothea Dix* was a notable exception, and there will be more about her and her observations about the state of corrections in 1845 in Chapter 3). Yet some of the themes that run through the practice of corrections apply to women and girls as well, but with a twist. Women have always represented only a small fraction of the correctional population in both prisons and jails, and the history of their experience with incarceration, as shaped by societal expectations of and for them, can be wholly different from that of men. As literal outsiders to what was the "norm" for inmates of prisons and jails, and as a group whose rights and abilities were legally and socially controlled on the outside more than that of men and boys, women's experience in corrections history is worth studying and will be more fully explored in Chapter 11.

PHOTO 2.1: In 1831, Alexis de Tocqueville, as a 26-year-old French magistrate, brought along his friend, Gustave de Beaumont, to study America's newly minted prisons.

What is clear from the Western history of corrections is that what was *intended* when prisons, jails, and reformatories were conceived and *how they actually operated,* then and now, were and are often two very different things (Rothman, 1980). As social critics ourselves, we can use the history of corrections to identify a series of "themes" that run through correctional practice even up to today. Such themes will reinforce the tried, yet true, maxim, "Those who cannot remember the past are condemned to repeat it" (Santayana, 1905, p. 284). Too often we do not know or understand our history of corrections, and as a consequence we are forever repeating it.

●●● THEMES: TRUTHS THAT UNDERLIE CORRECTIONAL PRACTICE

There are some themes that have been almost eerily constant, vis-à-vis corrections, over the decades and even centuries. Some of these themes are obvious, such as the influence that money, or the lack thereof, exerts over virtually all correctional policy decisions. Political sentiments and the desire to make changes also have had tremendous influence over the shape of corrections in the past. Other themes are less apparent, but no less potent, in their effect on correctional operation. For instance, there appears to be an evolving sense of compassion or humanity that, although not always clear in the short term, in practice, or in policy or statute, has underpinned reform-based decisions about corrections and its operation, at least in theory, throughout its history in the United States. The creation of the prison, with a philosophy of penitence (hence the *penitentiary*), was a grand reform itself, and as such it represented, in theory at least, a major improvement over the brutality of punishment that characterized early English and European law and practice (Orland, 1995).

Some social critics do note, however, that the prison and the expanded use of other such social institutions also served as a "social control" mechanism to remove punishment from public view while making the state appear to be more just (Foucault, 1979; Welch, 2004). This is not to argue that such grand reforms in their idealistic form, such as prisons, were not primarily constructed out of the need to control but rather that there were philanthropic, religious, and other forces aligned that also influenced their creation and design, if not so much their eventual and practical operation (Hirsch, 1992). Also of note, the social control function becomes most apparent when less powerful populations such as the poor, the minority, the young, and the female are involved, as will be discussed in the following chapters.

Other than the influence of money and politics and a sense of greater compassion/humanity in correctional operation, the following themes are also apparent in corrections history: the question of how to use labor and technology (which are hard to decouple from monetary considerations); a decided religious influence; the intersection of class, race, age, and gender in shaping one's experience in corrections; architecture as it is intermingled with supervision; methods of control; overcrowding; and finally the fact that good intentions do not always translate into effective practice. Although far from exhaustive, this list contains some of the most salient issues that become apparent streams of influence as one reviews the history of corrections. As was discussed in Chapter 1, some of the larger philosophical (and political) issues, such as conceptions of right and wrong and whether it is best to engage in retribution or rehabilitation (or both, or neither, along with incapacitation, deterrence, and reintegration) using correctional sanctions, are also clearly associated with correctional change and operation.

••• EARLY PUNISHMENTS IN WESTERNIZED COUNTRIES

Humans, throughout recorded history, have devised ingenious ways to punish their kind for real or perceived transgressions. Among tribal groups and in more developed civilizations, such punishment might include whipping, branding, mutilation, drowning, suffocation, execution, and banishment (which in remote areas was tantamount to a death sentence). The extent of the punishment often depended on the wealth and status of the offended party and the offender. Those accused or found guilty who were richer were often allowed to make amends by recompensing the victim or his or her family, while those who were poorer and of lesser status were likely to suffer some sort of bodily punishment. Whatever the approach, and for whatever the reason, some sort of punishment was often called for as a means of balancing the scales of justice, whether to appease a god or gods or, later, Lady Justice.

As D. Garland (1990) recounted, "Ancient societies and 'primitive' social groups often invested the penal process with a wholly religious meaning, so that punishment was understood as a necessary sacrifice to an aggrieved deity" (p. 203). As urbanization took hold, however, and transgressions were less tolerated among an increasingly diverse people, the ancients and their governing bodies were more likely to designate a structure as appropriate for holding people. For the most part, such buildings or other means of confining people were often used to ensure that the accused was held over for trial or sometimes just for punishment (Orland, 1975, p. 13). Fines, mutilation, drawing and quartering, and capital punishment were popular ways to handle those accused or convicted of crimes (Harris, 1973; Orland, 1975). Orland (1975) described practices in England:

> Although mutilation ultimately disappeared from English law, the brutality of Anglo-Saxon criminal punishment continued unabated into the eighteenth century. In the thirteenth century, offenders were commonly broken on the wheel for treason. A 1530 act authorized poisoners to be boiled alive. Burning was the penalty for high treason and heresy, as well as for murder of a husband by a wife or of a master by a servant. Unlike the punishment of boiling, that of burning remained lawful in England until 1790. In practice, and as a kindness, women were strangled before they were burned. The right hand was taken off for aggravated murder. Ordinary hangings were frequent, and drawing and quartering, where the hanged offender was publicly disemboweled and his still-beating heart held up to a cheering multitude, was not uncommon.
>
> In addition, until the mid-nineteenth century, English law permitted a variety of "summary" punishments. Both men and women (the latter until 1817) were flagellated in public for minor offenses. For more serious misdemeanors there was the pillory, which was not abolished in England until 1837. With his face protruding through its beams and his hands through the holes, the offender was helpless. Sometimes he was nailed through the ears to the framework of the pillory with the hair of his head and beard shaved; occasionally he was branded. Thereafter, some offenders were carried back to prison to endure additional tortures. (p. 15)

THE FIRST JAILS

Jails were the first type of correctional facility to develop, and in some form they have existed for several thousand years. Whether pits, dungeons, or caves were used or the detained people were tied to a tree, ancient people all had ways of holding people until a judgment was made or implemented (Irwin, 1985; Mattick, 1974; Zupan, 1991).

According to Johnston (2009), punishment is referenced in a work written in 2000 B.C. and edited by Confucius. The Old Testament of the Bible refers to the use of imprisonment from 2040 to 164 B.C. in Egypt as well as in ancient Assyria and Babylon. Ancient Greece and Rome reserved harsher physical punishments for slaves, whereas citizens might be subjected to fines, exile, imprisonment, or death or some combination of these (Harris, 1973). As Harris (1973) described,

> Ancient Roman society was a slave system. To punish wrongdoers, *capitis diminutio maxima*—the forfeiture of citizenship—was used. Criminals became penal slaves. Doomed men were sent to hard labor in the Carrara marble quarries, metal mines, and sulphur pits. The most common punishment was whipping—and in the case of free men, it was accompanied by the shaving of the head, for the shorn head was the mark of the slave. (p. 14)

Early versions of *gaols* (or jails) and prisons existed in English castle keeps and dungeons and Catholic monasteries. These prisons and jails (not always distinguishable in form or function) held political adversaries and common folks, either as a way to punish them or as a way to incapacitate them or hold them over for judgment by a secular or religious authority. Sometimes people might be held as a means of extorting a fine (Johnston, 2009). The use of these early forms of jail was reportedly widespread in England even a thousand years ago. By the 9th century, Alfred the Great had legally mandated that imprisonment might be used to punish (Irwin, 1985). King Henry II in 1166 required that where no gaol existed in English counties, one should be built (Zupan, 1991) "in walled towns and royal castles," but only for the purpose of holding the accused for trial (Orland, 1975, pp. 15–16). In Elizabethan England, innkeepers made a profit by using their facilities as gaols.

Such imprisonment in these or other gaols was paid for by the prisoners or through their work. Those who were wealthy could pay for more comfortable accommodations while incarcerated. "When the Marquis de Sade was confined in the Bastille, he brought his own furnishings and paintings, his library, a live-in valet, and two dogs. His wife brought him gourmet food" (Johnston, 2009, p. 12S). The Catholic Church maintained its own jails and prison-like facilities across the European continent, administered by bishops or other church officials.

In fact, the Catholic Church's influence on the development of Westernized corrections was intense during the Middle Ages (medieval Europe from the 5th to 15th centuries) and might be felt even today. As a means of shoring up its power base vis-à-vis feudal and medieval lords and kings, the Catholic Church maintained not only its own forms of prisons and jails but also its own ecclesiastical courts (D. Garland, 1990). Although proscribed from drawing blood, except during the Inquisition, the Catholic Church often turned its charges over to secular authorities for physical punishment. But while prisoners were in its care and in its monasteries for punishment, the Catholic Church required "solitude, reduced diet, and reflection, sometimes for extended periods of time" (Johnston, 2009, p. 14S). Centuries later, the first prisons in the United States and Europe, then heavily influenced by Quakers and Protestant denominations in the states, copied the Catholics' monastic emphasis on silence, placing prisoners in small austere rooms where one's penitence might be reflected on—practices and architecture that, to some extent, still resonate today.

COMPARATIVE CORRECTIONS   The Tower of London

© Mary Stohr

PHOTO 2.2: The infamous White Tower inside the Tower of London complex.

There are few international iconic prison images as prominent as that of the Tower of London, located on the River Thames in the center of London, England. Begun after 1066 when William the Conqueror captured the city of Saxon London in the Norman invasion, the centerpiece of this castle complex, the White Tower, was completed in roughly 1080 (Impey & Parnell, 2011). The Tower of London today has a number of buildings, including the White Tower, along with several towers and gates on its double walls. At one time it included a moat, which has since been filled in. Sited in Old London, today it is surrounded by modern buildings and near ancient structures alike. Over the centuries it has been added to by various kings and used to defend the city, as a royal palace and a symbol of power for royalty, as a mint for royal coinage, as an armory, as a treasury for the royal jewels, as a conservator of the King's Court's records, as a kind of zoo for exotic animals gifted to the royalty, as a tourist attraction for centuries, and (for our purposes) as a prison and place of execution.

The Tower of London's role as a prison began early in 1100, lasting until the 1820s, and then was a prison again during World War II (Impey & Parnell, 2011). For the most part, there were no separate prison quarters for its mostly exalted prisoners other than a shed constructed in 1687 for prison soldiers. Therefore, political and other prisoners were accommodated in whatever quarters were available. For instance, Anne Boleyn, who was Henry the VIII's second wife, was married at the Tower, executed there 3 years later in 1526, and buried there. The young Princess Elizabeth (Anne's daughter) was also held at the Tower by her half-sister Queen Mary I until Elizabeth attained the throne as Elizabeth I. Sir Thomas More (1478–1535) spent a year imprisoned in the Tower before his execution and Sir Walter Raleigh (1554–1618) spent 15 years imprisoned in the Tower, both allegedly for treason. Notably, William Penn, discussed in other parts of this book, was imprisoned at the Tower for 7 months in 1668–1669 for pamphleteering about his Quaker religion. Their incarceration in the Tower, as well as many others of rank and wealth, was not as hard as it would have been if they had been sent to public prisons of the time—and even sometimes included luxurious accommodations and servants. Torture did happen at the Tower (the use of the rack and manacles, etc.), but its use was relatively rare because it needed to be sanctioned by a special council. Executions occurred inside the walls of the Tower of London, but most occurred on nearby Tower Hill or elsewhere near the complex.

© Mary Stohr

PHOTO 2.3: Side view of the Tower of London as it appears today.

GALLEY SLAVERY

Another form of "corrections," **galley slavery**, was used sparingly by the ancient Greeks and Romans but more regularly during the late Middle Ages in Europe and England, and it stayed in use until roughly the 1700s. Under Elizabeth I in 1602, a sentence to galley servitude was decreed as an alternative to a death sentence (Orland, 1975). Pope Pius VI (who was pope from 1775 to 1799) also reportedly employed it (Johnston, 2009, p. 12S). Galley slavery was used as a sentence for crimes as a means of removing the poor from the streets. It also served the purpose of providing the requisite labor—rowing—needed to propel ships for seafaring nations interested in engagement in trade and warfare. For instance, galley slaves were reportedly used by Christopher Columbus (Johnston, 2009). The "slaves" were required to row the boat until they collapsed from exhaustion, hunger, or disease; often they sat in their own excrement (Welch, 2004). Under Pope Pius, galley slaves were entitled to bread each day, and their sentences ranged from 3 years to life (Johnston, 2009). Although we do not have detailed records of how such a sentence was carried out, and we can be sure that its implementation varied to some degree from vessel to vessel, the reports that do exist indicate that galley slavery was essentially a sentence of death. Galley slavery ended when the labor was no longer needed on ships because of the technological development of sails.

POVERTY AND BRIDEWELLS, DEBTORS' PRISONS, AND HOUSES OF CORRECTION

However, galley slavery could absorb only a small number of the poor that began to congregate in towns and cities during the Middle Ages. Feudalism, and the order it imposed, was disintegrating; wars (particularly the Crusades prosecuted by the Catholic Church) and intermittent plagues did claim thousands of lives, but populations were stabilizing and increasing and there were not enough jobs, housing, or food for the poor. As the cities became more urbanized, and as more and more poor people congregated in them, governmental entities responded in an increasingly severe fashion to the poor's demands for resources (Irwin, 1985). These responses were manifested in the harsh repression of dissent, the increased use of death sentences and other punishments as deterrence and spectacle, the increased use of jailing to guarantee the appearance of the accused at trial, the development of poorhouses or bridewells and debtors' prisons, and the use of "transportation," discussed below (Foucault, 1979; Irwin, 1985).

In 18th-century England, the number of crimes subject to capital punishment increased to as many as 225 for offenses such as rioting over wages or food (the Riot Act) and "blacking" one's face so as to be camouflaged when killing deer in the king's or a lord's forest (the Black Act) (Ignatieff, 1978, p. 16). New laws regarding forgery resulted in two-thirds of those convicted of it being executed. Rather than impose the most serious sentence for many of these crimes, however, judges would often opt for the use of transportation, whipping, or branding. Juries would also balk at imposing the death sentence for a relatively minor offense and so would sometimes value property that was stolen at less than it was worth to ensure a lesser sentence for the defendant. In the latter part of the 1700s, a sentence of imprisonment might be used in lieu of, or in addition to, these other punishments.

Bridewells, or buildings constructed to hold and whip "beggars, prostitutes, and nightwalkers" (Orland, 1975, p. 16) and later as places of detention, filled this need; their use began in London in 1553 (Kerle, 2003). The name came from the first such institution, which was developed at Bishop Ridley's place at St. Bridget's Well; all subsequent similar facilities were known as bridewells.

Bridewells were also workhouses, used as leverage to extract fines or repayment of debts or the labor to replace them. Such facilities did not separate people by gender, age, or

Galley slavery:
A sentence forcing convicted criminals to work as rowers on a ship.

Bridewells:
Workhouses constructed to hold and whip or otherwise punish "beggars, prostitutes, and nightwalkers" and later as places of detention.

What Would You Do?

You are the manager of a bridewell in 17th-century England. Most of the people you house are desperately poor and displaced people (people from the countryside who have moved into the towns with few skills or connections to help them). Your income derives from charging the inmates of your bridewell for their keep, but many of them do not have the funds to pay you, so you have some difficulty in paying your own bills and are in danger of defaulting on debts and ending up in debtors' prison yourself. Yet if you do not feed and clothe them, some of your charges are likely to die of starvation, exposure, or typhus (gaol fever). What do you do? What do you think John Howard would recommend that you do?

criminal/noncriminal status, their inmates were not fed and clothed properly, and sanitary conditions were not maintained. As a consequence of these circumstances, bridewells were dangerous and diseased places where if one could not pay a "fee" for food, clothing, or release, the inmate, and possibly his or her family, might be doomed (Orland, 1975; Pugh, 1968). The use of bridewells spread throughout Europe and the British colonies because it provided a means of removing the poor and displaced from the streets while also making a profit (Kerle, 2003). Such a profit was made by the wardens, keepers, and gaolers—the administrators of bridewells, houses of correction (each county in England was authorized to build one in 1609), and gaols, who, although unpaid, lobbied for the job because it was so lucrative. They made money by extracting it from the inmates. If an inmate could not pay, he or she might be left to starve in filth or be tortured or murdered by the keeper for nonpayment (Orland, 1975, p. 17).

Notably, being sent to "debtors' prison" was something that still occurred even after the American Revolution. In fact, James Wilson, a signer of the Constitution (and reportedly one of its main architects) and a Supreme Court justice, was imprisoned in such a place twice while serving on the Court. He had speculated on land to the west and lost a fortune in the process (Davis, 2008).

TRANSPORTATION

Yet another means of "corrections" that was in use by Europeans for roughly 350 years, from the founding of the Virginia Colony in 1607, was **transportation** (Feeley, 1991). Also used to rid cities and towns of the chronically poor or the criminally inclined, transportation, as with bridewells and gaols, involved a form of privatized corrections, whereby those sentenced to transportation were sold to a ship's captain. He would in turn sell their labor as indentured servants, usually to do agricultural work, to colonials in America (Maryland, Virginia, and Georgia were partially populated through this method) and to white settlers in Australia. Transportation ended in the American colonies with the Revolutionary War, but it was practiced by France to populate Devil's Island in French Guiana until 1953 (Welch, 2004). Welch (2004) noted that transportation was a very popular sanction in Europe:

> Russia made use of Siberia; Spain deported prisoners to Hispaniola; Portugal exiled convicts to North Africa, Brazil and Cape Verde; Italy herded inmates to Sicily; Denmark relied on Greenland as a penal colony; Holland shipped convicts to the Dutch East Indies. (p. 29)

Transportation: A privatized sentence exiling convicts and transporting them to a penal colony. The sentenced were sold to ship captains, and in turn their labor as indentured servants was sold to colonials by the same captain.

In America, transportation provided needed labor to colonies desperate for it. "Following a 1718 law in England, all felons with sentences of 3 years or more were eligible for transport to America. Some were given a choice between hanging or transport" (Johnston, 2009, p. 13S).

It is believed that about 50,000 convicts were deposited on American shores from English gaols. If they survived their servitude, which ranged from 1 to 5 years, they became free and might be given tools or even land to make their way in the New World (Orland, 1975, p. 18). Once the American Revolution started, such prisoners from England were transported to Australia, and when settlers there protested the number of entering offenders, the prisoners were sent to penal colonies in that country as well as in New Zealand and Gibraltar (Johnston, 2009).

One of the most well-documented such penal colonies was **Norfolk Island**, about 1,000 miles off the Australian coast. Established in 1788 as a place designated for prisoners from England and Australia, it was regarded as a brutal and violent island prison where inmates were poorly fed, clothed, and housed and were mistreated by staff and their fellow inmates (Morris, 2002). Morris, in his semi-fictional account of *Alexander Maconochie*'s effort to reform Norfolk, noted that Machonochie, an ex-naval captain, asked to be transferred to Norfolk, usually an undesirable placement, so that he could put into practice some ideas he had about prison reform. He served as the warden there from 1840 to 1844. What was true in this story was that "in four years, Maconochie transformed what was one of the most brutal convict settlements in history into a controlled, stable, and productive environment that achieved such success that upon release his prisoners came to be called 'Maconochie's Gentlemen'" (Morris, 2002). Maconochie's ideas included the belief that inmates should be rewarded for good behavior through a system of marks, which could lead to privileges and early release; that they should be treated with respect; and that they should be adequately fed and housed. Such revolutionary ideas, for their time, elicited alarm from Maconochie's superiors, and he was removed from his position after only 4 years. His ideas, however, were adopted decades later when the concepts of "good time" and parole were developed in Ireland and the United States. In addition, his ideas about adequately feeding and clothing inmates were held in common by reformers who came before him, such as John Howard and William Penn, and those who came after him, such as Dorothea Dix.

••• ENLIGHTENMENT—PARADIGM SHIFT

SPOCK FALLS IN LOVE

As noted in Chapter 1, the Enlightenment period, lasting roughly from the 17th century through the 18th century in England, Europe, and America, spelled major changes in thought about crime and corrections. But then, it was a time of paradigmatic shifts in many aspects of the Western experience as societies became more secular and open. Becoming a more secular culture meant that there was more focus on humans on Earth, rather than in the afterlife, and as a consequence the arts, sciences, and philosophy flourished. In such periods of human history, creativity manifests itself in innovations in all areas of experience; the orthodoxy in thought and practice is often challenged and sometimes overthrown in favor of new ideas and even radical ways of doing things (Davis, 2008). Whether in the sciences with Englishman Isaac Newton (1643–1727), philosophy and rationality with the Englishwoman Anne Viscountess Conway (1631–1679), feminist philosophy with the Englishwoman Damaris Cudworth Masham (1659–1708), philosophy and history with the Scotsman David Hume (1711–1776), literature and philosophy with the Frenchman Voltaire (1694–1778), literature and philosophy with the Briton Mary Wollstonecraft (1759–1797), or the Founding Fathers of the United States (e.g., Samuel Adams, James Madison, Benjamin Franklin, Thomas Paine, Thomas Jefferson), new ideas and beliefs were proposed and explored in every sphere of the intellectual enterprise (Duran, 1996; Frankel, 1996). Certainly, the writings of *John Locke* (1632–1704) and his conception of liberty and human rights provided the philosophical underpinnings for the Declaration of Independence as penned by Thomas Jefferson. As a result of the Enlightenment, the French Revolution beginning in 1789 was also about rejecting one form of government—the absolute monarchy—for something that was to be more democratic and liberty based. (Notably, the French path to

Norfolk Island: An English penal colony, about 1,000 miles off the Australian coast, regarded as a brutal and violent island prison where inmates were poorly fed, clothed, and housed and were mistreated by staff and their fellow inmates.

PHOTO 2.4: Philosopher John Locke's writings and his conception of liberty and human rights helped to provide the philosophical underpinnings for the Declaration of Independence.

ETHICAL ISSUE

democracy was not straight and included a dalliance with other dictators such as Napoleon Bonaparte, who came to power in 1799.)

Such changes in worldviews or paradigms, as Thomas Kuhn explained in his well-known work *The Structure of Scientific Revolutions* (Kuhn, 1962) when discussing the nonlinear shifts in scientific theory, usually come after evidence mounts and the holes in old ways of perceiving become all too apparent. The old theory simply cannot accommodate the new evidence. Such an event was illustrated on a micro, or individual, level in an episode of the original *Star Trek* television show when Spock (the logical, unemotional, and unattached first officer) falls in love with a woman for the first time after breathing in the spores of a magical flower on a mysterious planet. Those who experienced the Enlightenment period, much like reformers and activists of the Progressive Era (1880s–1920s) and Civil Rights Era (1960s–1970s) in the United States that were to follow centuries later, experienced a paradigm shift regarding crime and justice. Suddenly, as if magic spores had fundamentally reshaped thought and suffused it with kind regard if not love for others, humans seemed to realize that change in crime policy and practice was called for, and they set about devising ways to accomplish it.

JOHN HOWARD

John Howard (1726–1790) was one such person who acted as a change agent. As a sheriff of Bedford in England and as a man who had personally experienced incarceration as a prisoner of war himself (held captive by French privateers), he was *enlightened* enough to "see" that gaols in England and Europe should be different, and he spent the remainder of his life trying to reform them (Howard, 1775/2000; Johnston, 2009). Howard's genius was his main insight regarding corrections—that corrections should not be privatized in the sense that jailers were "paid" by inmates a fee for their food, clothing, and housing (an inhumane and often illogical practice because most who were incarcerated were desperately poor, a circumstance that explained the incarceration of many in the first place). Howard believed that the state or government had a responsibility to provide sanitary and separate conditions and decent food and water for those it incarcerated. His message of reform included these central tenets:

1. The fee system for jails should be ended.

2. Inmates should be separated by gender and offense (single cells would be optimal).

3. Inmates should be provided with sanitary conditions and clean and healthful food and water.

4. Staff should serve as a moral model for inmates.

5. Jails and prisons should have a set of standards and be independently inspected to ensure that these standards are maintained.

Howard's humanity was apparent in that he promoted these ideas in England and all over the European continent during his lifetime. He was able to do so because he inherited money from his father, his sister, and his grandmother and used that money to improve the lives of the tenants on his land and the inmates in correctional facilities. Howard's (1775/2000) major written work, *The State of the Prisons in England and Wales, With Preliminary Observations, and an Account of Some Foreign Prisons,* detailed the horror that was experienced in the filthy and torturous gaols of England and Europe, noting that despite the fact that there were 200 crimes for which capital punishment might be prescribed, far more inmates died from diseases contracted while incarcerated. (Note to reader: The Old English used by Howard in the following quote and that in the next paragraph sometimes substitutes the letter "f" for the letter "s.")

> I traveled again into the counties where I had been; and, indeed, into all the reft; examining Houfes of Correction, City and Town-Gaols. I beheld in many of them, as well as in the County-Gaols, a complication of diftrefs: but my attention was principally fixed by the gaol-fever, and the fmall-pox, which I faw prevailing to the deftruction of multitudes, not only of felons in their dungeons, but of debtors alfo. (p. 2)

PHOTO 2.5: John Howard (1726–1790) believed that the state or government had a responsibility to provide sanitary conditions and decent food and water for those it incarcerated.

Howard (1775/2000) found that gaol fever was widespread in all kinds of correctional institutions of the time—bridewells, gaols, debtors' prisons, and houses of correction. Notably, in larger cities there were clear distinctions among these facilities and who they held, but in smaller towns and counties there were not. In the neglect of inmates and the underfunding of the facilities, Howard found them all to be quite similar. He noted that in some bridewells there was no provision at all made for feeding inmates. Although inmates of bridewells were to be sentenced to hard labor, he found that in many there was little work to do and no tools provided to do it: "The prifoners have neither tools, nor materials of any kind; but fpend their time in floth, profanenefs and debauchery, to a degree which, in fome of thofe houfes that I have feen, is extremely fhocking" (p. 8). He found that the allotment for food in county jails was not much better, remarking that in some there was none for debtors, the criminals, or the accused alike. He noted that these inmates, should they survive their suffering, would then enter communities or other facilities in rags and spread disease wherever they went.

IN FOCUS 2.1

Modern-Day John Howard: Ken Kerle

The Corrections Section of the Academy of Criminal Justice Sciences (ACJS) established the "John Howard" Award in 2009 and gave the first one to a modern-day John Howard, Ken Kerle (retired managing editor of *American Jails* magazine). Kerle has spent much of his adult life trying to improve jail standards both here in the United States and abroad. As part of that effort, he has visited hundreds of jails in this country and around the world. He has advised countless jail managers about how they might improve their operations. He has increased the transmission of information and the level of discussion between academicians and practitioners by encouraging the publication of scholars' work in *American Jails* magazine and their presentations at the American Jails Association meetings and by urging practitioners to attend ACJS meetings. Kerle (2003) also published a book on jails titled *Exploring Jail Operations*.

In his census of correctional facilities (including debtors' prisons, jails, and houses of correction or bridewells) in England and Wales, Howard (1775/2000) found that about 16% of inmates were petty offenders, about 60% were debtors, and about 24% were felons (which included those awaiting trial, those convicted and awaiting their execution or transportation, and those serving a sentence of imprisonment) (Ignatieff, 1978, p. 25). Ironically, Howard eventually died from typhus, also known as gaol fever, after touring several jails and prisons in Eastern Europe, specifically the prisons of Tsarist Russia.

BENTHAM AND BECCARIA

As mentioned in Chapter 1, the philosophers and reformers *Jeremy Bentham* (1748–1832) in England and *Cesare Beccaria* (1738–1794) in Italy separately, but both during the Enlightenment period, decried the harsh punishment meted out for relatively minor offenses in their respective countries and, as a consequence, emphasized "certainty" over the severity and celerity components of the deterrence theory they independently developed. Beccaria (1764/1963), in his classic work *On Crimes and Punishment*, wrote,

> In order that punishment should not be an act of violence perpetrated by one or many upon a private citizen, it is essential that it should be public, speedy, necessary, the minimum possible in the given circumstances, proportionate to the crime, and determined by the law. (p. 113)

Beccaria argued that knowledge, such as that provided by the sciences and enlightenment, was the only effective antidote to "foul-mouthed ignorance" (p. 105).

Bentham (1789/1969) also proposed, in his *Plan of Construction of a Panopticon Penitentiary House* (although the funding of it was not signed off on by King George III), the building of a special type of prison. As per Bentham, the building of a private "prison"-like structure—the **panopticon**, which he would operate—that ingeniously melded the ideas of improved supervision with architecture (because of its rounded, open, and unobstructed views) would greatly enhance supervision of inmates. Such a recognition of the benefits of some architectural styles as complementary to enhanced supervision was indeed prescient in that it presaged modern jail and prison architecture. His proposed panopticon would be circular, with two tiers of cells on the outside and a guard tower in its center, with the central area also topped by a large skylight. The skylight and the correct angling of the tower were to ensure that the guard was able to observe all inmate behavior in the cells, although owing to a difference of level and the use of blinds the keeper would be invisible to the inmates. A chapel would also be located in the center of the rounded structure. The cells were to be airy and large enough to accommodate the whole life of the inmates in that the cells were to "serve all purposes: work, sleep, meals, punishment, devotion" (Bentham, 1811/2003, p. 194). Somehow, Bentham (1811/2003) noted in his plan without elaboration that the sexes were to be invisible to each other. He did not call for complete separation of all inmates, however, which becomes important when discussing the Pennsylvania and New York prisons in Chapter 3, but he did assert that the groups of inmates allowed to interact should be small, including only two to four persons (p. 195).

As an avowed admirer of John Howard, Bentham proposed that his panopticon penitentiary would include all of the reforms proposed by Howard and much more. Bentham (1811/2003) promised that inmates would be well fed, fully clothed, supplied with beds, supplied with warmth and light, and kept from "strong or spirituous liquors" and would have their spiritual and medical needs fulfilled, be provided with opportunities for labor and education ("to convert the prison into a school" and to incentivize the labor so that they got to "share in the produce"), be taught a trade so that they could survive once released, and be helped to save for old age (pp. 199–200). He would also personally pay a fine for every escape, insure inmates' lives to prevent their deaths, and submit regular reports to the "Court of the King's Bench" on the status of the prison's operation (pp. 199–200). Moreover, he proposed that the prison would be open in many respects

Panopticon:
A rounded prison design in which multi-tiered cells are built around a hub so that correctional staff can view all inmates without being observed.

not just to dignitaries but also to regular citizens, and daily, as a means of preventing abuse that might occur in secret. Bentham also recommended the construction of his prisons on a large scale across England, such that one would be built every 30 miles, or a good day's walk by a man. He planned, as he wrote in his 1830 diatribe against King George III wryly titled "History of the War Between Jeremy Bentham and George the Third—By One of the Belligerents," that "But for George the Third, all the prisoners in England would, years ago, have been under my management. But for George the Third, all the paupers in the country would, long ago, have been under my management" (p. 195).

Although his plan in theory was laudable and really visionary for his time, and ours, he hoped to make much coin as recompense for being a private prison manager—to the tune of 60 pounds sterling per prisoner, which when assigned to all inmates across England was a considerable sum (Bentham, 1811/2003, p. 195). What stopped him, and the reason why he was so angry with his sovereign, was King George's unwillingness to sign the bill that would have authorized the funding and construction of the first panopticon. Bentham alleged that the king would not sign because the powerful Lord Charles Spenser was concerned about the effect on the value of his property should a prison be located on or near it. Bentham's prison dream was dead, but eventually Bentham was awarded 23,000 pounds for his efforts (Bentham, 1811/2003, p. 207). It was left to others to build panopticon prisons in both Europe and the states during the coming years.

WILLIAM PENN

William Penn (1644–1718), a prominent Pennsylvania Colony governor and Quaker, was similarly influenced by Enlightenment thinking (although with the Quaker influence his views were not so secular). Much like Bentham and Beccaria, Penn was not a fan of the harsh punishments, even executions, for relatively minor offenses that were meted out during his lifetime. While in England, and as a result of his defense of religious freedom and practice, he was incarcerated in the local jails on more than one occasion, even in the Tower of London in 1669, for his promotion of the Quaker religion and defiance of the English crown. He was freed only because of his wealth and connections (Penn, 1679/1981). As a consequence, when he had the power to change the law and its protections, and reduce the severity of punishments, he did so. Many years later (in 1682) in Pennsylvania, he proposed and instituted his **Great Law**, which was based on Quaker principles and deemphasized the use of corporal and capital punishment for all crimes but the most serious ones (Clear, Cole, & Reisig, 2011; Johnston, 2009; Zupan, 1991). His reforms substituted fines and jail time for corporal punishment. He promoted Pennsylvania as a haven for Quakers, who were persecuted in England and Europe generally, and for a number of other religious minorities (Penn, 1679/1981). His ideas about juries, civil liberties, religious freedom, and the necessity of amending constitutions—so that they are adaptable to changing times—influenced a number of American revolutionaries, including Benjamin Franklin and Thomas Paine.

Many of Penn's contemporaries were not of the same frame of mind, however, and after his death the Great Law was repealed and harsher punishments were again instituted in Pennsylvania, much as they existed in the rest of the colonies (Johnston, 2009; Welch, 2004). But the mark of his influence lived on in the development of some of America's first prisons.

Much like Howard and Bentham, Penn was interested in reforming corrections, but he was particularly influenced by his Quaker sentiments regarding nonviolence and the value of quiet contemplation.

> **Great Law:** William Penn's idea, based on Quaker principles, deemphasizing the use of corporal and capital punishment for all crimes but the most serious ones.

Photos.com/Thinkstock

PHOTO 2.6: William Penn proposed and instituted his Great Law, which was based on Quaker principles and deemphasized the use of corporal and capital punishment for all crimes but the most serious ones.

The early American prisons known as the **Pennsylvania prison system (Walnut Street Jail, Western and Eastern Pennsylvania prisons)** incorporated these ideas (Johnston, 2009). Even the **New York prison system (Auburn and Sing Sing)**, often juxtaposed with Pennsylvania prisons based on popular depiction by historians (see Beaumont & Tocqueville, 1833/1964), included contemplation time for inmates and a plan for single cells for inmates that reflected the same belief in the need for some solitude.

••• COLONIAL JAILS AND PRISONS

The first jail in America was built in Jamestown, Virginia, soon after the colony's founding in 1606 (Burns, 1975; Zupan, 1991). Massachusetts built a jail in Boston in 1635, and Maryland built a jail for the colony in 1662 (Roberts, 1997). The oldest standing jail in the United States was built during the late 1600s and is located in Barnstable, Massachusetts (Library of Congress, 2010). It was used by the sheriff to hold both male and female inmates, along with the sheriff's family, in upstairs, basement, and barn rooms. Men and women were held in this and other jails like it, mostly before they were tried for both serious and minor offenses, as punishment for offenses or to ensure that they would be present for their own executions.

Such an arrangement as this—holding people in homes, inns, or other structures that were not originally designated or constructed as jails—was not uncommon in early colonial towns (Goldfarb, 1975; Irwin, 1985; Kerle, 2003). As in England, inmates of these early and colonial jails were required to pay a "fee" for their upkeep (the same fee system that John Howard opposed). Those who were wealthier could more easily buy their way out of incarceration, or if that was not possible because of the nature of the offense, they could at least ensure that they had more luxurious accommodations (Zupan, 1991). Even when jailers were paid a certain amount to feed and clothe inmates, they might be disinclined to do so, being that they were able to keep what they saved by not taking care of their charges (Zupan, 1991). As a result, inmates of early American jails were sometimes malnourished or starving. Moreover, in the larger facilities they were crammed into unsanitary rooms, often without regard to separation by age, gender, or offense, conditions that also led to disease and early death. Nonetheless, Irwin (1985) did remark that generally Americans fared better in colonial jails than in their English and European cousins because the arrangements were less formal and restrictive in the American jails and were more like rooming houses. Relatedly, Goldfarb (1975) remarked,

> Jails that did exist in the eighteenth century were run on a household model with the jailer and his family residing on the premises. The inmates were free to dress as they liked, to walk around freely and to provide their own food and other necessities. (p. 9)

Pennsylvania prison system (Walnut Street Jail, Western and Eastern Pennsylvania prisons): Prisons that emphasized silence and isolated inmates in their cells, restricting their contact with others and reinforcing the need for penitence.

New York prison system (Auburn and Sing Sing): Prisons that included congregate work and eating arrangements but silent and separate housing.

Old Newgate Prison, near Hartford. Conn.

PHOTO 2.7: Newgate Prison, a working copper mine, served as an early colonial prison.

As white people migrated across the continent of North America, the early western jails were much like their earlier eastern and colonial cousins, with makeshift structures and cobbled together supervision serving as a means of holding the accused over for trial (Moynihan, 2002). In post–Civil War midwestern cities, disconnected outlaw gangs (such as the Jesse James Gang) were treated in a harsh manner. Some communities even built *rotary jails*, which were like human squirrel cages. Inside a secure building, these rotating steel cages, segmented into small "pie-shaped cells," were secured to the floor and could be spun at will by the sheriff (Goldfarb, 1975, p. 11).

PERSPECTIVE FROM A PRACTITIONER

Marianne Fisher-Giorlando, Board Member of Louisiana State Penitentiary Museum Foundation

Position: Louisiana State Penitentiary Museum Foundation, commonly known as Angola Museum, Board Member; Education Committee, Chair; and Accession/Deaccession Committee Member.

Location: Angola, Louisiana

How long have you been working in this position?

I have been the chair of the Education Committee for approximately 5 years. However, I have been a member of the board since the museum officially opened in 1998.

What are your primary duties and responsibilities?

As chair of the Education Committee, I oversee the oral history project and the biannual symposium in addition to the ongoing project of developing education programs. I also do the research and sometimes write the narratives for new and rotating exhibits.

The purpose of the oral history committee is to collect oral histories from present and former employees of the Louisiana Department of Public Safety and Corrections, past and present prisoners, and those who have lived at Angola as free people. The interviews will be used to complement exhibits and be available to researchers.

Symposiums are designed to educate the public about the history and contemporary policies, practices, and programs of Louisiana's correctional system. Symposium topics have included the history of Angola, prison music at Angola, and a recent one for 2014, "Farming on the Farm: Agricultural Operations at the Louisiana State Penitentiary at Angola."

In general, what does a typical day working in this position look like?

My day is never typical. It can start with a text, email, or phone call request, sometimes before 7 in the morning. And I am involved in any one of the following activities or a bit of all of them in one day.

I work closely with the director of planning and development, Genny Nadler-Thomas, to schedule the exhibit calendar for the year. This plan is often revised depending on unanticipated events and opportunities. We just finished with a Smithsonian Museums on Main Street traveling exhibit, "The Way We Worked." From initial notice and training for that exhibit, other museum employees and I worked on it off and on for more than 2 years.

The museum has a website where people can make inquiries about Angola. Requests that are sent to me can vary anywhere from "Do you have a record of my ancestor who I just found out was incarcerated at Angola in the early 1900s?" to "I was born at Angola" to a request from Warden Burl Cain about how and why the present name of the convict cemetery is "Point Lookout." The ancestor requests oftentimes include very sparse information, with only a name and a wide range of potential dates. I love digging out this information for people. They are always so happy to receive information about their long-lost relatives.

Just recently I interviewed the first female warden at Angola, who was appointed in the late 1970s. She is a legend at Angola for many reasons. She not only supervised *The Angolite,* the prison newsmagazine, but she went back to school to take journalism classes to "do the best job possible."

I also co-wrote a $40,000 planning grant proposal to the National Endowment for the Humanities to digitize Angola's old Receiving Center's ID records and plan a research center for the museum's collections.

Finally, I coordinated the traveling exhibit, "Farming on the Farm" which was on display in 10 different libraries during 2013–2014.

What is the importance of corrections museums and the study of correctional history?

If we do not know our history, we are doomed to repeat it. In the United States, we cannot afford to repeat the dreadful practices and treatment of prisoners that was

(Continued)

(Continued)

our embarrassing history, especially now in light of such serious budget cuts for so-called frivolous things such as the arts and education in prisons.

Corrections museums can provide stimulating questions about why we did what we did historically and continue to question why we do what we do now in the field of corrections. If done well, corrections museums can portray both the "keeper" and the "kept" in more than the stereotypical representations of their roles generally portrayed in the community.

What would be your advice to someone either wishing to study, or now studying, criminal justice to become a practitioner in this career field?

I think you would find this field infinitely intriguing and rewarding. I do. I believe people starting in the field would be vital to a corrections historical museum as they bring new eyes to the same material. Because the nature of this work requires interactions with present and former employees of correctional institutions and present and former prisoners, the work is not limited to the museum space but requires almost daily visits to all corners of the prison. Therefore, the newcomer to this field would learn about the prison—keepers and kept—in a different manner than a typical new prison employee.

I am retired from teaching corrections in a criminal justice department for over 27 years, and I found this work makes use of the knowledge I have about the field but also expands my boundaries by asking me to use that knowledge in a distinctly different manner in planning exhibits and writing the narratives for the accompanying catalogues.

COMPARATIVE CORRECTIONS

Early European and British Prisons

Some early European versions of prisons bucked the trend of harsh physical punishments even for minor offenses. Others, but only a few, even classified their inmates not just by economic and social status but also by gender, age, and criminal offense. For instance, in the Le Stinche Prison built in Florence, Italy, during the 1290s, the inmates were separated in this way (Roberts, 1997). Later, the Maison de Force Prison in Ghent, Belgium (1773) placed serious offenders in a different section of the prison from the less serious offenders. A juvenile reformatory was even built in a separate wing of the Hospice of San Michele in Rome (1704) (Roberts, 1997). An architectural depiction of the Ghent prison shows an octagonal shape with a central court and then a partial view of separate living areas or courts for exercise and for women, vagrant men, and other men. Much like the American colonies and England, however, the early European prisons and jails classified inmates by their social status and their ability to pay, with the concomitant amenities going to the wealthier.

Incarcerated nobles who could pay the heftiest fees lived in comparative comfort with a modicum of privacy; less affluent prisoners were confined in large common rooms; the poorest inmates, and those who were considered the most dangerous, needed to endure squalid dungeons. It was not unusual for men, women, and children, the sane and the mentally ill, felons and misdemeanants, all to be crowded indiscriminately into group cells (Roberts, 1997, p. 5).

Another less enlightened type of prison existed in England in the form of the **"hulks,"** derelict naval vessels transformed into prisons for the overflowing inmates in England. Used in tandem with transportation and other forms of incarceration during the mid-1700s, and then increasing in use during the gap between the end of transportation to the American colonies with the Revolutionary War and the beginning of transportation of "criminals" to Australia, the last hulk was used on the coast of Gibraltar in 1875 (Roberts, 1997, p. 9).

The English even confined some prisoners of war in a Hudson River hulk during the American Revolution. Inmates of these hulks were taken off to labor during the day for either public works or private contractors. The conditions of confinement were, predictably, horrible. "The hulks were filthy, crowded, unventilated, disease-ridden, and infested with vermin. The food was inadequate and the discipline was harsh" (Roberts, 1997, p. 11). Some inmates housed on the lower decks even drowned from water taken on by these broken-down ships.

A major proponent of reform of English prisons, and also a Quaker, was *Elizabeth Gurney Fry* (1780–1845). She was an advocate for improved conditions, guidelines, training, and work skills for women inmates (Roberts, 1997). She provided the religious instruction herself to the women inmates.

PHOTO 2.8: Drawing of inmates in a hulk prison washroom.

Of course, without prisons in existence per se (we discuss the versions of such institutions that did exist shortly), most punishments for crimes constituted relatively short terms in jails, public shaming (such as in the stocks), physical punishments (such as flogging and the pillory), or banishment. Executions were also carried out, usually but not always for the most horrific of crimes such as murder and rape, although in colonial America many more crimes qualified for this punishment (Zupan, 1991). As in Europe and England at this time, those who were poorer or enslaved were more likely to experience the harshest punishments (Irwin, 1985; Zupan, 1991). Similar to Europe and England during this era, jails also held the mentally ill along with debtors, drifters, transients, the inebriated, runaway slaves or servants, and the criminally involved (usually pretrial) (Cornelius, 2007).

Although the Walnut Street Jail, a portion of which was converted to a prison, is often cited as the "first" prison in the world, there were, as this recounting of history demonstrates, many precursors that were arguably "prisons" as well. One such facility, which also illustrates the "makeshift" nature of early prisons, was the **Newgate Prison in Simsbury, Connecticut** (named after the Newgate Prison in London). According to Phelps (1860/1996), this early colonial prison started as a copper mine, and during its 54 years of operation (from 1773 to 1827) some 800 inmates passed through its doors. The mine was originally worked in 1705, and one-third of the taxes it paid to the town of Simsbury at that time were used to support Yale College (p. 15). "Burglary, robbery, and counterfeiting were punished for the first offense with imprisonment not exceeding ten years; second offence for life" (p. 26). Later, those loyal to the English crown during the U.S. Revolutionary War—or Tories—were held at Newgate as well. Punishments by the "keeper of the prison" could range from shackles and fetters as restraints to "moderate whipping, not to exceed ten stripes" (p. 26). The inmates of Newgate prison were held—stored, really—in the bowels of the mine during the evening (by themselves and with no supervision), and during the day they were forced to work the mine or were allowed to come to the surface to labor around the facility and in the community. Over the course of the history of this facility, there were several escapes, a number of riots, and the burning of the topside buildings by its inmates. Early versions of prisons also existed in other countries.

Hulks: Derelict naval vessels transformed into prisons and jails.

Newgate Prison in Simsbury, Connecticut: An early American version of a prison (1773–1827) and a working copper mine. The inmates slept in the mine at night (by themselves and with no supervision), and they were forced to work the mine or above ground during the day. During the Revolutionary War, some loyalists to the English Crown were held there.

SUMMARY

- Humans have been inventive in their development of punishments and ways to hold and keep people.

- Correctional history is riddled with efforts to improve means of correction and reform.

- Those accused or convicted of crimes who had more means were less likely to be treated harshly or punished severely.

- Sometimes the old worldviews (paradigms) are challenged by new evidence and ideas, and they are then discarded for new paradigms. The Enlightenment period in Europe was a time for rethinking old ideas and beliefs.

- Jeremy Bentham, Cesare Beccaria, John Howard, and William Penn were all especially influential in changing our ideas about crime, punishment, and corrections.

- Correctional reforms, whether meant to increase the use of humane treatment of inmates or to increase their secure control, often lead to unintended consequences.

- Some early European and English versions of prisons and juvenile facilities were very close in mission and operation to America's earliest prisons.

KEY TERMS

Bridewells, 29

Galley slavery, 29

Great Law, 35

Hulks, 38

Newgate Prison in Simsbury, Connecticut, 39

New York prison system (Auburn and Sing Sing), 36

Norfolk Island, 31

Panopticon, 34

Pennsylvania prison system (Walnut Street Jail, Western and Eastern Pennsylvania prisons), 36

Transportation, 30

DISCUSSION QUESTIONS

1. Identify examples of some themes that run throughout the history of corrections. What types of punishments tend to be used and for what types of crimes? What sorts of issues influence the choice of actions taken against offenders?

2. How were people of different social classes treated in early jails and bridewells?

3. We know that galley slavery ended because of the development of sails, which was an improvement in technology. Can you think of other types of correctional practices that have been developed, improved on, or stopped because of advances in technology?

4. What role has religion played in the development of corrections in the past?

5. What types of things have remained the same in corrections over the years, and what types of things have changed? Why do you think things have changed or remained the same?

6. Several historical figures mentioned in this chapter advanced ideas that were viewed as radical for their day. Why do you think such ideas were eventually adopted? Can you think of similar sorts of seemingly "radical" ideas for reforming corrections that might be adopted in the future?

⑨SAGE edge™

Review → Practice → Improve

Sharpen your skills with SAGE edge at **edge.sagepub.com/stohressentials3e**.

SAGE edge offers a robust online environment featuring an impressive array of free tools and resources for review, study, and further exploration, keeping both instructors and students on the cutting edge of teaching and learning.

FOR FURTHER EXPLORATION AND APPLICATION, TAKE A LOOK AT THE INTERACTIVE EBOOK FOR THESE PREMIUM RESOURCES:

- ▶ **Career Video 2.1** Court Administrator
- ▶ **Feature Video 2.1** Interactions With Law Enforcement
- ▶ **SAGE News Clip 2.1** Tom Mooney in Gaol
- ▶ **SAGE News Clip 2.2** Georgia Jail House
- ▦ **Journal Article 2.1** Early Use of Imprisonment as Punishment

3

Correctional History

The 17th to 20th Centuries

TEST YOUR KNOWLEDGE

Test your current knowledge of correctional history by answering the following questions. Check your answers on page 389 after reading the chapter.

1. What are the main differences between the Pennsylvania prison system and the New York prison system? Which system did most of America adopt and why?

2. Most scholars believe that the Walnut Street Jail, as refurbished, became the first American prison in 1790. (True or false?)

3. The Auburn Prison featured complete separation from other inmates. (True or false?)

4. The complete separation of inmates was abandoned under the New York system of prisons. (True or false?)

5. After visiting the Eastern Pennsylvania Prison, Charles Dickens was an advocate for the "silent and separate" system of the Pennsylvania prisons. (True or false?)

6. To maintain control during the early years at the Auburn and Sing Sing prisons, the liberal use of "the lash," along with other methods, was required. (True or false?)

7. Dorothea Dix favored the New York prison system over the Pennsylvania prison system. (True or false?)

8. The 1870 American Prison Congress was held to celebrate the successes of prisons. (True or false?)

9. The Elmira Reformatory used the marks system to encourage good behavior. (True or false?)

10. To be termed a correctional institution, a prison should have some rehabilitation programming for inmates. (True or false?)

LEARNING

- Describe the o. prisons

- Evaluate the two predomi. systems of the early 1800s an. strengths and weaknesses

- Summarize what the social critics (Beaumont, Tocqueville, and Dix) thought of the early prisons and why

- Explain why reform of prisons and jails was needed and how those reform efforts worked out

- Assess where we are today in America in terms of prison types and how we got there

- Describe the prevailing themes in correctional history

JIM CROW TREATMENT IN PRISONS

A black Folsom [prison] inmate named W. Mills complained about this [the racial segregation of prison jobs in the 1940s] in a letter to the Governor's Investigating Committee in 1943. "Our servitude here is limited to inferior work. The only work that is given to Negroes is such as porter work, digging in the ground and breaking rock or whatever else the white inmates don't want to do." Among the most powerful testimonies offered to racial segregation in the California Prison System came from Wesley Robert Wells, a black prisoner who contested the conditions of prison Jim Crow, and whose death sentence for throwing an ashtray at a guard became a rallying point for civil rights and radical labor advocates in the 1950s. Wells explained that racism abounded in the California Prison System when he arrived there in 1928. "There was a lot of jimcrow [sic] stuff in Quentin in those days—just like there is now, and if you objected you were a marked number. . . . I was young and I held my head up. I didn't take no stuff from prisoner, stoolie, or guard. As a result, I got it bad. I got the strap, the rubber hose, the club, the curses" (Blue, 2012, pp. 66–67).

••• INTRODUCTION: THE GRAND REFORMS

In this chapter, we review the attributes of the seminal prison models of the early 1800s known as the Pennsylvania prison system (including the Walnut Street Jail and the Western and Eastern Pennsylvania prisons) and the New York prison system (including the Auburn and Sing Sing prisons). We include the eyewitness accounts of the operation of such systems during their early years as these are provided by Beaumont, Tocqueville, and Dix.

Out of these two systems, the rampart for all American prisons, and many European prisons, was constructed. As it became clear that neither prison model accomplished its multifaceted goals, and that its operation was so distorted and horrific for inmates, changes were gradually made as new reform efforts ensued. The Elmira Prison in New York was perhaps the most ambitious of these efforts during the latter part of the 1800s, which in turn set the stage for the later development of **correctional institutions**. Although the implementation of the reform ideals at Elmira is much critiqued, it certainly was much more humane than the convict leasing system that operated at that time in the South. The Folsom Prison in California during the 1940s, with its racial segregation, men laboring in rock quarries for lack of better work, and little programming (as described by inmate Wells), is representative of the Big Houses that preceded more concentrated efforts at rehabilitation that came with correctional institutions of the 1960s and 1970s. (More about these topics is presented later in the chapter.)

What does become crystal clear from this two-chapter review of the history of corrections in the United States is that there are several themes that run through it. One such theme, of course, is the cyclical need for reform itself, but to what purpose it is not always clear.

Correctional institutions: Institutions that carefully classify inmates into treatment programs that address their needs and perceived deficiencies. They are also intended to be places where inmates can earn "good time" and eventual parole.

Walnut Street Jail: Originally constructed in 1773 in Philadelphia and remodeled in 1790 into arguably the first full-fledged prison. The fee system was dropped, inmates were adequately clothed and fed regardless of their ability to pay, and they were separated by gender and offense. However, because of problems in implementation, by 1816 the prison was reportedly operating no better than before the reform and remodel.

••• EARLY MODERN PRISONS AND THE PENNSYLVANIA AND NEW YORK MODELS

THE WALNUT STREET JAIL

The **Walnut Street Jail** was originally constructed in 1773 in Philadelphia and operated as a typical local jail of the time: holding pretrial detainees and minor offenders; failing to separate by gender, age, or offense; using the fee system, which penalized the poor and led to the near starvation of some; and offering better accommodations and even access to liquor and sex to those who could pay for it (Zupan, 1991). It was remodeled in 1790, however, and reconceptualized so that many correctional scholars, but not all, regard it as the first prison.

The remodeled cell house was of frame construction and was built for the inmates of the "prison" section of the jail, with a separate cell for each inmate. Based on the reforms that Howard (and later Bentham and Fry) had envisioned for English and European jails, several reforms were instituted in this prison; the fee system was dropped, inmates were adequately clothed and fed regardless of their ability to pay, and they were separated by gender and offense. Children were not incarcerated in the prison, and debtors were separated from convicted felons. Although inmates were to live in isolated cells (to avoid "contaminating" each other), some work requirements brought them together. In addition, medical care was provided and attendance at religious services was required. The availability of alcohol and access to members of the opposite sex and prostitutes were stopped.

The impetus for this philosophical change came from the reform efforts of the Philadelphia Society for Alleviating the Miseries of Public Prisons (or the Philadelphia Prison Society, currently known as the Pennsylvania Prison Society), led by *Benjamin Rush*, who was a physician, reformer, statesman, and signatory of the Declaration of Independence. Rush agitated for laws to improve the jail's conditions of confinement and a different belief about correctional institutions—namely, that they could be used to reform their inmates (Nagel, 1973; Roberts, 1997). Ideally, the Walnut Street Jail (prison) was to operate based on the religious

PHOTO 3.2: Drawing of the Walnut Street Jail (circa 1799).

beliefs of the Quakers, with their emphasis on the reflective study of the Bible and abhorrence of violence that was so prevalent in other correctional entities. In 1789, the General Assembly of Pennsylvania enacted legislation based on these recommendations and the Pennsylvania prison system was born (Nagel, 1973).

The Walnut Street Jail, as a prison, was also an entity with a philosophy of penitence that, it was hoped, would lead to reform and redemption. This philosophy was combined with an architectural arrangement shaped to facilitate it by ensuring that inmates were mostly in solitary cells. As Roberts (1997) aptly noted, the reason why the Walnut Street Jail's new wing was the first real prison, as opposed to the other prisons such as Newgate of Connecticut that preceded it or some of the early European prisons, was "because it carried out incarceration as punishment, implemented a rudimentary classification system, featured individual cells, and was intended to provide a place for offenders to do penance—hence the term 'penitentiary'" (p. 26).

But in reality, the Walnut Street Jail soon became crowded, reportedly housing four times its capacity. As Johnston (2010) noted, "At one point 30 to 40 inmates were sleeping on blankets on the floor of rooms [that were] 18 feet square" (p. 13). Moreover, the institutional industry buildings that provided work for inmates burned down, leading to idleness, and by 1816 the Walnut Street Jail (prison) was little different from what it had been before the reforms (Harris, 1973; Zupan, 1991).

As Beaumont and Tocqueville (1833/1964) commented in 1831, after visiting and analyzing several prisons and jails in the United States, the implementation of the Walnut Street Jail had "two principal faults: it corrupted by contamination [of] those who worked together. It corrupted by indolence, the individuals who were plunged into solitude" (p. 38).

NEWGATE PRISON—NEW YORK CITY

Yet another Newgate Prison, in New York City (1797), was modeled after the Walnut Street Jail prison (as were early prisons in Trenton, New Jersey [1798]; Richmond, Virginia [1800]; Charlestown, Massachusetts [1805]; and Baltimore, Maryland [1811]) and even improved on that model in some respects (Roberts, 1997). Thomas Eddy, the warden of Newgate, was a Quaker. The focus at the Newgate Prison in New York was on rehabilitation, religious redemption, and work programs to support prison upkeep; it did not use corporal punishment. The builders of Newgate even constructed a prison hospital and school for the inmates. Unfortunately, because of crowding, single celling for any but the most violent inmates was not possible, and a number of outbreaks of violence erupted (such as a riot in 1802).

THE PENNSYLVANIA PRISON MODEL (SEPARATE SYSTEM)

The Western Pennsylvania Prison (1821) was built in Pittsburgh, followed by the Eastern Pennsylvania Prison (1829) in Philadelphia, which was to replace the Walnut Street Jail prison (Nagel, 1973). The Western Pennsylvania Prison, built 8 years before the Eastern Pennsylvania Prison, is little remarked on or studied in comparison with Eastern. It was devised to operate in a solitary and separate fashion. Even labor was to be prohibited because it was thought that this might interfere with the ability of the criminal to reflect and feel remorse for his or her crime (Hirsch, 1992). Despite the lessons learned from the Auburn prison—namely, that complete separation without labor can be injurious to the person and expensive for the state to maintain (a point made by Tocqueville and Beaumont)—the Western Pennsylvania Prison was built to hold inmates in complete solitary confinement (hence the use of the term *separate system*), with no labor, for the full span of their sentence. However, as Beaumont and Tocqueville (1833/1964) remarked about the Western Pennsylvania Prison, reducing all communication, and thus contamination in the authors' view, was almost impossible at this prison:

> Each one was shut up, day and night in a cell, in which no labor was allowed to him. This solitude, which in principle was to be absolute, was not such in fact. The construction of this penitentiary is so defective, that it is very easy to hear in one cell what is going on in another; so that each prisoner found in the communication with his neighbor a daily recreation, i.e. an opportunity of inevitable corruption. As these criminals did not work, we may say that their sole occupation consisted in mutual corruption. This prison, therefore, was worse than even that of Walnut Street, because, owing to the communication with each other, the prisoners at Pittsburgh (Western Pennsylvania Prison) were as little occupied with their reformation, as those at Walnut Street. And while the latter indemnified society in a degree by the produce of their labor, the others spent their whole time in idleness, injurious to themselves and burdensome to the public treasury. (p. 44)

As a consequence of these problems of architecture and operation, the Western Pennsylvania Prison as a model was abandoned and the Eastern Pennsylvania Prison came to epitomize the "Pennsylvania System," as opposed to the "New York System," of building and operating prisons. At the Eastern Pennsylvania Prison, known as "Cherry Hill" for much of its 150 years of operation, the idea that inmates could be contaminated or corrupted by their fellow inmates was officially embraced.

Mike Graham/Flickr

PHOTO 3.2: The Eastern Pennsylvania Prison was the largest building in America during the 1820s. (Lithograph, circa 1855)

The Eastern Pennsylvania Prison was designed and built by the architect John Haviland, a relative newcomer from England. It cost three-quarters of a million dollars to build, which was an incredible expenditure for the time. It was the largest building in America during the 1820s (Alosi, 2008; Orland, 1975). The prison itself was huge, with seven massive stone spokes of cells radiating off of a central rotunda, as on a wheel. A 30-foot wall was constructed around the outside perimeter of the prison, thus physically and symbolically reinforcing the separation of the prison and its inhabitants

COMPARATIVE CORRECTIONS   The Pentonville Prison

Although most American prisons of the 19th century ended up copying the Auburn and Sing Sing (New York model) prisons in design and operation, the Pentonville Prison, opened in London, England, in 1842, was modeled on the Pennsylvania prisons (Ignatieff, 1978). Inmates were confined in their rather large cells for most of the day except for chapel (where they had their own solitary box) and recreation (where they had their own isolated yard). In their cells, inmates worked on crafts and at looms. As with the Pennsylvania prisons, at Pentonville silence was enforced and inmates were sent to solitary dungeon rooms for disobeying the rules. But also as with the Pennsylvania prisons, inmates devised ways to communicate between cells by tapping messages to each other at night. At first, as with the Pennsylvania prisons and initially with the Auburn Prison, inmates were confined completely to their cells for 18 months. However, as inmates experienced the predictable mental illnesses associated with this isolation, such periods were eventually reduced to 9 months for new inmates (Ignatieff, 1978).

from their community (Nagel, 1973). The cells were built large (15 by 7.5 feet with 12-foot ceilings), and those on the lowest tier had their own small outside exercise yard attached, so that inmates could do virtually everything in their cells (Harris, 1973; Orland, 1975). The cells had both hot water and flush toilets, reportedly the first public building in the country to have such amenities. There were 400 solitary cells in this prison (Orland, 1975). At first inmates were not to work, but that dictate was later changed and they were allowed to work in their cells (Harris, 1973). As Johnston (2010) explained,

> The solution to the problem of criminal contamination for the reformers was to be a regimen of near-total isolation and absolute separation of prisoners from one another, the use of numbers rather than names, and a program of work, vocational training, and religious instruction, all taking place within the inmate's individual cell. (p. 13)

The only contact inmates were to have with the outside was with the clergy and some vocational teachers: "The reading of the Scriptures would furnish the offender with the moral guidance necessary for reform" (Nagel, 1973, p. 7). They had no access to visitors, letters, or newspapers. Even their exercise yards were surrounded by a high stone fence. When they were brought into the prison and were taken for showers or to see the doctor, they needed to wear a mask or a draped hood so as to maintain their anonymity and to prevent them from figuring out a way to escape (Alosi, 2008). As to how else they could occupy their time, "They made shoes, wove and dyed cloth products, caned chairs, and rolled cigars. Those products were sold to defray prison costs" (Roberts, 1997, p. 33).

The stated purpose of the solitary confinement was to achieve reform or rehabilitation. Quakers believed that God resides in everyone, and for a person to reach God he or she must reflect. Silence is required for self-reflection, the Quakers thought. The Quakers also believed that because God was in everyone, all were equal and were deserving of respect (Alosi, 2008).

Solitary confinement as a practical matter remained in existence at the Eastern Penitentiary until after the Civil War, but it was not formally ended until 1913 (Alosi, 2008). When it was rigorously applied, there are indications that it drove some inmates insane. In fact, and tellingly, most of the European countries that copied the Eastern

ETHICAL ISSUE ?

What Would You Do?

You are a new pastor in the Eastern State Penitentiary when Charles Dickens, the celebrated English author, visits the prison in 1842. Your position is tenuous at the prison, and you have been told it is dependent on your meticulous adherence to the rule of silence for inmates. Although you are not a proponent of this kind of control of inmates, the warden has made it clear to you that your livelihood and that of your family (you have eight children) depend on your complete compliance. For some reason, Dickens chooses to visit inmate cells and observe them while they work making shoes or weaving. You have been instructed to report whether inmates speak or even look at Dickens (because they have been instructed not to do so under penalty of confinement in a segregation cell for months with only food and water). During the course of your rounds you note that Dickens routinely and secretively—presumably so as to protect inmates from punishment—attempts to engage inmates in conversation. In a few instances, you have overheard inmates whisper responses to his queries. You cannot be sure that a guard has not also observed this behavior and has seen you in the vicinity when it occurred. What would you do? Would you report the offense? Would you ask Dickens to stop speaking to inmates (or would you just ask for his autograph)?

Pennsylvania model and its architecture did not isolate the inmates for this reason. Moreover, at a minimum, solitary confinement debilitated people by making them incapable of dealing with other people. For instance, the wardens' journals for the Eastern Pennsylvania Prison during the early years indicate that it was not uncommon for an inmate to be released and then ask to be reinstated at Eastern because he or she did not know how to live freely. Some inmates, once released, would actually sit on the curb outside the prison because they said they no longer understood the outside world or how to function in it (Alosi, 2008).

Although the separation of inmates under the Pennsylvania prison system was to be complete, there are indications that it was not. In testimony before a special investigation by a joint committee of the houses of the Pennsylvania Legislature in 1834 (before the whole prison was even completed), it was noted that a number of male and female inmates (there were a small number of female inmates housed separately at the Eastern Pennsylvania Prison) were used for maintenance, cleaning, and cooking at the facility and roamed freely around it, speaking and interacting with each other and staff (Johnston, 2010). Moreover, there were indications from this testimony that inmates were tortured to maintain discipline; one prisoner had died of blood loss from the iron gag put in his mouth, and another went insane after buckets of cold water were poured on his head repeatedly. It was alleged that food and supplies meant for inmates were given to guards or community members by the prison cook (who was a wife of one of the guards). There were also indications of the use and abuse of alcohol by staff and inmates and of sexual improprieties involving the warden and his clerk, some male inmates, and the female cook. Although ultimately charges against the warden and his clerk related to these improprieties were dropped, the cook was blamed and the guards who testified about the scandal (the whistleblowers) were fired.

In addition to these problems of implementation at the Eastern Pennsylvania Prison, a debate raged among prison experts regarding the value of separation. As a result of the experiment with the Western Pennsylvania Prison and the early use of the Eastern prison and the Auburn prison (which we describe further on), the idea of "total separation" was under siege. As mentioned in the foregoing, it was observed that for those truly subjected to it, solitary confinement and separation caused serious psychological problems for some inmates. Despite these problems, about 300 prisons worldwide copied the Eastern Pennsylvania model, and tens of thousands of men and women did time there, including the 1920s gangster Al Capone. It was a famous prison worldwide because of its philosophy, its architecture, and its huge size. It even became a tourist attraction during the 19th century to the extent that famous English author Charles Dickens noted it as one of the two sights he wanted to see when visiting the United States (the other was Niagara Falls) (Alosi, 2008). It turned out, after a visit of a few hours and talking to inmates, keepers, and the warden, that Dickens was far from impressed with its operation (see In Focus 3.1).

AUBURN, SING SING, AND THE NEW YORK (CONGREGATE) SYSTEM

The New York model for imprisonment was preferred over the Pennsylvania system, and copied extensively by American prison builders, in part because it disavowed the solitary confinement that Dickens and others lamented in the Pennsylvania prisons. Beaumont and Tocqueville (1833/1964) commented that the use of solitary confinement as normal practice for all inmates was ended at Auburn because it drove inmates insane. But it is not that the builders and planners for the Auburn Prison in New York learned from the Pennsylvania system; rather, they learned from their own dalliance with solitary confinement. At first, the inmates of Auburn were housed in solitary confinement in their cells, a practice that was abandoned by 1822 because it led to mental anguish and insanity for inmates and it hampered the efficient production of goods that can be done only in the congregate. By 1822, a total of 5 prisoners had died, 1 had gone insane, and the remaining 26 were pardoned by the governor of New York because their mental faculties had deteriorated to such a great extent (Harris, 1973, p. 73). The governor ordered that inmates be allowed to leave their cells and work during the day, and a legislative committee in 1824 recommended the repeal of the solitary confinement laws (Harris, 1973).

Beaumont and Tocqueville (1833/1964) supported the practice of maintaining the solitude of inmates at night and their silence during the day as they worked because they believed, along with the Quakers of Pennsylvania, that solitude and silence led to reflection and reformation and also reduced cross-contamination of inmates. As to labor, they claimed, "It fatigues the body and relieves the soul," along with supplementing the income of the state to support the prison (p. 57).

The Auburn (New York) Prison cornerstone was laid in 1816. It received its first inmates in 1817, but it was not finished until 1819 (Harris, 1973). *Elam Lynds* (1784–1855), a strict disciplinarian and former army captain, was its first warden in 1821. Auburn has been in existence ever since (202 years at the time of this writing in 2017), although its name changed to the Auburn Correctional Institution in 1970.

Auburn's cells were built back to back with corridors on each side. The prison has always had a Gothic appearance, and its elaborate front and massive walls have been maintained up until today, with towers and a fortress facade.

The Auburn Prison has a storied history that spans the virtual beginning of prisons in the United States to the present day. As was already noted, Beaumont and Tocqueville visited Auburn and recommended it over the Pennsylvania prisons. Auburn opened with a solitary confinement system, which was very quickly abandoned, and replaced it with the congregate,

PHOTO 3.4: Auburn Prison, built in 1816, is still in operation today, although its name has changed to the Auburn Correctional Institution.

PHOTO 3.5: Sing Sing Prison, modeled after the Auburn Prison, was built by inmates from Auburn Prison in 1825.

IN FOCUS 3.1

Charles Dickens's Impressions of the Eastern Pennsylvania Prison and the Silent System in 1842

In its intention, I am well convinced that it is kind, humane, and meant for reformation; but I am persuaded that those who devised this system of Prison Discipline, and those benevolent gentlemen who carry it into execution, do not know what it is that they are doing. I believe that very few men are capable of estimating the immense amount of torture and agony which this dreadful punishment, prolonged for years, inflicts upon the sufferers; and in guessing at it myself, and in reasoning from what I have seen written upon their faces, and what to my certain knowledge they feel within, I am only the more convinced that there is a depth of terrible endurance in it which none but the sufferers themselves can fathom, and which no man has a right to inflict upon his fellow-creature. I hold this slow and daily tampering with the mysteries of the brain, to be immeasurably worse than any torture of the body: and because its ghastly signs and tokens are not so palpable to the eye and sense of touch as scars upon the flesh; because its wounds are not upon the surface, and it extorts few cries that human ears can hear; therefore I the more denounce it, as a secret punishment which slumbering humanity is not roused up to stay.

I was accompanied to this prison by two gentlemen officially connected with its management, and passed the day in going from cell to cell, and talking with the inmates. Every facility was afforded me, that the utmost courtesy could suggest. Nothing was concealed or hidden from my view, and every piece of information that I sought, was openly and frankly given. The perfect order of the building cannot be praised too highly, and of the excellent motives of all who are immediately concerned in the administration of the system, there can be no kind of question. . . .

Standing at the central point, and looking down these dreary passages, the dull repose and quiet that prevails, is awful. Occasionally, there is a drowsy sound from some lone weaver's shuttle, or shoemaker's last, but it is stifled by the thick walls and heavy dungeon-door, and only serves to make the general stillness more profound. Over the head and face of every prisoner who comes into this melancholy house, a black hood is drawn; and in this dark

PHOTO 3.3: Charles Dickens

shroud, an emblem of the curtain dropped between him and the living world, he is led to the cell from which he never again comes forth, until his whole term of imprisonment has expired. He never hears of wife and children; home or friends; the life or death of any single creature. He sees the prison-officers, but with that exception he never looks upon a human countenance, or hears a human voice. He is a man buried alive; to be dug out in the slow round of years; and in the mean time dead to everything but torturing anxieties and horrible despair. . . .

My firm conviction is that, independent of the mental anguish it occasions—an anguish so acute and so tremendous, that all imagination of it must fall far short of the reality—it wears the mind into a morbid state, which renders it unfit for the rough contact and busy action of the world. It is my fixed opinion that those who have undergone this punishment, MUST pass into society again morally unhealthy and diseased. (Dickens, 1842, n.p.)

but silent, system, which formally lasted until the beginning of the 20th century. It was the progenitor of such widely adopted practices as the "lockstep" walk for inmates, the striped prison uniforms and the classification system that went hand in hand with them, and the well-known ball and chain. Warden Lynds believed in strict obedience on the part of inmates and the use of the whip by staff to ensure it (Clear et al., 2011). Under his regime, inmates were forbidden to talk to or even glance at each other during work and meals. Solitary confinement and flogging were used for punishing and controlling inmates. As noted in the foregoing, except for a few years at the beginning of Auburn's history, inmates were single-celled at night and the cells were quite small, even coffin-like (7 × 7 × 3.5 feet), and during the day the inmates worked together, but silently, in factories and shops (Roberts, 1997).

The small cells like those at Auburn Prison were cheaper to build, and prisons could house more inmates in the same amount of space than prisons with larger cells. In addition, congregate work allowed for the more efficient production of more products, and thus more profit could be made (Roberts, 1997). However, putting all of these inmates together in one place presented some difficulties in terms of control and management. This is why the control techniques represented by the use of the lash, solitary confinement, and marching in lockstep and the requirement of silence came into play. As Roberts (1997) noted, "Ironically, whereas the penitentiary concept was developed as a humane alternative to corporal punishment, corporal punishment returned as a device to manage inmates in penitentiaries based on the Auburn System" (p. 44).

The Sing Sing Prison was modeled after the Auburn Prison architecturally in that the cells were small and there were congregate areas for group work by inmates, but its cell blocks were tiered and very long. Inmate management and operations exactly mirrored the Auburn protocols. In fact, Sing Sing was built by Auburn inmates under the supervision of Auburn's Warden Lynds.

The prison was built on the Hudson River, near the town of Sing Sing and Mount Pleasant (and for many years the prison was referred to as Mount Pleasant), from locally quarried stone. Products produced at the prison could be transported to local towns via the river. Inmates sent there would refer to it as being sent "up the river" because it is 30 miles north of New York City (Conover, 2001). Its name derives from the Indian phrase *Sint Sinks,* which came from the older term *Ossine Ossine* and ironically means "stone upon stone" (Lawes, 1932, p. 68).

Warden Lynds picked 100 men from the Auburn Prison to build Sing Sing Prison in 1825. The story of its construction, in silence, as relayed by Lewis Lawes, a later warden of Sing Sing, goes like this:

> Captain Lynds, then the foremost penologist of the day, was insistent, to the point of hysteria, on silence as the backbone of prison administration. "It is the duty of convicts to preserve an unbroken silence," was the first rule he laid down. "They are not to exchange a word with each other under any pretense whatever; not to communicate any intelligence to each other in writing. They are not to exchange looks, wink, laugh, or motion to each other. They must not sing, whistle, dance, run, jump, or do anything which has a tendency in the least degree to disturb the harmony or contravene to disturb the rules and regulations of the prison." . . . The sea gulls in the broad river, darting in large flocks here and there on the water, chirped raucously at these strange creatures sweating at their tasks in silence. Stone upon stone. (Lawes, 1932, pp. 72–73)

Once Sing Sing Prison was constructed, it was noticed that with some effort inmates could communicate between the closely aligned cells, but nothing was done to rebuild the cells. Moreover, because the inmates from the old New York Newgate Prison were moved to Sing Sing right away, as were additional inmates from Auburn Prison, the prison was full at 800 inmates by 1830 (Lawes, 1932).

Prison labor during the early years of prisons (before the Civil War) was contract labor and subject to abuse. Contractors would pay a set amount for inmates' labor and then would make sure they got the most work out of them, cutting costs where they could and bribing wardens and keepers when they needed to do so. Eventually, such contracts were ended because the cheap labor made prison-produced goods too competitive with products made by free workers (Conover, 2001).

When one thinks about old prisons, those castle-like fortress prisons, the image of Auburn and Sing Sing inmates and prisons come to mind, even unknowingly. So many U.S. prisons copied the New York design and operation of these prisons that even if one is not thinking of Auburn or Sing Sing per se, one is likely imagining a copy of them. By the time Beaumont and Tocqueville (1833/1964) visited the United States in 1831, they reported that the Auburn Prison had already been copied in prisons built in Massachusetts, Maryland, Tennessee, Kentucky, Maine, and Vermont.

It was not just the physical structure or the silent, but congregate, inmate management that was copied from Auburn and Sing Sing prisons; it was the inmate discipline system as well. Orland (1975) summarized the Connecticut prison regulations of the 1830s, which were borrowed from the New York model:

> Inmates were exhorted to be "industrious, submissive, and obedient"; to "labor diligently in silence"; they were forbidden to "write or receive a letter" or to communicate in any manner "with or to persons" without the warden's permission; they were prohibited from engaging in conversation "with another prisoner" without permission or to "speak to, or look at, visitors." (p. 26)

••• EARLY PRISONS AND JAILS NOT REFORMED

Lest one be left with the impression that all prisons and jails during the early 1800s in America were reformed, we should emphasize that this was not the case. Beaumont and Tocqueville (1833/1964) commented, for instance, on the fact that the New Jersey prisons, right across the river from the reformist New York system, were vice ridden and that Ohio prisons, although ruled by a humanitarian law, were "barbarous," with half of the inmates in irons and "the rest plunged into an infected dungeon" (p. 49). But in New Orleans, Louisiana, they found the worst, with inmates incarcerated with hogs. "In locking up criminals, nobody thinks of rendering them better, but only of taming their malice; they are put in chains like ferocious beasts; and instead of being corrected, they are rendered brutal" (p. 49).

As to jails, Beaumont and Tocqueville (1833/1964) noticed no reforms at all. Inmates who were presumed innocent, or if guilty had generally committed a much less serious offense than those sent to prison, were incarcerated in facilities far worse in construction and operation than prisons even in states where prison reform had occurred. During colonial times, inmates in American jails were kept in house-like facilities and were allowed much more freedom, albeit with few amenities that they did not pay for themselves. Dix (1843/1967) described many jails, particularly those that did not separate inmates, as a "free school of vice." However, as the institutionalization movement began for prisons, jails copied their large locked-up and controlled atmosphere without any philosophy of reform to guide their construction or operation (Goldfarb, 1975). By mid-century, some jails had employed the silent or separate systems popular in prisons, but most were merely congregate and poorly managed holding facilities (Dix, 1843/1967). Such facilities on the East Coast by the latter quarter of the 1800s were old, crowded, and full of the "corruptions" that the new prisons were trying to prevent (Goldfarb, 1975). In the end, Beaumont and Tocqueville (1833/1964) blamed the lack of reform of prisons in some states, and the failure to reform jails hardly at all, on the fact that there were independent state and local governments that handled crime and criminals differently: "These shocking contradictions proceed chiefly from the want of unison in the various parts of government in the United States" (p. 49).

PRISONS: "THE SHAME OF ANOTHER GENERATION"

The creation of prisons was a grand reform promoted by principled people who were appalled at the brutality of discipline wielded against those in their communities. Prisons were an exciting development supported by Enlightenment ideals of humanity and the promise of reformation. They were developed over centuries, in fits and starts, and had their genesis in other modes of depriving people of liberty (e.g., galley slavery, transportation, jails, bridewells, houses of corrections, early versions of prisons), but they were meant to be much better—so much better—than these.

It is not clear whether the problems arose for prisons in their implementation or in their basic conceptualization. In societies where the poor and dispossessed exist among institutions in which law and practice serve to maintain their status, it is no wonder that prisons, as a social institution that reflects the values and beliefs of that society, would serve to reinforce this status. All indications are that most prisons, even those that were lauded as the most progressive during an earlier age of reform, were by the mid-19th century regarded as violent and degrading places for their inmates and staff.

IN FOCUS 3.2

Lewis E. Lawes's Observations About Sing Sing History and Discipline

In 1920, Lawes began his tenure as Sing Sing Prison warden and later commented on how the severity of prison discipline had waxed and waned at this prison over the years. At first it was very severe, with the use of the "cat-of-nine-tails" whip. "It was made of long strips of leather, attached to a stout wooden handle, and was not infrequently wired at the tips. The 'cat' preferred its victim barebacked" (Lawes, 1932, pp. 74–75). Under a warden in 1840, however, the cat was retired and inmates could have a few visits and letters. A Sunday school and library were constructed, and the warden walked among the men. Within a few years, however, a new warden was appointed with a new political party in power, and all of the reforms were abandoned and the cat was resurrected. A few years later, when a reportedly insane inmate was literally whipped to death, the public was outraged and the use of the lash declined for men and was prohibited for women. The prison discipline was consequently softened, and this cycle continued for the rest of the 1800s, from severe to soft discipline. Lawes maintained, after reviewing all of the wardens' reports since the opening of Sing Sing, that escapes were highest during times of severe punishment despite the risks inmates took should they be caught.

He also observed that the prison had problems with management and control in other ways, noting that by 1845 an outside accountant found that the prison held 20 fewer female inmates and 33 fewer male inmates than it had officially on the books, that $32,000 was missing, and that there was no explanation as to where these people were or where the money had gone (Lawes, 1932, p. 82). The warden's and other official reports indicated that inmates were poorly fed and that diseases were rampant at Sing Sing. By 1859, some of Sing Sing's small cells became doubles to accommodate the overcrowding, and the punishments got worse. By 1904, the official report was that the prison was in a disgraceful condition. Lawes (1932) wrote, "Such was the Sing Sing of the Nineteenth Century. A hopeless, oppressive, barren spot. Escapes were frequent, attempts at escape almost daily occurrences. Suicides were common" (p. 88).

DOROTHEA DIX'S EVALUATION OF PRISONS AND JAILS

Dorothea Dix was a humanitarian, a teacher, and a penal and insane asylum reformer who, after 4 years of studying prisons, jails, and almshouses in northeastern and midwestern states, wrote the book *Remarks on Prisons and Prison Discipline in the United States* in 1843 (revised in 1845 and reprinted in 1967). The data for her book were assembled from multiple observations at prisons; conversations and correspondence with staff, wardens, and inmates in prisons; and a review of prisons' annual reports.

Dix tended to prefer the Pennsylvania model over the New York model because she thought inmates benefited from separation from others. However, she forcefully argued that both prison models that had promised so much in terms of reform for inmates were in fact abject failures in that regard. She found these and most prisons to be understaffed and overcrowded and with inept leadership that changed much too often. She noted that at Sing Sing Prison about 1,200 lashes, using the cat-of-nine-tails whip, were administered every month to about 200 men, an amount she thought was too severe even though she believed the use of the lash, especially in understaffed and overcrowded prisons like Sing Sing and Auburn, was necessary to maintain order (Dix, 1843/1967). In contrast, at the Eastern Penitentiary she commented that punishments included mostly solitary confinement in darkened cells, which to her appeared to lead to changed behavior of recalcitrant inmates. Dix (1843/1967) argued that, as far as inmate discipline goes, "Man is not made better by being degraded; he is seldom restrained from crime by harsh measures" (p. 4).

Thus, Dix argued against the long sentences for minor offenses that she found in prisons of the day (e.g., Richmond, Virginia; Columbus, Ohio; Concord, Massachusetts; Providence, Rhode Island) and the disparity in sentencing from place to place. She thought that such sentences not only were unjust but also led to insubordination by inmates and staff who recognized the arbitrary nature of the justice system. On the other hand, in her study of prisons, she found that the pardoning power was used too often, and this again led, she thought, to less trust in the just and fair nature of the system and to insubordination of its inmates.

PHOTO 3.6: Dorothea Dix was a humanitarian, a teacher, and a penal and insane asylum reformer who, after 4 years of study of prisons, jails, and almshouses in northeastern and midwestern states, wrote the book *Remarks on Prisons and Prison Discipline in the United States* in 1843.

Dix also remarked on the quality and availability of food and water for inmates in early correctional facilities. She found the food to be adequate in most places except Sing Sing, where there was no place to dine at the time of the second edition of her book (1845), and the water to be inadequate in most places except the Pennsylvania prisons, where it was piped into all of the cells. Her comments on the health, heating, clothing, cleanliness, and sanity of inmates were also detailed by institution and indicated that although there were recurrent problems with these issues in prisons of the time, some prisons (e.g., Eastern Penitentiary) did more than others to alleviate miseries by changing the diet, providing adequate clothing, and making warm water for washing available to inmates.

She did not find that more inmates were deemed "insane" in Pennsylvania-modeled prisons based on her data, or at least not more than one might expect, even in the Pennsylvania prisons. Given the history of the separate system being linked to insanity, she was sensitive to this topic. However, by 1845, when she published the second edition of her book, inmates at Eastern Penitentiary were not as "separate" from others as they had been, both formally and informally, and this might explain the relative paucity of insanity cases in her data. By this time, inmates were allowed to speak to their keepers (guards) and to attend church and school.

Dix also explored the moral and religious instruction provided at the several state prisons and county prisons (jails) that she visited. Except for the Eastern Penitentiary, she found all of them to be deficient in this respect and found that the provisions of such services were severely lacking in the jails.

Dix studied a peculiar practice of the early prisons—that of allowing visitors to pay to be spectators at the prisons. Adults were generally charged 25 cents and children were charged half price in some facilities. In Auburn in 1842, the prison made $1,692.75 from visitors; in Columbus in 1844, the prison made $1,038.78; and Dix (1843/1967) documented five other prisons that allowed the same practice, one she thought should be "dispensed with" because it "would not aid the moral and reforming influences of the prisons" (p. 43). Of course, this fascination with watching inmates continues today with reality-based television shows filmed in prisons and jails.

Finally, Dix (1843/1967) tried to explore the idea of recidivism or, as she termed it, reform. She wanted to know how many inmates leave their prison and are reformed or "betake themselves to industrious habits, and an honest calling; who, in place of vices, practice virtues; who, instead of being addicted to crime, are observed to govern their passions, and abstain from all injury to others" (p. 66). When she asked about how many inmates were reformed, she found that none of the prisons had records in that regard but that wardens tended to think most inmates were reformed because they did not return to those particular prisons. She was doubtful that this failure of inmates to return to the same prisons should be regarded as an indication of low recidivism because she suspected that inmates got out, changed their names, and dispersed across the countryside where they could return to crime undetected. In most respects, in all of these areas, she concluded from her study of several prisons that the Eastern Penitentiary was far superior to most prisons and that the Sing Sing Prison was far inferior, but she thought even the Eastern Penitentiary was far from perfect. Rather, she called for more focus on the morals and education of the young and on preventing crime as a means of improving prisons and reducing their use—a call that sounds very familiar today.

THE FAILURE OF REFORM IS NOTED

Dix's writings foretold the difficulties of implementing real change even if the proposal is well intentioned. Simply put, prisons during the latter half of the 19th century were no longer regarded as places of reform. As Rothman (1980) stated,

> Every observer of American prisons and asylums in the closing decades of the nineteenth century recognized that the pride of one generation had become the shame of another. The institutions that had been intended to exemplify the humanitarian advances of republican government were not merely inadequate to the ideal, but were actually an embarrassment and a rebuke. Failure to do good was one thing; a proclivity to do harm quite another—and yet the evidence was incontrovertible that brutality and corruption were endemic to the institutions. (p. 17)

Newspapers and state investigatory commissions by the mid-19th century were documenting the deficiencies of state prisons. Instead of the relatively controlled atmosphere of the Pennsylvania and Auburn prisons of the 1830s, there was a great deal of laxity and brutality (Rothman, 1980). Prisons were overcrowded and understaffed, and the presence of prison contractors led to corruption such as paying off wardens to look the other way as inmate labor was exploited; alternatively, the wardens and staff used inmates and their labor for their own illegal ends. At Sing Sing Prison, an 1870 investigation found that inmates were largely unsupervised, had access to contraband, and were unoccupied for most of their sentences (Rothman, 1980).

ETHICAL ISSUE **?**

What Would You Do?

You are Dorothea Dix, the American humanitarian and penal and insane asylum reformer, and you are visiting prisons and jails in the United States during the 1840s. The task you have set for yourself is to document what appears to be working, and what does not, in the facilities you visit. You pride yourself on maintaining high moral standards. You are not opposed to the use of the lash in some circumstances, but you think its overuse is counterproductive in that it turns men "into brutes" rather than reforming them. During the course of your visit to Sing Sing Prison, where the lash is used for the smallest offenses, you notice that an emaciated inmate steals a piece of bread off a tray. The warden, although known for his harsh treatment of inmates, has treated you with every courtesy and you know that he would expect you to report this offense. What would you do and why? Do you think that your decision is colored by the time period in which you live? Why or why not?

A lack of space and staff was likely to lead to more severe punishments to deter misbehavior. Therefore, when their keepers did pay attention to inmates, it might be to administer brutal, medieval-style punishments where inmates were hung by their wrists or their thumbs (the "pulley"), were forced to wear the iron cap or cage on the head that weighed 6 to 8 pounds, or were tied up by their hands so high behind them that they needed to "stand" on their toes, or where the guards resorted to the "lash and paddle" (Rothman, 1980, p. 19). Solitary confinement in a dark, dungeon-like cell was popular, too, especially with little sustenance (water and bread) and a bucket. A Kansas prison employed the "water crib":

> The inmate was placed in a coffin-like box, six and one-half feet long, thirty inches wide, and three feet deep, his face down and his hands handcuffed behind his back. A water hose was then turned on, slowly filling the crib. The resulting effect of this procedure was the sensation of slowly drowning, with the inmate struggling to keep his head up above the rising water line. (Rothman, 1980, p. 20)

••• THE RENEWED PROMISE OF REFORM

THE 1870 AMERICAN PRISON CONGRESS

The first major prison reform came about 50 years after the first New York and Pennsylvania prisons were built, and doubtless as a result of all those calls for change. The 1870 American Prison Congress was held in Cincinnati, Ohio, with the express purpose of trying to recapture some of the idealism promised with the creation of prisons (Rothman, 1980). Despite their promises of reform and attempts at preventing "contamination," the early prisons had become, by the 1860s, warehouses without hope or resources. All of the themes mentioned at the beginning of Chapter 2—save the desire for reform, and that was remedied with the next round of reforms to follow the Congress—applied to the operation of the 19th-century prisons; they were overcrowded, underfunded, brutal facilities where too many inmates would spend time doing little that was productive or likely to prepare them to reintegrate into the larger community.

Appropriately enough, then, the Declaration of Principles that emerged from the Prison Congress of 1870 was nothing short of revolutionary at the time and provided a blueprint for prisons we see today (Rothman, 1980). Some of those principles were concerned with the grand purposes of prisons—to achieve reform—while others were related to their day-to-day operation (e.g., training staff, eliminating contract labor, treating the insane) (American Correctional Association, 1983).

ELMIRA

As a result of these principles, a spirit of reform in corrections again spurred action, and the **Elmira Reformatory** was founded in 1876 in New York (Rothman, 1980). The reformatory would encompass all of the rehabilitation focus and graduated reward system (termed the **marks system**, as in if one behaves it is possible to earn marks that in turn entitle one to privileges). The marks system, as mentioned in Chapter 2, was practiced by Maconochie, and later by Crofton in Irish prisons, and was promoted by reformers. Elmira was supposed to hire educated and trained staff and to maintain uncrowded facilities (Orland, 1975).

Zebulon Brockway was appointed to head the reformatory, and he was intent on using the ideas of Maconochie and Crofton to create a "model" prison (Harris, 1973, p. 85). He persuaded the New York legislature to pass a bill creating the indeterminate sentence, which would be administered by a "board" rather than the courts. He planned on the reformatory handling only younger men (ages 16–30 years) because he expected that they might be more amenable to change. He planned to create a college at Elmira that would educate inmates from elementary school through college. He also sought to create an industrial training school that would equip inmates with technical abilities. In addition, he focused on the physical training of inmates, including much marching but also the use of massages and steam baths (Harris, 1973). The marks system had a three-pronged purpose: to discipline, to encourage reform, and to justify "good time" in order to reduce the sentence of the offender. Brockway did not want to resort to the use of the lash.

Much lauded around the world and visited by dignitaries, the Elmira Reformatory, and Brockway's management of it, led to the creation of good time, the indeterminate sentence (defined in Chapter 5), a focus on programming to address inmate deficiencies, and the promotion of probation and parole. "After Brockway, specialized treatment, classification of prisoners, social rehabilitation and self-government of one sort or another were introduced into every level of the corrections system" (Harris, 1973, pp. 86–87).

Unfortunately, and as before, this attempt at reform was thwarted when the funding was not always forthcoming, and the inmates did not conform as expected. The staff, who were not the educated and trained professionals that Brockway had envisioned, soon resorted to violence to keep control. In fact, Brockway administered the lash himself on many occasions (Rothman, 1980). It should not be forgotten, however, that even on its worst day the Elmira prison was likely no worse, and probably much more humane, than were the old Auburn and Sing Sing prisons.

THE CREATION OF PROBATION AND PAROLE

As indicated in Chapters 7 and 10, probation and parole were developed during the first half of the 19th century, and their use spread widely across the United States during the early 20th century. The idea behind both was that programming and assistance in the community, while supervising the offender, could result in the reduction in the use of incarceration and help the offender to transition more smoothly back into the community. Doubtless, the intent was good, but the execution of this reform was less than satisfactory; however, it did represent an improvement over the correctional practices that preceded it (Rothman, 1980). For a full discussion of the history and current operation of probation and parole, or community corrections, see Chapters 7 and 10.

Elmira Reformatory: Founded in 1876 in New York as a model prison in response to calls for the reform of prisons from an earlier era, it aimed to encompass all of the rehabilitation focus and graduated reward system for which reformers were agitating.

Marks system: A graduated reward system for prisons in which if one behaves it is possible to earn "marks" that in turn entitle one to privileges.

••• SOUTHERN AND NORTHERN PRISONS, THE CONTRACT AND LEASE SYSTEMS, AND INDUSTRIAL PRISONS

Southern prisons, because of the institution of slavery, developed on a different trajectory from that of other prisons. As indicated by Young's (2001) research, prisons were little used before the Civil War. In agriculturally based societies, labor is prized and needed in the fields, particularly slave labor, and that served as a basis for the southern economy. Once slavery was abolished with the Thirteenth Amendment to the Constitution, southern states during the Reconstruction period following the Civil War began incarcerating more people, particularly ex-slaves, and recreating a slave society in the corrections system. As Oshinsky (1996) documented for Mississippi prisons, blacks were picked up and imprisoned for relatively minor offenses and forced to work like slaves on prison plantations or on plantations of southern farmers.

The northern and midwestern states, and later the western states, built prisons somewhat on the Auburn model, but for the most part they abandoned the attempt to completely silence inmates. It was no longer emphasized because maintaining such silence required a large staff and constant vigilance, and these were usually not available in the under-staffed and overcrowded facilities (J. Jacobs, 1977). Inmates in such prisons worked in larger groups under private or public employers, and order was maintained with the lash or other innovations in discipline, as discussed in Chapter 2 (see also Lawes [1932] regarding the management of Sing Sing Prison). Although there was no pretense of high-minded reform going on in these prisons, their conditions and the accommodations of inmates were thought to be far superior to those provided in southern prisons of the time. Conditions under both the **contract and lease systems** could be horrible, but they were likely worse under the southern lease system, where contractors were often responsible for both housing and feeding inmates. Such contractors had little incentive for feeding or taking care of inmates because the supply of labor from the prison was almost inexhaustible.

INDUSTRIAL PRISONS

The contract system morphed into industrial prisons during the latter part of the 19th century and first few decades of the 20th century in several states. Inmates were employed either by outside contractors or by the state to engage in the large-scale production of goods for sale in the open market or to produce goods for the state itself. Eventually, as the strength of unions increased, and particularly as the Depression struck in 1930, the sale of cheap, prison-made goods was restricted by several state and federal laws, limiting the production of goods in prisons to just products that the state or nonprofits might be able to use.

Contract and lease systems: Systems devised to use inmates' labor, which was leased by prisons to farmers or other contractors.

Stateville Prison: Built in Illinois as a panopticon in 1925 in reaction to the deplorable conditions of the old Joliet prison built in 1860.

••• CORRECTIONAL INSTITUTIONS OR WAREHOUSE PRISONS?

In James Jacobs's classic book *Stateville: The Penitentiary in Mass Society*, the author describes the operation of and environmental influences on the **Stateville Prison** in Illinois (Jacobs, 1977). It was built as a panopticon in 1925 in reaction to the deplorable conditions of the old Joliet prison built in 1860. Joliet was overcrowded, and the Stateville Prison was also built to relieve that overcrowding, but by 1935 Stateville itself was full at 4,000 inmates and the population at Joliet had not been reduced at all.

In a reformist state such as Illinois at the time (the juvenile court reform began there, and it was one of the first states to initiate civil service reforms), Stateville Prison was conceived as a place where inmates would be carefully classified into treatment programs that would address their needs and perceived deficiencies and where inmates could earn good time and eventual parole. Inmates were believed to be "sick," and a treatment regimen provided by the prison would address that sickness and hopefully "cure" them so that they might become productive members of society. Thus, correctional institutions would use the "medical model" to treat inmates. Even though it was built as a maximum-security prison, Stateville's conception fit the definition of a correctional institution, where inmates were not to be merely warehoused but rather to be corrected and treated. However, although inmates in the Illinois system were classified and good time was available for those who adhered to the rules, there was little programming available, the prison was crowded, it was understaffed, and the staff who were employed were ill trained (J. Jacobs, 1977). Moreover, the first 10 years of operation were filled with disorganized management and violent attacks on staff and inmates in a prison controlled by Irish and Italian gangs.

In essence, and despite the intent to create a correctional institution, Stateville became what is termed a **Big House prison**. These facilities, according to Irwin (2005), are fortress stone or concrete prisons, usually maximum security, whose attributes include "isolation, routine, and monotony" (p. 32). Strict security and rule enforcement, at least formally, and a regimentation in schedule are other hallmarks of such facilities. The **convict code**, or the rules that inmates live by vis-à-vis the institution and staff, is clear-cut: "1. Do not inform; 2. Do not openly interact or cooperate with the guards or the administration; 3. Do your own time" (p. 33).

The next 25 years of the Stateville Prison (1936–1961) were marked by the authoritarian control of one warden (Joseph Ragen), the isolation of staff and inmates from the larger world, strict formal rule enforcement, and informal corruption of those rules. Some of the trappings of a correctional institution were present (i.e., good time for good behavior and parole), but for the most part inmates were merely warehoused and double- or triple-celled. Those inmates who were favored by staff and the warden were given better housing and a whole array of privileges. Corruption seethed under the surface with the relaxation of rules for tougher inmates, black market trade by both staff and inmates, and the warden turning his head when beatings of inmates by staff occurred. By the mid-1950s, Ragen, who had been appointed director of corrections for the state in 1941, was redefining its purpose as one of rehabilitation (J. Jacobs, 1977). So that his prisons would appear to be at the forefront of the move to a rehabilitative focus, the numbers of inmates in school and in vocational programming did increase, although staff, under the guise of providing vocational training, were able to use the inmate labor to repair their appliances and cars for free.

By the 1960s, Stateville and other Illinois prisons, much like those in the rest of the country, were under pressure internally by more career-oriented professionals interested in management of prisons and externally by greater racial consciousness and an emerging inmates' rights movement. Eventually, such prisons needed to open their doors to other ideas and perspectives, and sometimes the press, as well as court-mandated legal review of their practices (J. Jacobs, 1977).

The 1960s through the 1990s saw a boom in prison building across the country, most of the medium- and minimum-security variety, which were more likely to classify inmates according to both security and treatment needs, institute rehabilitative programming (although the amount and value of this have varied from state to state and by time period), and employ the use of good time and parole (except in those states that abolished

Medical model: Rehabilitation model that assumes criminals are sick and need treatment.

Big House prisons: Fortress stone or concrete prisons, usually maximum security, whose attributes include "isolation, routine, and monotony." Strict security and rule enforcement, at least formally, and a regimented schedule are other hallmarks of such facilities.

Convict code: Informal rules that inmates live by vis-à-vis the institution and staff.

it) as part of a determinate sentencing schema; see Chapter 4. Thus, by the 1960s and 1970s, the ideal of a correctional institution had been more fully realized in many parts of the country and in some prisons. However, the extent to which it truly was realized is in doubt. Staff hired to work in these prisons, other than the few treatment staff, tended to have only a high school diploma or GED and were not paid a professional wage. The prisons were understaffed. They were also often crowded, and educational and other treatment programs, even work programs, were limited. Good time was usually a given, although one could lose it. One did not in fact earn it; rather, one did time and got it. Parole was typically poorly supervised, and by the 1970s and through the 1980s and early 1990s several states and the federal government had eliminated it as they moved to determinate sentencing (see Chapter 5).

By the mid-1970s, a conservative mood regarding crime had gripped the country and skepticism had developed about the value of rehabilitative programming. The media and politicians played on the fear of crime, and despite the fact that overall street crime had been decreasing since the early 1980s and violent crime had been decreasing since the mid-1990s in the United States, a prison building boom ensued (Irwin, 2005). Prisons of the 1980s and 1990s and into the 2000s reflect all of these earlier trends and influences. The maximum- and super-maximum-security prisons of today (and possibly some medium- and minimum-security prisons) are merely warehouse prisons where inmates' lives and movement are severely restricted and rule bound. There is no pretense of rehabilitation in warehouse prisons; punishment and incapacitation are the only justification for such places. The more hardened and dangerous prisoners are supposed to be sent there, and their severe punishment is to serve as a deterrent to others in lesser security prisons.

These lesser security prisons, the medium- and minimum-security prisons that comprise roughly two-thirds of all prisons, do still have the trappings of rehabilitation programming, although it is limited in scope and funding, and they usually afford good time and even parole (most states still have a version of these). They, too, are often crowded and understaffed, and their staff are not as educated or well paid as one might wish. However, such prisons do approximate the original ideal of a correctional institution.

The rest of this book will be primarily focused on the correctional institution model as it is often imperfectly implemented in the United States. There are some who argue (e.g., Irwin, 2005) that the rehabilitative ideal is not realized in prisons and instead that programming is too often used to control inmates rather than to help locate for them another life path that does not involve crime. Correctional institutions intended to rehabilitate instead end up warehousing the "dangerous classes" (Irwin, 2005) or the poor and minorities. Of course, our history of corrections would lead us to be skeptical of any easy claims to rehabilitative change. (For a fuller discussion of rehabilitative programming, see Chapter 15.) As will be explored in this book, too often a plan, although well intentioned, is inadequately conceived and executed, and as a result nothing changes or, worse, we achieve precisely the opposite results.

Warehouse prisons:
Large prisons, of any security level, where inmates' lives and movement are severely restricted and rule bound. There is no pretense of rehabilitation; punishment, incapacitation, and deterrence are the only justifications.

●●● THEMES THAT PREVAIL IN CORRECTIONAL HISTORY

There are several themes interwoven throughout the history and current operation of corrections in the United States. The overriding one, of course, has been money. Operating a correctional institution or program is a costly undertaking, and from the first those engaged in this business have needed to concern themselves with how to fund it. Of course, the availability of funding for correctional initiatives is shaped by

PERSPECTIVE FROM A PRACTITIONER

Pat Mahoney, Alcatraz Corrections Officer

Position: Corrections Officer and Boat Captain

Location: Alcatraz Federal Penitentiary

How long were you a Corrections Officer on Alcatraz?

From 1956 to 1963, so 7 years—the best 7 years of my career. Alcatraz was a special place, from the guards to the convicts.

The primary duties and responsibilities of a Corrections Officer on Alcatraz were:

About 15 positions, from tower, to kitchen, to garbage truck, to prison industries, supporting food and water deliveries, and supervising convict efforts for cleanup and all the other daily requirements. It was surprisingly busy. Corrections officers also manned the gun gallery in the cell house. Roles were changed about every 3 months. I was originally a corrections officer; then I was promoted to boat captain. I was also always on call if any work had to be done. I also supervised a crew that did maintenance for the actual prison.

In general, a typical day for a Corrections Officer on Alcatraz included:

In the cell house, there were several in charge of convict teams that cleaned the cell house continuously. They supervised or conducted inmate counts. They also had to get convicts from their cells to visiting attorneys, to the barbershop, showers, meals, and work locations. The hours were always busy. Boredom was not ever a factor. Everyone had things to do at all times. The tower guards were the least active but had regular duties and communication with others. Tower guards also watched the bay and occasionally saw a boat in distress, so they became a primary communicator to the Coast Guard for boats around Alcatraz.

Life on the Rock was fun when not on duty. We had a social hall, two bowling lanes, commissary for food, a playground for the kids, a handball court, and regular family dinners. About every 3 weeks, we had an island-wide dinner for all guards and families at the social hall. The view from the island was always tremendous. We looked right on downtown San Francisco.

My advice to someone either wishing to study, or now studying, criminal justice to become a Corrections Officer would be:

The key is to be honest. If convicts think for a second that you are not honest, they will try to work you until you get fired or hurt. They can sense if someone is not honest. It is an exciting role, meeting some of the best and worst of society at Alcatraz. In the prison, there are no weapons for the guards on the floor. All know this, so there is a common respect. You need good people skills to work with some who may have issues.

Note: Words written by Steve Mahoney (born on Alcatraz) as given by Pat Mahoney (corrections officer and boat captain, Alcatraz).

the political sentiments of the time. Not surprisingly, schemes to fund correctional operations have often included ways to use inmate labor. Complementary themes that have shaped how money might be made and spent, and how inmates or clients might be treated, have included a move to greater compassion and humanity in correctional operation; the influence that the demographics of inmates themselves has had (e.g., race, class, gender); religious sentiments about punishment and justice; architecture as it aligns with supervision; the pressure that crowding places on correctional programs and institutions; and the fact that although reforms might be well intentioned, they do not always lead to effective or just practice. Again, this list of themes is not exhaustive, but it does include some of the prevailing influences that span correctional history in the United States and that require the attention of each successive generation.

SUMMARY

- Howard, Beaumont and Tocqueville, and Dix all conducted studies of corrections in their day and judged the relative benefits of some practices and institutions over others, based on their data.

- The Pennsylvania and New York early prisons were the models for most American prisons of the 19th century.

- The ideal conception of prisons was rarely achieved in reality.

- The Elmira Prison arose out of a prison reform movement that occurred roughly 50 years after the Auburn Prison was built.

- The southern and northern versions of prisons that followed the Civil War were not like Elmira and were instead focused on using inmate labor for the production of goods for private contractors.

- The Stateville Prison, although conceived as a correctional institution and all that implies, for the most part became a Big House prison.

- Correctional institutions, as a type of prison, do exist in a less than perfect form in the United States.

- Correctional institutions, as that term has been expanded to apply generically to jails, prisons, and some forms of community corrections, have been shaped by several themes throughout their history. These themes, although apparently constant, are a product of the times. For instance, the Eastern Penitentiary would not be built today as a *general use prison* because it would be considered cruel to isolate inmates from other human contact. Yet this kind of isolation, sometimes even with tiny cells, is seen as beneficial by those who today build and operate super-maximum-security prisons for "special uses" to control "incorrigible" inmates (Kluger, 2007).

- In the following chapters, we will see such themes and the history of corrections, as detailed here, dealt with again and again. However, although we continue to repeat both the mistakes and successes of the past, that does not mean we cannot make, and have not made, any progress in corrections. There is no question that on the whole the vast majority of jails and prisons in this country today are much better than those for much of the last 200 years, although the unprecedented use of correctional sanctions in the United States would be regarded by some as overly harsh and thus a regressive trend. These themes presented here represent ongoing questions (e.g., how much money, compassion, or religious influence is the "right" amount), and as such we are constantly called on to address them.

KEY TERMS

Big House prisons, 59

Contract and lease systems, 58

Convict code, 59

Correctional institutions, 44

Elmira Reformatory, 57

Marks system, 57

Medical model, 59

Stateville Prison, 58

Walnut Street Jail, 44

Warehouse prisons, 60

DISCUSSION QUESTIONS

1. Discuss the relative benefits and drawbacks of the Pennsylvania and New York models of early prisons. What did Beaumont and Tocqueville and Dix think of them and why? Which type of prison would you rather work in, or be incarcerated in, and why?

2. Why did prison and jail managers like to require silence, and why did they eventually end that requirement? Why is it so difficult to control human behavior?

3. How has the question of inmate labor shaped the development of prisons over time?

4. Note why there is often a disconnect between the intentions of reformers and the ultimate operation of their reforms. Why is it difficult for theory to be put

into practice? How might we ensure that there is a truer implementation of reforms?

5. How are the "themes" that run through the history of corrections represented in current practices today? Why do these themes continue to have relevance for correctional operation over the centuries?

$SAGE edge™

Review → Practice → Improve

Sharpen your skills with SAGE edge at **edge.sagepub.com/stohressentials3e**.

SAGE edge offers a robust online environment featuring an impressive array of free tools and resources for review, study, and further exploration, keeping both instructors and students on the cutting edge of teaching and learning.

FOR FURTHER EXPLORATION AND APPLICATION, TAKE A LOOK AT THE INTERACTIVE EBOOK FOR THESE PREMIUM RESOURCES:

- **Career Video 3.1** Corrections Sergeant
- **SAGE News Clip 3.1** Texas Prison Reform
- **SAGE News Clip 3.2** U.S. Senate Criminal Justice
- **Journal Article 3.1** Broken Beyond Repair: Rehabilitative Penology and American Political Development

4 Ethics and Corrections

TEST YOUR KNOWLEDGE

Test your knowledge about ethics and corrections by answering the following questions. Check your answers on page 390 after reading the chapter.

1. Ethics and morality are the same thing. (True or false?)

2. What is the difference between deontological and teleological approaches to ethics?

3. The ethical formalism framework includes the belief that there is a universal law that includes clear rights and wrongs. (True or false?)

4. Utilitarianism follows the principle that what is good is that which results in the greatest utility for the greatest number. (True or false?)

5. Most religions include a universal set of rights and wrongs. (True or false?)

6. Noble cause corruption is the idea that it is okay to do the wrong thing if it is for the right reasons. (True or false?)

7. A correctional officer who engages in unethical behavior for personal gain is practicing official deviance. (True or false?)

8. There are characteristics of correctional work that make it more susceptible to ethical violations. (True or false?)

Check your answers on page 390 after reading the chapter.

LEARNING OBJECTIVES

- Explain the differences between ethics and morality

- Describe the different ethical frameworks

- Analyze why people are motivated to commit ethical violations

- Identify why corrections workers might be prone to ethics violations and how such violations might be prevented

A NOVICE BOWS TO SUBCULTURAL PRESSURE

Mary K. Stohr

When I first started as a correctional officer at an adult male prison in Washington State, I was the second woman hired (and the first was hired a month before me). I was relatively well educated (two bachelor's degrees) and had worked at all kinds of jobs since age 10 but never in corrections. I was young (25), scared, and naïve. My first reports were rejected by my sergeant as too wordy, and I was thought to be too soft on the inmates. (I called the inmates Mr. this and Mr. that and treated them with courtesy.) After about 4 weeks on the job, and in an effort to help me, a well-meaning sergeant took me aside and said, "Stohr, I'm worried about you. I'm not sure you can do this job. You've got to learn to write better [meaning less and in a more sparse fashion—he might as well have said, 'Just the facts, ma'am'], and you've got to treat the inmates with less respect, or you aren't going to make it on this job."

We were in a back area of the control room, and he pointed to an inmate at the control room window—we'll call him Mr. Smith. He said, "That man Smith, he's a dirty baby raper [which I took to mean that Smith was a child molester]. He's been hanging around the window when you're here because you are too nice to him. You've got to treat him differently, or he'll take advantage of you." Essentially, he said that you don't have to be mean (he wasn't that kind of man), but you shouldn't be friendly either.

Well, I took this sergeant's advice to heart because I knew he was trying to help me and there were a few of the staff at the prison who wanted to see me and the other woman fail. I also paid attention to his advice because he was well respected and had welcomed me to the job. (He was an uncle of the first woman hired.) I diligently studied the reports of other officers and tried to imitate them. As a result, my reports were suddenly accepted. But the thing I did that was small, and that I regret, was that I treated Mr. Smith with less respect than he probably deserved; not that he wasn't a child molester (I read his file when I became a counselor and had access to it), but he was still a human being, he was in my care, and how I acted was not professional. The next time Mr. Smith came to the window for his meds, I did not meet his eyes; he became Smith without the Mr., and I was quite abrupt with him. This kind of behavior characterized most of our interactions from then on. The sympathetic sergeant witnessed this and literally patted my back and said, "Stohr, you'll be all right," and that was it; I was accepted into the subculture, at least by him, but I wasn't entirely happy about it or proud of myself.

••• INTRODUCTION: TO DO THE RIGHT THING!

As you likely gathered from Chapters 2 and 3 on the history of corrections, ethical abuses have always been a problem for corrections workers. Their jobs are largely hidden from public view, somewhat cloaked in secrecy, with enormous amounts of discretion, and they deal with people in their care who have few rights and protections. Moreover, as we will discuss throughout this book, these are jobs (e.g., correctional officers, sergeants, lieutenants, and captains; probation and parole officers; correctional counselors) that do not always have professional status in terms of pay, training, experience, or educational requirements (these problems all are particularly true for correctional officers, less so for the other positions listed here), which would ensure that the best people are always hired and that they use their discretion wisely. Therefore, unqualified people are sometimes in these demanding correctional jobs, and because of this they are more likely to make bad and sometimes unethical choices.

It cannot be overemphasized, however, that the vast majority of correctional staff, whether a correctional officer working in an adult facility or a probation officer working with youths in the community, are *ethical* in their work practices, meaning that they do the right thing. It is those few bad apples who leave a negative impression of corrections work and workers. Luckily, there are things an organization and its managers and workers can do to minimize abuse of power and resources by staff and to correct the misbehavior of some staff. The development of codes of ethics, the professionalization of staff, and the routinization of policies and procedures all are key to preventing ethical abuses. In this chapter, we review those efforts to reduce corruption and abuses in corrections that might be both unethical and illegal (see In Focus 4.1), but first we discuss what ethics is and is not and the source of ethical and unethical behavior.

DEFINING ETHICS: WHAT IS RIGHT (AND WRONG)?

As mentioned in the foregoing, **ethics** is the study of what is right and wrong, and to be ethical is to practice in your work what is "right" behavior. But you might ask (rightly!), "What is *right* behavior?" In a larger sense it is what is legal (what the law is), and in an organizational sense it is what is legal, too, but also what is allowed and not allowed according to codes of ethics and policies and procedures of that workplace. So a person could sexually harass others in the workplace (e.g., make negative comments about them or undermine their work because of their gender), but this behavior, although unethical and perhaps prohibited by the workplace code of ethics and policies and procedures, might not rise to the level of illegal behavior.

Ethics: The study of right and wrong professional conduct.

Morality, we should note, is not the same as ethics because it concerns what is right or wrong in the personal sphere, whereas ethics is concerned with the professional sphere. People tend to base their beliefs about what is right or wrong, ethical or unethical, and moral or immoral on what they have learned from any number of sources. For instance, it is not difficult to figure out what is the right thing to do in the case of the death of Jason Echevarria (as showcased in the In Focus 4.2 box) because what we have learned from our family, schools, religious teachings, workplace policies, and other sources has helped us to determine our own sense of right and wrong in such instances.

IN FOCUS 4.1

A Lack of Ethics: Florida's YSI Private Prisons for Youths

In Florida, all of the juvenile prisons in the state are operated by private companies, and Youth Services International (YSI), a for-profit company owned by former hotelier James F. Slattery, operates about 9% of them (Kirkham, 2013, p. 1). YSI also operates detention centers and boot camps. Slattery's company has been able to secure these contracts and many others in other states such as Georgia, Maryland, Nevada, New York, and Texas, worth more than $100 million in the Florida contracts alone, despite the fact that the Department of Justice has investigated complaints about them in several of these states. Auditors in Maryland found that YSI workers have encouraged fighting between inmates, and staff reportedly routinely fail to report "riots, assaults and claims of sexual abuse" (Kirkham, 2013, p. 2). A Bureau of Justice Statistics report indicated that a YSI facility in Palm Beach, Florida, had the "highest rate of reported sexual assaults out of 36 facilities reviewed in Florida" (Kirkham, 2013, p. 2). YSI had only 9% of the state contracts for youth beds in the state of Florida, but it had 15% of the cases of excessive force and injured youth (Kirkham, 2013, p. 8). Local public defender offices and the Southern Poverty Law Center have complained about the handling of youths and conditions at YSI facilities, with little response from the state. In an investigation by a *Huffington Post* reporter, where official records were reviewed and former employees were interviewed, Kirkham (2013) found the following:

- Staff underreported fights and assaults to avoid scrutiny and the possible loss of contracts.

- Staff abused youths in the facilities by hitting and choking them, sometimes to the point of fracturing bones.

- Turnover of staff was high.

- Food was restricted and prepared incorrectly or in an unsanitary manner, and youths were encouraged to gamble with others to win their food portions.

When the reporter asked why, with this dismal record of care, YSI was continually offered contracts, the answer he received from those concerned about the treatment of juveniles both inside and outside the state of Florida was that YSI supported the political campaigns of Florida's and other states' politicians with hefty donations. The company has donated more to politicians in Florida than two of the largest companies in the state,

> donating more than $400,000 to state candidates and committees over the last 15 years, according to the HuffPost's review. The recipient of the largest share of those dollars was the Florida Republican Party, which took in more than $276,000 in that time. Former Florida Senate President Mike Haridopolos, an avid supporter of prison privatization, received more than $15,000 from company executives during state and federal races. (Kirkham, 2013, p. 6)

According to sources cited in the article (Kirkham, 2013), margins are narrow in the operation of correctional facilities (i.e., there is not a lot of "fat" in publicly operated prisons or jails), so if private prison companies want to make money for their owners and investors, it means that they need to cut staff pay or benefits, slash programming, or feed people less, and it appears that all three of these things are happening at YSI facilities, indicating unethical (if not illegal) behavior by politicians, company managers, and correctional officers on the line.

Discussion Questions

1. Based on the above narrative, what factors led to the abuses reported in the YSI facilities?

2. What steps can be taken to reduce the incidence of such abuses in like facilities?

3. How is staffing tied up in the nature and amount of the abuse?

••• ETHICAL FOUNDATION FOR PROFESSIONAL PRACTICE

It is not clear how much of an ethical foundation most humans are born with, although it is clear that several institutions try to instill one in their members. The family is likely the most influential social institution to inculcate ethics and morality. Educational institutions, both K–12 schools and colleges, all in some way or another—and usually in many ways—discuss what is right and wrong in many different situations. Diverse religions all convey a sense of right and wrong, and a key concept emanating from many of them is the *golden rule,* or "do unto others as you would have them do unto you." Other institutions—such as the military, social and professional clubs, even kids' sports teams, and of course the work environment itself—all strive to instill a moral or ethical framework in their members. The larger culture and life experiences doubtless also contribute to one's sense of right and wrong.

> **Deontological ethical systems:** Systems concerned with whether the act itself is good.
>
> **Teleological ethical systems:** Systems focused on whether the consequences of the act are good.
>
> **Ethical formalism:** Determines morality based on a universal law that includes clear rights and wrongs.

Much of the research on ethics also reviews the theoretical bases for decisions involving ethics (Braswell, McCarthy, & McCarthy, 1991; Pollock, 1994, 1998, 2010; Rohr, 1989; R. Solomon, 1996). The philosophical touchstones that are referenced as guides to human decision making are ethical formalism, utilitarianism, religion, natural law, the ethics of virtue, the ethics of care, and egoism.

Moral behavior is shaped by both deontological and teleological ethical systems, and these touchstones are subsets of them. **Deontological ethical systems** are concerned with whether the act itself is good, and **teleological ethical systems** are focused on the consequences of the act. If the act itself is moral or ethical, then someone who is guided by a deontological framework is not concerned about the consequences of the act. It is enough to just act in a moral fashion. Someone who is guided by a teleological ethical system does not care so much about the rightness or wrongness of the act but instead cares about whether the consequences of the act are good. Pollock (1998, 2010) defined the ethical frameworks that derive from these ethical systems in her book *Ethics in Crime and Justice: Dilemmas and Decisions.*

PHOTO 4.1: A correctional officer opens a gate for an inmate. The security of an institution relies on the vigilance of officers' closing and locking gates.

ETHICAL FORMALISM

Pollock (1998) defined **ethical formalism** as "what is good is that which conforms to the categorical imperative" (p. 48). Under this system, there is the belief that there is a universal law that includes clear rights and wrongs. The philosopher Immanuel Kant (1774–1804) noted that there is a categorical imperative requiring that each person act as he or she would like all others to act (very much like the golden rule mentioned in the foregoing). Kant also believed that people must seek to be guided by reason in their decision making. Ethical formalism falls under a deontological system because the focus is on the act and its rightness (or wrongness) rather than on the consequences

IN FOCUS 4.2

Mentally Ill Inmate Dies at Rikers

In a series of articles appearing in the *New York Times,* reporter Michael Schwirtz documented the abuse and neglect suffered by mentally ill inmates incarcerated in the Rikers Island jails (Schwirtz, 2014a, 2014b). Rikers Island jails are a complex of 10 jails on an island in the East River of New York City. Since 2009, 20 officers from Rikers have been prosecuted for assaults on inmates. In mid-March 2014, a mentally ill inmate died from being left in an overheated cell at Rikers. But the particular subject of these articles was a 25-year-old inmate named Jason Echevarria, who was diagnosed with bipolar disorder. He was placed in a special mental health unit at Rikers because of his diagnosed mental illness and because he had behavioral problems when in the general population of the jail. He had a record of attempted suicides while incarcerated at Rikers (Schwirtz, 2014a, 2014b).

Because there were problems with raw sewage coming out of toilets, on August 18, 2012, inmates were given a packet of powdered detergent that they were to use to clean up their cells (Schwirtz, 2014a, 2014b). By policy, inmates were supposed to be given detergent that was diluted by several gallons of water, but an inexperienced officer instead gave the full packets to inmates. Echevarria swallowed the toxic detergent, and as a result his tongue and mouth skin were severely damaged as he vomited; he experienced extreme pain and expelled blood from his mouth over the course of several hours. A correctional officer claimed that he responded to Mr. Echevarria's cries for help by reporting his health problems to his captain, who told the correctional officer not to talk to him about this again unless the inmate was dead. Despite this warning, the correctional officer claimed that he reported to the captain twice more about the inmate's distress and even tried to call for medical assistance at least once but was prevented from doing so by the captain. Both the captain and the officer came off their shifts without getting any medical assistance for the inmate. Echevarria was dead the next morning. The captain was demoted to an officer position, was arrested

United States Geological Survey

PHOTO 4.2: An aerial view of the Rikers Island jail complex.

by the Federal Bureau of Investigation (FBI), and was prosecuted for violating the civil rights of Echevarria. The officer was fired and filed a wrongful termination suit, disputing the captain's claim that he was never told about Echevarria's health crisis.

An independent commission studying Rikers Island recommended on April 2, 2017, that it be shut down over a period of 10 years (Corasanti, 2017). New York City Mayor Bill de Blasio was supportive of this plan, as was the city council and the state governor. The hope is to reduce incarceration of those accused of low-level offenses in the jail (thus halving the city jail population) and then to construct five small jails in each of the five boroughs of the city.

Discussion Questions

1. Why aren't correctional facilities well suited to handle the mentally ill?

2. Instead of incarcerating the mentally ill, what should public policy be instead?

3. What advantages and disadvantages are there to shuttering Rikers Island?

of the act and their goodness (or badness). It is a position that does not account for gray areas; an act is either right or wrong. So some acts, such as murder, lying, and stealing, are always wrong even when the end of these acts is good.

UTILITARIANISM

Utilitarianism is defined as "what is good is that which results in the greatest utility for the greatest number" (Pollock, 1998, p. 48). So morality is determined by how many people were helped by the act. The philosopher Jeremy Bentham (1748–1832) believed that people will do a "utilitarian calculus" regarding how much pleasure or pain a given act will garner, and they will act on that to maximize pleasure. But when one's pleasure conflicts with the greater good for society, then one must bow to the greater good under a utilitarian perspective. Because utilitarianism is focused on the end—whether it is moral or immoral or is ethical or unethical—achieved by an act, it falls under the teleological system.

RELIGIOUS PERSPECTIVE

People who employ a **religious perspective** to guide their decisions believe that "what is good is that which conforms to God's will" (Pollock, 1998, p. 48). This is a perspective that weighs what is right or wrong based on one's religion and covers all facets of living and relationships with others. How one treats others, how one lives his or her life, and one's understanding of the meaning of life itself all are influenced by this religious perspective. Under this perspective, both the means and ends are foci of interest and are perceived through the lens of what one believes his or her god or gods would want. Most religions include a universal set of rights and wrongs, much like ethical formalism, and they have, as mentioned already, a form of the categorical imperative or the golden rule. Although there is widespread agreement across religions on some matters, there is much disagreement about social practices such as drinking alcohol, dancing, certain kinds of foods, behavior on holy days, how appropriate clothing is, and the political and social status of women and other minorities such as members of LGBTI (lesbian, gay, bisexual, transgender, and intersex) communities.

© iStockphoto.com/gece33

PHOTO 4.3: An elaborate cathedral front, symbolic of the wealth and artistry devoted to religious practice over the centuries.

Utilitarianism: "What is good is that which results in the greatest utility for the greatest number" (Pollock, 1998, p. 48).

Religious perspective: A perspective that weighs what is right or wrong based on one's religion.

Natural law: A framework whose adherents believe that what is good is what is known to be so.

NATURAL LAW

Adherents of an ethical framework based on **natural law** believe that "what is good is that which is natural" (Pollock, 1998, p. 48). Behavior is or should be motivated by what is universally understood to be right and wrong. Using reason, all humans can figure out these rights and wrongs. The major difference between a natural law believer and someone who is guided by a religious perspective is that in the latter case the supreme being(s) is the one who determines what is right and wrong, whereas under a natural law perspective these rights and wrongs are just clear and knowable through reason. Under this perspective, we know what truth and decency are, and so we just need to act on our natural inclination in that direction. These natural laws about what is right and wrong are believed to be cross-cultural and true over time; they are not relative to time or place. Moreover, out of these natural laws flow natural rights such as those accorded to citizens under the Constitution of the United States.

ETHICS OF VIRTUE

Believers in the **ethics of virtue** think that "what is good is that which conforms to the golden mean [the middle ground between positions]" (Pollock, 1998, p. 48). Instead of focusing on the nature of an action, the question here is whether the person is virtuous or good. The end to be achieved is to live a good and moral life by performing virtuous acts. Such virtues include "thriftiness, temperance, humility, industriousness, and honesty" (Pollock, 1998, p. 43). Models of virtue provide examples for those interested in living with integrity and according to a code of ethics.

ETHICS OF CARE

Relatedly, an **ethics of care** is centered on good acts. It is a deontological perspective. Those who subscribe to this framework believe that "what is good is that which meets the needs of those concerned" (Pollock, 1998, p. 48). Under this perspective, the care and concern for others is paramount. This is a perspective that is regarded as more "feminine" because it is believed that women, as a group, are more attuned to the needs of others. Carol Gilligan found in her research on moral development that women's perspective differs from men's perspective in this area (Gilligan, 1982). Women are more likely to be concerned about the care of others as guiding how they behave. Peacemaking and restorative justice are thought to derive from the ethics-of-care framework.

EGOISM

The last ethical framework that Pollock (1998) mentioned is one based on the individual—namely, **egoism**. Under this framework, the needs of the self are most important, so acting to satisfy one's own wants and needs under this framework is acting ethically. Because the act is the focus here, egoism falls under the deontological perspective. Even when acting on behalf of others, it is believed that one is acting out of *enlightened egoism,* or helping and caring for others so they will do the same for you when you are in need of assistance.

● ● ● WHY PEOPLE BEHAVE UNETHICALLY

Despite the influence of these ethical frameworks, there are several reasons why people behave unethically. The most obvious, and perhaps the most common, reason is for *personal gain* or *out of selfishness.* For instance, the owner of YSI, which manages private prisons for juveniles in Florida, clearly benefits financially from cutting staff salaries and inmate food (this must be unethical, right?), and not surprisingly the result is poorly operated and, at times, dangerous facilities (see In Focus 4.1). If the captain supervising the Rikers Island jail mental health unit when Echevarria died did what he is accused of doing—ignoring the desperate health needs of an inmate—then he behaved both criminally and unethically for selfish reasons; he did not want to be bothered (see In Focus 4.2 box). The remedy for such a motivation is multifaceted and is discussed momentarily.

OFFICIAL DEVIANCE

Another reason people in corrections might behave unethically is official deviance. **Official deviance** was defined by Lee and Visano (1994) as

Ethics of virtue: A framework that emphasizes the virtue of one's character over actions.

Ethics of care: A framework centered on good acts in which the care of and concern for others is paramount.

Egoism: Framework under which the needs of the self are most important, so acting to satisfy one's own wants and needs is acting ethically.

Official deviance: When officials act in a way that benefits their organization but violates laws or formal rules.

ETHICAL ISSUE ?

What Would You Do?

You are a new manager (2 weeks on the job) of a public correctional institution (jail) that has experienced several ethical crises during the last year. Your jail has been sued twice successfully during the last year for overcrowding and neglect of the mental health needs of inmates. You were hired to "clean up" the ethical environment of the facility, although you already recognize that the staff subculture in the jail is intransigent and resistant to change. What steps would you take to transform this jail to accomplish the desired change? What resistance do you expect to encounter, and how do you think it can be overcome?

actions taken by officials which violate the law and/or the formal rules of the organization, but which are clearly oriented toward the needs and goals of the organization, as perceived by the official, and thus fulfill certain informal rules of the organization. (p. 203)

Lee and Visano (1994) studied officials' behavior in both the United States and Canada, and they found that many deviant acts by criminal justice actors are not committed for personal gain but rather are committed to help the organization or to be in compliance with subcultural goals. If the subculture values secrecy and protection of fellow officers, as is true for subcultures in corrections, then one might be called on to lie, even on the witness stand and under oath, to protect an officer when he or she is charged with wrongdoing (Stohr & Collins, 2014). The important point here is that the organizational member who lies or engages in other acts of official deviance gains nothing from engaging in the deviance; it is the organization or other organizational members who benefit. The penalty for organizational members who refuse to engage in official deviance might be shunning, harassment, or even firing for unsubstantiated reasons. The remedies to reduce official deviance are noted in the following (after the discussion of noble cause corruption).

NOBLE CAUSE CORRUPTION

A third reason why criminal justice workers and corrections workers, in particular, might engage in unethical behavior might be that they are motivated by noble cause corruption. Crank and Caldero (2000) defined the **noble cause** for police officers as a

> profound moral commitment to make the world a safer place to live. Put simply, it is getting bad guys off the street. Police believe they're on the side of angels and their purpose in life is getting rid of bad guys. (p. 35)

Crank and Caldero (2000) identified two noble cause themes that explain police officer behavior: "the smell of the victim's blood" and "the tower" (p. 35). What they mean by the smell of the victim's blood is that police officers are motivated to act to protect and save victims. But in the course of trying to protect victims, they may step over an ethical line and lie, plant evidence, or abuse force so as to catch the "bad guy" by whatever means. And it is always the ends (e.g., catching the "bad guy") that are more important than the means (e.g., acting professionally and ethically) with noble cause corruption.

What Crank and Caldero (2000) meant by "the tower" is that police officers, when confronted with a shooter in a tower, will run to the tower (they will act in the face of danger) when everyone else is running from it. Because they are inclined to run to the tower—metaphorically at least—and also because their job requires that they *act* in dangerous situations, they may cross the ethical and legal line by overreacting or making rash decisions. They will "run to the tower" because they want to make things right. Crank and Caldero (2011) and others (e.g., Bartollas & Hahn, 1999; O'Connor, 2001) think that the police are motivated by their desire to make the world right. They tend to

Noble cause:
A profound moral commitment to make the world a safer place to live.

see the world in black and white, and when a suspect interferes with this perception the police might engage in unethical behavior because it is inspired by acting in the cause of "rightness." The problem is that the police are not always right, and they cannot always see what is right (as with all of us).

Noble cause corruption, as an explanation for unethical behavior by corrections workers, makes a great deal of sense. One of the authors, when working in a male prison as an officer many years ago, was told right away which inmates were in for "child molesting," although this information was supposedly confidential between the counselors and their clients (see the related story that appears at the beginning of this chapter). It was boldly stated that such inmates were not to be treated with respect by staff and were to be regarded with an additional dose of suspicion. Interactions with other correctional professionals over the years, in all kinds of correctional settings, reinforced this experience that correctional staff are motivated in their actions by "the victim's blood," especially when that victim is a child.

People who are attracted to work in corrections are also doers and people who want to make the world right. They will not hesitate to "run to the tower" to accomplish this feat either. The authors know of several stories of officers in federal prisons, state prisons, and jails who were thrilled to be called to engage in the quelling of altercations in corrections. These are stories of correctional staff who enthusiastically "ran to the tower" to "make the world right," but in at least a few of these cases those officers admitted that more force by staff was used to stop fights and put down disturbances than was strictly necessary. Once the fists started flying, the adrenaline took over and the sense that force was being used to do good made its use, even its excessive use, justified.

Noble cause corruption, as with official deviance and deviance for selfish ends, is all the more likely to occur in environments where the behavior of actors is hidden and little supervised and the clients are powerless. These factors all accurately describe correctional environments. Most correctional work is done in some isolation from the larger community, and this is particularly true of prisons and jails. Even community correctional officers operate in environments where the interactions are personal and their content is not documented. Supervisors' span of control is stretched, and they don't always have adequate time to review an individual actor's behavior. Correctional clients are some of the most powerless people in the United States. By law, they have very few rights and legal protections, and thus they are subject to the behavior of both ethical and unethical correctional personnel. Top all of these organizational and individual characteristics off with the fact that correctional staff have a great deal of **discretion** (defined here as the ability to make choices and to act or not act on those choices), and there is only one more ingredient necessary to make the perfect admixture for unethical behavior: the influence of a negative subculture.

SUBCULTURE

In fact, a key feature of correctional environments that would make staff and management more prone to engage in unethical behavior is the presence of a strong negative subculture. **Subcultures** are subsets of larger cultures with their own norms, values, beliefs, traditions, and history. They can be positive in their promotion of prosocial values and support of their members, but they can also be negative when they promote antisocial values and, in correctional work (and police work), unethical behavior. In an

PHOTO 4.4: Correctional staff confer in the yard next to a housing unit at the Corcoran State Prison in Corcoran, California. Effective and honest communication between officers is a key component of correctional institutions.

Discretion: The ability to make choices and to act or not act on them.

Subculture: A subset of a larger culture, with its own norms, values, beliefs, traditions, and history.

IN FOCUS 4.3

Subcultural Values of Probation and Parole Officers

In ethics training exercises in 1994 and 1995, probation and parole managers in a western state identified the subcultural values of the community corrections officers they supervised (Stohr & Collins, 2009). They were as follows:

1. Always aid your coworker.

2. Never rat on coworkers.

3. Always cover for a coworker in front of clients.

4. Always support the coworker over the client in a disagreement.

5. Always support the decision of a coworker regarding a client.

6. Don't be sympathetic toward clients. Instead be cynical about them (to be otherwise is to be naïve).

7. Probation/parole officers are the "us," and everyone else is the "them," including administration, the media, and the rest of the community.

8. Help your coworkers by completing your own work and by assisting them if they need it.

9. Since you aren't paid much or appreciated by the public or the administration, don't be a rate buster (i.e., don't do more than the minimal amount of work).

10. Handle your own work and don't allow interference. (p. 63)

Discussion Questions

1. Which of these subcultural values do you think makes the workplace better for staff but can lead to unethical behavior?

2. How might correctional managers and workers concerned about unethical behavior in the workplace prevent some of the most destructive of these values from being embraced in the workplace?

Source: *Criminal justice management: Theory and practice in justice-centered organizations,* by Stohr and Collins (2009, p. 63). By permission of Oxford University Press, USA.

ethics training course conducted by one of the authors and a colleague for probation and parole managers, the participants identified several barriers to ethical practice in their workplaces. Kauffman (1988, pp. 85–112) identified most of these barriers in his study of correctional officers, and Pollock (1994, p. 195) did so in her text on ethics and the negative side of subcultures (see In Focus 4.2).

●●● HOW TO PREVENT UNETHICAL BEHAVIOR AND PROMOTE ETHICAL WORK PRACTICES

As you can see, a few of these subcultural values are positive in that they provide support of coworkers, but the ones that support coworkers even if they are wrong or engaged in wrongdoing vis-à-vis their clients or the work, are negative and promote an unethical work environment. Most of the managers at that ethics training session reported that unethical behavior was common on the job and ranged from the routine, such as rudeness to clients and their families, to the rare, such as lying on reports and verbally and physically abusing clients. The subcultural values listed before, however, made it difficult for managers to address the unethical behaviors.

This is why the organizational and individual remedies to prevent unethical behavior, whatever its motivation and in spite of the subculture, are multifaceted and include at least these:

1. Hire people who are less likely to be motivated by personal gain. To do this, correctional organizations need a well-developed selection process with extensive background checks on potential hires (Stohr & Collins, 2014).

2. Pay people a professional wage because then they will be less likely to be tempted to engage in unethical behavior for personal gain.

3. Encourage professional development of employees through further education, training, and engagement in professional organizations because employees who are immersed in a professional and learning subculture are more likely to encourage positive change in others and improve the workplace, and they may be less likely to be tolerant of a workplace subculture that fosters unethical behavior.

4. Develop an ethics code with employee input and review it regularly in the department. By involving a cross section of staff in the development of an ethics code, more staff are likely to feel like they "own it" and therefore support it.

5. Require extensive training in ethics at the beginning of employment and throughout employees' careers. More and ongoing training will reinforce the need to behave ethically, and it will undercut negative subcultural influences.

6. Supervise people sufficiently and check up on what they are doing and how they are doing it.

7. Provide support for positive changes in the workplace that will enhance the ability of workers to do the job right. Sometimes, staff will claim that they cannot act ethically because there are not enough resources (e.g., time, staff) to do so; by ensuring that there are enough resources—and this is hard to do in the public sector these days—managers make it possible for employees to do the work the right and ethical way.

8. Discipline violators of ethics, and if the violations of the rules or laws are serious enough, fire them. Doing this will reinforce a positive subculture that is supportive of ethical work practice.

9. Promote those who behave ethically, and include ethics-related measures in evaluations. By doing this, managers will motivate all to support ethical practice.

10. Encourage whistleblowing (the reporting of wrongdoing or problems in the workplace), and make it possible for people to do so anonymously. Despite an ethical manager and workers' best efforts, there is sometimes illegal or unethical behavior going on in the workplace, and because of the power of subcultures, correctional workers need to be able to report this behavior without fear of reprisal.

11. Develop the means for all employees to provide input into the decisions that are made by and for the organization because doing so is more likely to be a check on management; uses the knowledge workers have; instills ownership of the work by those who do

PHOTO 4.5: Corrections officer interacting positively with inmates.

Mikael Karlsson/Alamy Stock Photo

IN FOCUS 4.4

The Abuse of Solitary Confinement in Florida

In March 2016, the Florida American Civil Liberties Union (ACLU) sent a letter to the U.S. Department of Justice's Civil Rights Division requesting a federal investigation into the overuse of solitary confinement (also known as restricted housing and isolation) by the Florida Department of Corrections (Simon & Wetstein, 2016). The ACLU noted that fully one in eight inmates in Florida prisons was held in solitary confinement. It also found that the numbers revealed a potential racial bias for male and female inmates and those diagnosed with a mental illness in Florida prisons given that African Americans were overrepresented among those in solitary when compared with the number of blacks in the general population. It also found that about 23% of those with a mental illness in Florida prisons were kept in solitary confinement. Notably, much of this information was obtained through Freedom of Information Act requests, not provided voluntarily by the Florida Department of Corrections. Finally, the ACLU detailed a number of cases, from several prisons, where mentally ill and other inmates placed in solitary died because of neglect or outright torture by correctional staff. Some of those cases from the ACLU letter (Simon & Wetstein, 2016) are summarized here:

Randall Jordan-Aparo died in 2010 "after being gassed three times while in a solitary confinement cell" (p. 4). He had been ill and was denied medical care despite the knowledge that he had a rare blood disorder.

Rommell Johnson died in 2010 after being gassed twice with chemical agents within a 5-minute span of time. He was asthmatic, and the medical examiner ruled that he died as a result of the gassing, which brought on a fatal asthma attack.

Darren Rainey died in 2012 "when he was tortured in a locked shower rigged to be controlled by guards from the outside, with its water temperature at approximately 180 degrees" (p. 4). Although his skin was literally falling off of his bones when he was found in the shower, the medical examiner ruled the death "accidental" and no one had been disciplined or fired as of March 2016.

Latandra Ellington died in 2014 alone in a solitary confinement cell, reportedly from heart disease. Her family claimed she had no heart problems. "She had been placed there after she filed a complaint alleging that Sgt. Patrick Quercioli had engaged in sex with another prisoner and threatened to kill Ellington" (p. 5). The family-sponsored autopsy found no heart disease "but found excessive bruising, and a lethal level of Amlodipine, a blood pressure medication, in her system" (p. 5).

Yalex Tirado died in solitary confinement in 2014 in a prison for juveniles with no explanation for his death provided by the facility. "This is a prison where, as *The Miami Herald* has reported, the sodomizing of inmates with broomsticks by other inmates has been common, and where nine guards have been charged over the last two years with battery or facilitating the entry of contraband" (p. 5).

Discussion Questions

1. How likely do you think it is that these deaths and the abuse of solitary are isolated incidents and not representative of regular practice in these Florida prisons? What evidence do you have to support your argument?

2. If you had witnessed abuses such as these, what action, if any, would you have taken to stop them?

3. If staff are found to be guilty in the deaths of these inmates, what punishments do you think they deserve? Do you think that the staff who witnessed these kinds of abuses but did not report them should also be disciplined in some way? Why or why not?

it; and leads to greater job satisfaction, less turnover, and more commitment to the job (Stohr & Collins, 2014).

12. Encourage involvement of outsider review and professional engagement (have an oversight board; support involvement in professional organizations; and provide

access to researchers, politicians, and the media) because more openness is more likely to reduce unethical behavior and defuse the power of negative subcultures.

By using these remedies, the correctional manager and, where applicable, the correctional worker are more likely to turn the subculture into a positive support system that promotes ethical behavior. The remedies are also likely to increase professionalism and reduce abuse of clients.

●●● WAR ON DRUGS = ATTACK ON ETHICS?

Wars are a popular thing for politicians to wage. Wars on poverty, crime, and drugs were the brainchildren of several presidents and carried on by others since the 1960s. The terminology of war is powerful and connotes a level of serious attention to a topic that few other terms convey. Campaigns, assaults, and offensives are waged in wars with some urgency behind them. A war means that all available resources and attention will be devoted to that effort, and those who do not agree—well, they are like traitors to a righteous cause. Yet these political wars, somewhat like wars waged with weaponry made of steel, are problematic because they are fighting social ills—poverty, crime, and substance abuse—that, although admittedly harmful, are somewhat intractable and very complex and therefore require sustained effort and multifaceted solutions. Because of the nature of the problems, wars on them never seem to end because the problems do not end. Although the Iraq War seemed to never end (lasting at least 8 years), consider that the war on drugs was first mentioned by President Richard Nixon in 1971 and has been waged by every president since then. We currently spend at least $51 billion each year on the war on drugs in this country, and that does not account for the millions of people who have passed through correctional doors as enemy combatants in the war and the billions of dollars it has taken to pay for their arrest, prosecution, and incarceration; nor does it account for the lost tax revenue and disrupted families and lives the war has left in its wake (the collateral damage). Many scholars, commentators, and even politicians now consider the war on drugs to be an abject failure in that it has not reduced the supply or use of illicit drugs and instead has galvanized the illegal drug trade and corrupted government officials in this country, Mexico, and Central and South Americas (Cullen, Jonson, & Stohr, 2014). According to the Drug Policy Alliance (2016, p. 1), an organization whose mission is to end the war on drugs, the following outcomes have resulted from the war on drugs:

- Amount spent annually in the United States on the war on drugs: **More than $51 billion**

- Number of people arrested in 2014 in the United States on nonviolent drug charges: **1.56 million**

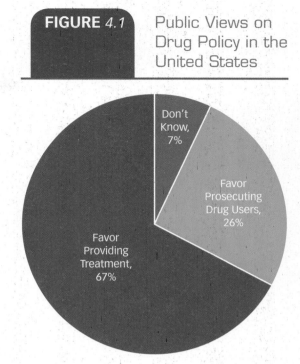

FIGURE *4.1* Public Views on Drug Policy in the United States

Don't Know, 7%

Favor Prosecuting Drug Users, 26%

Favor Providing Treatment, 67%

Source: "America's New Drug Policy Landscape," Pew Research Center, Washington, DC (April, 2014), http://www.people-press.org/2014/04/02/americas-new-drug-policy-landscape/4-2-14-1/

Note: Survey conducted February 14–23, 2014.

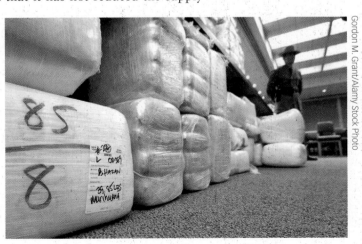

PHOTO 4.6: The war on drugs led to drug seizures like these.

- Number of people arrested for a marijuana law violation in 2014: **700,993**

- Number of those charged with marijuana law violations who were arrested for possession only: **619,809 (88%)**

- Number of Americans incarcerated in 2014 in federal, state, and local prisons and jails: **2,224,400 or 1 in every 111 adults**, the highest incarceration rate in the world

- Proportion of people incarcerated for a drug offense in state prison who are black or Hispanic, although these groups use and sell drugs at similar rates as whites: **57%**

- Number of people killed in Mexico's drug war since 2006: **100,000+**

- Number of students who have lost federal financial aid eligibility because of a drug conviction: **200,000+**

- Number of people in the United States who died from a drug overdose in 2014: **47,055**

- The Centers for Disease Control and Prevention found that syringe access programs lower HIV incidence among people who inject drugs by 80%. One-third of all AIDS cases in the United States have been caused by syringe sharing: **360,836 people**. U.S. federal government support for syringe access programs: **$0.00**, thanks to a federal ban reinstated by Congress in 2011 that prohibits any federal assistance for them.

ETHICAL ISSUE ?

What Would You Do?

You are a probation officer with a large caseload of low-level drug offenders (mostly pot smokers). Some might be addicted to marijuana, and others might not, but you need to monitor them and ensure that they attend programming and provide clean urinalysis (UA) samples. The department of corrections you work for is in transition, however, moving from a more law enforcement focus to a greater treatment orientation. The department has given you and other officers more leeway in decisions about whether to violate (write up) offenders who commit minor offenses. One of the UAs you take comes up dirty for marijuana, and you are faced with "violating" a client on your caseload who was convicted of felony drug possession (i.e., there was enough to sell). In all other ways, this client has done well in that she has made all the meetings, been employed, and attended drug programming. Would you write a violation on this offender? (Doing so may result in jail time or a trip to prison.) Would it make any difference in your decision making if your client has two dependent children who will be placed in foster care should she be incarcerated? Why or why not? Which ethical framework do you think best fits the decision you made?

So the point is that the war on drugs has been a huge resource suck, which has distracted our attention from drug treatment and real prevention, punished addicts, disproportionately incarcerated minority group members, and likely cost trillions of dollars over time. (It has been going on for 46 years at the time of this writing.) More to the point, it has challenged the ethical behavior of corrections officials by forcing them to overincarcerate some relatively minor offenders who got caught in its net. Correctional workers in prisons, jails, and detention centers or working in probation and parole, and even their managers, have little to no control over whom they are given to incarcerate or supervise in communities. But they are affected by the drug war because their facilities and caseloads have been crowded by such offenders, which has made carrying out their tasks very difficult and sometimes ethically challenging. They have been involved in drug monitoring and treatment to a much greater extent than if the war had not been waged. They have needed to supervise people who—compared with robbers and rapists—do not really merit the use of incarceration and perhaps even community supervision. Therefore, we would add one more remedy to the list that will help organizations to prevent unethical behavior, but this remedy must be understood by policymakers: Consider the likely outcomes of wars or other grand schemes on the ethics of the actors or soldiers tasked with carrying them out, and consider the larger social impact of waging war on your own citizens.

SUMMARY

- Ethical work practice is a messy business, sometimes clear-cut but often fraught with anxiety. The nature of corrections work and the organization's attendant subcultures often create situations where ethical dilemmas are common and their resolution is difficult. Moreover, the kinds of people hired in corrections work, those with a noble cause bent, are sometimes more susceptible to engaging in ethical abuses, although that is not their intent. Thankfully, there are things that organizations and individuals can do to prevent ethical abuses, but they require some resource commitment and resolve.

KEY TERMS

Deontological ethical systems, 68

Discretion, 73

Egoism, 71

Ethical formalism, 68

Ethics, 66

Ethics of care, 71

Ethics of virtue, 71

Natural law, 70

Noble cause, 72

Official deviance, 71

Religious perspective, 70

Subculture, 73

Teleological ethical systems, 68

Utilitarianism, 70

DISCUSSION QUESTIONS

1. Where do we learn our sense of right and wrong? Why do you think that some sources are more powerful in influencing people than others?

2. What makes the correctional workplace more susceptible to unethical behaviors than most workplaces? If you were to work in corrections, how would you make sure that you always made the "right decision"?

3. What can organizations do to prevent noble cause corruption? Do you think that you are a person who could be corrupted in this way?

4. Which ethical framework best describes your feeling about ethics? Why do you think that this is applicable to you?

5. Discuss how the drug war has affected corrections and how it has threatened the ethical practice of workers.

$SAGE edge™

Review → Practice → Improve

Sharpen your skills with SAGE edge at **edge.sagepub.com/stohressentials3e**.

SAGE edge offers a robust online environment featuring an impressive array of free tools and resources for review, study, and further exploration, keeping both instructors and students on the cutting edge of teaching and learning.

FOR FURTHER EXPLORATION AND APPLICATION, TAKE A LOOK AT THE INTERACTIVE EBOOK FOR THESE PREMIUM RESOURCES:

- ▶ **Career Video 4.1** Former Drug Investigator
- ▶ **Feature Video 4.1** Drug Use
- ▷ **SAGE News Clip 4.1** Rikers
- ▷ **SAGE News Clip 4.2** New York Corrections Officer
- ▤ **Journal Article 4.1** Ethics in a Mountain State County Jail

5

Sentencing

The Application of Punishment

TEST YOUR KNOWLEDGE

Test your current knowledge of the criminal sentencing process by answering the following questions as true or false. Check your answers on page 390 after reading the chapter.

1. Basic principles of justice mandate that the criminal justice system punish every person convicted of committing the same crime equally regardless of other differences.

2. The only concern at sentencing is the severity of the crime the defendant has committed.

3. Three-strikes laws are laws that allow states to possibly imprison for life a person who has been convicted of a third felony.

4. If a person is convicted of two different crimes committed on two different occasions, he or she must be sentenced to consecutive terms (one to be served after the other is completed) of probation or prison.

5. Because victims or their survivors can unfairly prejudice a judge against a defendant, with the exception of death penalty cases, victims or survivors cannot have any input into the sentencing decision.

6. Except for statutory limitations, judges basically must decide on an appropriate sentence for convicted felons without any guidance or advice.

7. Blacks and other minorities are frequently subjected to discriminatory sentencing.

8. Separate courts exist for criminals with special problems such as drug addiction.

9. All states use guidelines to help judges make sentencing decisions.

LEARNING OBJECTIVES

- Explain how modern sentencing engages Aristotle's notion of justice

- Describe the different types of sentencing and their rationales

- Define and explain the role of problem-solving courts

- Assess the issues surrounding sentencing disparity

- Identify the purpose of presentence reports and sentencing guidelines as well as the contentious issues surrounding them

VINDICTIVE VERSUS **SENSIBLE SENTENCING**

"Jane" is a 30-year-old mother of three children aged 8, 6, and 4. Her husband recently suffered a heart attack and died, leaving Jane with no money. Jane has only a 10th-grade education and cannot afford child care costs, so she was forced onto the welfare rolls. When Christmas came around, she had no money to buy her children any presents, so she took a temporary Christmas job at the local mega store where she earned $1,200 over a 2-month period. Jane did not report this income to the welfare authorities as required by law, and a welfare audit uncovered her

crime. The terrified and deeply ashamed Jane pled guilty to grand theft, which carries a possible sentence of 2 years in prison, and was referred to the probation department for a presentence investigation report (PSI).

"Jim" is a 32-year-old man with a lengthy record of thefts and other crimes committed since he was 10 years old. Jim also pled guilty before the same judge on the same day and was likewise referred for a PSI. Jim had stolen money and parts totaling $1,200 from an auto parts store during one of his brief periods of employment.

These two cases point to a perennial debate about the appropriate sentence for people who commit the same crime. Recall the classical and positivist schools of thought discussed in Chapter 1. Although both positions are ultimately about the role of punishment, the classical position maintains that punishment should fit the crime and nothing else. That is, all people convicted of identical crimes should receive identical sentences regardless of any differences they may have. The classical position maintains that Jane and Jim freely chose to commit the crimes, and the fact that Jim has a record and Jane does not is *irrelevant*. The positivist position is that punishment should fit the offender and be appropriate to rehabilitation. Jane and Jim's crimes were motivated by very different considerations; they are very different people morally, and blindly applying similar punishments to similar crimes without considering the possible consequences is pure folly. Think about these two cases and your own position on them as you read about the purpose of sentencing, the way sentencing guidelines are structured, and the uses of the PSI.

• • • INTRODUCTION: WHAT IS SENTENCING?

Sentencing refers to a post-conviction stage of the criminal justice process. A **sentence** is the punitive penalty ordered by the court after a defendant has been convicted of a crime either by a jury, in a bench trial by a judge, or in a plea bargain. Sentencing typically occurs about 30 days after conviction. The goals of sentencing are to implement one or more of the punishment philosophies discussed in Chapter 1: retribution, deterrence, incapacitation, or rehabilitation. In some states juries may be entitled to pronounce sentences, but in most states, and in federal court, sentencing is performed by a judge—except in death penalty cases, where it is the jury's responsibility. The penalties meted out at sentencing can include various forms of probation coupled with fines and restitution orders and/or treatment orders, house arrest/electric monitoring, work release, jail time, prison time, or the death penalty, all of which are discussed elsewhere in this book. The severity of the penalty depends on the crime or crimes of which the defendant is convicted and the extent of his or her criminal history, although other factors—both legitimate and illegitimate—may also come into play.

It is a major concern of the American criminal justice system that punishments received by defendants at sentencing should be consistent with justice. **Justice** is a moral concept that is difficult to define, but in essence it means to treat people in ways consistent with norms of fairness and in accordance with what they justly deserve by virtue of their behavior. Perhaps the best definition was provided by the Greek philosopher Aristotle many centuries ago: "Justice consists of treating equals equally and unequals unequally according to relevant differences" (cited in Walsh & Stohr, 2010, p. 133). In terms of sentencing, this means that those who have committed the same crime and have similar criminal histories are considered legal "equals" and should be treated equally. Those who have committed different crimes and have different criminal histories are considered legal "unequals" and therefore should be treated unequally; that is, one should be treated either more leniently or more harshly than the other.

You may ask what these "relevant differences" are and who defines them. Strictly speaking, the relevant differences in sentencing should be limited to legally relevant

Sentence: A punitive penalty ordered by the court after a defendant has been convicted of a crime either by a jury, by a judge, or in a plea bargain.

Justice: A moral concept about just or fair treatment consisting of "treating equals equally and unequals unequally according to relevant differences."

© iStockphoto.com/powerofforever

PHOTO 5.1: Fairness in sentencing is often a difficult goal to attain, with many factors to consider such as the type of crime committed, the criminal history of the offender, and the requirements of the judicial system.

factors (crime seriousness and prior record), but extralegal factors are often also brought into play such as gang affiliation, a history of substance abuse, and a person's rehabilitative potential (as the opening vignette suggested). Depending on what these factors are, justice is either served or not served by adding them. A judge who sentences a remorseful mother—whose children would become wards of the state if she were sent to prison—to probation rather than to prison is probably acting justly. This may be so even if the same judge sentences to prison an unremorseful single man who has committed the same crime and has an identical criminal record as the mother and, thus, the judge is treating legal equals unequally. On the other hand, if the judge sentences legal equals unequally only because one defendant is a woman and the other is a man, or only because one defendant is black and the other is white, then the judge is not acting justly.

••• TYPES OF SENTENCES: INDETERMINATE, DETERMINATE, AND MANDATORY

A prison sentence a person receives can be indeterminate or determinate. An **indeterminate sentence** is one in which the actual number of years a person may serve is not fixed but rather is a range of years, such as the person "shall be imprisoned for not less than 2 or 3 years to 10 years." More serious crimes move both minimum and maximum time periods upward. Indeterminate sentences were previously much more common than they are today, but a number of states still retain this system. Indeterminate sentences fit the positivist rehabilitation philosophy of punishment because they allow offenders to be released after they have served their minimum period if they demonstrate to the parole board's satisfaction that they have made efforts to turn their lives around. Such sentences are tailored to the offender and aimed at rehabilitation rather than tailored to the crime and designed to be strictly punitive.

The indeterminate sentencing model prevailed most strongly under the so-called medical model, whereby offenders were considered "sick" and in need of a cure. Because some criminals may be "sicker" than others, the time made available for the "cure" must be flexible. Offenders who behaved themselves in prison and could demonstrate that they were "reformed" could be rather quickly released; ill-behaved and stubborn offenders might need to serve the upper boundary (10 years in the above example) and be released whether "rehabilitated" or not. It has been precisely because of its flexibility that indeterminate sentencing has been accused of contributing to sentencing disparity. For instance, even if two offenders receive the same "2 to 10 years," one may serve only 2 years because he or she can keep out of trouble and knows how to play the rehabilitation/parole game while the other, who is more rowdy and does not play the game as well, may serve 2 or 3 more years. Supporters of the model, however, will reply that it is not the judiciary that is at fault (after all, both offenders were sentenced identically by judges); rather, it is the inmates themselves who caused the discrepancy by their different behaviors while incarcerated.

Prisoners released from state prisons in 1996 served an average of only 44% of their sentences under predominantly indeterminate sentencing structures (Ditton & Wilson, 1999). Rising crime rates during the 1980s and early 1990s saw a groundswell of opposition to what many saw as "mollycoddling" criminals, and there were many calls for longer sentences. In response to public demands, most states enacted **truth-in-sentencing laws**. These laws require that there be a truthful, realistic connection between the custodial sentences imposed on offenders and the time they actually serve and mandate that inmates serve at least 85% of their sentences before becoming eligible for release. In addition, many states restrict good time credit and/or parole eligibility.

Indeterminate sentence: A prison sentence consisting of a range of years to be determined by the convict's behavior rather than one of a fixed number of years.

Truth-in-sentencing laws: Laws that require there be a truthful, realistic connection between the sentences imposed on offenders and the time they actually serve.

Comstock/Thinkstock

PHOTO 5.2: A defendant listens as his sentence is announced by the judge.

Determinate sentences became more prevalent after the enactment of truth-in-sentencing laws. A **determinate sentence** means that convicted individuals are given a fixed number of years they must serve rather than a range. Under a determinate sentencing structure, the maximum prison time for a given crime is set by the state legislature in state statutes. This structure is more in tune with the classical notion that the purpose of punishment is to deter and that all who commit the same crime must receive a fixed sentence. This does not mean that everyone convicted of the same crime receives the same set penalty. For instance, the maximum time for burglary may be set at 15 years, and a repeat offender may be sentenced to the full 15 years. Another person who is a young first offender may receive only 5 years. Whatever the sentence, offenders know under this sentencing structure how much time they will need to serve. Longer and more determinate sentences satisfy the urge for greater punishment for offenders and serve an incapacitation function. However, time off for good behavior is still granted.

Another type of sentencing is **mandatory sentencing**, sometimes known as mandatory minimum sentencing. Mandatory sentencing can exist in the context of both determinate and indeterminate sentencing structures and simply means that probation is not an option for some crimes and that the minimum time to be served is set by law. It is set by law because legislative bodies in various states have decided that some crimes are just too serious for probation consideration (certain violent crimes) or have decided that there is a particular problem, such as drug trafficking or the use of a gun during the commission of a crime, that requires mandatory imprisonment as a deterrent.

Prison sentences imposed for two separate crimes, whether they occurred during the same incident (e.g., robbery and aggravated assault) or in different incidents (e.g., two separate burglaries), can be ordered to be served concurrently or consecutively. A **concurrent sentence** is one in which two separate sentences are served at the same time. If the robbery and aggravated assault crimes both carry sentences of 10 years, for instance, the offender's release date would be calculated on the basis of 10 years rather than 20 years. A **consecutive sentence** is one in which two or more sentences must be served sequentially (one at a time). If the robber/aggravated assaulter received two 10-year sentences to be served consecutively, his or her release date would be based on 20 rather than 10 years. Therefore, consecutive sentences increase the time a person spends in prison. The judge's decision to impose concurrent or consecutive sentences for persons convicted of two crimes may rest mainly on factors such as the seriousness of the crimes, criminal history, plea bargain arrangements, and offender cooperation. Some have suggested that judges may actually impose harsher sentences on those offenders with the audacity to demand a trial rather than accept a plea bargain because it makes extra work for the judge. This philosophy has been expressed as the judge's warning—"You take some of my time and I'll take some of yours" (Neubauer, 2008).

••• HABITUAL OFFENDER STATUTES

Habitual offender (or "three-strikes-and-you're-out") **statutes** are derived from the same punitive atmosphere that led to truth-in-sentencing statutes. These statutes

Determinate sentence: A prison sentence of a fixed number of years that must be served rather than a range.

Mandatory sentence: A prison sentence imposed for crimes for which probation is not an option, where the minimum time to be served is set by law.

Concurrent sentence: A sentence in which two separate sentences may be served at the same time.

Consecutive sentence: A sentence in which two or more sentences must be served sequentially.

Habitual offender statutes: Statutes mandating that offenders with a third felony conviction be sentenced to life imprisonment regardless of the nature of the third felony.

essentially mean that offenders with a third felony conviction may be sentenced to life imprisonment regardless of the nature of the third felony. This is a way of selectively incapacitating felons only after they have demonstrated the inability to live by society's rules. This all sounds fine until we factor in the financial costs of these sentences. Few of us would be against the lifetime incarceration of seriously violent offenders, but many states include relatively minor nonviolent crimes in their habitual offender statutes. For instance, the U.S. Supreme Court upheld the life sentence of a felon under Texas's habitual offender statute even though the underlying felonies involved nothing more serious than obtaining a total of less than $230 over a 15-year period by false pretenses (fraudulent use of a credit card and writing bad checks) in three separate incidents (*Rummel v. Estelle*, 1980). Very few of us would consider this a just sentence, and apart from the disproportionate nature of the sentence, the cost to the taxpayers of Texas of keeping Rummel in custody is many thousand times greater than the $230 he fraudulently obtained.

A life sentence still carries with it the possibility of parole, but some life sentences are imposed as **life without parole (LWOP)**. Such sentences may seem popular with the public at large until taxpayers get the bill. According to Nellis (2010), in 2008 there were 140,095 prisoners serving LWOP sentences in the United States, a 400% increase from 1984. LWOP sentences are usually imposed on those convicted of murder, but habitual property offenders have also been given such sentences. Long-term incapacitation of violent and/or habitual offenders is sound policy, but how much time is enough? In one large-scale study, only one-fifth of "lifers" who were released after long stays (15–30 years) in prison were rearrested within 3 years versus two-thirds of non-lifers who were released (Mauer, King, & Young, 2004). Old age is the best "cure" for criminal behavior that we have, so perhaps releasing lifers after 20 to 30 years of imprisonment is both humane and fiscally responsible. Given the ever increasing medical needs of people as they age, elderly inmates add a highly disproportionate financial burden on taxpayers.

●●● OTHER TYPES OF SENTENCES: SHOCK, SPLIT, AND NON-CUSTODIAL SENTENCES

Judges have many sentencing options open to them besides straight imprisonment. The fact is that more than 90% of sentences imposed in our criminal courts do not involve imprisonment (Neubauer, 2008). One type of sentence that does include imprisonment is shock incarceration, also called **shock probation**. This type of sentence is used to literally shock offenders into going straight by exposing them to the reality of prison life for a short period, typically no more than 30 days, followed by probation. Shock probation is typically reserved for young, first-time offenders who have committed a relatively serious felony but who are considered redeemable.

Split sentences are sentences that require felons to serve brief periods of confinement in a county jail prior to probation placement. Jail time may need to be served all at once or spread over a certain period such as every weekend in jail for the first year of probation placement. This is designed to show offenders that jail is a place to stay away from and thus to convince them that it would be a good idea to abide by all the conditions imposed by the court. Another form of split sentence is work release, whereby a person is consigned to a special portion of the jail on weekends and nights but is released to go to work during the day. Thus, these mainly non-custodial sentences typically mean a probation sentence coupled with certain conditions that must be followed in order to remain in the community. The conditions may involve such things as paying fines, paying restitution, attending drug and/or alcohol treatment programs, doing community service, remaining

Life without parole (LWOP): A life sentence with the additional condition that the person never be allowed parole.

Shock probation: A type of sentence aimed at shocking offenders into going straight by exposing them to the reality of prison life for a short period followed by probation.

Split sentences: Sentences that require convicted persons to serve brief periods of confinement in a county jail prior to probation placement.

ETHICAL ISSUE **?**

What Would You Do?

You are a prosecutor in a state with a strict three-strikes law. You have been assigned the case of 46-year-old Billy Banks, who has been arrested and charged with burglary. Billy has two previous felony convictions—one for auto theft and a previous burglary conviction—although you know he has committed many other crimes. Billy shoplifted merchandise worth $145 from a local department store. This amount is low enough to charge Billy with a misdemeanor petty theft, but because he admitted entering the store with the express purpose of shoplifting he was charged with a burglary, which is defined as "the unlawful entry of a structure to commit a felony or theft." What are the pros and cons of charging Billy under the three-strikes law? And with what crime would you charge him?

gainfully employed or be looking for work, and any number of other more specific conditions. These different non-custodial sentences and probation conditions will be discussed more fully in the chapters on probation, parole, and treatment.

VICTIM IMPACT STATEMENTS

In 1982, President Ronald Reagan created the President's Task Force on Victims of Crime. One of the outcomes of this was the inclusion of victim impact statements (VISs) at sentencing. A **victim impact statement** allows persons directly affected by the crime (or victims' survivors in the case of murder) to inform the court of the personal and emotional harm they have suffered as a result of the defendant's actions and, in some states, to make a sentencing recommendation. VISs are typically incorporated into PSIs written for the court by probation officers. The opportunity to provide input into the sentencing decision and the recognition that the harm is suffered by individuals, not the state, is considered a valuable aid in the emotional recovery of victims and may even aid the rehabilitation of some defendants by forcing them to confront the harm caused by their actions (Walsh, 1986).

VISs have been challenged as prejudicial and a return to a more conservative punitive stance toward punishment because such statements can lead to sympathy for the victim and hostility toward the defendant (Paternoster & Deise, 2011). However, in *Payne v. Tennessee* (1991), the U.S. Supreme Court upheld the constitutionality of VIS testimony in the sentencing phase of a trial, and all 50 states now include the use of VISs in the form of written or oral statements at sentencing. But how influential are they in terms of the actual sentence imposed? Overall, the evidence is ambiguous, although in capital cases—where juries rather than judges decide the sentences—they seem to be influential (Paternoster & Deise, 2011). Research in noncapital cases tends to show that VISs actually have little effect on sentencing decisions after accounting for the effects of legally relevant variables (seriousness of crime and prior record) (Walsh, 1986). This sometimes leads to resentment and dissatisfaction with the sentencing process when victims (or their survivors) believed that their recommendations would carry more weight than they did (Meredith & Paquette, 2001).

Victim impact statement: A statement made by persons directly affected by a crime (or victims' survivors in the case of murder) to inform the court of the personal and emotional harm they have suffered as a result of the defendant's actions and, in some states, to make a sentencing recommendation.

••• SENTENCING BY CIVIL COMMITMENT FOR SEX OFFENDERS

The animus that society has toward criminals is nowhere more obvious than in the case of sex offenders. In 1997, the U.S. Supreme Court upheld a Kansas statute (*Kansas v. Hendricks*, 1997) aimed at keeping sexual predators behind bars under civil commitment laws *after* they have served their prison terms if they demonstrate "mental abnormality." The decision paved the way for other states, and for the federal government, to pass similar involuntary commitment laws. Despite being placed in confinement against one's will, a civil commitment is not considered punishment in the eyes of the law because it is not a decision rendered in criminal court. Prior to 1990, civil commitments were limited to those individuals said to suffer from mental illness, but to cover sex offenders several states have loosened their criterion for commitment to "mental abnormality" as opposed to "mental illness."

The most notorious contemporary example is that of Nushawn Williams (aka Shyteek Johnson). Nushawn was convicted in 1997 of having unprotected sex with numerous girls and women, including a 13-year-old girl, in drugs-for-sex encounters, knowing that he was HIV positive. He was sentenced to 12 years in prison, but at the completion of his sentence the state of New York refused to release him due to its Mental Hygiene Law. In 2013, a jury determined that he was a dangerous sex offender with a mental abnormality and should be detained. In 2014, the New York State Supreme Court ordered that Williams be committed to a secure treatment facility as a sexual predator. According to Dennis Vacco, who was the New York attorney general when the state legislature passed the Mental Hygiene Law, "It was designed to keep the most vicious sexual predators from ever getting back out on the street, and in this instance, I couldn't think of anybody who is more eligible for the application of this statute than Nushawn Williams" (Ewing & Dudzik, 2014).

Whatever your thoughts are about sex offenders in general, Williams had demonstrated his wanton disregard for others, knowingly infecting his victims with a deadly virus. Such laws have created a category of individuals defined as "abnormal" who may be punished indefinitely for what they *might* do if released. Some people consider these laws to be wrong and discriminatory. Others laud them as protecting the public from predatory and dangerous individuals who can almost be guaranteed to offend again if released. What do you think?

••• PROBLEM-SOLVING COURTS

Problem-solving courts are alternatives to traditional criminal courts that cannot adequately address the problems of offenders with special needs and other issues such as drug, alcohol, domestic violence, and mental health problems. These courts originated during the late 1980s to early 1990s in response to burgeoning rates of incarceration, the financial costs of incarceration, the realization that many offenders needed treatment rather than jail or prison, and the woeful inability of the social services system to provide that treatment. The traditional criminal courts have long seen the same individuals with the same problems recycle through them time after time. Problem-solving courts are designed to address the underlying causes of a person's antisocial behavior under the assumption that it will cease or diminish with the alleged cause under control. These courts largely suspend the adversarial approach to justice in the interests of achieving a therapeutic outcome. In other words, the judge, prosecutor, *and* defense attorney are supposed to work together collegially along with treatment specialists and supervising probation/parole officers to achieve a common goal—the rehabilitation of the offender. These courts thus promote outcomes aimed at benefitting offenders, victims, and society as a whole by both saving jail and prison costs and minimizing the probability of reoffending. Problem-solving courts thus are novel responses to deal with problems that affect the probability of further criminal behavior. According to the Bureau of Justice Assistance (2013), problem-solving courts are characterized by the following:

- *Focus on Outcomes*: Problem-solving courts are designed to provide positive case outcomes for victims, society, and offenders (e.g., reducing recidivism, creating safer communities).

- *System Change*: Problem-solving courts promote reform in how the government responds to problems such as drug addiction and mental illness.

Problem-solving courts: Alternatives to traditional criminal courts that cannot adequately address the problems of offenders with special needs and other issues such as alcoholism and mental health problems.

- *Judicial Involvement*: Judges take a more hands-on approach to addressing problems and changing behaviors of defendants.

- *Collaboration*: Problem-solving courts work with external parties to achieve certain goals (e.g., developing partnerships with mental health providers).

- *Nontraditional Roles*: These courts and their personnel take on roles or processes not common in traditional courts. For example, some problem-solving courts are less adversarial than traditional criminal justice processing.

- *Screening and Assessment*: Use of screening and assessment tools to identify appropriate individuals for these courts is common.

- *Early Identification of Potential Candidates*: Use of screening and assessment tools to determine a defendant's eligibility for a problem-solving court usually occurs early in a defendant's involvement with criminal justice processing.

We concentrate on drug courts, which are the most prevalent type of problem-solving court, in this chapter.

●●● DRUG COURTS

Drug courts are by far the most common form of problem-solving court in the United States. In response to the growing drug problem, the first drug court was established in Miami–Dade County, Florida, in 1989. Twenty years later, there were 2,037 drug courts active in all 50 states, growth that suggests there is much that is positive about drug courts (Mackin, Lucas, & Lambarth, 2010). A referral to a **drug court** requires the offender to be involved in an intensive treatment program that lasts 2 years. Participants typically have pled guilty to a nonviolent drug-related felony charge. Under the supervision of the judge, probation officers, and other caseworkers, participants attend counseling groups and 12-step meetings, regularly appear before a judge, and must submit to random urine testing. If a participant successfully completes the program, in nearly all jurisdictions the criminal charges will be dismissed. The U.S. Department of Justice (Ashcroft, Daniels, & Herraiz, 1997) provided the 10-component model presented below for state and county agencies implementing their drug court systems:

1. Drug courts integrate alcohol and other drug treatment services with justice system case processing.

2. Using a non-adversarial approach, prosecution and defense counsel promote public safety while protecting participants' due process rights.

3. Eligible participants are identified early and promptly placed in the drug court program.

4. Drug courts provide access to a continuum of alcohol, drug, and other related treatment and rehabilitation services.

5. Abstinence is monitored by frequent alcohol and other drug testing.

6. A coordinated strategy governs drug court responses to participants' compliance.

7. Ongoing judicial interaction with each drug court participant is essential.

8. Monitoring and evaluation measure the achievement of program goals and gauge effectiveness.

Drug court: A special sentence for drug-related nonviolent offenders who must then complete an extensive drug treatment program.

9. Continuing interdisciplinary education promotes effective drug court planning, implementation, and operations.

10. Forging partnerships among drug courts, public agencies, and community-based organizations generates local support and enhances drug court effectiveness.

The drug court processes from arrest to final outcome (either graduation or termination and incarceration) are graphically shown in Figure 5.1 from the Albany, New York, drug court. The first stage of the process is a referral to the drug court, typically from an offender's attorney. With the receipt of the referral, members of the drug court team review the applicant's criminal history and police reports relevant to the current offense and other pertinent information. Violent offenders and offenders who have previously committed the same offense or who have failed other treatment programs before will not be accepted into most drug court programs. A standardized form containing all the gathered information is sent to members of the drug court team for review at a weekly staff meeting. After reviewing a case, members of a drug court team vote to accept or reject an offender's application. If the offender is accepted into a program, the case is referred to a probation officer, who then performs a prescreening interview. The officer will listen to the defendant and observe his or her behavior and attitudes in order to assess the level of desire to change his or her lifestyle. The officer will provide a rundown of the drug court program and ascertain an offender's willingness to abide fully with the program's guidelines in order to achieve sobriety. Most offenders, it should be understood, lack the personal skills associated with success in any endeavor, so the prospect of participating in an arduous treatment program in which they will be held strictly accountable is often daunting to them. Offenders who, by their words and actions, give the impression that they do not take responsibility for their behavior and have no desire to change will not be accepted.

As a result of their frequent interactions during court appearances, it is expected that participants will develop rapport with the judge, who speaks directly to them

FIGURE 5.1   Case Flow From Arrest to Court Termination in the Albany, New York, Drug Court

The Drug Court Process

Defendant is arrested or indicted on sealed indictment

Defendant is evaluated, file is reviewed and discussed by team

Defendant participates and is monitored throughout process

Defendant successfully completes drug court

Defendant returns to court

Defendant goes to court, qualifies for drug court, and agrees to participate

Defendant accepts plea to felony and signs drug court contract as part of plea

Defendant violates drug court agreement and the case returns to criminal court for sentencing

Source: Adapted from Albany County Judicial Center, http://albanycountyda.com/Bureaus/RevJohnUMillerOR/CommunityProsecution/drugcourtprocess.aspx

PHOTO 5.3: An offender listens to the judge in drug court.

in an informal way, asking about their progress and either exhorting them to try harder or praising their accomplishments. The judge will also remind them of the obligation to remain drug free and may impose sanctions for ongoing drug use or other behavior that impedes progress toward sobriety. These sanctions may include jail time and/or dismissal from the program, in which case the offender receives the agreed-on prison sentence. The judge will ultimately decide the defendant's fate—graduation or incarceration.

Graduation from drug court takes place with as much fanfare as a typical college graduation ceremony. Commenting on the graduation of 54 drug, DUI (driving under the influence), and veteran's treatment court graduates recognized at a ceremony in Tulsa, Oklahoma, Bland (2014) wrote,

> Drug Court saved Clark Dagnall's life. In return, the 26-year-old Sand Springs resident took the stage at the program's most recent graduation and promised to pay it forward by helping others. "My goal is just to help the next addict," he told the crowd of graduates' friends and family members. "Maybe I can get through to somebody that nobody else could."

Graduates received certificates of graduation for completing the nearly 2-year program. Bland (2014) also wrote that the graduates who spoke at the ceremony were grateful for the support and guidance they received in the program, and the drug court staff expressed their pride in the graduates. "'We watch these individuals transform and rise from the ashes,' said Lawrence Gilbert, Action Steps Counseling program coordinator."

Note the strong emphasis on interagency cooperation, the provision of services to participants, and the strict monitoring of their behavior. In addition to saving the states many millions of dollars in jail and prison costs, drug courts appear to be quite successful in reducing recidivism. For instance, the Baltimore County Juvenile Drug Court outcome analysis (Mackin et al., 2010) estimated that the program saved the county $8,762 per participant over 24 months because of lower recidivism rates and savings from incarceration. Figure 5.2 provides an illustration of recidivism outcomes for drug court graduates, participants who did not graduate, and the control group consisting of juveniles who fit the criteria for participation. Note that while the likelihood of rearrest increased for all groups over time, the graduates had a lower arrest rate at 24 months than the control group did at 6 months.

Roman's (2013) study of drug courts in 29 different U.S. jurisdictions showed that drug court participants were significantly less likely to test positive for drugs than other probationers (29% vs. 46%) and less likely to be rearrested (52% vs. 62%). Roman also noted that the cost per drug court participant was significantly higher per year ($15,326) for drug court participants than for comparison probationers ($7,191), but that was offset by lower costs in other areas such as the costs of further crime and victimization. Overall, the net financial benefit per participant spread over all 29 jurisdictions in Roman's study was $5,680 compared with control probationers. If there were only 100 participants, this would amount to an average saving of $1,360,000 over 2 years, which is the usual duration of such courts. This is without even considering the emotional costs of criminal victimization. Other studies have found that, compared with traditional probation, drug courts reduce overall recidivism by 12.4% to 13.0% for drug-related recidivism (Mitchell, Wilson, Eggers, & MacKenzie, 2012).

A meta-analysis of 201 different studies (Sevigny, Fuleihan, & Ferdik, 2013) found that drug courts reduce jail and prison incarceration by 32%. Putting this in a nationwide perspective, the researchers reported that this results in 9,911 fewer incarcerations among the estimated 52,777 annual drug court participants across the United States. However, these lower incarceration rates were offset by the longer sentences imposed on participants who fail. Nevertheless, in addition to saving the states many millions of dollars in jail and prison costs, drug courts appear to be quite successful in reducing recidivism.

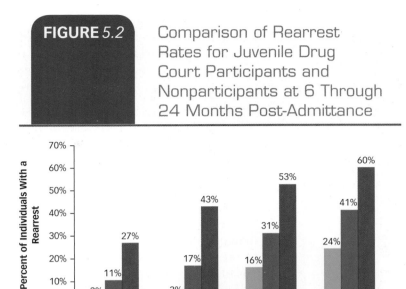

FIGURE *5.2* Comparison of Rearrest Rates for Juvenile Drug Court Participants and Nonparticipants at 6 Through 24 Months Post-Admittance

Source: Mackin, J., Lucas, L., & Lambarth, C. (2010). *Baltimore County Juvenile Drug Court outcome and cost evaluation.* Baltimore, MD: NPC Research.

●●● SENTENCING DISPARITY, LEGITIMATE AND ILLEGITIMATE

Sentencing disparity occurs when there is wide variation in sentences received by different offenders. This disparity is legitimate if it is based on considerations such as crime seriousness and/or prior record, but it is discriminatory if it is not. We think of sentencing disparity as discriminatory if there are differences in punishment in cases in which no rational justification can be found for them. The biggest concern is racial discrimination. There is no doubt that the American criminal justice system has a dark history of racial discrimination, but does this indictment still apply?

African Americans receive harsher sentences on average than white or Asian American offenders, a fact often seen as racist, but is it? Sentencing variation according to race is reasonable and just if the group being more harshly punished commits more serious crimes and does so more often than other groups, but it is discriminatory and unjust if that group does not. All data sources show that African Americans commit more crime, especially violent crime, than whites or Asians. For instance, the 2016 Uniform Crime Reports (Federal Bureau of Investigation [FBI], 2016) shows that African Americans were overrepresented in arrests for all crimes, especially violent crime, in 2015 except for DUI.

But the question is whether this racial disproportionality in offending is sufficient to account for the disparity in sentencing. One sentencing scholar concluded that it was not: "Racial bias continues to pervade the U.S. criminal justice sentencing system [although] the effects of this bias are somewhat hidden . . . or may even have less to do with the race of the defendant than with the race of the victim" (Kansal, 2005, p. 17). Another scholar concluded the opposite: "Although critics of American race relations may think otherwise, research on sentencing has failed to show a definitive pattern

Sentencing disparity: Wide variation in sentences received by different offenders that may be legitimate or discriminatory.

of racial discrimination" (Siegel, 2006, p. 578). Different researchers thus arrive at different conclusions, but there is widespread agreement on one point: The more stringent researchers are in controlling for the effects of legally relevant variables (crime seriousness and criminal record), the less likely they are to find racial discrimination (Siegel, 2006).

Sentencing research is complicated and typically reports average effects, among which are multiple interacting variables hiding specifics. Many extralegal factors (including race, ethnicity, and gender) play at least some role in sentencing. For instance, victim characteristics play a role; if the victim is a child, is elderly, has a disability, or is female, the sentence is typically harsher (Hatch & Walsh, 2016). The extent to which victims participate in sentencing via victim impact statements also generally leads to harsher sentences (Haynes, 2011). Political ideology also plays a role, with more conservative "law and order" jurisdictions sentencing more harshly (Ulmer, 2012). Wu and Walsh (2007) found that conservative probation officers recommended harsher sentences (regardless of race) than liberal officers and that judges followed the recommendations of both sets of officers closely. A study of the sentencing practices of 18 Ohio judges found that half of them took no extralegal facts into consideration at all, 5 judges sentenced blacks more leniently, and 4 judges sentenced blacks more harshly (Wooldredge, 2010). The harsh and lenient judges just cancel one another out if researchers look only at the overall record of all judges without examining the record of individual judges.

One study of more than 46,000 federal defendants in 23 states found no evidence of racial bias after controlling for legally relevant variables (Wang & Mears, 2010), although Jordan and Freiburger (2015) maintained that many studies (including their own) continue to show that minorities are sentenced more severely than whites. So, is there racial discrimination involved in sentencing? The short answer is that it depends on the quality of the data, where you look, how hard you look, and even what you expect to find based on your assumptions.

Table 5.1 shows the average length in months of felony sentences in state courts in 2006 broken down by race and gender (Durose, Farole, & Rosenmerkel, 2010). You can see that black males have longer sentences than white males and that males have longer sentences than females. Also note that for violent offenses white females receive longer sentences than black females. However, no conclusions about racial or gender bias can be drawn from the table because it tells us nothing about how serious each of the crimes was (some robberies, sexual assaults, and assaults are more vicious than others, for instance), nor does it tell us anything about the criminal histories of the men and women represented in the table.

One of the biggest concerns in the sentencing disparity literature is the huge difference in sentencing received by crack possession versus sentences imposed for possession of powder cocaine. Of particular concern was the difference in sentencing imposed on those who used or sold the cheaper crack cocaine, who tended to be minority group offenders, particularly African Americans, versus those who used or sold powder cocaine, which tended to be more expensive and more likely used and trafficked by white offenders. In 1988, Congress passed the Anti-Drug Abuse Act, which established a 100-to-1 quantity ratio differential between powder and crack cocaine. That act also specified that simple possession of crack cocaine was to be treated more seriously than simple possession of other illegal drugs. According to a U.S. Sentencing Commission Report to Congress in 1995, in 1986 Congress was reacting to media hype about how addictive crack was, with congressional members claiming that crack use was at "epidemic" levels, crack babies were severely impaired, and crime related to crack use was out of control in some cities. African American law professor Randall Kennedy informed us that the Congressional Black Caucus strongly supported the legislation and actually pressed for even tougher penalties (Kennedy, 1998). No one would call

TABLE 5.1	Average Length of Felony Sentences in 2006 by Offense, Race, and Gender (in months)

| | Mean Maximum Sentence Length for Persons Who Were: | | | |
| | White | | Black | |
Most Serious Conviction Offense	Male	Female	Male	Female
All offenses	40	25	45	25
Violent offenses	75	52	88	41
Murder/Nonnegligent manslaughter	265	225	266	175
Sexual assault	115	72	125	32
Robbery	89	61	101	54
Aggravated assault	42	30	48	29
Other violence	43	55	41	17
Property offenses	31	22	35	23
Burglary	41	29	50	34
Larceny	24	17	23	19
Fraud/Forgery	27	22	27	23
Drug offenses	31	22	36	22
Possession	21	17	25	15
Trafficking	39	26	40	27
Weapon offenses	34	24	34	24

Source: Durose, Farole, and Rosenmerkel (2010). Bureau of Justice Statistics.

black congresspersons anti-black racists. It is more sensible to conclude that they were deeply concerned about how crack was decimating black communities across the country with addiction and bloody turf wars over distribution territories. Nevertheless, at the time of this 1995 report, the U.S. Sentencing Commission (1995) knew that "88.3 percent of the offenders convicted in federal court for crack cocaine distribution in 1993 were Black and 7.1 percent were Hispanic," and critics were concerned that instead of fair and evenhanded sentences for all, the effect of the Anti-Drug Act was to be unfair and harsh in the sentencing of racial minorities (p. 1).

Criticisms of the different treatment of people convicted of possession of pharmacologically identical drugs resulting in the increased incarceration of minorities for longer periods of time mounted to the point where Congress needed to do something. In 2009, a **Fair Sentencing Act** was introduced and passed by Congress and signed into law by President Barack Obama on August 3, 2010. Under the act, the amount of crack cocaine subject to the 5-year minimum sentence is increased from 5 grams to 28 grams, thereby reducing the 100-to-1 ratio to an 18-to-1 ratio (28 grams of crack gets as much time as 500 grams of powder cocaine). Thus, there is still a large sentencing differential between possessors of crack and possessors of powder cocaine. This ratio probably reflects lawmakers' perceptions that crack is more intimately related to

Fair Sentencing Act of 2010: An act mandating that the amount of crack cocaine subject to the 5-year minimum sentence be increased from 5 grams to 28 grams, thereby reducing the 100-to-1 ratio to an 18-to-1 ratio (28 grams of crack gets as much time as 500 grams of powder cocaine).

violence (in territorial battles) and to a higher probability of addiction than the powder variety (Leigey & Bachman, 2007).

••• STRUCTURING SENTENCING: THE PRESENTENCE INVESTIGATION REPORT

To assist judges in sentencing, a **presentence investigation report** is commonly used. There are few documents as important to the defendant as the PSI. It is used for many other purposes besides sentencing such as treatment planning, classification to supervision levels in probation/parole departments and prisons, and parole decisions (Walsh & Stohr, 2010). A PSI is usually completed in 30 days or less so that the convicted individual can be sentenced in a timely manner. PSIs are usually written by probation officers informing the judge of various aspects of the offense for which the defendant is being sentenced as well as information about the defendant's background (educational, family, and employment history), gang ties, substance abuse, character, and criminal history. Because of plea bargaining, judges typically know very little about the circumstances of the offense or the offender. On the basis of this information, officers make recommendations to the court regarding the sentence the offender should receive. Because probation officers enjoy considerable discretionary power relating to how their reports are crafted to be favorable or unfavorable to offenders, many scholars view them as the agents who really determine the sentences that offenders receive (Champion, 2005). Other researchers, however, suggest that the high rate of judicial agreement with officer recommendations reflects an anticipatory effect, whereby officers become adept at "second guessing" a judge's likely sentence for a given case and recommend accordingly (Durnescu, 2008).

In Focus 5.1 is an example of a (fictional) PSI containing the usual required information. PSIs come in a variety of sizes, the smallest being a 1- or 2-page short-form report used in misdemeanor cases or less serious "run-of-the-mill" felony cases. For serious or complicated cases, we may see 10- to 15-page reports, although the trend is toward smaller reports. The report given here is an example of a mid-range report used for relatively serious crimes, although the trend is for shorter, more concise reports focusing primarily on legally relevant variables.

PSI CONTROVERSIES

Although the PSI has generally been considered a positive aid to individualized justice, it is not without its problems. Because the future of a defendant depends to a great extent on the content of the report, the information contained therein should be reliable and objective. All pertinent information must be verified by cross-checking with more than one source, and those sources should be reliable. The officer must be careful in the terms he or she uses to describe the offender. The use of phrases such as "morally bankrupt" and "sweet young lady" may reveal more about the officer's attitudes and values than the defendant's character.

If you were the subject of a PSI, would you not like to see what was in it so that you could challenge any erroneous information harmful to you contained in it? There have been a number of arguments for and against allowing defendants and their attorneys access to PSIs. It is feared that if victims and other informants from whom the investigating officer has sought information know that the offender will see their comments, they will refuse to offer their information; thus, the judge would not have complete information on which to make the sentencing decision. However, 16 states currently require full disclosure; other states require disclosure but erase information that may

Presentence investigation report: Report written by the probation officer informing the judge of various aspects of the offense for which the defendant is being sentenced as well as providing information about the defendant's background (educational, family, and employment history); character; and criminal history.

IN FOCUS 5.1

Modern-Day John Howard—Dr. Ken Kerle Example of a PSI

**Gem County Adult
Probation Department**

Williamstown, Iowa 74812

Name: Joan Place

Indictment No.: CR 6742

Age: 28

Race: white

Sex: female

Marital Status: divorced

Judge: Franklin Riley

Probation Officer: James Smith

Attorney: William Paley

Offense: forgery

Conduct (IRC #2908) two counts

Circumstances of the Offense:

On 8/10/94, Mr. John Smith, security operative for the Omaha Trust Company (OTC), reported to the police that the defendant cashed forged checks in the amount of $917.00 at various OTC branch banks. These checks were drawn against the account of one Mrs. Patricia DeValera, 4561 Black St. The defendant stole Mrs. DeValera's checks while employed by her as a nurse's aide. Mr. Smith also indicated that the defendant cashed forged checks in the amount of $575.00 on the account of Mr. Richard Blane, a former boyfriend of the defendant. The total loss to the Omaha Trust bank is $1,492.00.

Defendant's Version:

The defendant's written statement is reproduced verbatim below: "Took checks filled it out in amount I needed for drugs and signed it, forged a name and cashed the checks in Aug. of 1994. No, I did not pay back the person. I was so drug dependent that I took my boyfriends checks, Mrs. Devaleras checks too. All I could live for at the time was heroin and alcohol (mainly beer). I'm sorry I did these things, normally I wouldn't of forged the checks if I wouldn't of needed drugs. All I could do was live for drugs. I've been threw the withdrawals of drugs when I put myself in the treatment center on Wilson St." It is noted that the defendant places the blame for her criminal activity on her craving for heroin and alcohol. Her statements of remorse ring rather hollow in light of her new forgery arrest while undergoing presentence

investigation. She was arrested on this new charge on 2/22/95 and released on $1,000 bond (10% allowed). Upon learning of this new arrest, I rearrested her on 2/24/95 and placed her in the county jail, where she has been ever since.

Prior Record:

Juvenile: None known.

Adult:

8-18-94 OPD Forgery, 5 counts, amended to one count: Present Offense

11-6-94 OPD Forgery, 3 counts, pending under CR841234.

2-5-95 OPD Forgery, pending.

Above record reflects juvenile, OPD, BCI, and FBI record checks.

Present Family Status:

The defendant is the fourth of five children born to Ann and Frank Place. Her father passed away in January of 1991. On 6/17/85, the defendant married one James Fillpot. Mr. Fillpot was described as a heavy drug abuser and is now serving a life sentence on an aggravated murder charge (he was convicted of murdering the defendant's alleged lover). The defendant divorced Mr. Fillpot shortly after his 1989 conviction, and shortly thereafter (6/89), she married one Ralph Burke. Mr. Burke is an alcoholic with an extensive criminal record. After an extremely abusive 2 years of marriage, the defendant's second marriage ended in divorce on 5/12/92. No children were born to either of these marriages. At the time of her arrest, the defendant was living with her mother at the above listed address.

Present Employment or Support:

The defendant is unemployed at the present time and was existing on $76.00 in food stamps at the time of her arrest. She receives no general relief monies. Her last period of employment was as a nurse's aide for Mrs. DeValera, one of the victims of the present offense.

(Continued)

(Continued)

This employment was for the period encompassing March through August, 1993. The defendant's longest period of employment was with the Red Barron Restaurant, 3957 Laskar Rd, as a waitress from March 1988 through November 1991. This employer has not responded to our request for information as yet.

Health, Physical:

The defendant describes her current physical health as "O.K." She relates no significant hospitalizations, diseases, or current health problems with the exception of her substance abuse. Her substance abuse is quite extensive. She claims that she has used anywhere from $20 to $300 per day on heroin. Needle marks on her arms attest to her frequent usage. She also relates that she likes to consume 6 to 12 beers per night, which she claims that she receives free from boyfriends. Her substance abuse goes back to her first marriage 13 years ago when Mr. Fillpot introduced her to heroin. Her second husband, Mr. Burke, got her heavily involved in alcohol. She admits that she has experimented with many other drugs, but states that heroin and beer are her drugs of choice. This officer contacted the Wilson Street Drug Rehabilitation Facility regarding the defendant's claimed attendance there. It appears that she did voluntarily admit herself there, but left after the first 15-day phase. I also made an effort to get her into the ROAD drug rehabilitation program. However, after two interviews with ROAD personnel, the defendant was denied admission because they thought that her only motive for seeking admission was her current legal difficulties.

Health, Mental:

The defendant is a 1981 graduate of Borah High School. She graduated 287th out of a class of 348. She attained a cumulative GPA of 1.64 on a 4.0 scale. Although no IQ information is available, the defendant impresses as functioning well within the average range of intelligence as gauged by her written and verbal statements. She did indicate that she was easily led and that she does not think much of herself. Her choice of marriage partners (both very abusive to her) and her current boyfriends give the impression that she is attracted to men who will verify her low opinion of herself.

Statutory Penalty:

N.R.C. 2913.31

Forgery "shall be imprisoned for a period of 6 months, 1 year, or 1 and one-half years and/or fined up to $2,500."

Evaluative Summary:

Before the court is a 28-year-old woman facing her first felony conviction. However, she has numerous other forgery charges pending at this time. There would seem to be little doubt that the genesis of her criminal activity is her severe abuse of alcohol and drugs. She also appears to possess a low concept of herself as indicated by her very poor choice of marriage partners, both of whom were serious substance abusers and both of whom were physically abusive to her. She appears to be intimately involved in the drug subculture. I initiated the procedure to get the defendant admitted to the ROAD residential drug treatment center. However, after conducting two interviews with the defendant, personnel from the ROAD decided that her motivation for seeking treatment was her current legal difficulties and thus her application was denied. They did indicate that they would reconsider her application after the disposition of the present offense. Therefore, I recommend that the defendant be placed on probation, ordered to pay complete restitution, and to pursue entry into the ROAD. It is also recommended that she remain in the county jail after sentencing to reinitiate her application with ROAD.

Approved	Respectfully Submitted
_____	_____
James F. Collins	Joyce Williams
Unit Supervisor	Probation Officer

lead to retaliation such as the officer's recommendation and negative comments from informants. Despite objections and real concerns about confidentiality, the trend is to allow defendants access to their PSIs. For instance, in the federal system, Section 3552 of the U.S. Code states,

The court shall assure that a report filed pursuant to this section is disclosed to the defendant, the counsel for the defendant, and the attorney for the Government at least ten days prior to the date set for sentencing, unless this minimum period is waived by the defendant. The court shall provide a copy of the presentence report to the attorney for the Government to use in collecting an assessment, criminal fine, forfeiture or restitution imposed.

In the federal system and in some state systems, probation/parole officers no longer write PSIs. Rather, they merely complete sentencing guidelines and certain other assessment tools and calculate the presumed sentence (Abadinsky, 2009). This and a number of other factors may be signaling a move away from individualized justice (the idea that punishment should be tailored to the individual and be consistent with rehabilitation) and back to the classical idea discussed in Chapter 1 that the punishment should fit the crime and serve as a retributive or deterrent factor.

ETHICAL ISSUE

What Would You Do?

You are a probation officer writing a PSI on 29-year-old Robert Jackson, who was arrested for carrying a concealed weapon (CCW). Robert is very concerned about his arrest and fears going to jail, losing his job, and not being able to support his wife and two children. At the conclusion of the PSI interview, he shakes hands with you and passes on a $100 bill. Would you report this attempted bribe and make matters worse for Robert, or would you return the money with a stern lecture and then forget about it?

●●● STRUCTURED SENTENCING: SENTENCING GUIDELINES

We saw in Chapter 1 that a major concern of the Classical School of criminal justice was to make the law more fair and equal by removing a great deal of judicial discretion and providing standards set by the legislature for making punishment for equal crimes standard. Prior to 1984, federal judges enjoyed nearly unlimited sentencing discretion as long as they stayed within the statutory maximum penalties. This led to a lot of criticism regarding sentencing disparities and moved Congress to establish the **U.S. Sentencing Commission**. This commission was charged with the task of creating mandatory sentencing guidelines to rein in judicial discretion (Reynolds, 2009). **Sentencing guidelines** are forms containing scales with a set of rules for numerically computing sentences that offenders should receive based on the crime(s) they committed and on their criminal record.

Guidelines are devised by federal or state sentencing commissions and provide classifications of suggested punishments based on an offender's scores on those scales. Because guidelines are a set of rules and principles that are supposed to decide a defendant's sentence, they curtail the discretionary powers of judges, as was intended by Congress. Most people view this as a good thing because unbridled discretion can lead to wide sentencing disparities based only on a judge's subjective evaluations and whims. At one extreme we might get "hanging" judges, and at the other end we might get "bleeding heart" judges, so a defendant's fate may depend largely on the temperament or ideology of the judge by whom he or she has the good luck or bad fortune to be sentenced.

Guidelines thus provide structured predictability to criminal sanctions by taking Aristotle's definition of justice ("treating equals equally and unequals unequally according to relevant differences") and assigning numbers to these relevant

U.S. Sentencing Commission: A commission charged with creating mandatory sentencing guidelines to control judicial discretion.

Sentencing guidelines: Scales for numerically computing sentences that offenders should receive based on the crime(s) they committed and on their criminal record.

FIGURE 5.3 Continuum of State Sentencing Guidelines

		AL			DE	AK				OR		
OH		DC			UT	MA				KS		
WI	MO	TN	AR	LA	VA	MD	MI	PA	WA	MN	NC

| 1 | 2 | 3 | 4 | 5 | 6 | 7 | 8 | 9 | 10 | 11 | 12 |

← More Voluntary   More Mandatory →

Source: National Center for State Courts (2008).

differences. The sample guideline in Figure 5.3 illustrates how numbers are assigned to various aspects of a case that are considered relevant to sentencing. The guidelines used by the federal government and some states limit themselves to crime seriousness and prior record, while others are more comprehensive and assign points not only for the statutory degree of seriousness of the offense and prior record but also for the amount of harm done; whether the offender was on bail, probation, or parole at the time; prior periods of incarceration; and a number of other factors. These numbers are then applied to a grid at the point at which they intersect, which contains the appropriate sentence.

Given the usefulness of guidelines, it is unfortunate that not all states use them and that, among the states that do, they vary greatly in quality. In 2008, the National Center for State Courts (NCSC, 2008) evaluated the guidelines in all 21 states that use them and assigned them points based on a number of criteria. The most important of these criteria were whether or not the guidelines were voluntary or mandatory, whether or not compelling and substantial reasons were required for departures from guideline sentences, and whether or not written reasons must be provided for any such departures. The NCSC then ranked each state's guidelines from most voluntary (judges need not follow them) to more mandatory (there is a presumption that judges will abide by them). Figure 5.3 presents the NCSC's evaluation of the guidelines of the 21 states that had them in 2008 on a continuum from most voluntary to most mandatory.

Although guidelines were mandatory in the federal system for many years after their creation, currently they are only advisory. By mandatory, we mean that the sentences indicated by the guidelines must be imposed unless there are compelling reasons for not following them. Advisory guidelines are used simply to guide the judges' decisions by providing a uniform set of standards for them to consult if they wish. According to Lubitz and Ross (2001), sentencing guidelines have achieved a number of outcomes consistent with this classical ideal and with Aristotle's definition of justice. These outcomes include the following:

1. A reduction in sentencing disparity.

2. More uniform and consistent sentencing.

3. A more open and understandable sentencing process.

4. Decreased punishment for certain categories of offenses and offenders and increased punishment for others.

5. Aid in prioritizing and allocating correctional resources.

6. Provision of a rational basis for sentencing and increased judicial accountability.

Figure 5.4 is a sentencing guideline that takes into consideration many more factors than the seriousness of the offense and prior record and leaves quite a bit of room for subjective judgment, especially in the culpability, mitigation, and credits section. How would you complete this guideline for the Joan Place case outlined in our sample PSI (In Focus 5.1)? What degree of culpability/mitigation would you assign her, and what credits would you give her?

FIGURE *5.4*   Example of a Comprehensive Sentencing Guideline

FELONY SENTENCING WORKSHEET:

DEFENDANT'S NAME:_____   **CASE NO.:**_____

OFFENSE RATING

1. Degree of Offense:

Assess points for the one most serious offense or its equivalent for which offender is being sentenced, as follows: 1st degree felony = 4 points; 2nd degree felony = 3 points; 3rd degree felony = 2 points; 4th degree felony = 1point.   _____

2. Multiple Offenses:

Assess 2 points if one or more of the following applies: (A) Offender is being sentenced for two or more offenses committed in different incidents; (B) offender is currently under a misdemeanor or felony sentence imposed by any court; or (C) present offense was committed while offender on probation or parole.   _____

3. Actual or Potential Harm:

Assess 2 points if one or more of the following applies: (A) Serious physical harm to a person was caused; (B) property damage or loss of $300.00 or more was caused; (C) there was a high risk of any such harm, damage, or loss, though not caused; (D) the gain or potential gain from theft offense(s) was $300 or more; or (E) dangerous ordinance or a deadly weapon was actually used in the incident, or its use was attempted or threatened.   _____

4. Culpability:

Assess 2 points if one or more of the following applies: (A) Offender was engaging in continuing criminal activity as a source of income or livelihood; (B) offense was part of a continuing conspiracy to which offender was a party; or (C) offense included shocking and deliberate cruelty in which offender participated or acquiesced.   _____

5. Mitigation:

Deduct 1 point for **each** of the following, as applicable: (A) There was substantial provocation, justification, or excuse for offense; (B) victim induced or facilitated offense; (C) offense was committed in the heat of anger; and (D) the property damaged, lost, or stolen was restored or recovered without significant cost to the victim.   _____

NET TOTAL = OFFENSE RATING   _____

DEFENSE RATING

1. Prior Convictions:

Assess 2 points for each verified prior felony conviction, any jurisdiction. Count adjudications of delinquency for felony as convictions.   _____

Assess 1 point for each verified prior misdemeanor conviction and jurisdiction. Count adjudications of delinquency for misdemeanor as convictions. Do not count traffic or intoxication offenses or disorderly conduct, disturbing the peace, or equivalent offenses.   _____

2. Repeat Offenses:

Assess 2 points if present offense is offense of violence, sex offense, theft offense, or drug abuse offense, and offender has one or more prior convictions for same type of offenses.   _____

3. Prison Commitments:

Assess 2 points if offender was committed on one or more occasions to a penitentiary, reformatory, or equivalent institution in any jurisdiction. Count commitments to state youth commission or similar commitments in other jurisdictions.   _____

4. Parole and Similar Violations:

Assess 2 points if one or more of the following applies: (A) Offender has previously had probation or parole for misdemeanor or felony revoked; (B) present offense committed while offender on probation or parole; (C) present offense committed while offender free on bail; or (D) present offense committed while offender in custody.   _____

5. Credits:

Deduct 1 point for each of the following as applicable: (A) Offender has voluntarily made bona fide, realistic arrangements for at least partial restitution; (B) offender was age 25 or older at time of first felony conviction; (C) offender has been substantially law abiding for at least 3 years; and (D) offender lives with his or her spouse or minor children or both and is either a breadwinner for the family or, if there are minor children, a housewife.   _____

NET TOTAL = OFFENDER RATING   _____

(Continued)

FELONY SENTENCING WORKSHEET: (continued)

Indicated Sentence:

Circle the box on the chart where the offense and the offender ratings determined on the previous page intersect. This indicates a normal sentencing package. If the indicated sentence appears too severe or too lenient for the particular case, do not hesitate to vary from the indicated sentence. In that event, however, list the reasons for the variance in the space provided on the next page.

		OFFENDER RATING				
		0-2	**3-5**	**6-8**	**9-11**	**12 OR MORE**
OFFENSE RATING	**6 OR MORE**	Impose one of three lowest minimum terms **No probation**	Impose one of three highest minimum terms **No probation**	Impose one of three highest minimum terms **No probation**	Impose one of two highest minimum terms. Make at least part of multiple sentences consecutive. **No probation**	Impose highest minimum term. Make at least part of multiple sentences consecutive. **No probation**
	5	Impose one of three lowest minimum terms Some form of probation indicated only with special mitigation	Impose one of three lowest minimum terms **No probation**	Impose one of three highest minimum terms **No probation**	Impose one of three highest minimum terms **No probation**	Impose one of two highest minimum terms. Make at least part of multiple sentences consecutive. **No probation**
	4	Impose one of two lowest minimum terms Some form of probation indicated	Impose one of three lowest minimum terms Some form of probation indicated only with special mitigation	Impose one of three lowest minimum terms **No probation**	Impose one of three highest minimum terms **No probation**	Impose one of three highest minimum terms **No probation**
	3	Impose one of two lowest minimum terms Some form of probation indicated	Impose one of two lowest minimum terms Some form of probation indicated	Impose one of three lowest minimum terms Some form of probation indicated only with special mitigation	Impose one of three lowest minimum terms **No probation**	Impose one of three highest minimum terms **No probation**
	0 - 2	Impose lowest minimum term Some form of probation indicated	Impose one of two lowest minimum terms Some form of probation indicated	Impose one of two lowest minimum terms Some form of probation indicated	Impose one of three lowest minimum terms Some form of probation indicated only with special mitigation	Impose one of three lowest minimum terms **No probation**

Source: Ohio Bar Association.

PERSPECTIVE FROM A PRACTITIONER

Laura Kiehl, Presentence Investigator

Position: Presentence Investigator

Location: Boise, Idaho

Education: Boise State University, B.A. in sociology, minor in English. In progress—Master of Arts in criminal justice

The primary duties and responsibilities of a presentence investigator are:

The goal of the presentence investigator is to provide the court with a depiction of a criminal defendant once he or she has been found guilty of a felony offense. My goal is not only to document the defendant's version of the crime he or she committed but also to provide the court with an outline of who that person is as an individual. This information comes from a one-on-one interview with the defendant as well as from collateral contacts made with friends, family, employers, educators, and medical professionals. With this information, I prepare a PSI for the sentencing judge that contains information pertaining to the instant offense, criminal history, family/social history, educational background, employment history, and medical and substance abuse history and document the defendant's goals for the future. I also provide the court with a recommendation for sentencing. The recommendation includes my perception of the criminal defendant based on my interactions with him or her as well as my contacts with collateral sources. There are three main options for recommendations: probation; rider (retained jurisdiction—meaning that the offender will spend a short time, typically 90 days, in prison followed by probation); and prison. Within the three recommendations, I add specific treatment/programming guidelines that might benefit the defendant. The recommendations I make are based on the defendant's risk factors and criminal history combined with any additional concerning or protective factors I have determined through the investigative process.

One of the most important traits for someone to have as a presentence investigator is a desire to get to know people. The saying "You catch more flies with honey than with vinegar" goes a long way in this line of work. The defendant has already been convicted, and therefore it is not the job of the presentence investigator to interrogate. I find that my best interviews, which have gained the most information valuable to the court, were interviews where I made the defendants feel comfortable and feel that they could trust me to tell their stories in a fair and honest manner. An investigative mind is also beneficial as learning to "dig" for information is part of what makes this job fun and interesting on a day-to-day basis.

In general, a typical day for a presentence investigator includes:

My work days vary a great deal. We work a flexible schedule and are required to be in the office only 20 hours per week. One reason for the flexible schedule is due to our need to be at the jails or prisons in order to conduct interviews with defendants who are in custody awaiting sentencing. We are also able to type our reports from home or wherever we work best. Some days I will start at the office, go to the jail for an interview, and spend the rest of my day typing from home with my dog sitting beside me. Other days I will be in the office all day for out-of-custody interviews and making collateral contacts. Some days I have writer's block and take the day off, knowing that I will be more productive on a different day. The flexibility has allowed me to be more productive on a day-to-day basis.

My advice to someone either wishing to study, or now studying, criminal justice to become a practitioner in this career field would be:

If you want to be a presentence investigator, hone your writing skills. Ultimately, while this job is investigative in nature, the report should be the main focus and needs to be well written and detailed. Reports can take between 10 and 12 hours (or more) to complete. Also, you cannot be afraid to ask questions. I have heard some of the craziest stories from criminal defendants, some of which were extremely uncomfortable to hear. Defendants willing to open up and provide details about their lives need an investigator who is not afraid to keep asking questions. Be ready to be surprised on a daily basis! This job is never boring and is different and challenging every day with every different case.

IN FOCUS 5.2

Policy Statement of the American Correctional Association Regarding Sentencing

Because of changing sentencing policies (determinate, mandatory minimums, and particularly the policies driven by the "War on Drugs"), there has been a huge increase in the prison population in the United States. According to the American Correctional Association (ACA), sentencing policies should be aimed at controlling crime at the lowest cost to taxpayers, and offenders should be placed in the least restrictive environment consistent with public safety. The ACA strongly promotes and supports any policies that render sentencing fair and rational and has issued its 2009 official statement on sentencing policy reproduced below.

The American Correctional Association actively promotes the development of sentencing policies that should

A. Be based on the principle of proportionality. The sentence imposed should be commensurate with the seriousness of the crime and the harm done;

B. Be impartial with regard to race, ethnicity, and economic status as to the discretion exercised in sentencing;

C. Include a broad range of options for custody, supervision, and rehabilitation of offenders;

D. Be purpose-driven. Policies must be based on clearly articulated purposes. They should be grounded in knowledge of the relative effectiveness of the various sanctions imposed in attempts to achieve these purposes;

E. Encourage the evaluation of sentencing policy on an ongoing basis. The various sanctions should be monitored to determine their relative effectiveness based on the purpose(s) they are intended to have. Likewise, monitoring should take place to ensure that the sanctions are not applied based on race, ethnicity, or economic status;

F. Recognize that the criminal sentence must be based on multiple criteria, including the harm done to the victim, past criminal history, the need to protect the public, and the opportunity to provide programs for offenders as a means of reducing the risk for future crime;

G. Provide the framework to guide and control discretion according to established criteria and within appropriate limits and allow for recognition of individual needs;

H. Have as a major purpose restorative justice—righting the harm done to the victim and the community. The restorative focus should be both process and substantively oriented. The victim or his or her representative should be included in the "justice" process. The sentencing procedure should address the needs of the victim, including his or her need to be heard and, as much as possible, to be and feel restored to whole again;

I. Promote the use of community-based programs whenever consistent with public safety; and

J. Be linked to the resources needed to implement the policy. The consequential cost of various sanctions should be assessed. Sentencing policy should not be enacted without the benefit of a fiscal-impact analysis. Resource allocations should be linked to sentencing policy so as to ensure adequate funding of all sanctions, including total confinement and the broad range of intermediate sanction and community-based programs needed to implement those policies.

This Public Correctional Policy was unanimously ratified by the American Correctional Association Delegate Assembly at the Congress of Correction in St. Louis, August 10, 1994. It was last reviewed and affirmed at the 2014 Winter Conference in Tampa, FL, February 4, 2014.

Source: Reprinted with permission of the American Correctional Association, Alexandria, VA.

●●● THE FUTURE OF SENTENCING GUIDELINES

As useful as guidelines have proven to be for reducing sentencing disparity and curtailing judicial discretion, their future format and function are by no means ensured. As mentioned above, the federal guidelines are now only "advisory," meaning that judges can consult them and follow them or not, which has opened the door once again to unwarranted sentencing discrepancies that guidelines were supposed to rein in. The turnabout began with the recognition of the separation of responsibilities of the trial judge and the trial jury. The role of judges is to be finders of law; the role of juries is to be finders of facts. A famous case based on that principle came before the U.S. Supreme Court in 2005 (*United States v. Booker,* 2005).

The circumstances of the case are that Freddie Booker was arrested in 2003 in possession of 92.5 grams of crack cocaine. He also admitted to police that he had sold an additional 566 grams. A jury found Booker guilty of possession with intent to sell at least 50 grams, for which the possible penalty ranged from 10 years to life. At sentencing, the judge used additional information (the additional 566 grams and the fact that Booker had obstructed justice) to sentence Booker to 30 years. Booker's sentence would have been 21 years and 10 months based on the facts presented to the jury and proved beyond a reasonable doubt.

Booker appealed his sentence, arguing that his Sixth Amendment rights had been violated by the judge "finding facts" when that is the proper role of the jury. An earlier federal appeals court had ruled that the facts of prior convictions are the only facts judges can "find" as justification for increasing sentencing. In other words, anything other than prior record that is used to increase a criminal penalty beyond what the guidelines call for must be submitted to a jury and proved beyond a reasonable doubt. The Supreme Court agreed with Booker that his sentence violated the Sixth Amendment and sent the case back to district court with instructions either to sentence Booker within the sentencing range supported by the jury's findings or to hold a sentencing hearing before a jury (Bissonnette, 2006).

The remedial portion of the Supreme Court's opinion (what can be done to prevent this from happening again?) is much more controversial. The Court held that the guidelines were to be advisory only and therefore no longer binding on judges. However, the Court did require judges to "consult" the guidelines and take them into consideration, but there is no way of ensuring that judges comply. John Ashcroft, the U.S. Attorney General at the time, called the decision "a retreat from justice," and Congressman Tom Feeney decried that "the extraordinary power to sentence" was now afforded to federal judges who are accountable to no one and that the decision "flies in the face of the clear will of Congress" (Bissonnette, 2006, p. 1499). In fact, Booker was resentenced by the same judge to the same 30-year sentence that he originally received. Because the sentencing guidelines had then become merely advisory, the judge did not need to further justify his sentence because it was within the range of the statutorily defined penalty. The Court's ruling on guidelines currently applies only to the federal system.

COMPARATIVE CORRECTIONS

Sentencing in Comparison Countries

Sentencing in our four major comparison countries differs radically. The most brutal sentences are handed out in Saudi Arabia. Sentences are fixed and unalterable for crimes called *hudud* crimes because they are considered crimes against God as outlined in the Koran. These crimes (and their penalties) are adultery (death), fornication (whipping—80 lashes), false accusation of any of the foregoing crimes (whipping—100 lashes), alcohol consumption (whipping—varies; death is possible after a third offense), apostasy—conversion from Islam to some other faith (death), theft (amputation of hand), and robbery (amputation of alternate side hand and foot). Saudi criminal courts are religious courts, and judges have practically free rein in sentencing in non-hudud crimes and do not follow any uniform legalistic guidelines.

For crimes known as *qisas* crimes, the penalties are imposed in a literal "eye for an eye, and a tooth for a tooth" fashion but can be forgiven on the payment of "blood money" to the victim or the victim's survivors. For instance, a 14-year-old was sentenced to be surgically paralyzed because he had stabbed and paralyzed a companion in a fight. However, the boy's mother was able to raise enough blood money to spare him that fate (Knowles, 2013). The least serious crimes under Islamic law are called *ta'zir* (rehabilitation) crimes, which include consumption of pork, bribery, provocative dress, wifely disobedience, and traffic offenses. Penalties for these offenses are entirely discretionary and may include a dressing down by the judge, a short prison sentence, or some form of light corporal punishment, but sometimes a death sentence can be imposed (Walsh & Hemmens, 2014).

China is definitely tough on crime, albeit more lenient than Saudi Arabia. Chinese sentences are classified as community control, criminal detention, fixed-term imprisonment, life imprisonment, and the death penalty. Community control is imposed for minor offenses and is analogous to probation. Offenders under control continue to work but are continually under surveillance by the police and under the informal control of neighborhood committees.

Criminal detention is analogous to a jail sentence in the United States where offenders are sent to jail for a short time for committing relatively minor crimes. Offenders may be granted permission to go home 1 or 2 days each month and may be paid for work, which makes the sentence like a work release sentence in the United States. Fixed-term imprisonment ranges from 6 months to 15 years, and the step after that is life imprisonment. Individuals sentenced to fixed-term or life imprisonment are subjected to long periods of hard labor as long as they are physically able. The most serious sentence is one of death; we will discuss this in a later chapter.

In 2008, the Chinese courts introduced sentencing guidelines with the intention of introducing uniformity in sentencing. These guidelines contain the same criteria for determining sentences as do American guidelines and are mandatory (judges must follow them). Curiously, for the harshest of sentences—life imprisonment and death—judges retain full sentencing discretion (Chen, 2010).

Before its exit from the European Union (EU), the United Kingdom was bound by the EU Charter of Fundamental Rights, which demands "proportionality" in criminal sentencing (Albers et al., 2013). However, national governments retain a margin of discretion in such matters, and the United Kingdom now has full control over its own penal policies. There are four types of sentences in England and Wales: discharge, fines, probation, and prison. Sentences depend on whether the offenses were indictable or summary offenses, which are analogous to the felony/misdemeanor distinction in the United States. A convicted person may be discharged conditionally or absolutely for minor offenses if the court decides not to impose any punishment. Fines are the most common sentence imposed in magistrates' courts (analogous to municipal courts that deal with misdemeanors in the United States). Prison sentences for serious offenses are of fixed terms from 1 year to life and are passed down by the Crown Courts (analogous to U.S. district courts). There is no death penalty in the United Kingdom. The courts in England and Wales use a grid-based guideline much like those in fashion in the United States, and Parliament has mandated that the "courts 'must follow' definitive guidelines rather than merely 'have regard to' them" (Roberts, 2011, p. 997). PSIs are also written for cases in which probation or prison is being considered.

According to the official French government website (*Service Public Francaise*, 2013), offenses in France are divided into *crimes, délits,* and *contraventions.* Crimes are the most serious offenses. They are tried in assize court with judges and juries and are punishable by 15 to 30 years in prison or, in exceptional cases, for life. Examples of crimes are murder and rape. A délit is an offense punishable by imprisonment from 2 months to 10 years and is tried in a correctional court. Although délits are classified as "second-tier" crimes, they are very serious offenses such as robbery, aggravated assault, and sexual assault. Délits can become crimes with aggravating circumstances. Contraventions are minor offenses tried in police courts and punishable only by fines up to 3,000 euros (about $4,000). There is no death penalty in France.

Because the termination of a French trial results simultaneously in a verdict and a sentence, a PSI is not necessary. All the information typically included in a PSI is already known to the sentencing panel (typically, three professional judges and nine laypersons) because the investigatory process in France is more thorough than in the Anglo-American common law tradition; thus, the character of the defendant and all the relevant personal information regarding his or her background is well known (Walsh & Hemmens, 2014). Nor are there sentencing guidelines other than statutory penalties, leaving judges with excessive discretion that can lead to serious inequalities in sentencing (Padfield, 2011).

SUMMARY

- Sentencing is a post-conviction process in which the courts implement one or more of the punitive philosophies: retribution, deterrence, incapacitation, or rehabilitation. Sentencing decisions should be in accordance with justice.

- There are three major sentencing models: indeterminate (a range of possible years), determinate (a specific number of years), and mandatory (can exist under either of the above models but means that the person must be sent to prison; probation is not an option). Sentencing to a drug court is becoming increasingly popular in the United States.

- Truth-in-sentencing laws have led to longer sentences, a stronger move to determinate and mandatory sentencing, and to statutes such as habitual offender statutes.

- Sentencing disparity—sentences not accounted for by legally relevant variables—is a major concern in the criminal justice system. A big concern is whether African Americans' more severe sentences are accounted for by their greater involvement in crime or by racism. The sentences imposed for crack versus powder cocaine possession have been a contentious issue because of racial differentials in the possession and sale of crack versus cocaine.

- Efforts have been made to "individualize" justice by providing judges with presentence investigation reports, written by probation officers, that contain many factors about the people the judges are to sentence. A big controversy involving these reports is whether the defense should be able to view them.

- Sentencing guidelines are designed to eliminate sentencing disparity by submitting a person's crime seriousness and prior record (in some states additional information is included) to a scoring system. The person is then supposed to be sentenced the same way as every other person who receives the same score.

- Certain legal problems with sentencing under guidelines moved the U.S. Supreme Court to rule that the federal guidelines, which were previously mandatory, were now to be merely advisory. This opened up the door once again for wide levels of judicial discretion and thus for sentencing disparity.

KEY TERMS

Concurrent sentence, 84

Consecutive sentence, 84

Determinate sentence, 84

Drug court, 88

Fair Sentencing Act of 2010, 93

Habitual offender statutes, 84

Indeterminate sentence, 83

Justice, 82

Life without parole (LWOP), 85

DISCUSSION QUESTIONS

1. Is it ever just, right, and moral to sentence equals in terms of legally relevant variables unequally? Give an example.

2. If you are being sentenced for a felony, would you prefer to know when your date for parole consideration is to come, or would you prefer an indeterminate sentence where you could possibly "work your way out" and get released earlier?

3. What is your opinion of habitual offender statutes that lock people up for life if convicted of a third felony?

4. What research strategy is required to assess the racial sentencing disparity issue?

5. What are the pros and cons of allowing the defense access to the presentence investigation report? Where do you stand on the issue?

6. Sentencing guidelines were designed to rein in excessive judicial sentencing discretion, and most criminal justice personnel consider this a very good thing. Why did the U.S. Supreme Court throw a wrench into the works by making the federal guidelines advisory only?

$SAGE edge™

Review → Practice → Improve

Sharpen your skills with SAGE edge at **edge.sagepub.com/stohressentials3e**.

SAGE edge offers a robust online environment featuring an impressive array of free tools and resources for review, study, and further exploration, keeping both instructors and students on the cutting edge of teaching and learning.

FOR FURTHER EXPLORATION AND APPLICATION, TAKE A LOOK AT THE INTERACTIVE EBOOK FOR THESE PREMIUM RESOURCES:

▶ **Career Video 5.1** Victim Advocate

▶ **SAGE News Clip 5.1** Patz Sentence

▶ **SAGE News Clip 5.2** Texting Suicide

▣ **Journal Article 5.1** Race, Ethnicity, and Habitual-Offender Sentencing

6 Jails and Detention Centers

TEST YOUR KNOWLEDGE

Test your present knowledge of jails by answering the following questions as true or false. Check your answers on page 391 after reading the chapter.

1. Most jails are operated by states.

2. Jails for juveniles are usually referred to as detention centers.

3. Most inmates of adult jails have been convicted of crimes.

4. The drug war has disproportionately affected the number of minorities and women incarcerated in jails.

5. Jails have become the most likely social institution to hold the mentally ill in the United States.

6. Incarcerated women tend to have fewer medical problems than incarcerated men.

7. Female staff in jails are more likely to be the perpetrators of sexual victimization of male inmates than are male staff.

LEARNING OBJECTIVES

- Describe the origins of jails

- Identify the types of jails in operation

- Explain how jails process individuals

- Assess how jails affect and are affected by overcrowding, race, ethnicity, gender, age, and special needs of their inmates

- Describe the various approaches jails take to address medical problems of inmates

- Discuss how jails manage sexual violence, gangs, and suicides

- Explain the kinds of innovations happening in jails and how they are working out

A MENTALLY ILL INMATE IN THE DONA ANA COUNTY JAIL, NEW MEXICO

Stephen Slevin, 59, was an inmate for 22 months in the Dona Ana County Jail in Las Cruces, New Mexico ("$15.5 Million Settlement," 2014, p. 20). He was first booked into the jail on charges of driving while intoxicated and receiving or transferring a stolen vehicle in August 2005 (a friend had let him borrow the car to drive across the country). He had a history of suicide attempts and mental illness, so the jail officers in booking placed him in an empty padded cell for 2 days before he was assessed by the mental health unit. He was then eventually sent to solitary confinement, where he had no contact with a judge or medical personnel for the next 18 months. It was noted that on entering the jail, he had been a well-nourished and healthy male with a mental illness. After the 18 months in solitary confinement and a psychiatric evaluation, however, he smelled bad, had overgrown nails and hair, was malnourished at 133 pounds, and "complained of paranoia, hallucinations, bed sores and untreated dental problems" ("$15.5 Million Settlement," 2014, p. 21). Slevin had pulled out his own infected tooth while incarcerated because no dental care was provided to him. A month after this evaluation, he was again placed in solitary confinement but was finally released in June 2007, when the charges were dismissed. He sued in federal court, alleging a violation of his civil rights and false imprisonment, and a federal jury agreed and awarded him $22 million. When Dona Ana County appealed this decision, a federal judge affirmed the punitive and compensatory damages in the original award. To avoid further appeals by the county, however, Slevin settled with the county and its insurer for $15 million in 2013 ("$15.5 Million Settlement," 2014, p. 20).

••• INTRODUCTION: THE COMMUNITY INSTITUTION

The American jail is a derivative of various modes of holding people for trial that have existed in Western countries for centuries. Whether fashioned from caves, mines, or old houses or as separate buildings, **jails** were developed originally as a primary means of holding the accused for trial, for punishment (even execution), or in lieu of a fine. As was noted in Chapter 2, jails were called gaols in the England of the Middle Ages and were operated by the *shire reeve,* or sheriff, and his minions.

Jails have been in existence much longer than prisons, and their mission is much more diverse, especially now. These days, jails are usually local and community institutions that hold people who are presumed innocent before trial; they hold convicted offenders before they are sentenced; they hold more minor offenders who are sentenced for terms that are usually less than a year; they hold juveniles (usually in their own jails or separated from adults or before transport to juvenile facilities); they hold women (usually separated from men and sometimes in their own jails); they hold people for the state or federal authorities (there are some exclusively federal jails); and, depending on the particular jail population being served and the capacity of any given facility, they serve to incapacitate, deter, rehabilitate, punish, and reintegrate.

Although described as correctional afterthoughts by scholars, and despite their multifaceted and critical role in communities, jails have often received short shrift in terms of monetary support and professional regard (Kerle, 1991, 2003, 2011; Thompson & Mays, 1991; Zupan, 1991). The vast majority of jails are operated by county sheriffs, whose primary focus has been law enforcement rather than corrections. As a result, jail facilities have often been neglected, resulting in dilapidated structures, and jail staff have had less training and pay than probation and parole officers in communities or correctional staff working at the state or federal level in prisons. Jail staff also often receive less pay and training than deputy sheriffs working in the same organization (sheriff's office) as the jail. Research indicates that many in the general public may even view jails as more punitive than prisons (see, e.g., May, Applegate, Ruddell, & Wood, 2014). The late comic Rodney Dangerfield's perennial lament, "I [They] don't get no respect," surely applies to jails more than perhaps any other social institution.

In this chapter, we discuss how this forgotten social institution fulfills a vital community role, one that includes all of the functions described in the preceding paragraph as well as serving as a repository for people who are only nominally criminal and have nowhere else to go (e.g., the homeless, the mentally ill). The role of jails also includes the holding of some state or federal inmates when prisons are too full or prior to their transport to prison. In some larger counties, the holding of longer-term sentenced inmates or those who have numerous physical, mental, and substance abuse problems—not to mention educational deficits—has led to more programming and treatment in jails. Part and parcel of this interest in treatment is the emergence of community reentry programs, as will also be discussed in Chapter 10, as a means of preventing crime and addressing the multifaceted needs of ex–jail inmates. In this chapter, these emerging trends are explored, as are the challenges jails face, but first we discuss the types of institutions that constitute jails.

Jails: Local community institutions that hold people who are presumed innocent before trial; convicted people before they are sentenced; convicted minor offenders, who are sentenced for terms that are usually less than a year; juveniles (usually in their own jails, separated from adults, or before transport to juvenile facilities); women (usually separated from men and sometimes in their own jails); and people for the state or federal authorities. Depending on the particular jail population being served and the capacity of the given facility, they serve to incapacitate, deter, rehabilitate, punish, and reintegrate.

© Wikimedia/WhisperToMe

PHOTO 6.1: Travis County Jail

JAIL TYPES

The typical jail is operated by the sheriff of a county. However, some cities, states, and the federal government operate jails, and sometimes multiple jurisdictions combine resources to administer a jail that serves a region. Some counties have hired jail administrators to oversee the operation of the jail, taking it out of the hands of the local sheriff. Jails for adults are sometimes called detention centers, and jails for juveniles are almost always referred to as detention centers. Some American Indian tribes have their own jails, and many police departments have short-term lockup facilities to hold suspects or those accused of crimes. Currently, there are about 2,900 jails in the United States, and 68 jails are operated by American Indian tribes (Minton, 2014; Minton & Golinelli, 2014; Sabol & Minton, 2008). When a state or the federal government (or another governmental entity) has inmates for a jail but no facility of its own in a given vicinity, the entity will typically ask the county to hold that inmate. Counties are usually more than willing to do this because they are paid a fee that often exceeds the cost of holding inmates, which makes holding inmates for other jurisdictions a money-making enterprise.

Most jails are composed of one or two buildings in close proximity to each other. They are usually operated somewhat close to a city or town center except when located on reservations or at military facilities. Larger jail jurisdictions (more than 1,000 inmates) will often operate more than one jail.

Many jails have adopted technological changes that have greatly enhanced their ability to supervise and control inmates. The use of cameras, voice-operated and visual-check-operated doors by a control center, electronic fingerprint machines, and even video arraignments and visiting are revolutionizing the jail experience. Certainly, these changes are making the facility more secure, but they also, in the case of video visiting, may make it easier to maintain contact with the outside.

●●● JAIL INMATES AND THEIR PROCESSING

Jails operate 7 days a week, 24 hours a day, because crime does not take a holiday. They hold all kinds of inmates, from the serious convicted offender awaiting transport to a state or federal prison to the accused misdemeanant who cannot make bail. About 60% of jail inmates have not been convicted of the crime for which they are being held; they are awaiting court action (Minton, 2010; Minton & Golinelli, 2014, p. 1). Jails receive inmates from local, state, federal, and tribal police officers. In 2015, they processed 10.9 million inmates (down from a peak of 13.6 million in 2008), with most inmates in and out within a few days or a week, some within hours, although others might be held for more than a year, particularly if they are sentenced state or federal inmates (Minton, 2010; Minton & Zeng, 2016, p. 1). Because of their complicated and diverse role, and as a means of keeping track of the inmates they are responsible for holding, jails will often follow a

PHOTO 6.2: A double-bunk jail cell. The pink interior paint is meant to soothe detainees.

Getty Images/AFP PHOTO/Jeff Haynes

PHOTO 6.3: Inmates in the reception housing area of a California state prison. Prisons in California, like those in many states, have suffered from severe overcrowding during recent decades.

set procedure that is prescribed by both tradition and practice.

The first part of the typical processing of an inmate at a county or city jail is the delivery of the arrestee to the facility by a law enforcement officer. As is discussed in the following, many arrestees may be stressed, upset, mentally disturbed, or intoxicated and/or drug impaired. In the latter two cases, the officer may choose to administer a Breathalyzer and/or blood test at the jail. If the arrestee is injured, the jail's booking staff may require that the arrestee be taken by the police to the hospital to be checked out before he or she is admitted to the jail.

If not injured, the arresting officer will fill out the paperwork for admittance of the arrestee to the facility. Usually, the arrestee is still with the officer when this is occurring and often still in handcuffs. Once the required paperwork and processing are completed, the jail will accept the arrestee, search him or her, and begin its own paperwork for admitting the arrestee. At this juncture and depending on the alleged offense, the arrestee may be allowed to contact family and friends and/or a bail bondsman. The arrestee might be released directly into the community if the alleged offense is minor. However, if the alleged offense is serious enough, the arrestee will need to await arraignment by a judge to determine bail and, during the interim, might be booked into the jail.

During the booking process, jails will often—although not always—strip search arrestees (now inmates), take their property, and issue clothing and other essentials. If the new inmate is intoxicated or belligerent, booking staff may place him or her in a special holding cell. In the latter case, this might involve a padded room or a restraint chair. Once the inmate is sober and calm, he or she is then classified and moved to a more permanent housing area in the jail. Larger jails often keep new inmates in a separate area or cell before they place them in a general housing unit so that they can be observed and classified (based on their alleged offenses, alleged criminal coconspirators, criminal histories, gang involvements, health and other needs, etc.).

••• TRENDS IN JAIL POPULATIONS

OVERCROWDING

As indicated in other sections of this book, jails need to deal with the same kinds of overcrowding issues that have afflicted prisons. **Overcrowding** occurs when the number of inmates exceeds the physical capacity (i.e., the beds and space) available. Each year and over the last several decades, the number of jail beds needed by jurisdictions has increased, and they have been filled almost as soon as they have been built (see Figure 6.1; Minton, 2010). However, between 2008 and 2009, there was an unprecedented decrease in jail inmates of 1.1%. As of 2015 (the latest data available at the time of this writing), on average jails were operating at nearly 80% of their capacity, and the highest capacity for the last decade (2000–2009) was achieved in 2006 and 2007 at 96% (Minton, 2010, p. 5; Minton & Zeng, 2016, p. 7). Between 2014 and 2015, the amount of bed space increased (Minton & Zeng, 2016, p. 1). This percentage use of capacity is actually better than in past years, when jails of the 1980s and 1990s were operating at well over their rated capacities (Cox & Osterhoff, 1991; Gilliard & Beck, 1997; Klofas, 1991). In addition, and notably, even an average of 80% for 2015 means that half of the jails in the United States are operating at over that average.

Overcrowding: A phenomenon that occurs when the number of inmates exceeds the physical capacity (the beds and space) available.

Moreover, the percentages of capacity can be misleading when one considers overcrowding. Certain sections of jails are designated for specific types of inmates who cannot or do not mix well (males and females but also juveniles, arrestees, inmates with medical problems, gang members, etc.). The percentage capacity may indicate that the jail is not completely full, but any given section might be overwhelmed with inmates.

Such overcrowding limits the ability of the jail to fulfill its multifaceted mission; less programming can be provided, health and maintenance systems are overtaxed, and staff are stressed by the increased demands on their time and the inability to meet all inmate needs. From the inmates' perspective, their health, security, and privacy are more likely to be threatened when the numbers of inmates in their living units increase and the amount of space—and possibly the number of staff—does not. The jail staff also lose their ability to effectively classify and sometimes control inmates; they may be unable to keep the offenders convicted of serious crimes away from the presumed innocent unconvicted or more minor-offending inmates. Judges and jail managers will struggle over how to keep the jail population down to acceptable limits, and as a result even serious offenders may be let loose into communities as a means of reducing the crowding. Therefore, although the "get tough" laws in many states were passed with the explicit intent of incarcerating more people for longer times, their actual unintended effect in some jails may be to incarcerate serious offenders less (because there is no room) and all offenders in less safe and less secure facilities.

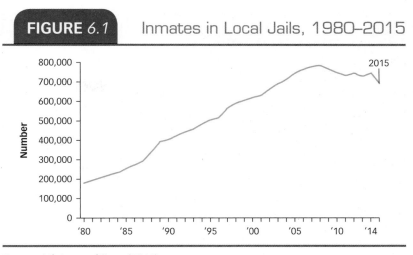

FIGURE 6.1   Inmates in Local Jails, 1980–2015

Source: Minton and Zeng (2016).

Although suits by jail inmates are usually not successful, some are. Welsh (1995) found, in his study of lawsuits involving California jails, that the issue courts gave greatest credence to was overcrowding. Perhaps this is because overcrowding is clearly quantifiable (the rated capacity is clear, and the inmate count is obvious), but it is likely that it was regarded as so important by courts because it can lead to a number of other seemingly intractable problems such as those just mentioned.

GENDER, JUVENILES, RACE, AND ETHNICITY

As indicated from the data supplied in Table 6.1, most jail inmates are adult minority males, although the number of whites represents the largest racial grouping of the men, and the number of whites as a proportion of the total men has increased markedly, particularly since 2010. Women comprised more than 12.2% of jail inmates in 2009, but that increased to nearly 15.0% by 2014 and 14.3% in 2015, both of which are more than in 2000 (11.4%) (Minton & Zeng, 2015, p. 4; Minton & Zeng, 2016, p. 5; see also Figure 6.2). The reason often cited for the overall increases in incarceration in jails and prisons, and the increases for women and minorities in jails and prisons in particular, has been the prosecution of the drug war since the 1980s and 1990s. The "get tough" policies, which have led to longer periods of incarceration in prisons, have also led to a greater propensity to catch and keep low-level drug offenders in jails (Irwin, 2005; Owen, 2005; Welch, 2005; Whitman, 2003). The focus of arrests in the drug war has often been on the low-level sellers, rather than on the buyers or the drug kingpins, and that has netted more minorities and women into the system. Mandatory sentences, juvenile waivers, and sentence enhancements for certain offenses have collectively led

PERSPECTIVE FROM A PRACTITIONER

Brian Cole, County Corrections Director

Position: Director of the county department of corrections

Location: Shawnee County Department of Corrections, Kansas

Education: B.A. in criminal justice and B.A. in psychology, Washburn University, 1989

What are the primary duties and responsibilities of a director of a county department of corrections?

Under administrative direction of the Board of County Commissioners, this position administers the adult and juvenile detention programs of Shawnee County, Kansas; ensures offenders placed in custody are housed in a safe and secure manner and that offenders receive appropriately fair and humane treatment by staff; monitors the overall security of the centers and regularly tours the facilities to ensure the highest security standards are maintained; proactively seeks to improve offender processes to enhance the security and efficiency of the agency; creates and expects a staff culture of integrity in the reporting of misconduct by other staff and offenders; and visits offender living units and speaks with offenders to gain a sense of morale of offenders and to monitor operations.

This position oversees programs to ensure compliance with federal, state, and local laws, regulations, and accrediting entity standards; plans and coordinates the annual budget, staffing, and program needs for the department; and ensures expenditures are within budget parameters and proactively seeks and implements methods by which the department can save funds.

This position also proactively recommends changes to the physical plant that will provide enhanced efficiency and security; creates future projections for physical plant expansion; develops and maintains positive working relationships with employees of other county agencies, other law enforcement agencies, colleges and universities, and other agencies and organizations as appropriate; delegates an appropriate amount of work to staff to encourage their professional growth

and seeks opportunities for professional self-growth; and seeks and completes public speaking engagements to promote positive community relations. The person holding this position is expected to respond to media requests, as appropriate, and attend community functions as a representative of the department.

What characteristics make a good director of a county department of corrections?

- Integrity
- Leadership
- Flexibility
- Initiative
- Sense of humor
- Compassion for staff
- Proactive
- Confidence
- Public speaking skills
- Good written and verbal communication skills

What is a typical day like for a director of a county department of corrections?

A typical day for me would be one that starts with meeting with staff and determining the priorities of the day. In corrections, you never have a "clean desk." As one project ends, you always are starting a new one. On a daily basis, I speak with my executive team to get a brief update on projects, personnel, budget, special-needs inmates, and physical plant issues. I also meet with our mental health team leader daily to review high-risk inmate statuses. Each day, I spend time researching current events and legal trends, trying to stay as proactive as possible to avoid complacency and litigation. I speak with inmates on a daily basis and respond to requests. I spend time meeting with the public to ensure our agency is meeting and exceeding citizen expectations, and I provide feedback to our commissioners.

What is your advice to someone either wishing to study or now studying criminal justice to become a practitioner in this career field?

Working in the field of corrections takes committed people. On a daily basis, you work with incarcerated individuals who have made (in some cases) some very bad life decisions. You have to be one who can separate emotion from your job and understand that you are managing people and managing problems. You have to have an appreciation for the environment you are working within. This is a stressful but very rewarding job. Corrections can be a career, not just another job. You make decisions each day that could mean the life or death of inmates, staff, and community members. You cannot take shortcuts. Learn as much as you can about your agency, the philosophy, and the culture that the leader of the organization has put in place. You have a great opportunity to help others, work as a team, and truly better your community.

What are the biggest challenges facing corrections?

Mentally Ill Inmates

Jails are becoming community mental health facilities for the mentally ill. With this being a trend in some parts of the country, a citizen has a better chance of receiving treatment in a jail than in his or her community. As directors, we must educate our staff to meet this challenge. One way is through crisis intervention team (CIT) training.

It is a fact that some people with mental illness will end up in jail. In some instances, this may be the safest and best option for them. However, inmates in jail go into crisis, and correctional staff must be able to handle these emergency situations. Through CIT training, our staff has been able to identify crisis situations, defuse these situations, communicate with the inmates in crisis, and—most of the time—see the incidents to positive resolutions that do not result in harm to the inmates or staff. The end result is officer and inmate safety, and then we will refer the inmate to mental health services for treatment. We have CIT training available two times a year for all staff.

Transgender Inmates

Historically, correctional institutions have classified inmates by their genitalia, not by their gender identity. Often transgender women are placed in male housing units, and transgender men are placed in female housing units. Transgender inmates have the right to be treated with dignity and respect and be free from harm and harassment.

A key federal court opinion out of the First Circuit Court of Appeals shed light on an issue that all correctional managers must be aware of. Increasingly, correctional managers must take the proactive steps to create and implement policy that begins with the early identification of transgender inmates, completion of medical and mental health evaluations and treatment (including gender reassignment surgery), proper housing, programs, and clear protocols for routine interactions such as showering and pat downs. As with every category of individual liberties, it is incumbent on correctional leadership to identify and address inmates' rights, as framed by legislative, executive, and judicial decisions.

to longer sentences for most offenders and backed up the numbers of offenders in some jails either awaiting transfer to state or federal prisons or doing their time in the jails rather than in the overcrowded prisons.

It is not clear why there have been recent declines in the numbers of minorities (particularly African Americans and Hispanics), vis-à-vis whites and women, incarcerated in jails, a particularly notable phenomenon in large-city jails (Minton, 2010; Minton & Golinelli, 2014; Minton & Zeng, 2015). It could just be a minor shift that will not become a trend, or it could signal a longer-term change in the use of jails due to the recession of 2007 to 2010, a rethinking in the prosecution of the drug war, or some other variable not yet identified by researchers. Longer-term trends do indicate that the number of adult males in jail from 1990 to 2006 nearly doubled while the numbers of adult females and juveniles nearly tripled. Percentage increases for women and juveniles are also large; in 1990 women represented only about 9% of jail populations and juveniles about 0.6%, whereas by 2000 women composed 11.3% and juveniles 1.2% of jail populations (Bureau

FIGURE *6.2*   Composition of Local Jails, 2015

Source: Minton and Zeng (2016).

Note: "Other" includes American Indians, Alaska Natives, Asians, Native Hawaiians, and other Pacific Islanders.

of Justice Statistics, 2000, 2007; see also Table 6.1). However, the percentage of inmates in adult jails who were juveniles decreased by half from 2000 to 2015 (from 1.0% to 0.5%) while the percentage of females increased by 3 percentage points during that same time period (see Table 6.1).

Across the two largest racial groupings (whites and African Americans) and the largest ethnic grouping (Hispanics), there have been significant increases in jail incarceration, but as indicated in Table 6.1, for both groups there have been decreases since at least 2000 and continuing through 2015 (the latest year for which we have data). The raw number of whites has increased from 1990 (when there were fewer whites incarcerated in jails than African Americans). Proportionate to their representation in the population, however, African Americans are much more likely to be incarcerated in American jails than are whites or Hispanics. As reported by the Bureau of Justice Statistics (BJS, 2008), for 2006, "Blacks were almost three times more likely than Hispanics and five times more likely than whites to be in jail" (p. 2). Again, this higher proportional rate of incarceration for African Americans, in particular, can likely be attributed to their greater concentration in impoverished neighborhoods and to the focus of the drug war that has tended to target such living areas and the selling and use of crack cocaine (see the discussion of enhanced sentences for crack cocaine in Chapter 5). But as the drug war has waned, in terms of not only crack cocaine sentences but also marijuana prosecutions, as both medical and recreational marijuana are decriminalized and legalized, the number of minorities has decreased as a percentage of jail populations, particularly among African Americans (from 41.3% in 2000 to 35.1% by year-end 2015; Minton & Zeng, 2015, p. 4; Minton & Zeng, 2016, p. 5), but also among Hispanics (see Table 6.1).

Thinkstock Images/Comstock

PHOTO 6.4: A female jail inmate awaits her cell assignment. Women comprised more than 12.2% of jail inmates in 2009 (Minton & Golinelli, 2014, p. 7).

| TABLE 6.1 | Inmates in Local Jails, by Characteristics, Midyear 2000 and 2005–2015 |

Characteristic	2000	2005	2006	2007	2008	2009	2010	2011	2012	2013	2014	2015
Sex												
Male	88.6%	87.3%	87.1%	87.1%	87.3%	87.8%	87.7%	87.3%	86.8%	86.0%	85.3%	85.7%
Female	11.4	12.7	12.9	12.9	12.7	12.2	12.3	12.7	13.2	14.0	14.7	14.3
Adults	98.8%	99.1%	99.2%	99.1%	99.0%	99.1%	99.0%	99.2%	99.3%	99.4%	99.4%	99.5%
Male	87.4	86.5	86.3	86.3	86.4	86.9	86.7	86.6	86.1	85.4	84.8	85.2
Female	11.3	12.6	12.9	12.8	12.6	12.1	12.3	12.6	13.2	13.9	14.6	14.3
Juveniles	1.2%	0.9%	0.8%	0.9%	1.0%	0.9%	1.0%	0.8%	0.7%	0.6%	0.6%	0.5%
Held as adults[a]	1.0	0.8	0.6	0.7	0.8	0.8	0.8	0.6	0.6	0.5	0.5	0.5
Held as juveniles	0.2	0.1	0.2	0.2	0.2	0.2	0.3	0.2	0.1	0.1	0.1	–
Race/Hispanic origin												
White[b]	41.9%	44.3%	43.9%	43.3%	42.5%	42.5%	44.3%	44.8%	45.8%	47.2%	47.4%	48.3%
Black/African American[b]	41.3	38.9	38.6	38.7	39.2	39.2	37.8	37.6	36.9	35.8	35.4	35.1
Hispanic/Latino	15.2	15.0	15.6	16.1	16.4	16.2	15.8	15.5	15.1	14.8	14.9	14.3
Other[b,c]	1.6	1.7	1.8	1.8	1.8	1.9	2.0	2.0	1.9	2.1	2.3	2.2
Two or more races[c]	–	0.1	0.1	0.1	0.2	0.2	0.1	0.2	0.2	0.2	0.1	0.2
Conviction status[b]												
Convicted	44.0%	38.0%	37.9%	38.0%	37.1%	37.8%	38.9%	39.4%	39.4%	38.0%	37.2%	37.3%
Unconvicted	56.0%	62.0%	62.1%	62.0%	62.9%	62.2%	61.1%	60.6%	60.6%	62.0%	62.8%	62.7%

Source: Minton and Zeng (2016).

Note: May not sum to total due to rounding. – = data not collected.

a. Includes juveniles who were tried or awaiting trial as adults.

b. Excludes persons of Hispanic or Latino origin.

c. Includes American Indians, Alaska Natives, Asians, Native Hawaiians, and other Pacific Islanders.

THE POOR AND THE MENTALLY ILL

The late corrections scholar John Irwin once referred to the types of people who are managed in jails as the "rabble," by which he meant "disorganized and disorderly, the lowest class of people" (Irwin, 1985, p. 2). These were not just the undereducated, the under- or unemployed, or even the poor and mentally ill. He meant to include all those descriptors as they related to the state of being disorganized and disorderly and as those designations might lead to permanent residence in a lower class, but he also meant that jail inmates tend to be "detached" and of "disrepute" in the sense that they offend others by committing mostly minor crimes in public places.

Mental Illness, Homelessness, Substance Abuse, and Poverty

Certainly, the fact of being homeless puts a person at a greater risk for negative contact with the police; lacking a home, private matters are more likely to be subject to public

IN FOCUS 6.1

High Schools in Jails

For many years, versions of high schools have existed in juvenile detention facilities. High school classes and the ability to earn high school credits and degrees have existed in America's prisons and larger jails. But the Five Keys Charter School in San Francisco, California, claims to be the first complete high school inside an adult jail (J. Tucker, 2014). Started in 2003, the Five Keys Charter School graduated 20 students in 2014, and 600 total have received a high school diploma or a certification of completion or equivalency diploma since its inception. "The school's philosophy is founded on the five keys to an inmate's success: connection to community; a focus on family; recovery from substance abuse; education; and employment" (J. Tucker, 2014, p. 1). Notably, these are the same areas that are a focus of other reentry programming. In a simple comparison of graduates' recidivism (44%) with other inmates'

recidivism (68%), the high school graduates do much better (J. Tucker, 2014, p. 1). If subsequent research includes matching of graduates with those who didn't graduate on key characteristics (such as criminal history, age, gender, and mental illness) and also finds reduced recidivism, this high school in an adult jail could save the public millions of dollars while creating safer communities.

Discussion Questions

1. Do you think that earning a high school diploma in a jail setting is likely to benefit inmates and their communities? Why or why not?

2. What are the likely barriers to completion of high school in most jails? How might such barriers be overcome?

viewing in public spaces, and this disturbs or offends some community members, which leads to police involvement. Those who are mentally ill are more likely to be homeless because they are unable to manage the daily challenges that employment and keeping a roof over one's head and food in one's mouth require (McNiel, Binder, & Robinson, 2005; Severson, 2004).

Jails in the United States are full of the mentally ill, the homeless, and the poor. Data from the BJS (based on interviews with local jail inmates in 2002) indicate that about 64% of jail inmates (75% of females and 63% of males) have a mental health problem (as compared with 56% of state prisoners and 45% of federal prisoners; see Figure 6.3) (James & Glaze, 2006, p. 1). In a later BJS study, it was determined that 26% of jail inmates had symptoms of "serious psychological distress" (Beck, Berzofsky, Caspar, & Krebs, 2013, p. 25). In contrast, about 10.6% of the U.S. population has symptoms of mental illness. Moreover, for virtually every manifestation of mental illness, more jail inmates than state or federal prisoners were likely to exhibit symptoms, including 50% more delusions and twice as many hallucinations (James & Glaze, 2006, p. 2). Of those jail inmates with a mental health problem, the specific diagnoses included mania (54%), major depression (30%), and psychotic disorder (24%) (James & Glaze, 2006, p. 2). The specific identification of a mental illness for each inmate by the BJS research team was based on a recent clinical diagnosis or symptoms that fit the criteria of the *Diagnostic and Statistical Manual of Mental Disorders* (*DSM-IV*).

A whole host of problems has been found to be associated with mental illness, including homelessness, greater criminal engagement, prior abuse, and substance use (McNiel et al., 2005). Among the findings from this BJS study of jails was that those jail inmates with a mental illness were nearly twice as likely to be homeless as those without a mental illness designation (17% as opposed to 9%) (James & Glaze, 2006, pp. 1–2). More inmates with a mental health problem had prior incarcerations than those without such a problem (25% as opposed to 20%). About three times as many jail inmates with a mental health problem had a history of physical or sexual abuse than those without such a problem (24% as opposed to 8%). Nearly three-quarters of the inmates with a mental health problem were dependent on or abused alcohol or illegal substances (74% as opposed to 53% of those without a mental health problem). In short, mental illness, along with poverty, was entangled in a whole array of societal issues for jail inmates.

Further evidence for this supposition was found by McNiel et al. (2005) in their study in San Francisco County. They found that mental illness, substance abuse, and jail incarcerations were inextricably connected as life events. Those who were mentally ill and homeless were also more likely to have a substance abuse problem, and it was also likely that jail incarcerations were part of their existence as well.

Mental Illness and Victimization

Moreover, in the BJS's National Inmate Survey—conducted in state and federal prisons, jails, Immigration and Customs Enforcement detention centers, and military and Indian country facilities and focused primarily on sexual victimization—the researchers found that those who are mentally ill are much more likely to be sexually victimized while incarcerated than inmates who are not (Beck et al., 2013). Among their important findings were the conclusions that inmates with serious psychological distress reported high rates of inmate-on-inmate and staff sexual victimization in 2011 and 2012 (pp. 6–8):

FIGURE 6.3 Percentage of Inmates With Mental Health Problems

Source: James and Glaze (2006).

- Among state and federal prison inmates, an estimated 6.3% of those identified with serious psychological distress reported that they were sexually victimized by another inmate. In comparison, among prisoners with no indication of mental illness, 0.7% reported being victimized by another inmate.

- Similar differences were reported by jail inmates. An estimated 3.6% of those identified with serious psychological distress reported inmate-on-inmate sexual victimization compared with 0.7% of inmates with no indication of mental illness.

- Rates of serious psychological distress in prisons (14.7%) and jails (26.3%) were substantially higher than the rate in the U.S. noninstitutional population age 18 or older (3.0%).

- For each of the measured demographic subgroups, inmates with serious psychological distress reported higher rates of inmate-on-inmate sexual victimization than inmates without mental health problems.

- Among inmates with serious psychological distress, nonheterosexual inmates reported the highest rates of inmate-on-inmate sexual victimization (21.0% of prison inmates and 14.7% of jail inmates).

What we might learn from these findings is that jails hold more inmates with psychological problems than do prisons, and—as with prisons—this mental illness makes them more vulnerable to sexual abuse. These data tell us that the likelihood of abuse is also heightened if the inmate is LGBTI (lesbian, gay, bisexual, transgender, or intersex) and has serious psychological problems.

Mental Illness and Solitary Confinement

Mental illness also makes jail inmates more likely candidates for the use of solitary confinement and targets of other violent inmates. In a study of the Rikers Island 10-jail complex by New York City, city health officials noted that a disproportionate number of inmates have a mental health diagnosis (Pearson, 2015). It was reported that the health care workers, who are employed by the city but are bound by medical ethics, are reticent to approve solitary confinement for such inmates because they know it can exacerbate their already precarious mental health status. Yet the mentally ill in these jails are more likely to be placed in solitary because of their behavior problems and/or as protection. In an earlier study of the Rikers Island jail complex by the Department of Justice and the *New York Times,* it was found that a culture of violence was predominant in these jails (particularly those for juveniles) and that too often the targets of this violence were adult and juvenile mentally ill inmates (Seabrook, 2014).

Calls for Reform in the Care of the Mentally Ill

The abuse and poor conditions for the mentally ill are not a problem reserved for the Rikers Island jail inmates. As A. Cohen (2013) documented in an article in the *Atlantic Monthly,* a number of reports emanating from the Justice Department, the American Civil Liberties Union, and a federal judicial decision indicate that the abuse is widespread and exists in both jails and prisons. "Prison [and jail] officials have failed to provide a constitutional level of care in virtually every respect, from providing medication and treatment to protecting the men from committing suicide" (p. 1). In fact, the problematic treatment of mentally ill jail inmates has risen to crisis status for the Council of State Governments. As a consequence, on May 6, 2015, it launched a national initiative to help counties address this issue in their jails (Council of State Governments Justice Center, 2015). Remedies, embodied in what is termed an evidence-based Stepping Up Program, will focus on diversion from jail to other services and the provision of treatment and better care for mentally ill inmates.

••• MEDICAL PROBLEMS

One of the social issues that is particularly problematic for jail inmates and the people who manage them is the relatively poor health of people incarcerated in jails. According to the 2011–2012 study of jail inmates by the BJS (Maruschak, 2015), half of jail inmates reported a chronic medical problem such as cancer or blood pressure or heart problems. According to an earlier iteration of this study (Maruschak, 2006, p. 1), most of these medical maladies preceded placement in jail and included the following (in order of prevalence): arthritis, hypertension, asthma, heart problems, cancer, paralysis, stroke, diabetes, kidney problems, liver problems, hepatitis, sexually transmitted diseases, tuberculosis, and HIV. A small percentage of inmates (2%) were so medically impaired that they needed to use a cane, walker, or wheelchair. Nearly 75% were overweight, and more than 60% were morbidly obese (Maruschak, 2015, p. 1).

ELDERLY INMATES

As one might expect, the elderly—and in prisons and jails, due to the premature aging of inmates, that can mean anyone over age 50—are much more prone to some of these medical maladies than are younger inmates (Hamada, 2015). In one BJS study, 61% of those over age 45 reported a medical problem (Maruschak, 2006, p. 1). With the exception of asthma and HIV, which tended to be more prevalent among younger inmates, the older inmates were much more likely to have the other medical problems tallied in this report; this means that older inmates are more costly to manage in jails because of their greater need for medical care.

FEMALE INMATES

Like the older inmates, women were much more likely to report medical problems to the BJS researchers (53% for women as opposed to 35% for men) (Maruschak, 2006, p. 2). They reported a rate of cancer that was nearly eight times that of men (831 per 10,000 female inmates compared with 108 per 10,000 male inmates), with the most common types being cervical cancer for women and skin cancer for men. In fact, of every medical problem documented in the study, the women reported more prevalence than the men, with the exception of paralysis, where they were even with men, and tuberculosis, where a slightly greater percentage of men reported more (4.3% for men as opposed to 4.0% for women) (Maruschak, 2006, p. 2).

JUVENILE INMATES

Incarcerated youths have their own set of potentially debilitating health problems that also present an immediate health risk to communities. In a study of adolescents in a juvenile detention center in Chicago, about 5% of the teens had contracted gonorrhea, and nearly 15% had chlamydia (Broussard et al., 2002, p. 8). Girls were more than three times more likely to have one of these diseases than were boys in this study.

RIGHTS TO MEDICAL CARE

According to the 1976 Supreme Court case *Estelle v. Gamble*, inmates have a constitutional right to reasonable medical care. The Court held that to be *deliberately indifferent* to the medical needs of inmates would violate the Eighth Amendment prohibition against cruel and unusual punishment. The Affordable Care Act of 2010 (ACA, commonly referred to as Obamacare) also requires that jails provide medical and mental health care within their facilities (Tally, 2015), although at the time of this writing during the spring of 2017 it was not clear whether the ACA would be repealed or not. Needless to say, treating such problems while providing care that meets the ACA mandate requires that a jail of any size have budgetary coverage for the salaries of nurses; contracts with a local doctor, mental health provider, and dentist; and an arrangement with local hospitals. Moreover, regular staff need basic training in CPR (cardiopulmonary resuscitation) and other medical knowledge (e.g., to know when someone is exhibiting the symptoms of a heart attack or stroke or the symptoms of mental illness) so that when problems arise staff recognize how serious they might be and know how to address them or whom to call (Kerle, 2011; Rigby, 2007).

Some jails are addressing these issues by contracting with private companies to provide medical services or using telemedicine as a means of delivering some services. The National Commission on Correctional Health Care recommends that if jails go the route of private provision of services, they should make sure that such programs are properly accredited so that the services provided meet national standards (Kerle, 2011). When such matters as obtaining and maintaining quality care are not attended to, as is sometimes the case in jails and prisons (Vaughn & Carroll, 1998; Vaughn & Smith, 1999), jail

© Scott Houston/Alamy

PHOTO 6.5: Female inmates line up for their medications.

inmates are likely to suffer the consequences in terms of continued poor health (Sturgess & Macher, 2005). In addition, jails may be sued for failure to provide care, and communities might be exposed to contagious diseases along with liability for legal bills (J. Clark, 1991; Macher, 2007; Rigby, 2007). Clearly, the provision of decent health care to incarcerated persons is important not just because the Supreme Court mandates it or because it is the moral thing to do for people who are not free to access health care on their own but also because the vast majority of jail inmates return to the community, most within 1 or 2 weeks (Kerle, 2011). Therefore, to prevent the spread of diseases and to save lives both inside and outside of jails, basic medical care would appear to be called for. Some jails are evidently expending energy to address this area of incarceration given that 4 in 10 of the inmates in the 2002 BJS study reported that they had had a medical exam since their admission (Maruschak, 2006, p. 1).

SUBSTANCE ABUSE AND JAILS

It is one of those oft-cited assumptions that people in prisons and jails have substance abuse problems, but this is one area of social commentary that actually fits social reality. According to a 2002 BJS study of jail inmates (the latest available data at the time of writing), fully 68% of jail inmates reported substance abuse or dependence problems (Karberg & James, 2005, p. 1). In fact, half of convicted inmates reported being under the influence at the time they committed their offense, and 16% said they committed the crime to get money for drugs. Female and white inmates both were more likely to report substance use at the time of the offense (Karberg & James, 2005, p. 5). For convicted offenders who used at the time of offense, alcohol was more likely to be in their system than drugs (33.3% for alcohol as opposed to 28.8% for drugs). The drugs of choice for abusers and users varied and included, by prevalence of use, marijuana, cocaine or crack, hallucinogens, stimulants (including methamphetamines), and inhalants (Karberg & James, 2005, p. 6). Not surprisingly, those who reported a substance abuse problem were also more likely to have a criminal record and to have been homeless before incarceration. White, Goldkamp, and Campbell (2006) found in their study conducted in New Mexico that many people who are arrested and subsequently come into contact with the local jail have "co-occurring disorders" such as mental illness and substance abuse problems (p. 303).

Violent offenders were more likely to use alcohol than other substances at the time of the offense. But violent offenders were also least likely, with the exception of public order offenders, to report being on drugs or alcohol at the time of the offense (Karberg & James, 2005, p. 6).

Fully 63% of those with a substance abuse problem had been in a treatment program before (Karberg & James, 2005, p. 1). Most such programs were of the self-help variety such as Alcoholics Anonymous and Narcotics Anonymous. However, 44% of these people had actually been in a residential treatment program or a detoxification program, had received professional counseling, or had been put on a maintenance drug (Karberg & James, 2005, p. 8).

Treatment for convicted offenders in jails, as of 2002, was at 6%. Notably, provision of treatment in jails is difficult because most inmates are out of the facility within a week, and about 60% are unconvicted, so as people who are presumed innocent, they cannot be coerced into getting treatment. Therefore, treatment programs are usually focused on those who meet all of the following criteria: They have a substance abuse problem, they are convicted, and they are longer-term inmates. Even having said this, the amount of treatment programming in jails does not fit the obvious need (Kerle, 2011).

••• SUICIDES, GANGS, AND SEXUAL VIOLENCE IN JAILS

SUICIDES

As indicated from the data presented above, those incarcerated in jails often enter them at some level of intoxication. Moreover, many have a mental disability, and if this is their first experience with jail, it might be exacerbated by the shock of incarceration. Most who are booked into jails are impoverished, and some are homeless. In addition, being booked itself may represent both the mental and physical low points of their lives. Such a combination of conditions may predispose some jail inmates to not just contemplate suicide but to actually attempt it (Winfree & Wooldredge, 1991; Winter, 2003).

In 1986, the National Center on Institutions and Alternatives (NCIA) did a study of suicides in jails. Twenty years later, in 2006, the National Institute of Corrections funded another NCIA study of the status of jail suicides. Based on 464 suicides that occurred in 2005 and 2006, the NCIA published the following findings regarding suicide victims in jails and characteristics of the suicides:

- Sixty-seven percent were white.
- Ninety-three percent were male.
- The average age was 35.
- Forty-two percent were single.
- Forty-three percent were held on a personal and/or violent charge.
- Forty-seven percent had a history of substance abuse.
- Twenty-eight percent had a history of medical problems.
- Thirty-eight percent had a history of mental illness.

- Twenty percent had a history of taking psychotropic medication.
- Thirty-four percent had a history of suicidal behavior.
- Deaths were evenly distributed throughout the year; certain seasons and/or holidays did not account for more suicides.
- Thirty-two percent occurred between 3:01 p.m. and 9 p.m.
- Twenty-three percent occurred within the first 24 hours, 27% between 2 and 14 days, and 20% between 1 and 4 months after incarceration. (Hayes, 2010, p. xi)

These data indicate that the profile of the suicide-prone inmate in jail is that of someone who is male, white, somewhat young (although the BJS data indicate both younger and older inmates are prone to committing suicide), in jail on a violent offense charge, with a history of substance abuse, and at the beginning of his jail incarceration. Other data from the BJS and other sources flesh out and contextualize these findings (see Figure 6.4).

Data obtained by BJS in a multi-year study (2000–2002) of deaths while in custody also suggest that age, gender, and race are important variables in predicting suicide along with jail size (Mumola, 2005). White males under age 18 and over age 35 and those inmates with a more violent commitment history were more likely to commit suicide than African American males or those in other age groups and who were not incarcerated for a violent offense (Mumola, 2005; Winter, 2003). Winter (2003) found in her study of 10 years of suicide data from jails in one midwestern state that those who committed suicide tended to be younger, were arrested for a violent offense, had no history of mental or physical illness, did not necessarily "exhibit suicidal tendencies," and were more likely to be intoxicated with alcohol when admitted (p. 138).

Moreover, according to the authors of the BJS study, the suicide rate for large, primarily urban jails, which tend to hold fewer whites, was about half that of the smaller jails (as cited in Mumola, 2005). Similarly, in a study by Tartaro and Ruddell (2006), the researchers also found that smaller jails (with less than a 100-bed capacity) had a two to five times greater prevalence of attempted and completed suicides than larger jails did (p. 81). In this study, crowded jails and those with "special-needs and long-term inmates" were also more likely to have a higher rate of suicide completion (p. 81). The shock of incarceration may be one explanation for jail suicide rates, although why this shock might be greater for those in smaller jails is not entirely clear. The BJS and NCIA data do indicate that about half of the suicides occur within the first 9 days—for women it was 4 days—and in the cell of the person committing the suicide (Mumola, 2005).

Larger jails, with their greater resources and higher level of training for staff, may be better equipped than their smaller counterparts to monitor and prevent suicides in their facilities. For instance, if younger inmates are fearful of being housed with and possibly abused by older adults, some less crowded and perhaps larger jails may have the luxury of segregating young men from older men and thereby lessening the fear that might precipitate some suicides. Winter's (2003) conclusion, after studying 18 years' worth of administrative data on suicides in a midwestern jail, is that keeping and accessing more complete records regarding suicides is critical to preventing them. It is possible that larger, more urban jails are better able to handle this responsibility. In their comparison study of rural and urban jails, Applegate and Sitren (2008) remarked on the greater capacity of urban jails, relative to rural jails, to provide services to inmates, which one assumes would directly and indirectly affect the rate of suicides in these jails.

However, large jails still have their share of problems with suicides. In a study by Selling et al. (2014) of suicides in the New York City jail system, the researchers found that between 2007 and 2011 there were eight deaths resulting from suicide and 2,514 cases of self-injury (out of yearly admissions of 80,000 and an average daily population of about 12,500) (p. 163). The self-injuries had increased in number during this time period. The methods of self-injury included, among others, "lacerations, ligatures tied around the neck, attempted overdose, and swallowed foreign objects" (p. 163). In response to this research, the jail managers (there are several New York City jails) improved the surveillance system and the electronic health records so they could better watch and document those who would be most likely to need help.

We do know that the rate of suicide among inmates in jails, despite its marked decrease over the last 9 years, is still twice as high as would be true for a comparable group of free citizens (Mumola, 2005). Jails have three times the rate of suicides that prisons do, although their homicide rates are comparable (Mumola, 2005). The good news, however, is that jail and prison deaths due to suicide (and homicide) declined precipitously from 1983 to 2002, with the rate of prison suicides declining by half during this time period and jail suicides by nearly two-thirds (Mumola, 2005, p. 2). In 1983 jail suicides were the major cause of death for inmates, but by 2002 illness had replaced suicide as the primary reason for death.

GANGS

Gangs present myriad management problems for jail and prison managers. Violence, including robberies, assaults, drug smuggling, and even murders, tends to naturally follow in their wake and prevents the orderly and safe operation of the facility for staff and inmates. Because gangs are more prevalent in large urban areas, they are more of a problem in large urban jails. Yet the estimates of their prevalence in large jail systems range from 16% to 25%, depending on the location of the jail (Tapia, 2014, p. 258). However, these estimates are likely to be low because gang members are usually not forthcoming about their membership in a correctional environment (Ruddell, Decker, & Egley, 2006). It is generally true that larger urban jails have more problems with gangs. Because jails are more likely to involve a short-term period of incarceration, however, they may be less likely to hold as many gang members as prisons (Alarid, 2000).

To counter the collective influence of gangs, jails will try to separate members in housing units, placing the most disruptive members in segregation (Tapia, 2014). Another tactic is to document those involved in gangs and to track them and their activities throughout the jail system. However, although gang members, by their definition, might appear to present a monolithic adherence to gang orthodoxy, there is some indication that not all gang members agree about how the gang should be operated and the tactics they should employ. For instance, in a study by Tapia (2014) of Latino gangs in Texas, it was found that there were intergenerational disputes on these matters, with younger inmates tending to organize themselves in more autonomous groups, which are as much support groups as criminal enterprises in jails. In that same research, however, the gangs identified by correctional officer respondents as most prevalent in Texas jails were the Texas Mexican Mafia, Aryan Brotherhood, Bloods, Texas Syndicate, Crips, Tango Blast, Tango Orejon, Aryan Circle, and Hermandad de Pistoleros Latinos (p. 262).

SEXUAL VIOLENCE

The **Prison Rape Elimination Act of 2003** mandated that the BJS collect data on sexual assaults in adult and juvenile jails and prisons and that it identify facilities with high

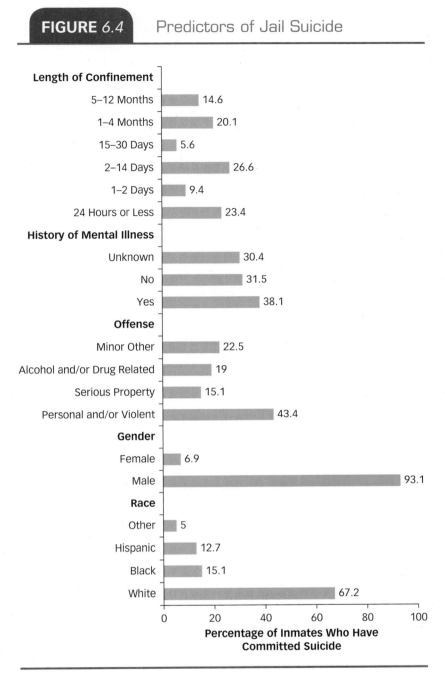

FIGURE 6.4   Predictors of Jail Suicide

Source: Based on data from Hayes (2010, p. xi).

Prison Rape Elimination Act of 2003: Act mandating that the Bureau of Justice Statistics collect data on sexual assaults in adult and juvenile jails and prisons and that it identify facilities with high levels of victimization.

ETHICAL ISSUE ?

What Would You Do?

You are a correctional officer who works in the booking area of a large urban jail. About once per month, the jail admits one or two transgender inmates. You notice that there is one male colleague named Joe who is particularly abusive of the transgender female inmates (calling them names, strip searching them, making them stand around naked in front of other staff and inmates while making derogatory comments about their body parts, doing unnecessary pat downs that focus inordinately on their breasts and genitals, referring to them by male pronouns, etc.). Although Joe is the primary instigator of this abuse, there are a few others, both male and female, who play along and others who try to ignore it (including you). You know your sergeant also has witnessed the abuse and has done nothing to stop it. You are unaware of any complaints being lodged by staff regarding Joe's or the others' behavior, although it is openly practiced in the booking area at least once or twice a month. You have heard that a lawsuit has been filed by a former inmate about Joe's and the other officers' treatment of her. As a booking officer, you are likely to be called to testify about what happened in her case (all of the abuse mentioned above). What will you do if called to testify? How will you explain your failure to report this abuse beforehand? What do you think will be the likely outcomes of the choices you made and make?

levels of victimization. According to the National Inmate Survey for 2011 and 2012 (which included 358 local jails and was conducted by BJS researchers), 3.2% of jail inmates (as opposed to 4.0% of prison inmates) reported experiencing sexual victimization perpetrated by other jail inmates or staff during the previous 12 months (Beck et al., 2013, p. 1). Extrapolating these sample findings to the national population of jail and prison inmates, the BJS researchers estimated that fully 80,600 inmates in prisons and jails experienced sexual victimization during this time period (Beck et al., 2013, p. 8). For jails, it was estimated that there were 25,100 victims; of these incidents, 11,900 were inmate on inmate and 13,200 were staff on inmate, and of these, 2,400 reported being victimized by both staff and inmates (Beck et al., 2013, p. 8). Notably, some of these victimizations were likely "consensual," although it is legally impossible for inmates, who occupy a powerless position vis-à-vis staff, to give consent to them.

Female inmates in jails (as well as in prisons) were more than twice as likely as male inmates to experience sexual victimization perpetrated by another inmate (3.6% for females as opposed to 1.4% for males) (Beck et al., 2013, p. 17). Male inmates in jails and prisons were slightly more likely to be victims of staff perpetrators. There was higher victimization among inmates who were two or more races or were white by other inmates and staff. In general, younger inmates (under 34 years) and those with a college degree were targeted more by both inmates and staff for sexual victimization.

As mentioned previously in this chapter, LGBTI inmates were much more likely to be victimized by both staff and inmates in both prisons and jails. In prisons, 1.2% and 2.1% of heterosexual inmates experienced inmate-on-inmate and staff-on-inmate sexual victimization, respectively, as compared with 12.2% and 5.4% of LGBTI inmates. In jails, the figures were similarly startling, with 1.2% and 1.7% of heterosexual inmates who experienced inmate-on-inmate and staff-on-inmate sexual victimization, respectively, as compared with 8.5% and 4.3% of LGBTI inmates (Beck et al., 2013, p. 18). In essence, in jails, the LGBTI inmates were seven times more likely to experience sexual victimization by other inmates and 2.5 times more likely to experience sexual victimization by staff than were heterosexuals.

In addition, as mentioned previously in this chapter, those with a mental illness were much more likely to experience sexual victimization than were inmates without such a malady (Beck et al., 2013). Mentally ill jail inmates experienced more inmate-on-inmate and staff-on-inmate sexual victimization than inmates without mental health problems.

In the Prison Rape Elimination Act–prescribed surveys of adult correctional authorities in prisons, jails, and other adult correctional facilities, it was found that the allegations of sexual victimization increased from 2009 to 2011, although the number of substantiated cases (those where an investigation found that the allegation was true) remained about the same since 2005 (Beck, Rantala, & Rexroat, 2014, p. 1). Notably, in an earlier

IN FOCUS 6.2

Prison Rape Elimination Act Controversy

As mentioned in the text of this chapter, the Prison Rape Elimination Act (PREA) of 2003 required that the Department of Justice and its subdivisions—the National Institute of Justice and the Bureau of Justice Statistics—study and report on the amount of sexual violence in adult and juvenile prisons and jails. In reaction to this reporting and court cases indicating that LGBTI inmates were particularly vulnerable to sexual abuse by inmates and staff, and after studying the matter, the National Prison Rape Elimination Commission, which was created by the PREA legislation, released its national standards in June 2009. These standards are extensive and require that states train staff differently, monitor inmates differently, report offenses, treat victims and offenders, audit themselves, and collect and keep relevant data related to sexual violence. The U.S. Attorney General was asked to release these standards and require that the Bureau of Prisons and each governor certify compliance with these standards or certify that they were working toward compliance. If governors did not do this, they risked losing 5% of any future Department of Justice grants (U.S. Department of Justice, 2015). As the date for certification of compliance neared during the spring of 2014, governors from at least seven states and one territory (Arizona, Florida, Idaho, Indiana, Nebraska, Texas, Utah, and the Northern Mariana Islands territory) ignored the certification deadline of May 15 or indicated that they would not certify compliance with these standards, some claiming that the standards were too cumbersome and expensive to comply with (Reilly, 2014, p. 1). On the other hand, a few states, including New Hampshire and New Jersey, certified compliance, while 46 states or territories promised to use their grant monies from the Department of Justice to work toward compliance with the federal standards (Reilly, 2014, p. 1). By spring of 2016, most states had certified or promised to move toward compliance.

Discussion Questions

1. What benefits would flow from certification by states for jail inmates?

2. How might non-LGBTQI inmates benefit from certification?

3. Why would states be reluctant to promise certification, and how might that reluctance be overcome?

---

have not gone away and will still be there when the inmate transitions back into the community. Therefore, in a community jail, those engaged in education, drug or alcohol counseling, or mental health programming will seamlessly receive such services while incarcerated and again as they transition out of the facility (Barlow et al., 2006; Bookman, Lightfoot, & Scott, 2005; National Institute of Corrections, 2008). Whether one is in and out of the facility within a few days or a few months, needs are met and services provided so that the reintegration into the community is smoother for the inmate and the community in question.

Managers of community jails also recognize that they cannot staff or resource the jails sufficiently to address every need of their inmates. Rather, community experts who are regularly engaged in the provision of such services are the appropriate persons to provide them whether the inmate is in a jail or free in the community; in both instances, it is argued, the inmate is a community member and entitled to such services (Barlow et al., 2006; Lightfoot et al., 1991).

Obviously, the development of community jails requires that some resources (particularly space) be devoted to the accommodation of community experts who provide for inmates' needs. Unfortunately, it is the rare jail that has the luxury of excess space for allocation to such programming. Therefore, the solution may lie in inclusion of

ETHICAL ISSUE ❓

What Would You Do?

You are a professor at a university, and you do research on jails. Some of your early research was on new-generation or podular direct-supervision (PDS) jails. One of the jails you profiled in that early research was a model PDS jail in that it practiced all of the principles of the best of such jails. You happen to visit that jail more than 20 years later, and other than the physical podular architecture, there is no longer anything new or progressive about the jail; there is no evidence that it is a PDS jail anymore. In fact, the supervision practices now seem to you to be abusive. Staff are no longer in the living units 7 days a week, 24 hours a day, and inmates are locked up in their double- and sometimes triple-celled small cells (made for one inmate) for up to 23 hours a day. Staff are not trained in how to be leaders in their living units because they are rarely in them, and inmates are not out of their cells to be led; instead, staff contact with inmates often includes yelling through the steel cell doors or the slight contact staff have with inmates when let out for their 1 hour of exercise. Inmates no longer have the support or services that typified PDS jails—and this jail—in the past. You are aware that fully 50% to 60% of the inmates in this jail have not been convicted of a crime, yet they are treated like they are serious offenders with behavior problems in a super-maximum-security prison. You know how this jail used to be operated, you know how it should be operated, and you know it is not being operated in this way. What would you do and why? Who might you talk to? What do you think would be the likely consequences of the action(s) you choose?

such space in jail architectural plans, although this certainly is not optimal given the immediacy of inmate needs discussed in the foregoing section.

The second problem that faces jail managers interested in creating community jails is convincing local service providers—and lawmakers if need be—that people in jails have a right to, and a continued need for, services and that the continued provision of such services by community experts benefits both those inmates and the larger community. Needless to say, making this case, as reasonable as it might sound, can be a "hard sell" to those social service agencies that already have scarce resources and to policymakers concerned that more tax dollars might be required to fund such resource provision in jails. For these reasons, larger jails and communities, with their economies of scale and a greater proportion of their populations in need of social services, might be better situated to operate community jails and thus achieve their purported benefits of less crime from the continuous provision of services in jails (Kerle, 2011; Lightfoot et al., 1991).

One interesting development on this front is how the Affordable Care Act is being implemented in jails. The ACA does not expressly prohibit jail inmates, as long as they are not convicted, from being able to sign up for Medicaid or qualified health plans while they are in jail. What this means is that a jail can embrace this community function by ensuring that its inmates are signed up. Evidence indicates that mentally impaired inmates with Medicaid coverage who reentered communities from jails were more likely to have a smooth transition to needed care than those who were not so covered (Robertson, 2014).

COEQUAL STAFFING

Another promising innovation in jails that has occurred during the last couple of decades in some sheriffs' departments has been the development of **coequal staffing**, which provides comparable pay and benefits to those who work in the jail with those who work on the streets as law enforcement (Kerle, 2003, 2011). Historically, jails have been a dumping ground (to use Irwin's [1985] terminology) not just for inmates but for staff as well. If a sheriff deemed that a staff person could not "make it" on the streets as law enforcement, he or she was given a job in the jail, where apparently the individual's lack of skills and ability was not seen as a problem. Moreover, jail staff were (and often still are) paid less and received less training than their counterparts working on the streets (Stohr & Collins, 2009). As a result, jails do find it difficult to attract and keep the best personnel, and even if they can attract the more talented applicants, jail jobs were (and often still are) used as "stepping stones" to better paying and higher status jobs on the law enforcement side of sheriffs' agencies (Kerle, 2011).

Coequal staffing:
Programs that provide comparable pay and benefits for those who work in the jail to that for people who work on the streets as law enforcement in sheriffs' departments.

Since the 1980s, however, many sheriffs' departments, although far from a majority, have recognized the problems created by according this second-tier status to those who work in jails (Kerle, 2011). Consequently, they have instituted programs whereby staff who work in the jails, who often are given deputy status, are trained and paid similarly to those who work in the free communities. Some anecdotal evidence from sheriffs' departments indicates that this change has had a phenomenal effect on the professional operation of jails (because they are better staffed) and on the morale of those who labor in them (Kerle, 2011).

REENTRY PROGRAMS FOR JAILS

Perhaps the newest "thing" in jails these days (and in prisons, too) is a rethinking about how to keep people out of them. (Reentry will be discussed in greater detail in Chapter 10.) Rather than focusing on deterrence or incapacitation so much (as during the 1980s and 1990s), jail practitioners are studying how to make the transition from jails to the community smoother and more successful so that people do not commit more crimes and return (Bookman et al., 2005; Freudenberg, 2006; McLean, Robarge, & Sherman, 2006; Osher, 2007). Research by Wodahl, Boman, and Garland (2015) indicates that community sanctions for probation and parole violations can be as effective as the use of jail and, at the same time, cost much less, so there is additional impetus for communities to try to move their jail inmates back into the community or to restrict their placement in the jail in the first place.

As indicated by the discussion in the foregoing material of all the medical, psychological, and social—not to mention educational—deficits that many inmates of jails have, this transition back into the community is likely to be fraught with difficulties. That is why any successful **reentry** program must include a recognition of the problems individual inmates may have (e.g., mental illness, physical illness, joblessness, homelessness) and address them systematically in collaboration with the client and the community (Freudenberg, 2006; McLean et al., 2006). In a study by Freudenberg, Mosely, Labriola, and Murrill (as cited in Freudenberg, 2006) conducted in New York City jails, the researchers asked hundreds of inmates what their top three priority reentry needs were. For adult women, they were housing, substance abuse treatment, and financial support; for adult men, they were employment, education, and housing; for adolescent males, they were employment, education, and financial support (Freudenberg, 2006, p. 15). Spjeldnes, Jung, and Yamatani (2014) also argued that women's and men's reentry needs may differ; these researchers found, in their study of a large urban jail, that more women than men reported chemical dependency and mental health needs and that women were more likely to value treatment programming.

Effective interventions to improve reentry, in the New York study, included everything from referral to counseling to drug treatment to post-release supervision, depending on the needs of the inmate, his or her unique reentry situation, and the services available in the community. Clearly, reentry is a complex process for people with multiple problems, and it requires that jail personnel prioritize the needs they will target and the interventions they will apply and then network with community agencies to provide the package of services most likely to further the goal of successful reentry (Freudenberg, 2006; McLean et al., 2006). In fact, Bookman and her colleagues (2005) argued that jail personnel should expect to engage in collaborative arrangements with community agencies (sounds a bit like community jails, doesn't it?) if they hope to succeed during the reentry process.

Reentry: The process of integrating offenders back into the community after release from jail or prison.

SUMMARY

- Jails in the United States are faced with any number of seemingly intractable problems. They are often overcrowded—or close to it—and house some of the most debilitated and vulnerable persons in our communities. They house the accused, the guilty, and the sentenced as well as low-level offenders and serious and violent ones. As with prisons, their mission is to incapacitate (even the untried), to deter, to punish, and even to rehabilitate. The degree to which they accomplish any of these goals is, in large part, determined by the political and social climate in which the jail is nested. Since the 1980s, the political climate has favored "harsh justice" meted out by policymakers and the actors in the criminal justice system and has led to the unrelenting business of filling and building prisons and jails across the country (Cullen, 2006; Irwin, 1985, 2005; Whitman, 2003).

- Jails have also served as a dumping ground for those who are marginally criminal and are unable or unwilling to access social services. Too often, the needs of such persons go unaddressed in communities, and as a result these unresolved needs either contribute to their incarceration (in the case of substance abuse and mental illness) or make it likely (in the case of homelessness) that they will enter and reenter the revolving jailhouse door.

- Sexual violence in jails remains problematic. It is likely true that the rate of violence between inmates and inmates or between staff and inmates has gone down during recent years. However, increased monitoring of this phenomenon is certainly called for and may serve to further reduce violence through the implementation of violence reduction techniques and training for staff. To that end, the implementation of the Prison Rape Elimination Act of 2003, with its reporting requirement for correctional institutions, represents a positive move.

- Thankfully, there have been some other hopeful developments on the correctional horizon. Jails in a position to do so have expanded their medical and treatment options to address the needs of inmates. Architectural and managerial solutions have been applied to jails in the form of new-generation jails and coequal pay for staff in sheriffs' departments, and some jails have even experimented with community engagement to ensure that the needs of people in communities are not neglected when such folks enter jails or reenter communities.

KEY TERMS

DISCUSSION QUESTIONS

1. Why are jails the "dumping ground" for so many people in our communities? What are the consequences of this social policy?

2. What is the best use for jails? What factors might make it difficult to operate jails so that they are able to focus on this best use?

3. What do you think are the best practices (most effective) in managing medically challenged or potentially suicidal inmates?

4. How can jail managers best reduce or eliminate sexual violence against inmates in jails? What do you think keeps managers from being successful at eliminating such violence?

5. What factors are likely to compromise the ability of podular direct-supervision jails to achieve their promise?

6. Why are jail staff in most facilities and sheriffs' departments still paid less than those on patrol? What argument can be made for the same or even higher pay for jail staff?

7. What are the relative advantages and disadvantages of community jails?

8. How might reentry programs prevent recidivism?

$SAGE edge™

Review → Practice → Improve

Sharpen your skills with SAGE edge at **edge.sagepub.com/stohressentials3e**.

SAGE edge offers a robust online environment featuring an impressive array of free tools and resources for review, study, and further exploration, keeping both instructors and students on the cutting edge of teaching and learning.

FOR FURTHER EXPLORATION AND APPLICATION, TAKE A LOOK AT THE INTERACTIVE EBOOK FOR THESE PREMIUM RESOURCES:

- **Career Video 6.1** Professor
- **SAGE News Clip 6.1** Alabama Prisons and HIV
- **SAGE News Clip 6.2** Prison Suicide Amid Hernandez News
- **Journal Article 6.1** Integrated Primary and Behavioral Health Care in Patient-Centered Medical Homes for Jail Releases With Mental Illness

7

Community Corrections

Probation and Intermediary Sanctions

TEST YOUR KNOWLEDGE

Test your current knowledge of probation by answering the following questions as true or false. Check your answers on page 391 after reading the chapter.

1. Probation in the United States began during the 1800s and was run by volunteers.

2. Probation is a popular punishment option among the American public.

3. Parole is another name for probation.

4. Probation is the most frequent sentence imposed by the courts in the United States.

5. Tough law enforcement–type probation officers achieve better results from their probationers than social work–type officers.

6. Work release programs are programs that allow tighter control of probationers than regular probation while allowing them to maintain their employment.

7. Hardened criminals would rather have any form of community supervision than a prison sentence.

8. Boot camps where offenders are treated with strict discipline are quite successful, especially with young offenders.

LEARNING OBJECTIVES

- Explain the origins and purpose of probation

- Describe the advantages of probation over incarceration for some offenders

- Describe the advantages of probation over incarceration for community offenders

- Analyze the probation officer role and models of probation supervision

- Explain the purpose of graduated sanctions for technical violations of probation

- Be able to describe the benefits of engaging the community in offender rehabilitation

- Identify the various intermediate community sanctions and what they have to offer

PTSD AND ESTABLISHING A VETERAN'S COURT IN BOISE, IDAHO

On July 28, 2009, a woman in Boise, Idaho, frantically dialed 911, saying that someone with a gun was pounding on her door and that he had fired one round at the lock. When the police arrived, they were confronted with a man holding a gun in a stairwell and fired 12 rounds at him without hitting him. The man surrendered without firing a shot and was charged with six felony counts. The man was 38-year-old sergeant George Nickel, a decorated (Bronze Star and Purple Heart) Iraq war hero who in 2007 suffered severe wounds in a bomb blast that killed three of his fellow soldiers. He told police that he hadn't slept for 3 days and had drank close to a full case of beer that day. He also told them that he was out looking for his dog, which he believed had been stolen, and was angrily trying to get it back.

Nickel suffered from posttraumatic stress disorder (PTSD) and "survival guilt" for surviving the blast in Iraq. He must have thought while in his jail cell that for all intents and purposes his life was over. However, under a plea agreement he was allowed to admit to one count of firing a weapon into an occupied residence and had the judgment withheld. A withheld judgment means that the charge would be purged from his record if he received mental health treatment and cooperated with law enforcement, which he did. Cooperation with law enforcement included sharing his harrowing experiences on videotape, which has been distributed to law enforcement agencies across the United States for training purposes.

Nickel's case was instrumental in the idea of establishing a veteran's court for Idaho, whereby people like Nickel can remain in the community with proper supervision rather than being sent to prison. Nickel subsequently earned a degree in social work from Boise State University and now works with other veterans to try to resolve their problems. Had it not been for the humane intervention of people like former Boise Police Chief Mike Masterson and Judge Deborah Bail, Nickel might have received up to 15 years in prison and still be left with his problems instead of becoming the upstanding citizen he now is. This is the kind of success story that all special problem-solving courts can claim—lives saved and turned around by considering the problem behind the act(s) that bring unfortunate souls before them. Such problem-solving courts have been one of the very few success stories in American corrections.

••• INTRODUCTION: THE ORIGINS OF PROBATION

This chapter focuses on **probation**, which is a sentence imposed on convicted offenders that allows them to remain in the community under the supervision of a probation officer instead of being sent to prison. The term *probation* comes from the Latin term *probare*, meaning "to prove." Because probation is a conditional release into the community, the probation period is a time of testing a person's character and his or her ability to meet certain requirements mandated by the court. That is, convicted persons must prove to the court that they are capable of remaining in the community and living up to its legal and moral standards. About 90% of all sentences handed down by the courts in the United States are probation orders (Kramer & Ulmer, 2009).

The practice of imprisoning convicted criminals is a relatively modern and expensive way of dealing with them. Up to 200 or 300 years ago, they were dealt with by execution, corporal punishments such as disfigurement and branding, or humiliation in the stocks. All these punishments took place as community spectacles and even with community participation in the case of individuals sentenced to time in the stocks. Assuming that a convicted person was not executed, he or she remained in the community enduring the shame of having offended it (think of Hester Prynne's punishment in Hawthorne's [1850/2003] *The Scarlet Letter*, briefly discussed in Chapter 1). The only kinds of offenders typically subjected to this kind of shaming today are sex offenders whose pictures are displayed on the Internet and who are frequently identified to their neighbors through community notification orders.

More enlightened ages saw punishments move away from barbaric cruelties and the emergence of the penitentiary, where offenders could contemplate the errors of their ways and perhaps redeem themselves while residing there. But as we have seen, penitentiaries were not very nice places, and some kind souls in positions to do so sought ways to spare deserving or redeemable offenders from being consigned to them. This practice had its legal underpinnings in the practice of **judicial reprieve** sometimes practiced in English courts in former times. A judicial reprieve was a delay in sentencing following a conviction, a delay that most often would become permanent if the offender demonstrated good behavior. In those days, there were no probation officers charged with supervising reprieved individuals; the nosey and judgmental nature of the small communities was more than adequate for that task.

Early American courts also used judicial reprieve, whereby a judge would suspend the sentence and the defendant would be released on his or her own recognizance. Today an "own recognizance" release is the release of an arrested person without payment of bail who promises to appear in court to answer criminal charges. In early America, it was granted to persons already convicted as a form of probation, although offenders received no formal supervision or assistance to help them mend their ways. The first real probation system in

Probation: A sentence imposed on convicted offenders that allows them to remain in the community under the supervision of a probation officer instead of being sent to prison.

Judicial reprieve: British and early American practice of delaying sentencing following a conviction that could become permanent, depending on the offender's behavior.

which a reprieved person was supervised and helped was developed in the United States during the 1840s by a Boston cobbler named John Augustus. Augustus would appear in court and offer to take carefully selected offenders into his own home where he would do what he could to reform them as an alternative to imprisonment. Probation soon became his full-time vocation, and he recruited other civic-minded volunteers to help him. By the time of his death in 1859, he and his volunteers had saved more than 2,000 convicts from imprisonment (Schmalleger, 2001). It should be noted, however, that Augustus worked only with first offenders and excluded the "wholly depraved" (Vanstone, 2004, p. 41), a luxury modern probation officers do not enjoy.

In 1878, the Massachusetts legislature authorized Boston to hire salaried probation officers to do the work of Augustus's volunteers, and a number of states quickly followed suit. This legislation grew out of the need to enforce the conditions of a suspended sentence as well as the need to help offenders change their lives (Vanstone, 2008). However, the probation idea nearly died in 1916 when the U.S. Supreme Court ruled that judges may not indefinitely suspend a sentence (*Ex Parte United States*, 1916). In this case, an embezzler was sentenced to 5 years of imprisonment, which the judge (Federal Judge John Killits) suspended contingent on the embezzler's good behavior. What Killits had done was place an offender on probation without there being such a system established by law. Probation was such a popular idea with legislators at this time, however, that this ruling led to the passage of the **National Probation Act of 1925,** allowing judges to suspend sentences and place convicted individuals on probation if they found that circumstances warranted it.

●●● NUMBER AND DEMOGRAPHIC CHARACTERISTICS OF OFFENDERS ON PROBATION

According to the Bureau of Justice Statistics (Kaeble & Bonczar, 2017), there were 3,789,800 adult Americans (1 in 61 adults in the United States) on probation in 2015. Table 7.1 provides highlights of the entries and exits from both probation and parole

National Probation Act of 1925: The act that initiated the legal use of probation in the United States.

TABLE 7.1	Highlights of Probation and Parole Population in 2015
• At year-end 2015, an estimated 4,650,900 adults were under community supervision, down by 62,300 offenders from year-end 2014.	• The adult parole population increased by 12,800 offenders from year-end 2014 to year-end 2015, to an estimated 870,500 offenders.
• Approximately 1 in 53 adults in the United States was under community supervision at year-end 2015.	• Parole entries increased for the first time in 7 years. Parole exits increased for the first time in 6 years.
• The adult probation population declined by 78,700 offenders from year-end 2014 to year-end 2015, falling to 3,789,800.	• Entries to parole increased from an estimated 461,100 in 2014 to 475,200 in 2015.
• Movement onto probation decreased from an estimated 2,065,800 entries in 2014 to 1,966,100 in 2015.	• Exits from parole increased from 450,800 in 2014 to 463,700 in 2015.
• Probation exits declined from 2,129,100 in 2014 to 2,043,200 in 2015.	

Source: Kaeble and Bonczar (2017).

FIGURE 7.1   Characteristics of Individuals on Probation, 2000–2014

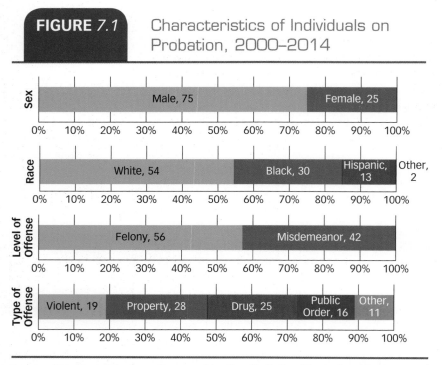

Source: Based on data from Bureau of Justice Statistics (November 2015), *Annual Probation Survey, 2000–2014*. Retrieved from https://www.bjs.gov/content/pub/pdf/ppus14.pdf

in 2015, and Figure 7.1 notes the demographic characteristics and level and type of offense for all people placed on probation in the United States from 2000 to 2014. In 2015, males constituted 75% of the adult probation population, 55% of adult probationers were white, 30% were black, 13% were Hispanic, and 4% were classified as "other," which is consistent with the previous years reported in Figure 7.1. The exit rate is the number of probationers who exit probation divided by the average probation population for the year. The exit rate for completion of probation was 53 per 100 probationers in 2015; of these, 33 per 100 successfully completed probation, 8 per 100 exited by incarceration, 1 per 100 absconded, and 9 per 100 for "other" reasons (Kaeble & Bonczar, 2017).

••• WHY DO WE NEED COMMUNITY CORRECTIONS?

Community corrections may be defined as any activity performed by agents of the state to assist offenders in establishing or reestablishing law-abiding roles in the community while at the same time monitoring their behavior for criminal activity. In theory, monitoring and assisting offenders while allowing them to remain in the community protects society from criminal predation without taxpayers shouldering the financial cost of incarceration. Even if as a society we were willing and able to bear the monetary cost of imprisoning all offenders, incarceration imposes other costs on the community. These costs can and must be borne where seriously violent and chronic criminals are concerned, but to send every felony offender to prison would be counterproductive. Yet the general public is not well disposed to the idea of probation because "it suffers from a 'soft on crime' image" and is seen as "permissive, uncaring about crime victims, and blindly advocating a rehabilitative ideal while ignoring the reality of violent, predatory criminals" (Petersilia, 1998, p. 30). However, allowing relatively minor felony offenders to remain in the community under probation supervision to prove that they can live law-abiding lives benefits their communities as well as themselves.

Community corrections: A branch of corrections defined as any activity performed by agents of the state to assist offenders in reestablishing functional law-abiding roles in the community while at the same time monitoring their behavior for criminal activity.

The general public's notion that a probation sentence is "getting away with it" is a notion not shared by many offenders. When a convicted felon is placed on probation, he or she actually receives a prison sentence. This prison sentence is then suspended during the period of proving that the probationer is capable of living a law-abiding life. This sentence hangs over probationers' heads like a guillotine ready to drop if they fail to provide that proof. It may be for this reason that a number of studies have found that "experienced" offenders who have done prison time, probation time, and parole time often prefer prison to the more demanding forms of probation such as day reporting and intensive supervision probation (Crouch, 1993; May, Wood, Mooney, & Minor, 2005).

Probation requires offenders to work, submit to treatment and educational programs, and do many other orderly things that many hardened criminals simply do not have the inclination to do. Numerous interviews with active "street criminals" (e.g., burglars, robbers, carjackers) show that such things are treated with disdain by them (B. Jacobs & Wright, 1999; Mawby, 2001; R. Wright & Decker, 1994). Serving time in prison is less of a hassle for many of them, and many know that they would end up there anyway because they would not live up to probation conditions (May et al., 2005).

Other less criminally involved offenders prefer a probation sentence so that they can retain their jobs and maintain connections to their families and communities. As we saw in Chapter 1, perceptions of the severity of a punishment, and thus its deterrent effect, is a function of the contrast between one's everyday life and life under punishment conditions (the contrast effect). With close to 4 million American adults on probation in 2012, 68% of them successfully completed their conditions of supervision and were released from probation (Maruschak & Bonczar, 2013). In the event of a failure to live up to the conditions of probation, the prison sentence may be imposed. Thus, while many fail the probation period, the majority succeed, so surely providing nonviolent offenders with the opportunity to try to redeem themselves while remaining in the community is sensible criminal justice policy. But what are the benefits for the community?

1. Probation costs far less than imprisonment. Note from Figure 7.2 provided by the U.S. Courts (2013) that it cost nearly nine times more (more for women, juveniles, and the elderly) for imprisonment than for community supervision. For each person placed on probation rather than incarcerated in 2012, taxpayers saved more than $25,000. Many jurisdictions require probationers to pay for their own costs of supervision, which means that the taxpayer pays nothing. However, while economic considerations are important for policymakers, they are not the primary concern of corrections; protecting the community is. Community-based corrections is the solution only for those offenders who do not pose a significant risk to public safety.

2. Employed probationers stay in their communities and continue to pay taxes, and offenders who were unemployed at the time of conviction may obtain training and help in finding a job. This adds further to the tax revenues of the community and, more important, allows offenders to keep or obtain the stake in the community that employment offers. A job also gives them the wherewithal to pay fines and court costs, as well as restitution to victims.

3. In the case of married offenders, community supervision maintains the integrity of the family, whereas incarceration could lead to its disruption and all the negative consequences such disruption entails.

4. Probation prevents felons from becoming further embedded in a criminal lifestyle by being exposed to chronic offenders in prison. Nearly all prisoners will leave the institution someday, and many will emerge harder, more criminally sophisticated, and more bitter than they were when they entered. Furthermore, they are now ex-cons, a label that is a heavy liability when attempting to reintegrate into a free society.

5. Many more offenders get into trouble because of deficiencies than because of pathologies. Deficits such as the lack of education, a substance abuse problem, and faulty thinking patterns can be assessed and addressed using the methods discussed in Chapter 15 on treatment. If we can correct these deficits to some extent, then the community benefits because it is a self-evident truth that whatever helps the offender to become a productive citizen also protects the community.

We do not wish to appear naive about this; there are people who are unfit to remain in the community and could not lead a law-abiding life even if given everything they needed to start over. We noted in Chapter 1 that for serious and violent offenders incarceration is cost-effective. Placing dangerous offenders on probation is putting the community

PHOTO 7.1: A probation officer meets with a probationer.

at risk, and they will mess up sooner or later and end up in prison anyway. For instance, according to the U.S. Marshals Service (2012), about 95% of those in the witness protection program (a program run by the U.S. Marshals Service to protect threatened witnesses and "snitches" during and after a trial) are criminals, and 17% percent commit further crimes under their new identities within a year despite being given jobs, housing, and basically a new start in life as part of the program. To use a medical metaphor, probation is "outpatient" treatment for the less seriously criminally afflicted; prison is hospitalization for people who cannot be successfully treated anywhere else.

••• THE PROBATION OFFICER ROLE

Probation and parole officers (the roles are combined in some states) have two common roles: to protect the community and to assist their probationers and parolees in becoming productive and law-abiding citizens. The dual roles mark them as law enforcement officers (this is their legally defined role in most states) and as social workers. The offenders they supervise may be on probation or parole, depending on their legal status. Probation is a judicial function meaning that they are under the ultimate supervision of the court. Probationers may or may not have served jail time prior to community supervision by a probation officer. Offenders who have served time in prison are placed on parole on release and are under the ultimate supervision of the executive branch of government, typically the state department of corrections.

Probation officers are officers of the court, and in this capacity they are responsible for enforcing court orders, which may require them to monitor probationers' adherence to programs such as drug and alcohol treatment and to develop plans to assist them in transitioning to a free society. They are also required to make arrests, perform searches, and seize evidence of wrongdoing. Officers might need to appear in court occasionally to present evidence of and violation of probation orders and to justify their recommendations for either termination of probation and imprisonment or continued probation with additional conditions. This is part of the officers' law enforcement role. Probation/parole officers work with criminal offenders who may be dangerous and often live in areas that may also be dangerous, which is why 35 states require their officers to carry a firearm (Holcomb, 2008). Nevertheless, it is important that officers spend a lot of time in those communities learning about their culture, customs and values, and resources available to assist with the rehabilitation of offenders.

••• MODELS OF PROBATION SUPERVISION

As is the case with all occupations, the effectiveness of probation/parole officers' performance ranges from dismal to outstanding. One of the biggest problems in probation and parole work is gaining the trust of their probationers or parolees and developing rapport with them. Most officers are white and middle class, whereas many of their "clients" are minorities, and whereas most probationers and parolees are male, about half of probation officers are female (Walsh & Stohr, 2010). It is very difficult for both officers and probationers to overcome the class, race, and gender divide and for each to understand and appreciate where the other is "coming from." Nevertheless, the job must be done as effectively as possible.

The measures of correctional effectiveness are how well the community is protected from the offenders on an officer's caseload (law enforcement role) and how well the offenders are able to resolve their criminogenic problems and become decent, law-abiding citizens (social work role). There is often tension between these supposedly contradictory roles (Skeem & Manchak, 2008), although there need not be, as one chief probation officer referred to in this so-called conflict in a question-and-answer session:

> When I'm asked at a meeting with probation officers, "Are we supposed to be cops or social workers?" I answered with another question— "How many of you are parents of teenagers?" I asked those who raised their hands, "Would you say you are a cop or social worker?" One of those that raised his hand said, "At different times, I was both." Bingo! (as cited in Klingele, 2013, p. 1030)

Some officers take on an exclusively law enforcement role and embrace working values, emphasizing strict compliance with probation conditions and holding offenders strictly accountable. Other officers take on a counselor role, providing offenders with whatever is available in the community to bring about behavior change. The extent to which officers follow these different models depends not only on the personalities and training of the individual officers but also on the overall supervision model dictated by whether their department's philosophy is punitive or rehabilitative, which in turn is dictated by the ideology of local politicians.

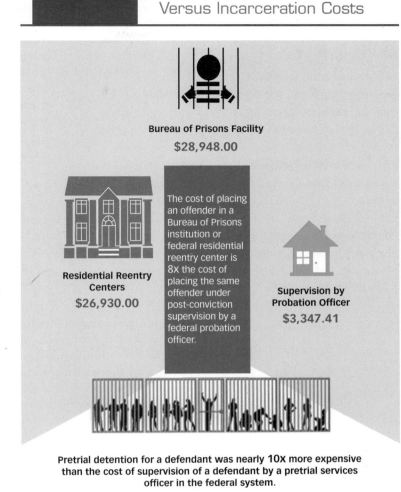

FIGURE 7.2 Community Supervision Costs Versus Incarceration Costs

Bureau of Prisons Facility
$28,948.00

Residential Reentry Centers
$26,930.00

The cost of placing an offender in a Bureau of Prisons institution or federal residential reentry center is 8X the cost of placing the same offender under post-conviction supervision by a federal probation officer.

Supervision by Probation Officer
$3,347.41

Pretrial detention for a defendant was nearly 10X more expensive than the cost of supervision of a defendant by a pretrial services officer in the federal system.

Source: U.S. Courts (2013). *Supervision costs significantly less than incarceration in federal system.* http://news.uscourts.gov/supervision-costs-significantly-less-incarceration-federal-system

A third group of officers combines the two roles and follows a "hybrid" approach, meaning that they follow both the law enforcement and social work models when appropriate. Skeem and Manchak (2008) viewed the law enforcer as authoritarian and the counselor as permissive but saw the hybrid officer as authoritative, the kind of parenting style that psychologists tell us the most effective parents adopt (Grusec & Hastings, 2007). Authoritarian officers are inflexible disciplinarians who require unquestioning compliance with their demands. Such a style often leads to hostility and rebelliousness among those to whom it is directed.

Permissive officers set few rules and are reluctant to enforce those that are set. This style often results in the perception among their probationers that the officer is a "pushover," and it practically invites lack of respect and noncompliance. Authoritative officers are hybrids who are firm enforcers but fair, knowing that boundaries must be set and consequences must be endured for venturing beyond them. They clearly describe those boundaries and the consequences for crossing them (the law enforcement role), but they also offer guidance and support to probationers (the social work role) so that they may be better able to stay within those boundaries.

How well do these different styles do with respect to the dual roles of community protection and offender rehabilitation? One study found that in terms of technical violations

ETHICAL ISSUE ?

What Would You Do?

You are a probation/parole officer assigned to write a presentence investigation report (PSI) on a burglary case that resulted in the loss of more than $1,000 in property and in which the house was trashed. On reading the police report, you realize that the house is that of a very close friend who was devastated by the experience. You realize that you can slant the report to put the offender in the worst possible light and recommend a stiff sentence for him, thereby exacting "revenge" for your friend. Would you do this, or would you still try to be as objective as possible and go ahead and write the report? Alternatively, would you realize your bias, tell your supervisor the circumstances, and request that the report be assigned to another officer?

such as failure to comply with some condition of probation, 43% of probationers supervised by a law enforcement–oriented officer, 5% of probationers supervised by a treatment-oriented officer, and 13% of probationers supervised by a hybrid officer received a technical violation (Paparozzi & Gendreau, 2005). These findings are as expected; law enforcers do not tolerate any violations, counselors tolerate nearly every violation, and hybrids, like good and concerned parents, tolerate selectively. New criminal convictions are a better measure of supervision effectiveness than technical violations, however, because while technical violations are largely in the hands of officers, new criminal convictions are out of their hands. Offenders with treatment-oriented social work officers were convicted of new crimes at twice the rate (32% vs. 16%) of those supervised by law enforcement–oriented officers, while only 6% of offenders supervised by hybrid officers were convicted of new crimes.

Further evidence for the effectiveness of the authoritative hybrid model comes from the success of Hawaii's Opportunity Probation with Enforcement (HOPE) program. According to the judge that initiated the program, it is based on the principles of effective parenting and on Beccaria's notion that consequences for misbehavior will be swift, certain, and proportionate to the severity of the misbehavior (as cited in Alm, 2013). HOPE begins with a formal warning that *no* violation of probation conditions will be tolerated and that any violation will *immediately* result in a short jail stay. The program has been shown to be so remarkably successful (it will be examined in greater detail in Chapter 15) that a number of states have implemented similar programs such as Delaware's Decide Your Time (DYT) program (O'Connell, Visher, Martin, Parker, & Brent, 2011).

••• PROBATION VIOLATIONS AND GRADUATED SANCTIONS

In these days of severe budget cuts and the concerns of cost-conscious politicians, there has been a tendency to turn to evidence-based research to see what can be done to reduce probation revocations (Klingele, 2013). After all, one of the advantages of probation is supposed to be saving the taxpayer money, and probation is hardly a cost cutter if it is simply a deferred incarceration. We have seen that 15% of probationers were ultimately incarcerated in 2012 (Maruschak & Bonczar, 2013), which amounts to nearly 600,000 individuals, and probation violators constitute about one-third of all individuals admitted to prison each year (Klingele, 2013). Probation officers enjoy a certain amount of discretion as to whether or not to formally violate someone's probation and the reasons why they will do so. A formal probation violation (PV) goes before the sentencing judge with a recommendation from the officer regarding whether or not the suspended prison sentence should be imposed.

One of the ways state legislatures and correctional departments have addressed the issue is by turning to actuarial assessment tools devised by criminal justice researchers to determine the circumstances for technical and, in some cases, minor criminal violations of probation. One such tool used by the Vermont Department of Corrections is presented in Table 7.1, which is designed to eliminate costly court appearances and incarcerations for offenders whose violations do not bear directly on their threat to the community or their rehabilitation.

PERSPECTIVE FROM A PRACTITIONER

Brian Fallock, Probation and Parole Officer

Position: Probation and Parole Agent for Pennsylvania Board of Probation and Parole

Location: Pennsylvania Board of Probation and Parole

Education: B.A. in Administration of Justice, University of Pittsburgh

What are your duties and responsibilities?

The primary responsibility of a probation/parole (P&P) agent is to ensure the safety of the community by supervising offenders on parole and probation released from a state correctional institution or county jail. While doing this, P&P agents also will assist offenders in adequately reentering into society through numerous techniques and programs to hopefully reduce recidivism and provide the offenders with the tools they need to stay out of jail. Agents refer offenders to outside agencies for specialized therapy in order to assist them in dealing with problems that need special attention such as employment, drugs, alcohol, and sexual and mental health problems. If an offender does violate, agents are responsible for requesting a warrant for his or her arrest through a superior and physically taking an offender into custody with the assistance of other agents or police agencies. P&P agents also participate in court proceedings, providing testimony on the adjustment of offenders in the community and answering questions concerning agency policy and procedures so that the court can make an accurate decision pertaining to an offender that has violated his or her supervision.

What are the characteristics and traits most useful in your line of work?

Strong interpersonal skills are recommended as you will be dealing with many offenders from different backgrounds as well as dealing with the offenders' families on a daily basis. Agents routinely work with various local and state law enforcement agencies, and being able to work with others to come to a common goal is encouraged. Good time management and organizational skills are a must as you will consistently have numerous issues to deal with simultaneously and will need to be able to keep track of them. Communication and writing skills are also required as there are various reports and notes that will need to be submitted on a regular basis.

Please describe your typical workday.

As a field agent, I am required to make field contacts with offenders, whether at their home, job, or elsewhere. Every offender is assigned a level of supervision that dictates policy regarding how often you are required to see that offender in a given supervision period. A typical workday will involve traveling through your assigned area of supervision, making attempts to see your offenders and their families to monitor their adjustment back into society. Agents will also communicate with various treatment agencies to ensure the offenders' compliance with the program they are enrolled in. If scheduled, agents will attend various court hearings to provide testimony and evidence proving any violations and detailing an offender's history while under supervision. When needed, agents will spend time in the district office writing reports, answering e-mails, and making phone calls.

What is your advice to someone who wants to enter your field?

Being a P&P agent can be challenging. P&P agents are often said to wear numerous hats, depending on the situation. One minute you could be wearing a "law enforcement hat" that will require you to violate offenders (determine they have violated parole) or take them into custody. The next minute you could be wearing a "social worker hat" where you are referring offenders to other agencies to get any help they need. To be successful in this type of work, you need to be flexible and hard-working. But you also need to keep in mind that these offenders can be dangerous, and you need to be cautious and on your toes at all times. You cannot become complacent, as there is no such thing as a "routine contact." Anything can happen, and you need to be prepared. But along with being challenging, being a P&P officer can be extremely rewarding. You will be able to provide guidance to offenders and give them the tools they need to be a contributing member of society, and hopefully they will complete their supervision successfully. Reducing recidivism is key, and if the offender is willing to change, P&P agents are on the front lines and can have a great effect on it.

ETHICAL ISSUE ?

What Would You Do?

You are 32-year-old Mary Mitchell's probation officer. She has been on your caseload for nearly 2 years since pleading guilty to shoplifting and drug possession. She has been a model probationer who has maintained employment, never missed an appointment with you, paid all her fines and court costs, and never tested positive for drug use. Now she has missed two appointments in a row and has not returned your phone calls. You go to her home to investigate and find her lying on a couch disheveled and obviously high. She tells you that she is deeply depressed because her mother passed away a month ago and that she cannot face the world without her. She begs you not to violate her probation since she has only 2 more months to serve. What are your options here, and what do you think you should or will do?

Note that both the violations and the sanctions attached to them have a three-level hierarchy of increasing seriousness of violation and increasing severity of punishment. Under this scheme, offenders are brought before a judge for technical violations only after a probationer reaches Level 3 violations and after all appropriate casework interventions have been exhausted. While state legislatures have designed these assessment tools primarily as cost-cutting devices, they also appear to be useful correctional tools by providing officers with a uniform way of responding to violations, thereby making authoritarian law enforcement–oriented officers less punitive and permissive social work–oriented officers less indulgent with offenders' transgressions.

••• PROBATION OFFICER STRESS

Supervising criminal offenders is not the easiest or most lucrative job in the world, although by today's job standards the pay and stability are excellent. According to the Bureau of Labor Statistics, in 2011 probation officers earned an average of $52,110 a year, but the median income (half earn below, half earn above) was closer to $47,840 a year. Officers with 5 to 10 years of experience earn between $31,470 and $61,460 a year, and those with 10 to 20 years on the job earn between $32,930 and $82,530. In addition, federal, state, and local benefits are much better than those typically provided by the private sector and include paid vacations, sick leave, pension, and health, dental, and life insurance plans.

In common with police officers and correctional officers, probation and parole officers are dealing with difficult human individuals on a daily basis, often without the tools and support needed to do the job as it should be done. Doing a demanding and sometimes dangerous job under less than adequate conditions can, and does, lead to stress (Slate, Wells, & Wesley Johnson, 2003). For instance, one study of officers in four states found that 35% to 55% reported that they had been victims of threatened or actual violence (Finn & Kuck, 2005). Stress is a physical and emotional state of tension as the body reacts to environmental challenges (stressors). No one can be expected to do a very good job while experiencing stress.

The most important job stressors identified by the officers surveyed by Slate et al. (2003) were poor salaries, poor promotion opportunities, excessive paperwork, lack of resources from the community, large caseloads, and a general frustration with the inadequacies of the criminal justice system. These stressors may eventually lead to psychological withdrawal from the job, meaning that probationers, and thus the community, are getting shortchanged. High stress levels in the department also lead to frequent absenteeism and high rates of employee turnover; thus, it is imperative that the issue of probation/parole officer stress be meaningfully addressed.

Slate et al. (2003) emphasized that an attempt to address the problem of probation officer stress should not be one of counseling officers on how to cope with stress because the problem is organizational (inherent in the probation system), not personal. They suggested that participatory management strategies be instituted so that each person in the department participates in the decision-making process and, thus, feels valued and empowered. The researchers found that personnel who did participate in decision making reported fewer stress symptoms and were happier on the job. Participatory management (workplace democracy) leads to a happier and more productive workforce even if nothing else changes—"contented cows give better milk."

TABLE *7.1*   Graduated Sanctions Guideline for Technical Probation Violations

Level 1 Violations	Level 1 Sanctions
➤ Failure to report as instructed	➤ Graduated Sanction Thinking Report
➤ Out of Place	➤ Apology (verbal or written)
➤ 1st positive drug/alcohol test	➤ Verbal warning
➤ Refusal of drug/alcohol test	➤ Develop Relapse Prevention Plan
➤ Missed treatment/programming group	➤ Written essay/educational activities
➤ Unemployment or failure to seek employment within 45 days	➤ Increase contacts for up to 30 days
➤ Failure to fulfill financial obligations	➤ Increase curfew restrictions for up to 30 days
➤ Failure to follow case plan/ORP	➤ Use of schedules for up to 30 days
➤ Failure to complete community service	➤ DOC work crew
➤ Curfew Violation	
Level 2 Violations	**Level 2 Sanctions**
➤ Multiple Level 1 violations	➤ Referral for treatment assessment
➤ Non-compliance with Special Conditions not indicated above	➤ Community Service Work for up to 80 hours
➤ Continued substance abuse or 2nd positive drug/alcohol test	➤ Community Restitution Work Crew for up to 10 days
➤ Continued missed treatment/programming group	➤ Curfew/Restriction to residence
➤ Failure to comply with Level 1 sanctions	➤ Increased reporting as directed for Alco-sensor, drug testing, employment search, or other related activity
➤ Contact with restricted persons (Non-Sex Offender/ Domestic Violence)	➤ Activities to address risk behaviors (self-help)
➤ Tampering with electronic monitoring equipment	➤ Loss of curfew/placed on schedule
	➤ Modification of the case plan to address risk-related behavior
	➤ Any Level 1 sanction
	➤ Use of Electronic Monitoring Equipment along with Level 1 sanction for up to 60 days
Level 3 Violations	**Level 3 Sanctions**
➤ Multiple Level 2 violations	➤ Use of Electronic Monitoring Equipment along with Level 2 sanction for up to 60 days
➤ Failure to comply with Level 2 sanctions	➤ Modified Conditions of Probation (risk-related)
➤ Non-threatening contact with victim	
➤ Suspension or placed on probation in treatment/ programming group	
➤ Misdemeanor behavior (Non-risk/Non-violent)	
➤ Out of Place for more than 24 hours	

Source: Vermont Department of Corrections (2010). *Graduated sanctions for technical violation of probation in lieu of court referral.* http://www.doc.state.vt.us/about/policies/rpd/rules/rpd/correctional-services-301-550/335-350-district-offices-general/docpolicy-347-graduated-sanctions-for-technical-violations-of-probation-in-lieu-of-court-referral

© SAGE/Jessica Miller

PHOTO 7.2: A probation officer's job is highly varied, ranging from interviewing police officers, victims, and family members of the defendant, as well as the defendant himself or herself, to making midnight raids on a probationer's home.

●●● ENGAGING THE COMMUNITY TO PREVENT RECIDIVISM

Although probation began as a voluntary community effort in the United States and Britain, community involvement in offender rehabilitation has faded in those countries with the professionalization of probation. Japan is a country in which probation volunteers still dominate. In Japan, there are about 50,000 volunteer officers but only 800 professional officers (T. Ellis, Lewis, & Sato, 2011).

Western countries probably cannot revive the old level of community involvement, and cultural differences preclude volunteerism at anywhere near Japanese levels (a volunteer probation officer position is highly sought in Japan because it confers high status [Gardner, 1996]). To achieve the average 2.5 ratio of probationers to volunteer probation officers that is enjoyed in Japan (only about 60,000 adults on probation there in 2010 [T. Ellis et al., 2011]) with the approximately 4 million probationers in the United States would require about 1.6 million volunteer officers. Nevertheless, we can engage our communities in the process of offender rehabilitation more than we are doing now, realizing that whatever helps the offender helps the community.

The criminological literature provides abundant support for the notions that social bonds (Hirschi, 1969) and social capital (Sampson & Laub, 1999) are powerful barriers against criminal offending. Social bonds are connections (often emotional in nature) to others and to social institutions that promote prosocial behavior and discourage antisocial behavior. Social capital refers to a store of positive relationships in social networks on which the individual can draw for support. It also means that a person with social capital has acquired an education and other solid credentials that enable him or her to lead a prosocial life. Those who have opened their social capital accounts early in life (bonding to parents, school, and other prosocial networks) may spend much of it freely during adolescence but, nevertheless, manage to salvage a sufficiently tidy nest egg by the time they reach adulthood to keep them on the straight and narrow. The idea is that they are not likely to risk losing this nest egg by engaging in criminal activity (the contrast effect again). Most criminals, on the other hand, lack social bonds, and largely because of this they lack the stake in conformity provided by a healthy stash of social capital.

If we consider the great majority of felons in terms of deficiency (good things that they *lack*) rather than in terms of personal pathology (bad things they *are*), we are talking about a deficiency in social capital. The community can be seen as a bank in which social capital is stored and from which offenders can apply for a loan. That is, the community is the repository of all those things from which social capital is derived such as education, employment, and networks of prosocial individuals in various organizations and clubs (e.g., Alcoholics Anonymous, churches, hobby/interest centers). Time spent involved in steady employment and with prosocial others engaged in prosocial activities is time unavailable to spend in idleness in the company of antisocial others planning antisocial activities. The old saying that "the devil finds work for idle hands" may be trite, but it is also very true.

Thus, good case management in community corrections requires community involvement. No community corrections agency is able to deliver the full range of offender needs (mental health, substance abuse, vocational training, welfare, etc.) by itself, and thus officers consider themselves intermediaries or brokers of community services. Probation and parole officers not only must assess the needs of their charges but also must be able

COMPARATIVE CORRECTIONS

Community Corrections in the United Kingdom

The probation concept is the child of the Christian missionary and temperance movements of the 19th century and grew rapidly during the late 19th and early 20th centuries. Between 1878 and 1920, probation statutes were in place in countries on every continent in the world (Vanstone, 2008). John Augustus can rightfully claim the title of "father of probation" (he coined the term for what he was doing), but in the very same year (1841) a British magistrate in Birmingham, England, named Matthew Davenport-Hill was laying the foundations for probation in Britain. Like Augustus, Davenport-Hill was a deeply religious man and an enemy of alcohol. Unlike Augustus, in addition to helping offenders overcome their problems, Davenport-Hill implemented the supervision of offenders and kept records of their behavior. He used what were known as police court missionaries, who were middle-class volunteers animated by strong Christian and temperance values and augmented by appointed police officers (Gard, 2007). The first full-time professional probation officers in England were appointed in 1907 (Gard, 2007).

As in the United States, probation is the most common disposition of a criminal case in the United Kingdom. The probation service in England and Wales (Scotland and Northern Ireland have separate correctional systems) underwent some broad-reaching changes in response to increasing crime levels during the 1990s. In 2004, the National Probation Service and Her Majesty's Prison Service were placed under a single umbrella in the form of the National Offender Management Service (NOMS). This change was justified in terms of maintaining offender supervision from prison to release in the community and consolidating correctional administration. Prior to consolidation, all probation officers held social work qualifications, but now probation officers are called "offender managers" and the social work aspect of the job is deemphasized. As G. Robinson and McNeill (2010) put it, "Probation officers in England and Wales . . . are no longer trained as social workers, and the context in which they work is no longer that of a social work agency, but rather a 'law enforcement agency'" (p. 744).

The probation service now seeks to hire ex-military personnel, which says a lot about the new emphasis. Probation officers-cum-offender managers still offer the same programs and services, but they deliver them in a more no-nonsense "pull up your socks, man" attitude than was previously the case. Counseling theories employed are now more the directive and confrontational type such as cognitive behavioral therapy. G. Robinson and McNeill (2010) quoted a NOMS official in 1999 regarding its new correctional policy framework: "We have put the focus firmly on outcomes—reducing reoffending and improving public protection. Success will be measured in those terms. The achievement of this common aim . . . must be first consideration for everyone engaged in delivering correctional policy, and not an afterthought" (p. 750).

By 2015, the U.K. government had outsourced probation services to private sector companies (contracted out on a payment-by-result basis) and to voluntary organizations. Public sector probation was scaled back and focused on supervising the most high-risk probationers and parolees and conducting presentence investigations (A. Travis, 2013).

to locate and network with the social service agencies that address those needs as their primary function. In fact, there are those who maintain that probation/parole officers' relationships with community service agencies are more important than their relationships with their probationers/parolees (Walsh & Stohr, 2010).

Figure 7.3 illustrates the central role of the probation (or parole) officer in community efforts to make the community safe. Officers receive all kinds of information (e.g., concerns, complaints) from people in the community that they need to assess and then decide on a method of action. If the officer decides that the concern is beyond his or her expertise, then the officer will refer it to the appropriate agency. Officers must be skilled at networking with the various agencies if they are to help provide offenders with the services they need. This brokerage function can be best achieved with fewer offenders who are intensively supervised on an officer's caseload than with many who are infrequently seen and haphazardly supervised.

FIGURE 7.3   Flow Chart of Referrals In and Out of Community Corrections

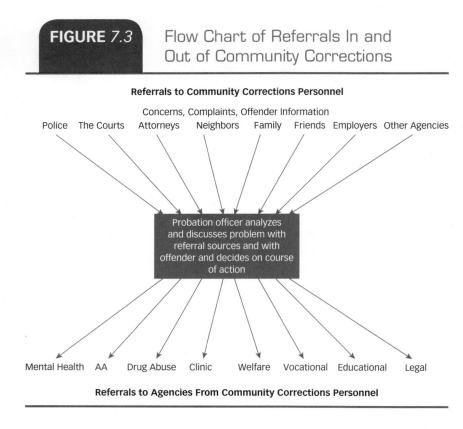

Referrals to Community Corrections Personnel

Concerns, Complaints, Offender Information

Police   The Courts   Attorneys   Neighbors   Family   Friends   Employers   Other Agencies

Probation officer analyzes and discusses problem with referral sources and with offender and decides on course of action

Mental Health   AA   Drug Abuse   Clinic   Welfare   Vocational   Educational   Legal

Referrals to Agencies From Community Corrections Personnel

••• INTERMEDIATE SANCTIONS

As we see in Figure 7.4, there are many sentencing options that are intermediate between prison and simple supervised probation. **Intermediate sanctions** refer to these alternative sentences that may be imposed in place of the traditional prison versus probation dichotomy. Such sanctions are considered intermediate because they are seen as more punitive than straight probation but less punitive than prison. They are a way of easing prison overcrowding and avoiding the financial cost of prison while providing the community with higher levels of safety through higher levels of offender supervision and surveillance than is possible with regular probation. As we will see, however, these supposed benefits are not always realized. We have already seen that many experienced offenders would choose prison over some of the more strict community-based alternatives. Furthermore, because offenders placed in some sort of alternative sanction program have recidivism rates not much different from those of offenders released from prison within the first year or subsequent years, the costs of state incarceration are deferred rather than avoided (Klingele, 2013; Marion, 2002).

The first alternative in Figure 7.4 is community detention (jail) and is addressed elsewhere in this book. Split sentencing is simply a period of probation preceded by a jail sentence of up to 1 year. The work release option is the first intermediate sanction we examine. Halfway houses and electric monitoring are examined in the next chapter.

WORK RELEASE

Work release programs are designed to control offenders in a secure environment while at the same time allowing them to maintain employment. Work release centers are usually situated in or adjacent to county jails, but they can also be part of the state prison system. Residents of work release centers have typically been given a suspended sentence and placed on probation with a specified time to be served in work release. Work release residents may also be parolees under certain circumstances such as the need to closely supervise a new parolee or a parole violator given another opportunity to remain in the community rather than being sent back to prison. Surveillance of work release residents is strict; they are allowed out only for the purpose of attending their employment and are locked in the facility when not working. The advantage of such programs is that they allow offenders to maintain ties with their families and with employers. Such programs also save the taxpayer money because offenders pay the cost of their accommodations with their earnings.

Although offenders given a work release order are generally the least likely of all community-based corrections offenders to be rearrested and imprisoned within 5 years

Intermediate sanctions: A number of innovative alternative sentences that may be imposed in place of the traditional prison/probation dichotomy.

Work release programs: Programs designed to control offenders in a secure environment while at the same time allowing them to maintain employment.

of successful completion, one study of a number of such programs found that 64% of offenders successfully released and 71% unsuccessfully released had further arrests within 5 years (Marion, 2002). Offenders chosen to partake in work release are typically chosen because, although they have committed crimes deemed too serious for regular probation, they are usually employed, although unemployed probationers can be placed in work release contingent on their finding employment within a specified time (Abadinsky, 2009). Being employed is incompatible with a criminal lifestyle (but, obviously from the above statistics, not completely), especially if the offender is a probationer rather than a parolee.

INTENSIVE SUPERVISION PROBATION

Intensive supervision probation (ISP) is typically limited to offenders who probably should not be in the community but have been allowed to remain either in the belief that there is a fighting chance they may be rehabilitated or in an effort to save the costs of incarceration. ISP officers' caseloads are drastically reduced (typically a caseload of 25) to allow officers to more closely supervise, often on a daily basis with frequent drug testing and surveillance. Burrell (2006) described ISP officers as "aggressive in their surveillance and punitive in their sanctions" (p. 4). Liberal critics of the tactics of ISP officers describe their model of supervision colorfully as one of "pee 'em and see 'em" or "tail 'em, nail 'em, and jail 'em" (Skeem & Manchak, 2008). This type of law enforcement surveillance is the kind of supervision required with high-risk offenders (Walsh & Stohr, 2010).

A study conducted by MacKenzie and Brame (2001) hypothesized that ISP coerces offenders into prosocial activities that in turn lead to a lower probability of their reoffending. Intensive supervision means that probation officers maintain more frequent contact with probationers and intrude into their lives more than is the norm with other probationers. Offenders on ISP are supervised at that level because they have the greatest probability of reoffending (they are high risk) and are the most deficient in social capital (they have high needs). Higher levels of supervision allow officers to coerce offenders into a wide variety of educational and treatment programs and other prosocial activities designed to provide offenders with social capital. MacKenzie and Brame found that ISP does result in offenders being coerced into more prosocial activities and that there was a slight reduction in recidivism. The issue the study left unresolved is whether participating in prosocial activities enabled offenders to acquire skills that provided them with social capital they could put to good use or whether intensive supervision per se accounted for their findings.

The term *coercion* has negative connotations for the more libertarian types among us ("You can lead a horse to water . . ." and all that), but the great majority of people being treated for problems such as substance abuse have very large bootprints impressed on their backsides. Probationers and parolees, almost by definition, will not voluntarily place themselves in the kinds of programs and activities we would like them to be in—they are simply not motivated in that direction. The criminal justice system must provide that motivation via the judicious use of carrots and sticks. Reviews of the U.S. literature (Farabee, Prendergast, & Anglin, 1998) and U.K. literature (Barton, 1999) on coerced substance abuse treatment concluded that coerced treatment often has more positive outcomes than voluntary treatment, probably because of the threat of criminal justice sanctions.

SHOCK PROBATION/PAROLE AND BOOT CAMPS

Shock probation was initiated in Ohio during the 1970s and was designed to literally shock offenders into desisting from crime by briefly exposing them to the horrors of prison. It was limited to first offenders who had perhaps been unimpressed with the realities of prison life until given a taste. Under this program, offenders were sentenced to prison and released after (typically) 30 days and placed on probation. In some states, a person may receive shock parole, which typically means that he or she has remained in prison longer than the shock probationer and is released under the authority of the parole commission rather than to the courts. Most of the research on this kind of shock

Intensive supervision probation (ISP): Probation that involves more frequent surveillance of probationers and that is typically limited to more serious offenders in the belief that there is a fighting chance that they may be rehabilitated (or to save the costs of incarceration).

FIGURE 7.4   The Continuum of Correctional Sanctions by Restrictiveness

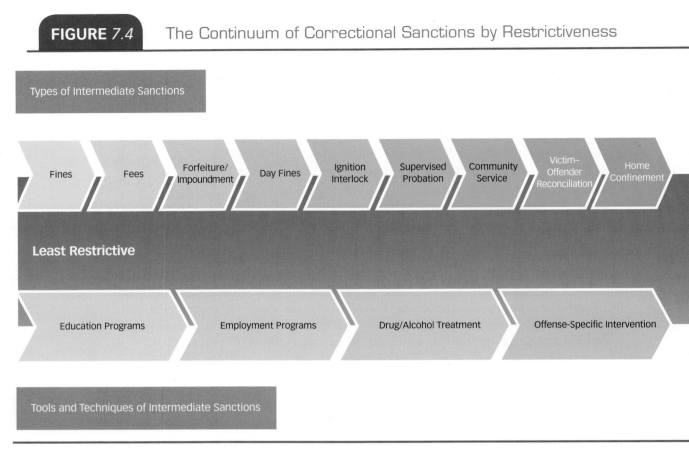

Source: Center for Community Corrections (1997). U.S. Department of Justice.

treatment was conducted during the 1970s and 1980s and concluded that shock probationers/parolees had lower recidivism rates than incarcerated offenders not released under shock conditions (Vito, Allen, & Farmer, 1981). This should not be surprising, however, given the fact that those selected for shock probation/parole were either first offenders or repeaters who had not committed very serious crimes.

When we hear of shock incarceration today, it is typically incarceration in a so-called boot camp. **Correctional boot camps** are facilities modeled after military boot camps. Normally only relatively young and nonviolent offenders are sent to correctional boot camps. They are usually there for short periods (90–180 days) and are subjected to military-style discipline and physical and educational programs. Boot camps are the most unpopular sentencing alternative with offenders. In May et al.'s (2005) analysis of "exchange rates," discussed earlier, offenders who had served time in prison would be willing to spend an average of only 4.65 months in boot camp to avoid 12 months in prison. Interestingly, judges and probation/parole officers also agree that boot camp is more punitive than prison, estimating that their charges would be willing to serve only 6.19 and 6.05 months, respectively, to avoid 12 months in prison (Moore, May, & Wood, 2008).

The idea of boot camps for young adult offenders was once a popular idea among the general public as well as among a considerable number of correctional personnel and criminal justice academics. Boot camps conjured up the movie image of a surly, slouching, and scruffy youth forced into the army who 2 years later proudly marched back into the old neighborhood with a crew cut, sparklingly clean, and properly motivated and disciplined. Yes, the drill sergeant with righteous fire and brimstone would do what the family and social work–tainted juvenile probation officers could never do.

Such magical transformations rarely happen in real life. The army merely provided many such youths with new opportunities to offend, and they spent much of their time either

Correctional boot camps: Facilities modeled after military boot camps where young and nonviolent offenders are subjected to military-style discipline and physical and educational programs.

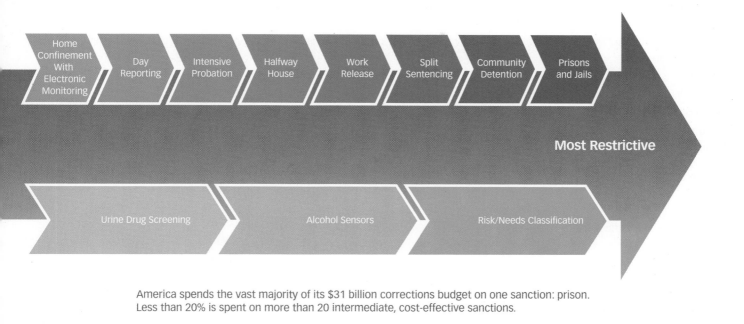

America spends the vast majority of its $31 billion corrections budget on one sanction: prison. Less than 20% is spent on more than 20 intermediate, cost-effective sanctions.

avoiding the MPs (military police) or lodged in the brig while awaiting their dishonorable discharges. Bottcher and Ezell's (2005) evaluation of offenders sent to correctional boot camp in California revealed the same sorry outcome. Specifically, they found no significant differences between their experimental group (boot campers) and a control group of similar offenders not sent to boot camp in terms of either property or violent crime reoffending. In other words, boot camps have joined the woeful list of correctional programs that have proven to be ineffective.

VICTIM–OFFENDER RECONCILIATION PROGRAMS

Victim–offender reconciliation programs (VORPs) are programs designed to bring offenders and their victims together in an attempt to reconcile ("make right") the wrongs offenders have caused and are an integral component of the **restorative justice** philosophy. This philosophy differs from models (retributive, rehabilitative, etc.) that are offender driven (what do we do with the offender?) in that it considers the offender, the victim, and the community as partners in restoring the situation to its pre-victimization status. Restorative justice has been defined as "every action that is primarily oriented toward justice by repairing the harm that has been caused by the crime . . . [and] usually means a face-to-face confrontation between victim and perpetrator, where a mutually agreeable restorative solution is proposed and agreed upon" (Champion, 2005, p. 154). Restorative justice is often referred to as a **balanced approach** in that it gives approximately equal weight to community protection, offender accountability, and offender competency.

Many crime victims are seeking fairness, justice, and restitution *as defined by them* as opposed to revenge and punishment. Central to the VORP process is the bringing together of victim and offender in face-to-face meetings mediated by a person trained in

Victim–offender reconciliation programs (VORPs): Programs designed to bring offenders and their victims together in an attempt to reconcile the wrongs offenders have caused.

Restorative justice: A system of justice that gives approximately equal weight to community protection, offender accountability, and the offender.

Balanced approach: A three-pronged goal of the juvenile justice system: (1) to protect the community, (2) to hold delinquent youths accountable, and (3) to provide treatment and positive role models.

IN FOCUS 7.1

Community Supervision and Recidivism

It is an article of faith among police officers that it is only a matter of time before a probationer or parolee commits another crime, but little is known about the probability of a person under community supervision being arrested versus someone not under supervision being arrested. An ambitious effort to find out was conducted by the Council of State Governments Justice Center (CSGJC, 2013) based on adult arrests occurring in four California jurisdictions (Los Angeles County, San Bernardino County, Sacramento County, and San Francisco County) from 2008 to 2011. The accompanying figure shows that probationers and

parolees combined accounted for just over 22% of the total arrests. However, 40% of arrestees not under supervision at the time had histories of prior criminal justice supervision. The 147,700 people under supervision were about 1% of the combined population of more than 14 million people residing in those counties. Thus, factoring out characteristics of individuals not likely to be arrested—such as the very young and the very old—probationers and parolees are at the very least 10 times more likely to be arrested than individuals in general. The crimes for which probationers and parolees were most likely to be arrested were drug related.

Comparing Probationer and Parolee Arrests With Arrests of People Not Under Supervision in Four California Counties, January 2008 to June 2011

Total Adult Arrests

Designation	Adult Arrests	% of Total
Total	476,054	100%
Parolees	40,476	8.5%
Probationers	66,251	13.9%
Not Supervised	369,327	77.6%

= Probationers

= Parolees

= Not on Supervision

Source: Council of State Governments Justice Center (2013). *The impact of probation and parole populations on arrest in four California cities*. http://www.cdcr.ca.gov/Reports/docs/External-Reports/CAL-CHIEFS-REPORT.pdf.

mediation theory and practice (Walsh & Stohr, 2010). Meetings are voluntary for both offender and victim and are designed to iron out ways the offender can make amends for the hurt and damage caused to the victim.

Victims participating in VORPs gain the opportunity to make offenders aware of their feelings of personal violation and loss and to lay out their proposals for how offenders can restore the situation. Offenders are afforded the opportunity to see firsthand the pain they have caused their victims and perhaps even to express remorse. The mediator assists the parties in developing a contract agreeable to both. The mediator monitors the terms of the contract and may schedule further face-to-face meetings.

VORPs are used most often in the juvenile system but are rarely used for violent crimes in either juvenile or adult systems. Where they are used, about 60% of victims invited to participate actually become involved, and a high percentage (mid to high 90s) of VORPs result in signed contracts (Coates, 1990). Umbreit (1994) summed up the various satisfactions reported by victims who participated in VORPs:

1. Meeting offenders helped to reduce their fear of being revictimized.

2. They appreciated the opportunity to tell offenders how they felt.

3. Being personally involved in the justice process was satisfying to them.

4. They gained insight into the crime and into the offender's situation.

5. They received restitution.

VORPs do not suit all victims, especially those who feel that the wrong done to them cannot so easily be "put right" and who want the offender punished (Olson & Dzur, 2004). In addition, the value of VORPs for the prevention of further offending has yet to be properly assessed.

PHOTO 7.3: Boot camps feature no-nonsense discipline and hard work modeled on military boot camps.

ZUMA Press, Inc./Alamy Stock Photo

SUMMARY

- Community-based corrections is a way of attempting to control the behavior of criminal offenders while keeping them in the community. Although conditional release (judicial reprieve) was practiced in ancient times in common law, probation wasn't really established until the 20th century. Although often considered too lenient, community corrections benefits the public in many ways. Probation helps the offender in many ways, and what helps offenders automatically helps the communities in which they live.

- There are many reasons to recommend probation over prison for many offenders, including saving the high cost of incarceration, allowing offenders to maintain family contacts and employment, and preventing them from becoming more embedded in a criminal lifestyle. However, there are many offenders who must be incarcerated for the safety of the community.

- Probation officers are both law enforcement officers and social workers. They follow a supervision style

consistent with their department's philosophy and their own personality. Some emphasize the law enforcement role, some emphasize the social worker role, and others emphasize one or the other when the occasion arises. The latter supervision style, dubbed the hybrid style, consistently gets the best results.

- For both cost-cutting and consistency concerns, many probation departments have initiated guidelines to determine officers' responses to technical violations. These guidelines graduate the severity of the sanctions imposed against offenders in accordance with the severity of their violations.

- Because of the dangers inherent in the job and officer perceptions of poor salaries, excessive paperwork, and large caseloads, among other things, probation officer stress is a major concern. However, the job can be interesting and exciting, and the median salary is about $10,000 more than the median salary of all occupations requiring a B.A./B.S. in a social science.

- Engaging the community in the task of rehabilitating criminals should be a major concern of community supervision agencies. Engaging the community involves officers paying close attention to concerns and complaints about offenders on their caseloads flowing in to them and being aware of the agencies outside their departments that offer services that may help offenders. It also means adopting effective volunteer probation officers' programs within their departments.

- Intermediate sanctions are considered to be more punitive than regular probation but less punitive than prison, although experienced criminals do not necessarily share that view. Some of these programs, particularly work release, show positive results,

although this may be more a function of the kinds of offenders placed in them rather than the programs themselves. Most participants in these programs, however, tend to recidivate at rates not significantly different from those of parolees.

- Victim–offender reconciliation programs are a fairly recent addition to community corrections. They consider the victim, the offender, and the community as equal partners in returning the situation to its pre-victimization status. This idea of restorative justice is mostly used with juvenile offenders and minor adult offenders.

KEY TERMS

Balanced approach, 151

Community corrections, 138

Correctional boot camps, 150

Intensive supervision probation (ISP), 149

Intermediate sanctions, 148

Judicial reprieve, 136

National Probation Act of 1925, 137

Probation, 136

Restorative justice, 151

Victim–offender reconciliation programs (VORPs), 151

Work release programs, 148

DISCUSSION QUESTIONS

1. Looking at all the pros and cons of community-based corrections, do you think probation is too lenient for felony offenders? If so, what should we do with them?

2. In your opinion, what is the single biggest benefit of probation for the community and its single greatest cost?

3. Studies show that about 95% of probation officers' sentencing recommendations to the courts are followed. Why do you think this is so, and is it a good

or bad thing that probation officers control the flow of information to judges?

4. Should probation/parole officers carry guns if they are supposed to be social workers as well as cops?

5. Boot camps have full and total control of offenders for up to 6 months, so why are they not able to change offenders' attitudes and behaviors?

6. Do you think police officers should be given the same powers of search and seizure as probation and parole officers for the purposes of controlling the activities of probationers and parolees?

ⓈSAGE edge™

Review → Practice → Improve

Sharpen your skills with SAGE edge at **edge.sagepub.com/stohressentials3e**.

SAGE edge offers a robust online environment featuring an impressive array of free tools and resources for review, study, and further exploration, keeping both instructors and students on the cutting edge of teaching and learning.

FOR FURTHER EXPLORATION AND APPLICATION, TAKE A LOOK AT THE INTERACTIVE EBOOK FOR THESE PREMIUM RESOURCES:

- ▶ **Career Video 7.1** Probation Officer

- ▶ **Feature Video 7.1** Experiences With Probation

- ▶ **SAGE News Clip 7.1** Prison Horticulture

- ▶ **SAGE News Clip 7.2** Prison Tech

- 📄 **Journal Article 7.1** Intermediate Sanctions in Probation Officers' Sentencing Recommendations: Consistency, Net Widening, and Net Repairing

- 📄 **Journal Article 7.2** The Effectiveness of Various Restorative Justice Interventions on Recidivism Outcomes Among Juvenile Offenders

Prisons and the Correctional Client

TEST YOUR KNOWLEDGE

Test your present knowledge of prisons by answering the following questions. Check your answers on page 391 after reading the chapter.

1. The incarceration rate in the United States remains the highest in the world. (True or false?)

2. Most inmates serve out their sentence in maximum-security prisons. (True or false?)

3. What factors describe a medium-security prison? How is it similar to and different from maximum- and minimum-security prisons?

4. What are *prisonization* and *importation* in the prison context?

5. What are gangs, and what role do they play in the prison subculture?

6. Why does violence exist in prisons?

7. Transgender inmates, particularly in men's prisons, are more likely to be sexually assaulted than any other group of inmates. (True or false?)

LEARNING OBJECTIVES

- Describe the differences between types of prisons

- Describe what factors affect the operation of prisons

- Explain what prisonization, mortification, importation, pains of imprisonment, and mature coping are and how they influence inmate behavior

- Evaluate the roles of inmates, staff, and prison gangs and why they exist in prisons

- Identify the reasons why violence, riots, and sexual assaults occur in prisons and some strategies for their reduction

- Describe the challenges of meeting the needs of aging, physically and mentally ill, and LGBTI (lesbian, gay, bisexual, transgender, and intersex) inmates in prisons

KITCHEN SUPERVISOR SEXUALLY ABUSES TWO MALE INMATES

The kitchen supervisor in a federal prison in Phoenix, Arizona, Carl David Evans, sexually abused two male inmates whom he supervised ("Kitchen Supervisor Gets Prison Time," 2014). He would separately take the two inmates into a food storage area of the kitchen and give one of them a package of cigarettes (which, in turn, the two could then sell for as much as $150 to other inmates) in exchange for sex. After the Federal Bureau of Investigation (FBI) learned of the abuse of one of these inmates, agents placed a video camera in the storage area and caught Evans and the inmates having sex.

Evans pleaded guilty to five of the federal charges against him in February 2013. He was sentenced to 36 months in prison, 3 years of supervised release, and a $5,000 fine ("Kitchen Supervisor Gets Prison Time," 2014, p. 20).

••• INTRODUCTION: THE STATE OF PRISONS

It has become axiomatic to say that correctional programs and institutions are over-crowded, underfunded, and unfocused these days. For the better part of 50 years, the drug war has raged on, mandatory sentencing has had its effect, and probation and parole caseloads and incarceration rates have spiraled out of control. As a consequence, although spending on corrections had, until recently, steadily and steeply climbed, it was and largely still is nearly impossible for most states and localities to meet the needs for programs, staff, and institutions. So they do not. As a consequence, the corrections experience for staff and offenders continues to be shaped by shortages.

However, during the last several years, there has been a reconsideration of the drug war: At the time of this writing (spring of 2017), recreational marijuana has been legalized in eight states (Alaska, California, Colorado, Maine, Massachusetts, Nevada, Oregon, and Washington) and Washington, D.C., and medical marijuana has been legalized in several others. It is likely that many more states will move to legalize marijuana in the near future. As was discussed in Chapter 5, a few years ago, Congress reduced the sentencing disparity between crack and powder cocaine. The effect of these two changes—marijuana legalization/medicalization and reduced sentences for crack cocaine—has been to reduce correctional populations. In addition, several states have rescinded their mandatory sentences for drugs and other crimes (e.g., three-strikes laws), which is also limiting time spent in prisons (Garland et al., 2014). The shift in correctional treatment away from retribution and deterrence as the sole justifications for prisons and other forms of corrections has also reduced populations. (Some things do work for some people, and often treatment works best in the community.) Finally, the cost of corrections for states and localities, particularly after the Great Recession of 2007 to 2010 hit, has caused those governmental units to shutter prisons and jails and to rethink the use of prisons, the most expensive correctional option (Cullen, Jonson, & Stohr, 2014). The collective effect of these changes in law and policy has been decarceration in several states and localities.

During the first months of 2017, Attorney General Jeff Sessions signaled that the federal government may move in the other direction from many of the states on harsher sentences. In May 2017, he issued a memorandum directing federal prosecutors to seek the longest sentences possible (mandatory minimums) even for low-level drug offenders (Ford, 2017). This memorandum marks a shift in policy under the Trump administration from the direction charted by the Obama administration and former Attorney General Eric Holder. The effect of the Sessions memo is likely to result in longer sentences for drug offenders in federal prisons but will have no effect on the more numerous state-level prisons.

Having written this about state-level corrections, and as has been discussed already in this text, it has always been somewhat true that the corrections experience has tended to be shaped by shortages. With the exception of the recent past, if it has been built or, in the case of probation and parole, it has been offered, they will come—because, as with all corrections sentences, they are forced to do so. Cases in point—almost immediately after the first American prisons were built, Walnut Street Jail (1790), Auburn Prison (1819), Western Pennsylvania Prison (1826), and Eastern Pennsylvania Prison (1829) were full, and within a few years they were expanded or new prisons were under construction.

PHOTO 8.1: A crowded dormitory at the Elmore Correctional Facility in Elmore, Alabama. Crowding makes the lives of inmates much harder, while it makes their supervision by staff more complicated and results in prisons that are much more dangerous.

AP Photo/Brynn Anderson

To say that crowding and corrections have always been linked, of course, is not to dismiss the negative effects of overfilling institutions. Certainly, despite some of the decarceration we are seeing across the United States, the combined incarceration rate for jails and prisons remains the highest in the Westernized world, at 670 per 100,000 U.S. residents, as of 2015 (Kaeble & Glaze, 2016, p. 4; Kaeble, Glaze, Tsoutis, & Minton, 2016; see also Figure 8.1). By way of comparison, this rate was 760 in 2007 and 2008 but has decreased since then (West, 2010, p. 4). Since 2007 (or the peak of the incarceration rate in this country so far), the raw number of inmates in prisons and jails has decreased by roughly 121,900 (Kaeble & Glaze, 2016, p. 3). All of this means that we are seeing some decreases in the use of incarceration, although from state to state or in the federal system the crowding of prisons is not necessarily a thing of the past.

In this chapter, we discuss the structure and operation of prisons. The inmate subculture that flourishes in prisons and the violence and gangs that bedevil them also are reviewed. The nature of the correctional experience for individuals incarcerated in prisons is somewhat different from what those in jails or community corrections encounter, and those differences are explored here.

••• PRISON ORGANIZATIONS

CLASSIFICATION

As inmates enter the prison system from the courts, they are usually assessed at a classification or reception facility based on their crime, criminal history, escape risk, behavioral issues (if any), and health and programming needs. Women and children are classified in separate facilities from adult males. This assessment includes the review of materials related to inmates by reception center personnel and tests and observation of inmates regarding their dangerousness and amenability to treatment. After being assessed by prison personnel for a period of weeks or months, inmates are sent to the prison that the personnel believe is the best fit based first on security needs, followed by space available, and finally inmates' needs. Inmates generally have no control over which prison they are sent to. Once they have done some time, inmates may request that they be moved to a facility that is closer to their family and friends, but such considerations are not a priority for classification and are more an option for adult males because the facilities available for transfer for adult females and juveniles are much more limited because there are fewer of them.

Prisons: Correctional facilities used for long-term and convicted offenders.

PRISON TYPES AND LEVELS

Prisons were and are used for long-term and convicted offenders who are to be simultaneously punished (experience retribution), deterred, and reformed (rehabilitated) while being isolated (incapacitated) from the community and, for most, reintegrated back into

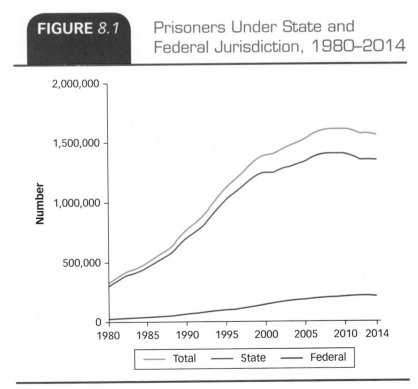

FIGURE 8.1 Prisoners Under State and Federal Jurisdiction, 1980–2014

Source: Bureau of Justice Statistics.

that community. As the number of prisons has expanded across the United States, their diversity has increased. Rather than just an all-purpose maximum- or medium-security prison, as was the norm when prisons were first built, there are state and federal prisons with myriad security levels, including super-maximum, maximum, medium, and minimum. There are prisons for men, women, men and women, children, and military personnel. Prisons come in the form of regular confinement facilities but also prison farms, prison hospitals, boot camps, reception centers, community corrections facilities (sometimes known as work release or day-reporting facilities), and others (Stephan, 2008).

By 2015, the number of inmates in federal prisons stood at 195,800, and those in state prisons totaled 1,244,400 (Kaeble & Glaze, 2016, p. 19; see also Figure 8.1). Of these federal prisoners, 26,000 were in private facilities, as were 91,300 state inmates (Kaeble & Glaze, 2016, p. 19). Private prisons held about 20% of inmates in six states as of 2015, but overall only 7% of state inmates are in private prisons, while 18% of federal inmates are (Bureau of Justice Statistics, 2016). Only 1,400 inmates were held in military prisons in 2015—the same number since 2010 and about 1,000 less than in 2000 (Kaeble & Glaze, 2016, p. 18).

As indicated in Figure 8.2, as of 2005 (the latest Census of State and Federal Correctional Facilities data available at the time of writing), there were 1,821 state and federal prisons in the United States, 1,406 of which were public and 415 of which were under private contract with either a state government or the federal government (Stephan, 2008, p. 2). Most prisons were operated by or under contract with the states (1,719) rather than the federal government (102). Although only about one-fifth of the prisons in the United States are designated as maximum security, because of their size, they hold about a third of the inmates incarcerated in this country (Stephan, 2008, pp. 2, 4). In contrast, medium-security prisons constitute about one-fourth of prisons but hold two-fifths of inmates—again, perhaps because of their relatively large size compared with minimum-security prisons, which are about one-half of all prisons but hold only about one-fifth of inmates (Stephan, 2008, p. 4). These data do indicate that the popular and academic depictions of maximum-security prisons as the norm in America are incorrect.

Supermax prisons:
High-security prisons that hold those who are violent or disruptive in other prisons in the state or federal system.

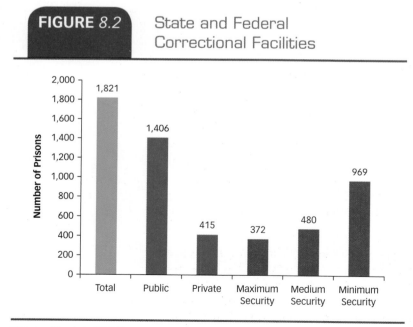

FIGURE 8.2 State and Federal Correctional Facilities

Source: Stephan (2008).

Supermax Prisons

When states were first building prisons, they tended to be a combination of a maximum- and medium-security type (think industrial and big house prisons). The exterior of these prisons was very secure, but internally inmates were given some freedom, although restricted, to move about and were often expected to do so for work, dining, and related purposes. **Supermax prisons** (the slang term for super-maximum-security prisons) developed later, and arguably the first of these was at the federal level, with Alcatraz Prison, which was built in 1934 to hold the most notorious gangsters of the era. Others argue that the first full-fledged supermaxes did not develop until the 1980s and were part of the "get tough on crime" movement

IN FOCUS 8.1

False Imprisonment as a Result of Wage Slavery

Sexual slavery and wage slavery are much in the news these days as organized crime and criminal entrepreneurs take advantage of desperate and vulnerable people who want to enter the United States and other relatively prosperous nations where demand for low-cost goods, even if that means poverty wages for some, is high. Unfortunately, the United States has allowed such wage slavery and sexual slavery entities a foothold on our shores, and local, state, and federal law enforcement are engaged in fighting another war on slavery during the 2010s. A key element of both types of slavery is *false imprisonment,* or illegally holding a person against his or her will.

In 2015, the Southern Poverty Law Center (SPLC), along with several firms donating their labor pro bono, won a coordinated lawsuit against a company that engaged in wage slavery. In this case, 500 Indian guest workers were lured to Mississippi in 2006 and 2008 with the promise of a well-paying job and a green card. One prospective worker paid a labor recruiter in India $12,000 for a chance at this opportunity. But when he arrived in the States, he instead discovered the horrific truth:

> There would be no green card, but rather a 10-month worker visa. He was packed into a guarded, isolated labor camp and forced to pay $1,050 a month to bunk with 23 other men in a space the size of a double-wide trailer. Their bags were regularly searched. No visitors were allowed. ("Jury Awards $14 Million," 2015, p. 1)

Because these guest workers were paid slave-like wages, housed in slave-like conditions, and prevented from quitting (one man tried to leave and was physically detained), a federal district jury awarded the five men who brought the case $14 million and found that Signal International, its lawyer, and the Indian recruiter had engaged in labor trafficking, forced labor, fraud, racketeering, and discrimination. In one case, they were also found guilty of false imprisonment. The company had reportedly made $8 million by treating the workers this way.

Discussion Questions

1. What do you think the appropriate sentence should be for people and companies who engage in forced labor and sex trafficking?

2. Why are such offenses increasing even in Westernized countries, and what can be done to stop their spread?

that promoted more severe punishment (e.g., see Mears, 2013). Today, supermax prisons at the federal and state levels are not all operated in exactly the same way, although certain characteristics do appear to be common (at least in theory). Inmates are confined to their windowless cells for 23 hours a day except for showers three times a week (where they are restrained) and solo exercise time a couple of times a week. They eat in their cells, and often the food is some form of "nutraloaf" (a bland but nutritious food that requires no utensils). If any limited rehabilitation is provided, the treatment personnel stand outside the cell and talk to the inmate within; physical contact is prohibited unless inmates are in restraints (Pizarro & Narag, 2008). Moreover, their confinement is usually lengthy, not for a day, a week, or even a month but rather for a year or longer (Mears, 2013).

Alcatraz closed in 1963, and other federal supermaxes in Marion, Illinois (opened in 1963 to take some of the Alcatraz inmates), and later Florence, Colorado (opened in 1994), took its place. States began building supermaxes in earnest during the 1980s and 1990s in reaction to the felt need to control more dangerous and disruptive inmates and to "get tough" with them (Mears, 2008, 2013; Olivero & Roberts, 1987; Richards, 2008). It is estimated that a total of 44 states, holding some 25,000 inmates, had some form of a supermax

AP Photo/Brennan Linsley

PHOTO 8.2: The supermax prison in Florence, Colorado, is considered a possible site for housing Guantanamo Bay detainees in the future.

(Mears, 2013, p. 684), although definitions of what a supermax is do vary across the states (Naday, Freilich, & Mellow, 2008). As with Alcatraz, these supermax prisons at the federal and state levels are supposed to hold the most dangerous offenders, violent gang members, those who cannot behave well in lower-security prisons, and those who pose an escape risk.

Because of the heightened security requirements, incarceration in a supermax is expensive, at about $50,000 per year, as compared with $20,000 to $30,000 to incarcerate an adult male in a lower-security prison (Richards, 2008, p. 18), and because of the materials used in their construction, supermaxes are at least two to three times more expensive to build than a "regular" prison (Mears, 2008). The research indicates that wardens believe that the presence of a supermax in a prison system deters violent offenders, increases order and control, and reduces assaults on staff in the other prisons in that system, not just in the supermax itself (Pizarro & Narag, 2008). Several states (e.g., Texas, Colorado, California) have claimed that violence decreased in their systems once they opened supermax prisons. Sundt, Castellano, and Briggs (2008) reported that inmate assaults on staff decreased in Illinois once the supermax was opened in that state, although there was no effect of inmate assaults on inmates. Clearly, there is room for more systematic examination of the data, as in this study, for these and other issues as they relate to supermaxes.

For instance, critics and some researchers claim that inmates' mental health is impaired after a stay in a supermax because of the sensory deprivation, and there is some evidence to support this assertion (Mears, 2013). There is also evidence that supermaxes are sometimes used to incarcerate those who are merely mentally ill or who have committed more minor infractions (Mears, 2008; O'Keefe, 2008). In addition, the effect of incarcerating less serious or mentally impaired offenders in a supermax, as King, Steiner, and Breach (2008) noted, can be a self-fulfilling prophecy, exacerbating inmate mental and behavioral problems through such secure and severe confinement. (Recall the story of the mentally ill inmate held in the Dona Ana County Jail, New Mexico, that appeared at the beginning of Chapter 6.) On the other hand, there are researchers who have found evidence that such a stay had a calming effect on inmates, allowing them to reflect on their wrongs and how they might change their behavior (e.g., see Ward & Kassebaum, 2009). Pizarro and Narag (2008) noted, however, that the evidence is weak on both sides of this argument and that more—and more rigorous—research is merited before we know the true effect of supermaxes on inmates or on prison systems.

Maximum Security

Maximum-security prisons: Prisons where both external and internal security are high and programs and contact with other prisoners and visitors are very limited.

State, federal, and military laws, traditions, and practices differ on how each type of prison operates, but some generalizations about how prisons with different security levels operate are usually accurate. Those prisons with the greatest internal and external security controls are the supermaxes, and next in security level are the **maximum-security prisons**. Inmates in supermaxes and, to a lesser extent, maximum-security prisons are often locked up all day, save for time for a shower or recreation outside of their cells, and they are ideally in single cells deprived of other sensory stimulation. Visits and contact with the outside are very restricted. The maximum and supermax exterior security consists of some combination of layers of razor wire, walls, lights, cameras, armed guards, and attack dogs on patrol.

Because the states that have a supermax usually only have one, maximum-security prisons are responsible for holding most of the serious offenders and those who could not handle themselves in the relatively freer environment of the medium- and minimum-security prisons. The latter type of inmate might be able to qualify for a medium- or minimum-security-level classification but instead is in maximum security because the inmate is unable to control his or her behavior.

In many states where the death penalty is legal, their death row is located at a maximum-security prison. Death rows are usually wholly separate areas of the prisons, sometimes in different buildings, and often have their own separate designated staff and procedures. (For a more involved discussion of the death penalty, see Chapter 16.)

Maximum-security prisons may have the same exterior security controls as supermaxes, but inside inmates are not locked down as much, although the treatment and work programming is much more constricted than in medium-security prisons. Maximum-security inmates may or may not be double-bunked, depending on the crowding in the institution, and unless they are under some special classification, they have some access to the yard (a large gathering area for inmates), the cafeteria, and the chapel. Visiting and contact with the outside world are less restricted than in supermaxes, and inmates are usually not in some kind of restraint when it occurs.

Medium Security

In **medium-security prisons**, the exterior security can be as tight as it is for supermax and maximum-security prisons, but internally inmates have many more opportunities to attend school, treatment, and church programming and to work in any number of capacities. There is also greater diversity in rooming options, from dormitories to single cells, with the preferred single and double cells used as a carrot to entice better behavior. Visiting and contact with the outside world are less restricted. Some medium-security inmates may even be allowed to leave the institution for work-related deliveries or on furloughs, although this is much more common in minimum-security prisons.

Medium-security prisons will hold a mix of people in terms of crime categories, all the way from the convicted murderer doing life but who programs well down to the lowly burglar or drug user who is awaiting transfer to a lower-security prison or who is engaged in the substance abuse programming that the prison affords. Medium-security prisons are more likely to have a college campus–type interior, with several buildings devoted to distinct purposes. There might be a separate cafeteria building, a separate programming and treatment building, a separate gym and recreation building, and separate work and housing buildings. Medium-security prisons are heavily engaged in industrial work such as building furniture, making clothing, and printing license plates for the state. In some cases and states, the goods produced in the prison are sold on the open market.

Minimum Security

Minimum-security prisons have a much more relaxed exterior security; some do not even have a wall or a fence. Inmates are provided with far more programming, either inside the

---

? ETHICAL ISSUE

What Would You Do?

You are a correctional officer in a supermax prison in a typical state. You understand the stated reasoning for such prisons in your state is "to house the worst of the worst"— inmates with behavioral problems—and to separate gang members. You have been on the job for a few years, and you generally like your colleagues and workplace. However, you have noticed that the mental stability of some of the inmates you supervise has deteriorated the longer they stay in this prison. You have reported these problems to the medical officer in charge of the medical unit for the prison, and she and your supervisor have discouraged you from making further reports because the medical unit is already full and understaffed, making the transfer of inmates out of supermax cells difficult. Is there anything else you can do? What do you think would be the best response to this problem and why?

Medium-security prisons: Prisons that have high external security but less restrictive internal security and more opportunities for programs and work.

Minimum-security prisons: Prisons with relaxed external and internal security created for lower-level felony offenders who are not expected to be an escape or behavioral problem.

IN FOCUS 8.2

Alcatraz: The United States' First Supermax

As Ward and Kassebaum (2009) noted in their book, *Alcatraz: The Gangster Years,* when Alcatraz was first opened as a federal prison in 1934, it was created in response to a perceived national crisis. This crisis involved gangsters and outlaws who were terrorizing communities with kidnappings, bank and train robberies, and organized crime. Moreover, there were a number of scandals where these gangsters and outlaws were effectively corrupting state and federal prison officials and staff through intimidation and with their money, contacts, and infamy.

Corrupt and poorly managed, state and federal prisons of the time were widely perceived as coddling influential felons by permitting special privileges and allowing them to continue involvement in criminal enterprises from behind bars while flaws in their security systems offered inmates opportunities for escape (Ward & Kassebaum, 2009, p. 2).

When Al Capone, one of the most notorious gangsters of this era, was incarcerated at Eastern State Penitentiary in Pennsylvania, he was provided by the warden with a single cell furnished like a home, a cushy library clerk job, unlimited visits by family and friends, and use of the telephone to contact his lawyer, crime partners, and politicians. Although he and his gang were implicated in a number of murders and graft of all sorts, he was able to evade prosecution for most of those crimes, and it was a tax evasion conviction that finally landed him in federal prison.

Alcatraz, on an island in the San Francisco Bay, was created to end the undue influence on incarceration that the "Capones" of the world exerted. "Surrounded by cold ocean currents, it was intended to hold the nation's 'public enemies' to an iron regimen, reduce them to mere numbers, cut them off from the outside world, and keep them locked up securely for decades" (Ward & Kassebaum, 2009, p. 2). News reporters were prohibited from interviewing Alcatraz staff or inmates, and staff were told that they would be fired if they talked to reporters. Visits were limited to a few blood relatives and then only once a month and through a guard-monitored telephone. Inmates were not allowed to talk about their life on the inside during those visits. That life was very controlled and monotonous and consisted of strict adherence to silence at night, work (when earned as a privilege), and not much

else. No effort was made to rehabilitate these inmates because they were supposed to be the most incorrigible troublemakers of all federal prisoners. There was no commissary, so there was no underground economy in goods. Inmates were out of their cells from 6:30 in the morning, if they had a job, until 4:30 in the afternoon. From then on, all they had were small crafts, reading, letter writing, and time for reflection.

In practice, over the 30 years of its existence (it closed in 1963), Alcatraz never lived up completely to its ideal, although Ward and Kassebaum (2009) claimed that it may have rehabilitated a number of inmates. The maintenance of silence, except at prescribed times, had long since been abandoned. Many inmates had attempted escape, inmates held strikes to protest conditions, and a few inmates and staff were assaulted—including a warden—or killed by inmates in fights and escape attempts. (It is possible that two men did succeed in escaping, but there is some debate about this.) The internal controls were never as harsh or effective as they were supposed to be either, although more than one inmate of the early years characterized incarceration there as tantamount to being buried alive (Ward & Kassebaum, 2009). Ex-inmates also talked to reporters once released, and the gunfire, fires, and sirens from the various events were noticed and speculated on by San Francisco reporters across the bay. Moreover, because there were not enough notorious and incorrigible inmates in the federal system to fill Alcatraz, about two-thirds of its inmates were less dangerous and influential than had been planned for (Ward & Kassebaum, 2009, p. 459). Yet Alcatraz became the model for other federal and state supermaxes that followed because, for the most part, it had avoided the corruption and violence apparent in other prisons and it had effectively controlled the gangsters and outlaws of its time (Ward & Kassebaum, 2009).

Discussion Questions

1. What events spurred the creation of the first supermax prison?

2. What made Alcatraz distinct from other prisons, and why did it become a model prison?

institution or outside in the community. The housing options are often as diverse as in the medium-security prisons, and inmates can usually roam the facility much more freely, availing themselves of programming, recreation, the yard, the chapel, and the cafeteria at prescribed times. With the recognition that inmates in a minimum-security prison will often be free within 1 or 2 years, visiting options are more liberalized so that the transition from prison to the community is smoother. Work is promoted, and inmates are often encouraged or, in the case of work release facilities with a minimum-security classification, are expected to work in the community.

PHOTO 8.3: Inmates in the yard at Mule Creek State Penitentiary in California. Prison yards provide a modicum of freedom for inmates but can be dangerous because the inmate-to-officer ratio is so high.

Inmates confined to minimum-security prisons are usually *short timers,* or people who are relatively close to a release date. These could be people who have been classified directly to this prison or work release facility because they received a sentence of 1 or 2 years and because they are not expected to be an escape risk or a behavioral problem. Whether they can work might also be a consideration in classification because this is often a central element of these prisons. Other inmates who might do time in a minimum-security prison or work release facility are more serious offenders who have moved through, or "down," the other classification levels and are relatively close to their release. Minimum-security prisons thus also hold the most serious offenders, including murderers, rapists, and child molesters, along with those convicted of burglary and substance abuse and trafficking offenses. The difference is that in minimum-security prisons all such offenders, no matter their offenses, are believed to be a good risk for behavior and in need of preparation for their imminent release.

PRISON VALUE?

Placing someone in prison is a very expensive decision, costing states and the federal government at least $20,000 per year for adult males and more than double that for women and children (Bureau of Justice Statistics, 2011). In the past, this cost was not always considered by policymakers intent on locking up those who had offended even in relatively minor ways. Instead, as discussed in preceding chapters, prisons and other means of "correcting" were created to achieve retribution, deterrence, incapacitation, rehabilitation, and reintegration. (Note that Cullen and Jonson [2012, pp. 10–12] would add restorative justice, or "reducing harm" for the victim, the community, and the offender, and early intervention, or "saving children," to this list of theoretical goals for correctional entities.)

Whether retribution is achieved by imprisonment and, if so, how much imprisonment is needed to achieve it are philosophical and ultimately subjective matters left to judges, juries, and social commentators. Achieving incapacitation is a much more tangible objective, however. When a person is removed and kept away from a community, as he or she is when incarcerated in a jail or prison or, to a lesser extent, when the individual's movements are restricted on probation or parole, it is obvious that incapacitation has been achieved. There is even evidence that incapacitation is related to reduced criminality in the range of three to six crimes per year for some criminals (Owens, 2009; Sweeten & Apel, 2007).

However, measuring whether corrections has had the effect of deterring or rehabilitating is not always obvious or easy to do. We do know that imprisonment for more than a year has not been consistently linked to reduced crime, and thus imprisonment does not appear to deter. Instead, it may prove to be criminogenic in that it exposes the incarcerated to deviant attitudes and beliefs and stigmatizes the individual, thus limiting his or her future employment and social opportunities (Nagin, Cullen, & Jonson, 2009). However, as will be discussed in the chapter on programming and treatment (Chapter 15). there is solid evidence that some treatment programs, even in prisons, can reduce recidivism when done correctly. Therefore, any positive "value" of imprisoning must be assessed based on what is a desirable outcome, the research on whether it can be achieved in a prison, and—in these trying economic times for public services—the financial cost of achieving that goal or those goals.

••• ATTRIBUTES OF THE PRISON THAT SHAPE THE EXPERIENCE

TOTAL INSTITUTIONS

Once classified to a given prison, whether maximum or otherwise, the inmate experience is shaped by several factors, including the *operation* of it. One central component of that operation is the "totality" of the organization.

As will also be discussed in Chapter 9 in reference to staff, Erving Goffman coined the term *total institution* to describe the nature of mental hospitals, as well as prisons, in the United States during the 1950s (Goffman, 1961). For 1 year, he served as a staff member (athletic director's assistant) and did ethnographic research in a federal mental health hospital in Washington, D.C. While avoiding sociable contact with staff, he immersed himself in the inmate world as much as he could without being admitted to the hospital, and what he observed allowed him to learn a great deal about that kind of institution and about roles for staff and inmates.

Goffman (1961) defined a **total institution** as "a place of residence and work where a large number of like-situated individuals, cut off from the wider society for an appreciable period of time, together lead an enclosed, formally administered round of life" (p. xiii). Another key component of this total institution is the defined social strata, particularly as those include "inmates" and the "staff" (p. 7). Specifically, there are formal prohibitions against even minor social interactions between these two groups in a total institution, and all of the formal power resides with one group (the staff) over the other group (the inmates).

This definition is directly applicable to prisons even today, although it more aptly described both prisons and jails of the past. For prison inmates, the institution is where they live—and often work—with people who are like themselves, not only in terms of criminal involvement but also largely in terms of their social class and other background characteristics. Although there is some ability to visit with others, the mode and manner of this contact with the outside world are quite limited in prisons and are also dependent on the security status of the institution (e.g., whether it is a work release facility or a maximum-security prison). The formal rules of prisons also closely control inmate behavior and movement. As already mentioned, another key formal attribute of total institutions governs interactions between staff and inmates. Simply put, staff are to restrict such interactions to business only and are to parcel out information only as is absolutely necessary. As Goffman (1961) put it, "Social mobility between the two strata is grossly restricted; social distance is typically great and often formally prescribed" (p. 7).

Total institution:
"A place of residence and work where a large number of like-situated individuals, cut off from the wider society for an appreciable period of time, together lead an enclosed, formally administered round of life" (Goffman [1961]).

How do these aspects of total institutions affect the lives of inmates? During the 1950s, Goffman (1961) believed that total institutions had the effect of debilitating their inmates. As he saw it, on entrance into the institution, the inmate may become *mortified* (known as **mortification**), or suffer from the loss of the many roles he or she occupied in the wider world (see also Sykes, 1958). Instead, only the role of "inmate" is available, a role that is formally powerless and dependent.

In addition, although each person entering a prison *imports* (known as **importation**) aspects of his or her own culture from the outside, to some extent inmates are likely to experience **prisonization**, whereby they adopt the inmate subculture of the institution (Carroll, 1974, 1982; Clemmer, 2001). Couple this mortification and subsequent role displacement with prisonization into the contingent inmate subculture, and you have the potential for the new inmate to experience a life in turmoil while he or she adjusts inside and to experience some difficulty when reentering the community.

PAINS OF IMPRISONMENT

Part and parcel of this inmate world are what Gresham Sykes—based on his research in a New Jersey maximum-security prison—described as the **pains of imprisonment**. Such pains include "the deprivation of liberty," "the deprivation of goods and services," "the deprivation of heterosexual relationships," "the deprivation of autonomy," and "the deprivation of security" (Sykes, 1958, pp. 63–83).

Deprivation of Liberty

Inmates in a prison (or jail) are not free to leave or even to move about the institution without the permission of their keepers (staff). But for Sykes, the worst of the liberty restrictions meant that inmates are cut off, for the most part, from family and friends. They cannot call whoever they like, or visit with whoever they want, when they wish to do so. Because many inmates are functionally illiterate and poor, they also have difficulty in writing letters and affording the postage. This deprivation of contact with family members, particularly their children, is a severe pain that many inmates experience when, as an artifact of their incarceration, they are unable to have regular interactions with their own children or to have any control over their children's environment on the outside (more about this in the chapter on women and corrections [Chapter 11]) (Gray, Mays, & Stohr, 1995; Stohr & Mays, 1993).

Deprivation of Goods and Services

As to the pain related to goods and services, inmates are required to surrender all of their property on entrance into the prison system, and in most cases they cannot have it back until they leave. The property they are allowed to legally possess is very limited and monitored closely by staff. Relatedly, they cannot choose who will cut their hair or where they will get their nails done, nor can they choose their doctor or schedule a visit. As Sykes (1958) noted—and this is perhaps even truer today in many prisons because of court intervention—most inmates' basic needs for food, shelter, space, and health care are met, yet it is the perception of deprivation in this material society that matters, too.

Deprivation of Sexual Relations

In light of the greater knowledge we have regarding sexual orientation of human populations today as opposed to 60 years ago, we might amend Sykes's (1958) "deprivation of heterosexual relations" to a more generalized *deprivation of sexual relations*. An inmate's access to significant others in the wider world is limited to visiting where touching is only minimally allowed (e.g., a brief kiss or hug at the beginning of the visit). Although much is made of conjugal visits for prison inmates, in reality there are few prisons that allow these, and even in those prisons a miniscule number of inmates are granted access to such visits.

Mortification: Process that occurs as inmates enter the prison and suffer from the loss of the many roles they occupied in the wider world.

Importation: When inmates bring aspects of the larger culture into the prison.

Prisonization: The adopting of the inmate subculture by prisoners.

Pains of imprisonment: The deprivation of liberty, goods and services, heterosexual relationships, autonomy, and security.

PHOTO 8.4: An inmate's access to significant others is limited to visitations where touching is only minimally allowed (e.g., a brief kiss or hug at the beginning of the visit).

Very few prisons allow conjugal visits between inmates and their gay or lesbian partners. Although, as with the free population, there are likely to be 3% to 5% of prison inmates who are gay or lesbian (see a brief discussion related to this topic later in this chapter), sexual intimacy between same-sex inmates is against the rules; however, it does occur. It is illegal as well between same- and opposite-sex staff and inmates.

Deprivation of Autonomy

Autonomy for inmates is also severely restricted in the rule-bound prison world. When, how, where, and with whom they live, eat, work, and play are all determined by the rules of the institution. Inmates can make few choices regarding their lives while imprisoned, and all of those choices are shaped by their imprisonment.

Deprivation of Security

Due to their imprisonment, inmates are thrown together with others, some of whom are aggressive and violent or become so in a prison environment, perhaps particularly in the maximum-security environment that Sykes (1958) studied. Because of the circumstances surrounding incarceration in a supermax, but also to a lesser degree in medium- and minimum-security prisons, inmates are deprived of their security, a basic human need, as defined by Maslow (1943/2001). Quoting an inmate in his study, Sykes (1958) repeated that "the worst thing about prison is you have to live with other prisoners" (p. 77), meaning that even if one is prone to violence or manipulation (termed an *outlaw inmate* by Sykes)—and not all inmates are—it is unnerving for even an outlaw inmate to need to live with others who are also so inclined. This lack of security, according to Sykes, can lead to anxiety on the part of inmates and the belief that at some point they, whether outlaws among outlaws or not, are likely to be forced to fight to defend themselves or to submit to the abuse of others.

Effects of Deprivation

Sykes (1958) argued that these pains, although not physically brutalizing, have the cumulative effect of destroying the psyche of the inmate. To avoid this destruction, inmates in prisons may be motivated to engage in deviance while incarcerated as a means of alleviating their pain. So bullying other inmates, involvement in gangs, buying items through the underground economy, and sexual relations all might be motivated, in fact, by the need for some autonomy, liberty, security, goods and services, and sexual gratification (Johnson, 2002). Extrapolating from this point, the extent to which female inmates form pseudofamilial relationships may be a means of alleviating the pain experienced due to the separation from children and other close family members (Owen, 1998).

One final note regarding the pains of imprisonment: Sykes (1958) did not believe that all inmates experienced or perceived these pains in the same way. He acknowledged that the way one experiences these pains does vary some by individual and background as well as by the prison in which one is incarcerated. However, he argued that, at least among the inmates he studied, there was a consensus that "life in a maximum security prison is depriving or frustrating in the extreme" (p. 63).

IN FOCUS 8.3

Prison Debate Project

By Amber Morczek and Roger Schaefer (written while doctoral students at Washington State University)

The Prison Debate Project was created in 2012 by Loretta Taylor and Johannes Wheeldon at Walla Walla Community College and Dr. Faith Lutze at Washington State University. The debate is structured to allow all members of the debate teams to participate in various capacities. Debate teams are composed of university student participants majoring in criminal justice and inmate student participants who work collaboratively to identify, develop, and deliver arguments supporting their side of the debate proposition (Pro or Con). Each team is assigned five speaking roles—introduction, fact, value, policy, and conclusion—that must be supported by research or academic literature. Speaking roles are agreed on by the team members and approved by course instructors.

The logistics of the program present unique challenges that demand routine coordination among university officials, prison staff and administration, and debate participants. University officials and prison administration work closely to address issues of risk in an effort to ensure safety. Custody and educational staff work together to promote safety while university students are at the prison. Criminal background checks are required for all individuals who enter the prison, including debate participants as well as university faculty or staff. The success of the prison tours, group meetings, and debate is a direct result of the collaborative work and preparation that occurs long before university students enter the prison.

The Diagrammatic Dialogue and Debate Model, developed and implemented by a group of scholars and instructors at Coyote Ridge Corrections Center in Connell, Washington, has emerged as a unique correctional and educational discourse (see Wheeldon, Chavez, & Cooke, 2013). Using this debate model, both university and inmate students are exposed to the human reality of disagreement and resolution, particularly within a traditionally rigid correctional environment. Within the context of correctional discourse, the Prison Debate Project empowers inmate participants to recognize opposing viewpoints and participate in respectful dialogue. From an educational perspective, the Prison Debate Project invites inmates to engage in an ongoing academic discussion on important social issues (e.g., gun control, gender and justice, jury selection). Overall, it is the structure of the debate that creates a foundation for prosocial self-actualization through critical thinking and respectful discourse.

Discussion Questions

1. How might this program reduce the pains of imprisonment for inmates?

2. How might this program benefit the college student participants?

3. How might this program benefit the prison in which it is hosted?

●●● THE PRISON SUBCULTURE

A *subculture,* or a subset of culture with its own norms, values, beliefs, traditions, and even language, tends to solidify when people are isolated from the larger culture and when members have regular and intense contact with each other for an extended period of time. In other words, it would appear that the total institution nature of prisons provides the perfect environment for a **prison subculture** to form. Accordingly, the degree to which a correctional environment fits the definition of a total institution will determine the extent to which a client subculture exists. It is also possible that the shared experiences of deprivation, as detailed by Sykes (1958), can further solidify a subculture for inmates.

Thus, research on inmate subcultures has tended to focus on prison inmates and specifically on medium- or maximum-security prison inmates. This is not to say, of course, that

Prison subculture: The norms, values, beliefs, traditions, and even language of the prison.

those in a jail or a minimum-security prison do not have distinguishable norms, values, beliefs, traditions, and language that set them apart from the wider community, but it is much less likely. By definition, the longer inmates are in an institution associating with others like them, and the more "total" the institution is in its restrictions on liberty and contact with "outsiders," the more subjected inmates are to the pains of imprisonment and the more likely they are to become prisonized in that they adopt the inmate subculture.

ROLES FOR INMATES AND STAFF

Indicators of such a subculture, as identified by prison researchers, include prescribed values and defined roles for inmates (Clemmer, 2001; Owen, 1998). For instance, Clemmer, in 1940 (reprinted in 2001), broadly defined criminal subcultural values, which include "the notion that criminals should not betray each other to the police, should be reliable, wily but trustworthy, coolheaded, etc." Also emphasized among these values are ultramasculinity and displays of toughness and solidarity among inmates and against staff (Lutze & Murphy, 1999; Sykes, 1958). Accordingly, the types of roles (inmate typology) that Sykes and Messinger (1960) and Sykes (1958) described for adult male prison inmates in their own argot, or language, are detailed in In Focus 8.4. Although these researchers identified these roles for inmates in prisons more than 60 years ago, current researchers still see them in prisons of today. Of course, any given inmate might be expected to change roles from time to time during his or her incarceration or to engage in more than one role simultaneously.

These roles are played out in the prison in a criminal subculture, which becomes a *convict subculture* for Clemmer (2001) when such inmates seek power and information so that they might get the goods and services they desire to alleviate those pains of imprisonment. Owen (1998) noted that some women engaged in a version of this subculture and these roles, although it might have been tempered by the relationships they had and the goods and services they needed (more about the different roles women inmates adopt in Chapter 11). Notably, both Clemmer and Owen found that a significant portion of inmates in the male and female prisons they studied were not at all interested in being involved in the convict subculture or the "mix" of behavior that can lead to trouble in prisons. Such inmates, in the argot identified by Sykes (1958) and Sykes and Messinger (1960), were *square johns*. These inmates either chose not to connect to the inmate subculture or held on to more traditional and legitimate values from the larger culture.

More recent research confirms that inmates are not as solidly aligned against staff as the early works indicated (Hemmens & Marquart, 2000; J. Jacobs, 1977; Johnson, 2002; Jurik, 1985a; Jurik & Halemba, 1984; Lombardo, 1982; Owen, 1998). Many inmates identify with free-world values as much as or more than inmate values and inmate subculture.

Other recent researchers and writers on prisons (e.g., Conover, 2001; Johnson, 2002; Rideau, 2010) find that staff and inmates engage in more personal and informal relationships with each other than is formally acknowledged, a reality that Sykes (1958) noted as well. The diversification of staff by race, ethnicity, and gender has changed the old dynamic between staff and inmates, making staff less dissimilar to inmates and the inmate world less "masculinized" than it was previously (for more involved discussions of these matters, see Chapter 11 on women and corrections and Chapter 12 on minorities and corrections), perhaps continuing to break down some of the more formal barriers between staff and inmates in a total institution.

Research, observations, and personal experience as a teacher, student-inmate, attendee, and governor (warden) in a male prison in the United Kingdom led Crewe, Warr, Bennett, and Smith (2014) to theorize that emotionally restrained "tough guy" depictions of inmates in prisons do not fully describe the *emotional geography* of such places. Rather, these

IN FOCUS 8.4

Inmate Roles Identified by Sykes (1958) and Sykes and Messinger (1960)

- **The right guy**: The inmate who fully supports and embraces the inmate code.

- **The rat or squealer**: The inmate who "snitches" on others to staff. Usually, such inmates are despised by other inmates because they violate the prohibition in the inmate code regarding this sort of behavior. Because they are so disliked, rats are vulnerable to attacks by other inmates.

- **The center man**: The inmate who agrees with the prison rules and procedures either because he is trying to curry favor from staff or because he believes that is the correct way to behave.

- **The tough**: The inmate who is aggressive, has anger issues, and is touchy and so is willing to fight at will.

- **The hipster**: The inmate who aspires to be a tough but who is really all talk and little action. He chooses his victims selectively to be sure he can, in fact, conquer them, whereas the tough will fight both the weak and the strong.

- **The gorilla**: The inmate who may be as aggressive as the tough but uses that aggression—or just the threat of it—to gain something from other inmates.

- **The merchant or peddler**: The inmate who engages in the underground black market to supply illicit goods and services to other inmates for material advantage.

- **The weakling**: The inmate who is vulnerable to exploitation by others and cannot stand up to them. He submits to the coercion—or threatened coercion—of the gorilla.

- **The fish**: The inmate who has just arrived and is not yet adjusted to the ways of the prison.

- **The wolf**: The inmate who aggressively and sexually pursues other inmates. He is believed to play a "masculine" role. There is no emotion or connection in the sexual act for the wolf; rather, he pursues men in the prison and rapes them.

- **The "fag"**: The inmate who plays the passive, although not unwilling, role in the sexual relationship with another inmate. He is believed to play a "feminine" role. (Note: The authors of this text acknowledge that the term "fag" is derogatory, and the assumption that male and female roles are tied to aggression and passivity is dated and limiting, but this term and these assumptions are the ones used by Sykes [1958] and Sykes and Messinger [1960], who were repeating the argot used by inmates of the late 1950s. As Sykes explained, inmate argot was often meant to be derogatory and inflammatory as it marked and labeled the roles of others.)

- **The punk**: The unwilling inmate who is coerced or bribed into the passive sexual role vis-à-vis other inmates. This inmate does not adopt the "feminine" role.

- **The ball buster**: The inmate who continually struggles against the system and staff despite the futility of it, often to the point of foolishness.

- **The innocent**: The inmate who repeatedly claims his innocence of the crime for which he is incarcerated.

- **The square john**: The inmate who does not become prisonized but instead identifies with the free-world values of staff and the outside community.

---

researchers claimed that there are certain subcultural zones where a wider range of emotions is allowed because the circumstances of such places allow it. One such zone in the prison is the visiting room, where interactions with families require more open emotional exchanges and allow for shows of vulnerability by inmates. Classrooms and the chapel were other areas where comradeship and the sharing of ideas, and even personal experiences and beliefs, broke down the typical emotional barriers that are present in prisons.

GANGS AND THE PRISON SUBCULTURE

Gangs, or groups of people with similar interests who socialize together and who may engage in deviant or criminal activities, are a common phenomenon in jails and

Gangs (prison): Groups of people with similar interests who socialize together and support each other but who also engage in deviant or criminal activities. Prison gangs have a hierarchical organizational structure and a set and often strict code of conduct for members.

prisons. According to the U.S. Department of Justice (2015) website, gangs in prisons and jails are, by definition, engaged in criminal activities and are connected through members and criminal involvement with communities. Prison gangs have a hierarchical organizational structure and a set and often strict code of conduct for members. As reported by the U.S. Department of Justice (2015),

> Prison gangs vary in both organization and composition, from highly structured gangs such as the Aryan Brotherhood and Nuestra Familia to gangs with a less formalized structure such as the Mexican Mafia (La Eme). Prison gangs generally have fewer members than street gangs and Outlaw Motorcycle Gangs (OMGs) and are structured along racial or ethnic lines. Nationally, prison gangs pose a threat because of their role in the transportation and distribution of narcotics. Prison gangs are also an important link between drug-trafficking organizations (DTOs), street gangs and OMGs, often brokering the transfer of drugs from DTOs to gangs in many regions. Prison gangs typically are more powerful within state correctional facilities rather than within the federal penal system. (p. 1)

Correctional scholars and practitioners believe that gangs are so ubiquitous in corrections because they meet the needs of inmates for security, goods and services, power, and companionship. They lessen the pains of imprisonment by providing protection in numbers and the potential to respond with force to any threats an inmate might face. They are conduits for the supply of illicit goods, such as tobacco, drugs, alcohol, and sex, in prisons and jails. They also provide some substitution for the diminished relationships that inmates have with their families and friends on the outside.

The history of gangs in prisons is a long one. Sykes (1958) noted that the first investigation of the New Jersey State Prison, in 1830, found what was called a "Stauch-Gang," which was firmly entrenched there and engaged in terrorizing both inmates and staff while also planning escapes (p. 92). Ward and Kassebaum (2009) also pointed out the importation and exportation of gang-related criminal activity between state and federal prisons and the streets during the 1920s. J. Jacobs (1977), in his history of the Stateville Prison in Illinois, observed that prison gangs had existed in that state for decades as imports from the streets of Chicago, although he thought that their ferocity and strength increased during the late 1960s and early 1970s.

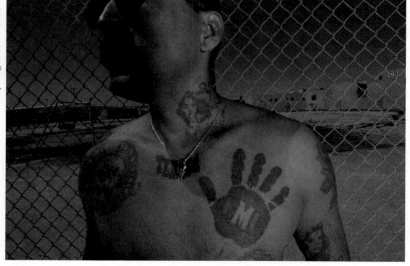

Getty Images/Bob Chamberlin

PHOTO 8.5: Mexican mafia tattoo on a member. Such tattoos provide a ready signal to other inmates and staff as to the gang membership of an inmate.

The prison gangs of today are almost too numerous for correctional authorities to keep track of, but they do tend to have in common a criminal focus. According to the Florida Department of Corrections (FDOC, 2014), most prison gangs these days recruit their membership based on ethnicity or race. Both the federal government and the FDOC report that gangs are much stronger in male prisons, and gangs will conspire with others, even rival gangs, so as to provide protection and increase their criminal reach. (For example, the Aryan Brotherhood might sometimes work with members of the Black Guerrilla Family despite the racial hatred of their members for each other if it will increase their drug sales.) The FDOC website identifies the six major prison gangs in the United States as follows:

1. Neta (Puerto Rican American/Hispanic)

2. Aryan Brotherhood (white)

3. Black Guerrilla Family (black)

4. Mexican Mafia (Mexican American/Hispanic)

5. La Nuestra Familia (Mexican American/Hispanic)

6. Texas Syndicate (Mexican American/Hispanic)

Because of their underground engagement in prison crime and the rivalries that develop between gangs, even those with members of the same ethnic backgrounds (e.g., the Mexican Mafia and La Nuestra Familia) are sworn enemies. Moreover, both the Mexican Mafia and La Nuestra Familia are rivals of the Texas Syndicate. Because of these rivalries, jails and prisons constantly need to consider gang membership in classification decisions. Whether it is fights over turf, protection of members, or some other issue, the presence of gangs and gang activities leads to disruption and even murder in prisons. For instance, according to the FDOC (2014), the Aryan Brotherhood (AB) disruptions of prisons include the following:

- The main activities of the AB are centered on drug trafficking, extortion, pressure rackets, and internal discipline.

- Prison activities include introduction of contraband, distribution of drugs, and getting past facility rules and regulations.

- Traditionally, targets have been non-gang inmates and internal discipline.

- From 1975 to 1985, AB members committed 40 homicides in California prisons and local jails as well as 13 homicides in the community.

- From 1978 to 1992, AB members, suspects, and associates in the federal system were involved in 26 homicides, 3 of which involved staff victims.

Because of the threat that prison gangs present for the security of the institution and the safety of staff and inmates, managers try to control or suppress gang involvement in their facilities. The first step in this process is the identification of gang members and their leaders. Once identified, correctional staff will try to separate members and leaders from each other. However, given the crowding of most prisons and prison systems, it is nearly impossible to always employ the separation tactic as a means of control and suppression. Therefore, what they are often left with is the monitoring of gang activity and, as much as possible, punishing deviance or neutralizing gang members and reducing their impact on a given system.

••• VIOLENCE

WHY PRISONS ARE VIOLENT

Violence is endemic to prisons. There is violence in prisons because incarcerated people are there unwillingly and forced to do things they normally would not do with people

---

? ETHICAL ISSUE

What Would You Do?

As an experienced counselor in the prison where you work, you are often given the more "difficult" inmates to work with. You are told by the prison intelligence officers that you may have a number of gang members on your caseload. One younger inmate by the name of Jacob, who you have spent some time with, has told you of his affiliation with one of the gangs in the prison. He has also emphasized that, although he is a member, he is not involved in any illegal activities. He is programming well and has a responsible job in the facility. As best as you can tell from your contacts with other inmates, Jacob is not involved in any criminal activities. You know that if you tell the intelligence officer about this inmate's affiliation, however, there is a good chance that Jacob will be placed in segregation or moved to another facility. What do you think would be the best response in this instance and why?

they might not like. Most important of all, some of them are inclined to be violent. According to Bureau of Justice Statistics (BJS) researcher Ann Carson, in 2013 about 54% of the state prison population was incarcerated for violent offenses (Carson, 2014). As was mentioned earlier, prisons as a whole are running at or over capacity. Maximum- and medium-security prisons tend to hold more inmates convicted of violent offenses or who have problems with following the rules in prisons, and as a result they are more likely to experience violent outbursts. Research by Meade and Steiner (2013), in which they used a representative national sample of adult male inmates, indicates that inmates who were exposed to violence or who were physically victimized prior to incarceration were likely to have more problems with adjustment while incarcerated. The researchers also found that having been abused as a child—not an uncommon experience for many inmates—was associated with maladjustment while in prison. Add to this mix the presence of gangs and their willingness to use force to achieve their criminal ends, and the possibility of violence in prisons rises.

THE AMOUNT OF VIOLENCE

With the exception of deaths due to violence, it is difficult to determine the exact amount of violence in prisons. Correctional institutions tend to underreport its incidence, and there is variation across facilities about what constitutes violence (Byrne & Hummer, 2008). Relatedly, inmates are reluctant to report the violence they experience or witness to staff. With these caveats regarding official statistics in mind, Stephan and Karberg (2003) found, using data collected from correctional institutions around the United States, that the number of assaults on staff and inmates increased in state and federal prisons from 1995 to 2000 and that the size of the increase was greatest for private institutions. They did note, however, that the rate of assaults on staff (or the number of assaults per staff person) decreased slightly during this time period. We also know, based on BJS data, that both the suicide and homicide rates in jails and prisons decreased from 1980 to 2003. More recent BJS data (2000–2013) indicate that the suicide rate in jails has continued to decline, while in prisons it has remained stable at 2002 levels (Figure 8.3) (Noonan & Ginder, 2013).

SEXUAL ASSAULTS

As was discussed in Chapter 6, the amount of sexual violence in prisons and jails, based on inmate surveys and official statistics, is becoming increasingly clear. The Prison Rape Elimination Act of 2003 (PREA) requires that the BJS collect data yearly on the amount of prison rape that occurs. In 2013, this meant that a 10% sample of the 7,600 jails, prisons, and community-based and juvenile facilities were included. The findings from this research indicate the following (BJS, 2014, p. 1):

- The allegations of sexual victimization increased from 2005 to 2011, more in prisons than in jails.

- In 2011, 10% of the allegations were substantiated (meaning that they were found to be true after an investigation).

- Whereas 52% of the substantiated incidents involved only inmates,

the other 48% involved staff and inmates.

- Injuries were reported in 18% of the inmate-only victimizations, whereas less than 1% of the staff and inmate victimizations involved injuries.

- Female staff committed more than half of the substantiated incidents of sexual misconduct.

The data indicate that 4.0% of prison inmates reported experiencing sexual victimization in 2011–2012 (63,400), which was perpetrated by either other inmates or staff (BJS, 2014, p. 3). Whether the number of such assaults is trending upward or downward and why it might be more prevalent in some facilities than in others are matters yet to be determined by more longitudinal research. Certainly, although horrific for the inmate

FIGURE *8.3*   Violence in Prisons, 2001–2013*

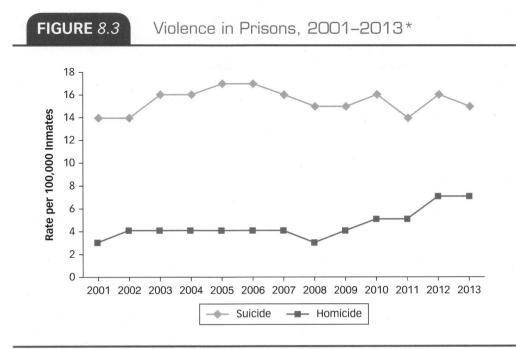

Source: Noonan, Rohloff, and Ginder (2015).

*Most recent data available.

experiencing it and keeping in mind the likely underestimation of victimization, a 4% sexual victimization rate does not fit the "myth" of sexual victimization that many people believe regarding prisons, a myth that predicts that everyone who goes to prison, particularly young males, will be raped (Fleisher & Krienert, 2009).

It might well be that this myth has more than a grain of truth to it in that prison rapes are underreported or that in the past it was much more common. The percentage of those raped or sexually assaulted may have declined, the same way the rate of prison assaults appears to have done (although not the number) over the years as corrections has become less "total" in its isolation and operation, as the courts have recognized some inmates' rights, and as training of staff has increased. As Byrne, Hummer, and Stowell (2008) noted, there are many factors (e.g., staffing levels, crowding) whose effect on violence is not yet established in the research.

Although it might be a myth that all who enter prisons—or even most—will be raped, the research by the BJS indicates that fully 80,600 inmates in prisons and jails were victims of sexual violence in 2011–2012 (Beck, Berzofsky, Caspar, & Krebs, 2013, p. 8). And it is true that certain groups are much more likely to be raped in prisons than other groups. As was discussed in the chapter on jails (Chapter 6), females, non-heterosexuals, and the mentally ill are much more likely to be victims of sexual assault in prisons and jails than are other inmates (see also Figure 8.4).

RIOTING

Rioting is another form of violence. It is group violence. Rioting presents a direct threat to the security of the institution and the inmates in it and is often met with reciprocal force by the staff and administration of the prison. Prison riots have existed as long as there have been prisons—in fact, before there were prisons. Recall the Newgate "prison" of Connecticut (see Chapter 2), where inmates were confined to a copper mine for much of their incarceration. Inmates at Newgate repeatedly rioted throughout the history of its operation. In fact, virtually every maximum- and medium-security prison with any longevity has experienced some form of rioting by inmates. Rioting—and

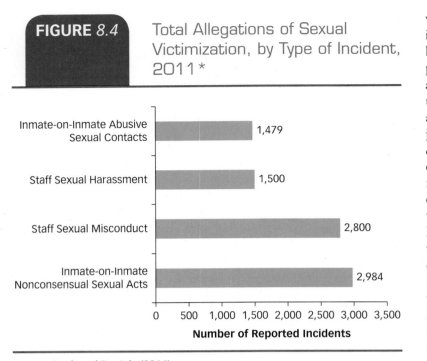

FIGURE *8.4*   Total Allegations of Sexual Victimization, by Type of Incident, 2011*

Source: Beck and Rantala (2014).

*Most recent data available.

violence in general—is engaged in by inmates to achieve some end, such as better food, better housing, or more power, or inmates might riot out of anger or frustration. When violence is used to achieve some end, it is known as *instrumental violence,* but when it is just an angry outburst, it is known as *expressive violence.* Of course, inmates engaged in violence or a riot could be involved for *both* instrumental and expressive reasons. An inmate who wants to protest the overcrowding of his or her institution may riot to let the world know about the conditions of confinement (instrumental violence), but he or she might also be angry about the effect that such crowding has on housing and the ability to sleep and become violent as a means of expressing it. When enough inmates engage in this violence together, it is called a riot.

The two most notorious instances of inmate rioting to date occurred in the **Attica Prison riot** of 1971 in New York and the **New Mexico Prison riot** of 1980. At Attica, the riot began with a spontaneous act of violence by one inmate against an officer when the officer tried to break up a fight. The violence spread when other inmates became involved the next day to avenge the punishment of the two fighting inmates (Deane & Bosch, 2000). The riot also spread because inmates were frustrated and angry about the overcrowded conditions and lack of programming for inmates, among other problems with the conditions of confinement; even showering and toilet paper were rationed. There were charges of racism by the mostly African American inmates regarding their treatment by the mostly white staff at Attica as well (Useem & Kimball, 1989). Add to this the student protests against the Vietnam War and the civil rights movement that had roiled the country outside of the Attica prison walls during the late 1960s and early 1970s, and it was clear why there was tension within them.

Because the prison staff were unprepared to respond to a riot, the inmates easily took over the Attica prison, burning some buildings and eventually congregating in one yard with their 40 hostages (Deane & Bosch, 2000). In the negotiations between the inmate leaders and the administration, the inmates asked for better food, better health care, and the ability to practice their religion. A number of observers, composed of politicians and media members, tried to intervene in the negotiations but to no avail. Some inmates killed three other inmates and one hostage, which also impaired the ability to negotiate. Moreover, Governor Nelson Rockefeller, who was considering a run for the White House at the time, did not want to appear soft on crime by being too soft on the rioting inmates.

In the end, the inmates and administrators could not come to an agreement (the inmates wanted amnesty for the rioters), and eventually, on Governor Rockefeller's orders, the prison was stormed by the state police and correctional staff. Tear gas was dropped from police helicopters into the occupied yard, and the inmates and their hostages were indiscriminately fired on with shotguns by the staff and police. As a consequence, 10 hostages and 29 inmates were dead or dying when the prison was secured, and another 80 inmates had gunshot wounds (Useem & Kimball, 1989). It was the bloodiest prison riot in American history. Inmates, even injured ones, were then beaten and humiliated (forced to stand naked in the yard for hours), and medical care was delayed or denied.

Attica Prison riot (1971): The bloodiest prison riot in American history. It ended when the prison was retaken by law enforcement, leaving 10 hostages and 29 inmates dead and 80 inmates wounded.

New Mexico Prison riot (1980): Prison riot over the conditions of confinement and crowding. The state eventually retook the prison. Over 3 days, 33 inmates were killed by other inmates.

The state indicted 60 inmates for a number of crimes, including sodomy and murder, arising out of the riot, but only 8 inmates were convicted (Gonnerman, 2001, p. 1). Years of legal wrangling eventually led to the $8 million award by the state of New York to the inmates who were beaten or tortured after the riot (Deane & Bosch, 2000). In 2005, the state paid out another $12 million to the survivors and families of employees killed in the aftermath of the riot (Kirshon, 2010).

In 1980, the New Mexico State Penitentiary also exploded in a riot over the conditions of confinement, which were deplorable, and crowding, which was at epidemic levels. Despite repeated warnings that a riot was going to occur, the administration and staff failed to adequately prepare. When a staff member slipped up in a security measure when locking down a dormitory for the night, he was grabbed, along with his keys, and inmates quickly advanced through the prison, taking control of several cellblocks, including the pharmacy and shops. Drugs and weapons were readily available as a result, and brutal inmate-on-inmate violence ensued. Some of this violence was particularly focused on inmate snitches and child molesters, who were housed in a separate cellblock. Rioting inmates broke into this cellblock, and gruesome and vicious assaults on and murders of these inmates were committed. The state eventually retook the prison without the resulting bloodshed that happened at Attica. However, over the course of 3 days, 33 inmates were killed by other inmates. Numerous other inmates, along with staff hostages, were beaten or raped, and millions of dollars in damage was done (Useem, 1985; Useem & Kimball, 1989). In the aftermath of this riot, New Mexico was sued several times. The state did build a number of medium- and minimum-security prisons following the riot, which eased the overcrowding at the main facility.

SOLUTIONS TO PRISON VIOLENCE
Strategies to Reduce Violence

There are some scholars and social commentators who argue that prisons and jails are naturally violent institutions, essentially for the same reasons why we wrote in the foregoing that they can be incubators for violence (e.g., they hold violent people involuntarily). But there is evidence that the degree of violence differs markedly from institution to institution and from group to group (Beck et al., 2013). If this is true—that one prison or jail is more or less violent than comparable institutions that hold similar types of inmates (i.e., security level and inmate history of engaging in violence)—then it is implied that it is not that violence is endemic to prisons or jails per se but rather that it is how the institution operates that creates and fosters violence. Therefore, it occurs to us that there are strategies that might be used to reduce violence such as the following:

- *Professional subculture:* Promote a professional environment or one where staff are well trained, well educated, paid decently, and versed in ethical behavior. Promote those who model these values up the career ladder for the institution (see Stohr & Collins, 2014).

- *Personnel:* Hire potentially professional people (people with education and ethical values), train them well, and pay them a wage that will entice them to stay. Training should include the latest research on how to spot and reduce violence in corrections (see Rembert & Henderson, 2014).

- *Supervision:* Promote ethical supervisors who have proven their abilities on the job. Value and facilitate further training, education, and development for them. Then, keep the *span of control* (the number of persons for whom a supervisor is responsible) within reason so that supervisors can know and influence what is going on around them. Discipline or fire those who violate ethical standards of the institution (see Stohr & Collins, 2014).

- *Classification:* Pay careful attention to inmate histories and proclivities for violence, and separate inmates based on this intelligence.

Neutralize criminal gangs so that their influence does not heighten the level of violence in the facility. As much as possible, classify inmates so that their needs can be met (e.g., work training, proximity to family and their communities, treatment to address their needs) (see Mears, Stewart, Siennick, & Simons, 2013).

- *Activities:* Provide opportunities for inmates to stay busy in prosocial activities such as work, education, treatment, recreation, art, religious engagement, and niches where they are more likely to experience prosocial values. This will benefit them and communities. In addition, provide opportunities for inmates to use their talents and abilities (see the discussion of mature coping and niches following, and see also research by Rocheleau, 2013; Wooldredge & Steiner, 2014).

- *Formal grievance procedures:* Ensure that there are formal grievance procedures in place where inmates can report on perceived deficiencies in the operation of the facility and that they can use to vent their concerns. Just having the ability to vent and knowing that one is heard can often be enough to alleviate anger and thus violence. Grievance procedures also provide the opportunity for inmates to report on real deficiencies in the prison operations (see Rembert & Henderson, 2014).

- *Ombudsman:* Larger facilities or prison or jail systems may be able to staff an ombudsman position; such a person can investigate serious complaints by staff or inmates and work to resolve them.

- *Open architecture:* When building a new jail or prison or when significantly remodeling one, try to improve the openness of the facility so that sight lines are clearer in living units because violence is more likely to occur when it cannot be seen (e.g., see the discussion of podular or direct-supervision jails in the chapter on jails [Chapter 6], and see research by Wooldredge & Steiner, 2014).

- *Official reporting:* Support the official reporting of violence to auditors at the local, state, or federal level. Note the discussion of PREA in the chapter on jails (Chapter 6) and the requirement of reporting sexual abuse and assaults in prisons and jails. Sometimes jail and prison managers do not know that their facilities are outliers in terms of the amount of violence that occurs there. Having official reports gets this information out into the sunlight and makes it more likely that there will be efforts to reduce the violence in facilities that have more of it.

- *Involvement of policymakers and the public:* Keep policymakers and the public apprised of the amount of violence that occurs and why it occurs, and enlist their support and assistance in solutions that would reduce it.

Mature Coping

Prison violence, whether by individuals or groups of rioters, occurs in part because some inmates are not capable of interacting, or do not know how to interact, with others without violence. In his research on corrections, Johnson (2002) noticed that despite the mortification, prisonization, and pains experienced to different degrees by incarcerated individuals, some were able to adjust prosocially, even to grow, in a prison setting. Although they were the exception rather than the rule, he noted that some inmates developed another means of adjusting. This alternative means of handling incarceration—or supervision in the case of probationers and parolees—is **mature coping**. As identified and defined by Johnson,

> Mature coping means, in essence, dealing with life's problems like a responsive and responsible human being, one who seeks autonomy without violating the rights of others, security without resorting to deception or violence, and relatedness to others as the finest and fullest expression of human identity. (p. 83)

Mature coping: The ability to adjust prosocially and to respond to problems responsibly and without resorting to violence.

IN FOCUS 8.5

The Story of Wilbert Rideau

Wilbert Rideau, an African American, grew up poor to laborer parents in Lawtell, Louisiana, during the 1940s and 1950s. The family moved around the segregated state, from small town to small town, looking for work, eventually settling in Lake Charles. His father drank, womanized, and abused his mother and later the children; he abandoned the family when Wilbert was a teenager, and his family went on welfare.

During the 1950s, Lake Charles was segregated and restricted the opportunities of African Americans to advance in any profession. After he was denied advancement at his low-paying job at a sewing shop, and as a means of leaving town for better opportunities, Wilbert Rideau attempted to rob a nearby bank. The robbery went horribly wrong. He kidnapped three bank employees, killing one and shooting another, in the botched bank robbery attempt. Once caught, almost immediately after committing the crimes, he was nearly lynched instead of being tried, his confession was coerced, the evidence presented was false, and he had inadequate counsel. But he admitted that he had committed the murder, shot another woman, and kidnapped three people.

In 1961, at the age of 19, Rideau was convicted and received a death sentence. He then spent 10 years on death row at the Angola Prison in Louisiana. He was eventually released to the general population of the prison when the *Furman v. Georgia* (1972) Supreme Court case invalidated death sentences around the country. He served the rest of his sentence, another 33 years, at the infamous Angola Prison and, during most of it, was the editor of *The Angolite,* an inmate newspaper.

In his book, *In the Place of Justice: A Story of Punishment and Deliverance,* Rideau (2010) discussed how, as an inmate, he grew—you might say he maturely coped—by finding a niche at *The Angolite* and doing work that was worthwhile. He won critical acclaim for the uncensored writing about prison life that he was allowed to present to the world by one forward-thinking warden. Once this pattern of an uncensored prison newspaper had been established, subsequent wardens were reluctant to shut him down, although they tried. Because his writing became known in the outside world, and several wardens even allowed Rideau to leave the prison to talk to community groups, he had a form of power that allowed him access to wardens and directors of prisons. According to Rideau, he used this access to help some inmates, to avert violence against inmates, and to steer wardens in the direction of treatment and programming. He also had plenty of time to regret his crimes and to reflect not only on the racism he had confronted in his life but also on his own racial stereotypes. He observed the workings of the inmate code in prison and learned to walk a fine line between upholding it and staying within the rules.

Rideau was released from prison in 2005 after a court found that his original trial had been mishandled. He had spent a total of 44 years in jails and prisons since his conviction, when the norm for his crime was less than 10 years. He lives with his wife, whom he met 20 years before on one of his speaking gigs outside of prison. She had spent many years of her life working to free him.

Discussion Questions

1. How did Rideau "grow" as a human individual while incarcerated?

2. How might such growth be increased for all inmates in prisons?

3. What are the chances that Rideau went on to live peaceably once released from prison?

As indicated by this definition, the offender needs to learn how to be an adult with some autonomy in an environment where the individual has little formal power (although the informal reality may be different) and his or her status is almost subhuman by wider community standards. Moreover, offenders must accomplish this feat without doing violence to others, although Johnson (2002) allowed that violence in self-defense may be necessary, and they need to exercise consideration of others in their environment.

Johnson (2002) noted that mature coping is relatively rare among the inmate population for a number of reasons. He argued that inmates are typically immature in their social relations to begin with, which of course is one of the reasons why they are in prison in the first place. Because of impoverishment; poor, absent, or abusive parenting; mental illness; abuse of drugs or alcohol at a young age; and/or schools that fail them or that they fail, offenders enter the criminal justice system with a number of social, psychological, and economic deficits. They are often not used to voluntarily taking responsibility for their actions, as one would expect of "mature" individuals, nor are they typically expected to "empathize with and assist others in need" (p. 93), especially in a prison or jail environment.

Second, Johnson (2002) argued that for inmates to maturely cope, it is helpful if they are incarcerated in what he termed a *decent prison*. Such a facility does not necessarily have more programming, staffing, or amenities than the norm, although he believed it might be helpful if it did; rather, such institutions or programs would be relatively free of violence and would include some opportunities so that inmates might find a *niche* (defined below) to be involved in. For inmates to find this niche, however, decent prisons need to include some opportunities for inmates to act autonomously.

Being secure from violence, like autonomy, is basic to human development. In fact, according to Maslow (1998), if the security need is not fulfilled, it will preoccupy offenders and motivate them to engage in behaviors (e.g., bullying, gang activity) that they normally might avoid if they were not feeling continually threatened (Johnson, 2002). Then, assuming that offenders perceive that they are relatively safe, there need to be prosocial activities, including work, school, athletics, church, treatment, and/or art programs, that provide some sort of means for positive self-value reinforcement. Such places were termed *niches* by Johnson (2002), and the opportunities they afford provide redress for the mortification and pains that offenders, particularly those who are incarcerated, experience.

••• SOCIAL SUPPORT

Social support is a necessary element to successful existence in this world. Humans, for the most part, are social animals in need of the assistance of others, such as families, friends, neighbors, schools, churches, nonprofits, and governments, to grow and thrive. Inmates in prisons and jails perhaps need more social support to succeed than most Americans. They usually come from poor backgrounds where their education was limited, they have few job skills, and socialization in prosocial behavior may have been lacking. On release, they will be dependent on family and friends, should they be lucky enough to have some, who are stretched financially and emotionally themselves. Former inmates will leave the prison relatively unskilled, with a GED (general educational development) or less, and the stigma of being an "ex-con." They will have financial obligations for their children and for fines imposed as part of their sentence, and often they will need to pay for their own supervision in the community. Their needs will be multifaceted and many, and to succeed they will depend on private and public sources of support.

Lin (1986) defined social support as "the perceived or actual instrumental and/or expressive provisions supplied by the community, social networks, and confiding partners" (p. 18). Cullen (1994) modified this definition to include both formal and informal delivery of this support. *Instrumental support* is material and includes the exchange of goods or money. *Expressive support* is more emotional and is the kind supplied by family and close friends. It is thought that the greater the degree to which inmates experience social support, whether instrumental or emotional, from whatever source while in prison, the more likely they are to change their behavior while incarcerated (fewer infractions of the rules and less violence) and in the larger community (reduced recidivism) (Woo et al., 2014). Currently, the research in this area is more suggestive than solid, but if evidence indicates that social support reduces the deviance of inmates while incarcerated, then it would make sense that correctional institutions develop ways to provide social support to inmates or allow others from the community to do so (Beare & Hogg, 2013; Hamilton, Kigerl, & Hays, 2015; Hochstetler, DeLisi, & Pratt, 2010; Lutze, Rosky, & Hamilton, 2013; Mears et al., 2013; Reisig, Holtfreter, & Morash, 2002).

••• SPECIAL POPULATIONS

ELDERLY INMATES

As mentioned in the chapter on jails (Chapter 6), the number of elderly people in jails and prisons is increasing at an exponential rate. As America ages, and mandatory sentences and other such laws lengthen sentences, correctional populations are graying. There are a number of collateral consequences that derive from this fact, most of them unintended:

1. The cost of incarceration increases to accommodate the extra medical care needed for older people.

2. Elderly inmates are less able to work in or for the prison, making them a further economic drain on the system.

3. Elderly inmates may require housing that is separate from younger inmates who may prey on them.

4. Elderly inmates, particularly those who have spent much or all of their adult lives in prisons, are less likely to have a supportive family or friends waiting for them on the outside, which makes the development of a parole or reintegration plan even more challenging for them.

Because elderly inmates necessarily present such a drain on state and federal correctional budgets, it might make sense for states to rethink the sentencing laws and correctional practices that led to the graying of prison populations nationally (more about this rethinking in the last chapter of the book [Chapter 17]). To not do so is to support the continued exponential growth in correctional budgets at the expense of all other budget priorities.

PHYSICALLY ILL INMATES

The number of ill people incarcerated in America's prisons and jails has grown in tandem with the number of elderly inmates (see Figure 8.5). At this juncture, about half of inmates in prisons and jails report an illness more serious than a cold or the flu (Maruschak, 2008, p. 1; see also Maruschak, 2006, 2015). According to a 2004 survey of state and federal prison inmates by the Bureau of Justice Statistics, the two most prevalent medical problems for prison inmates were arthritis and hypertension (as cited in Maruschak, 2008). Women and elderly inmates in prisons, as in jails, report more medical problems than do other inmates. Heart disease and suicide accounted for most of the deaths in jails, while cancer and heart disease claimed more than half of those who died in state prisons, in 2011 and 2012 (Noonan et al., 2015).

The extent of medical care provided for such inmates depends on the jurisdiction, with some larger counties, some states, and the Bureau of Prisons at the federal level providing better care than other jurisdictions. According to the 2004 study mentioned above, about 70% of the state and 76% of the federal prison inmates with medical problems reported seeing a medical professional at the prison about their illness, and more than 80% reported receiving a medical exam since their admission (as cited in Maruschak, 2008, p. 1). However, even in those jurisdictions that can afford to and do provide decent medical care, it is often minimal. Dentistry typically consists of pulling teeth rather than crowning or even filling them. Not much preventive medical care is provided, and the common response to complaints is the provision of medication.

Most larger jails have a section devoted to their inmates with medical complaints. Larger prisons or prison systems often have buildings or whole institutions devoted to inmates with medical maladies. The staffing of such sections, buildings, or institutions again varies by jurisdiction and the ability and willingness to pay the high cost for qualified staff (Vaughn & Carroll, 1998; Vaughn & Smith, 1999). Working in a jail or prison medical facility has not usually been the first choice of medical personnel, and so it is not surprising that it might be hard to recruit and keep the best personnel.

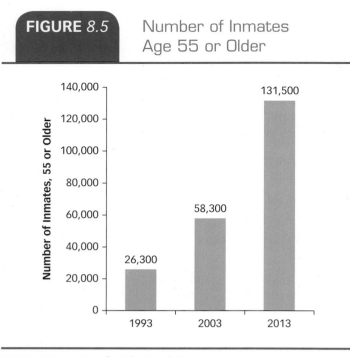

FIGURE *8.5*   Number of Inmates
Age 55 or Older

Source: U.S. Bureau of Justice Statistics.

MENTALLY ILL INMATES

The number of mentally ill inmates has also grown in America's prisons, although not to the same extent as it has in the jails (see Chapter 6). As jails became dumping grounds for the mentally ill after mental health hospitals closed during the 1970s, some of these inmates with chronic mental illnesses have found themselves in a prison environment (Slate & Wesley Johnson, 2008).

The **deinstitutionalization of the mentally ill** in the United States came about as a result of the civil rights movement and the related effort to increase the rights of powerless people (Slate & Wesley Johnson, 2008). Too many people were civilly committed to mental health institutions for years without any legal recourse or protection, it was thought. In addition, the pharmaceutical company Smith, Kline, & French (now GlaxoSmithKline) pushed its drug, Thorazine, as a potential "cure" for some mental illnesses with state legislators who were eager to save money by closing mental health institutions (Slate & Wesley Johnson, 2008). As legal restrictions on civil commitment of the mentally ill spread across the country, and as state legislators believed the claims (which turned out to be unfounded) of the pharmaceutical company, states and counties closed their mental health hospitals or reduced their capacities significantly. Congress passed the Community Mental Health Act in 1963, which ended much of the federal support for mental health hospitals. Instead, Congress was to fund less restrictive institutional alternatives, such as halfway houses, but outpatient facilities were either underfunded or shunted away by community members who did not want such facilities in their neighborhoods (Slate & Wesley Johnson, 2008). Thus, an unintended consequence of this deinstitutionalization movement was that there were few public services available in communities to assist the mentally ill and their families. Jails, and then prisons, became the de facto mental health patient dumping ground.

Unfortunately, as with those who have major medical problems, most prisons and jails are ill equipped and ill staffed to handle mentally ill inmates. There are difficulties in diagnosis, management of people who do not understand how to behave in a prison, programming and developing appropriate prison employment, and devising a reentry plan (Slate & Wesley Johnson, 2008). Any treatment programming available has a long waiting list. Sometimes staff need to be concerned that the mentally ill inmates require protection from predation, and to protect other inmates they will need to keep an eye on the violent outbursts of mentally ill patients because they might injure others (Wood & Buttaro, 2013). Some studies link posttraumatic stress disorder with an assault history, propensity for revictimization, violent behavior, substance abuse, and mental illness, so it is no surprise that there needs to be trauma-related treatments available for the mentally ill in prisons as well (Wood & Buttaro, 2013).

Needless to say, the cost of providing medical and mental health care to an aging and ill correctional population is cost-prohibitive. However, because these inmates are unable to access such services in communities due to their incarceration, such costs must be borne.

GAY, LESBIAN, BISEXUAL, TRANSGENDER, AND INTERSEX INMATES

The true number of gay, lesbian, bisexual, transgender, and intersex (LGBTI) inmates in corrections is not known. According to Gary Gates (personal communication,

Deinstitutionalization of the mentally ill: A result of the civil rights movement and the related effort to increase the rights of people involuntarily committed to mental hospitals.

PERSPECTIVE FROM A PRACTITIONER

Michael Klein, Former Correctional Officer

Position: Correctional Officer (2006–2009)

Location: Indiana Department of Corrections, Wabash Valley Correctional Facility

Education: M.A. in criminal justice; currently completing a Ph.D. in criminal justice

What is your previous experience in criminal justice?

I have worked as a juvenile correctional officer and in private security and social services.

What are the duties and responsibilities of a correctional officer?

Maintaining the safety and security of the facility, mediating offender disputes, ensuring one's personal security, ensuring the safety of offenders, and ensuring the safety of one's fellow officers.

What are the characteristics and traits most useful for a correctional officer?

Patience, courage, ability to work as a team member, understanding, ability to keep calm in disturbing situations, and a strong stomach.

What was your typical workday as a correctional officer?

First, I would enter the facility and go through a security check. I would then arrive at my post, greet the prior shift of officers, and sign into the logbook. I had several different positions within the Wabash Valley Correctional Facility, and my activities varied by position. If I worked in a cell house, there would be the initial rush of complaints, concerns, and questions from the offenders. I would then try my best to maintain a smooth shift as 100 offenders milled freely about me. If I worked in segregation, there was less offender contact, but there were a lot more messy situations to contain. The daily activities of a correctional officer are both banal and uncertain. You never really know what to expect.

What is your advice for future correctional officers?

Keep your cool, stay out of bad situations, and ask for help. Working in corrections is something that each officer has to figure out for himself or herself. Just be sure to think things through before making any rash judgments.

March 14, 2011), a demographer with the Williams Institute at the University of California, Los Angeles School of Law, estimates based on surveys that query people about their sexual orientation and **gender identity** (the gender one identifies with rather than the sex of one's genitalia when born) suggest that about 3% to 5% of the free community are gay, lesbian, or bisexual. Gates noted that the percentage of transgender (and likely intersex) people in the community is also unknown, but it is likely 1% or less. In a recent study published by the Williams Institute, the researchers estimated that, based on state-level surveys, about 0.6% of adults identify as transgender, or about 1.4 million people in the United States (Flores, Herman, Gates, & Brown, 2016, p. 1). Based on these estimates, we might reasonably expect that similar percentages for each group are represented in prisons. In addition, because heterosexual relations are formally restricted in prisons, there is some percentage of male and female inmates who engage in homosexual relations while incarcerated, although they may never have done so when they were free. Lieb and his colleagues (2011) found that the percentage of men who have ever had sex with men in the free community is around 6.4%. We might expect, therefore, that the percentage of men who engage in sexual relations with other men while in prison is likely around 6% or higher.

Gender identity: The gender one identifies with rather than the gender associated with the genitalia one is born with.

PERSPECTIVE FROM A FORMER INMATE

Rex E. Hammond, Former Inmate and Doctoral Student

Location: Indiana Department of Corrections

Education: M.A. in criminal justice; doctoral student in criminal justice

Previous experience in criminal justice: 27 years in juvenile and adult jails and prisons

Prison and Change

By Rex E. Hammond*

Quite often, people discuss the negative effects of incarceration, and there are a plethora of these to concentrate on: disrespecting prison staff; being treated like an animal by some correctional staff; engaging in fights, stabbings, and illegal gambling and drugs; learning new and different ways to commit crimes; and being oppressed, depressed, and separated from family and the larger society. However, I thought I would discuss a couple of the positive effects of spending more than 27 years (2 as a juvenile and 25 as an adult) behind concrete walls and razor wire fences.

Currently, I am a 51-year-old Ph.D. student. However, prior to this, I was a life course criminal. My crimes as a youth included the following: runaway, truancy, incorrigibility, theft, burglary, and armed robbery. As an adult, I took a deputy hostage in a county jail and was engaged in a series of armed robberies. My first run-in with the law was when I was 9 years old, and my last was at the age of 32; in between, I was repeatedly in and out of juvenile halls or adult jails and prisons. My last incarceration consisted of a 13.5-year stay in prison.

Students and professors may wonder what on Earth I could possibly have to say that is positive about spending more than half of my life imprisoned. Well, during a college presentation I gave, a female student asked me a question: "Have you ever thought about fate?" It was perhaps the best question I have ever been asked.

I had a brother who was 2 years older than me. He was my idol, and I looked up to him. He was a strong influence in my early life—introducing me to drugs, crime, and an uncontrollable temper; however, he never served prison time. He spent his life in the free community, only to become an alcoholic for more than 25 years. He was an ex-Marine, suffered from depression, was in and out

of volatile relationships, and was heavily addicted to gambling and prescription pills. Four months after my final release from prison, he committed suicide by parking on a country road, putting a handgun to his head, and pulling the trigger. So to answer the student's question, yes, since my brother's suicide, I have often thought of fate.

You see, had I not spent nearly my entire life incarcerated, the opportunities for me to become just like the brother I "idolized" would have greatly increased. I find that prison probably saved my life. Although it took me years to grow, understand, and mature, I was finally able to undergo enough self-reflection that I found the strength and self-determination to succeed. It was after getting my associate's degree in prison (2001), coupled with cognitive behavioral programming, that I was able to change the way I thought and then my behavior. Maybe this is very elementary, but early in my life I never knew that I could control the way I thought, thus changing my reactions and behavior. Throughout my life behind bars, I observed this to be true for many repeat or life course criminals. They think that they are reduced to reacting the way they have always reacted. Prison gave me the opportunity to alter my thinking process and to gain better control over my emotions.

When I first entered the adult Indiana prison system in 1983 at the age of 19, there were no college programs or cognitive behavioral programs. In addition, prisons were not designed for controlled offender movement, meaning inmates could move about the prison without accountability, oversight, or a particular schedule. This lack of control created plenty of opportunities for inmates to engage in violent acts against other inmates and other criminal behavior without detection. When I began my prison term, the only programming available was GED classes, vocational training, or work lines. While vocational training affords inmates the opportunity to learn an employment skill, it does nothing to help offenders make it through the strain and stressful situations they will encounter in society. It was not until the 1980s, after Dr. Stanton Samenow and Dr. Samuel Yochelson's studies of violent offenders, that the benefits of cognitive behavioral programming for prisoners became clear. Indiana's Department of Corrections began to adopt this change during the 1990s.

Life is all about being able to change and adapt. I began my incarceration as a young punk—engaging in unruly behavior, gambling, drugs, drinking homemade brew, tattooing, and fighting with prison staff, often finding myself spending months upon months in solitary confinement. Just like my brother, I was spinning out of control as each day passed. However, as the prison environment transformed, I found myself engaging in this adjustment and utilizing the opportunities that prison granted me. It gave me the opportunity to experience great personal growth. I also witnessed firsthand the way the Indiana prison system changed over a quarter of a century. Getting my college degree while imprisoned and participating in various cognitive behavioral programs afforded me the opportunity for self-development. While my brother spent 25 years sinking further into a darkened hole, prison gave me the chance to spend 25 years climbing out of one.

Discussion Questions

1. Do you think that if Rex (or inmates like him) had been afforded more programming earlier in his prison sentence, this might have changed his behavior earlier? Why or why not?

2. Is it possible that programming in the community could have been as helpful in changing Rex's behavior as it was in the prison?

3. What do you think would have happened if, instead of 25 years in prison, Rex's sentence was reduced to 10 or 15 years because of his successful completion of programming? In other words, what amount of time was sufficient punishment for his crimes and enough time for him to rehabilitate?

4. What can we learn about redemption and the renewal of one's spirit from Rex's story?

*Rex E. Hammond was a doctoral student in the Department of Criminal Justice and Criminology at Washington State University. He earned his bachelor's and master's degrees from the Department of Criminology and Criminal Justice at Indiana State University. Before that, he spent 27 years as an inmate in juvenile and adult jails and prisons.

As with gays and lesbians, the exact number of transgender and intersex people in communities is unknown because they often keep their feelings on this matter hidden, knowing that they might be marginalized (Tewksbury & Potter, 2005). In prisons, the number of transgender inmates is also difficult to know, although large male prisons will often house many (Sexton, Jenness, & Sumner, 2010). In their study of transgender female inmates in California prisons, Jenness and her colleagues (2007, as cited in Sexton et al., 2010) found that they are much more likely than other inmates (59% as compared with 4.4% for non-transgender inmates) to report being sexually assaulted while in prison (a report that is backed up by PREA-inspired research by the Bureau of Justice Statistics [Beck et al., 2013]).

Protecting sexual orientation and gender identity minorities in prisons presents a challenge for administrators, particularly in male prisons. Male bravado and posturing to show strength and ward off attacks is common in male prisons, which makes males who are unable or unwilling to put on such fronts targets for abuse or predation. If one is a transgender inmate in a male prison or a person who was once biologically male but through dress, hormonal treatment, and/or surgery is now female, the challenges mount. Not only must administrators be concerned about the safety of the inmate, but they also must figure out a way to accommodate her needs for privacy, medical treatment, and housing. As noted in the chapter on jails (Chapter 6), PREA regulations now require greater consideration of the privacy, respect, and medical needs of transgender and intersex inmates because they have been a particular target for abuse in jails and prisons, particularly transgender women in men's prisons (Routh et al., 2014; Sexton et al., 2010; Stohr, 2014).

In women's prisons, as with racial and ethnic minorities, there appears to be more acceptance of both lesbian and transgender inmates; part of this greater acceptance may have to do with the sense that women inmates have direct experience with marginalization and therefore are more understanding of those who vary from the norm in sexual orientation or gender identity. Or it might have to do with the lesser need of women in prisons to defend themselves physically from the predation of other inmates; the frequency of violent and sexual attacks in women's prisons by other inmates, as far as this can be determined, is much lower than it is in men's facilities (Britton, 2003).

SUMMARY

- Prisons come in various shapes and security levels.

- To varying degrees, inmates experience mortification and pain related to their status, and as humans they will behave in either pro- or antisocial ways to lessen that pain.

- Inmates adopt certain roles and engage in certain behaviors because they are prisonized and adopt the subculture or because they import aspects of the culture from the outside community into the prison.

- *Total institutions* exist to different degrees, depending on the security level and operation of prisons.

- Gangs and violence are one way that inmates "adjust" to their environment and have their needs met and their pain alleviated.

- Strategies to reduce violence exist and can be practiced by agencies interested in reducing violence.

- Mature coping is one way that correctional clients can fruitfully "adjust" and perhaps reform in that environment.

- Social support, even when inmates are on the "inside," may potentially have prosocial effects (e.g., reduce violence) while inmates are in the prison and after they leave.

- Special population inmates present unique challenges for administrators interested in meeting their needs and keeping them safe in the correctional environment.

KEY TERMS

Attica Prison riot (1971), 176

Deinstitutionalization of the mentally ill, 182

Gangs (prison), 171

Gender identity, 183

Importation, 167

Mature coping, 178

Maximum-security prisons, 162

Medium-security prisons, 163

Minimum-security prisons, 163

Mortification, 167

New Mexico Prison riot (1980), 176

Pains of imprisonment, 167

Prisonization, 167

Prisons, 159

Prison subculture, 169

Supermax prisons, 160

Total institution, 166

DISCUSSION QUESTIONS

1. Which prison, from our history of prison chapters, most reminds you of super-maximum-security prisons? What were the problems with this historical prison? Based on what we know of that prison from our history, what problems do you foresee arising with the supermax prisons of today?

2. Define what a *total institution* is and how it might vary by type of correctional arrangement (e.g., probation, parole, jail, prison) and inmate status.

3. Inmate subcultures are thought to be related to the concepts of prisonization, importation, and the pains of imprisonment. Discuss how and why this might be so.

4. What are the attributes of gangs that make them appealing to inmates in prisons? How might that appeal be reduced by prison managers?

5. What are some of the difficulties that correctional organizations might face in employing the strategies to reduce violence? Who would you expect to support these strategies, and who would not?

6. How might correctional clients configure their environment to ensure their own reform? How might we, as citizens, assist them in that endeavor?

7. What might be the most effective strategies for managing special populations in prisons?

CHAPTER 8 · PRISONS AND THE CORRECTIONAL CLIENT   **187**

$SAGE edge™

Review → Practice → Improve

Sharpen your skills with SAGE edge at **edge.sagepub.com/stohressentials3e**.

SAGE edge offers a robust online environment featuring an impressive array of free tools and resources for review, study, and further exploration, keeping both instructors and students on the cutting edge of teaching and learning.

FOR FURTHER EXPLORATION AND APPLICATION, TAKE A LOOK AT THE INTERACTIVE EBOOK FOR THESE PREMIUM RESOURCES:

- ▶ **Career Video 8.1** Defense Attorney
- ▶ **Feature Video 8.1** Prison Culture
- ▶ **SAGE News Clip 8.1** U.S. Prison Pizzas
- ▶ **SAGE News Clip 8.2** USA Prison Riot
- ▤ **Journal Article 8.1** Inmate Custody Levels and Prison Rule Violations

The Corrections Experience for Staff

TEST YOUR KNOWLEDGE

Test your current knowledge of work in corrections by answering the following questions. Check your answers on page 392 after reading the chapter.

1. Correctional officers are not called guards anymore. (True or false?)

2. Name three of the five characteristics of a profession.

3. Generally speaking, which job do you think pays the most and the least of these three (and why): police officer, correctional officer, or probation and parole officer?

4. Generally speaking, which job do you think requires the most education and which requires the least (and why): police officer, correctional officer, or probation and parole officer?

5. Television programs and movies tend to depict corrections work accurately. (True or false?)

6. A *role* is what a person does on the job every day. (True or false?)

7. What factors likely cause stress for correctional officers?

8. Unionized correctional officers make more money than nonunionized correctional officers. (True or false?)

LEARNING OBJECTIVES

- Compare what makes work a profession as opposed to just a job

- Describe the effect of growth in staff and clients or inmates

- Explain the importance of education and training in the correctional field

- Describe how and why demographic factors affect corrections

- Identify what correctional roles are

- Describe the influence of subculture and socialization on correctional officers

- Discuss why correctional staff might abuse power and experience stress and burnout

JOHN'S TRAGIC STORY

Mary K. Stohr

John was about 22 years old when I first met him as an inmate on my caseload at the adult male prison I worked at during the 1980s. I was his classification counselor and only a few years older than him at the time. He had a tragic life up until that point. He was abandoned, for the most part, by his father; his mother was hauled away to a mental institution in front of him when he was 5 years old; and foster care homes and struggling family members took care of him for the rest of his childhood. He was in and out of juvenile facilities, mostly for property crimes and joy riding, although he admitted that he had a problem in controlling his temper. He received very few visits because the people he loved (his girlfriend and sister) were poor and unable to make the trip often. His instant offense was one of those crimes (robbery)

that was technically serious, but the facts indicated it was really burglary. It was the 1980s, and the talk was all about being "tough on crime," and that meant criminals like John, too.

He would come in and talk to me at length once or twice a week about his life and his hopes (e.g., getting a job once released, staying out of prison, reuniting with his off-and-on estranged girlfriend). He seemed sincere and in need of a friend, but a correctional staffer can never cross the line or be "friends" with inmates, although he or she can be friendly to a point. One time, he came in to talk, and it was clear he had been crying; his dad was presumed to have killed himself by driving his truck into a lake on purpose and drowning. John was distraught, feeling that he had let down the father who had pretty much abandoned him. I talked to John for some time, and although upset, he seemed rational. Security staff wanted to put him in segregation, but I successfully argued against it. John continued to come to see me and seemed to need someone to talk to. Then, all of a sudden, about a month after his dad died, he stopped coming by. It was a Friday night, and I was getting ready to leave for the weekend and tracked him down at a Bingo game in the cafeteria. He was with one of his buddies, and when I asked him why I hadn't seen him during the last couple of weeks, he was noncommittal and uncharacteristically standoffish. I suspected something was wrong. In retrospect, I should have probed further and have always wondered if things would have turned out differently if I had.

The next morning, I came in and was told what had happened. John had escaped from the prison during the night (it was a restricted, minimum-custody prison with no fence) and stolen a motorcycle, ostensibly to try to see his girlfriend, who had recently broken up with him. He drove the bike wildly in downtown Vancouver, Washington, and attracted the attention of a police officer, who then gave chase. John refused to stop for the officer and instead sped up and seemingly purposefully drove straight into a concrete wall. He died instantly.

••• INTRODUCTION: WHAT IS A PROFESSION?

Work in corrections has changed a great deal from the *shire reeves* (the Old English name for sheriffs) who ran the jails in England during the Middle Ages and the guards who staffed the first Pennsylvania and Auburn prisons. For one thing, security staff in correctional facilities are no longer referred to as *guards,* because that title is thought to reflect a more primitive role, and are instead formally referred to as *correctional officers,* perhaps a reflection of the move to professional status for these staff.

Yet the public does not generally see corrections work as a profession. Other than probation and parole work (which, not coincidentally, usually requires more education and pays more), most college students do not identify work in jails or prisons as their career goal either. In addition, despite a century of effort by some determined correctional administrators, corrections organizations (such as the American Correctional Association [ACA], the American Jail Association, and the American Probation and Parole Association), and academicians, many correctional jobs are not structured like a profession. A **profession** is typified by five characteristics: (1) prior educational attainment involving college, (2) formal training on the job or just prior to the start of the job, (3) pay and benefits that are commensurate with the work, (4) the ability to exercise discretion, and (5) work that is guided by a code of ethics (Stohr & Collins, 2014). Yet most jobs in corrections still do not adequately meet the first three of these criteria for professional status, and although most correctional workplaces either have their own code of ethics or are nominally guided by that of a corrections organization (e.g., see the ACA's Code of Ethics in In Focus 9.1), there is no enforcement of this code as there is for medical doctors with the American Medical Association or for lawyers with the American Bar Association.

Profession:
Distinguished by prior educational attainment involving college, formal training on the job or just prior to the start of the job, pay and benefits that are commensurate with the work, the ability to exercise discretion, and work that is guided by a code of ethics.

In this chapter, we explore the nature of correctional work as it has evolved and as it is shaped by professionalism, the requirements of the job, and clients and inmates. We review the factors that lead to stress and turnover for officers and how those might be addressed. Although correctional work is often not the first choice of a college graduate, it does have its own appeal, and we discuss why that might be so and how it has grown during the last three decades.

••• THE STATE OF THE WORK IN CORRECTIONAL INSTITUTIONS AND PROGRAMS

GROWTH IN STAFF AND CLIENTS OR INMATES

In addition to exploding inmate and offender populations, the number of employees in corrections, albeit often undereducated, undertrained, and underpaid for their work, has grown astronomically during the last quarter century. From 1982 to 2006, there was a nearly 600% increase in direct expenditures for all criminal justice agencies (i.e., police, courts, and corrections). (For the latest data available at the time of this publication, see Figure 9.1.) During that same time period, just the expenditures for corrections increased by 660%. Surprisingly, employment in corrections more than doubled, from 300,000 to 765,466, during this time period, with the majority of those employees being correctional officers (66%) working in state and local correctional facilities and programs, both public and private (K. Hughes, 2006; Perry, 2008; Stephan, 2008, p. 4). By 2014, more than 686,000 people worked in state and local corrections alone (U.S. Census Bureau, 2014b, p. 1). At the state level, where most prisons and most adult probation and parole agencies are operated and funded, three-quarters or more of the correctional budget was spent on correctional institutions through 2011 (Kyckelhahn, 2014, p. 2). Most correctional spending occurs at the state level (57.3%), while about a third (32.5%) is spent by local governments and about 10.0% is spent at the federal level (Kyckelhahn, 2015, Table 201). Given the recession that began in 2007 and ended about 3 or 4 years later and the decarceration

we are seeing at the state and federal levels (Kaeble, Glaze, Tsoutis, & Minton, 2016), however, it is likely that these increases have not continued. In fact, as indicated by Figure 9.2, by far most employees of state and local governments are employed in education (either K–12 or higher education), by hospitals, or by the police.

Of these employees, in 2005 (the latest date for which we have figures), the majority, particularly those who work directly with inmates as correctional staff, were males by a 3-to-1 ratio (Stephan, 2008, p. 2). In federal facilities, the gender differences were largest, with 87% of correctional officers being male and only 13% being female. The smallest gender employment difference was in the 400-plus private facilities, where 52% were

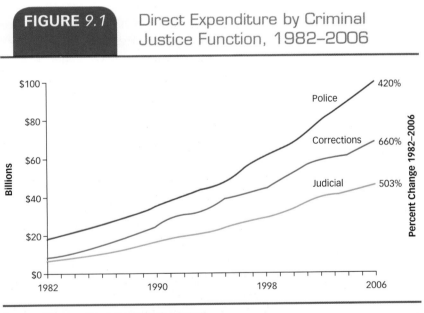

FIGURE 9.1   Direct Expenditure by Criminal Justice Function, 1982–2006

Source: Bureau of Justice Statistics (2008).

Note: Most recent data available.

male and 48% were female. In the more numerous state correctional facilities, there were 74% male correctional officers compared with 26% female (Stephan, 2008, p. 2). Notably, these gender differences by level and type of facility very closely align with pay differences. Among prisons, federal correctional officers, who are much more likely to be male, are the best paid, and private facility

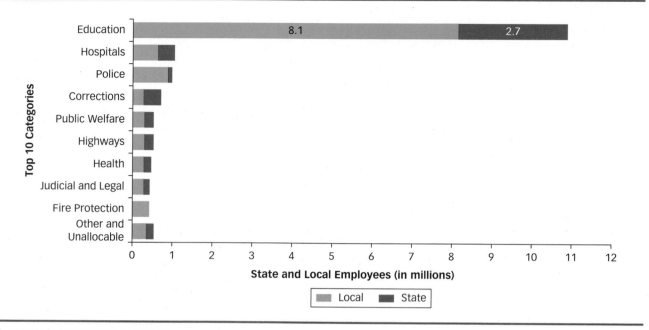

FIGURE 9.2   State and Local Government Employees by Field of Work

Source: U.S. Census Bureau (2014b).

correctional officers, who are almost as likely to be female, are paid the least (see Table 9.1 regarding private vs. public pay for correctional work).

Even with this growth in staff numbers overall, whether male or female, the proportional growth in inmates has been much larger. As a result, the ratio of inmates to staff in prisons grew significantly from 2000 to 2005, with the most inmates to correctional staff in federal prisons (10.3 in 2006 but decreasing to 4.4 in 2015) and private prisons (6.9 vs. 5.0 in public prisons) in 2005, as compared with state prisons (4.9) (Davidson, 2015, p. 1; Stephan, 2008, p. 5). Likewise, jails continue to hold in the neighborhood of 82% of their capacity (Minton & Golinelli, 2014, p. 3), and the caseloads of parole officers at the state level (data on state or federal probation officer caseloads and parole officer caseloads at the federal level were not available) range around 38 per officer (Bonczar, 2008, p. 1). Simply put, staff working in corrections are stretched very thin despite the growth in their numbers. In addition, as is indicated

TABLE 9.1   Median Annual Pay for Full-Time Workers

	Correctional Officers and Jailers	Probation Officers and Treatment Specialists	Police and Sheriffs
Public local, state, and federal	$45,320*	$54,080*	$61,270*
Private	$21,216^	Not available	$45,594^

Source: U.S. Department of Labor. *Occupational Employment Statistics* (2015).

*Data from 2015.

^Data from 2010.

in Figure 9.3, the employment of correctional officers in prisons and jails varies somewhat by state and locality, with states and local jurisdictions with larger populations employing the most.

Given these numbers of inmates and clients, one can appreciate the organizational problems that develop for correctional managers seeking to hire, train, and retain the best employees to do this difficult work. Perhaps in part because of this recognized need to get and keep the best employees, the management of correctional institutions and programs has shifted over the years as efforts to professionalize, democratize (allow more say in the work by those doing it), and standardize work in corrections has had some success.

In general, compensation that is commensurate with job requirements and skills is a clear indication of the value given to a particular profession. It is true that it would be difficult to regard some correctional institutions or programs or their staff as *professionals* because they do not meet the educational, training, and pay requirements of a profession. However, there are a number of correctional institutions and programs that have made much progress in this area, although the path to professionalization and the creation of a work environment that is conducive to employee growth and welfare are not always achieved.

So if we were to imagine a continuum of correctional professionalism across the field, we could probably generalize that community corrections officers (probation and parole officers) and their work are more professionalized—defined as having more education, training, and pay—than are prison and jail correctional officers (see Table 9.1). (We discuss ethics separately at the end of the chapter, and it was also covered in Chapter 4.) Next along that continuum would come correctional officers who work in public prisons

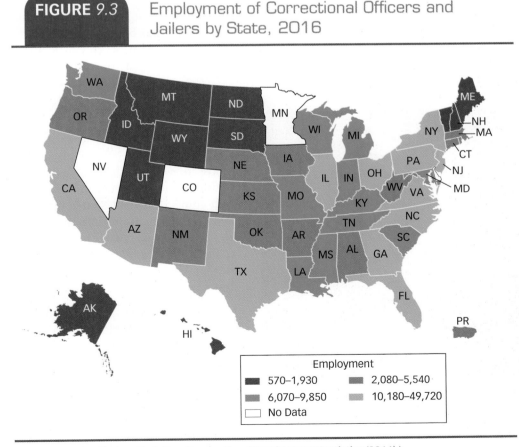

FIGURE 9.3   Employment of Correctional Officers and Jailers by State, 2016

Employment
- 570–1,930
- 2,080–5,540
- 6,070–9,850
- 10,180–49,720
- No Data

Source: Bureau of Labor Statistics. *Occupational Employment Statistics* (2016b).

and then those who work in public jails. Of course, these generalizations do not hold true for every institution or every locality. For instance, in some larger city jails, officers might be paid and trained as well as or better than prison officers or even adult probation and parole officers. Typically, jail officers in large counties are paid more than those in small counties and often—but not always—are paid less than state- and federal-level correctional officers. Usually, federal-level community corrections officers make more than prison officers at their level of government (e.g., at the federal or state level) (Stohr & Collins, 2014). These data do indicate that attempts to professionalize corrections, as it pertains to pay, need more effort in some areas than in others.

Note that police officers at both the state and local levels are paid about $18,000 more per year than correctional officers and more than $8,000 more than probation and parole officers in any given state (see Table 9.1). Therefore, it is not surprising that both local and state police officers, along with probation and parole officers, are more likely to require at least some college and possibly a college degree. Students of criminal justice tend to recognize this difference in that when asked what they want to do when they graduate, they are more likely to identify police or community corrections (probation and parole) jobs as desirable over work in a prison or jail.

Notably, the push to privatize correctional and law enforcement work since the 1980s has not resulted in better pay for staff. In fact, as is illustrated in Table 9.1, privately employed correctional and law enforcement officers' median pay is about $24,000 less for the former and $14,000 less for the latter than for comparable jobs in the public sector. (Notably, these data were not collected for the same year, and that might account for some of the difference.) If better pay is correlated with a more professional workforce, we can conclude that the privatization efforts are not moving us in that direction.

PERCEIVED BENEFITS OF CORRECTIONAL WORK

There are many reasons why people who work in corrections might find it gratifying. For one, people are attracted to correctional work because it has been a booming business for a number of decades, creating thousands of jobs in the process. Correctional work also provides a steady, if not lucrative, paycheck (U.S. Census Bureau, 2010; see Table 9.1).

© Marmaduke St. John/Alamy Stock Photo

PHOTO 9.1: Correctional staff in the control center at the Santa Ana, California, city jail. Control center staff have the challenging job of monitoring several screens at once and are responsible for the electronic unlocking and locking of most doors in the facility.

People who want to make a difference in other people's lives, to end the tragic circumstances that tend to produce a cycle of street-level criminals, might choose to work with juveniles in corrections or in treatment programming with adults or juveniles on community supervision or in institutions. When they see someone change for the better and know they might have contributed to that change, this is when correctional work can be personally fulfilling.

It is also possible that those who are attracted to correctional work are curious about the human psyche and how it operates. Working with people who have engaged in seriously deviant behavior enhances the understanding about why people behave the way they do. Some might also find it rewarding to be engaged in keeping these seriously deviant and violent offenders off the streets and, in that sense, to be part of the justice-dispensing machinery that is corrections.

COLLECTIVE BARGAINING

Correctional staff moved to unionize as a means of gaining power vis-à-vis administrators. As we know from our history of corrections, the wardens of earlier prisons (and this is still true, to some extent, today in some correctional institutions) often acted like dictators over their fiefdoms, the prisons (Bergner, 1998; Rideau, 2010). It was not only inmates who were their subjects but also staff, who were relatively powerless to voice their concerns or to earn a decent and livable wage. By unionizing, correctional staff working at the state and local levels were able to gain some collective power to bargain with administrators to improve their own work conditions. A *union worker* is defined by the U.S. Department of Labor (2010) as follows:

> Any employee in a union occupation when all of the following conditions are met: a labor organization is recognized as the bargaining agent for all workers in the occupation; wage and salary rates are determined through collective bargaining or negotiations; and settlement terms, which must include earnings provisions and may include benefit provisions, are embodied in a signed, mutually binding collective bargaining agreement. A nonunion worker is an employee in an occupation not meeting the conditions for union coverage. (p. 1)

A number of concerns regarding unionization have been raised, however, and these include the belief that unionization restricts the ability of administrators to fire incompetent people, that union contracts are too restrictive regarding the work that people can do, and that in some cases unions have worked to increase incarceration as a means of increasing job opportunities. Although some of these concerns may have merit, it is also true that those states with unionized correctional staff pay those staff more and provide more benefits for them (see Table 9.2), which is likely to increase the ability of those states to attract and keep better and more professional workers. If it is harder for administrators to fire incompetent unionized workers, it is also harder for administrators to fire people based on their politics or simply because they do not like them. Such contrarian voices in the workforce (those who disagree with administrative practices) often provide an important check on the power of administrators, and unions give such people protection from the wrath of those administrators who might want to retaliate against "contrarians."

Although the union for correctional officers in California did lobby to increase the number of institutions and jobs in corrections in that state during the 1990s, it is possible that union leaders were just representing the sentiments of their membership. Correctional staff tend to be somewhat conservative regarding crime issues and so would tend to support, like the general public of the 1980s, 1990s, and 2000s, the creation of more correctional institutions.

TABLE 9.2	Mean Hourly Wages of Union and Nonunion State and Local Correctional Workers and Law Enforcement	
	Union	**Nonunion**
Probation and parole	$27.69	$21.00
Correctional officers and jailers	23.36	14.74
Police	30.42	20.97

Source: U.S. Department of Labor (2010). Data taken from Table 13.

PHOTO 9.2: Stanford Prison Experiment "inmate"

••• WHY REQUIRE MORE EDUCATION AND TRAINING?

First of all—and unfortunately—most correctional institutions and programs do not have prior educational requirements that would elevate them to the level of a profession. Although it is true that many probation and parole officers must have a college degree or at least some college to qualify for the job, most jails, prisons (with the exception of federal correctional officers, who must have a bachelor's degree and experience), and even juvenile institutions (including those with a greater emphasis on rehabilitative programming) often do not require such a qualification from applicants.

STANFORD PRISON EXPERIMENT

Yet the oft-cited **Stanford Prison Experiment** provides a powerful argument for the value of formal education and training for correctional staff. In this 1971 experiment, volunteer students, with no training as officers and only their own expectations and beliefs to guide them, were divided into officers and inmates in a makeshift "prison" (Haney, Banks, & Zimbardo, 1981). The "officers" were outfitted in uniforms, including reflective sunglasses, and given nightsticks. The "inmates" were given sack-like attire. Neither "officers" nor "inmates" were told of any rules or policies to guide or restrict their behavior. Predictably, a few of these "officers" or "guards" engaged in verbal and psychological abuse of the "inmates." In the end, about a third of the "officers" engaged in the abuse, and others stood by while it was going on. The experiment was stopped after a few days and is often referenced as an example of how correctional work and the subcultures that develop as part of the job can foster corrupt behavior by officers.

The problem with the experiment, however, was that the "officers" were never given any education or training in corrections work. They were directed to exercise their discretion in controlling the inmates, but it was a discretion that was not necessarily anchored to any history or knowledge of "best practices" in corrections. Rather, the "choices" made by the "officers" in the absence of any education and training were likely shaped by the movies and popular press depictions of corrections that tended to reinforce the stereotypes of the institutions, programs, and work. Not knowing how best to "get people to do what they otherwise wouldn't" (Dahl's [1961] definition of **power**), the "guards" used what knowledge of corrections they had, even if it was all wrong.

ABU GHRAIB

The **Abu Ghraib** scandal of 2004, in which prisoners were tortured by mostly untrained "correctional officers" in the American-operated Abu Ghraib military prison in Iraq, tends to reinforce the lessons of the Stanford Prison Experiment, even contrived as those circumstances were. At Abu Ghraib, some correctional officers made inmates sleep naked, crawl on the floor, and pose in pyramids naked (while staff took pictures). A number of officers also deprived inmates of food and basic necessities and engaged in physical torture. The U.S. Army's investigation of the abuses at Abu Ghraib found that officers engaged in the following:

Breaking chemical lights and pouring the phosphoric liquid on detainees; pouring cold water on naked detainees; beating detainees with a broom handle and a chair; threatening male detainees with rape; allowing a military police guard to

Stanford Prison Experiment: A 1971 experiment conducted at Stanford University that used volunteer students divided into officers and inmates in a makeshift "prison." In the end, about a third of the "officers" engaged in the abuse of "inmates," and other "officers" stood by while it was going on.

Power: The ability to "get people to do what they otherwise wouldn't" (Dahl, 1961).

Abu Ghraib: An Iraq prison operated by the American military during the war in which prisoners were tortured by mostly untrained "correctional officers."

stitch the wound of a detainee who was injured after being slammed against the wall in his cell; sodomizing a detainee with a chemical light and perhaps a broom stick, and using military working dogs to frighten and intimidate detainees with threats of attack, and in one instance actually biting a detainee. (Hersh, 2004, p. 1)

While the U.S. Army wanted to blame the abuses that occurred at Abu Ghraib on untrained and rogue staffers at the prison (and six of them were prosecuted), the blame for the abuses extended up the chain of command to the Army Reserve brigadier general in charge of all Iraqi prisons—although she had had no previous experience or training in running prisons (she was relieved of command)—and perhaps as high as Defense Secretary Donald Rumsfeld:

> As the international furor grew, senior military officers, and President George W. Bush, insisted that the actions of a few did not reflect the conduct of the military as a whole. Taguba's report [Major General Antonio M. Taguba investigated what happened at Abu Ghraib], however, amounts to an unsparing study of collective wrongdoing and the failure of Army leadership at the highest levels. The picture he draws of Abu Ghraib is one in which Army regulations and the Geneva conventions were routinely violated, and in which much of the day-to-day management of the prisoners was abdicated to Army military-intelligence units and civilian contract employees. Interrogating prisoners and getting intelligence, including by intimidation and torture, was the priority. (Hersh, 2004, p. 4)

Simply put, the lesson from these incidents and countless corrections scandals over the years that have involved the systematic abuse of inmates by staff is that some people will not act professionally—or even decently—especially when they have no education or training in that profession. The training and education will not necessarily prevent all such abuses (at least two of the officers involved in Abu Ghraib had prior experience as correctional officers in Virginia and presumably some training in that state), but they will at least provide the officers with the knowledge and skills to do the job the way it should be done.

Correctional work often does not resemble other professions because the formal training provided for many new hires, including the number of hours required and the quality of that training, does not approach the level of other professions, which may schedule months of training (e.g., police departments with an average of 761 hours, or 19 weeks, of training for new recruits [Reaves, 2009]) or extensive internships, months or years in duration, in other fields (e.g., teachers, social workers, doctors).

The typical correctional job has lesser requirements for formal training or structured experience. For instance, in a *Corrections Compendium* (Clayton, 2003) survey, the researchers found that 31 of the reporting U.S. agencies required at least 200 hours of preservice training for those planning to work in a correctional institution. Likewise, in a quick survey of 150 directors and staff trainers, with responses received from 13 states or agencies in April 2004, the Juvenile Justice Trainers Association found that about 140 to 180 hours of preservice, academy-like training are required for most new hires in juvenile facilities (personal correspondence with B. Collins, May 2004).

Moreover, in some professions, the requisite college or professional degree is geared toward the

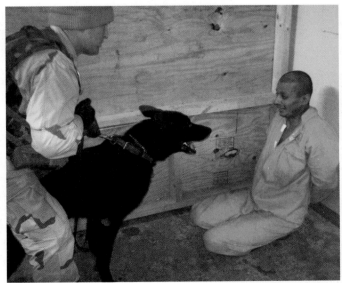

PHOTO 9.3: Inmate at the Abu Ghraib prison being terrorized by a staff dog.

work itself (e.g., computer programming, law school, master's in social work). Yet when a college degree is *required* for a job in corrections, it is rarely specifically a criminal justice degree but is typically one or more of the social science degrees, which might include no classes on corrections or the criminal justice system at all.

The American Probation and Parole Association (APPA) and the National Institute of Corrections, along with researchers affiliated with the Academy of Criminal Justice Sciences (ACJS), have been meeting for several years at ACJS trying to devise a college curriculum that fits the role of probation and parole officers in the community (B. Garland & Matz, 2017). After surveying ACJS, APPA, and American Society of Criminology members, B. Garland and Matz (2017) found the following:

> Results indicate that both groups, especially practitioners, gave the strongest preference to coverage of universally applicable job skills such as critical thinking, written and oral communication, and organizational and listening skills. Practitioners generally expected classroom learning to be more in depth and applied than faculty members. Some of the most substantial gaps in expectations were found for daily routine items such as interview skills with offenders, on-the-job decision-making, providing courtroom testimony, and stress coping. (p. 259)

B. Garland and Matz (2017) recommended that colleges and universities reconsider their offerings in criminal justice and criminology curricula in light of these findings to ensure that they provide the critical skills future employees need to succeed on the job. Notably, such skills as critical thinking, written and oral communication, and organizational and listening skills are essential for success in many lines of work and in life in general. The authors of this textbook would comment that they have never had a practitioner come into their class to talk about work in the system (not just corrections) who didn't remark on the need for all of these skills.

Of course, these deficits in formal education and knowledge base and in training leave correctional workers less suited to perform their job in anything approaching a historical or present-day, research-based context. When they have not studied corrections or been provided with sufficient training, they might not understand the reason why some practices are undertaken or why others are abandoned. They do not have the requisite tools to suggest changes or the background in research to know whether something "works" or not. Their ability to behave and develop as professionals is limited. So when they use their *discretion* (defined here as the ability to make choices and to act or not act on them), they could be making ill-informed choices that are not based on knowledge or experience and are overly influenced by their personal ideology, politics, or the media (Merlo & Benekos, 2000).

ETHICS

Not surprisingly, and as was discussed in this chapter and the chapter on ethics (Chapter 4), there have been numerous instances of documented ethical abuses by staff that include sexual assaults—beatings and rapes of clients on probation and parole as well as of inmates in jails and prisons in the United States (Amnesty International, 2004; Bard, 1997; Schofield, 1997; Serrano, 2006). As a means of preventing such abuses, correctional agencies will often adopt ethics codes, such as those promulgated by the ACA (see In Focus 9.1) and the American Jail Association, and train people on what is right and wrong behavior in corrections.

The importance of training correctional workers initially and throughout their careers on what constitutes ethical behavior cannot be overemphasized. Just as important as the

IN FOCUS 9.1

ACA Code of Ethics

Preamble

The American Correctional Association expects of its members unfailing honesty, respect for the dignity and individuality of human beings, and a commitment to professional and compassionate service. To this end, we subscribe to the following principles.

1. Members shall respect and protect the civil and legal rights of all individuals.

2. Members shall treat every professional situation with concern for the welfare of the individuals involved and with no intent to personal gain.

3. Members shall maintain relationships with colleagues to promote mutual respect within the profession and improve the quality of service.

4. Members shall make public criticism of their colleagues or their agencies only when warranted, verifiable, and constructive.

5. Members shall respect the importance of all disciplines within the criminal justice system and work to improve cooperation with each segment.

6. Members shall honor the public's right to information and share information with the public to the extent permitted by law subject to individuals' right to privacy.

7. Members shall respect and protect the right of the public to be safeguarded from criminal activity.

8. Members shall refrain from using their positions to secure personal privileges or advantages.

9. Members shall refrain from allowing personal interest to impair objectivity in the performance of duty while acting in an official capacity.

10. Members shall refrain from entering into any formal or informal activity or agreement that presents a conflict of interest or is inconsistent with the conscientious performance of duties.

11. Members shall refrain from accepting any gift, service, or favor that is or appears to be improper or implies an obligation inconsistent with the free and objective exercise of professional duties.

12. Members shall clearly differentiate between personal views/statements and views/statements/positions made on behalf of the agency or Association.

13. Members shall report to appropriate authorities any corrupt or unethical behaviors in which there is sufficient evidence to justify review.

14. Members shall refrain from discriminating against any individual because of race, gender, creed, national origin, religious affiliation, age, disability, or any other type of prohibited discrimination.

15. Members shall preserve the integrity of private information; they shall refrain from seeking information on individuals beyond that which is necessary to implement responsibilities and perform their duties; members shall refrain from revealing nonpublic information unless expressly authorized to do so.

16. Members shall make all appointments, promotions, and dismissals in accordance with established civil service rules, applicable contract agreements, and individual merit rather than furtherance of personal interests.

17. Members shall respect, promote, and contribute to a workplace that is safe, healthy, and free of harassment in any form.

Source: Reprinted from the ACA website (www.aca.org), with permission from the American Correctional Association, Alexandria, VA.

training, however, is ensuring that ethical people work in the organization. To do this, managers might consider using selection instruments and practices geared toward weeding out those who have little understanding of what is right and wrong and promoting only those people who exhibit that understanding in their daily work.

CORRECTIONAL WORK IS LITTLE UNDERSTOOD

It is possible that students and the general public might not view correctional work as a desirable career choice because they do not understand it. The truth is that probably few people outside of correctional work (or academe) know how institutions and community supervision actually operate, nor do they hold the roles of staff working in those agencies in very high regard. Students are acculturated by media preoccupied with violence that tend to depict correctional institutions as dark, corrupt places peopled by abusive or, at a minimum, cynical and distant "guards" (Conover, 2001; Johnson, 2002; O'Sullivan, 2006). In movies and television specials, prisons are almost always maximum security, old, and noisy; jails are crowded and huge monstrosities; and juvenile facilities are depressing and havens for child predators. Perhaps just as discouraging, community corrections, which is arguably—based on our criteria here—the most professionalized sector of corrections, is rarely depicted in the mass media at all (Lutze, 2014).

Unfortunately, the mass media are not alone in misleading the public and students of criminal justice and criminology about corrections and correctional work. Academics have also tended to focus much of their attention on only the biggest and "baddest" of correctional institutions and programs and the labor of their staff. Maximum-security institutions and, to a lesser extent, metropolitan city jails have been showcased, although they are not the norm for most corrections in this country (e.g., see Conover, 2001; Hassine, 1996; J. Jacobs, 1977; Johnson, 2002; Morris, 2002; Sykes, 1958). Research on these institutions tends to focus on the negative, or what the institutions or staff are doing wrong, rather than on what is working well. Of course, it is understandable that the "negative" shines through when these particular institutions and their type are the center of attention; given the makeup of their inmate population and the likelihood that they are overcrowded and understaffed, there is much that is amiss in such places.

Predictably, work in probation and parole, much like the study of jail staff, receives short shrift by academics who tend, like the media, to be preoccupied with what is "sexy," violent, and controversial (Lutze, 2014). Given these depictions by the media and academics, it is hard to discern the truth about correctional institutions and programs and work in them because it is clear that the work is underappreciated, little understood, and hampered by misguided perceptions of it.

••• INDIVIDUAL-LEVEL FACTORS THAT AFFECT THE CORRECTIONAL WORKPLACE

RACE OR ETHNICITY AND GENDER

Clearly, people who are unqualified for a job should not be hired, but if two people are roughly comparable in terms of skills and abilities, should the employer look for other personal features, such as race, gender, military background, and age, to determine who would be the best hire for the organization? Whether people will admit it or not, such matters do enter the calculus of who gets hired and promoted in organizations. (The topics of gender and race will be explored in greater detail in Chapters 11 and 12.) Left to their own devices and without the pressure that courts brought, the hiring of minorities and women did not occur in most criminal justice agencies to any extent until after the Civil Rights Act (CRA) of 1964 was passed and modified in 1972 to include gender (Stohr & Collins, 2014). Before the passage of this law and its modification, most employees in criminal justice agencies were very homogeneous in terms of race/ethnicity and gender, and today—about 45 years later—this is still true in some organizations but to a much

PERSPECTIVE FROM A PRACTITIONER

Michael Klein, Former Correctional Officer

It was a curious bit of the informal slang that makes up the diction of prison life. I first heard it when I was a new officer. I think that I had been out of training for maybe 1 or 2 weeks at the time, and I was working a cell house. It was time for nightly cell searches. I walked into my ordered cell, and I started to search. Contraband. Nothing major. The offenders in the cell had eight hardboiled eggs. It doesn't seem like a big deal to have eight hardboiled eggs, but that amount of hardboiled eggs could only have been smuggled out of the dining hall. I gathered up my booty and exited the cell. To be honest, I wasn't going to write the offenders up; I was just going to trash the eggs. So there I was, walking through the dayroom and holding my inconsequential find. All eyes were on me. One hundred offenders stared. I didn't really think much of it. I was new. I was used to offenders staring at me and sizing me up. An offender who we called "Shady" moseyed up to my workstation where I had just set the eggs.

"You're taking their food?" he asked.

I shrugged. "I guess."

"Why?"

"Because they're not supposed to have it."

Shady sighed.

"They don't have any money. They don't get any other zoom-zooms or wham-whams."

"What's that mean?" I asked.

"You know. Cakes. Commissary. Treats. Food. They don't get no other food. Don't take their eggs, man."

I then looked around the room. The offenders were staring at me in their curious way of looking while not looking.

It was my turn to sigh. "OK."

Shady smiled, picked up the eggs, and walked them back to the cell. I could feel a ripple of approval flowing through the room. In training, they would tell us that the offenders would try to "fish" or scam us. I don't think that's what happened. I don't think they were trying to scam me. I think that the offenders approved of me giving back the eggs because Shady was right. The offenders in that cell had no family or friends. They had no one to send them money for zoom-zooms and wham-whams. The offenders approved because I had treated the offenders like *people,* not inmates. It was the first time I realized that the offenders in the prison weren't animals or monsters. They were just people. They just wanted a cake, a cookie, or an egg. They just wanted that one moment of daily sweetness. We all need zoom-zooms and wham-whams. There are a lot of epiphanies when you work with offenders, and these sudden moments of realization come out of nowhere. Training might not prepare you, but I found that if you just realize that the offenders are people caught in a bad situation, it will make the job a whole lot easier.

lesser extent or not true at all in others. Correctional organizations, like other criminal justice agencies, did not hire women (except to work with other women or with children and in both cases for less pay) or minorities until they were forced to by the CRA and sometimes by lawsuits. One of the authors of this book worked as a correctional officer for an adult male prison in Washington State in 1983, and she was only the second woman hired there; the other woman had been hired only a month before. The warden told her that he had fought central office for years about hiring any minorities or women. When promoted to the counselor position the next year at that same prison, she was the first woman in the history of that institution to work as a counselor. At the time she worked there, only one Hispanic officer was employed and the warden did not want him there. The warden told the author that he would never hire a black man or woman for

PHOTO 9.4: A correctional officer addressing inmates. Correctional staff are often called on to lead inmates and to instruct them on how the organization works.

a correctional position. Fast forward 30 years, and women and minority group members have integrated the correctional workplace at all levels and in every position. There are women correctional officers in maximum-security prisons and working as juvenile probation officers. There are minority group members who serve as wardens and directors of corrections and who serve on the line in medium-security prisons. Is corrections fully integrated? The answer to that question is no, not fully, but the law and courts have made it possible for all qualified applicants to work in correctional organizations so that they better reflect the composition of their communities.

As the correctional workplace has diversified, so has the importance of race in that it might affect workers' perceptions of each other and their labor (Camp, Steiger, Wright, Saylor, & Gilman, 2013). Employees of different racial and ethnic groups perceive that their job opportunities are shaped by their race or ethnicity and the race or ethnicity of others in their workplace. Managers, therefore, need to be cognizant of these perceptions and sensitive to them as they hire, train, and promote people.

As much as race, the change in gender composition of the employee workplace has had an effect on correctional worker attitudes, perceptions, and behavior. We will discuss the effect of gender much more in Chapter 11, but suffice it to say here that some research has found that female staff are as capable as male staff and bring a different supervisory style to the work from that of men (Britton, 2003; Jurik & Halemba, 1984). When one of the authors of this book first started in corrections, she had several inmates and officers who approached her and remarked on how the language had become less harsh by staff and inmates since she and another woman had integrated the correctional officer workforce. She and the other female officer had done nothing to change the language; rather, those around them thought that the language should change because of their presence.

Regarding sexual harassment in the correctional workplace, the research indicates that female workers are more likely to be harassed by male coworkers or supervisors than are male workers to be similarly harassed by females (Stohr, Mays, Beck, & Kelley, 1998). However, when inmates are harassed by staff, the harassment is not merely restricted to female victims and male offenders, nor is it limited to just staff (Marquart et al., 2001). Recent research indicates that female officers are much more involved, particularly in the more minor and "consensual" versions of sexual harassment of male inmates, than are their male counterparts. In an example of a serious *boundary violation* in this regard, a female McNeil Island Prison (Washington State) nurse, hired in 2005, was fired in 2006 for allegedly having an intimate sexual relationship with a violent sex offender. Yet she continued to call him and have phone sex with him and visit him after her firing, and that was not even the worst of her behavior vis-à-vis this inmate: "In 2007 and 2008, she reportedly smuggled in 50 pornographic movies to the inmate and delivered crack cocaine to him 11 times" (Glenn, 2010, p. A4).

AGE

Correctional agencies will also consider the age of the applicant when making a hiring decision. None will hire below age 18, and many will require that the applicant be at least 21. Correctional agencies do not typically have an upper age limit for hiring as police departments legally do; rarely will police departments hire people in their 30s unless they have prior experience, and almost never will departments make a first hire of an officer who is in his or her 40s or older. Most of the time, the initial hires in corrections are people in their 20s and 30s. Depending on the job specified and the correctional clients worked with, correctional work can be a physically taxing and stressful job, which is why agencies will tend to target younger workers. When the job has fewer physical requirements (e.g., counseling, treatment programming, work as a probation or parole officer), the agency is much more likely to hire a worker in his or her 40s or older. What correctional and police agencies may fail to realize, however, is that more mature workers are able to bring a level of human experience and wisdom that might compensate for what they lack in physical agility in the management of inmates and clients.

PRIOR MILITARY SERVICE

Another personal characteristic, beyond race or ethnicity and gender, of workers that tends to shape the correctional environment is prior military service. Such experience is usually considered favorably by correctional agencies seeking to hire. Some agencies will state such a preference explicitly, and others will provide extra points for military service when applications are assessed. Whether such military service better prepares workers to handle jobs in corrections is not a settled matter either, although the militaristic accoutrements of correctional work (the uniform, military titles, command structure, etc.) would certainly make ex–military officers feel at home in some correctional workplaces.

••• CORRECTIONAL ROLES

THE ROLE DEFINED

Another aspect of the work that affects staff is the correctional role. The **role** of those working in a correctional workplace—or any other workplace—is determined by what those people do on the job every day. The role of staff in corrections is determined by their job description, their assigned duties, and the type of organization and clientele they work with. Therefore, correctional officers working in a living unit in a medium- security prison have a different role from that of probation officers working with lower-level offenders in the community. The first role involves constant supervision and interaction with inmates who live a very restricted lifestyle in a secure institution. The second role, that of probation officers, also involves supervision and interaction (although it is less intense because they are likely to see their clients less than daily) but also formally includes assistance to those they supervise. Both prison and probation officers usually work with convicted felons, but the prison inmates are more likely to be repeat felons and are usually convicted of more serious offenses. Although the first role involves the maintenance of both safety and security, for prison officers that usually means safety and security for other staff and other inmates, whereas for probation officers it usually means that they are concerned about community members their clients interact with. Both are likely involved in facilitating programming, but prison officers are most often watching inmates engaged in it or escorting them to it—although in some prisons officers help deliver it—whereas probation officers might recommend it or even run treatment groups. Prison officers might make recommendations regarding a person's placement in housing or work assignments in the secure facility, whereas probation officers will monitor a probationer's engagement in them or counsel him or her about how to find them.

Role: What a person does on the job every day.

ETHICAL ISSUE ?

What Would You Do?

As a district manager of a probation and parole district, you notice that several of your staff members seem burned out and stressed by their work. There are many more sick calls and more turnover than is normal for this size of workplace. You have bachelor's and master's degrees in criminal justice, and you know some of the research around these issues. You convene a meeting and note that your staff are reluctant at first to tell you what is wrong but then start complaining about working conditions and about how they are treated, not by inmates but rather by management and other staff. What do you think would be the best approach to alleviate the stress and burnout by staff? Will this involve the need for you and other supervisors to give up some power in the workplace? What obstacles do you anticipate getting in the way of any change? Despite these obstacles, should you still do it?

Both roles involve paperwork—loads of it—and both involve interactions with supervisors and accountability for what they do. For prison officers, they must adhere to the formal and informal rules that shape prison work as those are provided by state law, policies and procedures, their administrators, and the subcultural values of coworkers and clients (Lipsky, 1980). For probation officers, they also must work within these formal and informal strictures, but in addition they are often in constant contact with court actors, prosecutors, police officers, and jail workers, and these contacts, plus the clients on their caseloads and their families, can shape the role they play on the job.

We clearly have overgeneralized in our comparison here of how the role of correctional officers in a medium-security prison and that of probation officers in the community might differ and be similar. In those states and institutions where treatment is emphasized, some correctional officers are very engaged in providing treatment, not just supervising an inmate's involvement in it, for instance. Moreover, the role of some probation officers, particularly those who have an intensive supervision caseload with more serious offenders, may involve as much direct supervision as correctional staff provide in a prison. The point is that a role for staff is determined by many things, and it is defined by what people actually do in their work.

STREET-LEVEL BUREAUCRATS

A **street-level bureaucrat** (SLB) is what everyone who wants to work in a criminal justice agency starts out as. SLBs are, according to Lipsky (1980) (who first defined them), entry-level public-sector workers with too much work to do, too few resources to do it, and some discretion to choose how to do it. Police officers, public prosecutors and defenders, probation officers, and juvenile and adult correctional officers, along with teachers, social workers, and many other like jobs, are SLBs. They often have clients who are poor, uneducated, and relatively powerless who need public services. Although clients in the correctional environment are often involuntary, they still need the assistance of correctional staff in communities and institutions.

The reason why we are mentioning SLBs here is that the concept encapsulates the struggles correctional staff face. Although they have discretion, they often need to make Solomonic choices because their resources (time, treatment programming, space, etc.) are limited and yet they have so many clients in need. Many of us would then argue that we should just increase the resources that correctional staff have, and consequently there would be enough for all of the clients. Lipsky (1980), however, would argue that there will never be enough public-sector resources to meet all of the demand because other forces in the larger environment of corrections will obstruct this increase (e.g., taxation reduction groups). So demand will never be met by supply, and that puts SLBs in an untenable position, forced to choose who to provide resources to and whose needs to ignore while they do it.

Street-level bureaucrat: A public-sector worker with discretion who has too many clients with too many needs and not enough resources to meet those needs.

HACK VERSUS HUMAN SERVICE

The public may be less inclined to support the increased **professionalization** of correctional staff when the public thinks their role is limited to the use of brute force, a role termed a *guard* in old-style Big House prisons and defined as a **hack** by current scholars (Farkas, 1999, 2001; Johnson, 2002). If a correctional officer is viewed by the public as a hack, or as a violent, cynical, and alienated keeper of inmates in a no-hope warehouse prison, there would appear to be little need to encourage education or provide the training and pay that would elevate such officers to professional status. Yet there is reason to believe that most officers in prisons, jails, juvenile facilities, and community corrections actually regularly engage in **human service**, which serves as an alternative, more developed, and more positive role for correctional workers (Johnson, 2002; Lombardo, 2001).

Johnson (2002) defined human service correctional officers as those who provide "goods and services," serve as "advocates" for inmates when appropriate, assist them with their "adjustment" to prison, and use "helping networks" of staff to facilitate that adjustment (pp. 242–259). Such goods and services might involve food and clothing or medication, advocacy might include helping inmates to find jobs or apply for different housing or roommates, and adjustment assistance could include counseling them about how to handle difficult people or situations. Clearly, these kinds of activities are not necessarily in the job description of most officers who work in institutions, but they are often very much a part of what they do in reality and require that officers be skilled and knowledgeable. When the public does not know about, and the correctional organization does not recognize, the alternate human service work role performed by correctional or juvenile justice officers and probation and parole officers, again there is no perceived need to provide the training and pay that would be commensurate with that more developed professional role.

> **Professionalization:** In corrections, includes the enforcement of professional standards for new hires such as a required college-level educational background, sufficient training, pay that is commensurate with job requirements, training that sufficiently prepares people for the job, and a code of ethics that drives the work practice.
>
> **Hack:** A correctional officer in a prison who is a violent, cynical, and alienated keeper of inmates.
>
> **Human service:** A correctional officer who provides goods, services, advocacy, and assistance to help inmates adjust.

••• THE SUBCULTURE AND SOCIALIZATION

The staff subculture in corrections, much like the roles, varies by facility and by type of organization. A subculture might be defined as the norms, values, beliefs, history, traditions, and language held and practiced by a group of people. (A subculture is just a subset of a larger organizational culture.) In corrections, those aspects of a subculture are shaped by what kind of facility or organization you have, what kind of clientele you are dealing with, and how isolated the group of people is from the rest of the community. The more isolated and the more exclusive the interaction of the group, the more likely it is that the subculture's norms, values, and beliefs are distinct from those of the larger community.

Historically, staff literally lived on the prison grounds with the inmates in prisons that were not open to the public or the media (Ward & Kassebaum, 2009). In such institutions, a distinct

Getty Images/Christian Science Monitor

PHOTO 9.5: Correctional officer working with youths in a Toledo, Ohio, detention center.

subculture was more likely to form than it is in today's prisons, jails, or community corrections entities, where staff come and go with shifts and where visitors, lawyers, and the media have much more access than they did in years past. However, although correctional organizations of today are less likely to have as strong a staff subculture as they did in years past, this is not to say that they do not have a subculture.

SUBCULTURAL VALUES

Subcultural values in the correctional setting are likely to have an effect on what staff do. Even today, correctional organizations and the people who work in them are somewhat cut off from the larger society by the nature of what they do and the need to keep some matters private for legal and security reasons. Moreover, staff in corrections have very intense experiences together involving violence and strong emotions, experiences that are likely to bind staff together in an us-versus-them stance toward their clients and the larger society. It is for this reason that the role of staff in corrections is likely, for better or worse, to be influenced by the subcultural values of the group (e.g., see the discussion of subcultural values in Chapter 4).

Some subcultural values are positive in that they facilitate the ability of officers to do their work well (e.g., aiding your coworker, doing your own work). However, other subcultural values sound exactly like those expressed by inmates (e.g., "never rat," the us-versus-them mentality) and serve to isolate the work and the workers, making officers more likely to either participate in corrupt activities or turn their heads when they witness these activities and to reinforce negative attitudes toward clients and the work.

● ● ● STAFF INTERACTIONS WITH INMATES

THE DEFECTS OF TOTAL POWER

Many of those subcultural values are shaped by the power relationships between staff and inmates. In a classic work by Gresham Sykes, he described the relationship between staff and inmates in a maximum-security prison. Sykes (1958) noted that staff at this prison or any prison need inmates to comply with orders because it would be difficult, if not impossible, to force inmates to do "what they otherwise wouldn't" (the definition of power mentioned earlier [Dahl, 1961]). Use of force to get inmates to comply with basic commands or orders would be inefficient, impossible, and counterproductive. For instance, if an inmate refused to make his bed or several inmates refused, it would be difficult for an officer to call in the emergency response team every time this happened because it would mean that these team members would be pulled from their own duties. It would also make the officer in question, the one who could not get the inmate to do something as simple as make his bed, appear like he or she could not handle the supervision of inmates. Moreover, force is sometimes impossible to use, at least daily, because the inmates outnumber staff in living units by sometimes as much as 50 or 100 to 1. There are ways to lock down living units and use gas and other measures to suppress disruptions, but if this needed to be done on a regular basis, the prison would be in a constant uproar. And if force were used regularly for such trivial matters as making a bed, it is likely that inmates would align themselves more in opposition to staff, thus making the use of force counterproductive and perhaps requiring greater use of it.

It is for these reasons that Sykes (1958) found that staff *needed* inmate compliance in prisons as much as inmates needed staff assistance. However, gaining compliance from inmates is not always easy. Staff, according to Sykes, have relatively little that they can give to

IN FOCUS 9.2

Staff Stress, Burnout, and Turnover

Work in corrections can be taxing and troublesome. Most correctional work in institutions is shift work and, when first started, involves late nights, sometimes all-night shifts, and weekend and holiday work. Even parole and probation officers are often called on to visit clients in the evenings or on weekends. Needless to say, late-night shifts and weekend work play havoc with family life and children's school schedules, making family obligations challenging to meet.

It does not help matters that the people correctional staff supervise are often angry and upset or immature (Johnson, 2002). They are usually unhappy about being supervised and are sometimes unpleasant to those correctional staff engaged in supervision.

Relatedly, people who are incarcerated or supervised in the community have often led impoverished and tragic lives riddled with alcoholism, drug abuse, child abuse and neglect, unemployment, early deaths of loved ones, and homelessness. Many have inflicted serious harm on others, including not only their victims but also family and community members, and the guilt and regret they shoulder only exacerbate the negativity that surrounds them. Collectively, these tragic lives weigh heavily on the people experiencing them and can create a negative environment for themselves and for those who work with them (Johnson, 2002).

Correctional staff immersed in this environment and required to get unwilling people to do things they are not inclined to do often experience stress and the related consequences of it: burnout and turnover (Lambert, Hogan, & Tucker, 2009; Leip & Stinchcomb, 2013; Slate & Vogel, 1997; Stohr et al., 1994; Tewksbury & Collins, 2006). In a meta-analysis of studies on stress in prisons, Dowden and Tellier (2004) found that those who adopted a more human service work attitude experienced less stress on the job than those who had a more punitive (i.e., hack) and custody orientation. In a study of five jails by Stohr, Lovrich, Menke, and Zupan (1994), the authors found that those jails that invested in training and pay and that allowed staff to have a voice in how to do their work—all factors related to professionalism that we discussed earlier—were more likely to have greater job commitment by staff and less stress and turnover among them. Leip and Stinchcomb (2013) also discovered, in their analysis of data from a national survey of 1,924 line staff members, that intention to turnover was reduced when the organizational climate was positive; relationships between colleagues and supervisors were strong when correctional staff felt that they had a voice in how their workplace operated. Relatedly, in a study of a large county correctional system (nine facilities), Paoline, Lambert, and Hogan (2006) found that adherence to policies and standards (of the ACA, which emphasizes professionalism, safety, and humanity in supervision) and positive and noncompetitive work relations with coworkers decreased the stress of workers. In their review of the literature on stress and burnout in correctional work, Finney, Stergiopoulos, Hensel, Bonato, and Dewa (2013) found that the organizational structure and climate had the greatest effect on stress and burnout in corrections.

Discussion Questions

1. Why would the organizational structure and climate have an effect on stress and burnout?

2. Why would having a voice in how your job is done reduce stress?

3. How can correctional managers reduce stress for staff?

inmates to motivate them. They can sometimes get inmates better work or housing assignments, but the amount of these rewards is limited and their power to garner rewards for inmates may be likewise so. Moreover, staff do not have the ability to reward inmate compliance with what inmates want most: their freedom. Therefore, according to Sykes, given these realities, staff and inmates tend to engage in a "corrupted" relationship, whereby inmates comply with staff orders as long as staff overlook some violations, usually minor

ETHICAL ISSUE **?**

What Would You Do?

As an experienced counselor in a private, nonprofit, juvenile halfway house, you notice that a few of the staff members (whom you are buddies with) tend to denigrate some of the kids at the facility by calling them names (e.g., "little criminals" and worse), using profanity in reference to them, and even writing them up for minor issues when they try to object. You notice that a few of these kids seem depressed and lethargic lately, and you wonder whether it could have anything to do with how they are treated at the home. You don't think the supervisor of the house (who also supervises other houses around the state) is aware of what is going on. You need this job and don't want to alienate your friends, but you don't want to continue to work at a place where kids are abused. What do you think would be the best course of action in such a situation? What do you think would be the likely consequences of your action or inaction?

ones, by inmates. Such a relationship is most likely to develop between staff and those inmates who have the most power to control and gain compliance from other inmates.

Of course, Sykes (1958) was only describing the dynamics of the staff–inmate relationship in a New Jersey maximum-security prison during the 1950s, and much has changed since then, even in the most secure prisons. However, the informal side of the relationship between staff and inmates or clients in corrections is still there, and the need for an exchange relationship between the two is still part of that dynamic. In another classic work on public-service workers generally, Michael Lipsky also recognized the fact that formally, staff control inmates, but informally, in prisons, schools, and social-welfare departments, clients, even ostensibly powerless ones, also exercise some power over staff (Lipsky, 1980). By not complying with orders, failing to review information, or complaining about the service they receive, clients—even inmate clients—are able to force staff to adjust their behavior.

THE CORRECTIONAL ROLE WHEN SUPERVISING CHILDREN

An example of the variability of the correctional role would be the form it takes when officers and counselors supervise children. Inderbitzin (2006) found, in a 15-month ethnographic study of staff members supervising a cottage of boys in a juvenile training facility (the juvenile version of a prison), that they "serve as their adolescent inmates' guardians, keepers, counselors, and role models" (p. 431). Noting that the work with these serious and sometimes violent juveniles could be "frustrating, dangerous, often amusing, and occasionally rewarding" (p. 439), she argued that officers and counselors needed to be flexible and energetic in order to best cope with a volatile mix of duties that each day would bring. The tactics used by staff members to gain the boys' cooperation and to supervise them effectively ranged from the more punitive disciplinary actions all the way to reasoning with or cajoling them and using humor. Some staff members tended to emphasize certain tactics over others, and some staff members tended to vary their own behavior as the situation required. Inderbitzin concluded that the staff members who were most successful in their work, in that they were able to effectively supervise their charges, were those who took on a "people worker" role (p. 442), or the human service role that was described earlier in this chapter (Farkas, 2000). Such staff members were also the most flexible, kind, creative, and respectful in their work with the adolescents.

ABUSE OF POWER

There are plenty of instances, both historically and currently, of correctional staff abusing their power over inmates and clients. We discuss such instances in some depth in several chapters in this book. It is important to mention here, however, that the abuse of power is more likely to occur in environments where staff behavior is not supervised closely enough by administrators or those outside the work environment, where inmates have little or no ability to contact the outside, where staff are not sufficiently trained, where there is a higher concentration of young and inexperienced staff, and where there is a higher concentration of disruptive inmates (Antonio, Young, & Wingeard, 2009; Rideau, 2010; Stohr & Collins, 2009).

USE OF FORCE

The actual use of force—or being prepared to use such force—is part of correctional work. Correctional administrators interested in channeling its use in appropriate and legal ways ensure that staff are trained on when to escalate or deescalate its use based on the situation (Hemmens & Atherton, 1999). In such training, the officer is taught to pay attention to cues that will tell him or her when to increase the force level and when not to do so.

Having said this, the use of force in any correctional environment depends on the type of institution or agency, the clients or inmates served, and the way they are managed. Generally speaking, there is less call for force in probation and parole work with adults or juveniles, although when engaged in arrests it is not uncommon for community corrections officers to need to use force. Minimum-security prisons for adults or juveniles generally have less cause for use of force; inmates in such institutions are classified as less prone to violence and/or are on

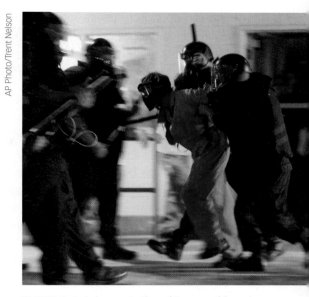

AP Photo/Trent Nelson

PHOTO 9.6: A demonstration of the use of force in a jail by the emergency response team in Montgomery County, Pennsylvania. Such teams are often called on to subdue violent or disruptive inmates.

their way out of the system and so are more likely to rein in any violent inclinations. As one proceeds up the correctional security ladder, from minimum to medium and then to maximum, the need to use force increases given the types of inmates incarcerated and the need to maintain stricter controls. It should also be mentioned, however, that in some prisons, under some wardens, the use of force is resorted to more frequently than under other wardens in similar prisons (Rideau, 2010). As Rideau (2010) observed after his 44-year incarceration in the Angola Prison in Louisiana and observing the management style of many wardens (see the description of Rideau's experience in Chapter 8), those wardens who allow more openness between staff and inmates and the outside and who have more transparency about their management decisions are less likely to experience the need for the use of force in their facilities. The more ready resort to force may be spurred by the type of inmates held (e.g., more violent) or the conditions of the facility (e.g., more crowded), but it could also just be a management tactic adopted by some wardens, as Rideau and others have argued (e.g., see Reisig, 1998).

SUMMARY

- The correctional experience for staff is fraught with challenges and much promise. It involves a diverse role that encompasses work with juvenile and adult inmates in institutions as well as with offenders or the accused in the community. It is not as narrow a role as is commonly perceived by the public, and it includes many opportunities to effectuate a just incarceration or community supervision experience for inmates and clients.

- Although many have worked long and hard to professionalize correctional work, there is every indication that most jobs in this area do not meet standard professional criteria.

- When correctional workers do not receive the requisite professional training and education they need to do their job in an appropriate manner, both clients and the community are likely to suffer.

- Many who labor in corrections undertake the *human service role,* focusing on the provision of goods and services; advocating for inmates, offenders, or clients; and assisting in their adjustment (Johnson, 2002).

- The research presented here would indicate that there are organizational factors that can be manipulated to improve this experience for staff so that they and their organization can realize their promise. In addition, better pay, benefits, and training can be used to foster the greater development of professional attributes, such as education, and the consequent reduction in role ambiguity, turnover, and stress and increase in job satisfaction. The organizational culture can also be assessed to determine whether certain characteristics are making it a more or less positive work environment for

staff and a safe, secure, and developmental one for inmates.

- This research also indicates that the organization can do much to reduce the problems associated with the greater diversification of its staff. It can be open in its promotion practices so that false impressions regarding unfair advantage are not perpetuated and do not have a demoralizing effect on the workforce. It is also within the correctional organization's power to prevent most sexual harassment, whether practiced by staff or inmates. In short, the promise of a positive correctional experience for staff is achievable, and as that perception seeps into the public consciousness, a correctional officer is much more likely to be perceived as a professional.

KEY TERMS

Abu Ghraib, 196

Hack, 205

Human service, 205

Power, 196

Profession, 190

Professionalization, 205

Role, 203

Stanford Prison Experiment, 196

Street-level bureaucrat, 204

DISCUSSION QUESTIONS

1. Explain why work in corrections is often not regarded as *professional* in comparison with other commonly referenced professions.

2. Note which jobs in corrections are most sought after and why. Discuss how all correctional work might become more appealing to educated workers.

3. Review the events surrounding the Stanford Prison Experiment. If you were going to conduct such an experiment now, how would you go about it? What questions would you like to address with the experiment?

4. Explain and discuss the "hack" versus human service role for staff. Which role do you think the public typically ascribes to correctional staff? Which role do you think is most commonly undertaken by staff?

5. Explain how the correctional organization can provide the right environment to reduce stress, turnover, and harassment of its staff.

6. Why is ethical behavior such a challenge in correctional work?

7. Consider the benefits and drawbacks of working in corrections. Do you plan on working in corrections? Why or why not?

$SAGE edge™

Review → Practice → Improve

Sharpen your skills with SAGE edge at **edge.sagepub.com/stohressentials3e**.

SAGE edge offers a robust online environment featuring an impressive array of free tools and resources for review, study, and further exploration, keeping both instructors and students on the cutting edge of teaching and learning.

FOR FURTHER EXPLORATION AND APPLICATION, TAKE A LOOK AT THE INTERACTIVE EBOOK FOR THESE PREMIUM RESOURCES:

- ▶ **Career Video 9.1** Police Captain
- ▷ **SAGE News Clip 9.1** Abu Ghraib
- ▷ **SAGE News Clip 9.2** U.S. Prison Stabbing
- ▤ **Journal Article 9.1** Is the Job Burning Me Out? An Exploratory Test of the Job Characteristics Model on the Emotional Burnout of Prison Staff

10 Community Corrections

Parole and Prisoner Reentry

TEST YOUR KNOWLEDGE

Test your current knowledge of probation by answering the following questions as true or false. Check your answers on page 392 after reading the chapter.

1. Parole began in an Australian penal colony during the 1830s.

2. Parole and probation both are under court supervision.

3. Parolees are always scrutinized by a parole board to determine eligibility.

4. Most parolees reoffend within 3 years of release.

5. The parolees most likely to recidivate are property offenders.

6. Researchers agree that incarcerating too many people from the same neighborhood is detrimental because it causes more crime in the long run.

7. Parole success is determined similarly in all states; that is, no recidivism.

8. Sanctions such as halfway houses and electronic monitoring cut costs and increase parolee surveillance.

LEARNING OBJECTIVES

- Understand the history and purpose of parole

- Know the difference between mandatory and discretionary parole and how they both differ from unconditional release

- Understand the roles and duties of probation officers and parole board members

- Understand the issues involved in prisoner reentry into the community and parolee recidivism

- Know what makes for a successful reentry

- Understand the principle of graduated sanctions

- Be able to identify and discuss halfway houses, house arrest, and electronic monitoring

THE PERILS OF PAROLE

On July 29, 1994, parolee Jesse Timmendequas lured 7-year-old Megan Kanka into his New Jersey home, where he beat, raped, and murdered her. Timmendequas, who was 33 years old at the time, had two previous convictions for sexually assaulting two young girls: one 5 years old and the other 7 years old. He was given probation on his first conviction but was sentenced to prison on his second. After his release from prison, Timmendequas lived with two other convicted sex offenders in Kanka's neighborhood. He confessed to investigating officers the next day and was arrested. He was subsequently convicted of kidnapping, aggravated assault, rape, and murder and was sentenced to death (commuted to life without parole in 2007 when New Jersey abolished the death penalty). The murder led to the introduction of Megan's Law, requiring law enforcement to disclose the location of registered sex offenders on probation or on parole.

What really upset people about this case (in addition to the brutal and needless death of a young girl) was that Timmendequas was a parolee who many thought should never have been released given his criminal record. It was cases such as this that led to efforts to eliminate parole, but short of locking up each and every offender until he or she dies, we need to have some way of reintegrating them into the community. The recognition of this brute fact and the need to protect the community from predators such as Timmendequas is the daunting task of parole board members and parole officers. How do the authorities deal with conflicting public demands for protection and for less tax money being spent on corrections, and how do they deal with the vexing problems of trying to turn around the lives of parolees who have demonstrated their inability to control their behavior time and time again? These are some of the frustrating and troublesome problems we discuss in this chapter.

PHOTO 10.1: The Norfolk (Australia) penal colony's superintendent during the 1830s, Alexander Maconochie, laid the philosophical foundation of parole, as applied to convicted criminals.

●●● INTRODUCTION: WHAT IS PAROLE?

The term *parole* comes from the French phrase *parole d'honneur*, which literally means "word of honor." In times when a person's word really meant something, parole was used by European armies to release captured enemy soldiers on condition (their word of honor) that they would take no further part in hostilities (Seiter, 2005). The practice also existed for a brief time during the American Civil War, but it was soon realized that neither side was honoring it because paroled soldiers were back in the fight weeks after release ("Civil War prisons and prisoners," 2002). Modern **parole** refers to the release of convicted criminals from prison under the supervision of a parole officer before the completion of their full sentences on their promise of good behavior. Parole is different from probation in two basic ways. First, parole is an administrative function practiced by a parole board that is part of the executive branch of government, while probation is a judicial function. Second, parolees have spent time in prison before being released into the community, whereas probationers typically have not. In many states, both parolees and probationers are supervised by state probation and parole officers or agents; in others, they are supervised by separate probation or parole agencies.

BRIEF HISTORY OF PAROLE

The philosophical foundation of parole, as applied to convicted criminals, was laid by the superintendent of the Norfolk Island penal colony off the coast of Australia during the 1830s. The superintendent was an ex-British naval officer and geography professor named Alexander Maconochie, who had experienced imprisonment himself as a captive of the French during the Napoleonic Wars after his ship was wrecked (Morris, 2002). The horrendous conditions in the colony offended the compassionate, such as Augustus and Davenport-Hill, and the deeply religious Maconochie, who was a firm believer in the primacy of human dignity. As prison superintendent, he operated on three basic principles: (1) cruel and vindictive punishment debases both the criminal and the society that allows it, making both worse; (2) the purpose of punishment should only be the reformation (today we would say rehabilitation) of the convict; and (3) criminal sentences should be seen not in terms of time to be served but rather in terms of tasks to be performed. To implement his programs, Maconochie required indefinite prison terms rather than fixed determinate terms so that convicts would have an incentive to work toward release. As we have seen, the type of sentence Maconochie advocated is known today as an indeterminate sentence.

Maconochie was a realist, not a bleeding-heart idealist. The philosophy behind Maconochie's correctional ideas and ideals is best stated by himself:

> I am no sentimentalist. I most fully subscribe to the right claimed by society to make examples of those who break its laws, that others may feel constrained to respect and obey them. Punishment may avenge, and restraint may, to a certain limited extent, prevent crime; but neither separately, nor together, will they teach virtue. That is the province of moral training alone. (as cited in Morris, 2002, p. xviii)

Parole: The release of prisoners from prison before completing their full sentences.

Steve Daggar

Maconochie's point was that retribution may deter some offenders and incapacitation is a temporary hold on a criminal career, but the real goal of corrections should be to correct or, in Maconochie's words, "teach virtue." With respect to the third principle (tasks performed rather than time served), Maconochie devised a *mark system* involving credits earned for the speedy and efficient performance of these tasks as well as for overall good behavior. When a convict had accumulated enough credits, he could apply for a *ticket of leave* (TOL), which was a document granting him freedom to work and live outside the prison before the expiration of his full sentence. TOL convicts were free to work, acquire property, and marry, but they needed to appear before a magistrate when required and church attendance was mandatory. Maconochie's system appeared to have worked very well. It supposedly was determined that only 20 of 900 of Maconochie's TOL convicts were convicted of new felonies (many more crimes were felonies during the 19th century than today),

ETHICAL ISSUE

What Would You Do?

As a probation and parole agent you become aware that one of your colleagues with whom you have a good relationship is sexually preying on his female probationers and parolees. He essentially waits for them to commit violations such as non-payment of fines, missed appointments, and providing dirty urine samples and then hints around that he will not violate their probation or parole status if they are forthcoming with sexual favors. You learn that he has been quite successful with this strategy and that he overlooks numerous violations. Would you (1) ignore this as none of your business, (2) talk to him and counsel him on the dangers of doing this and tell him to stop or you will report him (it is a crime for someone with legal authority over another to demand sexual favors), or (3) report him to his supervisor?

a recidivism rate of 2.2% that modern penologists are scarcely able to comprehend and many dismiss as too good to be true (R. Hughes, 1987). Nevertheless, and perhaps predictably, when Maconochie returned home to England and tried to institute his reforms there, he was accused of coddling criminals and relieved of his duties.

Nevertheless, the TOL system was adapted to the differing conditions in Britain under Walter Crofton, who devised the so-called **Irish system**. This system involved four stages, beginning with a 9-month period of solitary confinement, the first 3 months with reduced rations and no work. This period of enforced idleness was presumed to make even the laziest of men yearn for some kind of activity. The solitary period was followed by a period in which convicts could earn marks through labor and good behavior to enable their transfer to an open prerelease prison when enough marks had been accumulated and finally by a TOL. TOL convicts were supervised in the community by either police officers or civilian volunteers (forerunners of the modern parole officer), who paid visits to their homes and attempted to secure employment for them (Foster, 2006). Of the 557 men released on TOL under the Irish system during the 1850s, only 17 (3.05%) were revoked for new offenses (Seiter, 2005); again, if true, this is an extraordinary level of success.

Elements from both Maconochie's and Crofton's systems were brought into practice in the United States during the 1870s by Zebulon Brockway, superintendent of the Elmira Reformatory in New York. Brockway's system required indeterminate sentencing so that "good time" earned through good conduct and labor could be used to reduce inmates' sentences (Roth, 2006). However, there were no provisions for the supervision of offenders who obtained early release until 1930 when the U.S. Congress established the U.S. Board of Parole. Eventually parole came to be seen not as a humanistic method of dealing with "reformed" individuals but rather as a way of maintaining order in prisons by holding out the prospect of early release if convicts behaved well. It has also become a way of trying to reintegrate offenders back into the community by offering programs to prepare them for life outside the walls and as a partial solution to the problem of prison overcrowding. Because of these functions, parole became an essential and valued part of the American correctional system.

Irish system: A prison system used during the 19th century. This system involved four stages, beginning with a 9-month period of solitary confinement, the first 3 months with reduced rations and no work.

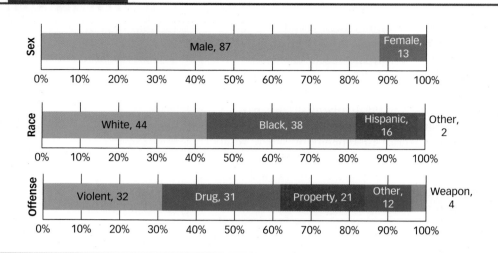

FIGURE 10.1   Characteristics of Parolees

Source: Kaeble and Bonczar (2017). Bureau of Justice Statistics.

THE MODERN PAROLE SYSTEM

There were 870,500 state and federal parolees in the United States in 2015. The demographic characteristics of parolees in 2015 are shown in Figure 10.1. These characteristics remained very stable from 2005 to 2015 (Kaeble & Bonczar, 2017). It is noted that although the number of parolees incarcerated for drug offenses has fallen since 2015, these crimes remain a major reason for the United States' huge level of incarceration.

The skyrocketing crime rates during the 1970s, 1980s, and early 1990s, many of the crimes committed by offenders on probation or parole, led to the "tough on crime" approaches to punishment discussed in the last chapter. The heinous kidnapping, rape, and murder of 13-year-old Polly Klaas by parolee Richard Davis and of 7-year-old Megan Kanka by parolee Jesse Timmendequas (in this chapter's opening vignette) led to calls for the abolition of parole from a fearful public and their representatives. Further fueling the fire was the case of Willie Horton. Horton was serving a life sentence for murder, supposedly without the possibility of parole, when he was granted a weekend furlough (a temporary leave of absence from prison) that he used to commit an armed robbery, rape, and assault. With public outrage at a fever pitch, the federal government and a number of states abolished parole, substituting the return of the fixed determinate sentence that Maconochie so disliked. This system means that essentially prisoners are unconditionally released after the completion of their sentences without supervision or reporting requirements. This type of release is known as **unconditional release**. Inmates who either are required to "max out" their time or choose to max out rather than be placed on parole have less incentive to enter rehabilitation programs or to abide by prison rules. A number of states had already made the switch to mandatory sentences for their own reasons prior to these hideous crimes committed by Davis, Timmendequas, and Horton.

Unconditional release: A type of release from prison for inmates who have completed their entire sentences. They are released unconditionally—with no parole.

Discretionary parole: Parole granted at the discretion of a parole board for selected inmates who have earned it.

Abolishing parole sounds very tough and goes over quite well politically, but the reality is something different. Prisoners are still released early for reasons of overcrowding and budgetary concerns, but there is much less rational control today over who is released than there was in the past. It is discretionary parole that has really been abolished in some states in favor of mandatory parole. **Discretionary parole** is parole granted at the discretion of a parole board for selected inmates who are deemed to have earned it. Prisoners earn discretionary parole by avoiding disciplinary infractions and engaging in programs that prepare them for reentry into the community. Discretionary parole also allows parole board members to assess the probability of a given offender's risk to society based on the crime for which he or she was incarcerated and on his or her criminal history, prison behavior, and psychological assessments.

Mandatory parole, on the other hand, is automatic parole for nearly all inmates in states that have a system of determinate (i.e., fixed) sentencing (Petersilia, 2000). This system is used by the federal government and about half of the states. Mandatory parole still has provisions for earning "good time" credits. Tragically, both Davis and Timmendequas were granted mandatory parole determined by mathematical norms generated by a computer based solely on time served, that is, without any kind of consideration of the risk these individuals posed to society. Had their cases gone before a parole board, where board members can peruse parole applicants' criminal history and target violent and dangerous criminals for longer incarceration, odds are that neither man would have been released (Petersilia, 2000). Davis, for instance, had been released after serving only one-half of his 16-year sentence because of his supposed "good behavior" while institutionalized for a previous kidnapping, robbery, and assault of a woman (Skolnick, 1993).

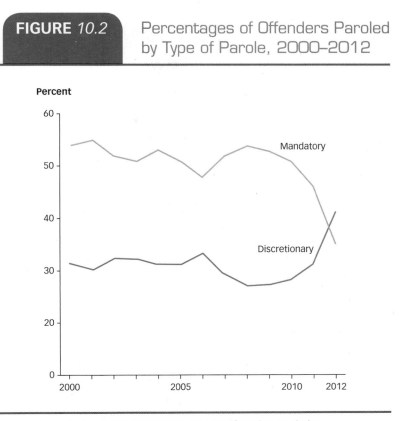

FIGURE 10.2   Percentages of Offenders Paroled by Type of Parole, 2000–2012

Source: Maruschak and Bonczar (2013). Bureau of Justice Statistics.

On the other hand, there is no such thing as mandatory furloughs, so what kind of "rational" discretion led to the decision to grant a vicious murderer like Willie Horton a weekend of freedom to go on a crime spree?

As we see from the graph in Figure 10.2, the percentage of offenders released on mandatory parole is dropping while discretionary parole releases are increasing. In 2012, 41% entered parole through discretionary release versus 35% who entered through mandatory release (Maruschak & Bonczar, 2013). This reverses the trend from 1980 to 1999, when mandatory parole releases exceeded discretionary releases by about 22% (T. Hughes, Wilson, & Beck, 2001). Both discretionary and mandatory release parolees are supervised post-release, but those 17% or 18% of inmates who are released at the expiration of their sentences (unconditional release) are not supervised. The graph in Figure 10.3 supports those who favor discretionary parole and the elimination of mandatory parole. Note that in 1999, about 52% of discretionary parolees successfully completed parole, while only about 32% of mandatory parolees did. This discrepancy was still very much in evidence in 2008 (Paparozzi & Guy, 2009).

PAROLEE RECIDIVISM

A nationwide study of parolee recidivism looked at nearly 300,000 parolees from 15 states released from prison in 1994 (Langan & Levin, 2002). Within 3 years of release, 67.5% were rearrested for a new offense, with the entire sample accumulating an astounding 744,000 new offenses during those 3 years. New arrests included 2,871 for murder, 2,444 for rape, 21,245 for robbery, and 54,604 for assault. Property offenders (over 70%) had the highest rate of recidivism, while murderers (40.7%) and sex offenders (41.4%) had the lowest recidivism rates. These rates do not mean, for instance, that 40.7% of murderers committed another murder—they mean a further arrest for any type of crime.

Mandatory parole: Automatic parole after a set period of time for nearly all inmates.

IN FOCUS 10.1

Example of Parole Conditions

When prisoners are released from prison and placed on parole, there are a number of strict conditions they must follow. Below are examples of these conditions from the state of Nevada. Conditions are pretty standard in all states, but the extent to which parolees are held to them, and the severity of consequences for not doing so, vary from jurisdiction to jurisdiction.

State of Nevada

Board of Parole Commissioners

PAROLE AGREEMENT

On the day of _____ _____ was sentenced by _____, District Judge of the _____ Judicial District Court in and for the County of _____, State of Nevada, to imprisonment in the Nevada State Prison System, for the crime of _____ for a term of _____.

The Board of Parole Commissioners, by virtue of the authority vested in it by the laws of the State of Nevada, hereby authorizes the Director of the Department of Prisons to allow said on the day of, or as soon thereafter as a satisfactory program can be arranged and approved by the Division of Parole and Probation, to go upon parole outside the prison buildings and enclosure, subject to the following conditions:

Reporting/Release: Upon release from the institution, you are to go directly to the program approved by the Division of Parole and Probation, and shall report to the Supervising Officer or other person designated by the Division. You are required to submit a written Monthly Report to your Supervising Officer on the first of each month on forms supplied by the Division of Parole and Probation. This report shall be true and correct in all respects; in addition, you shall report as directed by your Supervising Officer.

1. Residence: You shall not change your place of residence without first obtaining permission from your Supervising Officer, in each instance.

2. Intoxicants: You shall not drink or partake of any alcoholic beverages (whatsoever) (to excess).

Upon request by any Parole or Peace Officer, you shall submit to a medically recognized test for blood/breath alcohol content. Test results of .10 blood alcohol or higher shall be sufficient proof of excess.

3. Controlled Substances: You shall not use, purchase nor possess any narcotic drugs, nor any dangerous drugs, unless first prescribed by a licensed physician; you shall immediately notify your Supervising Officer of any prescription received. You shall submit to narcotic or drug testing as required by any Supervision Officer.

4. Weapons: You shall not possess, own, carry, or have under your control, any type of weapon.

5. Associates: You shall not associate with individuals who have criminal records or other individuals as deemed inappropriate by the Division. You shall not have any contact with persons confined in a correctional institution unless specific written permission has been granted by your Supervising Officer and the correctional institution.

6. Cooperation: You shall, at all times, cooperate with your Supervising Officer and your behavior shall justify the opportunity granted to you by this parole.

7. Laws and Conduct: You shall comply with all institutional rules, municipal, county, state and federal laws, and ordinances; and conduct yourself as a good citizen.

8. Out-of-State Travel: You shall not leave the State without first obtaining written permission from your Supervising Officer.

9. Employment/Program: You shall seek and maintain legal employment, or maintain a program approved by the Division of Parole and Probation and not change such employment or program without first obtaining permission.

10. Supervision Fees: You shall pay monthly supervision fees while under supervision of the Division.

11. Fines/Restitution: You shall pay all Court-ordered fines, fees and restitution on a schedule approved by the Division.

12. Special Conditions: _____

13. Search: You shall submit to a search of your person, automobile, or place of residence, by a Parole Officer, at any time of the day or night without a warrant, upon reasonable cause as ascertained by the Parole Officer.

14. Your Parole Expiration Date is:

15. Credits: You shall receive no credit, whatsoever, on this sentence should you be absent from supervision at any time and be considered an absconder.

This parole is granted to and accepted by you, subject to the conditions stated herein, and with the knowledge that the Board of Parole Commissioners has the power, at any time, in case of violation of the conditions of parole to cause your detention and/or return to prison. Your right to vote has been revoked and may be restored upon Honorable Discharge from parole.

APPROVED BY THE BOARD OF PAROLE COMMISSIONERS

Chief Parole Officer _____ **Dated:** _____

AGREEMENT BY PAROLEE

I do hereby waive extradition to the State of Nevada from any state in the United States, and from any territory or country outside the continental United States, and also agree that I will not contest any effort to return me to the United States or the State of Nevada.

I have read or had read to me, the conditions of my parole, and I fully understand them and I agree to abide by and strictly follow them. I fully understand the penalties involved should I, in any manner, violate the foregoing conditions.

Parolee _____

Officer Witness _____ **Dated:** _____

A Bureau of Justice Statistics study (Durose, Cooper, & Snyder, 2014) of recidivism among the 405,000 state prisoners released in 30 states in 2005 and followed for a 5-year period found almost identical results. Among the results were the following:

- About two-thirds (67.8%) of released prisoners were arrested for a new crime within 3 years, and more than three-quarters (76.6%) were arrested within 5 years.

- Within 5 years of release, 82.1% of property offenders were arrested for a new crime, compared with 76.9% of drug offenders, 73.6% of public order offenders, and 71.3% of violent offenders.

- More than a third (36.8%) of all prisoners who were arrested within 5 years of release were arrested within the first 6 months after release, with more than half (56.7%) being arrested by the end of the first year.

- About two in five (42.3%) released prisoners were either not arrested or arrested once during the 5 years after their release.

- A sixth (16.1%) of released prisoners were responsible for nearly half (48.4%) of the nearly 1.2 million arrests that occurred during the 5-year follow-up period.

- An estimated 10.9% of released prisoners were arrested in a state other than the one that released them during the 5-year follow-up period.

Solomon, Kachnowski, and Bhati (2005) analyzed a subset of 38,624 parolees for whom the type of release was known. There were surprisingly few differences between the parolees other than the fact that discretionary release parolees had a lower average number of prior arrests (7.5) than mandatory parolees (9.5) or unconditionally released parolees (9.6).

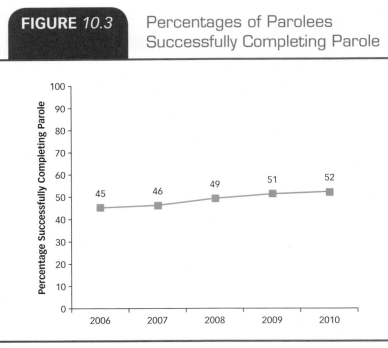

FIGURE *10.3* Percentages of Parolees Successfully Completing Parole

Source: Glaze and Bonczar (2011). Bureau of Justice Statistics.

Among those rearrested after release, unconditionally released parolees were rearrested an average of 9.9 months after release, mandatory parolees an average of 10.4 months, and discretionary parolees an average of 11.5 months. The average time served, as one would expect, was also noticeably different, with the unconditionally released parolees serving an average of 32 months; mandatory parolees an average of 18.5 months; and discretionary parolees an average of 21.3 months. This suggests that supervision is particularly vital at the early stages of the parole process, when parolees are still struggling to find their way back into their communities and are thus most susceptible to returning to their criminal ways.

Figure 10.4 provides an example of a mandatory parole release form showing the "word of honor" promises that parolees are supposed to abide by in Alaska. The listed conditions are fairly standard from state to state and are indistinguishable from the conditions set for probationers. These are general conditions with which all parolees must comply, but often there are additional conditions set for individual offenders. These conditions may be things such as requiring alcoholics or drug addicts to enroll in and attend certain programs and requiring sex offenders to avoid all contact with children or to refrain from Internet pornography. These additional conditions will likely be set by the parole board and/or by each individual parole officer after reviewing each parolee's case. It is then the responsibility of the parole officer to make sure that the parolee follows the conditions that have been mandated.

••• PAROLE BOARDS

Parole boards are required only in states that employ a discretionary system of granting parole. A **parole board** is a panel of people presumably qualified to make judgments about the suitability of a prisoner to be released from prison after having served some specified time of his or her sentence. This is termed an inmate's parole eligibility date, which is the earliest possible time that he or she can be released from prison. Board members are appointed by the governor for a fixed (renewable) term in most states. Some states mandate that a board appointee be well versed in criminology and corrections, while other states have no such requirement. Although many board members serve on a part-time basis and collect a minimal salary and per diem expenses, chairpersons and vice chairpersons are full-time salaried individuals in nearly all states (Abadinsky, 2009).

Parole board: A panel of people presumably qualified to make judgments about the suitability of a prisoner to be released from prison after having served some specified time of his or her sentence.

In making their decision of whether to grant or deny parole, board members assess a variety of information about the inmate and interview him or her at a parole hearing to discuss the assessed information and to gain some face-to-face insight about the inmate. Among the information considered by the parole board members to help them make their decision are the following:

FIGURE 10.4   Example of a Mandatory Parole Form

STATE OF ALASKA   **DEPARTMENT OF CORRECTIONS**

ORDER OF MANDATORY PAROLE

Parolee: _____ DOB: _____ OTIS# _____ Released: _____ Supv. Expires: _____

****

The following terms and conditions are effective on the release date shown on the CERTIFICATE OF GOOD TIME AWARD (AS 33.20.030) for all prisoners released pursuant to AS 33.16.010 or AS 33.20.040. I understand I am required by law to abide by the conditions imposed, whether or not I sign these conditions. The Parole Board may have me returned to custody at any time when it determines a condition of parole has been violated.

CONDITIONS OF MANDATORY PAROLE

1. REPORT UPON RELEASE: I will report in person no later than the next working day after my release to the P.O. located at: _____ and receive further reporting instructions. I will reside at: _____

    _____

2. MAINTAIN EMPLOYMENT/TRAINING/TREATMENT: I will make a diligent effort to maintain steady employment and support my legal dependents. I will not voluntarily change or terminate my employment without receiving permission from my Parole Officer (P.O.) to do so. If discharged or if employment is terminated (temporarily or permanently) for any reason, I will notify my P.O. the next working day. If I am involved in an education, training, or treatment program, I will continue active participation in the program unless I received permission from my P.O. to quit. If I am released, removed, or terminated from the program for any reason, I will notify my P.O. the next working day.

3. REPORT MONTHLY: I will report to my P.O. at least monthly in the manner prescribed by my P.O. I will follow any other reporting instructions established by my P.O.

4. OBEY LAWS/ORDERS: I will obey all state, federal and local laws, ordinances, and court orders.

5. PERMISSION BEFORE CHANGING RESIDENCE: I will obtain permission from my P.O. before changing my residence. Remaining away from my approved residence for 24 hours or more constitutes a change in residence for the purpose of this condition.

6. TRAVEL PERMIT BEFORE TRAVEL OUTSIDE ALASKA: I will obtain the prior written permission of my P.O. in the form of an interstate travel agreement before leaving the State of Alaska. Failure to abide by the conditions of the travel agreement is a violation of my order of parole.

7. NO FIREARMS/WEAPONS: I will not own, possess, have in my custody, handle, purchase or transport any firearm, ammunition or explosives. I may not carry any deadly weapon on my person except a pocket knife with a 3" or shorter blade. Carrying any other weapon on my person such as hunting knife, axe, club, etc. is a violation of my order of parole. I will contact the Alaska Board of Parole if I have any questions about the use of firearms, ammunition, or weapons.

8. NO DRUGS: I will not use, possess, handle, purchase, give or administer any narcotic, hallucinogenic, (including marijuana/THC), stimulant, depressant, amphetamine, barbiturate or prescription drug not specifically prescribed by a licensed medical person.

9. REPORT POLICE CONTACT: I will report to my P.O., not later than the next working day, any contact with a law enforcement officer.

10. DO NOT WORK AS AN INFORMANT: I will not enter into any agreement or other arrangement with any law enforcement agency which will put me in the position of violating any law or any condition of my parole. I understand that the Department of Corrections and Parole Board policy prohibits me from working as an informant.

Source: State of Alaska.

PHOTO 10.2: Charles Manson

- The nature of the offense for which the inmate is currently incarcerated.

- The criminal history of the inmate.

- Indications by word and/or deed that the inmate is repentant.

- The inmate's mental health via psychological and psychiatric reports.

- The original presentence investigation report.

- Reports of institutional conduct, including disciplinary reports and participation in religious and rehabilitative programs.

- The inmate's parole plan—for example, where does the inmate plan to reside, does the inmate have guaranteed or possible employment waiting, and does the inmate enjoy a good support system in the community?

- Statements made by others supporting (e.g., family members, counselors, ministers) or opposing (e.g., the victim, prosecutor, other criminal justice officials) the inmate's request for parole.

Of course, parole boards are composed of humans who have their own reasons for granting or denying parole. Although a majority vote wins the day, there are always members (especially chairpersons) who wield more influence than others. They can never be certain who will or will not fail on parole, but they know that on average about two-thirds will fail. They are thus likely to err on the side of caution (not releasing someone who would have made it successfully) than to endanger the public and embarrass themselves by releasing someone who then proceeds to commit heinous and highly publicized crimes such as those committed by Davis, Timmendequas, and Horton.

••• WHAT GOES IN MUST COME OUT: PRISONER REENTRY INTO THE COMMUNITY

Numerous commentators of all political persuasions consume an incredible amount of space writing about America's imprisonment binge, but rarely outside of the academic literature do we find much concern about the natural corollary of the binge: What goes in must come out. J. Travis (2005) introduced us to the idea of prison reentry in this way: "Reentry is the process of leaving prison and returning to society. Reentry is not a form of supervision, like parole. Reentry is not a goal, like rehabilitation or reintegration. Reentry is not an option. Reentry reflects the iron law of imprisonment: they all come back" (p. xxi). "They all come back" refers to prisoners returning to the communities from which they came.

Understanding the process of prisoner reentry and reintegration into the community is a very pressing issue in corrections. In 2012, 609,800 offenders entered American state and federal prisons and 637,400 left them (Carson & Golinelli, 2013). Except for those few who leave prison in a pine box or who make their own clandestine arrangements to abscond, all prisoners are eventually released back into the community. Unfortunately, among this huge number, one in five will leave with no post-release supervision, rendering "parole more a legal status than a systematic process of reintegrating returning prisoners" (J. Travis, 2000, p. 1). Pushing convicts out the prison door with $50, a bus ticket to the nearest town, and a fond farewell is a strategy almost guaranteeing that the majority of them will return. With the exception of convicts who max out, prisoners will be released under the supervision of a parole officer charged with monitoring offenders' behavior and helping them to readjust to the free world.

Because parolees have been in prison, and are thus on average more strongly immersed in a criminal lifestyle, we should expect them to be more difficult to supervise than probationers, and they are, and we should expect them to have lower success rates, and they do. While Glaze and Palla (2005) indicate a success rate of 60% for probationers in 2004, the same figure for successful completion of parole was only 46% (although note the difference between the success rates of discretionary versus mandatory release parolees in Figure 10.3 and the 58% success rate in 2012 noted earlier in this chapter).

The longer people remain in prison, the more difficult it is for them to readjust to the outside world. Inmates spend a considerable amount of time in prison living by a code that defines as "right" nearly everything that is "wrong" on the outside. Adherence to that code brings them acceptance by fellow inmates as "good cons." Over time, this code becomes etched into an inmate's self-concept as the prison experience becomes his or her comfort zone. When inmates return to the streets, they do not fit in, they feel out of their comfort zone, and their much sought-after reputation as a good con becomes a liability rather than an advantage. As prison movie buffs are aware, these readjustment problems were dramatically presented in the suicide of Brooks in *The Shawshank Redemption* and in the final crazy hurrahs of Harry and Archie in *Tough Guys*.

Brooks, Harry, and Archie all were old men who had served very long periods of incarceration and who had thoroughly assimilated the prison subculture by the time of their release into an alien and unaccepting world. Thus, one recommendation might be to reduce the length of prison sentences so that those unfortunate enough to be in them do not have time to become "prisonized." Such a recommendation gains support from statistics showing that the shorter the time spent in prison, the greater the chance of success on parole (J. Travis & Lawrence, 2002), but if we are looking for something causal in those statistics we are surely sniffing around the wrong tree. Shorter sentences typically go to those committing the least serious crimes and who have the shortest arrest sheets; such people are already less likely to commit further crimes than those who commit the more serious crimes and have long rap sheets. It is not for nothing that former U.S. Attorney General Janet Reno called prisoner reentry "one of the most pressing problems we face as a nation" (as cited in Petersilia, 2001, p. 370).

••• THE IMPACT OF IMPRISONMENT AND REENTRY ON COMMUNITIES

Because crime is highly concentrated in certain neighborhoods, a disproportionate number of prison inmates come from and return to those same neighborhoods. There are those who believe that although high incarceration rates may reduce crime in the short run, the strategy provides only a temporary reprieve and that it will eventually lead to higher crime rates by weakening families and communities and reduce the supervision of children (DeFina & Arvanites, 2002). According to this body of literature, the loss of individuals concentrated in certain communities reduces community organization and cohesion, disrupts families economically and socially, and adds many other problems that will eventually lead to more crime than would have occurred if offenders had been allowed to remain in the community. Clear, Rose, and Ryder's (2001) interviews with residents of high-incarceration neighborhoods is in this tradition. They hypothesized that when public control (incarceration) occurs at high levels, private control (informal control) functions at low levels and ultimately results in more crime. Clear and colleagues did not deny that neighborhood residents were better off and safer when the bad apples were pulled from the shelf and shipped off to prison. This implies the opposite of their hypothesis, however. That is, when private control functions at low levels, public control occurs at high levels.

There can definitely be many negative impacts on the community, especially financial impact on families, when working fathers are removed from it. However, a Bureau of Justice Statistics report (Mumola, 2000) showed that 48% of imprisoned parents were never married and that 28% of those who were ever married were divorced or separated and very few men lived with their children prior to imprisonment. Moreover, the majority of parents had been convicted of violent or drug crimes and 85% had drug problems, which makes it difficult to see how the presence of antisocial fathers in the community somehow contributes to private control rather than detracts from it (Rodney & Mupier, 1999). For instance, a longitudinal study of 1,116 British families showed that the presence of a criminal father in the household strongly predicted antisocial behavior of his children and that the harmful effects increased the more time he spent with the family (Moffitt, 2005). Another large-scale study found that when an antisocial father resides with the mother and offspring there is more risk to children than when the father does not because "children experience a double whammy of risk for antisocial behavior. They are at genetic risk because antisocial behavior is highly heritable [greatly influenced by genetic factors]. In addition, the same parents who transmit genes also provide the child's environment" (Jaffee, Moffitt, Caspi, & Taylor, 2003, p. 120).

PHOTO 10.3: A prison gate stands open both to admit new inmates and to allow them to leave when they have completed their time.

••• WHAT MAKES FOR A SUCCESSFUL REENTRY?

Reentry is a process of reintegrating offenders back into their communities regardless of whether or not they were integrated into it in a prosocial way before they entered prison. Part of that process is preparing offenders to reenter by providing them with various programs that target the risks they pose to the community (e.g., anger management classes) and their needs (e.g., educational and vocational programs). Unfortunately, one of the prices we have paid for the prison expansion during recent years is "a decline in preparation for the return to the community. There is less treatment, fewer skills, less exposure to the world of work, and less focused attention on planning for a smooth transition to the outside world" (J. Travis & Petersilia, 2001, p. 300). Yet there is always an abundance of suggestions about what we should be doing to prepare inmates to reenter free society. If these programs were to be actually implemented, and if they do what they are supposed to do, parolees may have a fighting chance of remaining in the community. The U.S. Department of Justice (Solomon, Dedel Johnson, Travis, & McBride, 2004) lists three programmatic phases believed necessary for reentry with a chance of success:

Phase 1—Protect and Prepare: The use of institution-based programs designed to prepare offenders to reenter society. These services include education, treatment for mental health and substance abuse issues, job training, mentoring, and a complete diagnostic and risk assessment.

Phase 2—Control and Restore: The use of community-based transition programs to work with offenders prior to and immediately following their release from jail or prison. Services provided in this phase include education, monitoring, mentoring, life skills training, assessment, job skills development, and mental health and substance abuse treatment.

Phase 3—Sustain and Support: This phase uses community-based, long-term support programs designed to connect offenders no longer under the supervision of the justice system with a network of social service agencies and community-based organizations to provide ongoing services and mentoring relationships.

The above programming strategy is an ideal rather than a reality most of the time, but many offenders released from incarceration do have access to some parts of each of these phases, and some manage to successfully complete parole. To be successful in Phase 1, offenders must be willing to apply themselves to the training and programming offered to them. They need to make a conscious decision to set long-term goals and convince themselves that a criminal career is not for them. Obviously, these are decisions that are typically only made by individuals not fully immersed in the criminal lifestyle. In Phase 2, they need to implement those decisions in the real world where it counts and not get sidetracked either by the frustration generated by the monitoring they are subjected to by their parole officers or by the criminal opportunities that may present themselves. Phase 3 may be the most difficult of all for some offenders who rely on authoritative figures to give their lives direction. This is why it is so important for community corrections officers to plug their clients into agencies outside the criminal justice system that are able to address parolee needs prior to termination of supervision.

Perhaps the most important tool for the successful reintegration of offenders who want to go straight is employment. Unfortunately, the typical offender is not prepared for much other than a low-skill manufacturing job, the kind of job that the United States has been losing in truly staggering numbers due to technological advances and/or companies moving operations overseas. Job prospects are thus fairly limited unless offenders can improve themselves educationally. A. Solomon and her colleagues (2004) reported that 53% of Hispanic inmates, 44% of black inmates, and 27% of white inmates have not completed high school or obtained a GED as opposed to 18% of the general population. In addition to their general lack of preparedness, employers are understandably reluctant to hire ex-convicts. Even taking into consideration lack of preparedness and employer reluctance to hire offenders, economists find that incarceration reduces employment opportunities by about 40%, wages by about 15%, and wage growth by about 33% (Western, 2003). There is no doubt that once offenders embark on a criminal career, it is extremely difficult for them to desist.

●●● DETERMINING PAROLE "SUCCESS"

Although one would not think so, defining parole success is difficult because there is no agreed-on standard by which we can judge success. Does it mean (1) a completed crime-free/technical violation-free period of parole, or does it mean (2) that the offender was released from parole without being returned to prison despite his or her behavior while on parole? It obviously means vastly different things in different states because parole "success" rates ranged from 19% in Utah to 83% in Massachusetts in

PERSPECTIVE FROM A PRACTITIONER

Lisa Growette Bostaph, Parole Commissioner

Current position: Parole Commissioner for Idaho Commission on Pardons and Parole

Education: Ph.D. in Criminal Justice from the University of Cincinnati

How long in current position and any previous criminal justice experience?

I have served as a parole commissioner for the past 2 years, which is a part-time appointment. My full-time position is Associate Professor of Criminal Justice and Graduate Program Coordinator for the Department of Criminal Justice at Boise State University in Boise, Idaho. Earlier in my career, I worked as a team member in a batterer treatment program; ran a crime scene crisis intervention program for victims of domestic violence, sexual assault, and child abuse; and worked as a victim/witness coordinator for a prosecutor's office, all in Minnesota.

What are the duties and responsibilities of being a Parole Commissioner?

A parole commissioner is charged with reviewing all applicable case material (police reports, presentence investigation reports, criminal history, previous supervision periods, institutional behavior, treatment case notes, and any applicable evaluations and/or assessments) in preparation for making a decision regarding parole during an open hearing with the offender. In addition, we review all offender requests for reconsideration of previous decisions and commutation of sentences plus all requests for pardons.

What are the characteristics and traits most useful in your line of work?

In terms of reviewing all of the documents, anyone serving on the commission needs to have a good attention span and be detail-oriented, empathetic, and nonjudgmental. Offenders come from all walks of life, backgrounds, and demographic categories. To be fair, you must be able to withhold any preconceived notions or stereotypes one may hold about people in any of these categories. This also applies to conducting the interviews during the hearings. To be a successful interviewer, you must be a good listener. Asking questions is not the most important aspect of interviewing; the ability to *hear* what is being said and respond appropriately is of utmost importance.

Please describe your typical workday:

In Idaho, the Parole Commission is a part-time body. There are five of us who serve in rotation on three-person panels hearing cases for 2 weeks of every month. Parole Commissioners in Idaho review case materials for all offenders eligible for parole, then conduct interviews of the offenders during open hearings. We also hear from supporters for the offender and from the victim(s) of the crime at these hearings. Once the interview and statements are completed, we deliberate in private to reach a unanimous decision regarding parole for the offender. We may make one of the following decisions: offer a parole date, deny parole and set another hearing at a later date for reconsideration, or deny parole and pass the offender to his or her full-term release date (meaning that the offender serves his or her entire sentence in prison). After reaching a decision, we reconvene the open hearing and announce our decision. In one day, we generally hear 25 cases, which translates into roughly 125 cases in the one week that each three-person panel serves during a month. If we cannot reach a unanimous decision, the hearing is continued to our quarterly hearings when all five commissioners hear cases (majority decision prevails in these hearings).

What is your advice to someone who wants to enter your field?

For most parole commissions or boards, you must be appointed by the governor, so it is not something that they advertise or for which you apply. That being said, performing well in whatever your chosen career is and serving on criminal justice-related boards and committees will demonstrate your commitment to the field.

1999 (J. Travis & Lawrence, 2002). Does this mean that Utah criminals are more than four times more resistant to taking the straight and narrow road than Massachusetts criminals or that Massachusetts has much better programming and professional parole officers? Of course not; it most likely means that conservative Utah follows our first definition of success, while liberal Massachusetts follows our second definition. Given the national average rate of 42% that year, it is plain that many parolees are forgiven many technical violations, or perhaps even a petty arrest or two, in most states. Thus, "success" has as much or more to do with the behavior of the parole authorities in different jurisdictions as it does with the behavior of parolees. When we speak of "success," then, we are generally speaking in middle-of-the-road terms in which certain parolee misbehaviors are forgiven occasionally in the interest of maintaining him or her on a trajectory that is at least somewhat positive.

●●● PAROLE VIOLATIONS AND GRADUATED SANCTIONS

During these days of tight budgets, a factor that may have played a large part in the increase in parole "success" rate—from 46% in 2004 to 58% in 2012, noted earlier—is the increasing reluctance of states to reincarcerate offenders for minor infractions than was heretofore the case. We saw in Chapter 7 that departments are taking a similar approach with probationers and are developing guidelines for officers to follow that are uniform across all officers' supervision styles. Figure 10.5 presents the Minnesota Department of Corrections guidelines for the restructure of parole conditions or for parole revocation.

Note that parole officers can restructure the conditions of parole without a formal hearing for any of the parole violations listed as Severity Level I or II, although if there are aggravating factors involved parole may be revoked and the offender incarcerated for the times indicated. Severity Levels III and IV automatically lead to revocation unless there are "multiple and/or significant mitigating factors." As noted in our discussion of the Vermont probation revocation guidelines in Chapter 7, the impetus to develop these guidelines was financial, but they are also useful correctional tools in that they provide officers with a uniform way of responding to violations, making authoritarian officers less punitive and permissive officers less tolerant of offender misbehavior.

HALFWAY HOUSES

An additional problem facing efforts to reintegrate parolees into their communities is not always knowing what works best, why, and for whom. In examining 32 studies that looked at the process of prisoner reentry, Seiter and Kadela (2003) identified programs that work, that do not work, and that are promising in helping prisoners in the long process of successfully reentering the community. In their research, they looked at transitional community programs such as halfway houses, work release programs, and programs that initiated treatment for inmate deficits (drug dependency, low education, poor life skills, etc.) while offenders were in prison and continued in the community after release. Programs that worked best were concrete programs that provided offenders with skills to compete in the workforce and intensive drug programs. Programs that were located in the community were more effective than prison-based programs.

As the name implies, **halfway houses** are transitional places of residence for offenders that are, in terms of strictness of supervision, "halfway" between the constant supervision of prison and the much looser supervision in the community. As with probation and parole, early halfway houses were organized and run by private religious and charitable organizations designed to assist released prisoners to make the transition back into free

Halfway houses: Transitional places of residence for correctional clients who are "halfway" between the constant supervision of prison and the much looser supervision in the community.

FIGURE *10.5*   Minnesota Department of Corrections Guidelines for Restructure/Revocation of Parole

Release condition severity level	Presumptive disposition
Severity Level I Restitution payments Unannounced visit/search Leaving state without permission	Restructure
Severity Level II Maintain contact with agent Follow instructions of agent Reside at approved residence Constructive daily activities Contact with law enforcement Use of intoxicants Misdemeanor conviction Subsequent level I violation	Restructure
Severity Level III Gross misdemeanor conviction Violation of special conditions (non-ISR) Violation of restructured release Subsequent level II violation	Revoke (120 days)
Severity Level IV Violation of special conditions (ISR) Felony conviction Report at residence/agent within 24 hours Offender apprehended out-of-state Assaultive behavior Contact with victims Firearms purchase/possession Subsequent level III violation	Revoke (150 days) Revoke (180 days) – Unamenable to supervision – Risk to public safety

Source: Minnesota Department of Corrections (2009).

society. The earliest such home was set up in New York City in 1845 by Quaker abolitionist Isaac T. Hopper (Conly, 1998). Also as with probation and parole, federal and state governments adopted the principles of halfway houses as a good idea. Many states use halfway houses as transition points between prison and full release into the community, and the federal prison system releases about 80% of its inmates into halfway houses ("Director Addresses Changes Within BOP," 2006).

In addition to being a transition between prison and the community, such places (also referred to as community residential centers) may serve as an intermediate sanction for offenders not sent to prison but needing greater supervision than straight probation or parole. The rationale behind halfway houses is that individuals with multiple problems such as substance abuse, lack of education, and a poor employment record may have a better chance to positively tackle these problems and to comply with court orders if they are placed in residential centers where they will be strictly monitored while at the same time being provided with support services to address some of the problems that got them there. Halfway houses may be operated by corrections personnel, but they are also likely to be operated by faith-based organizations such as the Salvation Army and Volunteers of America. Nevertheless, residents are still under the control of probation/parole authorities and may be removed and sent to prison if they violate the conditions of their probation or parole.

In times of rising costs and prison overcrowding, cost-conscious legislators tend to view community-based alternatives to prisons like diet-conscious beer drinkers—"prison lite." Community-based residential programs supposedly provide public safety at a fraction of the cost while allowing offenders to remain in the community and at work earning their own keep. Best of all, they are assumed to reduce recidivism. Halfway houses are also a valuable resource in that they provide offenders released from prison who would otherwise be homeless with an address for employment purposes.

Marion (2002) questioned some of these assumptions and generally painted a disappointing picture for those who believe that keeping offenders out of prison aids in rehabilitation. She saw programs such as halfway houses admitting individuals who would not have gone to prison anyway, meaning that such programs increase rather than decrease correctional budgets. Many residents are "unsuccessfully released" from halfway houses because they used alcohol or drugs while there, and even those successfully released in Marion's multi-year study, between 10.8% and 50.6% (depending on the year of release) were later imprisoned. However, Lowenkamp and Latessa's (2002) more comprehensive examination of 38 such facilities in Ohio found that while not all of them were effective, most were. They found that community-based programs were of no use for low-risk offenders (indicating that they didn't need them in the first place), but that the majority of them were effective in substantially reducing recidivism among medium- and high-risk offenders. Another review of the relative success of halfway houses concluded, "Relative to individuals discharged into the community without supportive living environments, those men and women who found residence in halfway houses had better substance abuse, criminal justice, and employment outcomes" (Polcin, 2009, p. 11).

Halfway houses should not be viewed as another way of coddling criminals. The "exchange rate" (i.e., how much time in an alternative sanction an offender is willing to serve to avoid 12 months in prison) for halfway house placement in the previously discussed study by May and his colleagues (2005) was an average of 12.77 months for offenders who had served time in prison (14.42 months for all offenders). "Experienced" offenders therefore see it as nearly as punitive as prison, despite the relative freedom that halfway residency affords offenders to reintegrate themselves into the community. Much of this has to do with the level of responsibility expected of residents of halfway houses. Living in a halfway house, offenders are expected to take more responsibility for their lives than prison inmates. Halfway house residents are

Community residential centers: Places where offenders (usually parolees) reside when correctional authorities deem them not yet ready to live completely freely.

expected to be in programming, expected to be working or looking for work, and subjected to frequent and random testing for drug/alcohol intake. Some halfway houses augment all this with electronic monitoring. None of these expectations is "suffered" by prison inmates (Shilton, 2003).

••• HOUSE ARREST, ELECTRONIC MONITORING, AND GLOBAL POSITIONING SYSTEMS

House arrest is a program used by probation and parole agencies that requires offenders to remain in their homes at all times except for approved periods, such as travel to work or school, and occasionally for other approved destinations. As a system of social control, house arrest is typically used primarily as an initial phase of intensive probation or parole supervision, but it can also be used as an alternative to pretrial detention or a jail sentence. As is the case with so many other criminal justice practices, house arrest was designed primarily to reduce financial costs to the state by reducing institutional confinement.

House arrest did not initially gain widespread acceptance in the criminal justice community because there was no way of ensuring offender compliance with the order short of having officers constantly monitoring the residence. It was also viewed by the public at large as being soft on crime—"Doing time in the comfort of one's home." However, house arrest gained in popularity with the advent of **electronic monitoring (EM)**. EM is a system by which offenders under house arrest can be monitored for compliance using computerized technology. In modern EM systems, an electronic device worn around the offender's ankle sends a continuous signal to a receiver attached to the offender's house phone. If the offender moves beyond 500 feet from his or her house, the transmitter records it and relays the information to a centralized computer. A probation/parole officer is then dispatched to the offender's home to investigate whether the offender has absconded or removed or tampered with the device. As of 2004, nearly 13,000 offenders were under house arrest, with 90% of them being electronically monitored (Bohm & Haley, 2007).

An even more sophisticated method of tracking offenders is that of the **global positioning system (GPS)**. GPS requires offenders to wear a removable tracking unit that constantly communicates with a non-removable ankle cuff. If communication is lost, the loss is noted by a Department of Defense satellite that records the time and location of the loss in its database. This information is then forwarded to criminal justice authorities so that they can take action to determine why communication was lost. Unlike EM systems, GPS can be used for surveillance purposes as well as detention purposes. For instance, it can let authorities know if a sex offender goes within a certain distance of a schoolyard or if a violent offender is approaching his or her victim's place of residence or work (Black & Smith, 2003). As of 2007, 28 states had legislation calling for some form of electronic monitoring of sex offenders (Payne, DeMichele, & Button, 2008).

Payne and Gainey (2004) indicated that detractors of electronic monitoring tend to criticize it as intruding too much into the realm of privacy and even as barbaric. Of course it is intrusive; that is the point. But it is far less intrusive than prison, and Payne and Gainey stated that offenders released from jails or prisons and placed in EM programs are generally positive about the experience (not that they enjoyed it, but rather that it was better than the

House arrest: Program that requires offenders to remain in their homes except for approved periods to travel to work, school, or other approved destinations.

Electronic monitoring (EM): A system by which an offender under house arrest can be monitored for compliance using computerized technology such as an electronic device worn around the offender's ankle.

Global positioning system (GPS): A system of probation/parole supervision whereby probationers/parolees are required to wear a tracking unit that can be monitored by satellites.

PHOTO 10.4: An electronic monitoring device, attached to an offender's ankle, sends a continuous signal to a receiver, which helps to ensure compliance without probation/parole officers needing to constantly monitor the offender.

COMPARATIVE CORRECTIONS

Chinese Community Corrections

Parole does not exist in China in quite the same sense as it exists in the United States. Each year, only a few dozen inmates are released from prison before the termination of their sentences, and then it is mostly for medical reasons. According to Jiang et al. (2014), an average of just under 2% of criminals were paroled between 2008 and 2010, and offenders convicted of murder, rape, robbery, kidnapping, arson, drug dealing, or organized violence, or those sentenced to more than 10 years, are not eligible for parole. In medical parole cases, offenders are considered on probation and can be returned to prison if or when their medical condition is resolved. For instance, in 1984, a 21-year-old man was sentenced to death for stealing a cap and public brawling, but later he was resentenced to life. He was medically paroled with a form of tuberculosis and fully recovered. In 2004, the police turned up on his doorstep and took him back into custody to serve the remainder of his sentence, although he never stopped reporting to his probation officer and complied with the conditions of his parole ("The Case for Freeing the Last Hooligan," 2011).

China's official criminal justice policy is "Integration of Leniency and Rigidity" (Liu, Zhao, Xiong, & Gong, 2012). China's promiscuous use of the death penalty and its treatment of the young man above points to rigidity, but where is the leniency? From the Chinese point of view, leniency resides in probation and public surveillance. Probation is granted only to first-time minor offenders, and relative to incarceration it is lenient. The Chinese Criminal Code states that "probation may be granted to a criminal sentenced to criminal detention or to fixed-term imprisonment of not more than three years if, according to the circumstances of his crime and his demonstration of repentance, imposing probation will not result in further harm to society" (as cited in Tursun, 2010, p. 288). Probation is typically granted for juvenile delinquency, dereliction of duty, and crimes of negligence; it cannot be applied to recidivists for any crime and is granted in only about 15% of criminal

cases (Liu et al., 2012). Chinese probation is viewed by many observers as the application of reintegrative shaming theory, whereby deviant acts are condemned (shaming) while leaving the door open to reacceptance into society on payment of one's debt to it (Deng, Zhang, & Cordilia, 1998).

Probation is not a formal legal sanction as it is in the United States and other Western countries; it is more an informal means of social control, although the offender is placed under the supervision of a probation officer (Tursun, 2010). Because of China's Confucian heritage, there has been a long tradition of informal social control via sanctioning mechanisms available to people's mediation committees that are organized in work and neighborhood groups (Walsh & Hemmens, 2014). Every adult in China belongs to one or more of these groups, and thus strong pressures toward conformity exist everywhere. Criminal behavior on the part of anyone in the community is seen as a bad reflection on the whole community and is intolerable to mediation committees.

Public surveillance is a sanction similar to probation but further requires that offenders be deprived of the freedom of speech, assembly, association, and demonstration "without the approval of the organ executing public surveillance" (Tursun, 2010, p. 290). Shaw (2010) described such an organ of surveillance with regard to parolees: "In local communities, individual administration of justice stations work with street, village, and other satellite government offices, keeping an inescapable net of surveillance, education, assistance, discipline, and control over former inmates" (p. 65). If a person under an order of public surveillance is deemed to be acting in a manner inconsistent with socialist principles, he or she is reported to the police and may then likely be imprisoned. The level of supervision and assistance afforded Chinese parolees is in stark contrast to the minimal supervision and assistance provided by U.S. parole services as well as by correctional services in other Western nations. This needs to be viewed in light of Western individualism and its concomitant concerns for privacy and individual rights.

jail or prison alternative). Their findings mirror those from a larger sample of offenders on EM programs in New Zealand (Gibbs & King, 2003). Many see it as jail or prison time simply served in a less restrictive and less violent environment (so much for the charge that it is barbaric), although the average experienced offender would exchange 11.35 months

ETHICAL ISSUE ?

What Would You Do?

You are a parole agent. Vice squad police officers with whom you have enjoyed a good relationship in the past have approached you to enlist your aid in setting up a parolee they badly want off the streets. Because you have more leeway than the police to enter the parolee's home and conduct searches, they want you to conduct an early morning raid on his house. They tell you that even if you don't find drugs, you should plant drugs they will provide for you. You know this parolee has been a major dealer in the past and that he has employed violent tactics to protect his territory. Although he hasn't given you any real trouble on parole so far, you agree that this man should not be on the streets. Discuss your options and what you believe you would end up doing.

on EM for 12 months in prison and offenders overall would exchange 13.95 months on EM for 12 months in prison (Moore et al., 2008). It would seem that from this and similar studies that inveterate offenders tend to prefer prison over virtually any other correctional sentence other than straight probation.

Researchers are positive about the alleged rehabilitative promise of allowing offenders to serve time at home and thus maintaining their links to family. A large study comparing 5,000 medium- and high-risk offenders on EM compared with 266,000 not on EM found a 31% decline in the risk of failure among EM offenders (National Institute of Justice, 2011). On the downside, although successful completion rates for EM programs are high, recidivism rates *after release from EM* were not any better than those of probationers/parolees not on EM programs matched for offender risk in several Canadian provinces (Bonta, Wallace-Capretta, & Rooney, 2000). This may be viewed positively, however, as a function of the greater ability to detect noncompliance with release conditions among those under EM supervision.

An additional problem with EM is that because its low cost relative to incarceration is alluring to politicians, it may be (and is) used without sufficient care being taken as to who should be eligible for it. While offenders can be monitored and more readily arrested if they commit a crime while on EM, EM does not prevent them from committing further crimes. Several high-profile crimes, including rapes and murders, have been committed by offenders who succeeded in removing their electronic bracelets (Reid, 2006). When cases such as these are reported, the public (which by and large would rather see iron balls and chains attached to offenders rather than plastic bracelets) responds with charges of leniency. This is unfortunate because EM does appear to have a significant impact on prison overcrowding and on reducing correctional costs. Of course, EM can be considered to reduce correctional costs only if it is used as a substitute for incarceration, not as an addition to normal probation and parole, in which case it is an added cost.

Several European nations have turned to EM to ease the burden of overcrowded prisons over the past 2 decades. The successful completion rates are fairly consistent across countries, and they are refreshingly high. This is possibly a function of the lower-risk offenders that are typically placed on EM in Europe. It is generally required that for an offender to be placed on EM, he or she must have a suitable residence, have a functional phone line, and be working (Havercamp, Mayer, & Levy, 2004). There is also a wide range of times to be served on EM, ranging from about 3 months in England and Wales for probationers to 13 to 23 months for parolees in France (Wennerberg & Pinto, 2009). One large-scale study conducted in Britain of parolees released under home detention curfew using electronic monitoring to enforce it provided very positive results (Dodgson et al., 2001). Six months after release, only 9.3% (118 of 1269) of the EM parolees were reconvicted of a new crime compared with 40.4% (558 of 1381) of the prisoners who were unconditionally released. Of course, all of this difference cannot be attributed to the EM program given that the groups were not matched for criminal history and those on the program were already considered to have a lower risk of reoffending. Nevertheless, the EM group was positive about the program (it got them early release from prison), and the net financial saving to the prison service over 12 months was estimated to be £36.7 million (about $60.9 million). The consensus in the European literature reviewed seems to be that electronic monitoring "works" and that it is here to stay.

••• CONCLUDING REMARKS ON REENTRY AND RECIDIVISM

We have learned that reentry into the community, whether on supervised parole or not, is an extremely difficult process. Everything appears to be working against offenders' successful reintegration, not the least of these factors being the offenders themselves. Many criminals are committed to their lifestyles and simply cannot, or will not, lead law-abiding lives. Numerous lines of evidence show that work and other normal responsibilities that go with the straight life do not mesh well with their "every night is Saturday night" lifestyles (B. Jacobs & Wright, 1999; Mawby, 2001; Rengert & Wasilchick, 2001). Nevertheless, correctional work is premised on the assumption that people can change, and not all criminals by any means are totally resistant to change. Although many offenders seem hell-bent on thwarting the best efforts of all to turn their lives around, many others can be reformed. When we find the best reentry programs (programs that have repeatedly been shown empirically to significantly reduce recidivism) and implement them, what kind of success can we expect? Joan Petersilia, the preeminent reentry researcher today, summed up the combined Canadian and American reentry "what works" literature and stated,

> They took place mostly in the community (as opposed to institutional settings), were intensive (at least six months long), focused on high risk individuals (with risk level determined by classification instruments rather than clinical judgments), used cognitive-behavioral treatment techniques, and matched therapist and program to the specific learning styles and characteristics of individual offenders. As the individual changed his or her thinking patterns, he or she would be provided with vocational training and other job-enhancing opportunities. Positive reinforcers would outweigh negative reinforcers in all program components. Every program begun in jail or prison would have an intensive and mandatory aftercare component. (Petersilia, 2004, pp. 7–8)

Petersilia (2004) went on to suggest that if we could design programs that combined all these things, we might be able to reduce recidivism by about 30%. So with all the best methods currently available, caring and knowledgeable counselors, legislators willing to provide budgets sufficient to meet the needs of all the identified programs, the best we can hope for is a 30% reduction in recidivism. Even this 30% figure is a "best guess" premised on Petersilia's faith in the efficacy of rehabilitative programs. As much as we would all love to find a way to turn offenders into respectable citizens, Petersilia's estimate reminds us that humans are not lumps of clay to be molded to someone else's specifications. Although correctional workers might regret that they cannot mold their charges' minds as they might wish to, the fact that they cannot do so without their owners' consent is a vindication of human freedom and dignity.

SUMMARY •———————————

- Parole is the legal status of a person who has been released from prison prior to completing his or her full term. The concept can be traced to the 19th century with Alexander Maconochie's ticket of leave system in Australia and Walter Crofton's Irish system. Parts of these systems were brought to the United States during the 1870s by Zebulon Brockway, superintendent of the Elmira Reformatory in New

York. Brockway's system required indeterminate sentencing so that "good time" earned through good conduct and labor could be used to reduce inmates' sentences.

- In the modern United States, we have two systems of parole—discretionary and mandatory. Discretionary parole is parole granted by a parole board based on its members' perceptions of the inmate's readiness to be released; mandatory parole is based simply on a mathematical formula of time served. Discretionary parolees are significantly more likely to successfully complete parole than are mandatory parolees.

- The reentry of prisoners into the community is a very difficult process. The ex-con stigma makes getting employment problematic, and the period of absence makes it tough to reestablish relationships. Successful reentry depends on several factors, not the least of which are the policies of the parole authorities, as the huge gap between the Massachusetts and Utah "success" rates indicates. Nevertheless, providing parolees with concrete help such as job skills and drug rehabilitation programs can go a long way in

helping them to remain crime free. This effort may be particularly fruitful if it is made in some form of community-based residential program.

- EM and GPS technology is increasingly used in corrections. It helps by increasing the level of offender monitoring and apprehension, but it cannot altogether prevent additional crimes while on the program, which is why candidates for this type of supervision must be chosen carefully. In sum, few programs can be said to work for most offenders if we define "work" unrealistically. Human nature is complicated, often ornery, and resistant to change. Even "ideal" programs such as those defined by Petersilia (2004) could be expected (according to her) to reduce recidivism by only about 30%.

KEY TERMS

Community residential centers, 229

Discretionary parole, 216

Electronic monitoring (EM), 230

Global positioning system (GPS), 230

Halfway houses, 227

House arrest, 230

Irish system, 215

Mandatory parole, 217

Parole, 214

Parole board, 220

Unconditional release, 216

DISCUSSION QUESTIONS

1. Compare the recidivism rates claimed for the ticket of leave parolees with those of modern American recidivism rates of parolees. What do you think may account for the huge differences?

2. Explore and discuss why it is that we still continue to use mandatory parole in the face of evidence that discretionary parole is a safer bet?

3. What do you think may be the single most difficult problem to overcome by a parolee, who has just been released after serving 5 years, in staying out of trouble?

4. Would it be a good thing to have a number of community-based residential facilities located in high-crime communities so that some of the problems noted by Clear et al. (2001) might be avoided?

5. Given that expert opinion says a 30% reduction in the recidivism rate is about the best we could accomplish if all treatment conditions were optimal, do you think that trying to rehabilitate criminals is a waste of time and that the money would be better spent on keeping them locked up?

$\circledS$SAGE edge™

Review → Practice → Improve

Sharpen your skills with SAGE edge at **edge.sagepub.com/stohressentials3e**.

SAGE edge offers a robust online environment featuring an impressive array of free tools and resources for review, study, and further exploration, keeping both instructors and students on the cutting edge of teaching and learning.

FOR FURTHER EXPLORATION AND APPLICATION, TAKE A LOOK AT THE INTERACTIVE EBOOK FOR THESE PREMIUM RESOURCES:

- ▶ **Career Video 10.1** Division Chief

- ▷ **SAGE News Clip 10.1** OJ Simpson Granted Parole

- ▷ **SAGE News Clip 10.2** California Manson Parole

- ▤ **Journal Article 10.1** The Electronic Monitoring of Offenders Released From Jail or Prison: Safety, Control, and Comparisons to the Incarceration Experience

11 Women and Corrections

© iStockphoto.com/Bill Oxford

TEST YOUR KNOWLEDGE

Test your current knowledge about women working in corrections and those under correctional supervision by answering the following questions as true or false. Check your answers on page 392 after reading the chapter.

1. The number of men and boys under correctional supervision almost always has exceeded the number of women and girls.

2. In early prisons, the correctional experience for women did not significantly differ from that of men.

3. Race shaped the incarceration of men and women in southern and northeastern prisons before and after the Civil War.

4. Female matrons were first hired, in part, to protect female inmates from sexual assault in prisons.

5. Street crimes are usually committed by women and girls and less commonly by men and boys.

6. Women are often considered *double deviants*.

7. Feminists have played an important role in improving corrections for women and girls.

8. A liberal feminist is someone who believes that women and girls should have the same jobs and educational opportunities as men and boys.

9. Male inmates' right to privacy has triumphed against women's equal employment rights in the courts.

LEARNING OBJECTIVES

- Summarize the history of women in corrections

- Identify how the experience of female correctional clients differs from that of males

- Describe the special challenges faced by women and girls in corrections

- Discuss the challenges that female staff have overcome in corrections and how they did so

SUPERVISING IS DIFFERENT **FOR WOMEN**

Mary K. Stohr

This is a story I often tell my students because it was an instance where merely my gender made such a difference in others' aggressive behavior in the correctional environment. The scene is a male prison control room. The sergeant is a very capable man who believes in the power of talking, as in "talking inmates down" from anger and aggression rather than using brute force. An inmate has been called to the office for the purpose of throwing him in segregation for suspicion that he has been "bull dogging" (I had reported him for taking other inmates' desserts at dinner [actually, the other inmates gave him their desserts when he came up to stand by their tables]), and the sergeant admits him to the control room

with two other male officers present in case there is trouble. And there is trouble. This inmate (we'll call him "Casey") is huge—as large as a door, with muscles bulging in his arms. Despite his size, he is not known to be the smartest of men and is prone to anger. The sergeant is wielding all of his verbal skills to reason with Casey, to no avail. Once the inmate refuses to enter segregation willingly and his fists are balling against his sides as he backs away from the sergeant and up against a wall, the sergeant begins calling in reinforcements.

A male counselor and I are in the back room watching this through a glass window. (The sergeant wanted me out of the way in case the inmate directed his anger at me.) When we can see, however, that things are getting out of hand, and knowing that the prison is understaffed, I move into the control room and face Casey. I don't say a word, but my plan is to grab and hold one of his limbs as we jointly wrestle him into segregation. But this plan doesn't become necessary, as Casey takes one look at me, unclenches his fists, and puts his hands out in front of him for the handcuffs. He goes peacefully to segregation. I am stunned, the sergeant is shocked, and the male correctional officers are staring at me as if I had some magic mojo, when all I had was the fact that I was female. I don't know why, but I believe that Casey didn't want to fight with or in front of a female, and for that we all were very grateful!

••• INTRODUCTION

As far back as anyone can remember, there have been fewer women and girls incarcerated or under correctional supervision than there have been men and boys. Of course, there have been exceptions for some crimes (e.g., prostitution for adult and juvenile females, status offending for girls), but correctional populations have always included more males. Although the percentage of women and girls in those populations has increased during recent years, it is still true that the vast majority of those under correctional supervision in the United States are male.

What this numerical "minority" status for girls and women has meant is that institutions and programming are and have been typically geared toward boys and men. As discussed in Chapter 2, the first prisons were built for men, although sometimes a section of them was set aside for women. The U.S. history of institution building illustrates this fact. What Young (1994) found from her research on the construction of juvenile facilities in the southern portion of the United States following the Civil War was that males, particularly white males, were much more likely to have juvenile prisons constructed specifically for them than were females. Women and girls accused (in the case of jails) or sentenced (in the case of jails or prisons) were much more likely to "do their time" in male facilities, initially as part of those facilities (e.g., in bridewells and other poorhouses) and later in separate sections of jails and prisons or completely distinct facilities and houses of refuge (Baunach, 1992; Belknap, 2001; Chesney-Lind & Shelden, 1998; Kerle, 2003; Pollock, 2002b, 2014; Rafter, 1985).

Part of what shaped the treatment of women and girls in the past was the numerical fact that they constituted fewer offenders and inmates than men and boys. As those numbers have increased, however, and as feminist beliefs regarding the value of women and girls have changed attitudes, concerns about how females are treated as clients and what their needs are and about female staff and their rights have reshaped correctional practice. In this chapter, we explore all of these issues, but we begin with a brief history of the female correctional experience.

••• HISTORY AND GROWTH

THE HISTORY OF WOMEN IN PRISONS

As mentioned in Chapter 2, the first American correctional facility—although it is not generally acknowledged as the first American prison—to hold felons only was Newgate Prison in Greenwich Village, New York City. Opened in 1797, it had a separate wing for women inmates, where they were housed in a group setting. As Rafter (2009) noted, putting the women together, although they had no matron, helped to provide protection from "lascivious turnkeys" or guards (p. 51). All indications are that the women at Newgate washed and sewed for the prison (while the male inmates were engaged in the production of goods for sale) and were situated close to other inmates.

When Newgate Prison closed, and the inmates were scheduled for transfer to the congregate but silent and strict discipline prisons of Auburn and Sing Sing, neither prison wanted to take the women, stating that they were difficult to manage (Rafter, 2009). While the matter was debated, the female inmates from New York City were held at the city's Bellevue Penitentiary, where the conditions in terms of food, housing, supervision, and classification were poor. Moreover, the silent requirement, so popular at the men's prisons, could not be enforced because of the congregate housing and the lack of a female matron. When a cholera epidemic hit the prison, 8 women died and 11 escaped (Rafter, 2009).

The New York women outside of New York City were sent to the new Auburn Prison in 1825 (Rafter, 2009). However, their treatment there was also subpar; they were housed in a cramped, unventilated attic above the kitchen without a matron until one was hired in 1832. Because of the congregate nature of their living and working conditions (they were engaged in sewing), it was once again difficult to enforce the silence requirement.

After discipline by the lash was used on a 5-months-pregnant inmate (who got pregnant while in prison) who later died, the state constructed a separate prison at Mount Pleasant for the women in 1839, the first women's prison in the United States (Rafter, 2009). Although it was close to Sing Sing Prison and was, in part, administered by it, **Mount Pleasant Prison** had its own buildings, staff, and administrator. This prison was built behind Sing Sing and overlooked the Hudson River. It was an Auburn-like building with Auburn- and Sing Sing-like sensibilities. It had a room for lectures, a chapel, and a nursery. The matron's quarters were also in the prison.

Ohio's development of prison facilities for women was similar to that of New York (Rafter, 2009). At first, women inmates were held in less secure facilities along with the men. Then, in 1834 Ohio built an Auburn-like prison called the Ohio Penitentiary, and in 1837 the state housed the women in a separate annex from the men. However, the standards for prison operation in Ohio were even worse than in New York, and disease and corruption were rampant. The annex for the women became crowded and fell into serious disrepair. The women had no matron, and thus discipline was nonexistent; moreover, the women were subject to sexual attack by male staff.

Among Tennessee prisons, when the first opened in Nashville in 1831, there was a progressive attitude toward standards and care, more like the New York model (Rafter, 2009). Women, however, were imprisoned in such small numbers before the Civil War that they were housed right with the men and worked with them in mines and on railroads. There were no matrons to protect them, and there were no separate accommodations for women in Tennessee prisons until the 1880s, and then they were placed in small, overcrowded quarters in the Nashville prison, with no room for work or exercise.

RACE IN EARLY PRISONS

Maryland opened its first prison, the Maryland State Penitentiary, in 1811 in Baltimore (Young, 2001). From its inception, it housed the women in a congregate fashion, in the same prison with the men, until 1921, although women were separated. At first, the races were not separated, but by the 1830s, black men and white men were separated at the prison, and later so were the women. Because Maryland was a *border state*—a slave state, although one caught between the slaveholding South and the free

PHOTO 11.1: A prison officer examines the knitting of an inmate.

Mount Pleasant Prison: The first prison constructed for women in the United States. Built in 1839 close to the Sing Sing Prison (New York) for men, it was in part administered by Sing Sing but had its own buildings, staff, and administrator.

North before the Civil War—administrators of its penitentiary wrestled with issues of slavery and free and enslaved blacks. The research on incarcerated black women indicates that they were disproportionately incarcerated in the Northeast and Midwest before the Civil War but that there were few blacks, male or female, incarcerated in the South before the war. After the war, however, black men and women were also disproportionately incarcerated in all prisons, but particularly in southern prisons, where slavery-like treatment and work requirements were imposed (Oshinsky, 1996; Rafter, 2009; Young, 2001).

In her study of the Maryland State Penitentiary between the years 1812 and 1869, Young (2001) found that 72% of the incarcerated females were black and that as the Civil War drew to a close, the proportion of black women only increased. This was also true regarding the incarceration of black women around the Civil War, especially during the antebellum stage, in Texas, Kansas, and Missouri. It is possible that a Maryland law, passed in 1858, that made black women who committed larceny subject to "sale" rather than prison resulted in less incarceration of black women before the Civil War in that state (Young, 2001).

Both black and white women in the United States of the 19th century tended to be incarcerated for property crimes, particularly larceny (Rafter, 2009; Young, 2001). Very few women were incarcerated for violent crimes—about 3% or 4% (Young, 2001). White women did tend to be incarcerated for "offenses against morality" more than black women were, perhaps because they were more "visible" to the police in white areas of town or because the police were more attentive to them (Young, 2001). But there were also convictions for other felonies, miscellaneous offenses, and vagrancy. Young (2001) also found that black female inmates were required to serve a greater proportion of their sentences than were white female inmates, and they tended to be pardoned less and to die while incarcerated more often than were white female inmates.

DISCIPLINE IN WOMEN'S PRISONS

As with male prisons during the 1800s, methods of discipline moved from the severe to the soft, depending on the availability of supervision, the facilities, the number of women incarcerated, and the inclinations of the keepers. Rafter (2009) reported that the lash was rarely used at Mount Pleasant Prison for women, but the gag was used all the time. At the Ohio prison, for instance, by the 1870s the discipline of women was quite severe, and women were beaten or placed in solitary confinement to enforce it (Rafter, 2009). By 1880, the "hummingbird" punishment was used in Ohio; it "forced the naked offender to sit, blind-folded, in a tub of water while steam pipes were made to shriek and electric current was applied to the body" (p. 53).

HIRING OF FEMALE MATRONS

A serious problem for many of the first prisons was the absence of a female matron to supervise and, in some cases, protect the women. Writing in 1845 (reprinted in 1967) after visiting several primarily male facilities that housed women, the reformer Dorothea Dix noted that matrons had been hired in several prisons where women were housed (e.g., Connecticut Prison, Sing Sing Prison, Eastern Penitentiary, and Maryland Prison) but not in many county jails or other prisons (Dix, 1845/1967).

Houses of refuge:
Facilities whose stated purpose was to remove impressionable youths, mainly boys but also girls, from the contamination that association with more hardened adult prisoners might bring.

HOUSES OF REFUGE FOR GIRLS AND BOYS

Developed in tandem with the adult prisons were juvenile facilities in larger states for delinquent, neglected, abandoned, and abused children. **Houses of refuge** were part of the Jacksonian movement (named after President Andrew Jackson) of the early 1800s to use institutions as the solution for social problems. The first was opened in New York in 1825, the second in Boston in 1826, and the third in Philadelphia in 1828 (Beaumont & Tocqueville, 1833/1964, p. 136). Their stated purpose was to remove impressionable youths, mainly boys but also girls, from the contamination that association with more hardened adult prisoners might bring. As Harris (1973) commented, such facilities for younger inmates had existed in Europe, particularly Holland, since the 17th century. The difference she noted between the American experiment with houses of refuge and the Dutch experiment was that the Dutch houses were used only for the delinquent and those thought likely to become so without intervention, and they were devised to achieve reform among their inmates.

From the first, the American house of refuge was a private institution. Such institutions were developed through private charity and subscription and were operated by people hired by private subscribers. The states sanctioned their development this way and paid "some pecuniary assistance" to them, but they had no part in their administration (Beaumont & Tocqueville, 1833/1964, p. 137).

The early American houses of refuge were to be a mix of prison and school. The keepers in such houses were guardians, and such guardianship continued until the children reached the age of 20. In some of the houses, the children were separated at night and worked or went to school together during the day. In others, they were in congregate situations both at night and during the day. The requirement of silence, imposed on adult institutions of the time, was not visited on the children because it was thought to be impossible to keep them completely quiet. In the New York and Philadelphia houses, the children labored in a workshop making shoes or cloth and as carpenters for 8 hours a day and spent

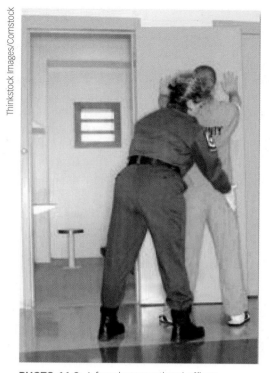

PHOTO 11.2: A female correctional officer searches a male inmate. Most correctional facilities try to perform same-sex searches, but that is not always possible.

another 4 hours in school. In the Boston house, they spent only 5.5 hours in the workshop, 4 hours in school, and 1 hour in religious study, and there were a few hours for play (Beaumont & Tocqueville, 1833/1964, p. 142). The workshops in the houses were operated by private contractors. Notably, the girls did all of the domestic work around the houses, including the cleaning, cooking, and sewing of clothes for themselves and the boys. The discipline used in the houses varied from deprivation of recreation, to solitary confinement, to restrictions on food and water, and sometimes to the use of corporal punishment or the use of stripes (lashes with a leather belt).

Because the children placed in houses of refuge were not always sent there for punishment, it was thought that their time needed to be indeterminate given that a magistrate could not tell at the beginning how long it would take to reform or correct the children. It was left to those who operated the institutions to decide when a child was ready to leave them. Moreover, if the child did not do as well as was hoped when released and was under age 20, the staff at the institution were still his or her guardians and had the right to call the child back into the house. Beaumont and Tocqueville (1833/1964) acknowledged that these absolute rights to deprive liberty might have led to abuse, but they pointed out that judges and parents did have some rights to oversee and protest the incarceration of these children in the courts.

In a recidivism study of the New York House of Refuge conducted by Beaumont and Tocqueville in 1831 (1833/1964), the authors found that of more than 500 children released, at least 200 of the boys and girls had been "saved from infallible ruin" (p. 151). As to the other children released, they found that their behavior since release was either doubtful, "bad," or "very bad" (p. 151). Of course, lacking a control group for these releasees, it is difficult to know how to interpret these findings, but it was an admirable attempt by these French observers to try to find evidence as to the effectiveness of such early houses of refuge.

Dorothea Dix, whose own research is described more fully in Chapter 3, also visited houses of refuge in Boston, New York, Philadelphia, and Baltimore and a farm school for children on Long Island (Dix, 1845/1967). Her impression of these facilities, 14 years after Beaumont and Tocqueville had visited some of them, was generally favorable. She liked that the children were employed in useful work, that the facilities were clean, and that the children were generally in good health. She noted that many houses of refuge provided schooling, training, and apprenticeships that would allow the children to succeed once they were able to leave. Some of the reports from the facilities that she reviewed indicated that children as young as 6 were incarcerated in these houses and that possible offenses that led to placement were being "stubborn" or "idle" along with other more common but usually minor criminal offending (Dix, 1845/1967, p. 91). Boys were often apprenticed to farmers and girls to domestic work once they reached their age of majority and so were able to leave the institution.

GROWTH IN NUMBERS OF WOMEN AND GIRLS

As mentioned in the foregoing, the number of incarcerated and supervised women under the correctional umbrella has never been larger, but it was not always so. In the past, the number of women inmates and supervisees was proportionately smaller. For instance, we know from U.S. Census reports that women constituted 3% or 4% of state and federal prison populations from 1910 through the 1970s (Cahalan, 1986, p. 65). In 1980, that proportion had risen to 5% and has only increased since then. According to Cahalan (1986), if you add in reformatories, women and girls accounted for, on average, about 5% of those incarcerated in correctional facilities from 1910 through 1959 (p. 66). Jail inmates were anywhere from 5% to 9% female from 1910 to 1983 (p. 91). Juvenile institutions averaged about 21.2% female residents (aged 15–19) from 1880 to 1980 (p. 130). Unfortunately, a gender breakdown of parolees and probationers is not available, but given the overall increase in the percentage of incarcerated women generally and women and girls on probation or parole currently, it is likely that historically they were not as subject to the criminal justice system as they are today either.

The best explanation for the historically low number of female offenders in the U.S. criminal justice system (as compared with males) has been the fact that they commit fewer street crimes that would garner this distinction. Most murders, robberies, rapes, burglaries, and even larcenies are committed by men and boys (Federal Bureau of Investigation [FBI], 2014). Even among corporate (or white-collar) and environmental crimes, the more likely offender is male, if for no other reason than the fact that more males are in a position to commit such crimes than are females. As mentioned in other chapters, the drug war of the past 30 years has brought more female offenders into the system, and this fact has resulted in their greater proportional growth among correctional populations, but even with this sort of offense they are in the clear minority.

••• WOMEN AND GIRLS IN CORRECTIONS TODAY

FEMALE CORRECTIONAL CLIENTS

More recently and by any measure, however, the number of women and girls as inmates or supervisees in corrections has grown exponentially over the past several years (see Figure 11.1).

In 2000 women comprised 11.4% of jail populations, but by 2014 that figure was nearly 15% (Minton & Golinelli, 2014; Minton & Zeng, 2015, p. 2). In 2000 women comprised 6.4% of prison populations, and by 2014 that figure was more than 7% (Carson,

2015, p. 2; Carson & Golinelli, 2013, p. 23). Girls confined in residential facilities increased from 13.6% of all juveniles in 1997 to 15.1% in 2003, although by 2010 they accounted for 13% again (Hockenberry, 2013, p. 11). But the largest growth, as far as correctional populations are concerned, has come in probation. Women constituted 22% of probation and 12% of parole caseloads in 2000, and by 2013 the percentage had increased to 25% for probation, although for parole it had stabilized at 12% (Herberman & Bonczar, 2015, pp. 17, 20). Although some of these percentage increases seem small (along with a few decreases), they represent increases, in the case of probation, of thousands of women on probation given that total caseloads in 2006 included 5 million people. For girls on probation, the increases do not even seem small. In 1985 girls constituted 19.3% of juveniles on probation, and by 2004 that percentage had grown to 27.2% and remained at 27% by 2009 (Livsey, 2012, p. 2; Puzzanchera & Kang, 2007). As indicated by the data contained in Figure 11.1, the overall

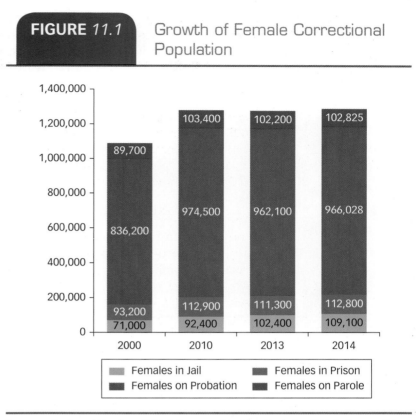

FIGURE *11.1* Growth of Female Correctional Population

Sources: Beck and Harrison (2001); Bureau of Justice Statistics (2001); Carson (2014, 2015); Glaze and Bonczar (2011); Glaze and Kaeble (2014); Guerino, Harrison, and Sabol (2012); Herberman and Bonczar (2015); Kaeble, Glaze, Tsoutis, and Minton (2016); Kaeble, Maruschak, and Bonczar (2015).

number of adult females under correctional control remained steady from 2010 to 2014; the only exception was the relatively large increase in women in local jails (an increase of 18.1%). Despite this increase, the majority of inmates for all correctional populations are still largely male, as shown in Figure 11.2.

FEMINISM

Women staff would not be employed at the level they are, and female inmates would not have the attention and programming they do (albeit usually less than men and boys), if not for the sustained efforts of feminist scholars and practitioners agitating for their rights and their needs (Pollock, 2002b, 2014; Rafter, 1985; Smykla & Williams, 1996; Stohr, 2006; Young, 1994; Zimmer, 1986, 1989; Zupan, 1992). As indicated by Rafter (1985), the proponents of change in female corrections during the last half of the 1800s and first half of the 1900s tended to be of two minds, as represented by the moralists and the **liberal feminists.**

There were those *moralists,* who were sometimes *social feminists* as Rafter (1985) termed them, who believed that women and girls involved in the criminal justice system were, in effect, morally impaired and therefore in need of religious and social remedies (prayers, efforts to keep them chaste, etc.). Women were crudely classified by these moralists either as "good," thus acting in conformance with societal expectations for their gender role (labeled the *madonna*), or as "bad," thus acting in opposition to their expected gender role (labeled the *whore*). This conceptualization and limited view of the possibilities for women and girls and its focus on sexuality were also shaped by social class and race/ethnicity. Those women who were of a higher class and who were white were believed to more closely approximate the madonna category—until, that is,

Liberal feminist: One who believes that the problem for girls and women involved in crime lies more with the social structure around them and that the solution lies in preparing them for an alternate existence so that they do not turn to crime.

FIGURE *11.2* Percentage of Male Versus Female Inmates, 2015

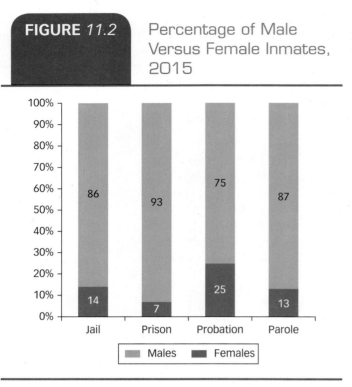

Sources: Carson and Anderson (2016); Kaeble and Bonczar (2017); Minton and Zeng (2016).

they violated societal expectations that they be docile homemakers with nary a thought in their heads. Should they violate these expectations regarding their gender role and social and legal prohibitions against the commitment of crime, then they were **double deviants**. (Rather than just being deviants, as men and boys who committed crime were, women and girls involved in crime were also deviants in terms of societal gender role expectations [Belknap, 2001].) Women of lower classes, but particularly women of color, were not expected to attain this madonna status. Women in the lower and even working classes, which described most women during the late 1800s and early 1900s, often worked outside of the home because they needed to in order to help support their families; thus, the belief—really a myth—that most women used to work only in the home applied only to the middle-class and wealthier women, not to the majority of women. Women of color, disproportionately represented in the lower classes (then and now), were seen as more sexual in nature, perhaps as a justification for their exploitation in this manner, and so could not even aspire to madonna status (Belknap, 2001).

There were others, those who espoused a *liberal feminist* perspective, who believed that the source of the crime problem for female offenders lay more with the social structure around these women and girls (e.g., poverty, lack of sufficient schooling or training, patriarchal beliefs) (Daly & Chesney-Lind, 1988). Liberal feminists believed that the solution to female crime lay in preparing those inclined to engage in it for an alternate existence—for work—and sometimes this involved "traditional women's work" so that they would not turn to crime (Rafter, 1985). Some of these early feminists believed, as liberal feminists do today, that men and women are inherently equal, and as such women and girls are entitled to the same rights, liberties, and considerations (e.g., in corrections, this would be programming, quality of institutions, and equal employment as staff) as men and boys (Belknap, 2001; Daly & Chesney-Lind, 1988).

The moralists triumphed, although not completely, in the argument over what lay at the heart of female criminality. As a consequence, we have had more than a century of correctional operation that has tended to be overly concerned with the sexuality of females (Giallombardo, 1966; Hefferman, 1972; Owen, 1998; Rafter, 1985). Another consequence of this triumph was that reform efforts were directed at training female inmates to be proper wives and mothers while forgetting that as members of the lower classes they would need to make a living for themselves and their children once they reentered their communities. Despite this morals-of-the-fallen-woman focus—the "soiled dove," if you will—feminist women and men were able to agitate for and sometimes get separate facilities for women and girls as well as other services (e.g., educational and job training) that were geared toward helping women and girls become independent and self-supporting in the free world (Hawkes, 1998; H. Yates, 2002).

Double deviants: Term often applied to women and girls when they engage in crime because they have violated societal gender role expectations and they have committed a crime.

Patriarchy: Involves the attitudes, beliefs, and behaviors that value men and boys over women and girls.

One societal obstacle to achieving equal treatment in corrections has been **patriarchy**. Patriarchy involves the attitudes, beliefs, and behaviors that value men and boys over women and girls (Daly & Chesney-Lind, 1988). Members of patriarchal societies tend to believe that men and boys are worth more than women and girls. They also believe that women and girls, as well as men and boys, should have certain restricted roles to play and that those of the former are less important than those of the latter. Therefore, education and work training that help one make a living and attain better pay are more important to secure for men and boys than for women and girls, who are best suited for more feminine—and by definition, in a patriarchal society, less worthy—professions. Feminist scholars have determined that many cultures, even today, hold such beliefs and engage in the practices that derive from them.

In the United States, much effort has been expended over the centuries, by male and female feminists, to address the patriarchal belief system, and there has been some success in this regard (Dworkin, 1993; S. Martin & Jurik, 1996; Morash, 2006; Whittick, 1979). In terms of corrections, feminists have been instrumental in pushing for more and better programming for incarcerated and supervised women and girls, for a reduction in the incarceration of girls for status offenses, for attention to the sexual abuse of women and girls while incarcerated, and for the greater employment of women in adult male and female correctional institutions.

MEETING FEMALE INMATES' NEEDS AND PROVIDING PROGRAMMING

In an article published in *American Jails Magazine*, Ney (2014) succinctly summarized some of the basic facts and differences between men and women in jails, with substantial application to prisons:

1. "Women pose a lower safety risk than men." What this means is that women do not riot and don't assault each other or staff as much, and when they do, they do less damage. They are less likely to be incarcerated for violent offenses.

2. "Women's pathways to criminal justice are different than men's." They are much more likely to be prior victims of abuse and to be impoverished before incarceration than men. They are more likely to have substance abuse problems and to have this problem intertwined with abuse and mental illness.

3. "Women's engagement in criminal behavior is often related to their connections with others." They commit crimes with crime partners, and usually, those are the men in their lives.

4. "Women entering jails and prisons often report histories of victimization and trauma, and continue to be vulnerable to victimization within correctional settings." This history makes them more susceptible to substance abuse, mental illness, and targeting by predators as future victims.

5. "Correctional policies and practices have largely been developed through the lens of managing men, not women." This means that the risk, needs, and responsivity issues that are so key to constructing programming that "works" are not adequately addressed for women.

6. "Jail and prison classification systems can result in unreliable custody designations and over-classification of female inmates." As a result, women will be held in more secure facilities and sections of facilities than is necessary.

7. "Gender-informed risk assessment tools can more accurately identify women's risk and needs." Some research is indicating that assessment might be more accurate—and thus result in more effective programming—if it fits the reality of women rather than men.

8. "Women are more likely to respond favorably when jail (and prison) staff members adhere to evidence-based, gender-responsive principles."

9. "Transition and reentry from jail to the community can be challenging for women." Reentry programming should therefore be geared to address their particular needs, which are often similar to men's but not always.

10. "The cost of overly involving women in criminal justice is high." Not only are we incarcerating or overly supervising people who are in less need of it, we are stymieing the ability of these women to grow and develop in a prosocial manner, we are depriving children of their mothers, and we are costing the taxpayers approximately twice the amount of money it takes to incarcerate men for someone who is usually less of a threat to the community. (pp. 8–10)

As a practical matter, then, if not just because women and girls have historically been valued less by this society (patriarchy) but perhaps because crime has generally been the purview of men and boys, correctional facilities and correctional practices have tended to focus on men. This focus led to disparate treatment that disadvantaged women and girls from the beginning and resulted in little concern for their needs, then or now, as Ney's (2014) summary indicates (Muraskin, 2003).

Yet women and girls are more likely to have mental and physical health problems than incarcerated men and boys (Morgan, 2013; Schaffner, 2014). They are also more likely to have substance abuse problems than their male counterparts. Moreover, they have the same kinds of educational and job training deficits and needs as men and boys (Gray et al., 1995; Morash, Haarr, & Rucker, 1994; Owen & Bloom, 1995; Pollock, 2002b). Their need for gainful employment is likely as great as, if not greater than, that of men and boys because they most often need to support themselves and their children, whereas fewer men have custody of their children before they are incarcerated (Owen, 2006); about 70% of women have custody of their children at the time of their incarceration (Henriques, 1996, p. 77). Moreover, a greater percentage of women, perhaps as high as 60%, were the victims of sexual abuse in the past, and this is likely to negatively shape their self-concept and their relations with others, thus necessitating more programming (Belknap, 2001; Blackburn, Mullings, & Marquart, 2008; Comack, 2006; Morash, 2006; Pollock, 2002b).

Given all of these needs, and assuming that policymakers would not want women and girls to reenter the system if for no other reason than they cost much more to incarcerate (because of their needs and a reduction in economies of scale—separate female institutions house fewer inmates but require nearly the same number of administrative and support staff as much larger male institutions), one would think that all of their needs would be met with adequate programming and health care. Unfortunately, this has been far from the case in most jurisdictions. Although there has been some recognition by the federal government of the need to develop programming that fits the needs of women and girls, it is unclear how much this has spread to state and local facilities (Morash, 2006; Morgan, 2013; Schaffner, 2014).

Although most of these needs are far from met in correctional environments, and far less than a majority of women are involved in meaningful programming, Pollock (2002b) noted that some states have made renewed efforts to address the needs of women and girls for educational, vocational, parenting, and substance abuse issues and their histories of past victimization. However, the numbers of these programs and their quality (very few are rigorously evaluated in terms of desired outcomes) leave much to be desired (Pollock, 2002a). In a longitudinal study of prison industries in federal women's prisons, Richmond (2014) found that involvement in this work had no effect on reducing rearrest or recommitment to federal prison. The author speculated that this lack of effect might be due to the fact that the work program was not suited to women and their needs. In a review of 155 programs designed to meet the reentry needs of women on community supervision in the 10 largest metropolitan areas, Scroggins and Malley (2010, p. 146) found that the programs were inadequate. The sad truth is that most women and girls

IN FOCUS 11.1

Orange Is the New Black (or Not)

The popular Netflix show *Orange Is the New Black* loosely features the sometimes hilarious and sometimes tragic experience of one woman (Piper) in jails and then a federal prison as a result of her drug courier involvement. In later episodes in the first and second seasons, the experience and life circumstances of several women in the same prison as Piper are also chronicled. The color orange in the title refers to the traditional color of the jumpsuit given to women (and men) in American jails (but rarely in prisons), although in reality their garb in jails varies depending on their security level and the preference of each facility, typically from orange, to white, to yellow, to red, to striped jumpsuits of various colors against a white background. In prisons, it is more likely that you'll find the women inmates in jeans and T-shirts than in an orange (or other colored) jumpsuit. Of course, the color black in the title refers to the classic color for women's wear (*basic black*), and so the title *Orange Is the New Black* might signify that imprisonment of women and the attendant orange wear is becoming much more common in our everyday lives than is the basic black of a woman in the free world. Or put another way, as per this show and the statistics cited in this chapter, prison is becoming a much more common experience for women, even white women with an upper-middle-class background like Piper,

PHOTO 11.3: Some of the cast of the show *Orange Is the New Black*.

but particularly for all of the working-class or poor women of color as well as those who are white, who are also featured in the show.

Discussion Questions

1. Why has the number of women in jails and prisons increased (metaphorically making orange the new black)?

2. Why do you think shows about imprisonment are so popular these days?

Getty Images/Jennifer S. Altman

who need programming in corrections are not able to access it, or if they are, it is sometimes of dubious worth (Morgan, 2013).

Researchers find that women and girls have programmatic needs and styles that determine whether some rehabilitative approaches are more effective than others (Loper & Tuerk, 2006; Staton-Tindall et al., 2007; E. Wright, Salisbury, & Van Voorhis, 2007). One type of programming with particular relevance for women, given that most had physical custody of their children prior to incarceration, is parenting programs. Loper and Tuerk (2006) found in their research on such programming that it is delivered in several prisons, but its purported value in terms of helping mothers and fathers become better parents has not been rigorously studied (see also Pollock, 2002a; Surratt, 2003). Craig (2009), in her past-to-present review of mother-and-child programs in prisons, found that many states and localities have had programs where infants or very small children may stay with their mothers, at least initially. However, most correctional facilities where women are housed do not have such programs, and the qualifications for their use, even in states that have them, vary widely.

In an interesting study of male and female inmates in 20 substance abuse treatment programs, Staton-Tindall and colleagues (2007) found that the females reported more psychosocial dysfunction (e.g., anxiety, depression), less criminal thinking (e.g., coldheartedness, entitlement, irresponsibility), and greater involvement in programming (e.g., willingness to participate, receptivity to input) than did the males. The authors maintained that these findings support other research indicating that programming for women must be shaped to fit their abuse histories and mental health needs.

Relatedly, in a study of 272 incarcerated women offenders in Missouri, E. Wright and her colleagues (2007) found that gender-responsive problems related to parenting, child care, and self-concept affect prison misconduct. Brown (2006), in her study of native and non-native Hawaiian women imprisoned in Hawaii, developed the alternate but parallel idea of *pathways* women traverse that can lead to crime. A pathway strewn with violence, trauma, and addiction, coupled with discrimination based on race, gender, and class, is more likely to end in criminal engagement for women. Such a pathway, Brown explained, may be related to poorer treatment outcomes for incarcerated women.

The health care needs of incarcerated women are tied up in needs specific to gender and in the particular pathway where many poor women tread. Women in jails and prisons have numerous gynecological, obstetrical, psychological, and psychiatric health ailments that are more specific to their gender along with health problems that are common to both genders. Because the health care needs of poor women and children in communities are going unmet, it is not surprising that similar circumstances apply to incarcerated women. Predictably, then, Moe and Ferraro (2003) found from their interviews of 30 women incarcerated in an Arizona jail that while basic needs were met in this jail, when the care required was of the long-term, extensive, or individualized type, it was lacking.

ABUSE

Unfortunately, abuse does not necessarily end at the corrections door. One of the primary reasons why women and girls were removed from facilities for men and boys during the 1800s and 1900s, and female staff were hired to supervise them, was that they were targets of sexual abuse by correctional staff and male inmates (Henriques & Gilbert, 2003; see also Figure 11.3). Although separation from male inmates has reduced their abuse, the sexual abuse by male staff—despite likely being much less prevalent than it once was, in part because of the inclusion of more female staff—has not been eliminated.

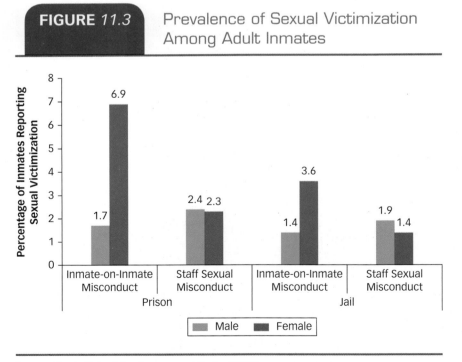

FIGURE *11.3*   Prevalence of Sexual Victimization Among Adult Inmates

Source: Beck, Berzofsky, Caspar, and Krebs (2013).

One of the authors of this book had occasion to serve as an expert witness for the plaintiffs in a civil suit in 2004 against a city in New Mexico whose judge and a few correctional officers for the local jail were involved in the sexual abuse of female inmates (*Salazar et al. v. City of Espanola et al.*, 2004). The male judge and a few male correctional staff members had an arrangement whereby female offenders whom the judge found attractive would be placed in the jail (whether their alleged offenses merited it or not), and then the judge would have access to them when they were sent over to "clean" his chambers. Inevitably, he would make passes at them, using the threat of more jail time, denied privileges, or a lengthened sentence as a way to coerce them into sexual activity with him. Meanwhile, a few of the correctional staff members were harassing the female inmates such as watching and commenting on their bodies as they showered, making sexual advances toward them, and touching them inappropriately. Two male officers were even involved in removing a few females from their cells and having sex with them in the control room at night, when no one else was around. There were no female staff on duty at the time of these sexual assaults and this abuse. After this kind of activity occurred for a period of time, and due to the concerted efforts of several ex-inmates and their attorneys, the judge was convicted of rape and the judge, correctional staff, and city lost a million-dollar lawsuit (*Salazar et al. v. City of Espanola et al.,* 2004).

In an even bigger case, *Tracy Neal v. Michigan Department of Corrections,* the plaintiffs alleged more than two decades of sexual abuse of women inmates in Michigan prisons (cited in Culley, 2012, p. 206). The history of abuse was compelling, as the combined jury verdicts in the case awarded $30 million for the plaintiffs and a settlement of $100 million.

Unfortunately, the sexual abuse of female inmates by male staff is not limited to adult facilities (see Figure 11.4). In 2003, the American Civil Liberties Union (ACLU) investigated reports of the abuse of juvenile girls by male staff in the Hawaii Youth Correctional Facility and reported that male staff observed the girls using the toilets and showers, made comments about their bodies, and threatened to rape them, and in fact several girls did have sex with the officers in exchange for cigarettes (Chesney-Lind & Irwin, 2006). A year later, one officer pled guilty to three counts of sexual assault and to threatening a female ward. A key circumstance that came out in the ACLU report was that there were no female officers on duty at night, when much of the abuse of the girls took place.

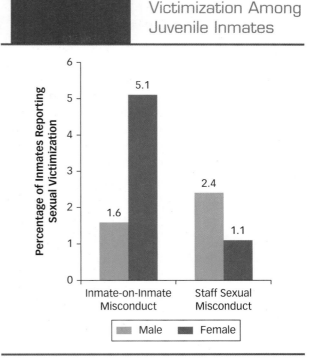

FIGURE *11.4* Prevalence of Sexual Victimization Among Juvenile Inmates

Source: Beck, Berzofsky, Caspar, and Krebs (2013).

Such abuse is particularly damaging when one considers that more than half of incarcerated women and girls have experienced some form of sexual abuse in the past (ACLU, 2015; Gray et al., 1995; Henriques & Gilbert, 2003). The Ninth Circuit Court (although not the Supreme Court), recognizing this fact, put some restrictions on body searches of female inmates by male staff, noting that such searches may serve to revictimize the women with sexual abuse histories (*Jordan v. Gardner,* 1993).

Efforts to reduce sexual abuse in correctional institutions have centered on ensuring that staff have the proper training and are supervised sufficiently to prevent abuse. Moreover, the value of disciplinary measures to reinforce appropriate practices cannot be overstated. Clearly, staff who violate the rights of their charges in a way that is as serious as sexual abuse should be fired and prosecuted, and there is some evidence emanating from the reporting required by the Prison Rape Elimination Act (PREA) that this may be occurring (see the discussion of PREA in preceding chapters on jails [Chapter 6] and prisons [Chapter 8]).

The hiring of more women officers to cover living units is another way that correctional agencies have worked to keep sexual predators from gaining access to relatively powerless female victims. There is no question, however, that lawsuits have been successful in spurring some of these needed changes in correctional practice. But the problem with lawsuits is that their application is hit or miss at best, and the success of plaintiffs

ETHICAL ISSUE ?

What Would You Do?

You are a female probationer living in the community. Your probation officer keeps coming on to you, but you aren't interested. Last week, at a family birthday you had a beer, and the next day your officer ordered a urinalysis. It came back "dirty" for alcohol. Now, your probation officer is saying that in exchange for sexual favors, he won't violate your probation. What do you think you should do? What are the likely consequences of any action you take?

is always iffy. For instance, although the *Neal* case referenced earlier was ultimately a success in the end, it took a 15-year battle to get the abuse to stop (Culley, 2012). Therefore, the best preventative measures are those that focus on hiring competent people, training them to behave professionally, supervising them carefully, rewarding them when they behave professionally, and punishing them (up to and including firing and prosecuting them) when they do not.

ADJUSTMENT, MISCONDUCT, AND PSEUDOFAMILIES

Women's adjustment in corrections is associated with their sometimes problematic personal relationships, separation from children, and greater propensity for mental health problems as well as the fact that in prisons women tend to be charged with infractions for more minor offenses (Owen, 2006). As Van Tongeren and Klebe (2010) found in their study of female inmate adjustment in a maximum-security prison in Colorado, adjustment is a multidimensional concept that encompasses an inmate's particular circumstances and environment, as well as his or her criminal thinking and adoption of the prison subculture. For instance, in a study of co-occurring disorders, or COD (mental illness and substance use disorder), of women inmates in Pennsylvania prisons, Houser and Welsch (2014) found that those inmates with COD were more likely to engage in misconduct than inmates without COD.

Beyond the mental illness and substance use disorders that some women prison inmates have, another circumstance they find themselves in, in most states, is being far from family and friends. There is still only one women's prison in most states, which is often located away from urban centers where most of the women come from. As a result, it is difficult to maintain familial relationships and friendships when a woman has a lengthy sentence. Poor families will find it much more difficult to visit their incarcerated family members because they will not have reliable or inexpensive transportation available. Moreover, incarcerated women do not have access to cell phones or computers to contact family and friends. The pay phones they do have access to are expensive to use for poor families, who must pay for the collect calls (even local calls). Because many of these women are incapable of writing a letter, and their children may be unable to read or be unreachable

PHOTO 11.4: Visits by family members are much appreciated by inmates of correctional facilities.

to these women, the ability to maintain contact is further impaired. The separation from children is particularly acute because the mothers lose control over their children's housing and care. Often, the children are placed with family members who have a history of abuse or in the foster care system, which in most states is overwhelmed (S. Sharp & Marcus-Mendoza, 2001).

As with males, females incarcerated or supervised in corrections must grapple with the pains associated with that status and find some way to adjust to its strictures. Early researchers in women's prisons (e.g., see Giallombardo, 1966) reported on the formation of *pseudofamilies* as a way for women to meet their needs for companionship, support, and love as well as sexual gratification. It was thought that women were

IN FOCUS 11.2

Gender Pathways to Community Corrections, Jails, and Prisons

For several years now, criminal justicians and criminologists have been researching and writing about the types of circumstances and choices that typify the life course of someone entangled in the criminal justice system. For girls and women, such circumstances include childhood poverty, low levels of education, poor neighborhoods and schools, abuse and neglect as children and abuse as adults, mental illness, substance abuse, and involvement with criminally engaged partners (Bloom, Owen, & Covington, 2003; Brown, 2006; DeHart, 2008; Owen, 1998; Simpson, Yahner, & Dugan, 2008). The effect of victimization on subsequent offending for such women is clear: Those who experience more victimization as children are also more likely to be involved in the criminal justice system—including corrections—earlier and are more likely to continue their own criminal engagement into adulthood.

Discussion Questions

1. Why would victimization as a child and as an adult lead to more involvement in crime?

2. Are men and women likely to differ in their pathways to crime? Why or why not?

3. What can be done to change the path to criminal involvement for girls and women?

importing these familial roles from traditional family structures and playing them out in the prison setting. In any given pseudofamily, there were inmates who took on the roles of fathers, mothers, grandmothers, daughters, aunts, and cousins. More recent research has shown that some women do indeed form "families" while in prison, but the strength of these relationships is perhaps more casual than was first reported (Owen, 1998). Moreover, as might be expected, women incarcerated for longer periods of time and who are further from their release dates may be more likely to maintain their pseudo-familial relations than those who are not as immersed in the subculture due to shorter incarcerations.

••• FEMALE CORRECTIONAL OFFICERS

FEMALE STAFF

The trajectory of employment of female correctional officers has not been as steep or as steady as it has been for those women and girls under correctional supervision. As already mentioned, women were employed as matrons, to a limited degree, to work with females in some of the earliest prisons and jails (Pollock, 2002b; Stohr, 2006; Zupan, 1992). However, they did not make significant inroads into the correctional profession until the 1964 Civil Rights Act was amended in 1972 and women began using that law to sue in courts to gain employment in both female and male correctional institutions. According to the Bureau of Labor Statistics (2016a, p. 4), in 2015, women occupied about 23.8% of correctional officer jobs in jails and prisons. As of 2005, only 13% of correctional officers in federal prisons, but 48% of correctional officers in private prisons, were women (Stephan, 2001, p. 8; Stephan, 2008, p. 4). As was mentioned in Chapter 9, it is probably no coincidence that the prisons that pay the most (federal) employ the fewest women as officers, and the prisons that pay the least (private) employ the most.

Staff demographic statistics regarding probation and parole officers for adults and children are not always readily available. According to a recent Bureau of Justice Statistics

PERSPECTIVE FROM A PRACTITIONER

Kay Heinrich, Correctional Program Manager

Position: Correctional Program Manager

Location: Washington State Department of Corrections

Education: M.A. in counseling and education, M.A. in criminal justice, and Ph.D. in criminal justice

What are your primary duties and responsibilities?

The Prison Division (PD) correctional program manager (CPM) is an integral part of the division's management team. This person is responsible for implementation of evidence-based principles (EBPs) policies that impact the PD. This includes assisting with staff development related to evidence-based interventions. The CPM provides operational oversight for evidence-based units and institutions, focusing on resource utilization and staff training needs and operationalizing evidence-based practices within the Washington State Department of Corrections (WSDOC) intensive-management, close-custody, medium, and minimum units.

This position contributes to the mission of the Department of Corrections (DOC) by ensuring that PD delivers EBPs consistent with resource allocations and established principles. These principles target offenders' risks and needs in order to achieve the DOC performance goals of improved public safety, decreased recidivism, and the operationalization of core correctional practices (CCPs). CCPs provide staff with tools to hold offenders accountable through effective interventions that contribute to changing offender behavior. The CPM position is responsible for assisting facilities in the operationalization of these principles. In coordination with established chains of command and other divisions, this position supports the fidelity of the EBP structure and delivery within the prisons by assessing data, observing operations at program sites, and interacting with staff and offenders.

Previously, for the WSDOC, I worked for 17 years as the clinical supervisor for the WSDOC Chemical Dependency Unit researching evidence-based practices, simultaneously designing, facilitating training for, and implementing chemical dependency (CD) programming treatment, including therapeutic communities, intensive outpatient programs, and a reentry continuum to the community for incarcerated, chemically addicted offenders.

What are the characteristics and traits most useful in your line of work?

- Perseverance and flexibility
- Honesty and integrity
- Practice what you preach
- Collaboration and communication skills
- Open-minded
- Ability to admit defeat and continue on while maintaining integrity
- Trustworthy
- Strong work ethic and ability to meet with staff during all three shifts
- Healthy boundaries between and within personal, professional, and offenders' borders
- Understanding of organizational development, culture, attitudes, and the stages of change within the institution and individuals, including offenders
- Getting along with others, which includes a diverse population of staff and offenders
- No matter how competent you are, if you cannot fit in, you will not be promoted
- Dealing with offenders' criminal histories and crimes, with the ability to remain objective in dealing with the offenders on a daily basis
- Dealing with offenders and managing staff

Please describe a typical workday.

There is no typical workday. Each day depends on the prison's level of security and the immediate needs of the institution to meet the safety and security of staff and offenders. For example, you may have meetings and training sessions planned, treatment groups scheduled, and individual priorities; however, if count is not cleared, there is an act of violence in the units or yard, or a medical or mental health emergency occurs, everything stops to accommodate correctional officers' responsibilities to maintain control and management of the prison.

When the prison is under "normal" status, responsibilities include traveling to the prisons where the evidence-based programs are facilitated to ensure that adequate staff are available and trained plus that staff are supported for working in a therapeutic role versus a custodial role. Labor unions, shift work, and a paramilitary environment are additional considerations that influence program implementation and facilitation, which make each day atypical. The prisons are scattered throughout Washington State, so travel is extensive, and use of GPS is mandatory. This position requires knowledge of each prison's administrative and management personnel and style, including the political hierarchical expectations from headquarters.

A CPM must have the ability to maintain neutrality in order to ensure that EBPs are facilitated with integrity and adherence to the model's curriculum. Neutrality extends toward each of the diverse offender populations (maximum to minimum offender classification), management styles, and cultures of every prison served according to the personalities, values, and attitudes of the superintendent and executive management team.

What is your advice to someone who wants to enter your field?

Stay away from the naysayers and negative staff. Don't get caught up in the politics at the prison or headquarters level. Don't get personally or intimately involved with fellow employees. Stick to your value system and the important role each position brings to achieving the overarching goal of offender change and public safety. Never lose your sense of humor, belief that people (staff and offenders) can change, hope in humanity, and belief that good always overcomes evil.

report, 49% of all state-level parole agency staff are women, but this figure includes all staff, not just parole officers (Bonczar, 2008, p. 3). Unfortunately, the Bureau of Justice Statistics does not supply this level of information regarding probation officers at the state or federal level. However, the Bureau of Labor Statistics (2016a, p. 3) reported that in 2015, 55.4% of probation officers and correctional treatment specialists in the country were women.

OVERCOMING EMPLOYMENT OBSTACLES

As with the accused and convicted women in the system, women have always constituted a minority in terms of correctional staff (see Figure 11.5). Although one would expect that women might comprise a greater percentage of staff given their representation in the larger community, the current figures actually represent a significant improvement over 30 or 40 years ago. At that time, women—with exceptions allowed for matrons in women's and girls' facilities working for lower pay than men working in male facilities—were prohibited by practice, tradition, or law from working in the more numerous men's and boys' correctional institutions or in probation and parole.

Although they were often prohibited from having an official and paid role in working with correctional clients, women were true partners in the work in America's early and rural jails. In what were termed *mom-and-pop jails*—rural jails from 1900 to 1970—Ruddell and Leyton-Brown (2013) found from their content analysis of newspaper articles covering the period that sheriffs' wives "admitted and supervised arrestees, thwarted jail escapes, apprehended escapees, and challenged lynch mobs" (p. 270).

However, as was mentioned earlier, it was not until the Civil Rights Act of 1964 was passed and amended in 1972 that women were given the legal weapon to sue for the right to work and be paid and promoted in all prisons, jails, detention centers, juvenile facilities, and halfway houses as well as in community corrections. Many women did in fact sue; they needed to if they wanted the same kinds of jobs and promotional opportunities

FIGURE *11.5*   Number of Male and Female
Correctional Employees, 1984–2005

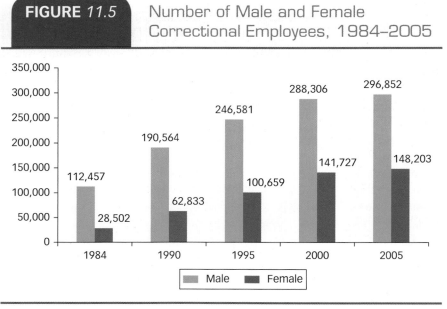

Sources: Stephan (1987, 1992, 1997, 2008); Stephan and Karberg (2003).

Note: Most recent data available. The data from the 1984 Census (Stephan, 1987) was for "state adult correctional facilities"; federal institutions were excluded.

then available only to men in corrections, policing, and law (Harrington, 2002; Hawkes, 1998; Stohr, 2006; H. Yates, 2002). As a result of this agitation and advocacy, slowly the available jobs and promotional opportunities became open to these pioneering women, resulting in the more diverse correctional workforce we see today.

CURRENT STATUS

As the number of women employed in corrections has increased, three issues have been particularly problematic for them in the workplace:

1. Whether women's rights to equal employment in male correctional facilities are more important than male inmates' rights to privacy in those same facilities

2. Whether women are physically and mentally suited to do correctional work with men

3. How to deal with sexual and gender harassment—primarily from other staff—while on the job

Equal Employment Versus Privacy Interests of Inmates

As mentioned before in this section, women achieved the legal right to equal employment in corrections through the law and lawsuits. Most of the jobs in institutional corrections or in communities are in dealing with male inmates or offenders. On the other hand, one can certainly understand the perspective of male inmates that they would like some privacy when engaged in intimate bodily functions such as using the toilet and showering. However, the courts, in this matter, have tended to side with the female employees' or prospective female employees' right to equal protection over the male inmates' right to privacy (Farkas & Rand, 1999; Maschke, 1996). Their reasoning was likely as much influenced by the fact that inmates in the United States have very limited rights while incarcerated, with no real right to privacy, as by the fact that correctional staff should be respectful and professional, no matter their gender, in their dealings with inmates.

Qualifications for the Job

The issue of whether women are physically and mentally qualified to work with male inmates has generally become a settled matter in most institutions, agencies, and states: They are. But when they were first making inroads into the correctional workplace, there were plenty of doubts about the ability of women to handle the work (Jurik, 1985b, 1988; Jurik & Halemba, 1984; Zimmer, 1986, 1989). Even regarding their propensity to use aggression in the course of their work, men and women correctional staff are similar (Tewksbury & Collins, 2006). However, the Supreme Court has left open the possibility that if there were a bona fide job requirement that women could not fulfill in a male prison, they could be excluded from that work (Bennett, 1995; Maschke, 1996).

In a qualitative study of female parole agents in California, Ireland and Berg (2006) noted that these agents reported subtle harassment in the form of less desirable shifts or assignments because of their gender. The women also felt that they were overlooked for promotions and an administrative career track. One 40-year veteran of the department observed that it was not the clients who harassed the women agents but rather their colleagues, who "often questioned [their] competence and treated [them] unprofessionally" (p. 140). In response to such bias and views, the women reported that they overcompensated, or did more than was expected of males on the job. Some female parole agents adapted by taking on stereotypically feminine roles such as acting helpless and in need of male assistance, flirtatious, and maternal. Still another adaptation by these agents was to refuse to acknowledge that there was any bias at all in the workplace; this latter group of women did not think that considerations of gender or race/ethnicity had hampered their ability to advance in their careers.

? ETHICAL ISSUE

What Would You Do?

As a new female correctional officer in a male prison, you are finding it difficult to gain acceptance from some of your older male colleagues. Of particular concern is whether you are tough enough to lead people who might not respect you as an officer. An older female officer advises you to act disrespectfully toward a few of the less well-regarded inmates (i.e., sex offenders) in front of those doubtful staff as a way of establishing your "toughness" credentials. Although you can appreciate that doing so may alleviate concerns by a few of these staff, it also requires you to do something you find abhorrent. What would and should you do in this instance?

Clearly, because of their biology, most women are not as physically strong as most men, and sometimes strength is called for in dealing with an unruly inmate. However, the use of brute force is rather rare in most correctional institutions and in the community when functioning as a probation or parole agent. Second, there are defensive (and offensive) tactics that give a trained and armed woman some advantage in a physical altercation with a male inmate. Third, there is some evidence that female staff may have a calming effect on male inmate aggression because they are more inclined to use their interpersonal and communication skills and are less likely to be seen as a threat (Jurik, 1988; Jurik & Halemba, 1984; Lutze & Murphy, 1999; Zimmer, 1986).

Some research has indicated that both male and female correctional officers value a service orientation over a security orientation in their work, so their work styles and preferences may be more similar than dissimilar (Farkas, 1999; Hemmens, Stohr, Schoeler, & Miller, 2002; Stohr, Lovrich, & Mays, 1997; Stohr, Lovrich, & Wood, 1996). Research in one state indicated that women correctional officers in prisons might be more fearful of victimization by inmates than are their male colleagues (Gordon, Proulx, & Grant, 2013). In research on attitudes of 192 male and female jail officers in a southwestern state's jail system regarding conflict resolution with inmates, Hogan and her colleagues (Hogan, Lambert, Hepburn, Burton, & Cullen, 2004) found that the genders reacted somewhat similarly in this area as well. When the gender of the inmate was female, male and female officers were likely to react equally aggressively. However, female officers perceived a greater physical threat from male inmates and were more likely to use force than male officers.

In research by Kim and colleagues (Kim, DeValve, DeValve, & Jonson, 2003) on the attitudes of male and female wardens, they found that 90 of the female wardens (out of a total of 641 male and female wardens surveyed) were more inclined to value programming and amenities in their prisons that promoted health, education, and other programming for inmates than were their male colleagues. However, these researchers also found that there were many more similarities than differences between the two genders as they viewed and appreciated their work.

PHOTO 11.5: Two female officers confer in a jail.

Taken in total, what all of this research on women's ability to do the work and on the differences and similarities in work styles between men and women indicates is that men and women mostly view and do correctional work similarly; that some women, perhaps more than some men, can calm an agitated inmate; and that some men, perhaps more than some women, are better at physically containing an agitated inmate.

Sexual and Gender Harassment

Unfortunately, the problem with gender and sexual harassment of female staff by male staff is not yet a settled matter. This is not to say, of course, that male staff are not harassed by female staff. This does happen and can be as debilitating for the male employee as it is for the female. But a number of studies have shown, over a period of years, that females are much more likely to be the victims of male harassment by bosses and coworkers in the workplace and that when men are victims they are as likely to be harassed by other men as by women (Firestone & Harris, 1994, 1999; Mueller, De Coster, & Estes, 2001; O'Donohue, Downs, & Yeater, 1998; Pryor & Stoller, 1994). Male institutions in particular, with their smaller percentages of women employees and managers and their traditions aligned with male power in the workplace, are more susceptible to this kind of behavior than are other correctional workplaces (Lawrence & Mahan, 1998; Lutze & Murphy, 1999; Pogrebin & Poole, 1997). The types of harassment that occur can be **quid pro quo sexual harassment** (something for something, as in you give me sexual favors and you get to keep your job) or the less serious, but still workplace-stultifying, **hostile environment** (when the workplace is sexualized with jokes or pictures or in other ways that are offensive to one gender).

Thankfully, there are remedies, imperfect and cumbersome though they might be, that can be employed to stop or at least significantly reduce such harassment. Initially, women needed to sue in order to stop the harassment because many managers of their workplaces simply would not do anything to stop it. In one mid-1990s case, one of the authors of this book served as an expert witness for the plaintiff against the State of California's San Quentin Prison. The female victim was awarded more than $1 million for enduring harassment by several male staff members and one inmate that started during the 1970s and ended when she quit in frustration during the 1990s; it was never stopped by the prison administration (*Pulido v. State of California et al.*, 1994). As successful as this case was, there was incontrovertible evidence of the harassment (as provided by memos, diaries, staffing logs, and witnesses), evidence that is usually not available to support most victims' stories. Moreover, the female victim, an African American woman, lost her job and needed to endure nearly 2 years of an uncertain legal battle before the case was tried and the judge ruled. Even then, the State of California appealed, and it took another year before the matter was finally settled in the plaintiff's favor.

What this story illustrates is that there are few true "winners" when sexual and gender harassment cases go to trial. Most such cases fail because there is not sufficient evidence of the abuse beyond a "he said, she said" scenario. Victims of such abuse suffer untold harm in terms of their psychological and physical well-being, both during the abuse and as they relive it during the legal process. Even when cases are successful at trial, taxpayers (not just the instigators of the abuse, who often do not have the "deep pockets" of their governmental employer) need to pay for the illegal practices of their own governmental entities and actors.

Quid pro quo sexual harassment: Involves something for something, as in you give your boss sexual favors and he allows you to keep your job.

Hostile environment: Occurs when the workplace is sexualized with jokes, pictures, or in other ways that are offensive to one gender.

In other words, there has got to be a better way—and there is. Researchers and correctional practitioners have agreed that there are proactive steps that managers and other employees can take to prevent or stop sexual and gender harassment in the correctional workplace. Such steps would involve hiring, training, firing, and promoting based on respectful treatment of other staff and clients. Training, in particular, can reinforce the message of a no-tolerance policy regarding harassment. But for it to be effective, employees need to see that people are rewarded when they adhere to the policy or are punished when they do not.

As a discussion of the current status of female staff working in corrections would indicate, women have made some significant advances in these workplaces. They have not just made gains in employment, but female supervisors and managers are also no longer anomalies in most states. Although nowhere near matching the numbers of men as staff and management in corrections, and while still grappling with the pernicious problem of sexual and gender harassment, nonetheless they have come a long way since the days of working as matrons, with lower pay and less respect, attributes that typified their work for most of the history of corrections.

SUMMARY

- The study of women and girls in corrections was not always a priority for scholars (Flavin & Desautels, 2006; Goodstein, 2006; Mallicoat, 2011). Patriarchal perceptions and beliefs, along with women's status as numerical minorities, have served to shape organizational and scholarly priorities in a way that favors men and boys. Since the 1970s, however, there has been more scholarly focus on the reality of women and girls who work, live, or are supervised under the correctional umbrella.

- Part of this shift in focus has occurred as the result of feminist efforts to equalize the work for women and the living and supervision arrangements for women and girls under correctional supervision.

- Recent research on women and girls under correctional supervision has highlighted the outstanding needs they have for educational, substance abuse, work training, parenting, and abuse survivor programming. Unfortunately, it has also shown that little programming is provided, in either jails, prisons, or the communities, to meet these needs.

- Female correctional officers have also faced a number of legal and institutional barriers to their full and equal employment in corrections.

- For the most part, many of these formal barriers have been removed as female officers have demonstrated their competencies in handling correctional work.

- Some researchers have even found a feminine style to officer work that employs the successful use of interpersonal communication skills to address inmate needs.

- However, there is still evidence that sexual and gender harassment and the sexual abuse of female inmates continues in some correctional environments. Although organizational remedies exist to "deal" with such abuse, they are not always employed by managers.

- Taken in tandem, the research presented in this chapter should shift our perspective from the much more numerous and normative studies of males over to females. By shifting our gaze to the female side, we are as likely to see the sameness of the genders as the contrasts that distinguish them (Rodriguez, 2007; Smith & Smith, 2005). We might also see that the life course of a woman or girl entangled in the criminal justice system (e.g., see Brown, 2006, and E. Wright et al., 2007) forms a predictable pattern that might be fruitfully addressed if we only had the will to do so.

KEY TERMS

Double deviants, 244

Hostile environment, 256

Houses of refuge, 240

Liberal feminist, 243

Mount Pleasant Prison, 239

Patriarchy, 244

Quid pro quo sexual
harassment, 256

DISCUSSION QUESTIONS

1. In what ways have women and girls occupied a minority status in corrections? How has that status affected how they are treated in the system?

2. What is feminism, and what do feminists advocate? How have they had an effect on the work of women and their (and girls') experience with incarceration?

3. What is patriarchy? What kind of effect did, and does, patriarchy have on corrections for women and girls? How might it negatively affect the experience of men and boys?

4. What sorts of factors are likely to lead to the greater abuse of female inmates in correctional institutions? How might such abuse be prevented?

5. What sorts of factors are likely to lead to sexual and gender harassment in correctional work? How might such harassment be stopped or prevented?

6. How might female officers' supervision styles differ from those of male officers? What might be the advantages of hiring women to work with men and boys in corrections? What might be the advantages of hiring men to work with women and girls in corrections?

Review → Practice → Improve

Sharpen your skills with SAGE edge at **edge.sagepub.com/stohressentials3e.**

SAGE edge offers a robust online environment featuring an impressive array of free tools and resources for review, study, and further exploration, keeping both instructors and students on the cutting edge of teaching and learning.

FOR FURTHER EXPLORATION AND APPLICATION, TAKE A LOOK AT THE INTERACTIVE EBOOK FOR THESE PREMIUM RESOURCES:

▶ **Career Video 11.1** Public Defender

▶ **Feature Video 11.1** Feminist Perspectives on Offending

▸ **SAGE News Clip 11.1** Florida Prison Dogs

▸ **SAGE News Clip 11.2** Tennessee Female Inmates

▤ **Journal Article 11.1** Women's Pathways to Serious and Habitual Crime

12

Minorities and Corrections

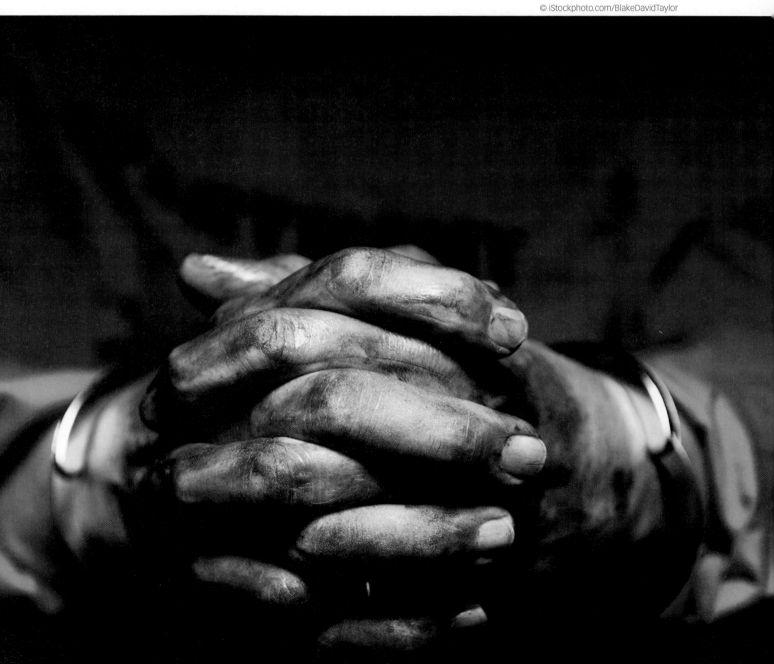

TEST YOUR KNOWLEDGE

Test your current knowledge about minority groups in this country and their experiences as staff and inmates in corrections by answering the following questions. Check your answers on page 393 after reading the chapter.

1. The race of a person is determined by his or her biology. (True or false?)

2. The ethnicity of a person is determined by his or her culture. (True or false?)

3. Explain what happened in the Scottsboro case and why it is considered emblematic of how African Americans were handled by the criminal justice system during the earlier half of the 20th century.

4. Name at least three facts that would indicate that racism still exists in the criminal justice system of today.

5. Very few Native Americans were in the Americas when Columbus landed. (True or false?)

6. Chinese and Japanese American immigration was widely supported during the 19th and 20th centuries. (True or false?)

7. Describe the reasoning for the internment of Japanese Americans in 1942. Why weren't German Americans also placed in such camps?

8. There is a connection among class, race/ethnicity, and crime. (True or false?)

9. The drug war has led to the increased incarceration of Hispanics and blacks in the United States. (True or false?)

10. Crack cocaine and powder cocaine are pharmacologically different. (True or false?)

11. Research shows that blacks and Hispanics use more drugs than whites. (True or false?)

LEARNING OBJECTIVES

- Define *race, ethnicity, disparity,* and *discrimination*

- Describe some of the history of minority group members in this country

- Identify the connection among class, race/ethnicity, and crime

- Explain the special challenges faced by minority group members in corrections

- Discuss how the criminal justice system has not been race neutral in its treatment of minorities

UNDOCUMENTED WORKERS **AND THEIR SIDE OF THE STORY**

One of the largest groups of cases before the federal courts and in some form of federal corrections (jails and prisons) involves unauthorized immigrants from Mexico and Latin America (Light, Lopez, & Gonzalez-Barrera, 2014). Yet although they violate U.S. immigration laws, De La Torre (2013), in her ethnographic research on Mexican migrants and

their version of their immigration story, found that these immigrants do not see themselves as criminals at all; rather, they see themselves as moral actors confronting impossible circumstances that require crossing the border in order to provide for themselves and their families. One can well imagine that refugees fleeing war-torn Syria for Europe in

2015, 2016, and 2017 would likely make the same argument.

The immigrants, in interviews, characterized coming to the United States as a moral act necessitated by the lack of decent living conditions and sparse opportunities in Mexico. As it was, they were unable to support their families in Mexico and did not see a future there:

> For instance, Juan Carlos, in his mid-20s, came to work in Chicago because he wanted a better economic position that would allow him to afford necessary things, among them, milk to feed his newborn daughter. His opportunities were limited as he struggled to provide for his family while living in Acapulco. Women also recounted how they had to sacrifice to feed families, raise their children, and take care of their elderly parents and relatives while engaged in paid work. For example, Araceli, in her early 30s, came to the USA because she was the only provider in her household, as her elderly parents could no longer work and her younger siblings started college in Guanajuato. In coming to the USA she sacrificed her own chance to attend college in Mexico. (De La Torre, 2013, p. 272)

But coming to the United States carries its own hazards and risks. One of them is incarceration and then expulsion from this country. As Light and his colleagues (2014) documented, "Among federal sentenced offenders in 1992, 12% were unauthorized immigrants. By 2012, that share had increased to 40%" (p. 1).

• • • INTRODUCTION

The races and ethnicities of America's population have shaped its law and practice from the beginning. At the very writing and ratification of the Constitution, full citizenship was denied to those who were not white and, for many decades, to those who were not male and in possession of significant amounts of property. The institution of slavery, the forcible seizure of American Indian lands, and the limitations on the immigration of non-whites and their rights while in the United States all have marked and marred this country. Accordingly, police agencies, courts, correctional institutions and programs, and their actors have historically treated people differently based on their race and ethnicity.

Minority group members were more likely in some parts of the country to be incarcerated when they were innocent or sentenced for periods that were longer than their white brothers and sisters. Once in the correctional system, minority group members were sometimes segregated into separate institutions, sections of institutions, and programs. At times, they were given less desirable jobs and housing in jails and prisons and were prevented from working in such places. Whether such discriminatory treatment continues today is a matter of some debate, but there are indications that some laws, police, courts, and correctional practices have the effect of maintaining a separate and unequal system for minority group members. In this chapter, we briefly discuss this history and use it as a context for current practices and experiences in corrections.

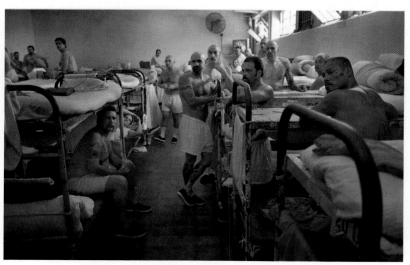

PHOTO 12.1: California inmates in Chino State Prison sitting in mixed-race groups.

••• DEFINING RACE, ETHNICITY, DISPARITY, AND DISCRIMINATION

RACE

Race is a term that refers to the skin color and features of a group of people. The extent to which different racial groups truly differ biologically is still being determined by scientists. Scientists are still putting together the collective pieces of our human history. However, the genotyping of the whole human race indicates that our species likely originated in Africa (Diamond, 1997; McAuliffe, 2010). Waves of migration then occurred, beginning at least 50,000 years ago and continuing over thousands of years, to Europe and Asia, resulting in variation in skin color and other features of racial groups, who in turn migrated to other continents and islands (Mann, 2006; McAuliffe, 2010). It is worth noting that even as these physical distinctions developed, there has been much intermingling, both historically and currently, among groups, resulting in populations that are substantially mixed rather than distinct in their "racial" heritage. For this reason, using racial designations, such as white, black, and Asian, might be necessary to ensure that one group is not advantaged over another, but we should recognize that they can be somewhat arbitrary designations because true racial differences, although visible to the eye, may be measured more in gradations than in clear distinctions, particularly in the most racially mixed communities.

ETHNICITY

Ethnicity, on the other hand, refers to the differences between groups of people based on culture. An ethnic group will often have a distinct language as well as distinct values and traditions and a shared religion and history. An ethnic group may be made up of several races and have a diverse national heritage. For instance, the term Hispanic is applied to an ethnic group in the United States that includes white, black, and Asian racial groups whose ancestors may hail from Cuba, Puerto Rico, Mexico, or Central or South America. Descendants of Italians, Irish, French, German, and other ancestral ethnic Europeans who immigrated to the United States are usually racially white but not always; while in Europe or after immigrating to the United States, those groups may have intermingled with Africans and Asians. For instance, people known as Creoles are both ethnically and racially differentiated by their white and African racial background and the French ethnic cultural influences in Louisiana. And who are "black Irish" Americans but primarily white ethnic Irish people who intermingled with Spanish Moorish people while in Europe (who were at least partially from North Africa) and who then immigrated as Irish to the United States. Among black people in the United States, there are distinct ethnic differences between those whose ancestors have been in the country for hundreds of years, either as free people or as those forcibly brought here through slavery, and those whose families are more recent immigrants from Africa or predominantly racially black areas of the world (e.g., immigrants from Caribbean Islands like Haiti). More recent immigrants from the Sudan, Nigeria, or Kenya are different ethnically; that is to say, they have a distinct culture, as well as nationality, from each other and from those blacks whose families have been in the United States for generations.

DISPARITY AND DISCRIMINATION

Clear, Cole, and Reisig (2011) defined **disparity** as "the unequal treatment of one group by the criminal justice system, compared with the treatment accorded other groups" (p. 527). In turn, they defined **discrimination** as "differential treatment of an individual or group without reference to the behavior or qualifications of the same" (p. 527). We would add that disparity can happen in many organizations and entities and is not just restricted to the criminal justice system, and often discrimination is linked in law

Race: Refers to the skin color and features of a group of people.

Ethnicity: Refers to the differences between groups of people based on culture. An ethnic group will often have a distinct language as well as particular values and traditions and a shared religion and history.

Disparity: Occurs when one group is treated differently and unfairly by governmental or other actors as compared with other groups.

Discrimination: Occurs when people or groups are treated differently because of who they are (e.g., race, ethnicity, gender, age, disability, religion, nationality, sexual orientation or identity, income) rather than because of their abilities or something they did.

to classes of people distinguished by race, ethnicity, gender, age, disability, religion, nationality, sexual orientation or identity, and income.

••• A LEGACY OF RACISM

The legacy of racism (or discriminatory attitudes, beliefs, and practices directed at one race by another) runs long and deep in the United States. Notably, sometimes the term racism is also applied when one ethnic group holds discriminatory attitudes or beliefs about, or engages in discriminatory practices against, another ethnic group. Correctional institutions and programs, as social institutions, are products of their larger social, political, and economic environments, and therefore the legacy of racism has affected and continues to affect their operation.

AFRICAN AMERICANS

In the United States, slavery historically involved the involuntary servitude of black Africans by white Europeans and was practiced almost from the settling of the United States (Davis, 2008). Many of the founding fathers were slave owners, and the practice of slavery was protected in the Constitution (through the three-fifths designation of slaves in Article I [the worth that slaves had for states that wanted to count them for representation in Congress] and Article IV [which caused fugitive slaves to be returned to the slave owners]).

Slavery was a lucrative business for ship owners in the colonial United States, both northern and southern, and for plantation owners in the South because it provided the backbreaking agricultural labor that built the southern economy. Although slavery officially ended with the Civil War between the northern and southern states and the subsequent adoption of the 13th Amendment in 1865, it lived on in civil society and law for 100 years through discriminatory laws and practices (see the discussion of Jim Crow laws later in this chapter).

Correctional institutions, particularly in the South following the Civil War, were devised to maintain the slave system, with newly freed and often unemployed blacks incarcerated for minor or trumped-up charges. Once incarcerated, their labor was leased out to southern farmers for work on the same plantations where they or their brethren had been slaves (Oshinsky, 1996; Young, 2001). During the same time period, in the North and Midwest, African American inmates were sometimes segregated from whites in prisons and jails and were given substandard housing and the least desirable work assignments (Hawkes, 1998; Joseph & Taylor, 2003).

IN FOCUS 12.1

Hate Groups in the United States

Unfortunately, as reported by the Southern Poverty Law Center (SPLC, a well-respected nonprofit organization that tracks hate groups and their activity in the United States), the number of hate groups in this country in 2017 stood at 917; this constitutes a doubling of such groups since 1999 when that number was 457 (SPLC, 2017, p. 1). Among these groups, there has been a 197% increase in anti-Muslim groups, and there are 130 Ku Klux Klan groups, 663 anti-government "patriot" groups, and 193 black separatist groups. Not surprisingly the number of hate crimes reported by the media has also risen, with the latest at the time of this writing (May 2017) being two white men killed on a train in Portland, Oregon, while trying to defend two Muslim women, by a white man involved in Klan activities who had racist views and who had been harassing and threatening those women (Piggott, 2017).

IN FOCUS 12.2

The Scottsboro Case

Nine African American teenage boys were hoboing in 1931 on a freight train headed to Memphis, Tennessee. The train was stopped, and they were arrested and accused of the rape of two white girls on the train. The case was first tried in Scottsboro, Alabama, where the boys received little representation, and the trial was rushed. All of the boys in this first trial, except the youngest (a 12-year-old), were convicted of rape and sentenced to death.

The case was appealed and made it all the way to the Supreme Court. In the famous decision *Powell v. Alabama* (1932), the Court ruled that the due process rights of the accused—in this case, their right to counsel in a capital case, particularly because these teenagers were indigent and illiterate—were violated. The Court reversed their convictions and sent their case back for retrial.

In the second trial, seven of the eight convictions were upheld by all-white juries. (Black voters in Alabama were purposefully excluded from lists for juries.) The reconvictions happened despite the fact that the case was moved to Decatur, Alabama, for retrial, and one of the two victims recanted her story, claiming that the story was made up and that the boys never touched either of them.

The Supreme Court, in 1935, again reheard the case in light of the all-white jury composition; the Court reversed again. The Alabama judge set aside the verdict and scheduled a new trial, where the accused were again found guilty.

Eventually, charges were dropped for four of the nine defendants, but the others received sentences of 75 years to death, and three of those five served prison time. The one who was sentenced to death was eventually pardoned in 1976 (Walker et al., 1996). This case is widely regarded by legal scholars as a gross miscarriage of

PHOTO 12.2: The Scottsboro accused meeting with their lawyer in jail.

justice and as emblematic of the way African Americans were treated in racist sectors of this country well after slavery was abolished.

Discussion Questions

1. Do you think the time and place of this event affected its outcome?

2. How does this case and how these teenage boys were treated compare with how young black men and boys are treated by the police today?

3. Is there room for improvement in race relations between the police and African American community members?

4. Why is it so difficult for racial and ethnic groups in this country to, as Rodney King asked, "just get along"?

The Scottsboro case exemplified the racist attitudes of communities and how those attitudes were translated into discriminatory practices by law enforcement, courts, and corrections (Walker, Spohn, & DeLone, 1996; see In Focus 12.2). The lynching of black men, fueled by mob rule and widespread Ku Klux Klan hate group activity, was also practiced in many states and communities following the Civil War and well into the 1900s (Keil & Vito, 2009). Lynching reinforced a culture of fear that prevented African Americans from achieving an equal and decent footing in communities. The Klan's avowed purpose was to target and persecute Catholics, Jews, and non-whites, especially blacks, particularly in

IN FOCUS 12.3

Fourteen Examples of Racism in the Criminal Justice System

By Bill Quigley*

The biggest crime in the U.S. criminal justice system is that it is a race-based institution where African Americans are directly targeted and punished in a much more aggressive way than white people.

Saying the U.S. criminal system is racist may be politically controversial in some circles. But the facts are overwhelming. No real debate about that. Below I set out numerous examples of these facts.

The question is—are these facts the mistakes of an otherwise good system, or are they evidence that the racist criminal justice system is working exactly as intended? Is the U.S. criminal justice system operated to marginalize and control millions of African Americans?

Information on race is available for each step of the criminal justice system—from the use of drugs, police stops, arrests, getting out on bail, legal representation, jury selection, trial, sentencing, prison, parole and freedom. Look what these facts show.

1. The U.S. has seen a surge in arrests and putting people in jail over the last four decades. Most of the reason is the war on drugs. Yet whites and blacks engage in drug offenses, possession and sales, at roughly comparable rates—according to a report on race and drug enforcement published by Human Rights Watch in May 2008. While African Americans comprise 13% of the U.S. population and 14% of monthly drug users, they are 37% of the people arrested for drug offenses—according to 2009 congressional testimony by Marc Mauer of The Sentencing Project.

2. The police stop blacks and Latinos at rates that are much higher than whites. In New York City, where people of color make up about half of the population, 80% of the NYPD [New York Police Department] stops were of blacks and Latinos. When whites were stopped, only 8% were frisked. When blacks and Latinos are stopped 85% were frisked according to information provided by the NYPD. The same is true most other places as well. In a California study, the ACLU [American Civil Liberties Union] found blacks are three times more likely to be stopped than whites.

3. Since 1970, drug arrests have skyrocketed, rising from 320,000 to close to 1.6 million according to the Bureau of Justice Statistics of the U.S. Department of Justice. African Americans are arrested for drug offenses at rates 2 to 11 times higher than the rate for whites—according to a May 2009 report on disparity in drug arrests by Human Rights Watch.

4. Once arrested, blacks are more likely to remain in prison awaiting trial than whites. For example, the New York State Division of Criminal Justice did a 1995 review of disparities in processing felony arrests and found that in some parts of New York, blacks are 33% more likely to be detained awaiting felony trials than whites facing felony trials.

5. Once arrested, 80% of the people in the criminal justice system get a public defender for their lawyer. Race plays a big role here as well. Stop in any urban courtroom and look at the color of the people who are waiting for public defenders. Despite often heroic efforts by public defenders, the system gives them much more work and much less money than the prosecution. The American Bar Association, not a radical bunch, reviewed the U.S. public defender system in 2004 and concluded, "All too often, defendants plead guilty, even if they are innocent, without really understanding their legal rights or what is occurring. . . . The fundamental right to a lawyer that America assumes applies to everyone accused of criminal conduct effectively does not exist in practice for countless people across the U.S."

6. African Americans are frequently illegally excluded from criminal jury service according to a June 2010 study released by the Equal Justice Initiative. For example in Houston County, Alabama, 8 out of 10 African Americans qualified for jury service have been struck by prosecutors from serving on death penalty cases.

7. Trials are rare. Only [3% to 5%] of criminal cases go to trial—the rest are plea bargained. Most African American defendants never get a trial. Most plea bargains consist of promise of a longer sentence if

a person exercises their constitutional right to trial. As a result, people caught up in the system, as the American Bar Association points out, plead guilty even when innocent. Why? As one young man told me recently, "Who wouldn't rather do three years for a crime they didn't commit than risk twenty-five years for a crime they didn't do?"

8. The United States Sentencing Commission reported in March 2010 that in the federal system black offenders receive sentences that are 10% longer than white offenders for the same crimes. Marc Mauer of The Sentencing Project reports [that] African Americans are 21% more likely to receive mandatory minimum sentences than white defendants and 20% more likely to be sentenced to prison than white drug defendants.

9. The longer the sentence, the more likely it is that non-white people will be the ones getting it. A July 2009 report by The Sentencing Project found that two-thirds of the people in the U.S. with life sentences are non-white. In New York, it is 83%.

10. As a result, African Americans, who are 13% of the population and 14% of drug users, are not only 37% of the people arrested for drugs but 56% of the people in state prisons for drug offenses (Marc Mauer, May 2009 congressional testimony for The Sentencing Project).

11. The U.S. Bureau of Justice Statistics concludes that the chance of a black male born in 2001 of going to jail is 32% or 1 in 3. Latino males have a 17% chance and white males have a 6% chance. Thus, black boys are five times and Latino boys nearly three times as likely as white boys to go to jail.

12. So, while African American juvenile youth [are] but 16% of the population, they are 28% of juvenile arrests, 37% of the youth in juvenile jails, and 58% of the youth sent to adult prisons (2009 Criminal Justice Primer, The Sentencing Project).

13. Remember that the U.S. leads the world in putting our own people into jail and prison. The *New York Times* reported in 2008 that the U.S. has [5%] of the world's population but a quarter of the world's prisoners, over 2.3 million people behind bars, dwarfing other nations. The U.S. rate of incarceration is five to eight times higher than other highly developed countries, and black males are the largest percentage of inmates, according to ABC News.

14. Even when released from prison, race continues to dominate. A study by Professor Devah Pager of the University of Wisconsin found that 17% of white job applicants with criminal records received call backs from employers, while only 5% of black job applicants with criminal records received call backs. Race is so prominent in that study that whites with criminal records actually received better treatment than blacks without criminal records!

So, what conclusions do these facts lead to? The criminal justice system, from start to finish, is seriously racist.

Discussion Questions

1. Have recent events involving videos of unarmed or lightly armed minority group members being shot by the police changed your mind about whether there are racist elements in the criminal justice system?

2. If so, what are the biggest challenges to changing that system?

*Note: Bill Quigley is legal director for the Center for Constitutional Rights and a law professor at Loyola University New Orleans College of Law. This excerpt was taken from an article he wrote for the *Huffington Post* (http://www.huffingtonpost.com/bill-quigley/fourteen-examples-of-raci_b_658947.html). Reprinted with permission.

the South and in the midwestern states. Membership was widespread among public and criminal justice officials during the first half of the 1900s and even included those who rose to such lofty heights as Supreme Court justices (e.g., Supreme Court Justice Hugo Black was a member during the 1920s) and members of Congress (e.g., Senator Robert Byrd of West Virginia was a member and defender of the Klan well into the 1950s).

There is little doubt that up until the civil rights movement and the implementation of laws and practices that reduced racism in public and private organizations, there was *institutional racism*—or racism practiced by many, if not most, institutional members—in criminal justice and other organizations. In correctional institutions, it was not until the civil rights movement morphed into the *prisoner rights movement* in jails and prisons that these practices were changed, and African American and white inmates were treated more similarly, or were legally required to be so treated, in correctional institutions (Belbot & Hemmens, 2010). But despite these reforms, African Americans constituted about 35% of total state inmates in 2013, although they composed only about 13% of the general population that year (Carson, 2014, p. 15; U.S. Census Bureau, 2014a, p. 1).

NATIVE AMERICANS/AMERICAN INDIANS

American Indians are another group of people who have been victims of racism in this country. Note that the terms *Native American* and *American Indian* both are used to describe the first peoples who lived in the Americas when Christopher Columbus landed on an island in the Bahamas in 1492. Columbus mistakenly thought he was in India and thus dubbed the native peoples "Indians." The name stuck, giving rise to the more recent use of the name *Native Americans* by those not wishing to associate these native peoples with Columbus. Other terms often used for native peoples in the United States are *indigenous peoples* and *first peoples*. The problem is that sometimes people who are not Indians have adopted the Native American term and might adopt the indigenous people term because they were born in the United States. The term *first peoples* is not much used in the United States, although it has gained currency in other countries as a term to describe indigenous peoples. However, the most common names used by natives and non-natives in the United States are American Indians and Native Americans, and they will be used interchangeably in this book (Mann, 2006).

At the time of the arrival of the first of Columbus's ships and the subsequent growth in European expansion to North, Central, and South America, there were reportedly as many as 20 million native people residing in North America (Colbert, 1997; Davis, 2008; Diamond, 1997; Mann, 2006). Emerging archeological evidence has established that complex cities and agriculture flourished in the Americas, particularly in South and Central America, thousands of years before this wave of Europeans arrived. (There are theories and some evidence that Africans, other Europeans, and Asians all made trips to the Americas and did so many times over the millennia and well before this latter foray by Columbus and the Spaniards [Awes & Awes, 2010; Mann, 2006].) Within a few short decades, those populations had been decimated by disease (mostly smallpox), wars, and massacres. Over the course of a few hundred years, only a small percentage of those original peoples survived, and they were overwhelmed by the influx of European immigrants who, through wars and treaties, relocated American Indians, often forcibly, off of their lands and onto reservations.

Such reservations, at least initially, were in essence forms of correctional institutions whose purpose was to incarcerate a whole people on a piece of land by restricting their movement away from the reservations. Such land was usually less desirable than the land the tribe originally resided on and was often inadequate to support the survival of that tribe. As a consequence, American Indian reservations of the 1800s and 1900s were populated by poor, underfed, and undereducated people with few prospects for regaining their land, wealth, or status (Blalock, 1967; Kitano, 1997; Stannard, 1992). Federal policy regarding American Indian tribes has shifted over time, from efforts to segregate them from white communities, to efforts to integrate tribal members into the larger community, to more current efforts to respect their identity, independence, and cultures.

As a result of this complicated history, the interplay of tribal, federal, and state laws is complex and depends on the time period and the state and tribe involved. Currently, there are 566 federally recognized tribes in the United States, and there are a number of tribes that have not received or sought this recognition (Bureau of Indian Affairs, 2014, p. 1943). On large reservations, more minor criminal offending by tribal members falls under the jurisdiction of that tribe, whereas felony offenses or off-the-reservation criminal activity by tribal members might be handled by the tribe, the state, or the federal government. Larger reservations maintain their own jails for tribal members accused of crimes, for minor offenders, and for those with shorter sentences of incarceration. Despite the existence of these separate legal and correctional systems on larger reservations, at least regarding less serious offending, the number of Native Americans in federal and state prisons is often disproportionate to their representation in the larger population of that state (Perry, 2004).

As reported in a recent Bureau of Justice Statistics publication regarding Indian jails (Minton, 2015, p. 1), there were 79 jails in Indian country in 2014, and the number of inmates confined in those jails has been increasing, although admissions decreased slightly between 2013 and 2014, and the percentage of people held for violent offenses also decreased in Indian jails.

HISPANICS/LATINOS/LATINAS

As mentioned previously, the term *Hispanic* is used to designate an ethnic group that spans many races and nations of origin, to the point where it might not be descriptive (Martinez, 2004). For this reason, other monikers are often used to describe Hispanics that may better represent who they are, such as the more general Latinos/Latinas (which can be used to describe those who originally hailed from Latin America or whose ancestors did) or terms that identify a particular national heritage—specifically—Mexican Americans, Cuban Americans, and so forth. Each of these groups of people has a history with a distinct American experience. Sometimes that history has included discrimination by criminal justice actors during incarceration.

IN FOCUS 12.4

Documented Lynchings of Mexican Americans

Lynching in America: Confronting the Legacy of Racial Terror, a publication of the Equal Justice Initiative (EJI, 2015), details an investigation into lynching in the South after the Civil War and up to World War II. There were 3,959 lynchings in southern states during this time period (1877–1950) (p. 1). According to the authors of this publication, the lynchings were public events, widely attended by whites, tolerated by state and local officials, and "used to enforce racial subordination and segregation" (p. 1). "Crimes" might include "bumping into a white person, or wearing their military uniforms after World War I, or not using the appropriate title when addressing a white person" (p. 1).

In a 2015 *New York Times* editorial, William D. Carrigan and Clive Webb described a little-known dirty American secret (derived from the same publication): "Blacks weren't the only victims of violence by white mobs" (Carrigan & Webb, 2015, p. A23). Although blacks were the most likely targets of lynching in America's past, particularly in the South, the authors noted that Mexicans and, to a lesser extent, Native Americans, Italians, and Chinese were also singled out in other parts of the country. From 7 Mexican shepherds hanged by white vigilantes near Corpus Christi, Texas, in 1878; to 547 newspaper-documented cases of lynchings of Mexicans and Mexican Americans in Arizona, California, New Mexico, and Texas from 1848 to 1928; to thousands killed by Texas Rangers and other law enforcement and vigilantes along the Mexican border from 1915 to 1918, the practice was reportedly widespread in the southwestern United States.

Discussion Questions

1. What do you think spurs people to lynch other people?

2. What makes the people who commit such atrocities, termed *acts of terror* by the EJI, think they can get away with it?

The history of Mexican Americans, the largest subgroup of Hispanics or Latinos/Latinas in the United States, has been one in which they and their land were forcibly made part of the American Southwest. As a result of the Mexican–American War, which lasted from 1846 to 1848, Mexico lost nearly half of its land—the area that has become the American Southwest, from Texas to California and all of the states in between. However, there is evidence that at least some of the Mexicans in these territories were willing to become citizens of the United States (Espinosa, Komatsu, & Martin, 1998).

Today, in border states, the number of Mexican Americans and Cuban Americans is so high, and their assimilation into the culture is so thorough (e.g., in New Mexico, Arizona, parts of Texas, California, and Florida) that the existence of a clear racial or ethnic majority group has disappeared or has become the Hispanic/Latino/Latina group itself. The increased numbers of Mexican Americans in these states and the immigrants crossing over the southern border into the United States have sparked a political debate over recent Mexican immigrants and whether or not they should be accorded citizenship rights. At the center of the debate is the passage by the state of Arizona of an immigration law that allows law enforcement there to demand papers from any person whom officers *suspect* might be in the country illegally without further cause (Archibold, 2010). Civil libertarians and civil rights groups allege that this law has resulted in discrimination against Hispanics in Arizona and creates the potential to fill jails, if not prisons, in that state. In the Supreme Court case *Arizona v. United States* (2012), the Court upheld the requirement that law enforcement verify immigrant status during lawful stops but struck down three other provisions of the law (National Conference of State Legislatures, 2012).

Whether in Arizona or in other states, however, and as with American Indians and African Americans, the representation of Hispanics in American prisons and jails is already disproportionate to their representation in the general population. In 2013, Hispanics constituted 21% of state inmates when their representation in the larger population was estimated at 17% for that year (Carson, 2014, p. 15; U.S. Census Bureau, 2014a, p. 1). Looking at just the number of inmates incarcerated tells an important story (Figure 12.1), but it is the rate of incarceration (Figure 12.2) that demonstrates more clearly the disparity in our correctional system.

ASIAN AMERICANS

As with most immigrants to America during the 1800s and 1900s, Japanese and Chinese immigrants (who collectively represent the largest group of Asian Americans but certainly not the only group [space prevents us from sufficiently exploring the Korean, Cambodian, Vietnamese, Laotian, Pacific Islander, and other East Asian experiences]) were looking for a better life for themselves and their families. Although they found such a life to varying degrees, their experience, like that of the other ethnic and racial minorities mentioned in this chapter, was tinged with racism. Originally settling primarily in western states during the 1800s and early 1900s, Chinese and Japanese immigrants were heavily involved in mining and agriculture in pioneer communities.

Chinese labor was crucial to the construction of the first transcontinental railroad (1863–1869). Later barred from owning property in some states and from voting in others, Chinese people made do by engaging in service professions (e.g., laundries, restaurants, herb shops) and settling together in parts of cities for both comfort and safety (J. Jones, 2016; Lennon, Angier, Tsui, Cheng, & Chin, 2003; Wei, 1999). When economies soured in some of those cities

Public domain

PHOTO 12.3: A cartoon that appeared in *Harper's Weekly* regarding the "Chinese Question," which depicts Lady Justice defending a Chinese man being persecuted by a racist mob.

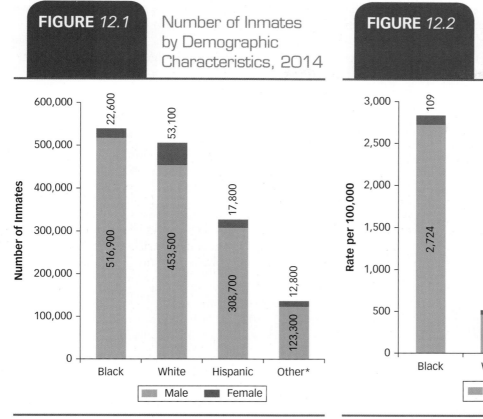

FIGURE 12.1 Number of Inmates by Demographic Characteristics, 2014

Source: Carson (2015, Table 10).

*Includes American Indians and Alaska Natives; Asians, Native Hawaiians, and other Pacific Islanders; and persons of two or more races.

FIGURE 12.2 Rate of Imprisonment by Demographic Characteristics, 2014

Sources: Carson (2015, Table 10); U.S. Census Bureau, Population Division (2016).

*Includes American Indians and Alaska Natives; Asians, Native Hawaiians, and other Pacific Islanders; and persons of two or more races.

or states, Asian immigrants were blamed for taking jobs from poor whites—much like the way blacks were blamed by poor whites in the South after the Civil War or recent Mexican immigrants are blamed by poor whites in much of this country today—and they were often run out of town. They were literally placed on ships and sent home even though they and their families may have lived in the United States for decades if not generations.

The first restrictive immigration law in the country, the Chinese Exclusion Act of 1882, was directed at reducing immigration from China (J. Jones, 2016; Wei, 1999). This act was not repealed until 1943. Some of the first drug laws, laws against opium dens dating from the 1870s onward, were passed because Chinese immigrants were thought to be corrupting the white population by spreading the use of the drug; such laws were ironic because opium was first introduced to China by Westerners (Lennon et al., 2003).

Much like Chinese immigrants, Japanese immigrants provided cheap labor as they were employed in the construction of railroads, as well as agriculture, restaurants, and many other businesses, primarily in the American West. In fact, when Chinese immigrants were excluded, Japanese immigrants filled the gap, beginning during the 1880s, until their own immigration was also restricted in 1908. Barred from owning their own land, many Japanese Americans earned their livings during the late 1800s and early 1900s by leasing land and growing beets in Oregon and Idaho, for instance. As their economic strength grew, however, they were regarded as a threat by the local white population, and there were numerous instances where they were forcibly run off of their land and out of town (Mercier, 2010).

> Despite the Issei's [another term for the first Japanese immigrants] hard work in the early twentieth century, envy and racial discrimination led to increasing anti-Japanese attitudes on the West Coast, much as the sentiment had developed against perceived Chinese competition. Residents of Mountain Home, Nampa, and Caldwell, Idaho, drove out Japanese workers, and white mobs near Coeur d'Alene and in Portland threatened Japanese railroad workers. Tensions led to the so-called "Gentleman's Agreement" between the U.S. and Japan that effectively limited after 1908 the numbers of laborers that could emigrate from Japan. Instead, the two governments allowed wives and brides to join earlier male immigrants in the United States, changing the character of the immigrant community. (Mercier, 2010, p. 10)

The internment of 120,000 Japanese Americans in 1942 in 10 inland concentration camps during World War II, along with the confiscation of their property, was not based on the actual threat they presented to the safety of western states—or at least no more, say, than the German Americans who were scattered all over the United States at the time and who were not incarcerated (Mercier, 2010, p. 1). The internment of whole Japanese American families in prison camps was instead based on racially tinged beliefs about who could be trusted and on ignorance regarding the allegiance that such citizens felt for this, their country.

As far as the incarceration of most Asian Americans these days goes, they tend to be underrepresented in correctional organizations in relation to their representation in the general population. It is not clear why such underrepresentation exists, but it is likely related to their tight-knit and supportive families and communities and the value those cultures have placed on education and achievement, resulting in higher incomes and education for many Japanese and Chinese American citizens (Mercier, 2010). Notably, successful integration into American society, as measured by economic and educational achievements, is not uniform across all Asian Americans. Those emigrating from war-torn Cambodia and Vietnam during the latter half of the 20th century were not always as "successful" or able to stay out of the criminal justice system and its correctional institutions.

••• THE CONNECTION BETWEEN CLASS AND RACE/ETHNICITY

Americans are often averse to recognizing the existence of a class system in the United States. In part, this dislike of class labels springs from our history of revolution, which was spurred, in part, by a desire to separate ourselves from the rigidity of the class system in England and Europe. In addition, our economic, political, and social systems have allowed people in lower classes to advance through ingenuity, education, or drive—or some mix of those—to the middle or upper classes. However, this upward mobility is hampered in any number of ways by poverty and related ills such as poor nutrition and schools, limited access to health care, and parents who are absent or neglectful. When poverty is combined with long-term and systematic discrimination against a people such that their families are destroyed, as occurred with the social institution of slavery and the continued discrimination against African Americans, recovery of communities can take generations. Not surprisingly, illegal drug use catches on in such poor communities, as do other forms of involvement in street criminality.

Certain racial and ethnic minorities are more likely to be poor and thus caught up in the criminal justice system and overrepresented in correctional institutions and programs (see Table 12.1). Race and traditions of discrimination against African Americans have stymied their ability to assimilate in many cases. Language barriers and discrimination regarding race have also prevented some Hispanics, American Indians, and Asians from moving to the middle and upper classes. Cultural differences have created a similar barrier for these groups. The drug war, which is discussed more fully in the following, has tended to target illegal drugs and their use and has had a disparate impact on minority groups such as Hispanics and African Americans. The drug war has led to the phenomenon of disproportionate representation by these minority groups in correctional organizations.

●●● MINORITIES: POLICIES AND PRACTICES THAT HAVE RESULTED IN INCREASED INCARCERATION

As has been mentioned in other chapters in this book, African Americans and Hispanics particularly, but also American Indians, are disproportionately represented as the accused or convicted in jails, prisons, and community corrections in the United States. Asian Americans are overrepresented in federal prisons. As already mentioned, most of these minority groups are also overrepresented among the poor in the United States and among those accused or convicted of street crimes (see Table 12.1). During the 1950s an estimated 70% of the inmates in America's prisons were white, but by the year 2013 about 56% of inmates in prisons were African American (35%) or Hispanic (21%) (Carson, 2014, p. 15). Yet according to the 2013 U.S. Census, only 13% of the population as a whole was black or African American and 17% was Hispanic or Latino of any race, whereas 78% was white (with other races constituting Asian [4.9%], Native Hawaiian or Pacific Islander [0.2%], and two or more races [2.3%]) (U.S. Census Bureau, 2014b, p. 1).

Stated another way, among the largest racial and ethnic groups in 2013, black non-Hispanic males had an imprisonment rate that was six times higher than white non-Hispanic males and 2.5 times higher than Hispanic males (Carson, 2014, p. 8). Likewise, black non-Hispanic females were imprisoned at twice the rate of white non-Hispanic females in 2013 (although the former's numbers had decreased from 2012) (Carson, 2014, p. 8). All of this means that no matter how one views the data, blacks or African Americans and Hispanics/Latinos/Latinas are disproportionately incarcerated in the United States when compared with their population composition.

THE DRUG WAR: THE NEW JIM CROW?

The rhetoric for the modern drug war was initiated by President Richard Nixon. He ran on a hardline law enforcement platform for president and, as a consequence, was interested in implementing tough-on-crime policies and practices. His efforts, however, were stymied by the fact that law enforcement was (and still is) primarily a responsibility of the states and their counties and cities. Ronald Reagan was the next president interested in enlarging the reach of the federal government into the states' business regarding law enforcement. His administration was responsible for declaring a war on drugs and for asking Congress to allocate money for prisons and law enforcement. Therefore, President Reagan is often credited (or blamed, depending on one's perspective) for starting the modern drug war.

TABLE 12.1 Number and Percentage of People in Poverty by Different Poverty Measures, 2016**

	Number in Thousands	Official				SPM				Difference	
		Number		Percentage		Number		Percentage			
		Estimate	Margin of Error (±)	Estimate	Margin of Error (±)	Estimate	Margin of Error (±)	Estimate	Margin of Error (±)	Number	Percentage
All people	320,372	40,706	735	12.7	0.2	44,752	810	14.0	0.3	*4,046	*1.3
Sex											
Male	156,939	17,739	396	11.3	0.3	20,693	438	13.2	0.3	*2,954	*1.9
Female	163,433	22,967	458	14.1	0.3	24,059	476	14.7	0.3	*1,092	*0.7
Age											
Under 18 years	74,047	13,344	366	18.0	0.5	11,281	349	15.2	0.5	*−2,062	*−2.8
18 to 64 years	197,051	22,795	473	11.6	0.2	26,303	571	13.3	0.3	*3,508	*1.8
65 years and older	49,274	4,568	198	9.3	0.4	7,168	235	14.5	0.5	*2,600	*5.3
Type of Unit											
Married couple	192,344	11,257	501	5.9	0.3	16,516	601	8.6	0.3	*5,260	*2.7
Cohabiting partners	24,994	6,576	345	26.3	1.0	3,261	284	13.0	1.0	*−3,314	*−13.3
Female reference person	42,758	11,647	510	27.2	1.0	11,655	498	27.3	1.0	7	0
Male reference person	15,030	1,814	196	12.1	1.2	2,635	258	17.5	1.6	*821	*5.5
Unrelated individuals	45,246	9,413	324	20.8	0.6	10,686	343	23.6	0.6	*1,272	*2.8
Race and Hispanic Origin											
White	246,310	27,174	546	11.0	0.2	30,717	617	12.5	0.3	*3,543	*1.4
White, not Hispanic	195,453	17,304	494	8.9	0.3	19,446	564	9.9	0.3	*2,142	*1.1
Black	42,040	9,248	388	22.0	0.9	9,086	390	21.6	0.9	−162	*−0.4
Asian	18,897	1,917	176	10.1	0.9	2,774	204	14.7	1.1	*857	*4.5
Hispanic (any race)	57,670	11,160	399	19.4	0.7	12,670	432	22.0	0.7	*1,511	*2.6
Nativity											
Native born	276,518	34,079	666	12.3	0.2	35,515	728	12.8	0.3	*1,437	*0.5
Foreign born	43,854	6,627	269	15.1	0.6	9,237	325	21.1	0.7	*2,609	*6.0
Naturalized citizen	20,409	2,045	143	10.0	0.7	3,205	171	15.7	0.8	*1,160	*5.7
Not a citizen	23,445	4,582	223	19.5	0.9	6,032	263	25.7	1.0	*1,449	*6.2

Source: Fox (2017).

†The margin of error (MOE) is a measure of an estimate's variability. The larger the MOE in relation to the size of the estimate, the less reliable the estimate. The MOE is the estimated 90% confidence interval. The MOEs shown in this table are based on standard errors calculated using replicate weights. For more information, see "Standard Errors and Their Use" at ftp://ftp2 .census.gov/library/publications/2014/demo/p60-252sa.pdf.

* An asterisk preceding an estimate indicates that change is statistically different from zero at the 90% confidence level.

** Latest data available at the time of this writing.

SPM = Supplemental Poverty Measure.

Riding this popular tough-on-crime rhetoric of the 1980s and 1990s, Presidents George H. W. Bush, Bill Clinton, George W. Bush, and Barack Obama each continued to fund—and, at times, expand the reach of—the federal drug war. The practical effect of this modern war, if not the intent of its architects, has been to incarcerate unprecedented hundreds of thousands of minority men and women, primarily African Americans and Hispanics, who would otherwise not be incarcerated in the correctional system (Lurigio & Loose, 2008).

M. Alexander (2010), in her book *The New Jim Crow: Mass Incarceration in the Age of Colorblindness*, asserted that the modern drug war has been focused on the poor and minorities while ignoring the fact that most drug users and drug dealers are white. She noted that in 2004 an estimated 75% of those incarcerated for drug offenses were black or Latino, while the majority of the drug users and dealers were white (p. 97). She argued the case that the drug war, as executed, has the practical effect of reinstating Jim Crow laws in the United States. She maintained that this is so because of the police sweeps of poor and minority neighborhoods, the law enforcement focus on small-time marijuana possession offenders, and the law's nonsensical emphasis on crack cocaine over powder cocaine even though they are similar in addiction and pharmacologically the same (see the following discussion of this topic and Chapter 5 on sentencing). Moreover, the implementation of the drug war has led to the erosion of civil liberties protections regarding search and evidence.

Jim Crow laws were devised by southern states following the Civil War, starting during the 1870s and lasting until 1965 and the civil rights movement, to prevent African Americans from fully participating in social, economic, and civic life. These laws restricted the rights and liberties of black citizens in employment, housing, education, travel, and voting. Interestingly enough, voter disenfranchisement, or preventing African Americans from voting, was a key part of the Jim Crow laws back then (M. Alexander, 2010). Today, a felony offense, gained through even a relatively minor drug possession conviction, can mean the loss of employability, access to public housing or food stamps, and the right to vote—much the same effect as the Jim Crow laws of a century ago.

CRACK VERSUS POWDER COCAINE

The concern over crack cocaine started during the 1980s. The sentencing disparity that occurred when crack cocaine possession was treated as 100 times worse than possession of powder cocaine in federal law was tied to the race and class of the persons associated with each drug (M. Alexander, 2010; Sentencing Project, 2011). Poorer and disproportionately black and Hispanic people tended to use the cheaper crack cocaine, whereas richer and disproportionately white people tended to use the more expensive powder cocaine. Although there was never any real evidence that crack was more harmful or addictive than powder cocaine, there were a number of stories sensationalizing news of "crack babies" and mothers—portrayed as *black* babies and their mothers—during the 1980s when the Reagan administration promoted the disparate sentencing. M. Alexander (2010) reported that the Reagan administration used the

---

ETHICAL ISSUE

What Would You Do?

You are a black male correctional officer in a jail, working in a living unit for inmates who are new to the facility. It is usually referred to as a *classification unit* because inmates in it are classified to other units by their conviction status, perceived dangerousness, and programming needs. After working in the unit for a few years, you notice that there are a few other staff members, although not most, who treat minority group inmates with less respect than white inmates. You also notice that some minority group inmates are classified with a higher security ranking than similar white inmates, and this means that minority inmates do not have as much access to reentry programming and to placement in the work release facility as do white inmates. What would you do to make sure that minority group inmates are treated and classified in the same way as other inmates?

Jim Crow laws: Laws devised by southern states following the Civil War, starting during the 1870s and lasting until 1965, to prevent African Americans from fully participating in social, economic, and civic life.

emergence of crack as a means of justifying the drug war and its focus on poor and minority people:

> They hired staff whose job it was to find reports of inner-city crack users, crack dealers, crack babies, and crack whores and to feed those stories to the media. The media saturation coverage of crack was no accident. It was a deliberate campaign that fueled the race to incarcerate. Legislators began passing ever harsher mandatory-minimum sentences in response to the media frenzy. (cited in A. Cooper, 2011, p. 7)

The harsher sentencing for crack cocaine possession is another example of a current criminal justice policy that even the U.S. Sentencing Commission concedes has had the practical and discriminatory effect of vastly increasing the incarceration of African Americans and Hispanics. Although the federal law was changed in 2010, crack cocaine sentences at the federal level are still much harsher than those for powder cocaine by a factor of 18 to 1 (rather than 100 to 1, as they were under the 1986 law). Even so, the U.S. Sentencing Commission (2011) estimated that 12,811 federal inmates would be affected by the retroactive application of the reduced sentences for crack cocaine and that 85% of those affected would be African Americans (p. 19). Despite efforts by Congress in

IN FOCUS 12.5

Harsh Justice and the Scott Sisters

In 1993, two sisters, Jamie Scott, 22, and her pregnant 19-year-old sister, Gladys, were convicted of using three teenage boys to set up the armed robbery of two men (Pitts, 2010). The Scott sisters supplied the shotgun to the teenagers. Only $11 was stolen during this robbery, and the victims were unharmed. For this crime, the sisters, who had no prior criminal history, were each given a double life sentence and, as of November 2010, had served 16 years of it.

The teenage boys, two of whom testified against the sisters as part of their plea bargains, each received a 2-year sentence, which they completed years ago. The Scott sisters claimed, and still claim, that they are innocent. The mother of the sisters argues that the harsh sentences were revenge for the family's willingness to testify against a corrupt sheriff (Pitts, 2010). As news columnist Leonard Pitts explained,

> Whatever the proximate cause of this ridiculous sentence, the larger cause is neon clear: The Scott sisters are black women in the poorest state in the union. And as report after report has testified, if you are poor or black (and God help you if you are both), the American justice system has long had this terrible tendency to throw you away like garbage. Historically, this has been especially true in the South. . . . How many other Scott sisters and brothers are languishing behind bars for no good reason, doing undeserved hard time on non-existent evidence, perjured testimony, prosecutorial misconduct or sheer racial or class bias? (Pitts, 2010, p. B6)

The Scott sisters did, finally, get some relief from their sentences. Due to the advocacy of Pitts and others, such as the National Association for the Advancement of Colored People, the original prosecutor of the sisters, the then-governor of Mississippi, Haley Barbour, suspended the sisters' sentences as long as Gladys donated a kidney to her sister Jamie, whose kidneys had failed (Diaz-Duran, 2010). They were released from prison in January of 2011.

Discussion Question

1. In what ways does the Scott sisters' treatment by the criminal justice system seem similar to and different from that experienced by the Scottsboro boys (see In Focus 12.2)?

2015 and 2016 to pass further sentencing reform at the federal level with an eye to reducing sentences for low-level drug offenses and the retroactive application, proponents of such efforts in Congress were unable to garner enough votes. Moreover, the degree to which state laws treating crack cocaine use more harshly than powder cocaine results in disproportionate incarceration of minority group members varies by state.

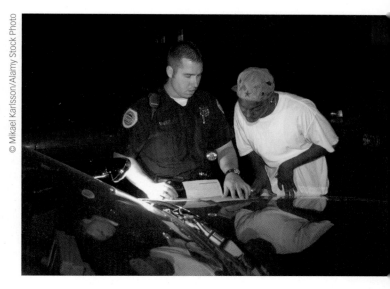

PHOTO 12.4: A white officer stopping a black driver. Critics argue that black and brown drivers are stopped more by the police than white drivers and that they are treated more harshly when they are stopped.

RACIAL PROFILING AND DRIVING WHILE BLACK OR BROWN

In addition to the drug war and its effect on increasing minority involvement as the accused or convicted in corrections, scholars note that racial profiling by the police can have a similar effect. DWB, which stands for **driving while black or brown**, refers to the police practice of focusing law enforcement attention on black- or brown-skinned drivers. The research in this area has been mixed, with some researchers finding that this practice affects arrests, while others are unable to establish the existence of this practice (Rice, Reitzel, & Piquero, 2005). Lundman's (2010) research also raised questions about the validity of police reports on the race or ethnicity of stopped drivers, noting that there were unaccounted for missing data on drivers from predominantly poor and minority neighborhoods in some research.

Police officers will tend to stop older vehicles, and such cars are often owned by poorer and minority group members. Having said this, Langan, Greenfield, Smith, Durose, and Levin (2001) found, in a review of Bureau of Justice Statistics data from a police and public national contact survey, that blacks and Hispanics were more likely to report being stopped by the police than were whites. Notably, in a presentation at the annual conference of the International Association of Chiefs of Police in October 2015, President Obama stated that he had been stopped for DWB. The researchers also found that minority group members were more likely to report negative criminal justice outcomes for themselves such as being ticketed, arrested, handcuffed, searched, or subjected to the use of force by officers when stopped. Rice and colleagues (2005) found, in their study of the perceptions of 700 randomly selected young adult (aged 18–26) New Yorkers, that the nuances of these stops might hinge on what shade one's skin is (p. 63). They found that blacks and black Hispanics were more likely to report that racial profiling was widespread and that they were racially profiled more than were whites or non-black Hispanics.

In a study of drug arrests in Seattle, Washington, Beckett, Nyrop, Pfingst, and Bowen (2005) found that the disparity in arrests between minorities and whites can be explained by racialized justice. The drug problem there was seen as a dangerous crack problem, which in turn was seen as a problem of use by blacks and Hispanics despite comparable use of illegal drugs by whites. Therefore, more minorities were stopped by the police because they were seen as more involved in illegal drug use.

Of course, the more such stops one is subjected to, the more likely that one is to run afoul of the law and to enter a correctional institution, such as a jail, or to find oneself on probation (Hawkins, 2005). Relatedly, these experiences are also more likely to result in the building of a record that, should one become entangled in the system again later, might be used to justify a conviction or a more severe sentence.

Driving while black or brown (DWB): Refers to the practice of police focusing law enforcement attention on black- or brown-skinned drivers.

EVIDENCE-DRIVEN PUBLIC HEALTH PROSECUTION USED TO REDUCE MINORITY GROUP CORRECTIONAL POPULATIONS

Prosecutors play a key role in determining what to charge and whether an offense will lead to significant jail or prison time for the offender. In recognition of this fact, the twice-elected district attorney for Milwaukee County, Wisconsin, John Chisholm, adopted what he terms an evidence-driven public health model for prosecution with a focus on the question, "What's the most effective way to keep a community healthy?" (Toobin, 2015, p. 27). Rather than being wholly concerned with winning or losing cases, this model puts primacy on keeping the public safe from violent offenders, but then for the more minor offenders, the model shifts to an effort to keep them out of the system. Proponents of the model argue that low-level offenders are likely to be harmed by placement in corrections and to bring that harm back into their communities in the form of more petty crimes by those who are low-skilled and undereducated, who are likely to remain unemployed and impoverished, along with their families. A disproportionate number of these low-level offenders in Milwaukee and the nation are minority group members.

In the Milwaukee experiment, an early intervention program in the prosecutor's office was established to assess whether the accused is a low-level offender and whether he or she is likely to reengage in crime (based on an eight-question assessment and a review of the rap sheet and police report) (Toobin, 2015). Respondents who score low on this assessment are given probation, and if they successfully complete it, they walk away with no record. Those who score high are further assessed and may garner a criminal record if convicted, but their charges might still be reduced. Other efforts related to the model include evaluations of repeat offenders, much like in a drug or other specialty court, and their program progress to determine whether new charges are warranted when violations of probation occur or if they just need other assistance to stay out of crime.

As a result of these efforts, there have been far fewer prosecutions of African Americans and whites for low-level drug offenses, including possession of drug paraphernalia, in Milwaukee County since the experiment began in 2006. The number of misdemeanor prosecutions has dropped by more than a third, and the number of African Americans sent to state prison from Milwaukee County has dropped by half (Toobin, 2015, p. 32). But the number of murders in Milwaukee and serious violent crimes like it have remained unusually high, and this, the district attorney concedes, is due to factors outside of his and his office's control in that it includes larger societal problems such as "poverty, hopelessness, lack of education, drug addiction, and the easy availability of guns" (Toobin, 2015, p. 32).

••• MINORITIES: EXPERIENCING INCARCERATION

Victor Hassine, a writer and inmate doing life since 1980 in Pennsylvania prisons for a capital offense, commented that race was and is an integral part of the prison life he has experienced and still does experience (Hassine, 2009). Segregation in housing and by gangs (both voluntary) and racial bias in treatment by staff were common in Graterford Prison, where he was an inmate during the 1980s. Most of the inmates in this prison were black, while most of the staff were white. (Notably, during the 1980s, in Graterford Prison the only choices for self-identifying inmate race *or* ethnicity were white and black.) Most of the staff in this prison identified as Christian, while a sizable proportion of the black inmates were Muslim. Added to these differences based on race and religion was their place of origin; many inmates tended to come from urban areas, while many staff were raised in more rural settings. Such differences between staff and inmates led to a difficult adjustment for minority inmates (see the following discussion of minority staff) and were cited as one of the complaints by inmates in the 1971 riot at Attica Prison in New York.

Wilbert Rideau, in his first-person account of incarceration in Louisiana prisons, described the setting for his third trial and the racial politics of the day in Baton Rouge in this way:

> In 1970, at the time of my third trial, the Klan was using the kind of intimidation for which it was famous. It invaded North Baton Rouge—the black part of town—and plastered the utility poles and other upright surfaces with signs showing a rearing white-hooded horse carrying a hooded white rider, his left hand holding aloft a fiery cross. Beneath the horse's feet was the Klan's motto: FOR GOD AND COUNTRY. The poster was dominated by the horse and rider and by the big, bold print in the upper left corner that read SAVE OUR LAND, and beneath the picture it read JOIN THE KLAN. (Rideau, 2010, p. 61)

Rideau (2010) encountered racism from some staff and inmates over the course of his long incarceration, but he noted that it lessened in degree and frequency as the years went on. Today, the racial mix of staff is more likely to reflect that of the community where inmates come from, which has tended to reduce race as a source of conflict between staff and inmates. However, Ross and Richards (2002) noted that a "color line" still divides prison inmates into at least these groups: blacks, whites, and Hispanics. Between and among these groups, there are different styles of living and means of surviving.

VICTIMIZATION BY RACE AND ETHNICITY

Regarding victimization in prisons, Wolff, Shi, and Blitz (2008) found that African Americans were more likely to report sexual or physical violence from staff than from other inmates, non-Hispanic whites were more likely to report victimization by other inmates than by staff, and Hispanics had above-average reporting of victimization by both staff and other inmates. When both types of victimization were accounted for, however, all three groups reported about the same amount of victimization, just from different sources.

PROBATION OR PRISON?

Some research indicates that black offenders may prefer prison over community alternative sentencing, whereas white offenders express the opposite preference. In a study by Wood and May (2003), the authors noted that blacks and whites "differed in their willingness to participate in alternative sanctions, in their preference for prison over alternatives, and in the amount of these alternatives they were willing to serve" (p. 624), with blacks being less willing to participate in alternatives or the number of alternatives and more likely to prefer prison over alternatives. There are several explanations for these differences discovered by these and other researchers.

? ETHICAL ISSUE

What Would You Do?

You are a white female counselor working in a privately owned juvenile detention facility, and you are interested in hiring a more racially and ethnically diverse staff to better match your community and clientele. Your company has an equal employment opportunity policy in place, but it has rarely been implemented in practice considering that nearly all of the staff are white, whereas almost all of the clients are black or Hispanic. You are on the selection team for a new position at the facility. After several interviews, you notice that at least one other member of the team—and possibly more—is not interested in hiring a minority group member given that this person consistently ranks such applicants' resumes and interviews lower than those of white applicants even though you do not think they merit it. The vote on the applicants is approaching, and there are three top candidates for the job who all seem similarly qualified for it. One of those applicants is a Hispanic male, and the other applicants are white. What would you do to ensure that this vote is fair and that the best applicant for the job gets the position?

PERSPECTIVE FROM A PRACTITIONER

James Watkins, Classification Counselor

Position: Classification Counselor (3), Washington State Department of Corrections

Location: Airway Heights Correction Center, Spokane, Washington

Education: North Idaho College and Spokane Community College

What previous criminal justice experience do you have?

I previously served as a correctional officer for 4.5 years, a sergeant for 1 year, and a classification counselor (2) for 4 years.

What are your primary duties and responsibilities?

- Supervise counselors on a behavior change unit

- Work with offenders to ensure correct classification levels

- Complete offender needs assessment per RNR (risk, need, and responsivity) model of offender classification

- Facilitate program services to include mental health services, education, chemical dependency, and evidence-based programs when available

- Provide inmates with information about reentry and release resources

- Engage offenders with programs to increase success on release

- Connect families through the facilitation of increased communication with families

- Mentor language, role-modeling prosocial behaviors for effective communication with staff and offenders

- Manage a caseload of adult criminal offenders who I am responsible for counseling and informing regarding community resources and problems they might encounter in their transition to work release, parole, or release

- Work with internal and external entities to facilitate offender reentry into the community, enforce court-ordered conditions, and impose DOC (Department of Corrections) conditions

- Participate in risk management with a multidisciplinary team

- Maintain communication with offenders to assist with attorney calls, child custody and child support hearings with DSHS (Department of Social and Health Services) and courts, and family contact through crisis/emergency situations

- Arrange translator services

- Evaluate offenders for early release

- Regularly review and update offender plans, needs assessment, and programming prioritization

- Make recommendations for offender program progression, earned time, and other incentives

- Exercise sound judgment, aligned with department policy, in decisions concerning sanctions, treatment, and education referrals

What are the characteristics and traits most useful in your line of work?

- Effective communication skills

- Honesty and integrity

- Flexibility and dependability

- Strong time management skills

- Stability, willingness to change, adaptability, and humor

- Do not take things personally, and be understanding of clientele.

- Thick skinned—withstand more than the average individual

- A superior mindset

- Understand that clients and staff are a diverse group of individuals and that inmates and staff come from a huge variety of social and economic backgrounds.

- Ability to accept individuals' beliefs that are far from your own and still be able to deal with those individuals

- Be levelheaded, not reactionary.

- Develop an ability to stand alone, stand on your morals and beliefs, and be very independent.

- Have positive avenues of relief outside the job environment.

- Ability to deal with difficult situations appropriately

- Be more rooted and grounded in who you are to overcome perceptions of others' beliefs about who you are.

- Ability to take the higher ground—as a minority, you need to show it more than others.

- Be independent because of the cultural perception of how you treat offenders within your same culture and race; you are under the spotlight more.

- Overcome the perception of giving preferential treatment to the same culture, race, and minority. That stereotype is always in the back of your mind—how others perceive your treatment of a minority and offenders of the same race.

- Do not compromise the self, and act even more professional. Coming from the Spokane area and becoming a part of the criminal justice system while living in the same community and having to withstand scrutiny and stereotyping, I had to maintain values, integrity, and goals regardless of my culture or race.

- Ability to deal with direct and indirect prejudicial statements from staff and references toward race, politics, community, and family

- Ability to deal professionally and maturely with the assumptions, stereotypes, and direct racism and indirect racist undertones

Please describe a typical workday.

- Come to work and check mail messages and calendar for the day

- Return phone calls and e-mails from DOC staff, offender families, offenders, criminal justice system attorneys, and judges

- Check on any information passed down from previous shifts pertaining to safety and security of unit staff and offenders

- Check list for classification case management issues and offender reviews and release dates

- EBC and unit responsibilities include program schedules, class facilitation, and specific unit and prison meetings.

- Meet with offenders; attend to classification issues, reentry/release, and security release; address offender jobs and programming

- Deal with insubordinate staff and offenders

- Maintain safety and security of unit in collaboration with unit supervisor

What is your advice to someone who wants to enter your field?

- Make sure to understand who you are. This is a job you want to perform well, but it isn't your life.

- Be prepared every day.

- Be very aware of who you are going to work for and what the job responsibilities are.

- You have to be very aware of the clientele with whom you are dealing on a day-to-day basis on both sides of the spectrum—that is, both the staff and the offenders.

- You need to be aware of how you will be perceived; go against the stereotype.

- You need to be aware of the stereotypes—for example, how you dress "like a gang member" versus going golfing, wearing identical clothes but being perceived differently, and how you conduct yourself at work and away from work. Stereotypical perceptions include that one is uneducated, is athletic, has low writing and language skills, or has an STG (security threat group, aka gang) affiliation.

- Prove that you are above the stereotypes; you may have to be patient. You want people to judge you on work performance, not by your race and culture.

- Unfortunately, the bigger burden is that how you conduct yourself influences others' perspectives of African Americans.

- Always take the high road. Fair isn't an option. You cannot think about what fair is or should be. You just have to follow your values, integrity, and beliefs and take the high road at all times.

- Have a "superior mindset," in the words of Professor Jigoro Kano, founder of judo.

PHOTO 12.5: An inmate being cuffed by an officer. Inmates in transit between institutions or who present a danger to staff are cuffed before they are removed from cells.

Crouch (1993) argued that blacks might be more able to accept prison and adjust to it over alternatives because they are more likely to find people they know housed there and are less likely to be threatened by prison life than whites given that they have suffered the violence and deprivations of the cities already. Wood and May (2003) added that it is possible that blacks may also prefer prison because the alternatives to it in the community may subject them to abuse and harassment and ultimate revocation of their probation anyway. Therefore, it is not likely true that blacks or whites "prefer" prisons or the alternatives (e.g., probation or other programming); they just disagree about which is the lesser evil.

MINORITIES WORKING IN CORRECTIONS

As with women, the employment of minority group men and women in correctional organizations did not increase until the Civil Rights Act of 1964 was passed and affirmative action plans were developed to encourage their employment. Today, however, the number of minorities employed in corrections, although not always reflecting their representation in the community (particularly regarding minority group women), has increased substantially. Although data in this area are not always consistent or up to date, we do know from the *Sourcebook of Criminal Justice Statistics* (Pastore & Maguire, 2000, Table 1.104; Pastore & Maguire, 2005, Table 1.101 and Table 1.107) that black non-Hispanics accounted for 23.7% of local jail correctional officer employees in 1999 (when their representation in the general population was about 12.2%, according to the U.S. Census for 2001); 19.5% of all employees in state, federal, and private prisons in 2004; and 24.3% of correctional officers in federal prisons in 2004. On the other hand, non-Hispanic whites and Hispanics are underrepresented among staff when compared with their representation in those communities. In 2001, whites constituted about 69.0% of the U.S. population and Hispanics constituted about 12.9% (U.S. Census Bureau, 2001). In these same data, whites were still the majority racial group employee (59.3%, 63.3%, and 60.6%, respectively) in these jails and prisons, and Hispanics constituted a substantial ethnic minority (7.7%, 7.3%, and 12.4%, respectively).

SUMMARY

- American history contains a racist past, which has affected the operation of correctional entities and the criminal justice system generally.

- Those who fall below the poverty line in the United States are also more likely to be enmeshed in street criminality. Some racial and ethnic groups who are more likely to be poor (e.g., African Americans,

Hispanics) are also more likely to be engaged in street crime.

- Police, courts, and correctional practices have had the effect of increasing the disproportionate incarceration of minority group members. Driving while black or brown, the drug war generally, and the harsh sentencing for crack cocaine specifically, along with the disenfranchisement that comes with a felony conviction (and in some states stays with a felony conviction), all serve to reinforce the disparity in treatment of racial and ethnic minorities by the criminal justice system.

- Physical and sexual victimization in prisons varies by type of victimization and by race and ethnicity, although the total amount of such victimization appears to be similar for these groups.

- The numbers of racial and ethnic minorities working in corrections has increased substantially over the years, and for African Americans, at least, it appears that they mirror their relative numbers in the community in a number of jurisdictions.

KEY TERMS

Discrimination, 263

Disparity, 263

Driving while black or brown (DWB), 277

Ethnicity, 263

Jim Crow laws, 275

Race, 263

DISCUSSION QUESTIONS

1. What sorts of criteria differentiate race and ethnicity? Why might it not always be clear what race or ethnicity a person is? Are there reasons to make such distinctions?

2. What evidence is there of disparity and discrimination against racial and ethnic minorities in the United States in the past?

3. What evidence is there of disparity and discrimination against racial and ethnic minorities in the United States currently?

4. How and why is adjustment in corrections affected by one's race and ethnicity?

5. Discuss how we might reduce the amount of disparity and discrimination against minorities in the United States. What specific steps can be taken in this direction? What are the likely barriers to accomplishing these changes?

$SAGE edge™

Review → Practice → Improve

Sharpen your skills with SAGE edge at **edge.sagepub.com/stohressentials3e**.

SAGE edge offers a robust online environment featuring an impressive array of free tools and resources for review, study, and further exploration, keeping both instructors and students on the cutting edge of teaching and learning.

FOR FURTHER EXPLORATION AND APPLICATION, TAKE A LOOK AT THE INTERACTIVE EBOOK FOR THESE PREMIUM RESOURCES:

▶ **Career Video 12.1** Legal Assistant

▶ **SAGE News Clip 12.1** U.S. Ferguson

▶ **SAGE News Clip 12.2** Arizona Racial Profiling

📄 **Journal Article 12.1** Race and Ethnicity Missingness in the Traffic Stop Data Reported by 308 Massachusetts Police Agencies

13

Juveniles and Corrections

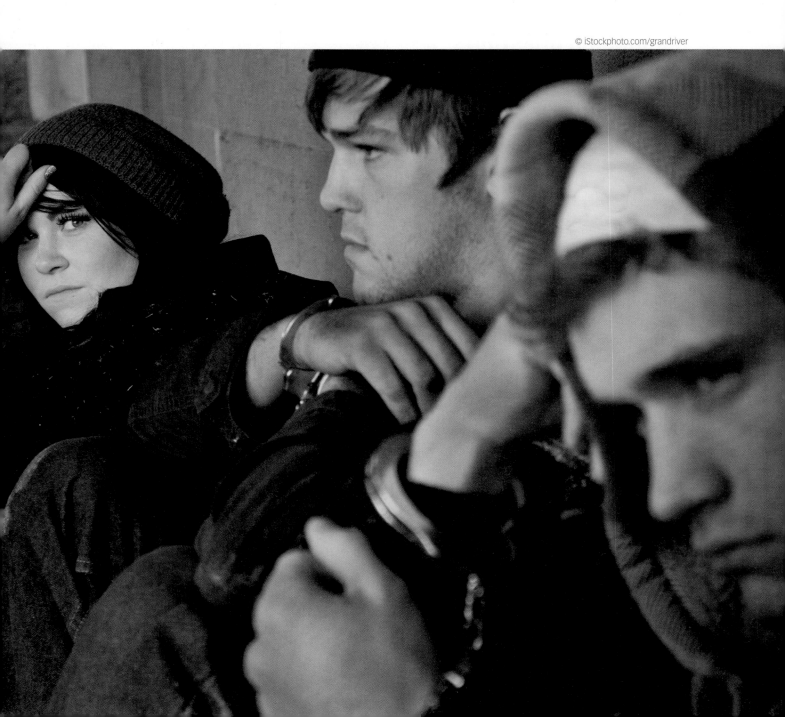

TEST YOUR KNOWLEDGE

Test your current knowledge of juvenile delinquency and juvenile corrections by answering the following questions as true or false. Check your answers on page 393 after reading the chapter.

1. Juveniles commit a disproportionate number of criminal acts.

2. Juvenile antisocial behavior is normal in that most adolescents engage in it.

3. Special juvenile courts began in England.

4. The ultimate source of responsibility for a juvenile's behavior is the state.

5. Juveniles can be tried in adult courts and sent to adult prisons in some circumstances.

6. Juveniles have always enjoyed the same rights as adults in criminal courts.

7. Juveniles can be sentenced to LWOP for any offense.

8. It was never permissible in the United States to execute those who committed murder while they were juveniles.

LEARNING OBJECTIVES

- Be able to explain the differences between delinquency and crime

- Understand why we see the age–crime curve in terms of adolescent development

- Know the history and philosophy of juvenile justice

- Understand the court cases that led to extending due process to juvenile offenders

- Gain a basic understanding of community and institutional juvenile corrections practices

- Be able to explain the processes involved in restorative justice

TOO YOUNG FOR LIFE

Joe Harris Sullivan was a 13-year-old tearaway when he and two other boys broke into the home of a 72-year-old woman in Pensacola, Florida, and stole jewelry and coins. One of the boys returned later and beat and raped her. Sullivan was convicted of the rape on the testimony of the other two boys (who received light sentences) and was sentenced to life without possibility of parole (LWOP). Sullivan's presentence report showed that he had committed 17 offenses (some serious, some not) prior to the burglary and rape. He was a troublemaker while in juvenile detention for previous offenses and assaulted other juveniles. Under Florida's sentencing guidelines, Sullivan scored 263 points above the minimum required to impose a life sentence.

In July of 2003, 16-year-old Terrance Jamar Graham and two accomplices attempted to rob a restaurant in Jacksonville, Florida. Graham was charged as an adult and placed on probation after he pled guilty. In December of 2003, Graham was arrested for a number of home invasion robberies and sentenced to LWOP for the robbery and probation violation when he was 17.

In both the Sullivan and Graham cases, the sentencing judges made certain remarks indicating that they were certain the boys were beyond hope of rehabilitation. Both boys were raised in abusive and neglectful homes (Graham's parents were both crack addicts) and lived in the worst ghettoes of their respective cities. While these circumstances cannot excuse their behavior, it makes it understandable. In appealing these boys' cases, their attorneys made much of neuroscience evidence relative to the immaturity of the adolescent brain. We all know that adolescence is a time of rebellion, but most of us limit that revolt to being a little experimental with our lives and being—from a parental point of view—a pain in the rear.

We will see, however, that there is a small subset of people who begin committing antisocial acts prior to adolescence and continue to do so over the life course.

Is LWOP the only solution to such predators, or can their deficiencies be addressed and the community be protected in some other way? Should Sullivan and Graham have been sentenced in adult court anyway? Are individuals who commit rapes and armed robberies "children" as we think of them, and should they be treated differently from adults? These are some of the things to think about as you read about the differences between the adult and juvenile justice systems in the United States.

••• INTRODUCTION: DELINQUENCY AND STATUS OFFENDING

The juvenile justice system generally falls under the broad umbrella of the civil law rather than criminal law. This placement emphasizes the distinction that the law makes between adults and juveniles who commit the same illegal acts. Juveniles who commit acts that are criminal when committed by adults are called **delinquents** rather than criminals, conveying the notion that the juvenile has *not* done something he or she *was* supposed to do (behave lawfully) rather than *done* something he or she *was not* supposed to do (behave unlawfully). This difference is a subtle one that reflects the rehabilitative, rather than punitive, philosophy of American juvenile justice.

Delinquents: Juveniles who commit acts that are criminal when committed by adults.

Status offenses: Offenses that apply only to juveniles such as smoking and disobeying parents.

Status offenders: Juveniles who commit certain actions that are legal for adults but not for children such as smoking and not obeying parents.

Juveniles are subject to laws that make certain actions that are legal for adults, such as smoking, drinking, not obeying parents, staying out at night to all hours, and not going to school, illegal for them. These acts are called **status offenses** because they apply only to individuals having the status of a juvenile, and they exist because the law assumes that juveniles lack the maturity to appreciate the long-term consequences of their behavior. Many of these acts can jeopardize juveniles' future acquisition of suitable social roles because they may lead to defiance of all authority, inadequate education, addiction, and teenage parenthood (Binder, Geis, & Bruce, 2001). If parents are unwilling or unable to shield their children from harm, the juvenile justice system becomes a substitute parent. Status offenses constitute the vast majority of juvenile offenses and consume an inordinate amount of juvenile court time and resources (Bynum & Thompson, 1999). Because of this, some states have relinquished court jurisdiction over status offenses to other social service agencies where terms such as "child in need of supervision" (CHINS) and "person in need of supervision" (PINS) are used to differentiate **status offenders** from juveniles who have committed acts that are crimes when committed by adults. In this chapter, we discuss the extent of juvenile delinquency and status offending, the likely causes of it, the history of dealing with children in corrections, and current processing of delinquents in the system.

© iStockphoto.com/Nikada

PHOTO 13.1: Immaturity of adolescent behavior is matched by the immaturity of the adolescent brain.

••• THE EXTENT OF DELINQUENCY

Figure 13.1 shows the juvenile proportion of all reported arrests in 2014. Juveniles (youths under 18) accounted for 11% of all violent crime arrests and 15% of all property crime arrests. According to the U.S. Census Bureau (2006), the percentage of the population between the age of responsibility (the age at which juveniles can be held accountable for their actions) and adulthood averaged across all states was about 11.5% in 2005. Juveniles are thus overrepresented in most of the crime categories in Figure 13.1.

Figures such as these are troubling, but antisocial behavior is normative (although not welcome) for juveniles; juveniles who do *not* engage in it are statistically abnormal (Moffitt & Walsh, 2003). Adolescence is a time when youths are "feeling their oats" and temporarily fracturing parental bonds in their own personal declaration of independence. Looking at data from 12 different countries, Junger-Tas (1996) concluded that delinquent behavior is a part of growing up and that the peak ages for different types of crimes were similar across all countries (16–17 for property crimes and 18–20 for violent crimes). Biologists tell us that adolescent rebellion is an evolutionary design feature of all social primates. Fighting with parents and seeking out age peers with whom to affiliate "all help the adolescent away from the home territory" (Powell, 2006, p. 867). As Caspi and Moffitt (1995) put it, "Every curfew broken, car stolen, joint smoked, or baby conceived is a statement of independence" (p. 500). The juvenile courts are thus dealing with individuals at a time in their lives when they are most susceptible to antisocial behavior.

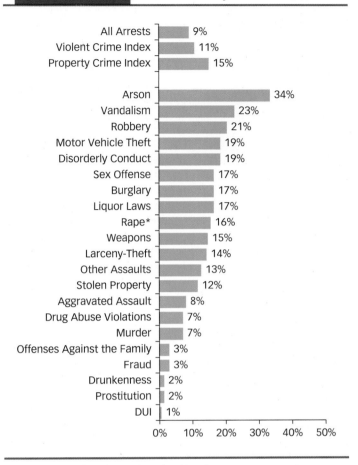

FIGURE *13.1*   Juvenile Proportion of Arrests by Offense, 2014

Offense	Percent
All Arrests	9%
Violent Crime Index	11%
Property Crime Index	15%
Arson	34%
Vandalism	23%
Robbery	21%
Motor Vehicle Theft	19%
Disorderly Conduct	19%
Sex Offense	17%
Burglary	17%
Liquor Laws	17%
Rape*	16%
Weapons	15%
Larceny-Theft	14%
Other Assaults	13%
Stolen Property	12%
Aggravated Assault	8%
Drug Abuse Violations	7%
Murder	7%
Offenses Against the Family	3%
Fraud	3%
Drunkenness	2%
Prostitution	2%
DUI	1%

Source: National Institute of Justice (2015).

*The new definition of rape went into effect in 2013. The revised definition expands rape to include both male and female victims and reflects the various forms of sexual penetration understood to be rape, especially nonconsenting acts of sodomy and sexual assaults with objects.

••• THE JUVENILE BRAIN AND JUVENILE BEHAVIOR

Figure 13.2 shows prevalence rates for criminal behavior over the life course from different times and different countries. This pattern is known as the **age–crime curve**. The age–crime curve is formed from the statistical count of the number of known crimes committed in a population over a given period mapped according to age. The curve reflects a sharp increase in offending beginning during early adolescence, a peak during mid-adolescence, and then a steep decline during early adulthood followed by a steadier decline thereafter. The peak may be higher or lower at different periods, and the peak age may vary by 1 or 2 years at different times or in different places, but the peak remains. This pattern has been noted throughout history of all cultures around the world and has been called "the most important regularity in criminology" (Nagin & Land, 1993, p. 330) and a "law of nature" (Gottfredson & Hirschi, 1990, p. 124).

The age–crime curve has long puzzled criminologists. Hirschi and Gottfredson (1983) noted, "The age distribution of crime cannot be accounted for by any variable or combination of variables currently available to criminology" (p. 554). However, with the tremendous advances made by the neurosciences over the past 3 decades, we are in a much better position to understand adolescent offending. Neuroscience research has thrown light on why there is a sharp rise in antisocial behavior during adolescence across time

Age–crime curve:
Formed from the statistical count of the number of known crimes committed in a population over a given period mapped according to age.

FIGURE *13.2*   Illustrating the Age–Crime Curve in Different Countries and Times

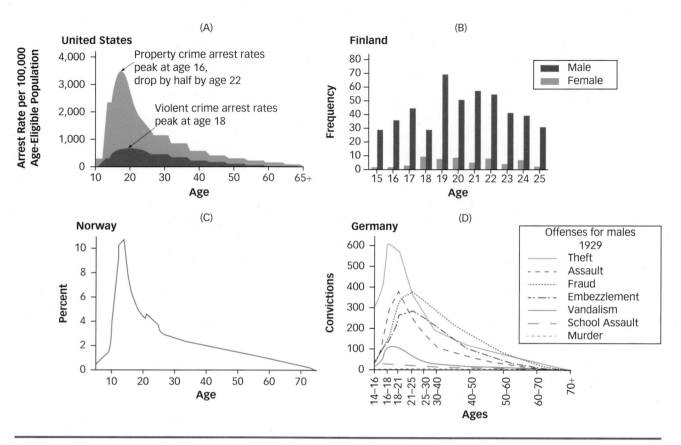

Source: Ellis and Walsh, *Criminology: A Global Perspective* (2000). Reprinted with permission.

and cultures, and some very important court decisions in juvenile justice (such as the abolition of the juvenile death penalty) have been influenced by this research (Garland & Frankel, 2006). What has emerged from this research is that the immaturity of adolescent behavior is matched by the immaturity of the adolescent brain. A. White's (2004) summation of the key messages from the 2003 conference of the New York Academy of Sciences (NYAS) made this quite clear:

1. Much of the behavior characterizing adolescence is rooted in biology intermingling with environmental influences to cause teens to conflict with their parents, take more risks, and experience wide swings in emotion.

2. The lack of synchrony between a physically mature body and a still maturing nervous system may explain these behaviors.

3. Adolescents' sensitivities to rewards appear to be different than in adults, prompting them to seek higher levels of novelty and stimulation to achieve the same feeling of pleasure.

4. With the right dose of guidance and understanding, adolescence can be a relatively smooth transition. (p. 4)

The onset of puberty also brings with it a 10- to 20-fold increase in testosterone in males, a hormone linked to aggression and dominance seeking (L. Ellis, 2003), and brain chemicals that excite behavior increase during adolescence while chemicals that inhibit it decrease (Collins, 2004; E. Walker, 2002). Many other events are reshaping the adolescent's body and brain during this period that lead to the conclusion that there are *physical* reasons why adolescents often fail to exercise rational judgment and why they tend to attribute erroneous intentions to others. When the brain reaches its adult state, a more adult-like personality emerges, with greater self-control and conscientiousness (Blonigen, 2010). It is important to understand these biological processes, and it is especially important to note the last of the NYAS's messages: "With the right dose of guidance and understanding, adolescence can be a relatively smooth transition" (as cited in A. White, 2004, p. 4). Indeed, by the age of 28, about 85% of all former delinquents have desisted from offending (Caspi & Moffit, 1995).

It has long been known that the vast majority of youths who offend during adolescence desist and that only a small number continue to offend during adulthood. Moffitt (1993) called the former adolescent limited (AL) offenders and the latter life course persistent (LCP) offenders. LCP offenders begin offending prior to puberty and continue well into adulthood. It is typically found that LCP offenders are saddled with neuropsychological and temperamental deficits that are manifested in low IQ, hyperactivity, inattentiveness, negative emotionality, and low impulse control that arise from a combination of genetic and environmental effects on brain development. LCP offenders constitute only about 7% of all delinquents but are responsible for at least 50% of all delinquent acts. Moreover, LCP offenders tend to commit serious crimes such as assault, robbery, and rape, whereas AL offenders tend to commit relatively minor offenses such as petty theft and vandalism (Moffitt & Walsh, 2003).

AL offenders, on the other hand, have developmental histories that place them on a prosocial trajectory that is temporarily derailed at adolescence. They are not burdened with the neuropsychological problems that weigh heavily on LCP offenders; they are "normal" youths adapting to the transitional events of adolescence and whose offending does not reflect any stable personal deficiencies. More teens than in the past are being diverted from their prosocial life trajectories because better health and nutrition have lowered the average age of puberty, while the average time needed to prepare for participation in an increasingly complex economy has increased. These changes have resulted in about a 5- to 10-year maturity gap between puberty and entry into the job market.

●●● HISTORY AND PHILOSOPHY OF JUVENILE JUSTICE

Up until about 300 years ago, the concept of childhood was not recognized; children were considered not much different from property, and no special allowances for children were recognized in matters of determining culpability and punishment. The minimum legal age of criminal responsibility was defined in early English common law as 7. In the United States today, it ranges from 6 in North Carolina to 10 in Arkansas, Colorado, Kansas, Pennsylvania, and Wisconsin, the same as it is in modern England (Snyder, Espiritu, Huizinga, Loeber, & Petechuck, 2003). Under the increasing influence of Christianity, English courts during the Middle Ages began to exempt children below the age of 7 from criminal responsibility, and children between the ages of 7 and 14 could be held criminally responsible only if it could be shown that they were fully aware of the consequences of their actions. The cutoff age between childhood and adulthood was 14 for the purpose of assigning adult criminal responsibility because individuals were considered rational and responsible enough at this age to marry (Springer, 1987).

Ever since the formation of the English chancery courts during the 13th century, there has been movement toward greater state involvement in children's lives. Chancery courts adopted the doctrine of **parens patriae**, which literally means "father of his country" but practically means "state as parent." Parens patriae gave the state the right to intercede *in loco parentis* ("in the place of parents") and to act in the best interest of the child or any other legally incapacitated person such as someone who is mentally ill. This meant that the state and not the parents had the ultimate authority over children and that children could be removed from their families if they were being delinquent and placed in the custody of the state (Hemmens, Steiner, & Mueller, 2003).

Despite parens patriae, the family was still considered the optimal setting for children to be reared in, and as such orphans or children with inadequate parents were assigned to foster families through a system known as binding out. Children whose parents could not control them or who were too poor to provide for them were apprenticed to richer families who used them for domestic or farm labor. This period saw the establishment of the first laws directed specifically at children, including laws that condemned begging and vagrancy (P. Sharp & Hancock, 1995). The concern over vagrancy led to the creation of workhouses in which "habits of industry" were to be instilled. The first one, called a bridewell, was opened in 1555, and in 1576 the English Parliament passed a law establishing bridewells, or workhouses (also discussed in Chapter 2), in every English county (Whitehead & Lab, 1996). These places were generally dank, harsh, and abusive, but the idea behind them was that if vagrant youths were removed from the negative influences of street life, they could be reformed by discipline, hard work, and religious instruction.

••• CHILDHOOD IN THE UNITED STATES

American notions of childhood and how to deal with childhood misconduct were imported whole from England. Based on the bridewell model, the New York House of Refuge was established in 1825 to house orphans, beggars, vagrants, and juvenile offenders. Several other cities, counties, and states soon established their own homes for "the perishing and dangerous classes," as they were viewed (Binder et al., 2001, p. 202). Children in houses of refuge (discussed in Chapter 11) lived highly disciplined lives and were required to work at jobs that brought income to the institutions. The indeterminate nature of children's residence allowed the institutions a great deal of latitude in their treatment. Children were required to work long hours, often received little or no training, and were frequently mistreated (Whitehead & Lab, 1996).

It was a frequent practice for poor parents to place their children in residence for idle and disorderly behavior, making it clear that the courts would need to create standards for admission. The courts did this in *Ex Parte Crouse* (1838). The subject of the case was a child named Mary Ann Crouse, who was placed in the Pennsylvania House of Refuge by her mother against the wishes of her father. Mary's father argued that it was unconstitutional to incarcerate a child without a jury trial, but the Pennsylvania Supreme Court ruled that parental rights are superseded by the parens patriae doctrine. This landmark decision established parens patriae as settled law in American juvenile jurisprudence (Del Carmen, Parker, & Reddington, 1998).

Parens patriae:
A legal principle giving the state the right to intercede and act in the best interest of the child or any other legally incapacitated persons such as the mentally ill.

TABLE *13.1*   Comparing Procedural/Event Terminology in Adult and Juvenile Court Systems

Procedure or Event	Adult System	Juvenile System
Police take custody of offender	Placed under arrest	Taken into custody
Official who makes initial decisions about entry into the court system	Magistrate/judge	Intake officer
Place accused may be held pending further processing	Jail	Detention
Document charging the accused with specific act	Indictment or information	Petition
Person charged with illegal act	Defendant	Respondent
Accused appears to respond to charge(s)	Arraignment	Hearing
Accused verbally responds	Enters a plea of guilty, not guilty, or no contest	Admits or denies
Court proceeding to determine whether accused committed the offense	Public jury trial	Adjudicatory hearing
Decision of the court as to whether accused committed the offense	Verdict of jury	Adjudication by judge; no jury; not public
Standard of proof required	Beyond a reasonable doubt	Beyond a reasonable doubt
Court proceeding to determine what to do with person found to have committed offense	Sentencing hearing	Dispositional hearing
Institutional confinement	Prison	Juvenile correctional facility
Community supervision	Probation; parole if had been imprisoned	Probation; aftercare if had been confined to juvenile correctional facility

● ● ● THE BEGINNING OF THE JUVENILE COURTS

Greater concern for children's welfare during the 19th century created an impetus for change in the way juvenile offenders were handled as it became increasingly obvious that adult criminal courts were not equipped to apply the spirit of the parens patriae doctrine. In 1899, Cook County, Illinois, enacted legislation providing for a separate court system for juveniles, and by 1945 every state in the union had established juvenile court systems (Hemmens et al., 2003). These courts combined the authority of social control with the sympathy of social welfare in a single institution and afforded judges a great deal of latitude in determining how "the best interests of the child" could be realized. The creation of a separate system of justice for juveniles brought with it a set of terms describing the processing of children accused of committing delinquent acts that differentiated it from the adult system. These terms reflect the protective and rehabilitative nature of the juvenile system, in contrast to the punitive nature of the adult system. Table 13.1 lists the terms used to describe the procedure or event from initial contact with authorities to the last one in both the adult and juvenile justice systems today.

• • • PROCESSING JUVENILE OFFENDERS

Figure 13.3 illustrates the flow of juvenile cases through the juvenile courts in the United States in 2009 (Knoll & Sickmund, 2012). We see that only 55% of the juveniles taken into custody ("arrested") or otherwise referred to juvenile court were petitioned (formally charged). Among those not petitioned, most had their cases dismissed, some are placed on informal probation (probation without a formal adjudication of delinquency, sometimes known as diversion), and "other sanctions"—this could be something as minor as a written apology to something as serious as placement in a mental institution.

When a petition has been filed by the juvenile court prosecutor, the court has to decide if it should take jurisdiction of the case. In about 99% of the cases, the court does accept jurisdiction, and about 66% of the time, the juvenile is adjudicated delinquent (found guilty). Note that in 32% of the cases without a finding of adjudication, 30% of those cases were not outright dismissed. In adult court, a finding of "not guilty" always means that the defendant is now a free person. Under the principle of parens patriae, however, the juvenile court has the power to intervene in a child's life as a proactive measure even though he or she has been found not guilty of any wrongdoing. If the juvenile court does not accept jurisdiction, it means that the case is waived to adult court, which is one of the most controversial issues in juvenile justice.

JUVENILES WAIVED TO CRIMINAL COURT

As noted earlier, juveniles can sometimes be *waived* (transferred) to adult criminal court, where they lose their status as minors, become legally culpable for their alleged crime, and are subject to criminal prosecution and punishments. A transfer to adult court is called a **waiver** because the juvenile court waives (relinquishes) its jurisdiction over the child to the adult system. Waivers are designed to allow the juvenile courts to transfer juveniles over a certain age who have committed particularly serious crimes, or who have exhausted the juvenile system's resources in trying to rehabilitate chronic offenders, to a more punitive system. Juveniles become increasingly likely to be waived if they are chronic offenders approaching the upper age limit of their state's juvenile court's jurisdiction. Note from Figure 13.3 that only about 1.0% of juvenile cases nationwide are waived to adult criminal court.

There are three primary (non–mutually exclusive) ways that juveniles can be waived to criminal court:

1. **Judicial waiver:** A judicial waiver involves a juvenile judge deciding after a "full inquiry" that the juvenile should be waived. (Currently, 48 states use this judicial discretionary model.) In some states, there are mandatory waivers for some offenses, but juvenile judges are involved in determining whether the criteria for a mandatory waiver are met. Currently, 12 states use a system of presumptive waivers in which the burden of proof is on juveniles to prove that they are amenable to treatment and therefore should not be waived; the burden of proof is not on the prosecutor to prove that they should.

2. **Prosecutorial discretion:** This model allows prosecutors to file some cases in either adult or juvenile court. In such cases (usually limited by age and seriousness of the offense), the prosecutor can file the case directly with the adult court and bypass the juvenile court altogether. Currently, 14 states and the District of Columbia allow prosecutorial discretion waivers.

3. **Statutory exclusion:** These are waivers in cases where state legislatures have statutorily excluded certain serious offenses from the juvenile courts for juveniles over a certain age, which varies from state to state. These automatic waivers are currently found in 31 states.

Waiver: Refers to a process by which a juvenile offender is "waived" (transferred) to an adult court because he or she has committed a particularly serious crime or is habitually delinquent.

Judicial waiver: Involves a juvenile judge deciding after a "full inquiry" that the juvenile should be waived to the adult system.

Prosecutorial discretion: Allows prosecutors to file some cases in either adult or juvenile court.

Statutory exclusion: Waivers in cases where state legislatures have statutorily excluded certain serious offenses from the juvenile courts for juveniles over a certain age, which varies from state to state.

FIGURE *13.3*	Juvenile Court Case Processing

Case Flow for a Typical 1,000 Delinquency Cases

Source: Knoll and Sickmund (2012), National Center for Juvenile Justice, Pittsburgh, PA.

Studies have shown that juveniles waived to adult courts are more likely to recidivate than youths adjudicated for similar crimes in juvenile court; however, remember that only the most delinquency-prone youths are waived, so this is no surprise (Butts & Mitchell, 2000). Neither does a waiver necessarily guarantee a more punitive disposition. Waived juveniles who commit violent crimes are likely to be incarcerated, but juveniles waived for property and drug offenses often receive more lenient sentences than they would have received in juvenile courts (Butts & Mitchell, 2000).

EXTENDING DUE PROCESS TO JUVENILES

Contrary to the "best interests of the child" philosophy, juvenile courts often punished children in arbitrary ways that would not be tolerated in the adult system, as illustrated in some famous juvenile cases presented below. Critics argued that the parens patriae doctrine allowed too much latitude for courts to restrict the rights of juveniles and that because the courts could remove juvenile rights to liberty, juveniles should be afforded the same due process protections as adults. Supporters of parens patriae countered that it was suitable and proper for the treatment of children and that any problems concerning juvenile court operation were problems of implementation, not philosophy (Whitehead & Lab, 1996).

The U.S. Supreme Court maintained a "hands off" policy with regard to the operation of the juvenile courts until 1966, when it agreed to hear *Kent v. United States*. In 1961, 16-year-old Morris Kent broke into a woman's apartment, raped her, and stole her wallet. Because of Kent's chronic delinquency and the seriousness of the offense, he was waived to adult court. The adult court found Kent guilty of six counts of housebreaking and robbery, for which he was sentenced to 30 to 90 years in prison. Had Kent remained in juvenile court, he could have been sentenced to a maximum of 5 years (the remainder of his minority, which was until age 21 at the time). Kent appealed, arguing that the waiver process had not included a "full investigation" and that his counsel had been denied access to the court files.

The Supreme Court remanded Kent's case back to district court, with Justice Abe Fortas stating,

> There is no place in our system of law for reaching a result of such tremendous consequences without ceremony—without hearing, without effective assistance of counsel, without a statement of reasons. . . . The admonition to function in a "parental" relationship is not an invitation to procedural arbitrariness. (n.p.)

Justice Fortas also noted that under the parens patriae philosophy, the child receives the worst of both worlds: "He gets neither the protections accorded to adults nor the solicitous care and regenerative treatment postulated for children" (n.p.). The *Kent* decision determined that juveniles must be afforded certain constitutional rights and, thus, began the process of formalizing the juvenile system into something akin to the adult system (Hemmens et al., 2003).

The Supreme Court heard a second case concerning juvenile rights 1 year later in *In re Gault* (1967). In 1964, 15-year-old Gerald Gault was adjudicated delinquent for making obscene phone calls and was sentenced to 6 years in the State Industrial School. An adult convicted of the same offense would have faced a $5 to $50 fine and a maximum of 60 days in jail. The Supreme Court used this case to establish five basic constitutional due process rights for juveniles—(1) the right to proper notification of charges, (2) the right to legal counsel, (3) the right to confront witnesses, (4) the right to privilege against self-incrimination, and (5) the right to appellate review—all of which had been denied to Gault.

A third significant juvenile case is *In re Winship* (1970). In 1967, 12-year-old Samuel Winship was accused of stealing $112 from a woman's purse taken from a locker. Winship was adjudicated delinquent based on the civil law's "preponderance of evidence" standard of proof (i.e., is it more likely than not that the person committed the act he or she is charged with?) and was sent to a state training school. On appeal, the Supreme Court ruled that when the possibility of commitment to a secure facility is a possibility, the "beyond a reasonable doubt" standard of proof must extend to juvenile adjudication hearings.

In *McKeiver v. Pennsylvania* (1971), the sole issue before the Supreme Court was, "Do juveniles have the right to a jury trial during adjudication hearings?" The Court ruled that they do not. The Court did not rule that the states cannot provide juveniles with this due process right, only that they are not constitutionally required to do so. And in *Breed v. Jones* (1975), the Supreme Court ruled that the prohibition against double jeopardy applied to juveniles once they have had an adjudicatory hearing (which is a civil process and not technically a trial). Breed had an adjudicatory hearing and was subsequently waived to adult court. The Court ruled that he had been subjected to the burden of two

PHOTO 13.2: Juvenile court, 1910: An 8-year-old boy charged with stealing a bicycle. Do you think a court would be more or less lenient on this boy today?

trials for the same offense and therefore the double jeopardy clause of the Fifth Amendment had been violated.

In the case of *Schall v. Martin* (1984), the issue before the Supreme Court was whether the preventative detention of a juvenile charged with a delinquent act is constitutional. The Court ruled that it was permissible because it serves a legitimate state interest in protecting both society and the juvenile from the risk of further crimes committed by the person being detained while awaiting his or her hearing. This ruling established that juveniles do not enjoy the right to bail consideration and reasserted the parens patriae interests of the state.

The last major juvenile case involves the two boys highlighted in this chapter's opening vignette—Sullivan and Graham. Their cases were consolidated as *Graham v. Florida* (2010), in which the majority opinion of the Supreme Court overturning the imposition of life without the possibility of parole for juveniles who have not committed homicide stated,

> The Constitution prohibits the imposition of a life without parole sentence on a juvenile offender who did not commit homicide. A State need not guarantee the offender eventual release, but if it imposes a sentence of life it must provide him or her with some realistic opportunity to obtain release before the end of that term. (n.p.)

JUVENILES AND THE DEATH PENALTY

The Supreme Court justices have also needed to wrestle with the moral issue of imposing the death penalty on individuals who committed their crimes as juveniles. From 1973 to 2003, a total of 22 such offenders were executed in the United States (Streib, 2003b). The death penalty has been applied only to juveniles who have murdered in particularly heinous and depraved ways.

The first such case was *Eddings v. Oklahoma* (1982). In 1977, 16-year-old Monty Lee Eddings and several companions stole an automobile. The car was stopped by an Oklahoma Highway Patrol Officer, and when the officer approached the car, Eddings shot and killed him. At Eddings's sentencing hearing, the state presented three aggravating circumstances to warrant the death penalty, but the judge allowed only Eddings's age in mitigation. The Supreme Court vacated Eddings's death sentence, ruling that in death penalty cases the courts must consider all mitigating factors (e.g., Eddings had been a victim of abusive treatment at home) when considering a death sentence.

Thompson v. Oklahoma (1988) involved 15-year-old William Thompson, who was one of four young men charged with the murder of his former brother-in-law. All four were found guilty and sentenced to death. Thompson appealed to the Supreme Court, claiming that a sentence of death for a crime committed by a 15-year-old is cruel and unusual punishment. The Court agreed, and using the "evolving standards of decency"

? ETHICAL ISSUE

What Would You Do?

You are an intake officer at juvenile court and have processed a 16-year-old boy named John with an IQ of 80 charged with a string of burglaries. The prosecutor has offered him a plea bargain stating that if he admits to the burglaries, he will receive 6 months' detention followed by probation until he reaches adulthood at age 18. If John refuses to admit the charges, the prosecutor indicates that she will seek a waiver to adult court where the presumptive sentence would be in the range of 36 to 48 months' imprisonment. In your professional judgment, John would be better off taking the plea, but he is adamant that he will not admit anything, which is his absolute right. You are convinced that his diminished capacity is contributing to his decision because all of the evidence shows that he did commit the burglaries. John's defense lawyer is ethically bound to abide by his decision to seek a waiver and be tried in adult court, but you are not sure whether you are similarly bound. How far will you go, if at all, to try and convince John to take the plea to save him from adult prison?

PERSPECTIVE FROM A PRACTITIONER

Skyler Brouwer, Juvenile Probation Officer

Position: Juvenile Probation Officer

Location: Omaha, Nebraska

Education: University of Nebraska at Omaha; criminal justice

How long have you been a juvenile probation officer?

Three years.

What are the primary duties and responsibilities of a juvenile probation officer?

To effectuate positive behavior change in an effort to reduce the likelihood of offenders' recidivating; to confirm that the offenders are in compliance with their court orders through face-to-face contact and from collateral information from treatment/mental health providers, drug testing, and school information; to assist the offenders and their families with finding resources in the community that they can benefit from while on probation and to motivate the offenders to lead law-abiding and successful lives (this is all done with building and maintaining positive rapport with the offenders, their family members, and the community support systems); and to update the court on progress, or lack of progress, through court reports, memos, e-mails, petitions, and face-to-face contact.

What are the characteristics and traits most useful for a juvenile probation officer?

- Honesty
- Confidence
- Excellent writing and communication skills
- Consistent
- Being able to think outside the box
- Empathetic
- Innovative
- Motivating
- Fair
- Resilient

Please describe your typical workday:

Conducting office and field visits with offenders, treatment providers, school administrators, counselors, and teachers to monitor compliance or noncompliance of the court order. Writing predispositional (presentence) and other reports occupies a considerable portion of a juvenile probation officer's time. Our department uses assessment instruments such as the Youth Level of Service/Case Management Inventory and the Adolescent Chemical Dependency Inventory. These instruments assist the probation officer with assessing the offenders' major needs, strengths, and barriers. The assessment breaks down into the following categories: prior and current offenses, education, substance abuse, family, personality/behavior, leisure and recreation, and attitudes/orientation. The Adolescent Chemical Dependency Inventory is an assessment that is a self-report test. This assessment obtains a lot of information in a short amount of time. The assessment screens the following: substance abuse and use, overall adjustment, and troubled youth concerns. Other duties include attending court hearings; communicating with formal and informal supports of the offender through voicemails, phone calls, e-mails, and memos; and ensuring the safety of the community and the offenders through the officer's efforts to assist them in their rehabilitation.

What is your advice to someone who wants to enter your field?

Be able to use your passion to think outside the box and assist people in becoming role models in their communities.

principle, it drew the line at age 16 under which execution was not constitutionally permissible.

Seventeen years later, in *Roper v. Simmons* (2005), the Supreme Court redrew the age line at 18 under which it was constitutionally impermissible to execute anyone. Christopher Simmons was 17 when he and two younger accomplices broke into a home, kidnapped the owner, beat her, and threw her alive from a high bridge into the river below, where she drowned. Simmons had told many of his friends before the crime that he wanted to commit a murder, and he bragged about it to them afterward. His crime was a "classical" death penalty case—premeditated, deliberate, and cruel—and he was totally unremorseful. Nevertheless, his sentence drew condemnation from around the world, with **amicus curiae briefs** ("friend of the court" briefs presented to the court arguing in support of one side or the other by interested parties not directly involved with the case) being filed in favor of Simmons by the European Union, the American and British Bar Associations, the American Medical and Psychological Associations, and 15 Nobel Prize winners, among others.

In a 5-to-4 opinion, Justice Anthony Kennedy noted that the United States was the only country in the world that gives official sanction to the juvenile death penalty (there are a number of countries that execute juveniles without giving the practice "official sanction"). He also noted the growing body of evidence from neuroscience about the immaturity of the adolescent brain. The majority opinion also cited *Atkins v. Virginia* (2002). In noting that the Supreme Court in *Atkins* had ruled the execution of the mentally disabled to be cruel and unusual punishment because of the lesser degree of culpability attached to the mentally challenged, it reasoned that such logic should be applied to juveniles. The Court also pointed out that the plurality of states (30) either bar execution of juveniles or have banned the death penalty altogether, thus citing state legislation as part of the impetus behind its decision.

Figure 13.4 presents a summary of important Supreme Court cases regarding juveniles' due process rights from *Kent* (1966) to *Miller* (2012). Taken as a whole, what these cases essentially mean is an erosion of the distinction between juvenile and criminal courts. On the positive side, these rulings have helped to create a juvenile court system that more closely reflects the procedural guidelines established in adult criminal courts. On the negative side, they have in effect criminalized juvenile courts. To gain due process rights enjoyed by adults, juveniles have surrendered some benefits such as the informality of solicitous treatment that they nominally enjoyed previously. Only time will tell if this convergence of systems results in more just outcomes for juveniles than they received under unmodified parens patriae.

ETHICAL ISSUE

What Would You Do?

You are an assistant district attorney who has been assigned a heinous murder case. In this case, a young man was burglarizing a house at night when the occupants were sleeping. The man of the house confronted the youth with a baseball bat, but the youth shot him. The man's wife screamed and ran into the bedroom to call the police, but the youth caught up with her, beat her, raped her, and then shot her also. The young man, who committed the offense on his 18th birthday, was caught later that night. You now need to decide whether you are to seek the death penalty, which is being demanded by an outraged community. Because the young man was only hours into adulthood when he committed the crime, you are urged by an anti–death penalty colleague not to seek it. What will you do and why?

••• JUVENILE COMMUNITY CORRECTIONS

As seen from Figure 13.5, juvenile corrections mirror the adult system in that the majority of adjudicated delinquents are placed into some form of community-based corrections and just over a quarter are sent to residential facilities. Juvenile community corrections offer a wide variety of options, all ostensibly designed to implement the three-pronged goal of the juvenile justice system: (1) to protect the community, (2) to hold delinquent youths accountable, and (3) to provide treatment and positive role models for youths. This is known as the balanced approach to corrections (K. Carter, 2006).

When juveniles are taken into custody, a complicated process of determining how to best deal with them with the above goals in mind is initiated. Juveniles may be released

Amicus curiae briefs: "Friend of the court" briefs presented to the court, arguing in support of one side or the other, by interested parties not directly involved with the case.

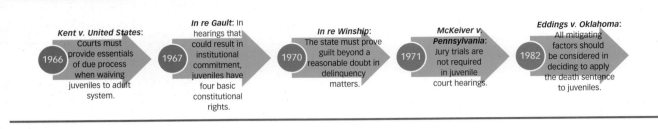

FIGURE 13.4   Supreme Court Cases Altering Juvenile Justice, 1966–2012

1966 — **Kent v. United States**: Courts must provide essentials of due process when waiving juveniles to adult system.

1967 — **In re Gault**: In hearings that could result in institutional commitment, juveniles have four basic constitutional rights.

1970 — **In re Winship**: The state must prove guilt beyond a reasonable doubt in delinquency matters.

1971 — **McKeiver v. Pennsylvania**: Jury trials are not required in juvenile court hearings.

1982 — **Eddings v. Oklahoma**: All mitigating factors should be considered in deciding to apply the death sentence to juveniles.

to their parents or detained in a detention center until this determination is made. The most lenient disposition of a case is known as **deferred adjudication**. Depending on the jurisdiction, a deferred adjudication decision can be made by the police, the prosecutor, a juvenile probation officer, or a juvenile magistrate/judge. A deferred adjudication means that an agreement is reached between the youth and a juvenile probation officer, without any formal court appearance, that the youth will follow certain probation conditions. This form of disposition is used only for status offenses or minor property offenses, and as long as the juvenile has no further charges, he or she is discharged from probation within a short time period. No formal record of the proceedings of the case is made in deferred adjudications.

Deferred adjudication: A decision made by certain criminal justice personnel to delay or defer formal court proceedings if a youth follows probation conditions.

Predisposition report: A report done in juvenile courts that is analogous to a presentence investigation report in adult courts.

Other juveniles may be placed on formal probation after adjudication in court by a juvenile judge. In such cases, there are records of the proceedings and probationers are more strictly monitored. As in the adult courts, juvenile judges typically make their dispositional decisions based on recommendations made by probation officers. Juvenile probation officers write **predisposition reports** (analogous to the adult presentence investigation reports) and will have a variety of classification instruments very similar to those used in the adult system, and discussed in Chapters 7 and 15, to help them formulate their recommendations.

Once a youth is placed on probation, under the doctrine of parens patriae, the probation officer becomes a surrogate parent to the youth. But with probation officers being saddled with a nationwide average of about 42 cases (Taylor, Fritsch, & Caeti, 2007), they can do very little "parenting." Probation officers might see their charges only once a month for perhaps 30 minutes, whereas the juveniles' natural parents see them (or should see them) every day. Juvenile probation officers therefore insist on parental support in working with their children because parental involvement in the rehabilitative effort of juveniles is considered a "must" (Balazs, 2006). It is a must because while probation serves the positive goal of keeping youths in the community and thus avoiding the stigma of institutionalization and the exposure to other

FIGURE 13.5   Juvenile Delinquency Probation Caseload, 1985–2009

Since 1997, the number of cases in which juveniles were placed on probation has declined steadily.

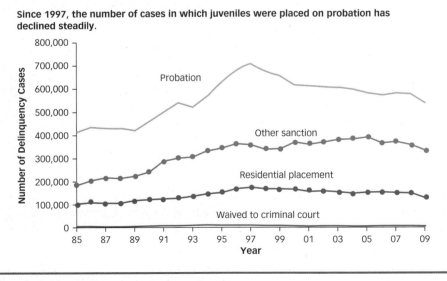

Source: Livsey (2012). U.S. Department of Justice.

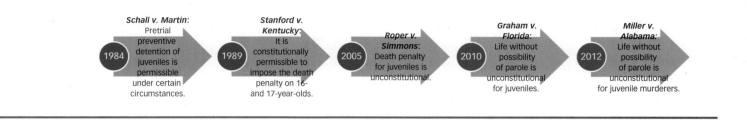

Schall v. Martin: Pretrial preventive detention of juveniles is permissible under certain circumstances. **1984**

Stanford v. Kentucky: It is constitutionally permissible to impose the death penalty on 16- and 17-year-olds. **1989**

Roper v. Simmons: Death penalty for juveniles is unconstitutional. **2005**

Graham v. Florida: Life without possibility of parole is unconstitutional for juveniles. **2010**

Miller v. Alabama: Life without possibility of parole is unconstitutional for juvenile murderers. **2012**

seriously delinquent youths, the potential danger is that the probationer may view the disposition as a slap on the wrist and return with more confidence to the old ways that led to his or her adjudication.

If the child comes from an antisocial family rife with substance abuse and criminality, officers are not likely to get any sort of positive support. Even if juvenile probationers come from prosocial two-parent families, there is often resistance by parents to juvenile authorities "poking their noses" into family affairs and "picking on" their children, who of course are victims of "bad company" (Walsh & Stohr, 2010, p. 457). If parents are eager to help their children, however, there are some excellent parent effectiveness training programs out there. The relatively short-term *Prosocial Family Therapy System* described by Bleckman and Vryan (2000) is a good comprehensive system with some very encouraging results reported.

••• INTENSIVE PROBATION

There will always be some juveniles who require more extensive supervision and treatment than others. To meet their needs and the needs of community protection, a variety of methods have been devised. One such method is intensive supervision probation (ISP), described in Chapter 7. ISP is usually imposed on youths as a last chance before incarceration. Juvenile probation officers with an ISP caseload typically supervise only 15 to 20 juveniles and may carry a gun (Taylor et al., 2007). Officers may make daily contact with their charges, visiting them at home, school, and work to monitor their behavior and progress in these settings. Officers will also enlist the help of other agencies (both public and private) that can provide probationers with more specialized and concrete help of the kind outside the purview of the juvenile court. These agencies will include mental health clinics, substance abuse centers, educational and vocational guidance centers, and welfare agencies (to help juveniles' families). ISP officers know that they cannot possibly provide all the needs of their probationers themselves and that efficient case management consists of their delivering services by using networks of collaborative providers. Delany, Fletcher, and Shields (2003) pointed out the importance of collaborative efforts to assist youths with multiple problems: "Without some level of collaboration among agencies, the odds of relapse and recidivism, which often leads to repeated institutionalization, are high" (p. 66).

Other forms of more intense supervision include electronic monitoring and/or house arrest. These sanctions were discussed in Chapters 7 and 10, and because they operate for juveniles exactly as they do for adults, they are discussed again here.

Youths who commit property crimes are frequently made to pay restitution to their victims to compensate for the victims' losses. This both compensates the victim and holds the youth accountable for his or her actions. To compensate the community as a whole, adjudicated delinquents may receive a **community service order**, which is part of a disposition requiring probationers to work a certain number of hours doing some kinds of tasks to help their communities. This work can range from cleaning graffiti from walls to picking up trash along highways or in parks. Restitution and community service orders can go a long way to help juveniles develop a sense of responsibility and the ability to accept the consequences of their actions without rancor. For these reasons, community service and restitution have been called "integral components of the restorative justice philosophy" (Walsh & Stohr, 2010, p. 455).

Restorative justice may be defined as "every action that is primarily oriented toward justice by repairing the harm that has been caused by the act" and "usually means face-to-face confrontation between victim and perpetrator, where a mutually agreeable restorative solution is proposed and agreed upon" (Champion, 2005, p. 154). Restorative justice defines delinquency as an offense committed by one person against another rather than against the state, and by doing so it personalizes justice by engaging the victim, the offender, and the community in a process of *restoring* the situation to its pre-offense status. Restorative justice thus gives equal weight to the needs of offenders, victims, and the community and focuses equally on each of these rather than being driven solely by offenders ("What do we do with them now?") (K. Carter, 2006). Victims or their representative are included in the justice process with the sentencing procedure addressing the needs of the victims, including their need to be heard and to be restored to wholeness again as far as possible.

Just as the retributive model reemerged after the alleged failure of the medical model, the restorative justice model has emerged with the apparent failure of "get tough" programs (Welch, 1996). However, the restorative model might not suit all victims because many victims understandably feel that things cannot be "put right" so easily and want the offenders punished. However, it would be a mistake to see it as a New Age "touchy-feely" approach to corrections. It holds offenders fully accountable for their actions by applying appropriate punishment and adds the additional dimensions by requiring offenders to accept responsibility for taking action to repair the harm done (Bazemore, 2000).

A meta-analysis found that restorative justice programs had a weak-to-moderate positive effect on victim satisfaction, a weak positive effect on offender satisfaction and recidivism, and a moderate effect on restitution compliance (Latimer, Dowden, & Muise, 2005). These findings should be viewed in light of the fact that both victims and offenders select themselves into such programs.

••• RESIDENTIAL AND INSTITUTIONAL JUVENILE CORRECTIONS

One of the dispositional sanctions that can be imposed on adjudicated delinquents is placement in some sort of program in a residential facility. A *residential facility* or *residential treatment center* is not analogous to an adult prison but rather more like a halfway house. Boot camps, discussed in Chapter 7 on adult probation, are one example of such facilities. Another one is *wilderness* or *survival programs*. These are more self-discipline programs designed to test delinquents' characters and coping skills by providing them with structured challenges. Overcoming these challenges is said to build youths' confidence and self-esteem, showing them that they are capable and not simply victims of circumstance. In such programs, there are no drill instructors bawling and spitting in their faces and belittling them; rather, there are guides who set adventurous challenges for them and provide encouragement. Wilderness programs do seem to be better than boot camps at reducing recidivism, although it is probably true that, on the whole, fewer serious offenders are assigned to wilderness

Community service order: Part of a disposition requiring probationers to work a certain number of hours doing tasks to help their communities.

programs than to boot camps. Nevertheless, one review of 22 studies of wilderness effectiveness found that wilderness participants recidivated at a rate of 29% versus 37% for comparison participants (S. Wilson & Lipsey, 2000).

Another alternative is a group home. *Group homes* are typically operated by private organizations that contract with juvenile authorities. These group homes tend to specialize in some form of programming such as drug treatment or treatment for "troubled girls." Youths in these homes remain in their communities and attend school and all the other normal functions of school-age children, but they live with perhaps 10 to 30 other youths at the home.

A commitment to a juvenile institutional corrections facility is a serious matter and is typically the disposition reserved for juveniles who have committed violent offenses or for chronic repeat offenders. There are two broad categories of institutional correctional facilities: long-term and short-term facilities. Short-term facilities include reception and detention centers (the equivalent of adult jails) where children may be held while awaiting release to parents, court adjudication, or release to youth shelters. Long-term facilities are those used for housing juveniles after adjudication. They include secure detention centers/training schools (the equivalent of an adult prison) and boot camps and less secure youth centers/ranches and adventure forestry camps.

PHOTO 13.3: Meagan Grunwald (*right*) enters court for her preliminary hearing. She faces murder charges for helping her boyfriend, who fatally shot a Utah deputy. What rights would she have during this preliminary hearing?

Juveniles sent to long-term, secure correctional facilities tend to have committed very serious delinquent acts or are chronic offenders. A study of juveniles sent to long-term secure facilities found that 35% were committed for violent offenses and the remaining 65% for property, drug, or status offenses (Sickmund & Wan, 2003). Minority youths are even more overrepresented in secure juvenile correctional facilities than minority adults are in adult prisons. G. Martin (2005) reported that whereas there were 204 white juveniles per 100,000 population in secure facilities, there were 1,018 African American juveniles per 100,000 population, and about 70% of those being held in custody for violent offenses were minorities (p. 247).

Steiner and Giacomazzi (2007) examined recidivism among juveniles waived to adult court and placed into a boot camp program compared with a control group of juveniles who were also waived to adult court but placed on probation rather than into a boot camp program. They found no difference between the boot camp and control groups on rates of recidivism, but boot camp juveniles were significantly less likely to be reconvicted, which may be one bright spot in an otherwise dark performance of boot camps.

Other important differences between juvenile and adult facilities are that juvenile facilities are almost always much smaller (rarely more than 250 juveniles), the costs associated with incarceration are considerably higher, and much more money is spent on programming relative to security (Taylor et al., 2007). For instance, the California Youth Authority spends 52% of its budget on academic and vocational training, case planning, counseling, and skills training as opposed to only 13% on custody and security (Taylor et al., 2007). Nevertheless, many of the same problems seen in adult prisons are also seen in juvenile facilities, especially in the larger institutions with a low staff-to-resident ratio. As in adult prisons, gangs form along racial/ethnic and neighborhood lines, and there is always the danger of violence and sexual assault against the unaffiliated (G. Martin, 2005).

COMPARATIVE CORRECTIONS   Juvenile Justice Philosophies

There are a variety of philosophies regarding juvenile justice around the world, which Reichel (2005) classified into four families or models: welfare, legalistic, corporatist, and participatory models. The models reflect broad generalities, and there is much overlap among the countries used to exemplify each. The *welfare* model reflects a concern for the well-being of children at the expense of legalities in which "troubled youths" are funneled through a series of non-judicial agencies designed to address the problem. Police cautions (a warning by a senior police officer) and restorative justice constitute a big part of this model, which Reichel saw the Australian and New Zealand systems as exemplifying. Sweden is even deeper into the welfare model given that it does not even have a juvenile court system. The police turn over offenders under age 20 to social boards that proceed very informally and only rarely refer a case to the criminal courts. The Swedish government has even abolished imprisonment for youths. All of this is designed to reduce stigma and support treatment, but it has led to youths knowing that they can commit criminal acts almost with impunity (Terrill, 2003).

The *legalistic* model emphasizes the law over treatment, although this does not necessarily mean that the model is less humanistic. Reichel used Italy as an example of this model. Legalism comes in with the realization that there is a need to treat juveniles differently in the criminal code. (Individuals cannot be held responsible for criminal actions in Italy until they reach age 14.) When an individual over age 14 commits a criminal act, he or she is treated procedurally just like an adult except for the purposes of punishment. In other words, all due process rights afforded adults are also afforded juveniles. Reichel saw the welfare and legalistic models as opposites in which the problem with the former is the lack of legal protections and the problem with the latter is the lack of compassion and flexibility.

Reichel saw the *corporatist* model, exemplified by England and Wales, as being a compromise between the extremes of the welfare and legalistic models. This model seeks the middle ground between realizing the lack of maturity of juveniles, and thus wanting to "treat" them, and at the same time asserting the need to hold them responsible for their actions, and thus wanting to "punish" them. Juvenile justice in the United Kingdom is primarily the responsibility of Youth Justice Boards (YJBs), which are locally managed social institutions set up in 1998 that operate semi-autonomously from the government. There is a great reliance on restorative justice programs in YJBs, but every dispositional option available in the United States, including incarceration, is available in the United Kingdom. Despite huge sums of money being poured into juvenile crime prevention in the United Kingdom, a 10-year evaluation of the progress made by YJBs found that they have had zero to minimal impact on youth offending (E. Solomon & Garside, 2009).

Whereas the welfare, legalistic, and corporatist models are all examples of efforts to control antisocial behavior through *formal* social control, the final model—the *participatory* model—seeks to control behavior more via informal social control. This model assumes that reform is best achieved if youthful offenders are dealt with outside of the formal court system and enlists the aid of family, school, and various neighborhood "committees" to control juvenile behavior. This system is popular in communist/socialist countries that (theoretically) see no division between the state and the people. Such a model would obviously work best in traditional societies where there was relatively little geographic mobility and relatively little racial/ethnic diversity. In other words, it would work best in a community where everyone more or less knew everyone else, and had known each other for a long time, and where everyone held the same values and attitudes. It does not, therefore, seem like a model that would work in modern Western societies.

SUMMARY

- The juvenile justice system in the United States is based on civil law and deals with status offenses (those applicable only to juveniles) and delinquency (crimes if committed by adults).

- Juveniles commit a disproportionate number of both property and violent crimes, and this has always been true across time and cultures. Recent scientific evidence relates this situation to the hormonal surges of puberty and a brain undergoing numerous changes. Although most adolescents commit antisocial acts, only a small proportion continue to do so after brain maturation is completed.

- The history of juvenile justice has three distinct periods. Originally, Western culture relied heavily on parents to control children. As society has changed, so have the expectations regarding juvenile delinquency. Institutional control of wayward youths was the model from the mid-1500s until the inception of the juvenile courts in the United States during the late 1800s/early 1900s. The juvenile court follows the doctrine of parens patriae, but recently there has been a movement away from the broad discretion formerly accorded to juvenile courts to a model more closely reflecting the constitutional protections afforded adult offenders. Much of this change has issued from the increased waivers of juveniles to adult courts and from the often arbitrary control that juvenile justice authorities have exercised over juveniles.

- The juvenile justice system in the United States has gradually changed from a totally paternalistic system governed by civil law procedures to one that now affords juveniles the same rights as adults. However, some have seen this as criminalizing the juvenile justice system. The greatest success of neuroscience research into the adolescent brain has been the elimination of the juvenile death penalty. We have also seen how the U.S. Supreme Court has ruled life without possibility of parole to be unconstitutional for juveniles who have not committed murder.

- Much of what constitutes juvenile corrections mirrors what we have written about in other sections of this book; thus, we have only briefly highlighted differences between the juvenile and adult systems. Major differences include a greater emphasis on rehabilitation, as exemplified by the ratio of programming to security spent in juvenile correctional facilities and the lesser likelihood of juveniles being sent to secure facilities relative to adults.

KEY TERMS

Age–crime curve, 287

Amicus curiae briefs, 297

Community service order, 300

Deferred adjudication, 298

Delinquents, 286

Judicial waiver, 292

Parens patriae, 290

Predisposition report, 298

Prosecutorial discretion, 292

Status offenders, 286

Status offenses, 286

Statutory exclusion, 292

Waiver, 292

DISCUSSION QUESTIONS

1. Discuss the development of the concept of childhood in Western culture.

2. Discuss the doctrine of parens patriae in relation to the development of the juvenile court system in the United States.

3. Do you think that restorative justice is workable? In what circumstances would it be or not be?

4. Which of the models of juvenile justice outlined by Reichel (2005) do you favor? Give your reasons.

5. Do you think that a highly dangerous person such as Terrance Jamar Graham should ever be released back into the community just because he committed his crimes as a juvenile?

$SAGE edge™

Review → Practice → Improve

Sharpen your skills with SAGE edge at **edge.sagepub.com/stohressentials3e**.

SAGE edge offers a robust online environment featuring an impressive array of free tools and resources for review, study, and further exploration, keeping both instructors and students on the cutting edge of teaching and learning.

FOR FURTHER EXPLORATION AND APPLICATION, TAKE A LOOK AT THE INTERACTIVE EBOOK FOR THESE PREMIUM RESOURCES:

- ▶ **Career Video 13.1** Juvenile Court Counselor

- ▶ **Feature Video 13.1** Experiences of Juvenile Offenders

- ▶ **SAGE News Clip 13.1** Woman Who Sent Texts Urging Suicide Found Guilty

- ▶ **SAGE News Clip 13.2** Colorado School Lockdown

- ▣ **Journal Article 13.1** Adult Crime, Adult Time? Benchmarking Public Views on Punishing Serious Juvenile Felons

PRACTICE AND APPLY WHAT YOU'VE LEARNED

▶ edge.sagepub.com/stohressentials3e

CHECK YOUR COMPREHENSION ON THE STUDY SITE:

- Mobile-friendly **eFlashcards** strengthen understanding of key terms and concepts.

- Mobile-friendly practice **quizzes** allow for independent assessment by students of their mastery of course material.

- **Learning objectives** reinforce the most important material.

- Carefully selected chapter-by-chapter **video and multimedia content** enhance classroom-based explorations of key topics.

- EXCLUSIVE! Access provided to certain full-text **SAGE journal articles** that have been carefully selected for each chapter. Each article supports and expands on the concepts presented in the chapter.

⑤SAGE edge™

14

Legal Issues in Corrections

TEST YOUR KNOWLEDGE

Test your current knowledge of legal issues pertaining to the rights of people under correctional supervision by answering the following questions true or false. Check your answers on page 393 after reading the chapter.

1. Prison inmates were not afforded any legal protections until the mid-20th century.

2. The First Amendment freedom of religion is as absolute for prisoners as it is for the rest of us.

3. The majority of lawsuits filed by inmates today have to do with claims of innocence.

4. Prison inmates have no Fourth Amendment protections against unreasonable search and seizure.

5. The mortality rate of prison inmates is lower than that of the U.S. population as a whole.

6. Prisoners are the only group of individuals in the United States with a constitutional right to medical care.

7. Sex offenders can be involuntarily placed in mental institutions after serving their full prison sentences.

8. Probationers and parolees are pretty much subjected to the same curtailment of rights as prison inmates.

LEARNING OBJECTIVES

- Understand what relevance Packer's (1997) two models of criminal justice have for prisoners' rights

- Know the different legal "periods" identified in terms of prisoners' rights

- Identify issues and cases involving the First, Fourth, Eighth, and Fourteenth Amendments

- Identify issues involved with the civil commitment of sex offenders

- Know how and why prisoners' petitions have been curtailed

PRISON WITHOUT LAW

Prisons are not nice places; they were never meant to be. This does not mean that society is ever justified in treating prisoners in less than humane ways. This message never reached at least two of Arkansas' state prison farms that used inmates' labor to produce crops and dairy products bringing in average yearly profits of $1.4 million. In 1967, a report was released detailing horrifying conditions at the Tucker and Cummins state penal farms, including widespread sexual assault, floggings, and extortion by the armed prisoners who were placed in positions of power by prison authorities to save spending money on correctional officers. A federal judge hearing a case stemming from Arkansas prison conditions called the entire Arkansas prison system a "dark and evil world." In addition to such medieval tortures as having testicles crushed and needles inserted under the fingernails, a more

"modern" method of torture was the Tucker telephone. The use of this device involved a prisoner being wired by the big toe and the genitals and an electric current applied by cranking an old-fashioned telephone. Depending on the offense, an inmate would receive a local or "long-distance" call.

Worse yet, a number of bodies of former inmates who had been listed as "successful escapees" were dug from unmarked graves on the orders of the new warden, Tom Murton (played by Robert Redford in the movie *Brubaker* based on the scandal). The scandal eventually became too much for the state governor as more bodies were exhumed, and Murton was fired and told that he had 24 hours to leave the state or be arrested for grave robbing. Thus, even prison reform-minded administrators such as

Governor Winthrop Rockefeller circle the wagons and block further investigations and reforms if they become threatening to the authorities. Who will protect inmates from exploitation, torture, and even murder if the executive branch of government will not? Only an independent body relatively free of concerns about the personal consequences of doing the morally right thing can be trusted to safeguard the rights of prisoners. As you read this chapter and perhaps become annoyed at what you may consider legal mollycoddling of "dirtbags," think about how the prison system would be without some sort of judicial oversight, which is precisely the way it was in the not-so-distant past.

••• INTRODUCTION

Winston Churchill once said that a civilization could be judged by the way it treated its prisoners (Morris, 2002). We do not treat them very well and never have, but many members of the public see them getting better treatment than they deserve, as summed up in the line, "If you can't do the time, don't do the crime." Convicted criminals are perhaps the most despised group of people in any society because they are generally viewed as evil misfits who prey on decent people, so why worry about what happens to them while in custody paying their debt to society? With an estimated 1 in every 100 adults in jails or prisons in the United States in 2008 (Robertson, 2010), however, issues relating to how these people are treated while incarcerated become more pressing. The only system capable of monitoring the treatment of people under criminal justice supervision, other than the criminal justice system itself, is the court system. The courts have changed their attitudes toward the treatment of prisoners over the history of the United States. These attitudes have ranged from complete indifference to almost attempting to micromanage a state's entire prison system. In this chapter, we review how convicted prisoners in prisons and jails and unconvicted detainees awaiting trial in jails were legally viewed in the past up to how they are legally protected today. Although much has changed in this regard, the trend during recent years has been to remove some of those legal protections and access to courts that inmates gained during the latter half of the 20th century.

••• THE RULE OF LAW

When we discussed Packer's (1997) crime control/due process model of criminal justice in Chapter 1, we were essentially asking, "How do we best achieve justice for all concerned—that is, both for society and those who offend against it?" The only way we can be reasonably assured that justice resides within a legal system is to determine the extent to which it adheres to the **rule of law**. The idea of the rule of law first appeared in Plato's *Laws* (2008, Book IV), written some four centuries before the birth of Christ. Plato wanted to determine what constitutes a just state and concluded, "I see that the state in which the law is above the rulers, and the rulers are the inferiors of the law, has salvation, and the very blessings which the Gods can confer." In other words, the law should be the supreme authority in a state and should constrain the behavior of government officials. The rule of law involves the notion that every member of society, including lawmakers, presidents, and prime ministers, is subject to the law. The rule of law has been called "the most important legal principle in the world" (Goff, 1997, p. 760), and according to Reichel (2005) it contains three irreducible elements:

1. A nation must recognize the supremacy of certain fundamental values and principles.

2. These values and principles must be committed to writing.

3. A system of procedures to hold the government to these principles and values must be in place.

Rule of law: The principle that laws, not people, govern and that no one is above the law.

All organized societies recognize a set of fundamental values that they hold supreme, whether the ultimate principles are secular or religious. Likewise, all literate societies put these values and principles in writing in their holy books or national constitutions. However, the third element is more problematic because it shows whether or not a country honors its fundamental values in practice as well as in theory. The law is just words on paper if it is not respected by human actors. If the law is to be consistent with justice, it can be so only if the procedures followed by its agents are perceived as just by everyone. The procedures designed to hold the government to its written principles are articulated by the concept of due process.

When we speak about something that is due to us, we are referring to something to which we are rightly entitled. Due process of law is owed to all persons whenever they are threatened with the loss of life, liberty, or property at the hands of the state. It is essentially a set of instructions informing agents of the state how they must proceed in their investigation, arrest, questioning, prosecution, and punishment of individuals who are suspected of committing crimes. The individuals charged with monitoring the behavior of agents of the state with respect to their adherence to due process principles are the judiciary. If the judiciary is corrupt, lax, or the puppets of politicians or public opinion, then the rule of law, especially as it applies to society's least valued citizens, is likely to be ignored. This was the case in the United States up until the early 1960s.

PHOTO 14.1: During the "hands-off" period, inmates often resided in dilapidated and overcrowded facilities where they might be overworked, underfed, and mistreated by the state and correctional officials.

••• THE HANDS-OFF PERIOD: 1866–1963

The general public's attitude of indifference has also been the general attitude of the courts throughout much of American history, as is evident in their so-called **hands-off doctrine**. This doctrine basically articulated the reluctance of the judiciary to interfere with the management and administration of prisons—to keep their "hands off." The doctrine rested primarily on the status of prisoners who suffered a kind of legal and civil death on conviction. Most states had **civil death statutes**, which meant that those convicted of crimes lost all citizenship rights such as the right to vote, to hold public office, and—in some jurisdictions—to marry. The philosophical justification for civil death statutes, ironically, came from the text of the Thirteenth Amendment to the U.S. Constitution, which abolished slavery in the United States. The Thirteenth Amendment reads,

> Neither slavery nor involuntary servitude, except as a punishment for a crime whereof the party shall have been duly convicted, shall exist within the United States, or any place subject to their jurisdiction.

Thus, slavery was abolished "except as a punishment for crime." This enabled prison officials (such as those in Arkansas in the opening vignette) to lease prisoners to local businesses for profit and to use them as unpaid labor to maintain the financial self-sufficiency of prisons—in short, to treat them like property (Call, 2011).

In affirming the ruling of a lower court in *Ruffin v. Commonwealth* (1871), the Virginia Supreme Court made plain the slave-like status of convicted offenders:

> For the time being, during his term of service in the penitentiary, he is in a state of penal servitude to the State. He has, as a consequence of his crime, not only forfeited his liberty, but all his personal rights except those which the law in its humanity accords to him. He is for the time being the slave of the State. He is civiliter mortuus [civilly dead]; and his estate, if he has any, is administered like that of a dead man.

Hands-off doctrine:
An early American court-articulated belief that the judiciary should not interfere with the management and administration of prisons.

Civil death statutes:
Statutes in former times mandating that convicted felons lose all citizenship rights.

Ruffin was a state case, and thus not binding on other states, but the case was consistent with the earlier U.S. Supreme Court case *Pervear v. Massachusetts* (1866). *Pervear* was the foundational case that first clearly enunciated the lack of concern for prisoners' rights contained in the hands-off doctrine. Pervear had been sentenced to 3 months' hard labor and a large fine for failing to obtain a license for his liquor store and challenged his sentence on the basis of the "cruel and unusual" clause of the Eighth Amendment. The Supreme Court made plain the slave-like status of prisoners, ruling that they did not even enjoy the protections of the Eighth Amendment. Convicted felons thus found themselves at the mercy of prison officials and fellow prisoners without any constitutional protection provided by judicial oversight.

The hands-off doctrine also prevailed because the courts viewed correctional agencies as part of the executive branch of government and did not wish to violate the Constitution's separation of powers doctrine. Correctional officials were considered quite capable of administering to the needs of prisoners in a humane way without needing to deal with the complicating intrusions of another branch of government. Besides, if prisoners have been stripped of any rights under civil death statutes, there is nothing that the courts have to monitor and protect.

••• THE PRISONERS' RIGHTS PERIOD: 1964–1978

The convict-as-slave approach slowly gave way to the approach by the courts that prisoners did retain a modicum of constitutional rights, but it was the business of the executive and legislative branches of state government to honor them. States' rights and fear of an overbearing federal government were more deeply felt concerns in the past than they are today, and the federal courts were still reluctant to move too far in the direction of limiting states' rights or further fueling citizens' distrust of the federal government.

We need to realize that the Bill of Rights was intended only to apply to actions of the federal government and was added to the Constitution to appease the fears of supporters of states' rights. It was not until the 20th century that federal courts began to apply the rights in the Bill of Rights to state actions in a process known as incorporation (Walsh & Hemmens, 2014). Incorporation essentially means that due process rights such as free speech, which formerly needed to be respected only by the federal government, now needed to be respected by the states as well.

As part of a growing trend toward an overall greater respect for individual rights during the mid-20th century, as African Americans, women, gays and lesbians, and other disadvantaged groups strongly agitated for them, the courts began to enter into the area of prisoners' rights. The major issue in prisoner litigation has been the conditions of confinement, but the first significant case was *Ex parte Hull* (1941), which dealt with the denial by prison officials of a Michigan inmate's petition for an appeal of the legality of his confinement (the term *ex parte* refers to situations in which only one party appears before the court). Although Hull's petition was denied (Hull had committed a statutory sexual offense, had violated his parole, and was returned to prison to serve out his original sentence), the U.S. Supreme Court ruled that inmates had the right to unrestricted access to federal courts to challenge the legality of their confinement. This ruling was the beginning of the end of the hands-off doctrine, although as we will see, there is growing evidence of its return (Federman, 2004).

The technical term for a challenge to the legality of confinement is a writ of habeas corpus. **Habeas corpus** is a Latin term that literally means "you have the body" and is basically a court order requiring that an arrested person be brought before it to determine the legality of his or her detention. Habeas corpus is a very important concept in

Habeas corpus: Latin term meaning "you have the body." It is a court order requiring that an arrested person be brought before it to determine the legality of detention.

common law that precedes even the Magna Carta of 1215, although its precise origins are unknown. It has been called the "Great Writ" and was formally codified into English common law by the Habeas Corpus Act of 1679. Indicative of the respect in which habeas corpus was held by the Founding Fathers of the United States is that it is only one of three individual rights mentioned in the U.S. Constitution (the other two are the prohibition of bills of attainder [imposing punishment without trial] and the prohibition of ex post facto laws [legislation making some acts criminal after the fact]). The other individual rights that Americans enjoy were formalized in the first 10 amendments to the Constitution (the **Bill of Rights**) almost as an afterthought. A writ of habeas corpus is not a direct appeal of a conviction but rather an indirect appeal regarding the legality of a person's confinement or the conditions of confinement. In *Coffin v. Reichard* (1944), the Sixth Circuit Court of Appeals widened habeas corpus hearings to include conditions of confinement, but this had little impact for 20 years.

Two cases signaled the end of the hands-off period: *Jones v. Cunningham* (1963) and *Cooper v. Pate* (1964). In *Jones*, the Supreme Court went further than it did in *Hull* and ruled that prisoners could use a writ of habeas corpus to challenge the conditions of their confinement as well as the legality of their confinement. This went beyond the original meaning of habeas corpus, which was only meant to address the pre-conviction issue of the legality of a petitioner's detainment. In *Cooper*, the Court went even further and ruled that state prison inmates could sue state officials in federal courts under the Civil Rights Act of 1871, which was initially enacted to protect southern blacks from state officials. This act is now codified and known as 42 USC § 1983, or simply as **section 1983 suits**, and any deprivation of rights grievance filed under it is called a **civil rights claim**. The relevant part of the act reads as follows:

> Every person who under color of any statute, ordinance, regulation, custom, or usage of any state or territory, subjects or causes to be subject, any citizen of the United States or other person within the jurisdiction thereof to the deprivation of any rights, privileges, or immunities secured by the Constitution and laws, shall be liable to the party injured in an action at law.

What had been a mere trickle of habeas petitions before *Cooper* quickly became a flood that threatened to drown the federal courts with grievances ranging from the petty to the deadly serious. The most serious petition led to a federal appeals judge declaring the entire prison system of Arkansas unconstitutional and a "dark and evil world" when he placed it under federal supervision (*Holt v. Sarver*, 1969). As we saw in the opening vignette, Arkansas institutions were horrific places where inmates were routinely subjected to brutal conditions. This case gave birth to what has come to be known as a "conditions of confinement lawsuit." From then on, the federal courts became very much involved in the monitoring and operation of entire prison systems. The vast majority of habeas corpus grievances filed today are about the conditions of confinement, not the legality of inmates' confinement. Inmates filing petitions challenging their confinement face an uphill battle because the state's defense against such a claim is based on inmates' convictions, which is the obvious legal basis for their confinement!

● ● ● THE DEFERENCE PERIOD: 1997–PRESENT

Convicted criminals are no longer considered civilly dead while under correctional supervision. However, after a short time in which prisoners' rights were granted and extended, there began an era that correctional scholars have called the **deference period**. This time period was a partial return to the hands-off period and basically refers to the courts' willingness to defer to the expertise and needs of prison authorities. The courts have come to the conclusion that it is necessary to place restrictions on prisoners' rights that

Bill of Rights: The first 10 amendments to the U.S. Constitution.

Section 1983 suits: A mechanism for state prison inmates to sue state officials in federal court regarding their confinement and their conditions of confinement.

Civil rights claim: A "section 1983" claim that a person has been deprived of some legally granted right.

Deference period: The period of time when there was a partial return to the hands-off approach. It refers to the courts' willingness to defer to the expertise and needs of the authorities.

PERSPECTIVE FROM A PRACTITIONER

Barbara Beldot, Attorney

Position: Professor at the University of Houston–Downtown

Through the 1980s and 1990s, the Texas state prison system (Texas Department of Criminal Justice, TDCJ) operated under several court orders issued by federal Judge William Wayne Justice in the case *Ruiz v. Estelle,* a lawsuit in which prisoners successfully challenged living conditions in TDCJ-ID. Judge Justice created a special team to monitor the state's progress in implementing the reforms he mandated. I served as an attorney on that team, the Office of the Special Master, from 1986 to 1990. My assignment was to monitor progress related to conditions in administrative segregation, including how inmates were assigned to that status, the inmate disciplinary system, and conditions on death row.

I spent countless hours meeting with administrative segregation and death row inmates, walking up and down cellblocks and talking with them through their cell doors as well as meeting with correctional officers assigned to those blocks. I reviewed paperwork and attended meetings related to assigning inmates to administrative segregation. I observed hundreds of disciplinary hearings. I received thousands of letters from inmates requesting that I investigate their specific complaints. Our team had open access to all state prison units and could come and go at any time of day. We could speak to anyone we determined could help us gather relevant information.

I met scary prisoners who had committed violent crimes, notorious prison gang members, as well as inmates who had done something stupid and were doing their time as best they could. I met correctional staff who were consummate professionals and those stuck in a job they obviously didn't like.

After spending several days at a prison, I wrote a long, detailed report to the judge documenting the unit's progress toward meeting the court mandates that I monitored. Other team members monitored health care delivery, access to courts, use of force, job safety, and issues related to overcrowding.

Court orders are meaningless unless they are implemented. That takes a long time and a shift in the culture in a complex organization such as a prison system, almost 20 years for TDCJ. The staff in the Office of the Special Master served as the judge's eyes and ears during those years.

It was the most fascinating job I've ever had.

---

do not apply to non-offenders because of the need to balance the rights of offenders and the legitimate needs and concerns of correctional authorities, particularly the safety and security needs of prisons and jails. In other words, prisoners' rights must be secondary to the maintenance of institutional order and security and the safety of inmates and staff. The basic stance of the U.S. Supreme Court on this matter has not changed since it was first enunciated in *Bell v. Wolfish* (1979), the case widely considered to be the one that signaled the onset of the deference period:

> Simply because prison inmates retain certain constitutional rights does not mean that these rights are not subject to restrictions and limitations. There must be a "mutual accommodation between institutional needs and objectives and the provisions of the Constitution that are of general application." Maintaining institutional security and preserving internal order and discipline are essential goals that may require limitation or retraction of the retained constitutional rights of both convicted prisoners and pretrial detainees. (n.p.)

We begin by looking at certain fundamental rights guaranteed by the First, Fourth, and Fourteenth Amendments to the Constitution and how they apply to convicted felons.

••• FIRST AMENDMENT

The First Amendment to the Constitution reads,

> Congress shall make no law respecting an establishment of religion, or prohibiting the free exercise thereof; or abridging the freedom of speech, or of the press; or the right of the people peaceably to assemble, and to petition the government for a redress of grievances.

The **First Amendment** thus guarantees freedom of religion, speech, press, and assembly. It goes without saying that in a prison setting these freedoms cannot extend to activities and materials that jeopardize prison

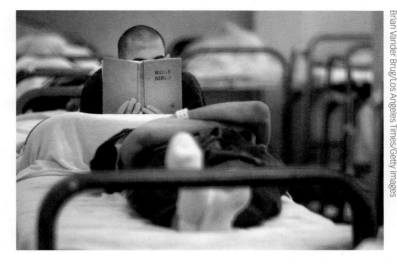

PHOTO 14.2: Inmates retain some First Amendment rights, including the right to practice their religious beliefs, if doing so does not unduly interfere with prison security.

safety or security. The *Cooper v. Pate* (1964) case discussed earlier was essentially a First Amendment issue because Cooper, a Black Muslim, alleged that he was denied certain religious publications solely on the basis of his religion. Prison authorities claimed that Black Muslim literature was dangerous and jeopardized the safety and security of the prison because it preached violent revolution and sought to recruit new members. The Supreme Court acknowledged that such literature may have an incendiary effect but ruled that Cooper's right to free exercise of his religion trumps what might result in security problems. Such free access to written materials need not extend to non-religious materials such as a manufacturer's guide to prison security locks, pornographic materials, and hate literature.

Religious freedom cannot extend to demanding alcohol or exotic foods to satisfy real or invented religious requirements. But the law is more an ideological exercise than a science. As if to prove our point, two federal circuit courts came to opposite conclusions in the same year (2008) regarding Muslim inmates' right to a *halal* diet (a diet that prohibits eating pork and shellfish and in which animals must be slaughtered in a certain way—closely akin to a Jewish kosher diet). The Eighth Circuit Court ruled that the non-provision of a halal diet did not place an undue burden on the inmate and that there were alternative means of obtaining such a diet. The more liberal Ninth Circuit Court ruled in a different case that the prison's refusal to supply a Muslim inmate with a halal diet impinged on the free exercise of religion clause of the First Amendment (Robertson, 2010).

Restrictions on inmates' rights to free speech can exceed those necessary to ensure safety and security. In *Smith v. Mosley* (2008), the plaintiff made a statement in a grievance that prison authorities saw as insubordinate and false for which he received disciplinary sanctions. The inmate sought relief in the federal court, claiming that he had been punished for exercising his right to free speech. The court disagreed, ruling that while filing a grievance is considered protected speech, the statements made within it were not, and therefore the imposition of sanctions was constitutionally permissible. Freedom of speech or expression can also be limited on moral or ethical grounds. For instance, inmates can write and publish their thoughts or sell personal memorabilia, but "notoriety-for-profit" statutes enacted by the federal government and most states forbid inmates from profiting monetarily from those activities (Walsh & Hemmens, 2014).

The right of assembly allows for attendance at religious services and for visitation from family and friends, but it obviously cannot be construed as allowing inmates to assemble

First Amendment:
Guarantees freedom of religion, speech, press, and assembly.

PHOTO 14.3: The inside of a sparsely furnished single cell.

at a tattoo conference outside the prison walls. Federal courts have also ruled that while Black Muslim groups had the right to assemble for worship, their right to hold religious services could be denied if prison administrators considered such services to constitute potential breaches of security (Inciardi, 2007).

••• FOURTH AMENDMENT

The **Fourth Amendment** reads,

> The right of the people to be secure in their persons, houses, papers, and effects, against unreasonable searches and seizures, shall not be violated, and no warrants shall issue, but upon probable cause, supported by Oath or affirmation, and particularly describing the place to be searched, and the persons or things to be seized.

The right to privacy is a paramount concern of the Fourth Amendment, and so it guarantees the right to be free from unreasonable searches and seizures. Does this mean that inmates have the right to privacy in their cells and to be "secure in their houses, papers, and effects" that people on the outside have and that corrections officers should obtain warrants before searching their cells for suspected contraband and/or weapons? What is reasonable inside prison walls is, of course, quite different from what is reasonable outside them. For all practical purposes, inmates have no Fourth Amendment protections because their prison cells are not "homes" of personal sanctuary deserving of privacy (*Hudson v. Palmer,* 1984).

The one area in which Fourth Amendment rights have not been completely extinguished for inmates is that involving opposite-sex body searches. The courts have needed to wrestle with conflicting claims on this issue. One is the equal employment claim of female corrections officers who want to work in male institutions where, because of their size and scope, promotion prospects are greater than they are in female prisons. Working in all-male prisons necessarily means that women officers will occasionally view inmates undressed or using toilet facilities, and sometimes they may be required to perform pat downs and visual body cavity searches (physical searches of body cavities may be performed only by medical personnel). A frequent inmate claim is that cross-gender searches are "unreasonable" within the meaning of the Fourth Amendment.

Bennett (1995) noted that the great majority of cross-gender search complaints are filed by males, which is not surprising given that males constitute about 94% of all state prison inmates (Bohm & Haley, 2007). On the other hand, it is surprising given the frequent complaints from female officers that some male inmates seem to take every opportunity to expose themselves and to behave in a sexual manner in their presence (Cowburn, 1998). Of course, this does not mean that many inmates are not genuinely embarrassed and offended by needing to bear the indignity of female officers observing them using the toilet. However, ever since the doors were opened in *Hull,* the filing of all sorts of complaints has become a sort of inmate hobby for some that serves the purpose of relieving boredom, getting "one over" on prison authorities, and possibly getting one or two rides into town to attend court (McNeese, 2010). There are many legitimate

Fourth Amendment: Guarantees the right to be free from unreasonable searches and seizures.

IN FOCUS 14.1

Any Complaints This Morning?

"Any complaints this morning?" was the drill sergeant's daily cynical question to newly drafted soldiers during World War II. Of course, none of the draftees confined in the sweltering barracks were ever bold enough to make any complaint, although living conditions were such that they would not be tolerated by the courts if they existed in our prisons today. We wonder what these old soldiers would say about the following.

In dismissing a lawsuit in one case, the Supreme Court noted that the majority of prisoner petitions are frivolous and/or malicious, cost taxpayers millions of dollars, and waste precious court time. Florida Attorney General Bob Butterworth asserted, "My office spends nearly $2 million a year defending that state against inmate suits, most of which contain ridiculous charges or demands" (Butterworth, 1995, p. 1). Similarly, Idaho Deputy Attorney General Timothy McNeese noted that fully 27% of all litigation in Idaho's federal district courts involve inmate petitions, most of which are "meritless," are "downright frivolous," and "no doubt are filed by inmates out of frustration and anger and desire to get even with a correctional employee or the 'system'" (McNeese, 2010, p. 321). Presented below are some examples of frivolous and/or malicious petitions gleaned from Butterworth and McNeese that judges must wade through to get to prisoner petitions that are really deserving of attention. The sheer audacity of these examples may put a smile on your face, but they are no laughing matter to the courts, prison administrators, taxpayers, and prisoners with real grievances whose petitions are lost in the pile:

> Prisoner starts a riot, shatters glass in his cell, and files an Eighth Amendment suit claiming cruel and unusual punishment because he cut his foot on the glass.

Prisoner sends for information about prison security and locks and sues because the warden refused to give him the mail containing the information.

Prisoner sues because his ice cream was half melted when it was served to him.

Prisoner sues over unsatisfactory haircut.

Prisoner sues because jailers cut her sausage into small pieces because she had been caught previously masturbating with a whole sausage.

Prisoner sues because he was required to eat off a paper plate.

Prisoner files more than 140 actions in state and federal court over finding gristle in his turkey leg.

Prisoner sues to receive fruit juice at meals and an extra pancake at breakfast.

Prisoner who murdered five people sues because he was forced to watch network television programs after lightning knocked out the prison's satellite dish. These programs contained violent material that this multiple murderer said was objectionable.

Prisoner sues over the inferior brand of sneakers issued to him.

Prisoner loses a suit claiming his rights as a Muslim were violated because the prison put "essence of swine" in his food, then converts to Satanism and demands tarot cards and "doves' blood."

Prisoner sues because the disciplinary cell he was placed in had no electrical outlet for his television set.

---

prisoner complaints, but Dilworth (1995) reported that 75% of prisoner petitions are dismissed by courts' own evaluations, 20% are dismissed in grants of states' motions, and about 2% result in trials where fewer than half result in a favorable verdict for the prisoner. Thus, less than 1% of prisoner complaints are considered legitimate. Examples of some frivolous and malicious petitions are given in In Focus 14.1.

In *Turner v. Safley* (1987), the Supreme Court enunciated what has come to be known as the *balancing test*, which means that the courts must balance the rights of inmates against the

ETHICAL ISSUE ?

What Would You Do?

You are a prosecutor in a jurisdiction that is determined to stamp down hard on crime. You have a case before you of a one-legged man charged with stealing the left boot of a pair of cowboy boots worth $300, making the theft a felony. The defendant has two prior felony convictions, and this would be his third if convicted. You want to dispose of the case quickly via a plea bargain and offer to reduce the charge to a misdemeanor if the defendant will plead guilty. You also tell him that if he does not take the plea, you will charge him as a habitual offender under the state's three-strikes law. The defendant refuses to plea, saying the theft should be a misdemeanor anyway because he stole only one boot. What will you do? After you have decided, take a look at *Bordenkircher v. Hayes* (1978) and see what the prosecutor decided and how this case was actually decided by the Supreme Court (yes, it actually happened).

interests of penological concerns of security and order. In ruling that lower courts were wrong in applying the strict scrutiny standard of review (a standard of review used by the courts if a "fundamental right" [anything in the Bill of Rights] or a "suspect classification" [race, religion, or national origin] is involved) to inmates' constitutional complaints, the Court ruled that these cases require a lesser standard and involve the issue of whether a prison regulation that impinges on inmates' constitutional rights is "reasonably related" to legitimate penological interests. This "reasonableness" revolves around a number of factors, including whether there is a valid and rational connection between the regulation and a legitimate government interest that is justified in the name of staff and inmate safety and security.

According to the balancing test, then, the viewing of opposite-sex inmates is constitutionally valid "if it is reasonably related to legitimate penal interests." Bennett (1995) told us how lower courts have interpreted "reasonableness" and concluded that while female officers conducting or observing strip searches of male inmates is tolerated in emergency situations, similar observation and searches by male officers of female inmates are considered unreasonable. This double standard has been justified on the two grounds that (1) males do not experience loss of job opportunities if they are forbidden to frisk female inmates and (2) intimate touching of a female inmate by a male officer may cause psychological trauma because many female inmates have histories of sexual abuse.

Farkas and Rand (1999) also supported gender-specific standards for cross-gender searches on the basis of prior sexual abuse that an inmate may have suffered and stated, "Cross-gender searches have the very real potential to replicate that suffering in prison" (p. 53), and further abuse would constitute cruel and unusual punishment. This raises the question of the possible legal validity of complaints about same-sex body searches if the complainant can show prior sexual abuse by a same-sex person. For instance, will such a person then be in a position to demand an opposite-sex body search?

Inmates' privacy rights have allowed them the freedom to file fraudulent tax returns claiming millions of dollars in refunds. In 2004, more than 18,000 false tax returns were filed claiming $68.1 million in refunds, which rose to nearly 45,000 filed in 2009 claiming $295 million in refunds. The Internal Revenue Service (IRS) catches most of these frauds, but refunds issued to these prisoners in 2009 amounted to more than $39 million (Department of the Treasury, 2010). Some prisoners (such as those working in prisoner industries) earn income and thus must file an annual income tax return to the IRS. Because this income information is considered private, prison officials cannot inspect returns for fraudulent claims.

●●● EIGHTH AMENDMENT

The **Eighth Amendment** reads,

Eighth Amendment:
Constitutional amendment that forbids cruel and unusual punishment.

Excessive bail shall not be required, nor excessive fines imposed, nor cruel and unusual punishments inflicted.

The pertinent part of the Eighth Amendment for us is the part that addresses cruel and unusual punishment. According to the U.S. Supreme Court, cruel and unusual punishment is punishment applied "maliciously and sadistically for the very purpose of causing harm" (*Hudson v. McMillian,* 1992), although the inmate is responsible for proving that the punishment was so applied. Eighth Amendment protections are denied by prison officials not only if they do something to inmates that they should not but also if they fail to do something that they have a duty to do. Prison officials must provide inmates with the basic amenities of life such as food and medical attention, and they must provide them with protection from the physical and sexual predations of other inmates, many of whom have histories of "maliciously and sadistically" causing harm to others.

Liability attaches to prison officials for inmate–inmate assaults if officials display deliberate indifference to an inmate's needs (Vaughn & Del Carmen, 1995). The courts have struggled to make plain what "deliberate indifference" means, but basically it occurs when prison officials know of, but disregard, an obvious risk to an inmate's health or safety (*Wilson v. Seiter,* 1991). In other words, prison officials must not turn a blind eye to situations that obviously imperil the health or safety of

? ETHICAL ISSUE

What Would You Do?

You are a district judge in a state that allows gay marriage. Two male inmates claiming to be in love have filed a suit demanding to be allowed to marry and be housed in the same cell. They also claim that prison authorities have purposely housed them in separate units so that they have no contact with each other. You know that the Prison Rape Elimination Act of 2003 (PREA) has been a potent tool for the selective sanctioning of inmates for any sexual expression at all. The state claims that prison officials must limit sexual interactions among inmates because of their potential liability regarding allegations of prison rape under PREA. The state also claims that such a thing is unprecedented and could lead to all kinds of unrest in the prison. The inmates claim that they are genuinely in love, that heterosexual inmates may marry, and that to deny their request is discriminatory and a violation of their human rights of sexual expression. How will you rule and why?

inmates entrusted to their care. Purposely placing a slightly built and effeminate young male in a cell with a known aggressive sexual predator is an example of a violation of the deliberate indifference standard for which prison authorities would be liable for any injuries suffered. For inmates to prevail in suits involving deliberate indifference claims, they must prove that (1) they suffered an objectively serious deprivation or harm and (2) prison officials were aware of the risk that caused the alleged harm and failed to take reasonable steps to prevent it. *Wilson* is seen as a key decision favoring correctional agencies because of these stringent proof requirements.

Despite movie depictions and public perceptions of jails and prisons as places where sexual assault is rife, the rate of sexual assault in prisons is 0.40 per 1,000 inmates, which is much lower than sexual violence rates on the outside (Beck & Harrison, 2007). In 2012, the forcible rape rate in the free community was at 0.53 per 1,000 females (Federal Bureau of Investigation [FBI], 2013), and this does not include all other sexual misconduct offenses of the kind included in the Beck and Harrison (2007) report. The Beck and Harrison report also noted that 38% of the allegations involved staff misconduct, sometimes referred to as "romance" between staff and inmate. The majority of forceful sexual assault was inmate on inmate (Robertson, 2010).

Inmate medical care is also covered by the concept of deliberate indifference. F. Cohen (2008) wrote,

> Our jails and prisons have increasingly become the de facto clinical depositories for hundreds of thousands of inmates who are very sick and who require all manner of specialty medical, dental, and mental health care. Prisons are not only the new mental asylums; they are the community hospitals and emergency wards for certain segments of the poor. (p. 5)

The medical needs of inmates in today's prisons are as well addressed as those of the average free person of roughly similar class background presenting with similar health problems. Indeed, inmates are the only group of people in the United States with a constitutional right to medical care. According to a Bureau of Justice Statistics report on inmate mortality in state prisons, prisoners between 15 and 64 years of age had a mortality rate 19% lower than that of the U.S. general population (Mumola, 2007). The majority of the difference was attributable to African American male inmates under 45 who had a mortality rate 57% lower than the rate of black males of similar age in the general population. Of course, not all of this difference is attributable to the medical care inmates receive, and no one claims that such care is better than, or even equal to, the average level of medical care available to most people on the outside. The lower mortality rate is most likely due to the fact that incarceration lowers the probability of being murdered, being exposed to drugs, having access to alcohol and tobacco, and other risks to a person's health and safety that those who pursue a criminal lifestyle face every day on the outside.

••• FOURTEENTH AMENDMENT

The **Fourteenth Amendment** is a long one with five sections; we cite only the first section here:

> All persons born or naturalized in the United States, and subject to the jurisdiction thereof, are citizens of the United States and of the State wherein they reside. No state shall make or enforce any law which shall abridge the privileges or immunities of citizens of the United States; nor shall any State deprive any person of life, liberty, or property, without due process of law; nor deny to any person within its jurisdiction the equal protection of the laws.

This is the due process clause of the Fourteenth Amendment and is the legal basis for granting limited procedural rights to individuals under correctional supervision. The due process clause was first applied to inmates facing disciplinary action for infractions of prison rules in *Wolff v. McDonnell* (1974). In *Wolff*, the Supreme Court declared that while inmates are not entitled to the same due process rights as an accused but unconvicted person on the outside, they are entitled to some. These rights are (1) to receive written notice of an alleged infraction, (2) to be given sufficient time (usually 24 hours) to prepare a defense, (3) to have time to produce evidence and witnesses on their behalf, (4) to have the assistance of non-legal counsel, and (5) to have a written statement outlining the disciplinary committee's findings.

In *Sandin v. Conner* (1995), the Supreme Court clarified and trimmed back inmate rights. The Court declared that the above due process rights are triggered only by any disciplinary action that may result in the loss of "good time," which amounts to an extension of an inmate's sentence. Conner had been given 30 days of punitive segregation for making foul and abusive comments to an officer while being subjected to a strip search. The Court ruled that due process rights are not triggered by actions that result in temporary placement in a disciplinary segregation unit, which does not amount to an extension of sentence. The Court also concluded that disciplinary segregation is not an atypical hardship relative to the ordinary hardships of imprisonment.

Fourteenth Amendment: Contains the due process clause, which declares that no state shall deprive any person of life, liberty, or property without due process of law.

••• THE CIVIL COMMITMENT OF SEX OFFENDERS

The idea that people who engage in socially disapproved behavior are sick and require treatment is seen as particularly applicable to sex offenders. In 1997, the Supreme Court upheld Kansas's Sexually Violent Predator Act (SVPA), which allowed for keeping sex offenders in state custody under civil commitment laws *after* they have served their full prison terms if they demonstrate "mental abnormality" or are said to have a "personality disorder" (*Kansas v. Hendricks,* 1997). The federal government and many other states have since passed similar involuntary confinement laws for sex offenders. Prior to *Hendricks,* civil commitments were limited to individuals suffering from mental illness, but seemingly for the express purpose of covering sex offenders, states have loosened the mental illness criterion in favor of the "mental abnormality" criterion (R. Alexander, 2004). The term *mental abnormality* can, of course, be used to cover almost anything society may disapprove of and serves as a justification for imprisonment in ways "reminiscent of Soviet policies that institutionalized dissidents" (Grinfeld, 1997, p. 2). There is no doubt that Leroy Hendricks was a repeat predatory pedophile and a thoroughly nasty piece of work, but while many applaud his incapacitation, what concerns civil libertarians is that the *Hendricks* decision created a special category of individuals defined as "abnormal" who may be punished indefinitely for what they *might do* if released.

Hendricks appealed his confinement on double jeopardy (no person can be prosecuted twice for the same offense) and ex post facto (a person cannot be punished for acts that were not crimes at the time he or she committed them) grounds. The Supreme Court ruled that Hendricks's confinement was not double jeopardy because the commitment proceedings of the SVPA under which he was confined were civil rather than criminal and thus did not constitute a second prosecution. Likewise, Hendricks's ex post facto claim was rejected because the ex post facto clause of the U.S. Constitution relates only to criminal statutes. The Court declared that because Hendricks was committed under a civil act, his commitment did not constitute punishment. The majority of Supreme Court justices seemed to have believed that putting a different name on state confinement against the will of the confined changes how that person experiences it.

In his analysis of civil commitment of sex offenders, R. Alexander (2004) listed a number of ways that he believed the Supreme Court erred in its rulings in *Hendricks* and subsequent cases dealing with the same issue. The gist of most of these criticisms is that the ruling offended Alexander's ideas of social justice and did not accomplish any of the goals of state confinement (deterrence and rehabilitation) other than retribution and incapacitation. Farkas and Stichman (2002) also argued that what they called the "culture of fear" generated by atypically brutal sex offenses has resulted in laws that are constitutionally questionable and that have negative consequences for the treatment of sex offenders, the criminal justice system, and society in general. The popularity of the laws with the general public, and the extremely negative view of sex offenders that it holds, makes it unlikely that these laws will be changed in the near future. It should be noted that only between 1% and 2% of sex offenders are confined under civil commitment orders (R. Alexander, 2004).

••• CURTAILING PRISONER PETITIONS

According to Federman (2004), two congressional acts signed into law in 1996—the Prison Litigation Reform Act (PLRA) and the Antiterrorism and Effective Death Penalty Act (AEDPA)—have severely curtailed prisoner access to the courts. Both acts were passed in part to reduce the thousands of lawsuits filed by inmates that clog the federal courts. In the year of the passage of these acts, inmates filed 68,235 civil rights lawsuits in the federal courts compared with less than 2,000 in the early 1960s (Alvarado, 2009). By 2000, the number of such lawsuits dropped to 24,519 (Seiter, 2005), a 64% decrease from the 1996 figure. Despite claims that these acts are "silencing the cells" (Vogel, 2004), the number of lawsuits filed is still more than 12 times what it was

FIGURE *14.1*   Comparison of Prisoner Petitions Filed in U.S. District Courts and Other Civil Cases, 2011–2015

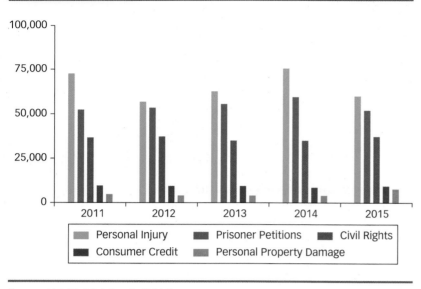

Source: U.S. District Courts (2016).

during the 1960s. Figure 14.1 is from a U.S. District Courts (2016) report comparing all kinds of prisoner petitions to federal courts with other types of cases. In 2015, there were 52,531 prisoner petitions, indicating that they are climbing dramatically again to more than double what they were in 2000, but they are still fewer than in 1996.

The primary intention of the PLRA was to free prisons and jails from federal court supervision as well as limit prisoners' access to the federal courts. Both intentions have largely succeeded. Among the requirements of the PLRA is one that state inmates cannot bring a section 1983 (civil rights) lawsuit in federal court unless they first exhaust all available administrative remedies such as filing a written grievance with the warden. The PLRA also states that inmates claiming to be unable to afford the required filing fee for the lawsuit may still need to pay a partial fee, which will be collected whenever money appears in their inmate accounts. This provision may limit the airing of genuine grievances in federal court because of financial difficulties.

The issues raised by the passage of the PLRA reached the Supreme Court in *Jones v. Bock* (2007). The specific issue in *Jones v. Bock* (2007) was whether the PLRA requires inmates bringing a federal civil rights suit to show they have exhausted all administrative remedies before suing rather than requiring the defense to prove that administrative remedies were not exhausted. In a unanimous opinion written by Chief Justice John Roberts, the Court ruled that the exhaustion of administrative remedies was not required by the PLRA and that prisoners could bring civil rights lawsuits without the need to demonstrate that they have exhausted all administrative remedies. The opinion did not ignore the flood of frivolous suits but intimated that this concern was secondary to the genuine complaints prisoners may have. In *Jones,* Justice Roberts wrote,

> Prisoner litigation continues to "account for an outsized share of filings" in federal district courts. In 2005, nearly 10 percent of all civil cases filed in federal courts nationwide were prisoner complaints challenging prison conditions or claiming civil rights violations. Most of these cases have no merit; many are frivolous. Our legal system, however, remains committed to guaranteeing that prisoner claims of illegal conduct by their custodians are fairly handled according to law. The challenge lies in ensuring that the flood of nonmeritorious claims does not submerge and effectively preclude consideration of the allegations with merit.

As the name implies, the AEDPA is mostly about antiterrorism and the death penalty rather than an act specifically designed to limit habeas corpus proceedings. It was passed in response to the bombing of the Murrah Federal Building in Oklahoma City, Oklahoma, with the reform of habeas corpus law being a rider to it. The AEDPA does not eliminate inmates' rights to habeas corpus, but it does restrict its availability (Alvarado, 2009). It does so by limiting successive petitions and judicial review of evidence and may now apply only to inmates who have sought, but have been denied, state court remedies available to them. The AEDPA thus takes habeas corpus partially back along the road to again becoming the pre-conviction remedy against unlawful imprisonment that it was initially.

A review of Supreme Court decisions on habeas corpus since the AEDPA found that they have upheld the reforms largely as intended by Congress (Scheidegger, 2006). Although civil rights groups such as the American Civil Liberties Union tend to decry both statutes, the Court's attitude toward them is probably a good thing for all involved for a number of reasons. First, it frees up the federal courts to deal with pressing inmate issues that are really repugnant to the Constitution as well as the numerous other matters it must deal with. Second, we all know that "crying wolf" too often leads to the dismissal of genuine claims, and if the situation continued as it was before the 1996 reforms, the solution may just have been the return to a complete hands-off policy. Third, it saves the taxpayers literally millions of dollars in frivolous legal exercises whose benefits were only to relieve the boredom of mischievous inmates (again, this does not mean that there are no substantively meaningful claims filed). Many states, aware that the courts could swing back to more active involvement, and of the high cost of defending lawsuits, have established internal mechanisms to more effectively deal with inmate concerns such as outside mediators and the creation of ombudspersons. Although the PLRA and AEDPA have limited inmate access to the courts, in a roundabout way they have given inmates more immediate and local ways to make their grievances known.

••• LEGAL ISSUES IN PROBATION AND PAROLE

The prisoners' rights period also extended rights to offenders under community supervision. Probation and parole are statutory privileges granted by the state in lieu of imprisonment (in the first case) or further imprisonment (in the second case). Because of their conditional privilege status, it was long thought that the state did not need to provide probationers and parolees with any procedural due process rights in the granting or revoking of either status. Today probationers and parolees are granted some due process rights, although like inmates there are restrictions on them that are not applicable to citizens not under correctional supervision.

The first important case in this area was *Mempa v. Rhay* (1967). Mempa was a probationer who committed a burglary, to which he admitted, 4 months after he was placed on probation. His probation was revoked without a proper hearing or the assistance of legal counsel; he was sent to prison. The issue before the Supreme Court was whether probationers have a right to counsel at a deferred sentencing (probation revocation) hearing. The Court ruled that under the Sixth and Fourteenth Amendments, they do because Mempa was being sentenced and the fact that sentencing took place subsequent to a probation placement does not alter the fact that sentencing is a "critical stage" in a criminal case. The Court further stated that probationers facing revocation should have the opportunity to challenge evidence by cross-examining state witnesses (typically only the probation officer), present exculpatory witnesses, and testify themselves.

A further advance in granting due process rights to offenders on conditional liberty status came in *Morrissey v. Brewer* (1972). Morrissey was a parolee who was arrested by his parole officer for a number of technical violations and returned to prison without a hearing. Morrissey's petition to the Supreme Court claimed that because he received no hearing prior to revocation, he was denied his rights under the due process clause of the Fourteenth Amendment. The Court agreed that when a **liberty interest** is involved, certain processes are necessary (a liberty interest refers to government-imposed changes in someone's legal status that interfere with the person's constitutionally guaranteed rights

Liberty interest: Refers to an interest in freedom from governmental deprivation of liberty without due process.

to be free of such interference). The ruling by the Court in *Morrissey* noted that parole revocation does not call for all the rights due to a defendant who is not yet convicted but that there were certain protections under the Fourteenth Amendment to which the defendant is entitled. These rights were laid out by the Court as follows:

a. Written notice of the claimed violations of parole

b. Disclosure to the parolee of evidence against him

c. Opportunity to be heard in person and to present witnesses and documentary evidence

d. The right to confront and cross-examine adverse witnesses (unless the hearing officer specifically finds good cause for not allowing confrontation)

e. A "neutral and detached" hearing body such as a traditional parole board, members of which need not be judicial officers or lawyers

f. A written statement by the fact finders as to the evidence relied on and reasons for revoking parole

While individuals are on probation or parole, they have limited constitutional rights and their probation/parole officers have broader powers to intrude into their lives than do police officers. Because probationers and parolees waive their Fourth Amendment search and seizure rights, probation/parole officers may conduct searches at any time without a warrant and without the probable cause needed by police officers. Evidence seized by probation/parole officers without a warrant can be used in probation or parole revocation hearings, but not as trial evidence in a new case (*Pennsylvania Board of Probation and Parole v. Scott*, 1998). The Supreme Court ruled that to exclude evidence from a parole hearing would hamper the state's ability to ensure the parolee's compliance with conditions of release and would yield the parolee free of consequences for non-compliance. This "special needs" (of law enforcement) exception to the Fourth Amendment has been extended to the police under certain circumstances. The Court has held that if a probation order is written in such a way that provides for submission to a search "by a probation officer or any other law enforcement officer," then the police gain the same rights to conduct searches based on less than probable cause as do probation and parole officers (*United States v. Knights*, 2001).

SUMMARY

- The only way we can be reasonably assured that justice resides within a legal system is to determine the extent to which it adheres to the rule of law. That is, a nation must recognize the supremacy of certain fundamental values and principles that have been committed to writing, and there must be a system of procedures to hold the government to these principles and values.

- The courts have moved through three general periods with respect to inmates' rights: the hands-off period, a short period of extending many rights to prisoners, and the current retreat to a limited hands-off policy.

- During the hands-off period, prisoners were considered slaves of the state and had no rights at all. During the period of extending prisoners' rights, the federal courts extended a number of First, Fourth, Eighth, and Fourteenth Amendment rights to them, although these rights were obviously not as extensive as they would be outside prison walls. (However, inmates are the only group of Americans with a constitutional right to medical treatment.)

- Because of the granting of these rights, the federal courts became clogged with section 1983 suits challenging the conditions of their confinement, the great majority of which were demonstrably frivolous.

- A major source of concern for civil rights activists is the civil commitment of some sex offenders after they have served their prison sentences. These offenders are liable to be locked up because of something they might do rather than because of something they have done.

- The U.S. Congress passed the Prison Litigation Reform Act (PLRA) in 1996, limiting prisoner access to federal courts and loosening the grip of the courts on state correctional systems because of these excessive suits. Congress also passed the Antiterrorism and Effective Death Penalty Act (AEDPA) in the same year, with a rider limiting inmates' habeas corpus rights. Numbers of prisoners' petitions to the federal courts dropped substantially for the first few years after the passage of the PLRA and AEDPA, but they are now climbing back up.

- The courts have been active since the 1960s in providing rights to offenders under community supervision also. The Supreme Court has ruled that probationers have a right to counsel at a deferred sentencing hearing and that probationers and parolees have a right to minimal due process rights (a fair hearing to establish cause) at revocation hearings. The Court has also extended the greater search powers of probation/parole officers to police officers under certain circumstances.

KEY TERMS

Bill of Rights, 311

Civil death statutes, 309

Civil rights claim, 311

Deference period, 311

Eighth Amendment, 316

First Amendment, 313

Fourteenth Amendment, 318

Fourth Amendment, 314

Habeas corpus, 310

Hands-off doctrine, 309

Liberty interest, 321

Rule of law, 308

Section 1983 suits, 311

DISCUSSION QUESTIONS

1. What were the two main reasons or justifications behind the hands-off doctrine?

2. Why does the concept of habeas corpus have such a revered place in common law?

3. In what way did the Supreme Court in *Jones v. Cunningham* (1963) go beyond the original meaning of habeas corpus?

4. Do you think that the majority of male inmate complaints about female officers searching them or viewing their nakedness are genuine indications of outrage?

5. What do you think of laws permitting the civil commitment of some sex offenders? Are there any potential dangers for widespread abuse in the practice?

6. With what sort of latitude should the law permit prisoners to file lawsuits without any obvious merit?

Review → Practice → Improve

Sharpen your skills with SAGE edge at **edge.sagepub.com/stohressentials3e**.

SAGE edge offers a robust online environment featuring an impressive array of free tools and resources for review, study, and further exploration, keeping both instructors and students on the cutting edge of teaching and learning.

FOR FURTHER EXPLORATION AND APPLICATION, TAKE A LOOK AT THE INTERACTIVE EBOOK FOR THESE PREMIUM RESOURCES:

- ▶ **Career Video 14.1** Supreme Court Librarian
- ▶ **Feature Video 14.1** The Effects of Anger
- ▶ **SAGE News Clip 14.1** U.S. Lethal Inject QA
- ▶ **SAGE News Clip 14.2** U.S. Firing Squad
- **Journal Article 14.1** The U.S. Supreme Court and the Civil Commitment of Sex Offenders

15

Correctional Programming and Treatment

TEST YOUR KNOWLEDGE

Test your current knowledge of correctional programming and treatment by answering the following questions true or false. Check your answers on page 394 after reading the chapter.

1. Trying to rehabilitate criminals is mollycoddling them and costs society too much; therefore, we should stop trying.

2. Programs to treat offenders and prevent recidivism are the biggest budget items in corrections after salaries.

3. Even the best-run treatment programs reduce recidivism by only about 5%.

4. Personal experience will give you a better understanding of what will or will not work with criminals.

5. Because addiction is a brain disease, the major way of attacking it in corrections is through pharmaceutical means.

6. Sex offenders are less likely to reoffend than almost any other type of offender.

7. Most people arrested in major cities test positive for some kind of illegal drug.

8. There are more mentally ill individuals in U.S. jails and prisons than in mental hospitals.

LEARNING OBJECTIVES

- Understand what rehabilitation is and why it is imperative

- Know the principles of evidence-based practices

- Understand the risk, needs, and responsivity model of treatment

- Learn something about cognitive-behavioral therapy

- Understand the functions of therapeutic communities in corrections

- Know the special treatment modalities applied to sex offenders

LIFE'S TURNING **POINTS**

Kathy Gardener was born to an "all-American" family in Dayton, Ohio. Her parents sent her to a Catholic girls' school, where she did well in her studies. All seemed to be going well for Kathy until she was 16 years old, when she went to a local air force base with two older friends from the neighborhood to meet the boyfriend of one of the girls. The boyfriend brought along two of his friends, and the six of them partied with alcohol, drugs, and sex. It was Kathy's first time experiencing any of these things, and she discovered that she liked all of them. Thus began a 9-year spiral into alcohol, drug, and sex addiction and into all the crimes associated with these conditions such as drug trafficking, robbery, and prostitution.

When Kathy was 25 years old, she was involved in a serious automobile accident in which she broke her pelvis, both legs, and an arm and suffered a concussion. She was charged with a probation violation, drunken driving, and possession of methamphetamine for sale. Kathy spent 10 months recuperating from her injuries, during which she was drug, alcohol, and sex free. Because of her medical condition, she was placed on probation. Her probation officer (PO) was a real "knuckle-dragger" who demanded full and immediate compliance with all conditions of Kathy's probation but who also became something of a father figure to her. While she was recuperating, she was often taken care of by a male nurse she described as "nerdy but nice." Her parents, who had been estranged from her for some time, became reacquainted with her, and her PO and nurse taught her to trust men again. She also occupied her time taking online college courses on drug addiction and counseling. She eventually married her "nerdy nurse" with her parents' blessing, and one of the guests was the "knuckle-dragger."

Kathy's story illustrates some core ideas in this chapter. No matter how low a person sinks into antisocial behavior, he or she is not destined to continue the downward spiral. There are a number of treatment programs available for all sorts of problems that get people into trouble with the law. Of course, not everyone is confronted with such a dramatic turning point in his or her life as a major automobile accident, leaving the person plenty of time to ruminate about life and where he or she is going. Kathy's addictive personality got her into all kinds of trouble, and she knew it. People must come to this realization, and when they do there must be programs in place to help them turn their lives around or else they will probably fail and the community will suffer.

● ● ● INTRODUCTION: THE RISE AND FALL (AND RISE AGAIN) OF REHABILITATION

As we have seen, there are five primary goals of the correctional system: deterrence, incapacitation, retribution, rehabilitation, and reentry. This chapter deals with the fourth of these goals—rehabilitation. The term *rehabilitation* means to restore or return to constructive or healthy activity (habilitation), but many offenders never experienced anything close to habilitation in the first place, so there is little to restore. Correctional treatment or programming needs to begin at the beginning and try to provide some of the things previously missing from the lives of offenders. Such programming obviously cannot supply the warmth and nurturing so critical during the early years of life or the deep sense of attachment and commitment to social institutions that comes from such experiences. However, programming and treatment can provide some of the concrete rewards, such as an education and job training, that most of us have had largely thanks to the attachments to the family and other social institutions we enjoyed as children, and it can do its best to change the destructive thinking patterns that infect criminal minds.

We try to rehabilitate criminals with the realization that whatever helps offenders helps the community. As former U.S. Supreme Court Chief Justice Warren Burger opined, "To put people behind walls and bars and do little or nothing to change them is to win a battle but lose a war. It is wrong. It is expensive. It is stupid" (as cited in Schmalleger, 2001, p. 439). In this chapter, we look at various ways that treatment personnel have been fighting the war. When reading this chapter, keep in mind that the vast majority of money assigned to correctional agencies is spent on surveillance and control functions. According to the National Center on Addiction and Substance Abuse (2010), among the 1.5 million inmates in jails and prisons nationwide in 2006, only 11.2% had received professional treatment since admission.

The American Prison Association (now the American Correctional Association, ACA) declared its commitment to rehabilitation in the following excerpt from its *Declaration of Principles* written nearly a century and a half ago (see In Focus 11.1).

Influenced by British pioneers Alexander Maconochie and Walter Crofton, rehabilitation was the goal of the early American prison reformers such as Zebulon Brockway. The ideal of rehabilitation reached the pinnacle of its popularity from about 1950 through the 1970s when the medical model of criminal behavior prevailed. The medical model viewed crime as a moral sickness that required treatment, and prisoners were to remain in custody under indeterminate sentences until "cured." Consistent with the switch from a punishment role to a more rehabilitative corrections role, classification systems, individual and group counseling, therapeutic milieus, and college classes were added to the usual rehabilitative fare of labor, basic education, and vocational training (Cullen & Gendreau, 2001).

IN FOCUS 15.1

The American Correctional Association's 1870 Declaration on Treatment

Corrections is responsible for providing programs and constructive activities that promote positive change for responsible citizenship.

Opportunity for positive change or "reformation" is basic to the concept of corrections because punishment without the opportunity for redemption is unjust and ineffective. Hope is a prerequisite for the offender's restoration to responsible membership in society.

Sound corrections programs at all levels of government require a careful balance of community and institutional services that provide a range of effective, humane, and safe options for handling juvenile and adult offenders.

Corrections must provide classification systems for determining placement, degree of supervision, and programming that afford differential controls and services for juvenile and adult offenders, thus maximizing opportunity for the largest number.

Corrections leaders should actively engage the community to assist in the restoration and reintegration of the offender.

Offenders, juvenile or adult, whether in the community or in institutions, should be afforded the opportunity to engage in productive work, participate in programs including education, vocational training, religion, counseling, constructive use of leisure time, and other activities that enhance self-worth, community integration, and economic status.

Source: American Correctional Association (2013). Reprinted with the permission of the American Correctional Association, Alexandria VA.

The rehabilitative goal was questioned and then fell apart with the publication in 1974 of Robert Martinson's article, "What Works? Questions and Answers About Prison Reform," in which the author concluded that "with few and isolated exceptions the rehabilitation efforts that have been reported so far have no appreciable effects on recidivism" (Martinson, 1974, p. 25). Unfortunately, the rhetorical question "What works?" got translated into a definitive "Nothing works" and became a taken-for-granted part of corrections lore. Before we can decide whether something does or does not work, we need to define thresholds for what we mean. If we demand 100% success, then we can be sure that "nothing works." A program designed to change people is not like a machine that either works or does not. Human nature being what it is, nothing works for everybody, some things work for some people some of the time, and nothing will work for anybody all of the time. High failure rates existed in many fields at their inception, but as practitioners in those fields learned from their mistakes and their successes, failure rates inevitably dropped.

●●● THE SHIFT FROM "NOTHING WORKS" TO "WHAT WORKS?"

Many of the correctional programs Martinson (1974) surveyed sought to change behaviors unrelated to crime, used programs that were not intensive enough, and used staff who were not adequately skilled. Few programs were based on the proper assessment of offender risks and needs, and programs often were faddish "Let's see what happens" programs, including everything from acupuncture to Zen meditation. While both these practices are beneficial in their own right, they are hardly useful for changing criminal lifestyles. One probation department actually insisted that male offenders should "get in touch" with their feminine side by requiring them to dress in female

ETHICAL ISSUE ?

What Would You Do?

You are the chairperson of your state's financial appropriation committee. The director of state corrections is again asking for a substantial increase in the prison budget for new treatment counselors in the state's five prisons. Given a realistic reduction in recidivism of about 10%, and given other pressing needs the state has, would you recommend appropriating the money or simply deny the request without taking it to the committee?

clothes, and another required "poetry therapy" (Latessa, Cullen, & Gendreau, 2002). Correctional resources are scarce and should be expended only on programs that have proven themselves useful in reducing recidivism.

How have Martinson's (1974) conclusions stood up over the last 30 years? Gendreau and Ross (1987) reviewed a number of studies of treatment programs and concluded, "It is downright ridiculous to say that 'Nothing works' . . . Much is going on to indicate that offender rehabilitation has been, can be, and will be achieved" (p. 395). Others have stated that properly run community-based programs could result in a 30% to 50% reduction in recidivism (Van Voorhis, Braswell, & Lester, 2000), although on the basis of major literature reviews, reductions in the 10% to 20% range are more realistic expectations (Cullen & Gendreau, 2001). A "success rate" is the difference in recidivism between a treatment group and a control group. A review of studies from prison, jail, probation, and parole settings conducted by Pearson, Lipton, Cleland, and Yee (2002) found that 55.7% of the subjects in treatment groups did not reoffend versus 43.3% of control group subjects. This difference translates into an average of 22.3% decrease in offending for treatment group members (55.7 − 43.3 = 12.4/55.7 = 22.3). Although there are still plenty of failures, if treatment programs managed only half this success rate, the financial and emotional savings to society would be truly enormous.

Lipsey and Cullen (2007) reviewed numerous studies of a variety of correctional intervention programs conducted from 1990 to 2006 and concluded that treatment works moderately well in reducing recidivism. Lipsey and Cullen believed that the biggest problem in offender treatment is not that "nothing works" but rather that correctional systems do not use the available research to determine what works—and then implement it. Rather, they tend to rely on convenience ("Who is available and what methods do they use?"), custom ("We've always done it this way and see no reason to change"), and ideology ("Criminals are scumbags; why waste time and money on them?").

••• EVIDENCE-BASED PRACTICES

Moving from the medical model to the just deserts/risk management model in corrections did not mean the death of the rehabilitation goal, but terms such as "assessment" and "programming" have replaced medical terms such as "diagnosis" and "treatment." The main concern of corrections is to reduce the risk that offenders pose to society, not to improve offenders' lives. Of course, the two goals are not incompatible; if more offenders can be taught to walk the straight and narrow, the risk of community members being victimized by them is reduced proportionately. Even though programs are run on a financial shoestring, prison officials like programming because it keeps inmates busy and out of trouble. Inmates also like it because it gives them something to do outside of their cells and looks good on their parole board records.

Evidence-based practices (EBP): Movement in which in order to reduce recidivism, corrections must implement practices that have consistently been shown to be effective.

The movement to a "what works" frame of mind has resulted in the most progressive agencies moving to **evidence-based practices (EBP)**. EBP simply means that in order to reduce offender recidivism, corrections must implement practices that have consistently been shown by rigorous empirical assessment to be effective in that endeavor. Extensive research has identified the following eight principles of evidence-based programming as formulated by the National Institute of Corrections and illustrated in Figure 15.1:

1. **Assess Actuarial Risk/Needs**—Assessing offenders' risk and needs (focusing on dynamic and static risk factors and criminogenic needs) at the individual and aggregate levels is essential for implementing the principles of best practice.

2. **Enhance Intrinsic Motivation**—Research strongly suggests that "motivational interviewing" techniques, rather than persuasion tactics, effectively enhance motivation for initiating and maintaining behavior changes. Motivational interviewing is a method of prompting behavior change by helping clients to explore and resolve discrepant thinking, that is, the ambivalent feelings of wanting, and not wanting, to change. The task of the counselor is to facilitate and engage intrinsic motivation on the assumption that if people can resolve the ambivalence themselves, they will value it more than if it is resolved by others, and they will develop a "can do" attitude.

3. Target Interventions

    a. **Risk Principle**—Prioritize supervision and treatment resources for higher risk offenders.

    b. **Needs Principle**—Target interventions to criminogenic needs.

    c. **Responsivity Principle**—Be responsive to temperament, learning style, motivation, gender, and culture when assigning to programs.

    d. **Dosage**—Structure 40% to 70% of high-risk offenders' time for 3 to 9 months.

    e. **Treatment Principle**—Integrate treatment into full sentence/sanctions requirements. Take a proactive approach to treatment using cognitive-behavioral therapy.

4. **Skill Train With Directed Practice**—Provide evidence-based programming that emphasizes cognitive-behavior strategies and is delivered by well-trained staff.

5. **Increase Positive Reinforcement**—Apply four positive reinforcements for every one negative reinforcement for optimal behavior change results.

6. **Engage Ongoing Support in Natural Communities**—Realign and actively engage prosocial support for offenders in their communities for positive reinforcement of desired new behaviors.

7. **Measure Relevant Processes/Practices**—An accurate and detailed documentation of case information and staff performance, along with a formal and valid mechanism for measuring outcomes, is the foundation of EBP.

8. **Provide Measurement Feedback**—Providing feedback builds accountability and maintains integrity, ultimately improving outcomes.

Taking a closer look at some of these principles, the psychosocial assessment of offenders typically begins with the **risk, needs, and responsivity (RNR) model**. The RNR model is the premier treatment model in corrections today in the United States and in many other countries (Ward, Melser, & Yates, 2007). The **risk principle** refers to an offender's probability of reoffending, and those with the highest risk are targeted for the most intense treatment ("dosage" under Principle 3). The **needs principle** refers to offenders' needs, the lack of which puts them at risk for reoffending, and suggests that these needs receive high

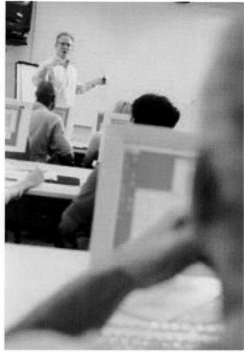

PHOTO 15.1: In addition to basic educational courses and vocational training, college classes are also offered as part of the rehabilitative role of correctional programs.

Risk, needs, and responsivity (RNR) model: A treatment correctional model that maintains that offenders and the community are better served if offenders' risks for reoffending and their needs (their deficiencies, such as lack of job skills) are addressed in a way that matches their developmental stage.

Risk principle: A principle that refers to offenders' probability of reoffending and maintains that those with the highest risk should be targeted for the most intense treatment.

Needs principle: A principle that refers to an offender's prosocial needs, the lack of which puts him or her at risk for reoffending, and that suggests these needs should receive attention in program targeting.

| FIGURE *15.1* | Integrated EBP Model Illustrated |

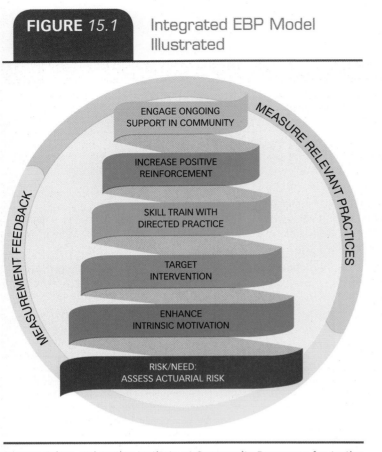

Source: Crime and Justice Institute at Community Resources for Justice (2009). United States Department of Justice.

priority. The **responsivity principle** maintains that if offenders are to respond to treatment in meaningful and lasting ways, counselors must be aware of their different development stages, motivation, and learning styles as well as their need to be treated with respect and dignity (Andrews, Bonta, & Wormith, 2006). The crux of these three principles is that we can no longer rely on "one size fits all" models, and treatment must be tailored to individual offenders' risks and needs.

Offenders' risks and needs are assessed by two separate scales: one for risk and one for needs. These scales are used to make predictions about offenders' success/failure based on **actuarial data** (Principle 1), that is, what has actually occurred and been recorded over many thousands of cases. It has been found time and time again across many professions that decisions made on the basis of actuarial statistical norms trump decisions based on the insight of individuals the great majority of the time (Andrews et al., 2006). **Offender risk** refers to the probability that a given offender will reoffend and thus the threat that he or she poses to the community. This is assessed by assigning numerical scores to the scale according to the extent that the offender evidences factors known to correlate with recidivism. Risk factors are either static or dynamic. *Static risk factors* are those that cannot change (gender, age, ethnicity, and other background variables). *Dynamic risk factors* (e.g., substance abuse, attitudes, values, behavior patterns) are factors that are targeted for change.

Offender needs refer to deficiencies in offenders' lives that hinder their making a commitment to a prosocial pattern of behavior. Scores on the risks and needs sections of the scale tend to be highly correlated—offenders with high risk tend to have high needs. Table 15.1 identifies and describes risks and dynamic needs that must be addressed; note that identifying needs mirrors the identification of risk. The other principles of EBP are either self-explanatory or addressed elsewhere in this book.

Responsivity principle: A principle maintaining that if offenders are to respond to treatment in meaningful and lasting ways, counselors must be aware of their different developmental stages and learning styles and offenders need to be treated with respect and dignity.

Actuarial data: Data relating to what has actually occurred and been recorded over many thousands of cases. Evidence-based treatment modalities are based on actuarial data.

Offender risk: The probability that a given offender will reoffend and thus the threat that he or she poses to the community.

●●● COGNITIVE-BEHAVIORAL THERAPY

The therapeutic concepts and methods that proponents of the RNR model find most useful in addressing offender risks and needs are cognitive-behavioral (Ward et al., 2007). Most of today's programming consists of **cognitive-behavioral therapy (CBT)**. CBT is an approach that tries to solve dysfunctional cognitions, emotions, and behaviors in a relatively short time through goal-oriented, systematic procedures and has been called "the most overtly 'scientific' of all major therapy orientations" (McLeod, 2003, p. 123). CBT combines the principles of operant psychology, cognitive theory, and social learning theory. Operant psychology asserts that behavior is determined by its consequences (rewards and punishments). Cognitive theory asserts that at a more proximal level, self-defeating behaviors are the result of unproductive thought patterns relating to our history of rewards and punishments (D. Wilson, Bouffard, &

| TABLE *15.1* | Major Risk and/or Need Factors and Promising Intermediate Targets for Reduced Recidivism |

Factor	Dynamic Need	Risk
History of antisocial behavior	Early and continuing involvement in a number and variety of antisocial acts in a variety of settings	Build noncriminal alternative behavior in risky situations.
Antisocial personality pattern	Adventurous, pleasure seeking, weak self-control, restlessly aggressive	Build problem-solving skills, self-management skills, anger management, and coping skills.
Antisocial cognition	Attitudes, values, beliefs, and rationalizations supportive of crime; cognitive emotional states of anger, resentment, and defiance; criminal versus reformed identity	Reduce antisocial cognition, recognize risky thinking and feeling, build up alternative less risky thinking and feeling, adopt a reform and/or anti-criminal identity.
Antisocial associates	Close association with criminal others and relative isolation from anti-criminal others; immediate social support for crime	Reduce association with criminal others; enhance association with anti-criminal others.
Family and/or marital	Two key elements are nurturing and/or caring and monitoring and/or supervision	Reduce conflict, build positive relationships, enhance monitoring and supervision.
School and/or work	Low levels of performance and satisfaction in school and/or work	Enhance involvement, rewards, and satisfactions.
Leisure and/or recreation	Low levels of involvement and satisfaction in anti-criminal leisure pursuits	Enhance involvement, rewards, and satisfactions.
Substance abuse	Abuse of alcohol and/or other drugs	Reduce substance abuse; reduce the personal and interpersonal supports for substance-oriented behavior; enhance alternative to drug abuse.

Source: Andrews, Bonata, and Wormith (2006, p. 11). Reprinted with permission of SAGE Publications.

Mackenzie, 2005). We can do nothing about past experiences, but we can do something to put the way we think about those things into proper perspective. Finally, social learning theory is a sociological view of socialization that asserts behavior is learned by modeling and imitation as well as by our history of rewards and punishments.

A. Ellis (1989) claimed that the great religious leaders of the past were cognitive-behavioral therapists because they were trying to get people to change their behavior from self-indulgence to temperance, from hatred to love, and from cruelty to kindness by appealing to their rational long-term self-interest. The common message imparted by religion is the need for personal change and the rewards that such change brings with it: "Do these things and you will feel good about yourself now, and you will be eternally rewarded." This is what CBT tries to do: change offenders' antisocial and self-destructive behavior into prosocial and constructive behavior by changing the way offenders think and by showing them that it is in their best interests to do so.

The first lesson of CBT is that criminals think differently from the rest of us. Yochelson and Samenow (1976) and Samenow (1999) pioneered treatment theories based on challenging criminal thinking errors when they realized that modalities based on "outside circumstances" theories did not work. The task is to understand how criminals perceive and evaluate themselves and their world so that we can change them. Criminal thinking

Offender needs: Deficiencies in offenders' lives that hinder their making a commitment to a prosocial pattern of behavior.

Cognitive-behavioral therapy (CBT): A counseling approach that tries to address dysfunctional cognitions, emotions, and behaviors in a relatively short time through goal-oriented, systematic procedures using a mixture of operant psychology, cognitive theory, and social modeling theory.

is destructive; it lands offenders in trouble with family, friends, employers, and the criminal justice system. Habitual offenders tend to perceive the world in fatalistic fashion, believing that there is little that they can do to change the circumstances of their lives. To illustrate this fatalism and other criminal thinking patterns, B. Sharp (2006) cited a cartoon in which one of the characters named Calvin says,

> I have concluded that nothing bad I do is my fault. . . . I'm a helpless victim of countless bad influences. An unwholesome culture panders to my undeveloped values and it pushes me into misbehavior. I take no responsibility for my behavior. I'm an innocent pawn of society. (p. 3)

Criminals think like Calvin in the context of a society where many people prefer to claim victimhood rather than personal responsibility ("McDonald's made me fat," "cigarette companies made me smoke," etc.). Many mainstream criminological theories locate the blame for crime on external factors such as poverty and peer pressure rather than on allowing criminals the dignity of owning responsibility for their behavior. Criminals are eager to jump on authoritative pronouncements that excuse their behavior, and defense lawyers are equally quick to argue them in court. All of this reinforces the patterns of criminal denial that treatment providers find so frustrating (B. Sharp, 2006; Walsh & Stohr, 2010). Challenging and changing maladaptive thought patterns takes on a central role in treatment as corrections workers strive to impress on offenders that whatever influences external factors may have on behavior, before they can affect behavior they need to be evaluated by individuals. The frustrations we experience do influence our behavior, but the important thing is not their presence but rather whether we deal with them constructively or destructively. The task of correctional workers is to teach criminals to stop blaming outside circumstances for their problems, how to take responsibility for their lives, and how to deal constructively with adversity.

CBT methods are used to address issues relating to self-control, victim awareness, relapse prevention, critical reasoning, and anger control (Vanstone, 2000). CBT literally "exercises the thinking areas of the brain and thereby strengthens the [neuronal] pathways by which the thinking brain influences the emotional brain" (Restak, 2001, p. 144). Receive a high enough "dosage" of CBT, and it can literally reorganize the brain's wiring patterns (Vaske, Galyean, & Cullen, 2011). A number of brain imaging studies show that CBT changes brain processes exactly the way that drugs such as Prozac do (Linden, 2006). A systematic review of brain imaging studies revealed neurobiological changes in people undergoing CBT. These studies show that CBT modifies the brain circuits involved in the regulation of negative emotions and fear extinction in treatment subjects. In short, CBT is able to change dysfunctions of the brain (Porto et al., 2009). However, these studies have been conducted only with individuals with problems such as depression, anxiety, and obsessive–compulsive disorder in which patients, unlike most criminals, are intensely motivated to overcome their problems.

●●● SUBSTANCE ABUSE PROGRAMMING

Alcohol is at the same time our most popular and most deadly way of drugging ourselves. Police officers spend more than half of their law enforcement time on alcohol-related offenses. One-third of all arrests (excluding drunk driving) in the United States are for alcohol-related offenses, about 75% of robberies and 80% of homicides involve a drunken offender and/or victim, and about 40% of other violent offenders in the United States were drinking at the time of their offenses (Mustaine & Tewksbury, 2004).

Alcohol is a very powerful and addictive drug and is the biggest curse of the criminal justice system despite the system's current obsession with illegal drugs. Illegal drug use presents almost as big a problem, with about 67% of state prisoners and 56% of federal prisoners being regular drug users prior to their imprisonment (Seiter, 2005). Clearly, mind-altering substances, both legal and illegal, are strongly associated with criminal behavior, and as such the tendency of many criminals to over-indulge in them must be addressed by correctional agencies.

Substance abuse problems are extremely difficult to treat because individuals most at risk for becoming addicted share many of the same traits associated with chronic criminal behavior, with many of these traits being strongly genetic (Vaughn, 2009). For instance, alcoholism researchers divide alcoholics into two types: Type I and Type II. Type II alcoholics start drinking and using other drugs earlier, become more rapidly addicted, and exhibit many more character disorders, behavior problems, and criminal involvement, both prior and subsequent to their alcoholism, than Type I alcoholics (Crabbe, 2002). Genetic researchers maintain that genes are much more heavily involved in Type II alcoholism than in Type I alcoholism (Crabbe, 2002).

It has been shown that drug addiction and criminality are part of a broader propensity to engage in many forms of deviant and antisocial behavior (Fishbein, 2003; Vaughn, 2009). For instance, the U.S. government's Arrestee Drug Abuse Monitoring (ADAM) program collects urine samples from arrestees across the country to test for the presence of drugs. Figure 15.2 shows the percentage of adult arrestees in five large U.S. cities who tested positive for illicit drugs over a 3-year period. The numbers show that

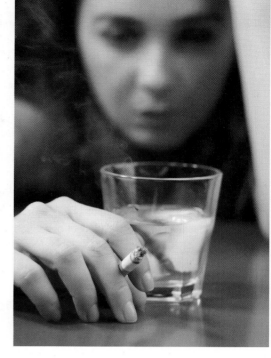

PHOTO 15.2: Substance abuse often contributes to poor decision making and criminal engagement for inmates.

illicit drug abuse is clearly strongly *associated* with criminal behavior, but the association is not necessarily a *causal* one. A large body of research indicates that drug abuse does not appear to *initiate* a criminal career, although it does increase the extent and seriousness of one (Menard, Mihalic, & Huizinga, 2001). In other words, research seems to point to the fact that chronic drug abuse and criminality are part of a broader tendency of some individuals to engage in a variety of deviant and antisocial behaviors. Numerous studies have shown that traits characterizing antisocial individuals such as conduct disorder, impulsiveness, and psychopathy also characterize drug addicts (Fishbein, 2003; McDermott et al., 2000). The large body of research indicating a strong genetic vulnerability to alcoholism/drug addiction helps to explain why many millions who drink and/ or experiment with drugs do not descend into the hell of addiction and why others are "sitting ducks" for it (Walsh, Johnson, & Bolen, 2012).

DRUG TREATMENT WITH SWIFT CONSEQUENCES FOR FAILURE: HAWAII'S HOPE PROGRAM

The state of Hawaii has a drug treatment program highly touted by the National Institute of Justice (NIJ, 2012) called Hawaii's Opportunity Probation with Enforcement (HOPE). The results of this program are based on 493 drug-using probationers with an elevated risk of violating probation, two-thirds of whom were randomly assigned to the HOPE program, with the rest being assigned to regular supervision. The program emphasizes a "no nonsense" delivery of both treatment and "swift and certain" punishment for violations. HOPE probationers are more closely monitored for drug use and other violations than control probationers. Figure 15.3 shows that this program had very positive results after 12 months. For instance, HOPE participants were 55% (47 − 21 = 26/47 = 55.3%) less likely to be arrested and 72% less likely to have used drugs. This experiment needs to be repeated in other locations with larger samples, and if results of any further studies come close to Hawaii's, there is real cause for optimism.

PERSPECTIVE FROM A PRACTITIONER

Margaret Jackson, Drug Treatment Specialist

Position: Drug Treatment Specialist

Location: Phoenix, Arizona

Education: Northern Arizona University, B.S., criminal justice; Boise State University, M.A., criminal justice administration; Rio Salado University, drug and alcohol counseling courses

How long have you been a drug treatment specialist (DTS)?

I have been a drug treatment specialist for 3 years; I have been in the correctional field for a total of almost 5 years.

The primary duties and responsibilities of a drug treatment specialist:

My primary duties are to provide drug abuse treatment to inmates in the federal prison system. I provide individual and group counseling/therapy to drug-/alcohol-addicted inmates incarcerated in the federal prison system. The Federal Bureau of Prisons provides a voluntary but criteria-based program called Residential Drug Abuse Program (RDAP), a 9-month (minimum of 500 hours of direct treatment) modified therapeutic community (TC). I provide clinical services using CBT techniques and introduce community as method to the inmates and develop a working system of a therapeutic community. The first step in working with inmates in this process is to determine their eligibility to receive counseling/therapy; one of the tools I use for this is a psychosocial assessment. If an inmate is eligible for treatment, I will use the psychosocial assessment to create an individual treatment plan for the inmate. Once eligibility and an assessment for treatment have been conducted, a team of three other therapists and I are responsible for providing residential treatment to the offenders. The inmates are assigned a series of workbooks and attend daily meetings. I construct the inmates' individual therapeutic treatment plans, reviews, and recommendations for further treatment on release from federal prison.

The qualities/characteristics that are most helpful for one in a probation or parole career:

- Be fair and consistent
- Have good judgment
- Be aware of population at hand
- Know your craft well
- Be reliable
- Be a team worker
- Be able to communicate with multiple agencies
- Be attentive to detail when writing reports and preparing inmate charts

In general, a typical day for a drug treatment specialist in corrections:

Monday through Friday, the TC starts with a morning meeting called "community meeting." This meeting is an inmate-run self-help meeting, with drug treatment staff supervising. During the treatment meetings/groups, inmates are learning and demonstrating therapeutic language and actions in a public "community" setting. After community meeting, inmates are separated into their appropriate phase groups, based on the date they entered treatment. RDAP, similarly to other TCs, uses a hierarchical form for the 9 to 12 months inmates are in treatment. Program participants typically have 3.5 hours of treatment daily; during this time, I am working directly with the inmates providing therapy. Therapy consists of using their RDAP workbooks and a facilitator guide to treat the inmates' addictions/behaviors. In RDAP, there are three phases of treatment, with new inmates entering treatment every 3 months (approximately 25 inmates per phase). With inmates phasing in and out of treatment, creating individual treatment plans, review of progress, and treatment summaries of each inmate are my responsibility to maintain and develop.

My advice to someone either wishing to study, or now studying, criminal justice to become a practitioner in this career field:

It would be important to understand the population for which you are providing therapy. In this regard, being an intern in a correctional setting would be beneficial to someone becoming a practitioner due to the nature of working inside a prison. Finally, practice development and presentation of lectures/seminars to groups as this will be a skill used often when providing group therapy.

Disclaimer: Opinions expressed in this article are those of the author and do not necessarily represent the opinions of the Federal Bureau of Prisons or the Department of Justice.

THERAPEUTIC COMMUNITIES

Therapeutic communities (TCs) are residential settings for drug and alcohol treatment that use the community spirit generated by the influence of peers and various group processes to help individuals overcome their addiction and develop effective social skills. Most such communities offer long-term (typically 6–12 months) residence, in which opportunities for attitude and behavioral change operate on a hierarchical model, whereby treatment stages reflect increased levels of personal insight and social responsibility. The interactions of the residents are both structured and unstructured, but they are always designed to influence attitudes and behaviors associated with substance abuse (Litt & Mallon, 2003). TCs provide dynamic "mutual self-help" environments, in which residents transmit and reinforce one another's acceptance of and conformity with the highly structured and stringent expectations of the TC and of the wider community. Life in a TC is extremely hard on people who have never experienced any sort of disciplined expectations from others, and as a consequence there are many dropouts; some residents withdraw voluntarily, and others are removed by TC staff for non-compliance.

TCs also operate within prison walls and are most often known as **residential substance abuse treatment (RSAT)** communities. These RSATs typically last 6 to 12 months and are composed of inmates in need of substance abuse treatment and whose parole dates are set to coincide with the end of the program. RSAT inmates are separated from the negativity and violence of the rest of the prison and are provided with extensive cognitive-behavioral counseling and attend Alcoholics Anonymous (AA) and Narcotics Anonymous (NA) meetings as well as many other kinds of rehabilitative classes (Dietz, O'Connell, & Scarpitti, 2003). Most participants in these RSATs are positive about most aspects of their experience, with most inmates listing cognitive self-change programs as the most positive aspect of their treatment (Stohr, Hemmens, Shapiro, Chambers, & Kelly, 2002). Dietz et al. (2003) also found that most inmates in prison-based TCs were positive about the program and that they had significantly fewer rule violations

Therapeutic communities (TCs): Residential communities providing dynamic "mutual self-help" environments and offering long-term opportunities for attitude and behavioral change and the learning of constructive, prosocial ways of coping with life.

Residential substance abuse treatment (RSAT): A community that typically lasts 6 to 12 months and is composed of inmates in need of substance abuse treatment and whose parole dates are set to coincide with the end of the program. RSAT inmates are separated from the negativity and violence of the rest of the prison and are provided with extensive cognitive-behavioral counseling and attend Alcoholics Anonymous (AA) and Narcotics Anonymous (NA) meetings as well as many other kinds of rehabilitative classes.

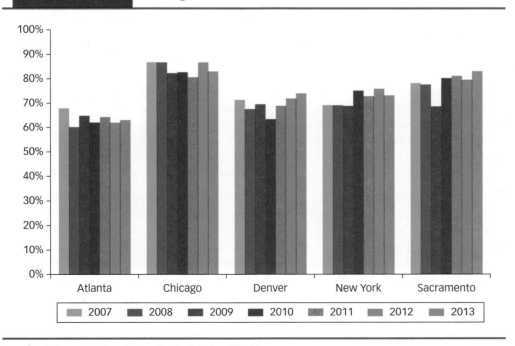

FIGURE 15.2   Percentage of Arrestees Testing Positive for Drugs in Five U.S. Cities, 2007–2013

Legend: 2007, 2008, 2009, 2010, 2011, 2012, 2013

Cities: Atlanta, Chicago, Denver, New York, Sacramento

Source: Office of National Drug Control Policy (2014).

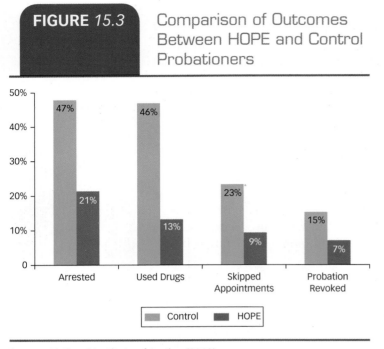

FIGURE *15.3* Comparison of Outcomes Between HOPE and Control Probationers

Source: National Institute of Justice (2012).

and rates of grievance filing than inmates in the general population.

An interesting program implemented in a prison setting and transitioning into the community is the Delaware Multistage Program (Mathias, 1995). In the beginning stage, offenders spend 12 months in a prison-based TC called Key; in Phase 2, they spend 6 months in a pre-release TC called Crest; and finally, in Phase 3, they receive an additional 6 months of counseling while on parole or in work release. Figure 15.4 compares drug use and arrest outcomes for offenders completing all phases (Key, Crest, and Key-Crest) 18 months after release from prison and a comparison group of offenders who did not participate in any of the phases. We see that 76% of Key-Crest members remained drug free, and 71% remained arrest free compared with only 19% and 30%, respectively, of the control group. Put another way, three times as many Key-Crest participants were drug free after 18 months than the comparison group, and 2.37 times more Key-Crest participants were arrest free than the comparison group.

Inciardi, Martin, and Butzin (2004) followed this same group 5 years after release from prison. As expected, the greater the time lapse between treatment and evaluation, the greater the relapse rate. Over the 5-year period, it was found that 71% of drug abusers who went through a residential treatment program and who received additional treatment on release (the Key-Crest group) had relapsed and 52% had been rearrested. However, the contrast with the comparison group still makes the Key-Crest program impressive. Among the comparison subjects, 95% had relapsed and 77% had been rearrested. This study shows how extremely difficult it is to battle addiction even after a long period of forced abstinence and extensive psychosocial treatment.

PHARMACOLOGICAL TREATMENT

Leshner (1998) informed us that addiction is a brain disease and a "prototypical psychobiological illness, with critical biological, behavioral, and social context elements" (p. 5). Because **addiction** is basically a brain chemistry problem, pharmacological treatment with drug antagonists (drugs that work by blocking the effects of other drugs) stabilizes brain chemistry and renders addicts more receptive to psychosocial counseling. Proponents of pharmacological treatment emphasize that it is not a magic bullet and that it augments, not replaces, traditional treatment methods.

There are many drug antagonists, but only one has claimed success in curbing both alcohol and drug addiction—naltrexone. Naltrexone reduces craving among alcohol/drug abstinent addicts and reduces the pleasurable effects of those who continue to use (Schmitz, Stotts, Sayre, DeLaune, & Grabowski, 2004). A study of drug addicts on federal probation found that about one-third of probationers who received naltrexone plus counseling relapsed as opposed to two-thirds of those who only received counseling (Kleber, 2003). A new drug called Vivitrol is a slow-release version of naltrexone (it releases the drug into the blood stream slowly over a period of days) that controlled clinical trials have shown to be effective not only in preventing drug abuse relapse but also in diminishing the

Addiction:
A psychobiological illness characterized by intense craving for a particular substance.

cravings that drive it. "Vivitrol is the first non-narcotic, non-addictive, extended release medication approved for the treatment of opioid dependence—marking an important turning point in our approach to treatment" (Volkow, 2010).

Proponents of pharmacological treatment claim that the effects of such treatment are more effective and immediate and wonder why the correctional system is relatively uninterested in pharmacological treatment (Kleber, 2003). It could be that corrections professionals received their training primarily in the social sciences, and there are some who have genuine ethical problems regarding chemical treatments for behavioral problems. However, according to the National Institute on Drug Abuse (2006), while medication is important for treating many addicts because medication helps them to stabilize their lives, it must be combined with counseling.

FIGURE *15.4*   Delaware Multistage Correctional Treatment Program 18 Months After Release From Prison

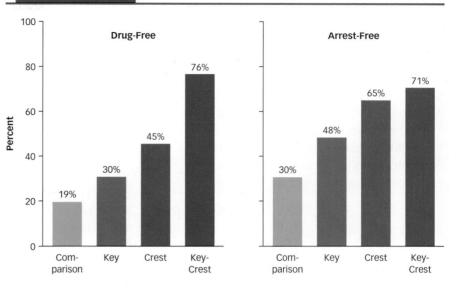

Source: Mathias (1995). National Institute on Drug Abuse and Addiction.

●●● ANGER MANAGEMENT

A central component of many treatment programs in corrections is anger management, particularly in violent, drug, and sex offender treatment programs. **Anger management programs** consist of a number of CBT techniques by which someone with problems in controlling anger can learn the cause and consequences of anger to reduce the degree of anger and avoid anger-inducing triggers. Anger is often central to violent criminal behavior, and given the frustrations resulting from being in custody or under correctional supervision in the community, it often leads to violence. Anger is a normal and often adaptive human feeling that is aroused when we feel that we have been offended or wronged in some way. The tendency to undo that wrongdoing by retaliating is motivated by anger and is adaptive in the sense that it warns those who have offended or wronged you that you are not to be treated that way. The problem, however, is not anger per se but rather the inability of some to manage it. These individuals often become excessively angry over minor real or imagined slights to the point of rage.

Anger management classes are taught in groups and designed to increase offenders' responsibility for ownership of their emotions (anger) and their reactions to them. Offenders often become frustrated and angry because they think that life is not fair to them ("I'm a victim of circumstances") and the world owes them a living. This kind of destructive thinking must be challenged and replaced by individual responsibility. Anger management classes also teach such skills as rational thinking ("Did this person really mean to diss me?") to increase offenders' ability to react to frustration and conflict in assertive rather than aggressive ways and to develop effective communication skills (Jolliffe & Farrington, 2009). There appears to be a growing consensus that

Anger management programs: Programs that consist of a number of techniques by which someone with problems in controlling anger can learn the causes and consequences of anger to reduce the degree of anger and avoid anger-inducing triggers.

ETHICAL ISSUE   ?

What Would You Do?

You are the chief psychologist in the largest state prison in the state. One of your counselors hasn't recommended that any inmate be put on a program of pre-release in 6 months, and you get a lot of complaints about his "hard-nosed" attitude. The counselor tells you that he operates from a therapeutic theory with a "no nonsense, no excuses" framework and that he's not going to let these "trailer trash out of here until they've completed their full minimums." What would be your response to this counselor?

properly conducted anger management programs reduce inmate violence and reduce violent recidivism for program completers versus control subjects by about 8% to 10% (Jolliffe & Farrington, 2009; Serin, Gobeil, & Preston, 2009). Although this seems like a small return on a corrections investment, even an 8% reduction in violent offenses prevents much needless suffering and millions of dollars in expenses.

••• SEX OFFENDERS AND THEIR TREATMENT

The American public harbors all sorts of very negative images of sex offenders. We lock them up under civil commitment orders after they have completed their prison terms, and all 50 states have sex offender registration laws (Talbot, Gilligan, Carter, & Matson, 2002). However, the term *sex offender* defines a very broad category of offenders ranging from "flashers" to true sexual predators, just as property offenders include everyone from petty shoplifters to career burglars. At least 98% of all sex offenders are either in the community on probation or parole or will be some day (Carter & Morris, 2002), making the issue of sex offender treatment of the utmost importance.

Although it is part of popular lore that sex offenders are untreatable and will never stop their offending, as a category of offenders they are actually less likely to reoffend than any other category. Looking at many years of British crime statistics, it was found that burglars are the most likely of all criminals to be reconvicted (76%) within 2 years of being released from prison, with sex offenders being the least likely (19%) (Mawby, 2001, p. 182). A review of 61 studies of sex offender recidivism found an average rate of reconviction for sexual crimes of 13.4% over a 4- to 5-year follow-up (Hanson & Bussiere, 1998). Perhaps the most instructive study of recidivism conducted to date was a study by the Bureau of Justice Statistics, whose researchers tracked 9,691 sex offenders released from prisons in 15 states in 1994 (Langan, Schmitt, & Durose, 2003). Over the 3-year period of the follow-up, sex offenders had a lower rearrest rate (43%) than 272,111 non–sex offenders released at the same time in the same states (68%). Rearrest rates included all types of crimes and technical violations such as failing to register as a sex offender and missing appointments with their parole officers. Only 3.5% of the sex offenders were reconvicted of a new sex crime during the follow-up period. Because recidivism rates include only those offenders who have been caught, in common with other types of offenders, the above figures should be considered bare minimums.

State-of-the-art treatment of sex offenders must include a thorough assessment of psychosocial problem areas, deviant arousal patterns, and polygraph ("lie detector") assessment (Marsh & Walsh, 1995). Deviant arousal patterns are assessed by a device called a penile plethysmograph (PPG), which measures blood flow in the penis (the level of the swelling of the penis) when exposed to deviant sexual images. These measures are then compared with measures in response to consensual adult sexual images. If, for instance, a man achieves a 10% erection viewing non-deviant heterosexual pornography, but achieves a 75% erection viewing sex involving young boys, we know where his sexual tastes are—the penis finds it difficult to lie. Of course, the PPG is far from foolproof.

Counselors are in agreement that effective treatment is impossible until the full extent of the offender's sex offending history is acknowledged by him or her and known to treatment personnel (Walsh & Stohr, 2010). But sex offenders are notorious for hiding their sexual histories, so polygraph assessment is needed to access their sexual histories. In comparing self-reports pre- and post-polygraph testing across 2 decades of research, it was found that child molesters underreport the number of sex crimes they have committed by about 500% and overreport their own childhood sexual victimization (the "I'm a victim too" excuse) by about 250% (Hindman & Peters, 2001). The polygraph therefore may be seen as a very useful tool if the first goal of treatment is to honestly acknowledge one's sexual history.

PHOTO 15.3: Group work is often used in offender programming both inside and outside of correctional facilities.

Unlike treatment for other problems in corrections, there has been a great deal of interest in the pharmacological treatment of sex offenders. Numerous researchers have concluded that optimal treatment (following a thorough psychosocial and physiological assessment) combines the biomedical and cognitive-behavioral approaches (Walsh & Stohr, 2010). The biomedical approach involves so-called chemical castration with a synthetic hormone called Depo-Provera, which is also sold as a method of female birth control. Depo-Provera works in males to reduce sexual thoughts, fantasies, and erections by drastically reducing the production of testosterone, the major male sex hormone. Depo-Provera prevents testosterone production, and it is testosterone activating a part of the brain called the hypothalamus that controls the male sex drive. Depriving the brain of testosterone allows offenders to concentrate on their psychosocial problems without the distracting fantasies and urges (Marsh & Walsh, 1995).

Following the State of California in 1997, several states now mandate chemical castration ("castration" is reversible on withdrawal from the drug) for repeat offenders. Not all sex offenders should be treated with this drug because there are sometimes negative side effects, and treatment can be provided only by a medical doctor. However, a number of reviews of the literature from Europe and America show that anti-androgen drugs such as Depo-Provera result in recidivism rates for repeat rapists and child molesters that are remarkably low (in the 2%–3% range) when compared with offenders treated with only psychosocial methods (Maletzky & Field, 2003). A review of 11 meta-analyses covering 353 separate studies from 1943 to 2009 found that surgical castration had the strongest effect on lowering recidivism, followed by chemical castration (B. Kim, Benekos, & Merlo, 2016). Insight-oriented therapies such as psychoanalysis had essentially no effect, while CBT had a significant effect, but much less if not combined with some form of anti-testosterone medication.

Chemical castration: A biomedical treatment for chronic sex offenders in which a synthetic hormone called Depo-Provera is administered. Depo-Provera works in males to reduce sexual thoughts, fantasies, and erections by drastically reducing the production of testosterone, the major male sex hormone.

••• MENTALLY ILL OFFENDERS

As graphically indicated in Figure 15.5 from the Council of State Governments Justice Center (2014), mental illness lurks behind many factors that are linked to criminal behavior. Mentally ill offenders under correctional supervision present a particularly difficult treatment problem. Alcoholics and drug addicts ingest substances that alter the functioning of their brains in ways that interfere with their ability to cope with everyday life, although their brains may be normal when not artificially befuddled. Mentally ill persons also have brains that limit their capacity to cope, but that limitation is intrinsic to their brains, not attributable to intoxicating substances. Studies around the world have found that mentally ill persons (mostly schizophrenics and manic depressives) are at least three to four times more likely to have convictions for violent offenses than persons in general (Fisher et al., 2006). Most mentally ill persons, however, are more likely to be victims than victimizers, and many of them make their problems worse by abusing alcohol and/or drugs (Walsh & Yun, 2013). It is because of their substance abuse and greater propensity for violence, in addition to mental hospital deinstitutionalization, that the mentally ill are overrepresented in the correctional system.

Torrey and his colleagues (2014) told us that there were an estimated 356,268 inmates with severe mental illness in prisons and jails in the United States in 2012 and approximately 35,000 severely mentally ill patients in psychiatric hospitals. In addition, the Bazelon Center for Mental Health Law (2008) estimated that 16% of individuals on probation or parole have some form of mental illness. This state of affairs results from the deinstitutionalization of all but the most seriously ill patients from mental hospitals that occurred during the 1960s. For instance, there were 559,000 persons in U.S. mental hospitals in 1955; in 2000 (with a U.S. population about 80% greater), there were only 70,000 (Gainsborough, 2002), and as we have seen, it was down to 35,000 in 2012. Deinstitutionalization of the mentally ill from mental hospitals has shifted to their institutionalization in jails and prisons, which in essence has resulted in the criminalization of mental illness (Lurigio, 2000). Table 15.2 presents the highlights of a Bureau of Justice Statistics report on the mental health problems of prison and jail inmates (James & Glaze, 2006).

Mentally ill offenders in jails and prisons are often victimized by other inmates, who call them "bugs" and exploit them sexually and materially (stealing from them), although most inmates seek to avoid them. Mentally ill offenders are also punished by corrections officers for behavior that, while not pleasant, is symptomatic of their illness. These behaviors include such things as excessive noise, refusing orders or medication, self-mutilation, and poor hygiene. Obviously, correctional facilities are not the ideal place for providing mental health treatment, even assuming that the staff are aware who the mentally ill are among their charges. Few correctional or probation/parole officers have any training about mental health issues, and one nationwide survey of probation departments found that only 15% of them operated special treatment programs for the mentally ill (Lurigio, 2000). It is not that anyone expects correctional workers to become treatment providers because that's a job for psychologists and psychiatrists. However, they should be expected to recognize signs and symptoms of mental illness, know how to effectively deal with situations involving mentally ill persons, and have a basic understanding of the causes of and treatment for the major mental illnesses.

Treatment for the mentally ill in prisons and jails consists primarily of antipsychotic and antidepressive medication, typically administered by a nurse. Many mentally ill individuals, especially paranoid schizophrenics, often refuse to take their medication. It is permissible in a number of states to forcibly treat mentally ill inmates if they meet state-specific criteria, which is typically if inmates pose a risk to others or themselves. This is determined on a case-by-case basis by a review

FIGURE *15.5* Mental Illness Lurks Behind Many Other Problems

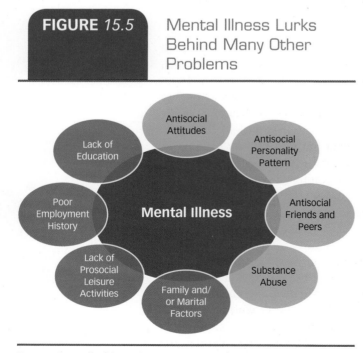

Source: Council of State Governments Justice Center (2014).

TABLE *15.2*	Prevalence of Mental Health Problems Among Prison and Jail Inmates

	Percentage of Inmates in . . .			
	State Prison		**Local Jail**	
Selected Characteristics	**With Mental Problem**	**Without**	**With Mental Problem**	**Without**
Criminal record				
Current or past violent offense	61%	56%	44%	36%
Three or more prior incarcerations	25%	19%	26%	20%
Substance dependence or abuse	74%	56%	76%	53%
Drug use during month before arrest	63%	49%	62%	42%
Family background				
Homelessness during year before arrest	13%	6%	17%	9%
Past physical or sexual abuse	27%	10%	24%	8%
Parents abused alcohol or drugs	39%	25%	37%	19%
Charged with violating facility rules*	58%	43%	19%	9%
Physical or verbal assault	24%	14%	8%	2%
Injured in a fight since admission	20%	10%	9%	3%

Source: James and Glaze (2006). U.S. Department of Justice.

*Includes items not shown.

committee composed of correctional and medical professionals (Torrey et al., 2014). Of course, just because such procedures are authorized by the state does not mean that they are used or that the inmate will be treated. According to Torrey and his colleagues (2014),

> Given the many legal difficulties in providing treatment for individuals with serious mental illness in prisons and jails, it is not surprising that many of them, including those who are most severely ill, receive no treatment whatsoever. This leaves corrections officers with few options for controlling mentally ill inmates' psychotic, often violent behavior. One option is seclusion, which often makes the inmate's mental illness worse. (p. 10)

What is both morally and fiscally required of the criminal justice system is to provide offenders with mental illness the support and structure they need to avoid further criminal behavior. One of the ways this is attempted is through mental health courts modeled on drug courts in use across the nation (and discussed in Chapter 5). As with drug courts, mental health courts seek to divert offenders from jails and prisons by facilitating their access to services, providing intensive judicial monitoring, and promoting collaboration among the court, probation, mental health service, and social service providers.

COMPARATIVE CORRECTIONS | Offender Treatment

The treatment of criminal offenders in modern Western nations is fairly uniformly centered on the RNR model. Countries that care little about the civil rights and treatment of their citizens in general obviously are not very concerned about the humane treatment of their prisoners. A modern country concerned with rehabilitation, but with some different assumptions about how to achieve it, is Japan. A large cultural difference between Japan and Western nations such as the United States is that whereas the latter emphasizes individualism and a great degree of personal freedom, the Japanese emphasis is on collectivism and individual conformity to community norms. Unlike the general tendency in American criminology to shift the blame for crime away from the individual and onto "society," the Japanese place responsibility for criminal behavior squarely on the shoulders of the individuals who commit it.

Western CBT counselors tend to play down introspection (gaining insight into one's self) as too time-consuming and believe that criminals need the participation and direction of counselors in order to benefit. Japanese correctional counselors, on the other hand, see their role as a kindly guide on the edge rather than as a trainer at the center providing definite directions (Bindzus, 2001). One type of counseling favored in Japanese corrections is called *Naikan,* which means "inside looking" and is designed to get offenders to see themselves as others see them. According to Kanazawa (2007), inmates undergoing Naikan therapy will spend many hours alone asking themselves three questions: "What has my mother (and other significant persons in my life) done for me?"; "What have I done for her (and other significant persons in my life) in return?"; and "What problems have I caused her (and other significant persons in my life)?" (p. 762). Thinking about these things is supposed to generate feelings of remorse, sadness, empathy, guilt, and consciousness of responsibility. The counselor will enter the offender's cell every hour or so to check on progress. Only if the offender displays tendencies to blame outside forces for his or her criminal behavior, or has not adequately explored the questions, will the counselor intervene to clarify.

Could such introspective methods work with Western prisoners who exist in cultures that seem to have little respect for individual responsibility? Bindzus (2001) expressed "doubts about the physical and psychological ability of European prisoners to stick through NAIKAN for a one-week period, with daily sessions up to sixteen hours" (p. 266). What works in one cultural context might not work in others for a variety of reasons. Of course, inmates require some sort of concrete help as well as introspective self-knowledge even in Japan. Indeed, Eskridge (1989) listed a large number of vocational training courses available in Japanese penal institutions, ranging from auto mechanics, to seamanship, to welding.

SUMMARY

- Although the vast majority of the correctional budget is spent on security, rehabilitation efforts have not completely ceased. The success rates of many rehabilitation programs are low, but outcomes are significantly better for treated offenders than for similarly situated offenders who did not receive treatment.

- Successful treatment programs implement evidence-based practices (EBP) that proceed by conducting a thorough assessment of offenders' risks and needs and then address these issues using cognitive-behavioral techniques along with the principles of responsivity. Treatment is best accomplished for severe substance abusers in therapeutic communities, although even then there is a significant percentage of failure. Much of this failure has to do with the intense psychological craving for the substance of abuse, which is something that may be significantly alleviated by certain alcohol/drug antagonists such as naltrexone.

- Similar observations were made about sex offenders who have difficulty in refraining from acting out their sexual fantasies with inappropriate targets. Repeat sex offenders treated with Depo-Provera combined with cognitive-behavioral counseling have much lower recidivism rates compared with offenders treated only psychologically.

- Mentally ill individuals are represented in the correctional system by a factor of at least 3 or 4 times their prevalence in the general population. The correctional system is not equipped to deal with mentally ill people, who are often victimized by other jail/prison inmates or disciplined by corrections officers for exhibiting behavior that is basically part of their mental disease syndrome.

KEY TERMS

Actuarial data, 332

Addiction, 338

Anger management programs, 339

Chemical castration, 341

Cognitive-behavioral therapy (CBT), 332

Evidence-based practices (EBP), 330

Needs principle, 331

Offender needs, 332

Offender risk, 332

Residential substance abuse treatment (RSAT), 337

Responsivity principle, 332

Risk, needs, and responsivity (RNR) model, 331

Risk principle, 331

Therapeutic communities (TCs), 337

DISCUSSION QUESTIONS

1. In your estimation, are the time, effort, and finances spent on rehabilitative efforts worth it given the low success rates? Would longer periods of incarceration better protect the public?

2. Cognitive-behavioral approaches stress thinking and rationality. How about emotions? Do you think that human behavior is motivated more by emotions than by rationality?

3. Given the greater involvement of genes in Type II alcoholism, in what ways would you treat Type II alcoholics differently from Type I alcoholics if you were a treatment provider? How about if you were a probation/parole officer?

4. Should all sex offenders undergo Depo-Provera treatment? What are the ethical problems of such invasive treatment?

5. Discuss the various component parts of the responsivity principle.

$SAGE edge™

Review → Practice → Improve

Sharpen your skills with SAGE edge at **edge.sagepub.com/stohressentials3e**.

SAGE edge offers a robust online environment featuring an impressive array of free tools and resources for review, study, and further exploration, keeping both instructors and students on the cutting edge of teaching and learning.

FOR FURTHER EXPLORATION AND APPLICATION, TAKE A LOOK AT THE INTERACTIVE EBOOK FOR THESE PREMIUM RESOURCES:

- ▶ **Career Video 15.1** Internal Affairs Investigator

- ▶ **Feature Video 15.1** Rehabilitation Efforts

- ▶ **SAGE News Clip 15.1** U.S. Jails Mentally Ill

- ▶ **SAGE News Clip 15.2** Drug Treatment

- **Journal Article 15.1** Defining Probability in Sex Offender Risk Assessment

16 The Death Penalty

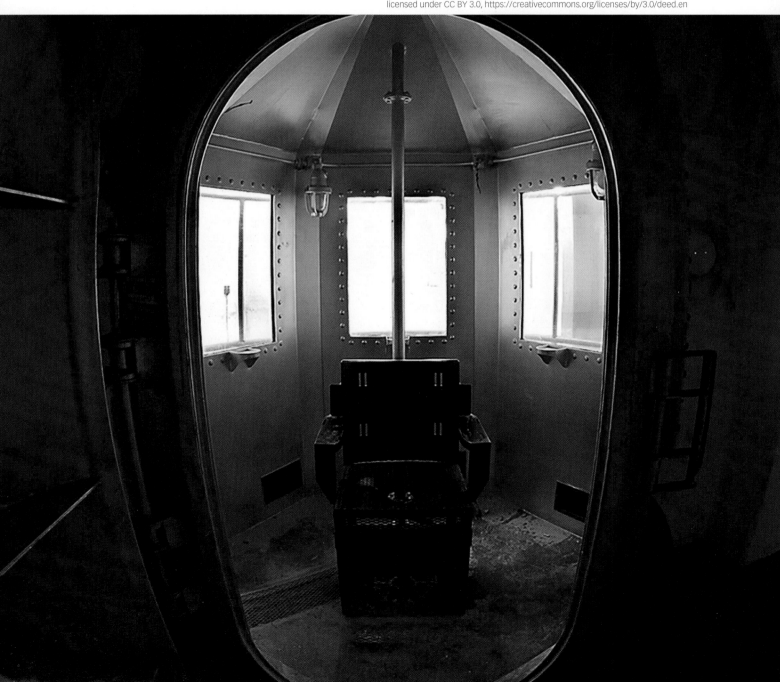

TEST YOUR KNOWLEDGE

Test your current knowledge of the death penalty by answering the following questions true or false. Check your answers on page 394 after reading the chapter.

1. Most Americans support the death penalty.

2. The United States is the only democratic country that currently uses the death penalty.

3. A white murderer is proportionately more likely than a black or Hispanic murderer to be sentenced to death and to be executed.

4. The gas chamber is still the favorite method of execution today.

5. Nearly all academics who study the death penalty believe that it has no deterrent effect.

6. The death penalty is cheaper than life in prison without the possibility of parole.

7. Women who commit heinous murders are far less likely to receive the death penalty than men who commit such acts.

8. In the United States, it is permissible to execute a person with a history of mental illness, but not one with a mental disability (i.e., low IQ).

LEARNING OBJECTIVES

- Explain the impact of public opinion on the retention or abolition of the death penalty

- Know the trends in the administration of the death penalty

- Identify the major Supreme Court death penalty cases

- Discuss the financial cost/benefit ratio of the death penalty

- Explain the difficulty in determining whether the death penalty is a deterrent

- Analyze the nuances relating to racial disparity and the death penalty

- Describe the innocence revolution and what it means

- Understand the issues surrounding the use of genetic and neuroimaging technology for determining exoneration and mitigation

A VERY UNUSUAL, VERY EXPENSIVE SERIAL KILLER

Charles Chi-Tat Ng is unique in a number of respects. He is the only known Asian American serial killer of the 20th century, he was a partner with Leonard Lake of one of the few documented serial killing teams, he precipitated a legal wrangle between the United States and Canada over the status of the death penalty, and his trial was the costliest criminal trial in American history at nearly $11 million.

Ng was born to wealthy parents in 1960 in Hong Kong. Ng was a troubled teen who was expelled for a variety of reasons from several schools, and when he was arrested at the age of 15 his father shipped him off to a boarding school in England. He did not last long there, being expelled for stealing, and returned to Hong Kong. Ng moved to the United States at age 18 to attend a university in California, but he dropped out after being involved in a hit-and-run. He then joined the U.S. Marines, but shortly thereafter he was caught

stealing machine guns and attempted desertion and served 3 years in prison. On his release in 1982, Ng moved in with a fellow ex-marine, Lake, and the two began a campaign of kidnapping, rape, torture, and murder. The pair is suspected of killing between 11 and 25 people.

Their orgy of murder ceased when Ng's compulsive stealing got him arrested for shoplifting in San Francisco in 1985, which eventually led to the arrest of Lake (who committed suicide). After Lake's arrest, the police went to the ranch shared by Lake and Ng and found the grisly evidence of their murders. Meanwhile, Ng ran off to Canada, where his stealing once again led to his downfall. He was arrested in Calgary for shoplifting and wounding a security guard and was sentenced to prison. While in Canadian custody, California embarked on a legal battle with Canada to get Ng extradited to the United States. Canada does not have the death penalty, and Ng argued that it would be in breach of his human rights to send him back. Ng finally lost the battle, and in 1991 he was shipped back to the United States. He was convicted in 1999 of the murders of six men, three women, and two infants and was sentenced to death. As of October 2017, he was still on San Quentin's death row.

Ng's case is a "classic" death penalty case. His murders (as many as 25) were horribly cruel, heartless, and remorseless. His guilt was never in doubt, and he never attempted to deny it. He was arrested in 1991 and convicted in 1999, so why is he still alive after California paid close to $11 million to see him executed? Many believe that we should not execute him or anyone else regardless of the heinousness of their crimes; others believe that execution is the only solution to such evil but may object to the death penalty for financial reasons. These are some of the things to think about as you read this chapter.

••• INTRODUCTION: THE DEATH PENALTY AND PUBLIC OPINION

The most controversial issue in corrections is the penalty of death. Given the emotional and philosophical issues surrounding the death penalty and particularly its finality (there is no way to put right an execution of someone later found to be innocent), it is understandable that it has been subjected to intense legal and ethical scrutiny. This has not always been the case, however. Throughout much of human history, the death penalty has been considered a legitimate, appropriate, and necessary form of punishment. As indicated in Figure 16.1, a clear majority of the American public still favors its retention. However, if life without parole (LWOP) is provided as an alternative to a death sentence, the percentage favoring the death penalty falls to about 46% (Gallup, 2013).

Note from Figure 16.1, illustrating trends in public opinion from 1936 to 2016, that in 1966 there were actually more people against the death penalty (47%) than for it (42%) ("no opinion" answers account for why the percentages in the figure never add

FIGURE 16.1 Results of Gallup Poll on Public Attitudes About the Death Penalty

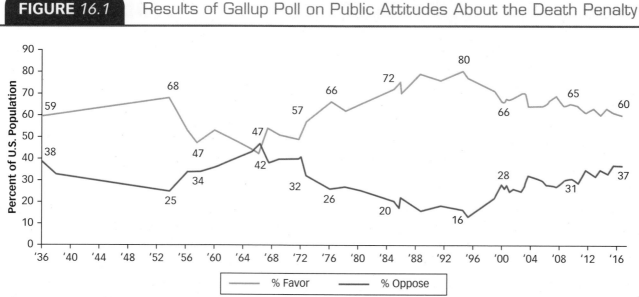

to 100%). Note also that support for the death penalty was the greatest during the 1980s and 1990s, with 1994 marking the highest level of support (80%) in the Gallup Poll's history. Why these large fluctuations? The most reasonable answer is that public opinion is swayed substantially by the crime rate—as crime goes up, so does support for the death penalty. According to Uniform Crime Report (UCR) data, the violent crime rate in 1994 was 713.6 per 100,000 population, which is 3.25 times higher than the 1966 violent crime rate of 220 per 100,000 (Federal Bureau of Investigation [FBI], 2013).

Public support for the death penalty is a major factor in its retention in the United States. It influences lawmakers, prosecutors, and judges, who fear electoral retaliation if they fail to show that they are "tough on crime." For example, former California Supreme Court Chief Justice Rose Bird, Justice Reynoso, and Justice Groin all were given their marching orders by the electorate, which felt frustrated over the Bird Court's reversal of more than 90% of capital cases (Traut & Emmert, 1998). Public support for capital punishment in California was notably strong in 1986 (83% favored) when the three justices were up for reelection.

Even the justices on the U.S. Supreme Court—who have nothing to fear from public reprisal arising from their decisions because they have lifetime tenure—are influenced by public opinion. In 1986, Supreme Court Justice William Rehnquist stated, "Judges need not 'tremble before public opinion' in the same way that elected officials may, but it would be remarkable indeed if they were not influenced by currents of public opinion" (as cited in J. Yates, 2012, p. 10).

The "currents of public opinion" doubtless contribute to the number of states that have retained the death penalty because legislators are more influenced by those currents than are judges. As seen in Figure 16.2, 31 states, the federal government, and the U.S. military retain the death penalty, while 19 states have abolished it. Executions are down 75% since 1996, and only five states executed anyone in 2016 (Death Penalty Information Center, 2017b). The fact remains, however, that only the United States, Japan, and South Korea, among the world's democracies, retain the death penalty.

Figure 16.3 is a graph of the annual number of executions in the United States from the mid-1970s, when states were coming to terms with the Supreme Court's *Furman v. Georgia* (1972) decision, which precipitated a brief moratorium on the death penalty from 1972 to 1976. By October 2017, 1,463 executions had taken place in the United States.

●●● METHODS OF EXECUTION USED IN THE UNITED STATES

The United States has historically used a variety of methods of execution. Table 16.1 lists methods used in the 20th century, the number of people executed by each method since 1976, and the jurisdictions authorizing each method. A short description of each method follows.

Hanging. The most common form of execution in the United States historically has been hanging. Although hanging seems fairly simple and "low tech," a number of factors need to be considered to ensure a relatively painless death. The condemned person's height and weight must be measured, the rope must be lubricated, and the noose must be placed

Hanging: A method of execution in which the condemned is hanged, causing either the neck to break or death by asphyxiation.

FIGURE *16.2* States With and Without the Death Penalty as of 2017

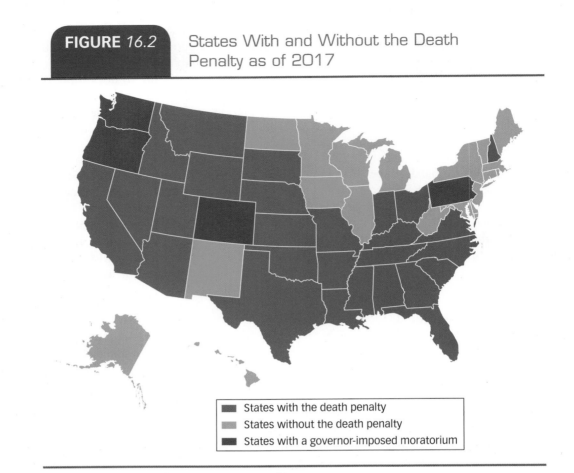

- States with the death penalty
- States without the death penalty
- States with a governor-imposed moratorium

Source: Death Penalty Information Center (2017b).

around the neck with the knot behind the left ear. If all is done correctly, the drop should cause a rapid dislocation of the neck; if all is not done correctly, the condemned may suffer slow asphyxiation.

Electrocution. The electric chair was introduced during the late 19th century as a more humane method of execution than hanging. A person undergoing execution by this method is firmly strapped to the chair with belts across the chest, groin, legs, and arms. A saline-moistened sponge is placed on the condemned person's shaved scalp, and an electrode skullcap is attached over it. Electrodes are also attached to the person's shaved legs. The executioner then engages the electrical power supply and delivers a 15- or 30-second jolt (depending on a state's protocol) of between 500 and 2,450 volts, after which the current is turned off to allow a physician to determine whether the person is dead. If the person is not dead, a further jolt is administered.

Gas Chamber. The use of cyanide gas to execute was considered more humane than electrocution. To execute by this method, the condemned person is placed in an airtight chamber and strapped to a chair, below which is a bucket containing sulfuric acid. Sodium cyanide is then released into the bucket, causing a chemical reaction that releases hydrogen cyanide gas. Once the prisoner breathes the gas, he or she dies shortly thereafter because this method shuts off oxygen to the brain.

Firing Squad. For a firing squad execution, the prisoner has a hood pulled over his or her head and is tied to a chair surrounded by sandbags. Five correctional officers, one of whom is issued a blank round, fire simultaneously at the inmate, thus causing death.

Electrocution:
A method of execution in which the person is strapped to the chair and electrodes are attached to his or her body. The person is then subjected to a 15- to 30-second jolt of between 500 and 2,450 volts of electricity.

Gas chamber: The use of cyanide gas to execute someone placed in an airtight chamber and strapped to a chair.

Firing squad:
A method of execution in which the condemned is strapped to a chair and shot by a firing squad.

FIGURE *16.3*   Number of Executions in the United States From 1976 to October 2017

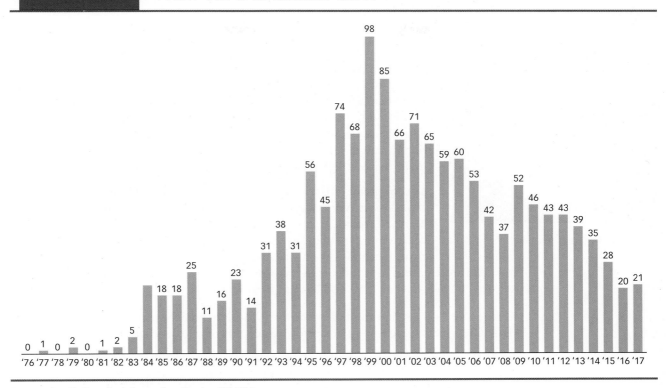

Source: Death Penalty Information Center (2017b).

Lethal Injection. As we see from Table 16.1, lethal injection is currently the preferred method of execution in all states, even if other methods are available as options. Using this method, the condemned person is strapped to a gurney and two needles are then inserted into the veins in his or her arms. These needles are connected to intravenous drips, one of which contains sodium thiopental, which puts the condemned person to sleep. The next drip is then released containing drugs that paralyze the muscular system and stop the person's breathing, followed by a drip of potassium chloride that stops the heart.

••• LEGAL CHALLENGES TO THE DEATH PENALTY

There have been a number of legal challenges to the death penalty revolving around the Eighth Amendment's prohibition of cruel and unusual punishment. These were typically about the constitutionality of the method of execution, not the penalty per se. The first case to successfully challenge the penalty itself was *Furman v. Georgia* (1972). William Henry Furman had shot and killed a homeowner during the course of a burglary and was sentenced to death. Furman challenged the constitutionality of his sentence, and the Supreme Court agreed in a 5-to-4 vote. The Court decided that the death penalty per se was not unconstitutional but rather the arbitrary way in which it was imposed was unconstitutional. The Court argued that because the death penalty

Lethal injection:
A method of execution in which the condemned person is administered drugs that paralyze the muscular system and stop the person's breathing, followed by another drug that stops the heart.

PHOTO 16.1: The electric chair

is so infrequently imposed, it serves no useful purpose, and that when it is imposed, judges and juries have unbridled discretion in making life-and-death decisions. Furman was paroled in 1984. He is currently serving 20 years in prison for a 2004 burglary.

Because of the Supreme Court's decision, states began the process of changing their sentencing procedures. Some states introduced bifurcated (two-step) hearings, the first to determine guilt (the trial) and the second to impose the sentence after hearing aggravating circumstances (circumstances that increase the heinousness of the offense) and mitigating circumstances (circumstances that decrease culpability) to determine whether death was warranted. Other states removed sentencing discretion (because this seemed to be the Supreme Court's problem with it) and made the death penalty mandatory for some murders.

The Supreme Court decided against mandatory death sentences in *Woodson v. North Carolina* (1976). In this case, the Court rejected the North Carolina statute mandating that all persons convicted of first-degree murder should receive the death penalty as excessive and unduly rigid. James Woodson was involved in an armed robbery in which a convenience store cashier was killed and a customer was seriously wounded. Woodson was released from prison in 1993 and has not been rearrested since.

Georgia revised its statute and opted for the bifurcated hearing. Using this process, Troy Gregg was sentenced to death for two counts of murder and two counts of armed robbery. In *Gregg v. Georgia* (1976), the Supreme Court upheld the constitutionality of the bifurcated hearing and thus of Gregg's death sentence. Gregg escaped from prison the day before his scheduled execution, but he was beaten to death in a bar fight that same night.

In *Coker v. Georgia* (1977), the Supreme Court ruled that the death penalty for rape was unconstitutional. Ehrlich Coker had escaped from prison, where he was serving time for murder, rape, and kidnapping, and promptly proceeded to commit another rape and kidnapping. Nevertheless, the Court struck down the Georgia statute authorizing death for rape under certain circumstances as "grossly disproportionate" and thus repugnant to the Eighth Amendment. Coker is currently serving multiple life sentences in Georgia.

Other legal challenges to the death penalty have to do with issues such as racial discrimination; the execution of juveniles, the mentally disabled, and the mentally ill; and challenges to the method of execution. These issues are addressed later in the chapter or were discussed in the chapter on juvenile corrections (Chapter 13).

••• DOES THE DEATH PENALTY DETER?

The death penalty is unique in that it is the only punishment required to demonstrate its deterrent effect to validate its constitutionality. We take it for granted that penalties applied to other crimes have a general deterrent effect, if not necessarily the desired specific effect. We have seen that the major argument for punishing wrongdoers is to deter a specific wrongdoer from repeating the act and to prevent potential wrongdoers from committing a similar act. If murderers are executed, it is obvious that they will not be able to harm anyone else, so specific deterrence is not an issue; rather, the issue is about general deterrence. It is also obvious that the threat of the death penalty fails to deter every time a murder is committed, and we can easily document the number of these failures. On the other hand, it is just as evident that we cannot count the times the

TABLE 16.1	Methods of Execution in the United States by State	
Method	**Number of Executions Since 1976 as of October 2017**	**Jurisdictions Authorizing the Method**
Lethal injection	1,288 executed	Alabama, Arizona, Arkansas, California, Colorado, Connecticut*, Delaware, Florida, Georgia, Idaho, Indiana, Kansas, Kentucky, Louisiana, Maryland, Mississippi, Missouri, Montana, Nebraska, Nevada, New Hampshire, New Mexico*, North Carolina, Ohio, Oklahoma, Oregon, Pennsylvania, South Carolina, South Dakota, Tennessee, Texas, Utah, Virginia, Washington, Wyoming, U.S. Military, U.S. Government (New Mexico abolished the death penalty in 2009, and Connecticut abolished it in 2012. However, the laws were not retroactive, leaving 2 and 11 people, respectively, on death row. Maryland abolished its death penalty in 2013.)
Electrocution	158 executed	Alabama, Arkansas, Florida, Kentucky, Oklahoma, South Carolina, Tennessee, Virginia (All have lethal injection as the primary method)
Gas chamber	11 executed	Arizona, California, Missouri, Wyoming (All have lethal injection as the primary method)
Hanging	3 executed	New Hampshire, Washington (Both have lethal injection as the primary method)
Firing squad	3 executed	Oklahoma, Utah (Both have lethal injection as the primary method. Utah no longer offers the firing squad but allows it for inmates who chose it prior to its elimination. Oklahoma offers the firing squad only if lethal injection and electrocution are found unconstitutional.)

Source: Adapted from Death Penalty Information Center (2017b).

death penalty threat may have succeeded because we cannot count non-events. That is, we cannot know how many (if any) people who might otherwise have committed murder did not do so for fear of losing their own lives. The question thus becomes, "Will the presence of the death penalty deter some unknown number of individuals from committing murder?" The question does not apply to all murders; it applies only to the heinous kinds of murder for which the death penalty is an option.

The deterrence argument generates an enormous amount of heat by those who state "conclusively" (mostly economists) that it deters and those who state just as "conclusively" that it does not (mostly criminologists and sociologists). Radelet and Lacock (2009) polled 77 leading criminologists, asking them whether they believed that the death penalty is a deterrent to further murder; fully 88.2% agreed or strongly agreed that it was not a deterrent, 6% replied that they were "not sure," and the remainder believed that it was a deterrent. We are not aware of any surveys of economists on this issue, but according to Shepherd (2005), while "all modern studies that use panel data [comprehensive data from all 50 states and/or across time periods] find a deterrent effect, . . . in contrast to economics studies, most of the sociological studies find no deterrence" (pp. 214–218).

Bushway and Reuter (2008) told us, "Economists and criminologists have actively butted heads over the topic of deterrence almost since economists began studying the topic [and] have clashed heatedly over empirical research on the death penalty since the 1970s" (pp. 390–391). The different discipline ideologies, training, and theoretical assumptions play a huge part in the argument. Economists assume a human nature that is rational and self-serving (the view of the classical scholars discussed in Chapter 1); that

PHOTO 16.2: The execution chamber in the Walls Unit in Huntsville, Texas. Texas has executed more than 460 inmates since the death penalty was reinstated in 1982.

is, humans respond to incentives and disincentives to maximize their pleasure and to minimize their pain. The deterrent effect of punishment is thus almost taken for granted by economists. On the other hand, most criminologists are sociologically trained (Cooper, Walsh, & Ellis, 2010) and thus may tend to be either agnostic about human nature or deny that such a thing exists.

Some criminologists and sociologists argue that capital punishment has a **brutalizing effect** rather than a deterrent effect. That is, executions are perceived by some as saying that it is acceptable to kill people who have offended us, and that a segment of those who perceive it this way will act on that perception, and thus executions increase the number of homicides. Once again, economists disagree: "The brutalization idea is not one that economists have given much credence" (Cameron, 1994, p. 206). Most (81.2%) of the anti-death criminologists surveyed by Radelet and Lacock (2009) joined economists on this issue, either disagreeing or strongly disagreeing that the death penalty has a brutalizing effect.

Shepherd (2005) found evidence for both deterrent and brutalizing effects of capital punishment, depending on the number of executions. Shepherd's model was based on 3,054 counties in states with capital punishment and covered the years 1977 through 1996. She found a threshold effect, whereby states with a deterrent effect (5 states) had an average of 32 executions over the time period, states with no effect (25 states) had an average of 6.7 executions, and states with a brutalization effect (6 states) had an average of 8.6 executions. These effects differed across time periods, but there was an overall deterrent effect of 4.5 fewer murders per execution in her study.

These contradictory opinions and research findings are confusing to those who want definitive "yes/no" answers to their questions. It is difficult to tease any deterrent effect out of the death penalty for a number of reasons. First, it is extremely rare; only about 2% to 6% (depending on jurisdiction) of murders are tried as capital cases (Berk, Li, & Hickman, 2005). Second, of that small number, only 15% of people sentenced to death since the death penalty was reinstated in 1976 have actually been executed (Nagin & Pepper, 2012). If a person is sentenced to death, the time lapse between conviction and execution increased from an average of 14.4 months during the 1950s to an average of 14.5 years in 2010 (Snell, 2011). As we have seen, the deterrent effect of punishment depends on its certainty, swiftness, and severity. While the death penalty is certainly severe, it is far from being certain or swift. Third, there are so many other variables to consider for inclusion in statistical models, and the inclusion or exclusion of any one may completely change the results (Nagin & Pepper, 2012).

These difficulties led the National Academy of Sciences to convene a subcommittee (the Committee on Deterrence and the Death Penalty [CDDP]) of criminologists, sociologists, economists, and statisticians to try to reach a conclusion. The CDDP examined the results of all credible death penalty studies up to 2011 and concluded that the evidence is ambiguous. The committee's conclusion reads as follows:

> The committee concludes that research to date on the effect of capital punishment on homicide is not informative about whether capital punishment decreases, increases, or has no effect on homicide rates. Therefore, the committee

Brutalizing effect:
The assumption that executions, rather than deterring homicides, actually increase homicides following the executions.

of the U.S. population, blacks are underrepresented based on their arrests and convictions for murder" (Robinson, 2008, p. 191).

There seems to be an emerging consensus that although African Americans are executed disproportionately more often in relation to their numbers in the general population, whites are disproportionately more likely to both receive a death sentence and be executed compared with the number of death-eligible homicides they commit. An early post-*Furman* study (Kleck, 1981) found that from 1930 onward in the northern states, whites were more likely to receive the death penalty, and that the discrimination evidenced against blacks in death penalty cases during earlier years in the South disappeared during later years. Greenfeld and Hinners (1985) looked at 1,405 prisoners under sentence of death and found that 15.8 per 1,000 white murderers were sentenced to death versus 11.6 per 1,000 black murderers. A large study by Gross and Mauro (1989) looked at death sentences in more than 14,000 cases and found that whites received a death sentence in 26.5% of the cases involving felony circumstances and in 1.4% of the cases with non-felony circumstances. On the other hand, 17.2% of blacks convicted in felony

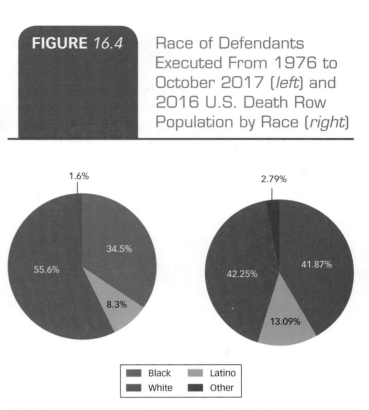

FIGURE *16.4* Race of Defendants Executed From 1976 to October 2017 (*left*) and 2016 U.S. Death Row Population by Race (*right*)

Source: Death Penalty Information Center (2017a).

circumstances and 0.4% convicted in non-felony circumstances received a death sentence (calculated by McAdams [1998] from Gross & Mauro's [1989] data). A U.S. Department of Justice (2001) study of federal death-eligible cases reached a similar conclusion:

> United States Attorneys recommended the death penalty in smaller proportions of cases involving Black or Hispanic defendants than in those involving White defendants; the Attorney General's capital case review committee likewise recommended the death penalty in smaller proportions of cases involving Black or Hispanic defendants. . . . In the cases considered by the Attorney General, the Attorney General decided to seek the death penalty for 38% of the White defendants, 25% of the Black defendants, and 20% of the Hispanic defendants.

Blume, Eisenberg, and Wells (2004) looked at data from the 31 states that sentenced 10 or more individuals to death from 1977 through 1999 (5,953 death sentences) and compared the proportion of blacks convicted of murder in each state with the proportion of black inmates on death row. In California, Nevada, and Utah, the percentages of murders committed by blacks were 33.8%, 30.2%, and 8.6%, and the percentages of blacks on death row in these states were 35.3%, 33.1%, and 10.5%, respectively. African Americans were thus overrepresented by narrow margins in these three states but were substantially underrepresented in the 28 other states. They were most underrepresented in Tennessee, Mississippi, and Missouri. The percentages of murders committed by African Americans in those states were 60.4%, 77.7%, and 62.6%, and the percentages of blacks on death row in those states were 33.3%, 59.0%, and 44.1%, respectively.

THE ISSUE OF VICTIM'S RACE

Recall that the concern in the *McCleskey* case was not discrimination against black defendants but rather discrimination against black victims (or in favor of white victims).

IN FOCUS 16.1

Karl Marx on Capital Punishment and Brutalization

Most contemporary criminologists might not put much stock in the brutalization effect hypothesis, but one of the founders of modern sociology, Karl Marx, did. Marx earned his keep for a while as a journalist. He wrote the article below for the *New York Daily Tribune* on February 17–18, 1853:

It has often been remarked that in this country a public execution is generally followed closely by instances of death by hanging, either suicidal or accidental, in consequence of the powerful effect which the execution of a noted criminal produces upon a morbid and unmatured mind.

Of the several cases which are alleged by *The Times* in illustration of this remark, one is that of a lunatic at Sheffield, who, after talking with other lunatics respecting the execution of Barbour, put an end to his existence by hanging himself. Another case is that of a boy of 14 years, who also hung himself.

The doctrine to which the enumeration of these facts was intended to give its support, is one which no reasonable man would be likely to guess, it being no less than a direct apotheosis of the hangman, while capital punishment is extolled as the ultima ratio of society. This is done in a leading article of the "leading journal." *The Morning Advertiser,* in some very bitter but just strictures on the hanging predilections and bloody logic of *The Times,* has the following interesting data on 43 days of the year 1849:

Executions of Murders and Suicides	
Millan	March 20
Hannah Sandles	March 22
M. G. Newton	March 22
Pulley	March 26
J. G. Gleeson—4 murders at Liverpool	March 27
Smith	March 27
Murder and suicide at Leicester	April 2
Howe	March 31
Poisoning at Bath	April 7

W. Bailey	April 8
Landick	April 9
J. Ward murders his mother	April 13
Sarah Thomas	April 13
Yardley	April 14
Doxey, parricide	April 14
J. Bailey kills his two children and himself	April 17
J. Griffiths	April 18
Charles Overton	April 18
J. Rush	April 21
Daniel Holmsden	May 2

This table, as *The Times* concedes, shows not only suicides, but also murders of the most atrocious kind, following closely upon the execution of criminals. It is astonishing that the article in question does not even produce a single argument or pretext for indulging in the savage theory therein propounded; and it would be very difficult, if not altogether impossible, to establish any principle upon which the justice or expediency of capital punishment could be founded, in a society glorying in its civilization. Punishment in general has been defended as a means either of ameliorating or intimidating. Now what right have you to punish me for the amelioration or intimidation of others? And besides, there is history—there is such a thing as statistics—which prove with the most complete evidence that since Cain the world has neither been intimidated nor ameliorated by punishment. Quite the contrary. From the point of view of abstract right, there is only one theory of punishment which recognizes human dignity in the abstract, and that is the theory of Kant, especially in the more rigid formula given to it by Hegel. Hegel says:

"Punishment is the right of the criminal. It is an act of his own will. The violation of right has been proclaimed by the criminal as his own right. His crime is the negation of right. Punishment is the negation of this negation, and consequently an affirmation of right, solicited and forced upon the criminal by himself."

With white defendants being sentenced to death and executed more often than black defendants, the race issue with regard to the death penalty has largely become "victim centered"; that is, the focus has moved from bias against black *defendants* to bias against black *victims.*

To address this bias issue, we first need to realize that only a very small fraction of murders are committed in a fashion that makes perpetrators eligible for the death penalty. For a murder to be eligible for the death penalty, it must satisfy a number of elements, including such things as being premeditated and purposeful, being particularly brutal, involving multiple victims, being committed during the commission of some other felony such as robbery or rape, or involving the killing of a law enforcement officer during the commission of his or her duties. A prior homicide conviction is also highly relevant.

Nearly all studies do show that before controlling for aggravating and mitigating factors, killers of whites (regardless of the race of the killer) are more likely to receive the death penalty than killers of blacks. To assess the issue of victim race in federal cases, the National Institute of Justice commissioned three different studies by three independent teams. In a 209-page report examining these findings, Klein, Berk, and Hickman (2006) showed that, without controlling for case characteristics, the death penalty is more likely when victims are white. However, racial disparities disappeared in all three studies when adjustments were made for the heinousness of the crimes. In other words, after controlling for all aggravating and mitigating factors that influence sentencing, there was no evidence of a race effect regardless of whether they were examining just the race of the victim, the race of the offender, or the interaction between victim's and defendant's race.

The case characteristics that make victim race disparities disappear were analyzed from the Georgia data used in *McCleskey v. Kemp* (1987) by statistician Joseph Katz. Katz (2005) found 141 cases that involved a white victim and a black perpetrator (W/B) among the sample of 1,082 homicide defendants. In 67.1% of W/B cases, the victim was killed during the course of a robbery compared with 7.4% in black victim cases, and 70.6% of the time the victim was a stranger compared with 9.6% in black victim cases. Katz also indicated that "white victim homicides show a greater percentage of mutilations, execution style murders, tortures, and beaten victims, features which generally aggravate homicide and increase the likelihood of a death sentence" (p. 405).

Just as there are contradictory findings about the deterrence issue among different groups of scholars, there are also contradictions on this issue. For instance, criminologists Paternoster and Brame (2003) looked at 1,130 death-eligible homicide cases in Maryland and found no race-of-defendant bias but found significant race-of-victim effects. In cases where the offender was black and the victim was white, they found that defendants were about 3.5 times more likely than any other offender/victim pairing to receive a death sentence. Statisticians Berk et al. (2005) looked at *the exact same data* and arrived at the opposite conclusion: "When race surfaces, cases with a black defendant and white victim or 'other' racial combinations are *less* likely to have death sentences imposed" (p. 381). With the death penalty being such an emotional issue about which many people have strong views, it may be wise to heed Scheidegger (2012): "Many academics who do research on the death penalty reliably produce results that favor one side, raising a suspicion of partisan bias" (p. 161).

The most recent study at the time of this writing (Sharma, Scheb, Houston, & Wagers, 2013) looked at all first-degree murder convictions in Tennessee from 1976 to 2007. Prosecutors sought the death penalty for 76% of white defendants and 62.6% of black defendants, and 37.3% of white defendants for whom the death penalty was sought received it versus 23.6% of black defendants. Prosecutors sought the death penalty in 64% of the cases where the victim was white and in 33% of the cases where the victim was black. When controlling for a variety of aggravating and mitigating factors, as well as demographic and evidentiary variables, they found that the killing of a law enforcement officer, prior violent offenses, and evidentiary (scientific, co-perpetrator testimony, confession, and strong eyewitness testimony) variables were by far the strongest predictors of receiving a death sentence. Victim's race did not play any significant independent part, but victim's sex (female) did. The racial makeup of the crime (black offender/white victim; white offender/white victim, etc.) had no significant independent effect, but race of the defendant did, with whites being 2.26 times more likely to receive the death penalty than blacks over the 30-year period.

••• WOMEN AND THE DEATH PENALTY

Both women and men commit murder, but women have constituted only about 2% of persons executed in the United States since the inception of capital punishment (Robinson, 2008). As of October 1, 2016, there were 54 women on death row, or 1.86% of the total death row population of 2,902 persons. Women have accounted for only 16 (0.9%) of persons (12 white and 4 black) actually executed since 1976 (DPIC, 2017a, 2017b). According to the U.S. Census, women constituted 53% of the U.S. population in 2012, which means that they have been, and are, massively underrepresented as persons executed or on death row.

Is this indicative of pro-female bias? It would be if females committed approximately the same number of death-eligible homicides as males, but they consistently commit only about 10% of all homicides each year. Many of these homicides are committed against spouses and lovers in self-defense situations, and only rarely do we find women committing the heinous kinds of murders that draw down the death penalty (Walsh, 2011). However, Bohm (2003) estimated that 4% to 6% of women murderers would receive death sentences "if women and men were treated equally [and if] no factor other than the offense was considered" (p. 211).

THE CHIVALRY HYPOTHESIS

The most obvious extralegal factor that leads to reluctance to impose the death penalty on women vis-à-vis men is the chivalrous or paternalistic attitudes about women that tend to prevail in our society (Reza, 2005). Reza (2005) cited the example of a petition to the governor of California signed by male inmates of San Quentin prison in 1941 to prevent the execution of Juanita Spinelli, a career criminal, ex-wrestler, and knife thrower, who murdered a 19-year-old gang member she feared would inform on her. Such an execution, they wrote, would be "a blot on the reputation of the state and repulsive to the people of California because of *her sex and her status as a mother*" (p. 183, emphasis added).

Such chivalry is still in evidence today. The pending 1998 execution of Karla Faye Tucker, a rock groupie, prostitute, and drug abuser convicted in 1984 of the pickax murder of a man and a woman when she was 23, produced a spate of protests even from pro-death penalty sources. Colonel Oliver North exclaimed in opposition, "I don't think chivalry can ever be misplaced," and television personality Geraldo Rivera said, "Please don't let this happen. This is—it's very unseemly. Texas manhood, macho swagger. . . . What, are ya' going to kill a lady? Oh jeez. Why?" (as cited in Robertson, 2008, p. 205). Then there is the case of Susan Smith, who in 1994 strapped her two young sons, ages 3 years and 14 months, into their car seats and rolled the car into a lake, drowning them both. Smith was attempting to reunite with her lover, who objected to the presence of her children. Smith was sentenced to life rather than death for her cold-blooded killings because, according to Reza (2005), she was viewed by the jury as a jilted victim "and loving mother with severe emotional issues" (p. 188).

THE EVIL WOMAN HYPOTHESIS

But chivalry does not always prevail because, as we have seen, 13 women have been executed since 1976. To account for these, we have the "evil woman" counterpart to the chivalry hypothesis. Both Tucker and Smith were fairly good-looking young women who came across to television audiences as matching the stereotype of femininity and "sweetness" despite having committed heinous acts. The evil woman hypothesis avers that females who defy traditional gender roles by not enacting a feminine identity invite the wrath of the male-dominated criminal justice system (Reza, 2005). Such women tend to be unattractive and "unladylike" in their general demeanor and very much out of their proscribed gender roles by acting "manly" and being "man hating." Two women executed since 1976—Wanda Jean Allen and Aileen Wuornos—fit this description and were lesbians. Juanita Spinelli, for whose life her fellow male inmates begged earnestly, deviated from gender role expectations in many ways. Clinton Duffy, warden of the prison housing Spinelli, called her the "coldest, hardest character, male or female" and added that she was "a hag, evil as a witch, horrible to look at" (as cited in Shatz & Shatz, 2011, p. 2).

PHOTO 16.3: Juanita Spinelli was the first woman executed at the San Quentin Prison gas chamber on November 21, 1941. She and her gang committed a robbery–murder, and then she helped murder one of the gang members they were afraid would tell others about the crime.

If female murderers on the whole are treated more leniently on the basis of their sex, then men are being discriminated against in a system that claims fairness and neutrality. Victor Streib, a strong opponent of the death penalty, warned that if women want to be treated as men's equals, then if men are eligible for the death penalty, women should be, too: "Otherwise, women are lumped with juveniles and the mentally retarded as not fully responsible human beings" (Streib, 2003a, p. 322). Similarly, Elizabeth Reza opined,

> When women commit similar [death-eligible] crimes, we should not withhold capital punishment simply because the murderer is a mother, sister, or wife. . . . The American judicial system must equalize the capital punishment system so that all, regardless of gender, are punished in a manner society and the legal system has deemed appropriate to impose on those who callously take the lives of others.
>
> For those who believe in the death penalty, the only answer to the sentencing equity issue is to execute more women convicted of death-eligible murders until they attain parity with men convicted of similar crimes who are executed or to reduce the number of men executed. For those who oppose the death penalty, the only answer to the issue is to execute no one. (Reza, 2005, p. 211)

••• THE DEATH PENALTY AND MENTAL DISABILITY

Mental disability is "a lifelong condition of impaired or incomplete mental development. According to the most widely used definition of mental retardation, it is characterized by three criteria: significantly subaverage intellectual functioning; concurrent and related limitations in two or more adaptive skill areas; and manifestation before age 18" (Mandery, 2005, p. 352). A subaverage level of intellectual functioning is defined as an IQ of 70 or below, a score that puts an individual

ETHICAL ISSUE ?

What Would You Do?

You are an assistant prosecutor who favors the death penalty. You have been assigned the case of John Franks, who has admitted molesting and killing at least five girls ranging in age between 4 and 12. The community is outraged and demands the death penalty. The problem is that Franks's IQ averaged over three tests while in school is 68, and it is constitutionally impermissible to execute anyone with an IQ lower than 70. You could argue that IQ scores are subject to a 5-point margin of error, and so John's "true" IQ could be 73 (it could just as easily be 63). Will you seek the death penalty for Franks's heinous crimes in accordance with your beliefs and with public demand based on this flimsy point, or would you select a non–death penalty option? What are the ethical issues involved?

at the bottom 2% of the general population. An 18-year-old with an IQ of 70, for instance, is functioning at the mental level of a child 12 to 13 years old. This does not mean that the mentally disabled cannot be held responsible for their actions; it only means that they should be held to a lower level of culpability than persons operating at higher intellectual levels.

In 1979, paroled rapist Johnny Penry was sentenced to death for a brutal rape and murder in Texas. Penry appealed to the Supreme Court on Eighth Amendment grounds that it is cruel and unusual to execute a mentally disabled person. Penry claimed that the jury was not instructed that it could consider his low IQ (between 50 and 63) as mitigating evidence against imposing the death penalty. The Supreme Court held in *Penry v. Lynaugh* (1989) that the jury should have been instructed it could consider mental retardation a mitigating factor when deciding Penry's sentence, but imposition of the death penalty on a mentally retarded defendant is not per se a violation of the Eighth Amendment.

However, in 2008 Penry's sentence was commuted to life imprisonment in light of *Atkins v. Virginia* (2002).

In *Atkins v. Virginia* (2002), the Supreme Court overruled itself with regard to executing the mentally disabled. The Court concluded that there was a national consensus (public opinion again) against executing the mentally disabled and that because they are less capable of evaluating the consequences of their crimes, they are less culpable than the average offender. The Court also noted that mentally disabled individuals are more prone to confess to crimes they did not commit and therefore are more prone to wrongful execution. Six of the justices concluded that the overwhelming disapproval of the world community must be considered a relevant factor in the Court's deliberations regarding the constitutionality of imposing capital punishment on the mentally disabled.

••• THE DEATH PENALTY AND MENTAL ILLNESS

Mental illness and mental disability are two different conditions. It is constitutionally impermissible to execute the mentally disabled but permissible to execute the mentally ill. This is because mental retardation is permanent and unalterable, but mental illness is not (in many cases), and while mental disability cannot be faked (because there is a long history documenting each case from early childhood), mental illness can. By adhering to a correctly prescribed medical regimen, most mentally ill individuals can be restored to sanity and lead meaningful lives.

The execution of the "presently insane" is not permitted under the U.S. Constitution. The phrase "presently insane" is not the same as saying "insane at the time of the crime." In earlier times, if a person was insane "at the time of the crime," that person would also be insane "presently" because there was no method of restoring a person to sanity. With a number of effective antipsychotic medications available today, new Eighth Amendment and due process issues have arisen. The primary legal issues the courts need to resolve with both mental deficiency and mental illness are the following: (a) Is this person competent to stand trial? (b) Did this person at the time of the crime have the requisite ability to form *mens rea* (guilty mind)? (c) Does this person's mental condition warrant a more lenient sentence than would normally attach to this crime? (Dillard, 2012).

Although not a death penalty case, the Supreme Court ruled in *Jackson v. Indiana* (1972) that it is constitutionally impermissible to hold a defendant in custody indefinitely based on his or her incompetence to stand trial. It also ruled that a defendant must either be civilly committed (committed by a non-criminal court) or released from criminal detention. This decision forced the states to undertake efforts to restore competency at a time when effective psychotropic drugs were becoming available.

The restoration of sanity was an issue in *Ford v. Wainwright* (1986). Career criminal Alvin Ford had been sentenced to death for the cold-blooded execution of a wounded police officer responding to a robbery being committed by Ford. There were no competency issues raised during Ford's trial, but he later claimed to have descended into insanity while on death row. Although prosecutors viewed Ford's claim of insanity to be a convenient ploy used just as his appeals were running out, three of four psychiatrists who examined him concluded that he was psychotic (Mello, 2007). In *Ford*, the U.S. Supreme Court held that the Eighth Amendment prohibits execution of the insane. The Court also ruled that Ford would still need to prove that he was mentally ill (insanity is an affirmative defense in which the burden of proof lies with the defendant) (Mello, 2007). Ford died of natural causes in 1991, 28 years after his crime.

In *Ford*, the Supreme Court ruled that society's retributive goals are served only if persons are aware of the punishment they are about to suffer and why they will suffer it. In *Panetti v. Quarterman* (2007), the Court was again confronted with the issue of the execution of the mentally ill. Panetti, who killed his mother-in-law and father-in-law in 1992, had a long history of mental illness for which he was taking medication. Despite his undisputed mental illness and claim of mental incompetence, he was found competent to stand trial and to waive legal counsel (he defended himself). While the Court recognized that the Eighth Amendment forbids the execution of the insane, it declined to overturn Panetti's death sentence or to offer guidance for setting up standards for determining mental competence beyond what it called the "rational understanding" test. This test goes beyond the "mere awareness" standard for sanity set in *Ford*. "Rational understanding" essentially means that the condemned must have a sane, logical, and coherent grasp of why he or she is being executed in order to show the requisite competence to be executed (Sewell, 2010). The difference between the two standards is that while one might be fully aware that one is going to be executed ("mere awareness"), he or she might lack a "rational understanding" of why. For instance, such a person may believe that he or she is being executed because of religious or political views rather than because of a heinous murder. As of October 2017, Panetti was still on death row in Texas.

The law on competency and execution is still murky and in need of further clarification, but currently it boils down to the fact that condemned individuals can be executed as long as they are mentally coherent enough to know they are about to die and to rationally understand the reason why. If someone is deemed currently incompetent to be executed, that person can be rendered competent with medication. The issue then becomes whether the state can forcibly administer antipsychotic drugs to insane inmates facing execution. Neither *Ford* nor *Panetti* touched on this issue, although in

ETHICAL ISSUE

What Would You Do?

You are a prison physician with no strong beliefs for or against the death penalty. Justin Williams, who is on death row in your prison, is a schizophrenic on medication. You need to declare Justin sane enough to be executed, and although you now believe that he is, you start feeling like a farmer fattening up his turkeys for the Thanksgiving slaughter. You can do your legal and medical duty and continue to medicate Justin. You can lie to prison officials about his insanity, or you can slowly reduce his medication until his insanity again becomes apparent to everyone, and thus you would have no need to lie. Which option do you think is the ethical one, if any?

COMPARATIVE CORRECTIONS

The Death Penalty in China and Saudi Arabia

Both China and Saudi Arabia boast low crime rates relative to the United States, the United Kingdom, and France (France and the United Kingdom do not have the death penalty). Perhaps one of the reasons we see few chronic criminals in China and Saudi Arabia is their frequent use of the death penalty. Both countries apply the death penalty to numerous crimes other than murder.

China

China is the world's leader in the number of executions it performs each year. The death penalty may be applied for 55 different offenses (down from 68 prior to 2011), including murder, rape, economic crimes committed by high-level officials, counterrevolutionary offenses, and hooliganism (Liu et al., 2012). "Hooliganism" was struck from the statutes in 2011 but formerly consisted of a grab bag of offenses such as gang fights and indecent exposure.

According to the Chinese human rights organization Dui Hua (2013), there were 3,000 executions in China in 2012, but because the actual number is a state secret, it could be many more. The 3,000 figure is still nearly 70 times more executions than occurred in the United States (43) in the same year in absolute terms and 18 times greater in proportional terms (DPIC, 2013). Amnesty International (2013) reported,

> Thousands of people were executed in China in 2011, more than the rest of the world put together. Figures on the death penalty are a state secret. Amnesty International has stopped publishing figures it collects from public sources in China as these are likely to grossly underestimate the true number.

There are two types of death sentence: immediate and delayed. A delayed sentence is a 2-year suspension of sentence during which defendants must show that they are reformed. If a person is considered rehabilitated, the sentence is usually changed to a long period of incarceration; if not, he or she is executed. An immediate sentence is carried out within 7 days of imposition of the penalty. Such a sentence is imposed when, in the court's opinion, the defendant is beyond rehabilitation. Execution is by a single shot at the base of the skull or, more recently, by lethal injection, and the condemned person's family is informed of the execution only after the fact (Dui Hua, 2013). China carries out these executions in specially equipped mobile death vans that move from jurisdiction to jurisdiction and often "harvest" valuable body parts (kidneys, corneas, etc.) from the executed persons. The Northwestern Law Center for International Human Rights (2011) claimed that 65% of organ transplants originating from China are from executed prisoners.

Saudi Arabia

Unlike other legal systems that categorize the seriousness of crimes and the punishments they entail by the severity of the damage they cause to the victim and/or to society, Saudi law characterizes offenses by the types of punishment they engender. If a punishment is prescribed by the Koran, it tends to be more severe than if it is not, regardless of the seriousness of the crime as Westerners might view it. A publication called *Information Pack for British Prisoners in Saudi Arabia*, which the British embassy in Saudi Arabia issues to British nationals arrested there, provides a frightening picture of the punishment individuals may expect if convicted:

> The Saudi courts impose a number of severe physical punishments. The death penalty can be imposed for a wide range of offences including murder, rape, armed robbery, repeated drug use, apostasy, adultery, witchcraft and sorcery and can be carried out by beheading with a sword, stoning or firing squad, followed by crucifixion. (British Foreign Office, 2013, p. 9)

The crimes mentioned above are *hudud* crimes, the most serious crimes in Islamic law. Oddly, murder is not a hudud crime. It is a *qisas* crime, which means "equal harm" or "retaliation" and in principle means an eye for an eye and a tooth for a tooth. Qisas crimes are crimes against individuals rather than against God. Thus, although the death penalty is prescribed for murder (equal harm), the crime may be forgiven in exchange for *diyya* ("blood money") paid to the victim's survivors. Saudi Arabia recently raised the diyya for killing a Muslim male to 300,000 riyals (about $80,000) for accidental deaths and 400,000 riyals ($106,666) for purposeful murder. Because a woman's worth is considered half of a man's worth, the diyya for killing a Muslim woman is one-half that for killing a Muslim man.

Saudi Arabia shares China's more frequent use of the death penalty. Saudi Arabia "officially" executed 82 people (it is suspected that there are many secret executions also) in 2012—a rate of 3.15 per 1 million inhabitants (Amnesty International, 2013). To put this in perspective, the United States executed 43 in 2012—a rate of 0.139 per 1 million. Thus, Saudi Arabia's rate of execution is at least 23 times higher than the U.S. rate. Alahmed (2013) reported,

Hundreds of people are executed in Saudi Arabia every year—because executions are carried out in secret, no one knows the real numbers. In 2007, the newspaper *Arab News* reported that 400 people remained on death row in the province of Makka alone. There are 12 other regions in the kingdom, so the total number of people awaiting execution could easily reach several thousand.

Washington v. Harper (1990) the Supreme Court ruled that in a prison environment an inmate may be involuntarily medicated "if the inmate is dangerous to himself or others, and the treatment is in the inmate's medical interest" (Sewell, 2010, p. 1292). To the extent that medication is voluntary, the insane on death row are confronted with a horrible choice: madness or execution. To the extent that it is not voluntary, prison physicians are presented with an ethical dilemma in that if they medicate someone "in the inmate's medical interests," they are simultaneously rendering the person "sane enough" for execution.

••• THE INNOCENCE REVOLUTION

The huge advances made by the genomic and brain sciences over the past 3 decades have revolutionized death penalty discourse in the United States. Abolitionist arguments used to center on such things as legalities, morality, fairness, financial cost, and deterrence issues. While these arguments are still forcefully made, the new and more powerful issue that now dominates abolitionist arguments is innocence. These arguments appear to have penetrated and influenced public opinion far more than other arguments because guilt and innocence have substance and are far more easily grasped than legal, statistical, and philosophical arguments. As Marshall (2004) stated, "Unlike other challenges to the fairness of capital proceedings, which have failed to stimulate widespread public outrage, evidence of the system's propensity to factual error has the power to open closed minds and trigger reexamination of the costs and benefits of capital punishment" (p. 579). Indeed, evidence of possible actual innocence was central in the decision not to reinstate the death penalty in New York in 2004, the repeal of the death penalty in New Mexico in 2009, and Governor George Ryan's clearing of Illinois' death row shortly before leaving office in 2003 (Aronson & Cole, 2009).

The Innocence Project is an organization founded in 1992 by lawyers Barry Scheck and Peter Neufeld and has taken advantage of modern science to provide scientific and legal expertise for cases (mostly sexual assault cases) in which false convictions may have occurred. The innocence movement received a large boost when President George W. Bush signed the Justice For All Act into law in 2004. This act includes a subsection called the Innocence Protection Act, granting federal inmates the right to petition a federal court for DNA testing to support a claim of innocence. The act provides for funding to encourage states to take measures to preserve organic evidence and to make DNA testing available to convicts claiming innocence. The law also requires states that are provided funding to certify the existence of government experts to monitor crime laboratories where allegations of misconduct and/or negligence have been made. The Innocence Project's website provides a list of all DNA exonerations in the United States; as of December 2012, it included 305 cases, 18 of which were death penalty cases (Innocence

Project, 2013). In nearly 50% of DNA exoneration cases, the actual perpetrator was identified by DNA; thus, this technology has been used to convict the guilty as well as to exonerate the innocent.

SOME CONCERNS WITH DNA TECHNOLOGY

A problem confronting death penalty opponents is that despite all the celebrations surrounding the DNA exonerations of numerous inmates (death row and otherwise), it may breathe new life into arguments supporting the death penalty. That is, if the fear of executing an innocent person is a major argument against the use of the death penalty, and if the "certainty of DNA" is the tool that prevents it, then pro–death penalty advocates can now rely on that same "certainty" and say that we have removed the major obstacle (the possibility of executing the innocent) and can move forward with a more just death penalty. Thus, touting DNA as some sort of truth device is a double-edged sword—if it can be used to exonerate the innocent with apparent certainty, it can be used to condemn the guilty with the same apparent certainty. This kind of "certainty" can provide what advocates of the death penalty might describe as a "foolproof" death penalty. This of course upsets those who oppose the death penalty on moral grounds regardless of certainty of guilt.

As wonderful as modern genetic and neuroscience technology is, the evidence supplied by it should not be accepted uncritically. There is an old saying that "statistics don't lie, but liars lie with statistics." Similarly, we can say that "DNA doesn't lie, but people can (wittingly or unwittingly) lie with DNA." DNA samples must be meticulously handled so as not to become contaminated, and there are sometimes problems in interpreting lab results as well as problems beyond technical difficulties involving human errors, incompetence, and downright fraud.

A number of police labs have been accused and found guilty of falsifying and fabricating DNA. Others have been shown to be incompetent in their use of the technology and/or in interpreting results and to have cross-contaminated and mislabeled sample DNA (Aronson & Cole, 2009). Many of these things are to be expected when dealing with complicated technical matters, and humans are expected to make errors, take shortcuts, and even fudge the data to conform to the desired conclusion. In a police lab, the "desired conclusion" is of course a match between the evidence DNA and the accused's DNA. Even without a biasing context, experts come to different conclusions. For instance, Dror and Hampikian (2011) presented "mixed" DNA evidence (DNA from two or more sources) from a sexual assault case to 17 different DNA analysts, omitting the biasing contextual criminal case information. Dror and Hampikian found that only 1 of the 17 reached the same conclusion ("defendant cannot be excluded") as the original analysts in the criminal case, while 12 concluded "exclude" and 4 concluded "inconclusive." Out-and-out fraud is a rarity, but the fact that it happens and the fact that experts often disagree in their interpretations of DNA evidence should be enough to stop us from thinking about DNA as the holy grail of guilt and innocence. However, the consequences of disregarding DNA evidence of someone's innocence are too far-reaching to doubt it, although a healthy skepticism in terms of it supplying the sole evidence of someone's guilt is a good thing.

Neuroimaging is typically used as evidence for mitigating punishment rather than exoneration. The workhorse of neuroimaging is **functional magnetic resonance imaging (fMRI)**. fMRI scans compare blood flow in the brain as it uses the oxygen to energize itself. Data from fMRI testing are based on aggregating these responses from a number of individuals. Because fMRI results emerge from data averaged over a group of subjects, they are problematic when applied to specific individuals. As O. Jones and Shen (2012) put it, "Just because a particular pattern of neural activity is associated, on average at the group level, with impaired decision-making, it does not necessarily follow that a defendant before the court whose brain scans produce the same neural patterns necessarily has a cognitive deficit" (p. 356).

Functional magnetic resonance imaging (fMRI): The workhorse of neuroimaging used to assess the functioning of a person's brain while engaged in some task.

PERSPECTIVE FROM A PRACTITIONER

Ginny Hatch, Investigator for Idaho Innocence Project

Position: Investigator for Idaho Innocence Project, Lecturer in Department of Criminal Justice at Boise State University

Location: Boise, Idaho

Education: Master of arts in criminal justice, Boise State University

How long have you been working with the Innocence Project?

7-plus years.

What are your primary duties and responsibilities with the Innocence Project?

Investigate claims of innocence and wrongful conviction cases.

In general, what does a typical day working with the Innocence Project look like?

When you work for the Innocence Project, there are no "typical days." Each day is different and presents new challenges. This type of work is unique because I investigate cases that have already been investigated and processed through the criminal justice system. The Innocence Project typically takes cases during the post-conviction phase(s), after most or all of the appeals have been exhausted. This can be particularly frustrating because I am not in control of what has happened in the past and oftentimes the previous professionals presiding over the case (prosecution and/or defense) are responsible for the errors that have led to the wrongful conviction.

In the early phases of investigation, I spend quite a bit of time reading and abstracting important documents associated with the case (trial transcripts, appellate briefs and decisions, discovery, etc.). If my investigation leads me to believe that someone is truly innocent, I must try to figure out how the conviction resulted. In doing so, I spend a lot of time rereading the case file. After I have a working knowledge of a case, I look for any discrepancies among or between witnesses. If inconsistencies are found, they are followed up on accordingly. I often interview witnesses that testified during trial as well as witnesses that have not yet been interviewed by the original investigators. Witnesses sometimes change their testimony, and they do so for a variety of reasons. It is my job to listen to their story and document it. Sometimes I learn of things that are helpful to my case and sometimes not, but at the end of the day I am only interested in the truth.

There are many factors that lead to wrongful convictions, including problems with eyewitness identification, false confessions, government misconduct, bad science, snitches/informants, and bad lawyers. Luckily, there is an abundance of academic literature on these issues to aid investigators and legal professionals in wrongful conviction cases. This research helps me to understand how an innocent person can be convicted of a crime that he or she did not commit. We often enlist the help of expert witnesses to explain to the court what went wrong in a particular case. After all of the investigative work is completed, what really matters is the battle that takes place in the courtroom—where justice is meted out! If I have learned nothing else from working with the Innocence Project, it is that our justice system is not infallible and we must always fight injustice of any measure.

What would be your advice to someone either wishing to study or now studying criminal justice to become a practitioner in this career field?

Innocence Project work requires profound dedication, a passion for justice, and an inordinate amount of patience. The job is complex and can almost always be described as an uphill battle. It is extremely difficult to prove a person's innocence after he or she has been found guilty in our criminal justice system. In doing so, you are essentially admitting that our justice system makes mistakes, and no one likes to think that innocent people may be incarcerated.

I strongly recommend that students who are interested in working as an investigator complete an internship for the organization or agency of interest to them. Most agencies are looking for experience in their field, so every bit helps. It is beneficial to have a bachelor's degree in criminal justice, but this is certainly not required. The type of educational background needed for an investigator position really depends on the type of agency one wishes to work for.

National Institute of Mental Health

PHOTO 16.4: Neuroscience researcher examining fMRI images.

SOME CONCERNS WITH NEUROIMAGING TECHNOLOGY

The neuroimaging evidence relating to which parts of the brain are activated under what conditions, and which parts are responsible for what behaviors, is both consistent and strong. But we must understand that neuroimages are maps of the terrain, not the terrain itself, and are generated mathematically (not direct pictures as in an X-ray) from numerous signals coming from the fMRI machine. They are indirect rather than direct evidence of increased neural activity because they are based on a statistical aggregate forming a correlation between a particular trait, behavior, or brain process and neurological responses in a particular area. A correlation is a trend in a given direction, and that correlational trend in brain scans is not entirely true of all brains tested and certainly not in terms of the wide variations in strength of brain responses of different people to identical stimuli.

Even given this, it is a big jump from talking about "impaired judgment" inferred from mistakes subjects make on tasks they are asked to perform in the laboratory and a brutal murder performed in the real world. Just how impaired is the defendant's brain compared with the average level of those subjects said to be impaired, and how many of these subjects similarly impaired have committed murder?

Another matter is that imaging of a defendant's brain is typically performed many years after the crime was committed. Today's brain is not yesterday's brain, and the images jurors may see in court might be vastly different from what they may have seen at the time of the crime for which the defendant is seeking mitigation. Scans of a killer's brain taken 5, 10, or 15 years after a murder may show that the person is a psychopath, but they tell us nothing about his or her state of mind when the person committed the murder, nor do they show that the person was incapable of controlling his or her behavior. Neuroimaging is vitally important in medicine and neuroscience research, but it cannot read minds, particularly mind states that occurred years prior to the scanning. Scanning tells us the probable state of the subject's mind at the time of the scan; it cannot settle matters of legal responsibility.

SUMMARY

- The majority of Americans support capital punishment, but their opinions fluctuate with the crime rate and with the availability of life without parole (LWOP).

- Because the United States stands almost alone among democracies in retaining the death penalty, the issue has generated much debate and numerous court cases questioning its constitutionality.

- A variety of methods of execution have been used in the United States, but lethal injection is used almost exclusively today in all states with the death penalty.

- The death penalty is often defended for its deterrent effect, but there is heated disagreement about whether it deters. A committee of experts who examined all death penalty studies up to 2011 concluded that we do not really know whether or not it is a deterrent.

- Seeking the death penalty for a murderer is immensely more costly than seeking LWOP, and even those given the death penalty are rarely executed.

- Historically, African Americans have been executed disproportionately not only to their numbers in the population but also to their numbers of murderers. However, today black murderers are proportionately less likely to be sentenced to death and to be executed than white murderers.

- The debate has now swung away from discrimination against black defendants to discrimination against black victims because killers (regardless of their race) of whites are more likely to receive the death penalty than killers of blacks. However, once aggravating and mitigating circumstances are taken into account, there is disagreement over whether this bias is still in evidence.

- Women have constituted only 2% of persons executed in the nation's history. They commit far fewer death-eligible murders than men, but it is estimated that if they were treated the same as men they would have constituted between 4% and 6% of those executed in the United States.

- The chivalry hypothesis has been advanced to explain why we executed fewer death-eligible female murderers than death-eligible male murderers, and the evil woman hypothesis has been advanced for females who are executed.

- It is constitutionally impermissible to execute the mentally disabled (defined as an IQ less than or equal to 70) in the United States, but it is permissible to execute the mentally ill. The reasoning is that mental disability cannot be changed or faked, while mental illness can. It is impermissible to execute the "presently mentally ill," but they can be restored to sanity with drugs and then executed.

- Advances in the genomic and brain sciences have led to an innocence revolution in death penalty discourse. DNA testing has resulted in many wrongly convicted persons being freed and the guilty being convicted. DNA is not a panacea for death penalty opponents, however, because death penalty advocates now say that with this advance we can go forth with an "error-free" death penalty.

KEY TERMS

Brutalizing effect, 354

Death Penalty Information Center, 355

Electrocution, 350

Firing squad, 350

Functional magnetic resonance imaging (fMRI), 366

Gas chamber, 350

Hanging, 349

Lethal injection, 351

DISCUSSION QUESTIONS

1. Why do you think that the United States retains the death penalty when nearly all other democracies eliminated it long ago? Should we eliminate it? Why or why not?

2. Argue your case for whether the death penalty does or does not deter.

3. If you are for capital punishment on the grounds of just deserts, do you think it is justified in financial terms? Why or why not?

4. What do you think accounts for the fact that prosecutors today seek the death penalty proportionately more often for whites than for minorities—a reversal of past practices?

5. Regardless of your stance on capital punishment, should women be treated the same as men if they commit the same crime? Why or why not.

6. Describe the reasoning behind the fact that the mentally ill may be executed but the mentally disabled may not.

7. If DNA evidence helps to reduce the possibility of executing an innocent person, can we also say that it has thereby presented us with an "error-free" death penalty?

$SAGE edge™

Review → Practice → Improve

Sharpen your skills with SAGE edge at **edge.sagepub.com/stohressentials3e**.

SAGE edge offers a robust online environment featuring an impressive array of free tools and resources for review, study, and further exploration, keeping both instructors and students on the cutting edge of teaching and learning.

FOR FURTHER EXPLORATION AND APPLICATION, TAKE A LOOK AT THE INTERACTIVE EBOOK FOR THESE PREMIUM RESOURCES:

- ▶ **Career Video 16.1** Director of IT and Electronic Security

- ▶ **SAGE News Clip 16.1** Tennessee Electric Chair

- ▶ **SAGE News Clip 16.2** Utah Firing Squad

- 📄 **Journal Article 16.1** Competing Pressures and Complex Choices
  African Americans and the Death Penalty

PRACTICE AND APPLY WHAT YOU'VE LEARNED

▶ edge.sagepub.com/stohressentials3e

CHECK YOUR COMPREHENSION ON THE STUDY SITE:

- Mobile-friendly **eFlashcards** strengthen understanding of key terms and concepts.

- Mobile-friendly practice **quizzes** allow for independent assessment by students of their mastery of course material.

- **Learning objectives** reinforce the most important material.

- Carefully selected chapter-by-chapter **video and multimedia content** enhance classroom-based explorations of key topics.

- EXCLUSIVE! Access provided to certain full-text **SAGE journal articles** that have been carefully selected for each chapter. Each article supports and expands on the concepts presented in the chapter.

$SAGE edge™

17 Corrections in the 21st Century

TEST YOUR KNOWLEDGE

Test your current knowledge about the likely future of corrections in this country by addressing the following questions. Check your answers on page 394 after reading the chapter.

1. Based on the chapters you have already read in this book, what do you think are likely to be trends in corrections over the next several years?

2. Decarceration is likely related to state budgets. (True or false)

3. Privatization of corrections leads to greater professionalism of staff. (True or false)

4. Privatization of corrections leads to more safety and security for inmates, staff, and communities. (True or false)

5. Correctional work is fully professionalized. (True or false)

6. Resource use and waste production by correctional institutions should be a serious concern for communities. (True or false)

LEARNING OBJECTIVES

- Identify the connection between punitive policies and the overuse of corrections

- Describe what decarceration is and what is causing it

- Understand why we might be entering an age of penal help and exiting a period of penal harm

- Evaluate the value of relationships and innovation in corrections

- Discuss the potential problems with privatization

CAN WE CURE CRIMINALITY?

Alex DeLarge is the product of a society in which no one takes personal responsibility for his or her actions and a culture that panders to our basest human instincts. He is the leader of a gang that is into what its members call "ultraviolence," with strong sexual undertones. Alex engages in all kinds of crime, especially sadomasochistic rape. Betrayed by his associates, he was eventually caught by police after raping and murdering a woman. Two years into his sentence for murder, Alex volunteered as a test subject for an experimental treatment based on aversion therapy. Alex was given drugs and forced to watch violent images while becoming nauseated by the drugs. After 2 weeks of "therapy," Alex became incapable of fighting back against a man who attacked him. The mere thought of violence and sex now made him retch violently. He was then released from prison as "successfully cured" in order to reduce the financial burden of imprisonment. Only when he finally freely chooses to desist from crime does he do so.

Some of you may recognize that this is the storyline of the dystopian futuristic novel *A Clockwork Orange*. The book is about efforts to "cure" criminality and its ultimate failure given that Alex reverted to his former self after the "cure" wore off. Another book (this time based on a futuristic utopian society) called *Walden Two* contains a similar theme. One of the characters in the book explains the goal of such a society: "You see, we want to do something—we want to find out what's the matter with people, why they can't live together without fighting all the time. We want to find out what people really want, what they need in order to be happy, and how they can get it without stealing it from somebody else" (Skinner, 1948/2005, p. 4). Efforts to "do something" this time were based on the principles of behaviorist psychology, principally on positive reinforcement, instead of aversion therapy.

Both books resonate with the perpetual problem of corrections—effectively identifying and treating the sources of criminality. We still need to "allot a portion of ground for a prison," as Nathaniel Hawthorne predicted in the opening vignette of Chapter 1. The financial cost of prisons is prohibitive, but we will always need them, barring some "miracle cure" awaiting us in the distant future. The great physicist Niels Bohr once said, "Prediction is very difficult, especially about the future," so we do not speculate about that here. And as Bill Clinton said in his successful campaign for the presidency, "It's the economy, stupid." Economic considerations will always drive corrections policy, as they always have driven it. We enact mandatory sentencing laws that imprison people who perhaps should not have been imprisoned when state budgets allow, and then we release prisoners early who should not have been released when state coffers are low. This generates public anger as victims' tormentors are released, and thus renewed calls to "get tough" are generated and the whole process recycles. Perhaps legalizing drugs and saving the prisons for folks like Alex is the only current solution. These are some of the things to think about as you read this last chapter.

●●● INTRODUCTION: LEARNING FROM THE PAST SO THAT WE HAVE HOPE FOR THE FUTURE

Americans have a tendency to revisit old themes, efforts, and programming every generation or so, even when such endeavors were clear failures and rejected by generations past. Perhaps it is because we are a relatively new nation and are seemingly remade as new generations of immigrants flood our shores, bringing their histories and cultures that do not include memories of past reform efforts made in this country. Perhaps we keep retrying old endeavors because of the media influence that reduces very complex problems to a brief and simplistic message, and as a consequence we do not understand that despite the fancy packaging and marketing, we have been there and done that before. Or maybe it is hand-in-glove collusion by the media and politicians in this reductionism of complex topics and collective memory loss.

Whatever the reason, we do not seem to learn much from the experience of those who have come before us, at least as that is related to correctional practice. Or more accurately, we certainly could learn more from our past than we have learned! It is an oft-cited truism, courtesy of the philosopher Santayana and as already mentioned in this book, that those who do not know their history are doomed to repeat it. This adage bears repeating because it clearly applies here regarding correctional programs, operations, and practices.

In this chapter, we try to prognosticate about what we expect to happen in the world of corrections in the not-too-distant future. Not surprisingly, some of our best estimates in that regard are based on our recent past. So for instance, if decarceration is a recent trend, we would expect that it might be a continuing trend. Therefore, we explore some of these current and, we expect, future trends in corrections—some that have been mentioned before in this book and are only highlighted again here and others that are brand new.

●●● PUNITIVE POLICIES YIELD OVERUSE OF CORRECTIONS

To illustrate this point about the importance of history, all we need to do is consider the efforts of the last two decades that are declining in popularity—namely, the drug war, mandatory sentencing, supermax prisons, and the abandonment of treatment programming. Spurred by punitive sentiments that swept the political, social, and economic systems, the statutes, declarations, and practices that derived from these efforts profoundly changed corrections as Americans experienced it (Cullen et al., 2014; Whitman, 2003).

First, they vastly increased the use of all forms of corrections in this country. Our imprisonment rate (just for prisons, not including jails) was stabilized at about 125 persons per

100,000 residents for 50 years (1920–1970) until the drug war, mandatory sentences, and other punitive policies increased it (Ruddell, 2004). At the end of 2009, this number had risen to 502 persons per 100,000 residents, or more than four times the imprisonment rate of that 50-year period. In raw numbers, the offenders sentenced to prison increased by more than 500%, from 319,598 in 1980 to 1,613,740 in 2009 (West, Sabol, & Greenman, 2010, p. 1). Notably, the number of people held in prison had decreased by 2013 to 1,574,700, but this still yielded a roughly 492% increase from 1980 to 2013 (Carson, 2014, p. 2).

A comparable steady and swift increase in the use of jails has occurred since punitive policies were put in place. In 1986 the incarceration rate for jails in the United States was 108 persons per 100,000 residents, and by 2009 it was 250, or nearly a 250% increase in the use of jails during more recent years, although it had decreased to 234 by 2014 (Minton, 2010, p. 4, Minton & Zeng, 2015, p. 1). Put another way, the number of persons incarcerated in America's jails more than quadrupled, or increased by 405%, from 183,988 in 1980 to 744,600 in 2014 (Minton & Zeng, 2015, p. 2).

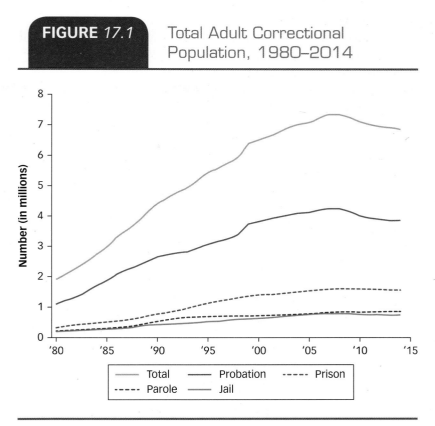

FIGURE 17.1   Total Adult Correctional Population, 1980–2014

Source: Kaeble, Glaze, Tsoutis, and Minton (2016).

Similarly astounding increases can be found in the use of probation and parole because of punitive practices. From 1980 to 2009, the number of people on probation more than tripled, with an increase of 376% (1,118,097 in 1980 to 4,203,967 in 2009) (Glaze, Bonczar, & Zhang, 2010, p. 2), although it decreased to 345% when the 1980 and 2014 figures for probation (3,864,100) are compared (Kaeble et al., 2015, p. 2). Likewise, the number of persons on parole nearly quadrupled during this time period (from 220,438 in 1980 to 856,900 in 2014) because most people in prisons and jails do eventually return to their communities (Kaeble & Bonczar, 2017). In sum, what all of these numbers and Figure 17.1 indicate is that because of punitive policies, the use of corrections—prisons, jails, and community corrections—has increased by almost unimaginable numbers from a generation ago, and although it is no longer increasing as much, it is not decreasing by much yet either.

Yet, as best we can tell (and as was mentioned in Chapter 1), we do not have proportionately more crime these days than at any other period in our history (see Figure 17.2). In fact, based on victimization and police reports, it appears that by 2014 we had the lowest rate of victimization since the National Crime Victimization Survey began in 1973. As indicated in Figures 17.1 and 17.2, crime—even violent crime—has been decreasing at the same time as use of corrections has been increasing.

In addition, our use of corrections is not in sync with what other countries are doing. We have similar crime rates (Farrington, Langan, & Tonry, 2004), yet our incarceration rate (by 2012) was more than 14 times that of Japan; 5 to 7 times that of France, Canada, China, and England and Wales; and 3 to 4 times that of Saudi Arabia and Chile (Walmsley, 2013). Russia is the only other developed nation that gets close to our

FIGURE *17.2*   Violent and Property Victimization, 1993–2014

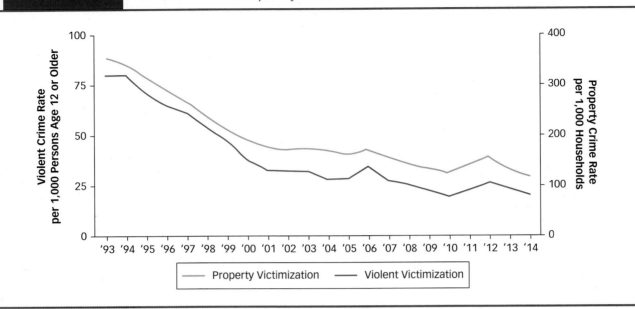

Source: Truman and Langton (2015, p. 1).

incarceration rate, and the United States still outpaces that nation, with 1.5 times its incarceration rate.

Second, interestingly enough, these punitive policies have not had the effect of increasing sentencing length. The average sentence to prison in state courts in 1992 was 6.5 years as compared with 5.5 years in 2009 (Bonczar, 2011, p. 1). It is not clear why sentencing length has decreased at the same time that more punitive policies are in effect. It is possible that decreased sentence length might be one of those unintended consequences of the overuse of incarceration. The capacity of prisons and jails, along with probation and parole caseloads, has been vastly increased over the past 20 years, but it might not have increased enough to accommodate the numbers of processed felons in the courts. What this means is that courts are forced to adjust their sentences to the lower relative capacity of prisons, and parole boards are pressured to release inmates as prisons and jails fill up.

Third, punitive policies, as was discussed in other chapters, have led to an explosion in the number of women and minority group members who are incarcerated or under some form of correctional supervision (Bureau of Justice Statistics, 2006; Carson, 2015; Irwin, 2005; Pollock, 2004). Until the current version of the drug war was resurrected—yes, there were others in American history (Abadinsky, 1993)—the proportion of women to men and of racial and ethnic minorities to whites in prisons, in jails, and on parole and probation was somewhat stable (Bureau of Justice Statistics, 2006).

Fourth, such policies have favored the use of more isolation, "punishment," and warehousing to deal with both bulging correctional populations and recalcitrant inmates. The number of supermax facilities has exploded, as has the number of supermax inmates, as management of the number of inmates turned to favoring punishment and warehousing over treatment (Irwin, 2005).

As a result of such policies, a fifth outcome has been the abandonment of a core principle of some correctional institutions and practices (e.g., probation, parole, minimum-security institutions, work releases)—namely, treatment—based on insufficient evidence. Some correctional programs and institutions were formulated on the premise that treatment is a major goal of corrections. Although the public has continued to believe this (Applegate, Cullen, & Fisher, 2001), for all intents and purposes, real efforts at treatment—beyond basic Alcoholics Anonymous, Narcotics Anonymous, religious groups, and GED programs—in prisons, jails, and community corrections received little funding and virtually disappeared for 20 years in many places (from the mid-1970s to the mid-1990s).

Although some of these endeavors and efforts, such as the drug war and mandatory sentencing, continue and even grow in some communities, for the most part scholars and some policymakers have deemed the former a failure and the latter a spectacular waste of money. Furthermore, although the

PHOTO 17.1: The number of persons incarcerated in America's jails more than quadrupled, or increased by 405%, from 183,988 in 1980 to 744,600 in 2014.

number of supermaxes has grown during the recent past, there is not nearly the hype about their promise for eliciting inmate reform. Finally, all indications are that the belief in and embrace of treatment programming, albeit programs that can demonstrate their worth, is on the upswing both in correctional institutions and in communities. Although all of these changes in attitudes and perceptions are positive, it is frustrating to realize that we knew—or should have known from our own past—that drug wars, mandatory sentencing, isolation, and pure punishment in the form of warehousing are not likely to reduce crime in this country, let alone reform those under correctional control. The long and the short of it is that we should have known better because it had all been done before.

••• DECARCERATION

As indicated in the foregoing, the numbers of persons incarcerated in jails and prisons and supervised in community corrections has been declining recently. By 2015, we had seen 8 years of declines of about 1.0% per year, with many of the declines being in probation populations, but for 5 of those years there were either decreases in incarceration at the state or federal level or only relatively small increases (Kaeble et al., 2016, p. 2). These declines were generally at the state level, but there have also been decreases at the federal level (we should caution that Attorney General Jeff Sessions called for harsher sentences at the federal level in the spring of 2017, so we may see more incarceration there in the immediate future). In most states, by 2014 a greater proportion of their correctional population was on community supervision than had been the case previously. As indicated by the data contained in Figure 17.3, from 2000 to 2014, there was a decline in the number of people on probation and decreases in the numbers of people in jails and prisons, although the steepest decline was in probation populations (Kaeble et al., 2016). But these decreases in correctional populations came during the second half of that time period (from 2007 to 2014), whereas from 2000 to 2007 there were just increases. Parole populations have been the exception to these decreases in correctional populations; they only increased from 2000 to 2014. These more recent decreases (and increases in parole) have not been uniform across the states or by region (Glaze & Herberman, 2013). In only three northeastern states—New York, New Jersey, and Maryland—were these declines a discernible trend over the last decade, although in Illinois, Michigan, Delaware, and Texas, the 2009 declines were

| FIGURE *17.3* | Rate of Persons Supervised by U.S. Adult Correctional Systems |

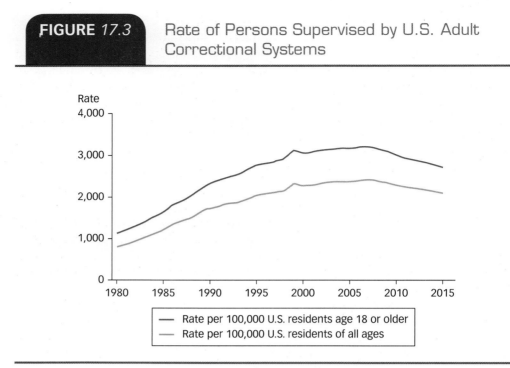

Source: Bureau of Justice Statistics, Key Statistics, Adult correctional supervision rate, 1980–2015, at www.bjs.gov

preceded by anemic growth rates earlier in the decade (West et al., 2010). Nor have all states experienced such declines. The difference about the time period we are in, however, is that for the first time in a long time, we are seeing some steady, if not dramatic, declines in the use of corrections.

EXPLANATIONS FOR THE DECLINE IN THE USE OF CORRECTIONS

What might these declines in the use of corrections be attributed to? Is it possible that declining crime, particularly violent crime, has actually begun to affect the use of prisons in some states? Is it possible that enforcement of the drug war has waned as 29 states and Washington, D.C., had legalized medical marijuana and 8 states (Alaska, California, Colorado, Maine, Massachusetts, Nevada, Oregon, and Washington state) and the District of Columbia had legalized recreational marijuana by November 2016— and the drug hype tied to criminality (e.g., the hysteria over crack mothers producing crack babies) has receded in the minds of the public, politicians, and criminal justice practitioners? Is it possible, in the case of the northeastern states, that declines are tied to reduced state populations, particularly of young people, who are most engaged in street crimes? Could it be that the reduced use of incarceration for some of these states is a consequence of the recession that hit the United States in 2007 and the consequent declining tax revenues and increasing debts faced by states and localities that can no longer afford the bill for spiraling imprisonment?

We think that it is possible that all of these scenarios have some value in explaining the decreased use of incarceration in some states during the last few years and for a few states over the last several years. We know that overall the number of admissions and parole violators returned to state prisons declined in 2010, signaling a change in the number of people before the courts, a change in sentencing by court actors, a change in parole agents' behavior, or some combination of these (West et al., 2010).

We also know that about 60% of inmates in state prisons these days are violent offenders, perhaps signaling greater attention to them rather than to drug offenders (West et al., 2010, p. 7). Finally, we know that despite their greater contribution to the composition of prisons, these violent offenders were actually "doing" less time. In 2000 the mean length of stay for violent offenders was 46 months, but by 2008 this mean had declined to 44 months—a seemingly small effect, but when multiplied by hundreds of thousands of people, this lower mean can have a huge impact on some prison systems (West et al., 2010, p. 8). Reduced length of stay may be related to the effect of declining state revenues on state prisons.

THE RECESSION, COST CUTTING, AND THE DECREASED USE OF CORRECTIONS

In 2009, the Pew Center on the States published a report subtitled *The Long Reach of American Corrections* in which the authors made the case that "more prison spending brings lower public safety returns" (Saylor & Iwaszko, 2009, p. 17). They argued that over the previous 20 years we had incarcerated too many first-time and nonviolent offenders who never needed to be incarcerated. Doing so has cost us billions of dollars, with no collateral decrease in crime because most of these people would either not reoffend or could have been handled in a much less expensive and intrusive way in the community. Moreover, the more we incarcerate, the less we achieve the ideal of incarcerating the serious repeat offenders (there are far fewer of these); the more the lower-level offenders are "replaced," leading to greater involvement of more people in crime; and the less likely we are to deter current criminals given that the research does not show that longer sentences deter more effectively. Although Saylor and Iwaszko (2009) acknowledged that the huge incarceration increase was likely responsible for somewhere between 10% and 35% of the decrease in violent crime since the mid-1990s (depending on which researcher you listen to and which model and assumptions he or she adopts), the authors noted that most of the drop in crime was likely attributable to factors outside of incarceration. It makes no sense financially, they argued, to continue to incarcerate low-level, aging, and less criminogenic offenders.

There are some recent examples from the news indicating that some states and localities came to the same conclusion. Washington State, for instance, in April 2011 closed the 135-year-old McNeil Island Prison because of the need to cut that state's budget (the cut was projected to save the state $12.7 million) (Mulick, 2010, p. 1). Likewise, for the first time in state history, Oregon in October 2010 closed a minimum-security facility for the same reason (the cut was projected to save the state $33.8 million) (Zaitz, 2010, p. 1). In both the Washington and Oregon instances, department of corrections officials claimed that none of the inmates would be released early because of the closures.

In another example from Washington State, this time involving a county jail and its finances (Thurston County), the county manager declined to open the newly built, $45 million facility, at least for a year, because the county could not afford to staff it or pay for its operation (Hulings, 2010, p. A4). In addition, the county manager noted that the new jail was not needed as much because of the declining jail population in the county, which happened after the jail's construction had begun.

These examples from Washington and Oregon came at a time when those states were still grappling with the Great Recession, but Texas closed three prisons between 2010 and 2014 and decided to invest some of the savings in treatment programming, both in prisons and in communities (Kruger, 2014, p. 1). Florida and New York were closing prisons in 2014 and 2015 and were turning those vacant facilities into homeless shelters or reentry centers (Couch, 2015, p. 1). The rationale for these closures is not cost cutting to deal with the recession but rather just cost cutting in general and the belief that locking up low-level offenders does not result in less crime. Such a shift in perspective has led to changes in sentencing and, consequently, fewer inmates to fill prison beds in many states and localities.

PHOTO 17.2: An empty hallway in a prison cell block

And notably, as a phenomenon, this decreased use of incarceration appears to have some international legs. In Germany, The Netherlands, and Sweden, the number of inmates in prisons is decreasing. In Germany and The Netherlands, those decreases have been 20% and 36%, respectively (Zachariadis, 2013, p. 1). In Sweden, four prisons were closed in 2012, resulting in a 6% drop in inmates in 1 year alone. Instead of prison time, these countries are using fines or probation. When in prison, inmates have much more liberal visitation policies, have more freedom to move around within the prison, and are rarely sentenced to solitary confinement.

Moreover, in a report by the Sentencing Project (Porter, 2016, p. 1), the author revealed that in 2015, 30 states continued the trend of reforming sentencing policies and reducing the use of imprisonment. In the past, such policy changes have included medical marijuana laws, reduced penalties for drug and property offenses, increased parole eligibility and reduced revocations, "ban the box" laws that delay questions regarding the criminal history of a job applicant until he or she is interviewed, and modified policies regarding juveniles to reduce their incarceration and the severity of it (Porter, 2011, p. 3). Porter (2011) noted that developing alternatives to prison contributed to a 20% drop in incarceration from 1999 to 2009 in both New York and New Jersey. She argued that although several of these changes in state policies were done to reduce current and future budgets, they were also adopted because policymakers were no longer convinced of the efficacy of mass incarceration as a public safety measure. In fact, in three states that cut their incarceration rate by more than the national average—New York and New Jersey (between 2009 and 2012) again but also California (between 2006 and 2012)—their violent crime rates dropped by more than the national average (Mauer, 2014, p. 2).

Will decarceration continue? That is anybody's guess, but a betting man or woman might increase his or her odds by considering the recent attempts to reduce correctional populations at the local, state, and federal levels and then note the national mood, which has turned against the overuse of corrections. Again we would caution that it appears that the Trump administration may be moving in the opposite direction toward greater use of incarceration at the federal level if statements made by the Attorney General in the spring of 2017 are any indication.

IMPLICATIONS OF DECARCERATION AND THE NEED FOR A PLAN OF ACTION

Should these early indications of decarceration turn into a flood of releases—dare we say *mass decarceration*—there will be many positive outcomes such as less incarceration of low-level offenders, resulting in a greater sense of justice for community members; less incarceration of minority men and women, also resulting in a greater sense of justice for all; fewer tax dollars being devoted to incarcerating people; a reduction in the growth of the corrections–industrial complex, at least at the institutional level (see a discussion of the complex later in this chapter); and more opportunities for people to age out of crime and contribute in a meaningful way to their communities. However, there are likely some negative outcomes that will result from decarceration, such as greater unemployment, more low-level crime, and increased use of drugs and alcohol by ex-inmates, that could occur if policymakers and correctional officials do not plan appropriately. There are also likely to be those working in corrections who oppose the closure of correctional institutions and programming because it will threaten their livelihoods (Garland et al., 2014). Clearly, money will be saved through decarceration, but some of these monies will likely be needed to fund reentry programs in corrections and work and training programs for the decarcerated in communities along with the expansion of drug and alcohol treatment in communities so that decarcerated people have the opportunity to rebuild their lives.

PENAL HELP VERSUS PENAL HARM

Another explanation for the decreased use of incarceration may be the increased use of treatment programming that addresses the appropriate risk, needs, and responsivity levels and types of offenders. As indicated in other chapters, there is a well-established science behind some of the best-formulated and best-implemented programs. There is evidence that these programs may be effectuating a decrease in criminal engagement, further convincing correctional managers that expenditures on programming may be a better bet for reducing crime and costs than the building of more institutions.

Some scholars have argued that this move to treatment over punishment may portend a move away from the **penal harm** movement of the last several decades to an age of reform embodied by the term **penal help** (Stohr, Jonson, & Cullen, 2014). The reform of state laws to liberalize marijuana use, the repeal of harsh sentences, and the reduction in the use of incarceration and correctional supervision generally, coupled with the increase in the use of rehabilitation, restorative justice, and reentry programming, all signal a sea change in the nature of the justice system and in corrections in particular. Taken together, they indicate that there has been a societal shift toward penal help over penal harm (Mauer, 2014; Pollock, Hogan, Lambert, Ross, & Sundt, 2012; Stohr et al., 2014; Tucker, 2014).

●●● PROFESSIONALIZATION AND INNOVATION

As we look to the future, there are a number of problems, in addition to the amount of incarceration, that should preoccupy those of us concerned about correctional practice. One issue that affects almost all areas of practice is that of professionalism. As indicated in other chapters of this book, the effort to professionalize corrections has not yet yielded consistent fruit around the country. Some correctional institutions and programs have moved to enforce professional standards for their new hires such as required college-level educational background, sufficient training, and pay that is commensurate with job requirements. However, most correctional organizations, perhaps primarily because of a lack of resources, have failed to move in a similar direction.

Yet hiring and keeping a professional staff is key to moving correctional institutions into the 21st century; it is key to the appropriate delivery of those treatment programs that are now valued in this age of penal help. When the correctional practitioner does not have the kind of education that acquaints him or her with the history, background, concepts, and research regarding corrections, the correctional organization is simply ill prepared to meet the challenges it faces. Moreover, when turnover is high because training and pay are insufficient, the organization becomes less stable and less equipped to problem solve regarding pressing concerns. Therefore, if we ever hope to move beyond the past and failed correctional endeavors and perspectives, the ranks of correctional practitioners need to be professionalized.

Penal harm: Movement in corrections based on retribution in sentencing and the infliction of greater harm while inmates are under correctional supervision.

Penal help: Movement that includes the reform of laws to liberalize marijuana use, the repeal of harsh sentences, and the reduction in the use of incarceration and correctional supervision generally coupled with the increase in the use of rehabilitation, restorative justice, and reentry programming.

PHOTO 17.3: Inmate Liz Louie feeds a Taylor's checkerspot honey water from a Q-tip. Doing "green" work in a correctional setting has benefits for both inmates and correctional facilities.

CORRECTIONS IS A RELATIONSHIP BUSINESS

The correctional experience for clients, offenders, or inmates and staff and the success of treatment and probation and parole programming all hinge on the relationships among the people in these organizations. It is often said that the greatest expense for any public-service organization is its staff. A collateral expense for correctional institutions and programs is the care of their inmates and/or clients. Notably, these expenses wax and wane, to some degree, based on the relationships among the actors. If those relationships are characterized by respect and concern among staff and respect and care (coupled with a healthy degree of control) between staff and clients or offenders, then there are less likely to be costly lawsuits, staff turnover, riots, and general stress that produces discord in the workplace.

In his groundbreaking work on less explored and identified types of intelligence—emotional and social—Goleman (1995, 2006, p. 4) argued that scientific research on the brain indicates that we are "wired to connect" to others, which means that every time we engage with other humans, we affect and are affected by their thoughts and, consequently, their behavior. Those relationships that are the most prolonged and intense in our lifetimes are most likely to affect us, not just socially or emotionally but also biologically.

To a surprising extent, then, our relationships mold not just our experience but also our biology. The brain-to-brain link allows our strongest relationships to shape us on matters as benign as whether we laugh at the same jokes or as profound as which genes are (or are not) activated in T cells, the immune system's foot soldiers in the constant battle against invading bacteria and viruses (Goleman, 2006, p. 5).

Goleman (2006) identified a "double-edged sword" in relationships in that those that are positive are healthful, but those that are negative can lead to stress, fear, frustration, anger, and despair, all emotions that can manifest themselves in physical ailments (p. 5). Of course, correctional environments are chock-full of stressed, fearful, frustrated, angry, and despairing people, and we are not just referring to the inmates here! So this means that unless correctional environments can foster some positive relationships between and among staff and clients or inmates, all will suffer psychologically and physically.

Recognition of the need to provide opportunities for inmates to "maturely cope" while under correctional supervision (as discussed in Chapter 8) would appear to be an acknowledgment that something positive can come out of the decent incapacitation of offenders. Moves to democratize workplaces and give people a voice and choice in their work may serve to reduce some of the negative emotions associated with working in corrections. More recent attempts to "treat" rather than just "warehouse" inmates in institutions and offenders on probation and parole, or efforts at penal help, also represent a move to more positive relationships and so a better future for corrections. As indicated by the findings from the research presented in the preceding chapters on these matters, there is reason to believe that some treatment and supervision tactics can work to help offenders as they endeavor to deal with their substance and other abuse issues.

GREEN PRISONS AND JAILS

An emerging issue in corrections is the idea of reducing the environmental impact of jails and prisons by reducing the consumption of resources and creating healthier living spaces for inmates. Prisons and jails have been characterized as "environmental hogs" (Stohr & Wozniak, 2014). They are often huge buildings or sets of buildings with outsized electrical needs because of their "24/7" lighting and security systems. Their inmates produce tons of waste in concentrated areas and, in turn, consume food, clothing, and numerous other products at levels that sometimes rival small cities. In recognition of these realities and, at times, in the name of cost cutting, some prisons and jails have turned to solar panels to supplement their energy sources and have turned to composting and gardening to increase soil health, reduce waste, and improve the diets of their inmates. Some prisons in Washington State have even begun programs that benefit other species (e.g., the Taylor's Checkerspot Butterfly Rearing Program at the Mission Creek Corrections Center; see Sustainability in Prisons Project, n.d.). It is thought that these **green prisons and jails** are likely to yield a number of benefits in the form of reduced costs, waste, and energy consumption and the improvement of the overall environment for the humans incarcerated in prisons and other species as well. An ancillary benefit may be the preparation of inmates for jobs in emerging green industries (Stohr & Wozniak, 2014).

••• PRIVATIZATION

THE PROFIT MOTIVE IN CORRECTIONS

Privatization in corrections is not a new phenomenon. As was discussed in the first chapters of this book, transportation and the convict lease system both were based on privatization. The privatization of parts of prison operations (e.g., health care, food service, work programs) continues in many public prisons. Since the 1980s, however, the number of completely private prisons has grown at both the state and federal levels. Several of those prisons have experienced problems with escapes, violence, staff turnover, inexperienced staff and deficient staff training, and brutality and abuse by staff along with inadequate physical facilities (Camp & Gaes, 2002).

In her 1973 book, *Kind and Usual Punishment: The Prison Business,* Jessica Mitford detailed the misuse of public monies for prisons; instead of improving the diets and opportunities of inmates after the Attica Prison riot (causes of the riot), for instance, millions of dollars were used by prison officials in New York to purchase riot gear and technology as well as to hire more staff. Her argument is that closed-off institutions, like prisons and jails with their relatively powerless inmates, are particularly susceptible to graft and corruption of both the legal and illegal sorts. Mitford (1973) noted that state legislatures are particularly susceptible to contributions by private entities that want to do business with corrections.

Forms of corruption and abuse of monies, of the illegal sort, are easy to spot but are not always stopped. Mitford (1973) complained, "Convicts will tell you about profitable deals made with local merchants for supplies in which the warden pockets a handsome rakeoff, unexplained shortages in the canteens, the disappearance of large quantities of food from the kitchen" (p. 172). It is the legally sanctioned graft in corrections, however, whereby money from state legislatures is intended for one type of purchase but is diverted to another—such as the hiring of more administrators rather than the provision of adequate food—that fascinated her and caused her to characterize the operation of public-sector corrections in this country during the 1970s as a "business." She charged that correctional institutions, in many states, were out to make a profit for administrators

Green prisons and jails: Correctional facilities that seek to reduce waste and energy consumption and focus on providing a more healthful environment for their staff and inmates.

Privatization: Occurs in corrections when services or whole correctional institutions are provided or operated by private businesses or corporations.

PHOTO 17.4: A for-profit prison, operated by Corrections Corporation of America, houses men awaiting trial on immigration matters.

and their supporters (among vendors and state legislatures), not to attend to their core mission of holding people decently and securely while assisting them in their reform.

More than 40 years later, if anything the operation of corrections in the United States has become even more business-like in the worst way, with some commentators characterizing the system as the **corrections–industrial complex** (Welch, 2005). In his last speech, President Dwight Eisenhower warned the nation about the development of the *military–industrial complex,* or the collusion among politicians, defense contractors, and leaders in the military regarding the value of war and military spending as a money-making and power-generating enterprise for all three (Mills, 1956). Similarly, Welch (2005) argued that corrections has become such an enterprise for state legislatures, governors, and city and town leaders (politicians), who receive contributions from prison and jail contractors, vendors, and private-prison corporations (businesses), and for directors and secretaries of corrections, wardens, sheriffs, and probation and parole managers (criminal justice officials), who participate in contracting with businesses. The criminal justice officials contract with the private-sector businesses, not necessarily because they provide better services or even less expensive services than the public sector but rather because they are pressured to do so by the politicians who appoint or select and fund them or they receive kickbacks themselves in terms of remuneration or jobs when they leave public service for the private sector.

IDAHO'S OWN PRIVATE PRISON

One of the largest private-prison corporations, the Corrections Corporation of America (CCA) with earnings of $1.7 billion in 2012, was voluntarily removed as the operator of a private medium-security prison that it had been operating near Boise, Idaho, since the 1990s (Boone, 2013a). CCA made $29 million from this Idaho contract alone (Boone, 2013b). CCA was accused of defrauding taxpayers by severely understaffing positions that it was paid for and was under investigation by the Federal Bureau of Investigation for this and the level of violence at the prison. As a result, inmates claimed that they are less safe. Counselors and case managers were used to fill security positions, thus making it difficult for them to help inmates with programming or reentry planning. The Idaho Department of Corrections reportedly knew of this understaffing for years because its own auditors reported on it. There were lawsuits from inmates claiming understaffing and excessive violence as a result. In fact, the Idaho Department of Corrections auditor found that the CCA prison had nearly three times the number of inmate-on-inmate assaults as other publicly operated prisons in the state. As a result of an inmate lawsuit regarding the staffing and violence brought by the American Civil Liberties Union (ACLU), CCA settled and promised more staff, and it reported that the mandatory staff positions were filled, but it turned out that CCA was falsifying those documents and those staff positions were vacant. The only way this problem came to light was that an Associated Press request for staffing and payroll information from CCA spurred the company to confess the truth to the Idaho Department of Corrections.

Corrections–industrial complex: The collusion among politicians, business, and criminal justice officials to make money for themselves and their organizations from correctional services, construction, and operations.

IN FOCUS 17.1

Privatization and the Walnut Grove Correctional Facility

The perfect example of how this kind of collusion among politicians, business, and criminal justice officials in this corrections–industrial complex can lead to gross injustices can be found in a small Mississippi town. One hour's drive east of Jackson, Mississippi, is the Walnut Grove Correctional Facility for boys and young men (the facility officials incarcerate up to age 22 to increase the number and, thus, the profit the private corporation can make) in the town of Walnut Grove. It is the largest juvenile prison in the country, housing 1,200 juveniles and young men. The state of Mississippi pays the private corporation GEO Group to operate the prison, which the company does for a profit. Before August 2010, the prison was operated by another private-prison corporation, Cornell Companies. (August was when GEO Group bought Cornell Companies and so acquired the contract to operate the Walnut Grove facility.)

In a two-part investigation of the Walnut Grove facility by National Public Radio (NPR), Burnett (2011) found that violence was set up and encouraged by the correctional officers. NPR also found that sexual abuse of the young male inmates by female officers was rife. In 2011, the prison was under investigation by the U.S. Department of Justice and was being sued on behalf of 13 inmates by the Southern Poverty Law Center (SPLC) and the ACLU.

> "When we began investigating conditions inside this facility and seeing how these kids were living with the beat downs and the sexual abuse and violence and corruption, it became a no-brainer. It became something we had to do," said Sheila Bedi, the lead attorney on the case and deputy legal director for the SPLC. (Burnett, 2011, p. 1)

According to Burnett (2011), the crux of the problem at Walnut Grove was the correctional officers. There were too few of them, there was little supervision of them, some were gang members themselves, and others were inclined to abuse the inmates, either physically or sexually. The national average of officers to inmates for juveniles is 1 to 10, but the 2009 audit at Walnut Grove determined that the ratio was only 1 to 60 there. Because staff are the most expensive item for any correctional entity to fund, cutting staff and their salaries is one way to ensure profits for a money-making enterprise like this prison (the GEO Group is traded on the New York Stock Exchange and made $1 billion in 2010) (Burnett, 2011, p. 1). According to the audit done in 2009, "There were three inmate injuries a day. In the first six months of 2010, there was more than one fight a day, an assault on staff at least every other day, and nine attempted suicides" (Burnett, 2011, p. 1).

NPR found, after a review of public records, that the warden and deputy wardens at Walnut Grove were receiving supplemental checks from the federal government for administering educational grants for the juveniles in the amount of $2,500 to $5,000 when they were already paid by GEO (Burnett, 2011, p. 1). The town of Walnut Grove also "makes money" out of the existence and growth of the prison. The mayor of Walnut Grove claimed that it funds the local police department. "'It's been a sweet deal for Walnut Grove,' Sims [the mayor] said. Indeed, every month, the prison pays the town $15,000 in lieu of taxes—which comprises nearly 15 percent of its annual budget" (Burnett, 2011, p. 1). In addition, a vending company owned by the mayor has 18 machines inside the prison. Moreover, the correctional authority that sends the Walnut Grove prison its grant money is given $4,500 per month by GEO. Left unexplored in the investigation was the question of why the Mississippi state legislature and governor's office authorized the private operation of the Walnut Grove Correctional Facility in the first place.

Discussion Questions

1. Why do you think the Mississippi state legislature and governor's office authorized the private operation of the Walnut Grove Correctional Facility?

2. If you were governor of Mississippi, what would you do to reduce corruption and the abuse of office in such prisons as Walnut Grove?

ETHICAL ISSUE

What Would You Do?

You are an auditor for a state public-prison system, and it is your job to make sure that all of the prisons in that system, both public and private, are using state funds appropriately and operating as they should be. Your office has filed more than one negative audit report in your state on a private prison that appears to have an abnormally low staff-to-inmate ratio. In those reports, you have noted that this understaffing has likely contributed to the high number of inmate-on-inmate and inmate-on-staff assaults and the relatively high number of medical- and psychiatric-related complaints filed by inmates at this prison. Unfortunately, despite your arguments that the problems in your reports should be attended to, your supervisors have paid them little mind because the political atmosphere in the state is very pro-privatization. You know that a lawsuit has been filed by staff at the prison alleging that the understaffing endangers both them and inmates, and the staff attorneys have contacted you, although they are unaware of the content of your audit reports. Should you talk to them? If so, what will you tell them? What do you think are the likely outcomes of your action?

On January 3, 2014, Idaho Governor Butch Otter, a big fan of prison privatization and someone who once suggested that more private-prison operators should be able to operate in Idaho, ended the contract with CCA, saying, "We had better hopes for outcomes in privatization" (Russell, 2014, p. B1). In May 2016, a federal appellate court upheld a contempt-of-court ruling against CCA, which means that the company will need to pay "higher-than-normal" attorneys' fees to the ACLU for its defense of inmates who brought suit because of the falsified staffing reports by CCA (Boone, 2016, p. 3A).

THE EXTENT OF PRIVATIZATION AND ITS PROBLEMS

In a related report by an NPR reporter, it was noted that 8% of all inmates in prisons are held in private prisons, and in federal prisons that proportion rises to 16% (Shahani, 2011, p. 1). As the recession deepened and state budgets tightened from 2009 through 2011, the projection was for the use of private prisons to grow and for private corporations to diversify into the "alternatives-to-corrections" market. Although private prisons do not cost less to operate—in fact, they might be more expensive when all costs are accounted for such as lawsuits and monitoring and assistance from publicly funded police and fire departments—they are easier and faster to build because they do not require the authorization of bonds from state legislatures (Camp & Gaes, 2002; General Accounting Office, 1996).

In a study of private prisons at the state and federal levels by Camp and Gaes (2002), the researchers, who were employees of the Federal Bureau of Prisons at the time, found that "the private sector experienced significant problems with staff turnover, escapes, and drug use" (p. 427). For instance, in 1999 secure-facility private prisons experienced 18 escapes, whereas out of all the Bureau of Prison facilities—a system that was larger than all of the private secure prisons combined—there was only 1 escape that year (p. 433). The researchers concluded, "The failures that produce escapes or illegal drug use can result from problems in policy and procedures, in technology, and in staff capabilities" (p. 445). As the two recent examples of private-prison failures provided in this chapter—the Walnut Grove facility in Mississippi and the CCA prison in Idaho—would indicate, when profit competes with professional staffing and just operation of prisons and jails, profit considerations often win out, with dire consequences for inmates and staff in such facilities.

In a surprising reversal of a 30-year trend toward greater privatization of corrections, and in recognition of the recent history of abuses and scandals involving private prisons, the Department of Justice under the Obama administration released a statement in summer 2016 indicating that the federal government would begin the process of ending the use of private prisons, claiming that they are "less safe and effective" than public prisons (Zapotosky & Harlan, 2016, p. 1). This decision was reversed, however, by the Department of Justice under the Trump administration in February 2017 (Zapotosky, 2017). Notably, neither of these decisions to use or not use private prisons at the federal level affects what happens in the states.

••• CONCLUDING THOUGHTS

It is a stunning realization that much of the future looks like the past, but it is true in a way. Current trends in corrections mimic those themes we laid out in the early chapters of this book. However, as has been demonstrated by the research presented throughout this book, there is also great progress in refining how we handle correctional practice and programming.

There is little doubt that most correctional experiences for clients or inmates are not tinged with violence or brutality. The vast majority of correctional staff, whether in communities or institutions, act professionally, whether the attributes of their work fit that designation or not. Basic health care, clean housing, and nutritious food are provided to most incarcerated persons in the United States. Probation and parole officers do provide referrals to their clients when time permits, and programs are available. Despite crowded caseloads, these officers usually make every effort to carefully watch the most dangerous of their charges. Jails, although often overcrowded or, at least, overused, are generally helpful at ensuring the safety of suicide-prone or mentally disturbed inmates or people detoxing from drug- or alcohol-induced highs. Jails might not represent the best places for such people, but they are usually safer than the streets and do provide a minimum of much-needed services for them. There is much more programming for those incarcerated in prisons and even jails and available to probationers and parolees than there was even 15 years ago, an indication that we have entered an age of penal help. In short, although we tend to repeat our past mistakes, there has been some learning from them as well, as that is manifested in improved correctional practice.

SUMMARY ●━━━

- The current decarceration trend in some states, and now at the federal level, is also hopeful in that prisons can then be reserved for the truly violent and serious offenders, with the effects of increasing public safety, reducing minority community disruption, making the system fairer and more just (with the punishments fitting the crimes), increasing the likelihood of successful reentry by offenders, and reducing the monetary costs of corrections for the public.

- A key component of this movement toward greater justice, if there is one, is the progress made in providing worthwhile treatment and programming—what might be termed the penal help movement in corrections. Should correctional managers and policymakers continue to support and increase funding for such initiatives, we may witness a true age of reform in this generation.

- Other trends that might catch fire in the near future are a greater understanding of emotional intelligence as it influences corrections, more green initiatives in corrections as cost-cutting and environment-saving efforts, and a continued push to professionalize.

- Another currently popular movement—privatization—should give us pause, however. As a number of studies and infamous examples indicate, private prisons tend to have more problems in the decent incarceration of inmates and the level of professionalism of their staff. For these reasons, and given the susceptibility of these institutions (and state legislatures and all political entities) to corruption and profiteering, privatization of whole institutions should be reconsidered.

- As the political winds shift away from purely punishment-oriented corrections, it will be interesting to see how correctional organizations, programs, and their actors will adjust in terms of privatization, professionalism, and decarceration.

KEY TERMS

Corrections–industrial complex, 384

Green prisons and jails, 383

Penal harm, 381

Penal help, 381

Privatization, 383

DISCUSSION QUESTIONS

1. Discuss the evidence indicating that our correctional practices do not fit the amount of crime in the United States. Note how we compare with other countries in terms of the use of incarceration.

2. Review the attributes of a professional and why and how the presence of those characteristics would serve to "improve" correctional operation.

3. What problems do "get tough" policies create for correctional operations? What benefits, if any, do they provide?

4. What is the connection between biology and environment in correctional operation? How do positive and negative environments affect the "biology" of those who work in corrections and those who are clients and inmates within and outside of them?

5. What are the indicators that a penal help perspective may come to guide corrections in the future? What are the indicators that a penal harm perspective is very much alive in present-day corrections?

6. Why do you think that private prisons have more problems with the operation of their facilities in terms of both inmate and staff management? Would you argue that we, as a country, should continue to authorize the construction and operation of private prisons and privatization in corrections? Why or why not?

7. In your opinion, what current initiatives in corrections offer the most promise for the future? Support this opinion with research and readings provided in this chapter or in the rest of the text.

$SAGE edge™

Review → Practice → Improve

Sharpen your skills with SAGE edge at **edge.sagepub.com/stohressentials3e**.

SAGE edge offers a robust online environment featuring an impressive array of free tools and resources for review, study, and further exploration, keeping both instructors and students on the cutting edge of teaching and learning.

FOR FURTHER EXPLORATION AND APPLICATION, TAKE A LOOK AT THE INTERACTIVE EBOOK FOR THESE PREMIUM RESOURCES:

▶ **Career Video 17.1** Case Manager

▶ **SAGE News Clip 17.1** Idaho Prison Abuse

▶ **SAGE News Clip 17.2** Stanford Latest

▤ **Journal Article 17.1** Revisiting Prison Privatization: An Examination of the Magnitude of Prison Privatization

ANSWERS TO TEST YOUR KNOWLEDGE

••• CHAPTER 1

1. True. We have seen that we justify punishment in terms of retribution, deterrence, incapacitation, rehabilitation, and reintegration.

2. False. The strongest deterrent against crime is the certainty of punishment.

3. False. While the severity of the crime is the most important consideration, the defendant's prior record and certain other considerations come into play.

4. True. The brain's pleasure centers light up when wrongdoers are punished, indicating that they have received a shot of rewarding dopamine.

5. True. Every legal system in the world assumes this.

6. True. Philosophies of punishment depend on concepts of human nature.

7. False. Specific deterrence rarely works, as recidivism rates aptly demonstrate.

8. True. The United States incarcerates people at a higher rate than any other country in the world.

••• CHAPTER 2

1. True. There are multiple themes that appear throughout the history of corrections.

2. True. The wealthy and powerful were often able to escape most punishments, and when that was not possible, they were often able to "buy" their way out of physical punishments.

3. Jails. Some form of a jail has existed as long as some form of a court.

4. True. The development of sails negated the need for human power to propel ships.

5. False. Transportation was a means of filling the colonies of Great Britain with the poor and the criminally inclined.

6. His work reforming jails.

7. False. The concept of the "panopticon," devised by Jeremy Bentham, included a rounded architecture to enhance the ability to see inmates in their cells and therefore to supervise them more effectively (or that was the plan anyway).

8. True.

••• CHAPTER 3

1. The main difference between the Pennsylvania and New York models for prisons was that in Pennsylvania inmates were required to be "silent and separate" from other inmates at all times, and in New York inmates were required to be "silent and congregate" in that they could work together and do other activities together, but they must be silent. The New York model was mostly adopted in the United States because it allowed inmates to work together, and they were able to make more and thus offset the cost of incarceration more than inmates under the Pennsylvania model, who were laboring alone in their cells.

2. True. First built and operated as a jail, a section of the Walnut Street Jail in Philadelphia, Pennsylvania, was remodeled with individual cells for inmates, separated by gender and offense, where they could do penance.

3. False. The Auburn Prison, whose cornerstone was laid in 1816 and which is still in operation today, was part of the New York system of

"congregate but silent" prisons. Inmates worked together but were housed separately and were to maintain silence no matter whether together or apart.

4. True. This was done because some inmates were psychologically harmed by the complete

separation and because inmates could produce more when they worked together.

5. False. Charles Dickens thought that keeping inmates completely separate from others created "morally unhealthy and diseased" humans.

6. True. Because inmates could be together for work and sometimes for worship but needed to be "silent," it was difficult to always control them. Therefore, Auburn and Sing Sing staff used the lash frequently, along with solitary confinement and marching in lockstep.

7. False. Dorothea Dix favored the Eastern State Penitentiary (or the Pennsylvania system) over the New York system because of the separation that prevented contamination in the former type of prison. However, she found both types of prisons and most prisons to be understaffed, overcrowded, and with inept leadership that turned over too quickly. She particularly disliked the overly harsh discipline (too much use of the lash) at the Auburn and Sing Sing prisons and the overly long sentences for relatively minor offenses that she observed in communities.

8. False. The 1870 Prison Congress was held because the promise of the early prison reformers had not been realized, and as a consequence attendees of this congress called for another round of reform.

9. True. Inmates were rewarded with "marks" for good behavior that entitled them to other privileges.

10. True. Correctional institutions are supposed to "correct" and therefore include some programming geared toward achieving that goal.

••• CHAPTER 4

1. False. The only difference is that one is concerned with what is right and wrong in the private sphere (morality), and the other is concerned with what is right and wrong in the public sphere (ethics).

2. Deontological ethical systems are concerned with whether the act itself is good, and teleological ethical systems are focused on the consequences of the act.

3. True.

4. True.

5. True.

6. True. Noble cause corruption is concerned with the end (serving the noble cause) over the means to get there. Correctional organizations tend to employ persons who are moved by the plight of the victims ("the smell of the victim's blood") and by the need to act to make the world right ("running to the tower").

7. False. Official deviance is unethical or illegal acts that are done to benefit the organization or organizational members, not the person committing the act.

8. True. The isolated, secretive nature of much of the work with clients who are powerless, and workers who have a great deal of discretion, makes correctional work more susceptible to ethical violations.

••• CHAPTER 5

1. False. Basic principles of justice mandate that the criminal justice system punish only similarly situated offenders (equals) with the same punishment.

2. False. Other things include prior record, gang affiliation, and treatment considerations.

3. True. Three-strikes laws are laws that allow states to imprison a person who has been convicted of a third felony for life.

4. False. He or she may be sentenced to serve concurrent sentences.

5. False. Victims or survivors can have input into the sentencing decision in all 50 states if they wish in the form of a victim impact statement.

6. False. Judges receive guidance or advice in the form of presentence investigation reports (PSIs) written by probation officers and in the form of sentencing guidelines.

7. False. Most studies find that once legally relevant variables are taken into account, it is rarely found

that minorities are subjected to discriminatory sentencing.

8. True. Separate courts do exist for criminals with special problems such as drug addiction.

9. False. Some states do and some states do not.

••• CHAPTER 6

1. False. Most adult jails are operated by counties, although a few states and the federal government administer them as well.

2. True. Most jails for juveniles are referred to as detention centers, and some adult jails are called this, too.

3. False. About 60% of inmates in adult jails have not been convicted of a crime.

4. True. The drug war has netted more women and minority group members because the war has focused on low-level offenders (not the drug kingpins) and because it has focused on impoverished areas of cities that are disproportionately occupied by minorities.

5. True. Jails hold more of the mentally ill than other social institutions in this country because the mental health hospitals have steadily decreased their populations over the past 40 years, leaving no place else for the police to take people.

6. True. Incarcerated women tend to have more medical problems than incarcerated men.

7. True. Female staff are more likely to be the perpetrators of sexual victimization of male inmates than are male staff. Notably, there are about 10 times more male inmates in jails than there are females, making it more likely that female staff will supervise male inmates than that male staff will supervise female inmates.

••• CHAPTER 7

1. True. Probation did start during the 1800s and was run by volunteers.

2. False. Most members of the public consider it "soft on crime."

3. False. Parole occurs after a period in prison; probation is in lieu of prison.

4. True. As many as 90% of cases are granted probation.

5. True. Law enforcement–type officers achieve better results than social work–type officers, but both do less well than "hybrid" officers.

6. True. Work release programs perform both functions.

7. False. Most hardened criminals would rather have prison than almost any form of community supervision other than straight probation.

8. False. Boot camps have proven ineffective in rehabilitating criminals of any age.

••• CHAPTER 8

1. True. Despite some real reductions in incarceration at the state and local levels over the past few years, the United States still has the highest incarceration rate in the world.

2. False. Although large by comparison with minimum-security prisons, about three-fifths of all inmates are held in medium- and minimum-security prisons, with medium-security prisons holding more inmates overall than maximum- and minimum-security prisons.

3. In medium-security prisons, the exterior security can be as tight as it is for the supermax and maximum-security prisons, but internally the inmate has many more opportunities to attend school, treatment, and church programming and to work in any number of capacities. There is also greater diversity in rooming options, from dormitories to single cells, with the more preferred single or double cells used as a carrot to entice better behavior. Visiting and contact with the outside world are less restricted. Some medium-security inmates may even be allowed to leave the institution for work-related deliveries or on furloughs, although this is much more common in minimum-security prisons.

4. Importation occurs when inmates entering a prison *import* aspects of their own culture from the outside. Prisonization occurs when inmates adopt the inmate subculture of the institution.

5. Gangs are groups of people with similar interests who socialize together and who may engage in deviant or criminal activities; they are a common phenomenon in jails and prisons. They may serve

to reinforce the prison subculture by providing for the needs of inmates and thereby reducing their deprivations and pains. Prison gang members are thought to be more likely to engage in crime and violence while incarcerated.

6. There is violence in prisons because incarcerated people are there unwillingly; people are forced to do things they normally would not do with people they might not like; and, most important, some of them are inclined to be violent.

7. True. Transgender inmates, particularly in men's prisons, are more likely to be sexually assaulted than any other group of inmates.

●●● CHAPTER 9

1. True. Calling a correctional officer a "guard" can be perceived as demeaning the role and thus as an insult.

2. The five characteristics of a profession are (1) prior educational attainment involving college, (2) formal training on the job or just prior to the start of the job, (3) pay and benefits that are commensurate with the work, (4) the ability to exercise discretion, and (5) work that is guided by a code of ethics.

3. Generally speaking, police jobs pay the most, then probation/parole officer jobs, and then correctional officer jobs.

4. Generally speaking, probation and parole officer jobs often require a bachelor's degree, policing jobs usually require some college if not an associate's or bachelor's degree, and correctional officer jobs rarely require a bachelor's degree or even some college.

5. False. Most depictions of corrections on television and in the movies show a distorted view of what corrections is and what correctional staff in institutions and communities do.

6. True.

7. Stress for correctional staff comes from many sources: shift and evening work that interferes with sleep and family relationships; a working environment with people who are experiencing a negative time in their lives; lack of power, control, and voice in their work; low pay and training; a hack rather than a human service role; and competitive and non-supportive coworkers.

8. True.

●●● CHAPTER 10

1. True. Parole began in an Australian penal colony during the 1830s.

2. False. Parole is an executive branch function.

3. False. Many parolees are released on mandatory parole.

4. True. At least two-thirds reoffend within 3 years.

5. True. The parolees most likely to recidivate are property offenders.

6. True or false. There is broad disagreement on this.

7. False. Parole success is determined differently in different states.

8. True and false. Sanctions such as halfway houses and electronic monitoring (EM) cut costs only if they are used appropriately, and they increase parolee surveillance only relative to ordinary parole—not relative to prison.

●●● CHAPTER 11

1. True.

2. False. In the early prisons, women were an afterthought because these prisons were not built for them. Therefore, they were often placed in attics or out-of-the-way places. They were not separated like the men because there wasn't enough room to do so. They tended to be preyed on by male staff and inmates before they were guarded by female matrons.

3. True. Race shaped the incarceration of men and women in southern and northeastern prisons before and after the Civil War because it determined where, how, and whether certain racial groups were incarcerated.

4. True.

5. False.

6. True. Women offenders are sometimes treated as double deviants because they are criminal deviants (because it is thought that most people don't commit crimes [there is some debate about this]) and because they are gender deviants (in that they do not conform to traditional gender expectations).

7. True. Feminists have advocated for equal treatment and gender-specific programming in corrections.

8. True.

9. False.

••• CHAPTER 12

1. True.

2. True.

3. Nine teenage black boys riding a train in 1931 were accused of raping two white girls. They were tried several times, and most were found guilty by all-white juries of rape, sometimes without the assistance of counsel, and their convictions kept getting overturned. At least one of the white girls recanted and said the rapes were a fabrication. Four of the youths did prison time. This case was emblematic of how African Americans were handled by the criminal justice system during the first half of the 20th century because it demonstrates how racism permeated every part of the system from police, to prosecutor, to judge, to jury, to corrections.

4. As Bill Quigley indicates, facts indicating that racism still exists in the criminal justice system include how the war on drugs has been prosecuted, driving while black or brown (DWB), more arrests of minority group members for drug offenses, longer waits for trial while incarcerated for accused minority group members, underfunded defense attorneys who serve disproportionately minority group members, minority group member exclusion from jury service, the fact that trials are rare, longer sentences for minority group members, disproportionately more of the longest sentences for minority group members, and disproportionate incarceration of minority group adults and youths.

5. False. Some estimates put the number at 20,000.

6. False. Chinese and Japanese immigration was opposed in law and in practice, particularly after the railroads were built.

7. In 1942, Japanese Americans were interned in reaction to the bombing of Pearl Harbor and the fear that they might conspire to help the Japanese government win the war. German Americans were not interned, although Germany had started the war and German Americans were widely dispersed across several states. One explanation for the differential treatment is racial discrimination.

8. One basic connection among class, race/ethnicity, and crime is that most people who commit street crimes are poor, and a disproportionate number of minority group members are poor.

9. True.

10. True.

11. False.

••• CHAPTER 13

1. True. Juveniles do commit a disproportionate number of criminal acts.

2. True. Juvenile antisocial behavior is normal in that most adolescents engage in it.

3. False. Special juvenile courts began in Cook County, Illinois.

4. True. This is the principle of parens patriae.

5. True. Juveniles can be tried in adult courts and sent to adult prisons.

6. False. Only relatively recently have they been afforded nearly all the same rights as adults.

7. False. The Supreme Court has ruled that juveniles cannot be sentenced to life without parole (LWOP) for any crime other than homicide.

8. False. It was permissible in the United States to execute those who committed murder while they were juveniles until 2005.

••• CHAPTER 14

1. True.

2. False. There are limits on it based on security concerns of the prison.

3. False. The vast majority of lawsuits filed by inmates are frivolous.

4. True. Their prison cells are not "homes."

5. True.

6. True.

7. True. Involuntary commitment to mental institutions is accomplished by civil law.

8. True. Probationers and parolees are subjected to the same curtailment of rights as prison inmates as far as search and seizure go, in particular.

●●● CHAPTER 15

1. False. The more criminals we can rehabilitate, the more society is protected.

2. False. The biggest budget outlay in corrections after salaries is for control and surveillance.

3. False. Many well-run programs expect to reduce recidivism by 10% to 20%.

4. False. Actuarial data supply a better understanding of what does and does not work.

5. False. Correctional officials have been reluctant to use pharmaceutical treatment for addicts.

6. True. Sex offenders are less likely to reoffend than all offense categories other than murder.

7. True. In all major cities studied, well over 50% of arrestees test positive for some kind of illegal drug.

8. True. There are more mentally ill individuals in jails and prisons than in mental hospitals in the United States.

●●● CHAPTER 16

1. True. Most Americans support the death penalty.

2. False. Japan and South Korea also retain the death penalty.

3. True. A white murderer is proportionately more likely than a black or Hispanic murderer to be sentenced to death and to be executed.

4. False. Lethal injection is used almost exclusively today.

5. False. Academics are split on the issue; economists tend to think it deters, while sociologists and criminologists do not.

6. False. The death penalty is far more expensive than life in prison.

7. True. Women are much less likely than men to be sentenced to death for committing a similar crime.

8. True. It is permissible to execute a person with a history of mental illness, but not one with a mental disability (IQ of 70 or below).

●●● CHAPTER 17

1. Answers will vary.

2. True, at least in part, but there are other reasons why correctional populations have been incrementally decreasing.

3. False. Privatization of corrections leads to less professionalism of staff because staff are paid less and trained less, so educated people are not attracted to the work and it is harder to keep good people who behave ethically.

4. False. Privatization of corrections does not lead to more safety and security for inmates, staff, and communities because the staff are less likely to be professional.

5. False.

6. True, and it rarely is considered by governmental or private agencies that operate corrections or by the general public.

GLOSSARY

Abu Ghraib: An Iraq prison operated by the American military during the war in which prisoners were tortured by mostly untrained "correctional officers."

Actuarial data: Data relating to what has actually occurred and been recorded over many thousands of cases. Evidence-based treatment modalities are based on actuarial data.

Addiction: A psychobiological illness characterized by intense craving for a particular substance.

Age–crime curve: Curve formed from the statistical count of the number of known crimes committed in a population over a given period mapped according to age. The curve reflects a sharp increase in offending beginning during early adolescence, a peak during mid-adolescence, and then a steep decline during early adulthood followed by a steadier decline thereafter. The peak may be higher or lower at different periods, and the peak age may vary by 1 or 2 years at different times or in different places, but the peak remains.

Amicus curiae briefs: "Friend of the court" briefs presented to the court, arguing in support of one side or the other, by interested parties not directly involved with the case.

Anger management programs: Programs that consist of a number of techniques by which someone with problems in controlling anger can learn the causes and consequences of anger to reduce the degree of anger and avoid anger-inducing triggers.

Attica Prison riot (1971): Prison riot that began with a spontaneous act of violence by one inmate against an officer who had tried to break up a fight. The violence quickly spread because inmates were frustrated and angry about the overcrowded conditions, lack of programming, and other conditions of confinement. There were charges of racism by the mostly African American inmates regarding their treatment by the mostly white staff. As negotiations broke down, the prison was stormed by the state police and correctional staff. As a consequence, 10 hostages and 29 inmates were dead or dying when the prison was secured, and another 80 inmates had gunshot wounds. It was the bloodiest prison riot in American history.

Balanced approach: A three-pronged goal of the juvenile justice system: (1) to protect the community, (2) to hold delinquent youths accountable, and (3) to provide treatment and positive role models.

Big House prisons: Fortress stone or concrete prisons, usually maximum security, whose attributes include "isolation, routine, and monotony" (Irwin, 2005, p. 32). Strict security and rule enforcement, at least formally, and a regimented schedule are other hallmarks of such facilities.

Bill of Rights: The first 10 Amendments to the U.S. Constitution.

Bridewells: Workhouses established in every English county during the 16th century. They were constructed to hold and whip or otherwise punish "beggars, prostitutes, and nightwalkers" and later as places of detention; their use began in London in 1553 (Orland, 1975, p. 16).

Brutalizing effect: The assumption that executions, rather than deterring homicides, actually increase homicides following the executions.

Chemical castration: A biomedical treatment for chronic sex offenders in which a synthetic hormone called Depo-Provera is administered. Depo-Provera works in males to reduce sexual thoughts, fantasies, and erections by drastically reducing the production of testosterone, the major male sex hormone.

Civil death statutes: Statutes in former times mandating that convicted felons lose all citizenship rights.

Civil rights claim: A "section 1983" claim that a person has been deprived of some legally granted right.

Classical School: School of penology/criminology that was a non-empirical mode of inquiry similar to the philosophy practiced by the classical Greek philosophers—that is, "armchair philosophy."

Coequal staffing: Practice involving the use of personnel processes that provide comparable pay and benefits for people who work in jails to that for people who work on the streets as law enforcement in sheriff's departments.

Cognitive-behavioral therapy (CBT): A counseling approach that tries to address dysfunctional cognition, emotions, and behaviors in a relatively short time through goal-oriented, systematic procedures using a mixture of operant psychology, cognitive theory, and social modeling theory.

Community corrections: A branch of corrections defined as any activity performed by agents of the state to assist offenders in reestablishing functional law-abiding roles in the community while at the same time monitoring their behavior for criminal activity.

Community jails: Jails organized so that those inmates engaged in education, drug or alcohol counseling, or mental health programming in the community will seamlessly receive such services while incarcerated (primarily from community experts in those areas) and again as they transition out of the facility.

Community residential centers: Places where offenders (usually parolees) reside when correctional authorities deem them not yet ready to live completely free.

Community service order: Part of a disposition requiring a probationer to work a certain number of hours doing tasks to help the community.

Concurrent sentence: A sentence in which two separate sentences may be served at the same time.

Consecutive sentence: A sentence in which two or more sentences must be served sequentially.

Contract and lease systems: Systems devised to use inmates' labor. Inmate labor under southern states' lease systems was leased by the prisons to farmers or other contractors. Inmates under a contract system in northern and midwestern prisons worked in larger groups under private or public employers.

Contrast effect: The effect of punishment on future behavior depending on how much the punishment and the usual life experience of the person being punished differ or contrast.

Convict code: Informal rules that inmates live by vis-à-vis the institution and staff and include "1. Do not inform; 2. Do not openly interact or cooperate with the guards or the administration; 3. Do your own time" (Irwin, 2005, p. 33).

Correctional boot camps: Facilities modeled after military boot camps where young and nonviolent offenders are subjected to military-style discipline and physical and educational programs.

Correctional institutions: Institutions (prisons) that carefully classify inmates into treatment programs that address their needs and perceived deficiencies. They are also intended to be places where inmates can earn "good time" and eventual parole. Correctional institutions use the medical model to treat inmates who are believed to be "sick" and in need of a treatment regimen, provided by the prison, which will address that sickness and hopefully "cure" the inmates so that they might become productive members of society. (This term originally applied only to prisons but now can refer to jails as well.)

Corrections: A generic term covering a wide variety of functions carried out by government (and increasingly private) agencies having to do with the punishment, treatment, supervision, and management of individuals who have been accused (in the case of some jail inmates) or convicted of criminal offenses.

Corrections–industrial complex: The collusion among politicians, business, and criminal justice officials to make money for themselves and their organizations off of correctional services, construction, and operations.

Crime control model: A model of law that emphasizes community protection from criminals and stresses that civil liberties can have real meaning only in a safe, well-ordered society.

Death Penalty Information Center: Major (partisan) source of information on the death penalty in the United States.

Deference period: The period of time when there was a partial return to the hands-off approach. It refers to the courts' willingness to defer to the expertise and needs of the authorities.

Deferred adjudication: A decision made by certain criminal justice personnel to delay or defer formal court proceedings if a youth follows probation conditions.

Deinstitutionalization of the mentally ill: A result of the civil rights movement in the United States and the related effort to increase the rights of people involuntarily committed to mental hospitals.

Delinquents: Juveniles who commit acts that are criminal when committed by adults.

Deontological ethical systems: Systems concerned with whether the act itself is good.

Determinate sentence: A prison sentence of a fixed number of years that must be served rather than a range.

Deterrence: A philosophy of punishment aimed at the prevention of crime by the threat of punishment.

Discretion: The ability to make choices and to act or not act on them.

Discretionary parole: Parole granted at the discretion of a parole board for selected inmates who have earned it.

Discrimination: Occurs when people or a group are treated differently because of who they are (e.g., race, ethnicity, gender, age, disability, religion, nationality, sexual orientation or identity, income) rather than because of their abilities or something they did.

Disparity: Occurs when one group is treated differently, and unfairly, by governmental actors as compared with other groups.

Double deviants: Women and girls who are deviant because they engage in crime and because they have violated societal gender role expectations.

Driving while black or brown (DWB): Refers to the practice of police focusing law enforcement attention on black- or brown-skinned drivers.

Drug court: A special sentence for drug-related, nonviolent offenders who must then complete an extensive drug treatment program.

Due process model: A model of law that stresses the accused's rights to a fair trial more than the rights of the community.

Egoism: A framework under which the needs of the self are most important. Acting to satisfy one's own wants and needs under this framework is acting ethically.

Eighth Amendment: Constitutional amendment that forbids cruel and unusual punishment.

Electrocution: A method of execution in which a person is strapped to the chair and electrodes are attached to the person's body. The person is then subjected to a 15- to 30-second jolt of between 500 and 2,450 volts of electricity. The electric chair was introduced as a more humane method of execution than hanging.

Electronic monitoring (EM): A system by which offenders under house arrest can be monitored for compliance using computerized technology such as an electronic device worn around the offender's ankle.

Elmira Reformatory: Founded in 1876 in New York as a model prison in response to calls for the reform of prisons from an earlier era. The inmates were to be younger men. It would encompass all of the rehabilitation focus and graduated reward system (termed the marks system) for which reformers were agitating. The lash was not to be used. Elmira was supposed to hire an educated and trained staff and to maintain uncrowded facilities (Orland, 1975). The operation of Elmira led to the creation of good time, the indeterminate sentence (defined in Chapter 5), a focus on programming to address inmate deficiencies, and the promotion of probation and parole. Ultimately, in practice, it was not the model reformers had hoped it would be.

Enlightenment: Period in history when a major shift in the way people began to view the world and their place in it occurred, moving from a supernaturalistic worldview to a naturalistic and rational worldview.

Ethical formalism: "What is good is that which conforms to the categorical imperative" (Pollock, 1998, p. 48).

Ethics: Right or wrong behavior on the job.

Ethics of care: A framework centered on good acts. It is a deontological perspective. Those who subscribe to this framework believe that "what is good is that which meets the needs of those concerned" (Pollock, 1998, p. 48).

Ethics of virtue: A framework that emphasizes the virtue of one's character over actions.

Ethnicity: The differences between groups of people based on culture. An ethnic group will often have a distinct language as well as particular values, religion, history, and traditions. Ethnic groups may be made up of several races and have a diverse national heritage.

Evidence-based practices (EBP): Movement in which in order to reduce recidivism, corrections must implement practices that have consistently been shown to be effective.

Fair Sentencing Act of 2010: An act mandating that the amount of crack cocaine subject to the 5-year minimum sentence be increased from 5 grams to 28 grams, thus reducing the 100-to-1 ratio to an 18-to-1 ratio (28 grams of crack gets as much time as 500 grams of powder cocaine).

Firing squad: A method of execution by which the condemned is strapped to a chair and shot by a firing squad.

First Amendment: Constitutional amendment that guarantees freedom of religion, speech, press, and assembly.

Fourteenth Amendment: Constitutional amendment containing the due process clause, which declares that no state shall deprive any person of life, liberty, or property without due process of law.

Fourth Amendment: Constitutional amendment that guarantees the right to be free from unreasonable searches and seizures.

Functional magnetic resonance imaging (fMRI): The workhorse of neuroimaging used to assess the functioning of a person's brain while engaged in some task.

Galley slavery: Used as a sentence for crimes or as a means of removing the poor from the streets. Galley slavery also served the twin purpose of providing the requisite labor—rowing—needed to propel ships for seafaring nations interested in engagement in trade and warfare. It was used by the ancient Greeks and Romans and during the Middle Ages, roughly ending sometime during the 1700s.

Gangs (prison): Groups of people with similar interests who socialize together and support each other but who also engage in deviant or criminal activities. Prison gangs have a hierarchical organizational structure and a set, and often strict, code of conduct for members.

Gas chamber: The use of cyanide gas to execute someone placed in an airtight chamber and strapped to a chair.

Gender identity: The gender one identifies with rather than the sex of one's genitalia when born.

General deterrence: The presumed preventive effect of the threat of punishment on the general population—that is, deterrence aimed at potential offenders.

Global positioning system (GPS): A system of probation/parole supervision whereby probationers/parolees are required to wear a tracking unit that can be monitored by satellites.

Great Law: William Penn's idea, based on Quaker principles, deemphasizing the use of corporal and capital punishment for all crimes but the most serious ones.

Green prisons and jails: Correctional facilities that seek to reduce waste and energy consumption and focus on providing a more healthful environment for their staff and inmates.

Habeas corpus: Latin term meaning "you have the body." It is a court order requiring that an arrested person be brought before it to determine the legality of detention.

Habitual offender statutes: Statutes mandating that offenders with a third felony conviction be sentenced to life imprisonment regardless of the nature of the third felony.

Hack: A correctional officer in a prison who is a violent, cynical, and alienated keeper of inmates.

Halfway houses: Transitional places of residence for correctional clients who are "halfway" between the constant supervision of prison and the much looser supervision in the community.

Hands-off doctrine: An early American court-articulated belief that the judiciary should not interfere with the management and administration of prisons.

Hanging: A method of execution in which the condemned is hanged, causing either the neck to break or death by asphyxiation. It is the most common form of execution in the United States historically.

Hedonism: A doctrine maintaining that all goals in life are means to the end of achieving pleasure and/or avoiding pain.

Hedonistic calculus: A method by which individuals are assumed to logically weigh the anticipated benefits of a given course of action against its possible costs.

Hostile environment: Occurs when the workplace is sexualized with jokes, pictures, or in other ways that are offensive to one gender.

House arrest: Program that requires offenders to remain in their homes except for approved periods to travel to work, school, or other approved destinations.

Houses of refuge: Part of the Jacksonian movement (named after President Andrew Jackson) of the early 1800s to use institutions as the solution for social problems. Their stated purpose was to remove impressionable youths, mainly boys but also girls, from the contamination that association with more hardened adult prisoners might bring.

Hulks: Derelict naval vessels transformed into prisons and jails.

Human agency: The capacity of humans to make choices and their responsibility to make moral ones regardless of internal or external constraints on their ability to do so.

Human service: A correctional officer who provides "goods and services," serves as an "advocate" for inmates when appropriate, and assists them with their "adjustment" and through "helping networks" (Johnson, 2002, pp. 242–259).

Importation: Occurs when inmates bring aspects of the larger culture into the prison.

Incapacitation: A philosophy of punishment that refers to the inability of criminals to victimize people outside prison walls while they are locked up.

Indeterminate sentence: A prison sentence consisting of a range of years to be determined by the convict's behavior rather than one of a fixed number of years.

Intensive supervision probation (ISP): Probation that involves more frequent surveillance of probationers that is typically limited to more serious offenders in the belief that there is a chance that they may be rehabilitated (or to save the costs of incarceration).

Intermediate sanctions: A number of innovative alternative sentences that may be imposed in place of the traditional prison/probation dichotomy.

Irish system: A prison system used during the 19th century. This system involved four stages, beginning with a 9-month period of solitary confinement, the first 3 months with reduced rations and no work. This period of enforced idleness was presumed to make even the laziest of men yearn for some kind of activity.

Jails: Local community institutions that hold people who are presumed innocent before trial; convicted people before they are sentenced; convicted minor offenders who are sentenced for terms that are usually less than a year; juveniles (usually in their own jails or separated from adults or before transport to juvenile facilities); women (usually separated from men and sometimes in their own jails); and people for the state or federal authorities. Depending on the particular jail population being served and the capacity of any given facility, they serve to incapacitate, deter, rehabilitate, punish, and reintegrate.

Jim Crow laws: Laws devised by southern states following the Civil War, starting during the 1870s and lasting until 1965 and the civil rights movement, to prevent African Americans from fully participating in social/economic and civic life. These laws restricted the rights and liberties of black citizens in employment, housing, education, travel, and voting. Voter disenfranchisement, or preventing African Americans from voting, was a key part of the Jim Crow laws.

Judicial reprieve: British and early American practice of delaying sentencing following a conviction that could become permanent, depending on the offender's behavior.

Judicial waiver: Involves a juvenile judge deciding after a "full inquiry" that the juvenile should be waived to the adult system.

Justice: A moral concept about just or fair treatment consisting of "treating equals equally and unequals unequally according to relevant differences."

Lethal injection: The preferred method of execution in all states today. Using this method, the condemned person is administered drugs that paralyze the muscular system and stop the person's breathing, followed by another drug that stops the heart.

Liberal feminist: One who believes that the problem for girls and women involved in crime lies more with the social structure around them (e.g., poverty, lack of sufficient schooling or training, patriarchal beliefs) and that the solution lies in preparing them for an alternate existence so that they do not turn to crime.

Liberty interest: An interest in freedom from governmental deprivation of liberty without due process.

Life without parole (LWOP): A life sentence with the additional condition that the person never be allowed parole—"life" means life for those receiving an LWOP sentence.

Mandatory parole: Automatic parole after a set period of time for nearly all inmates.

Mandatory sentence: A prison sentence imposed for crimes for which probation is not an option, where the minimum time to be served is set by law.

Marks system: A graduated reward system for prisons, developed by Maconochie, in which if one behaves, it is possible to earn "marks" that in turn entitle one to privileges.

Mature coping: Occurs in prisons when the inmate deals "with life's problems like a responsive and responsible human being, one who seeks autonomy without violating the rights of others, security without resorting to deception or violence, and relatedness to others as the finest and fullest expression of human identity" (Johnson, 2002, p. 83).

Maximum-security prisons: Prisons where both external and internal security are high. Inmates are often locked up for all or a large part of the day, save for showering or recreation outside of their cell, and they are ideally in single cells, deprived of much contact with others. Programming is limited or nonexistent. Visits and contact with the outside are restricted. The exterior security consists of some combination of layers of razor wire, walls, lights, cameras, armed guards, and attack dogs on patrol. Inmates in maximum security tend to be those who have committed very serious offenses or those who have problems with adhering to the rules in prisons. Death rows, if states have capital punishment, are usually located in maximum-security prisons.

Medical model: Rehabilitation model that assumes criminals are sick and need treatment.

Medium-security prisons: Prisons that hold a mix of people in terms of crime categories but who program well. Medium-security prisons have high external security, but inmates are able to move around more freely within the "walls." Some are built like a college campus, with several buildings devoted to distinct purposes.

Minimum-security prisons: Prisons created for lower-level felony offenders and those who are "short timers," or people who are relatively close to a release date. Those sent here are not expected to be an escape or behavioral problem. The ability and willingness to work is often a prerequisite for classification to this type of facility.

Mortification: Process that occurs as inmates enter the prison and they suffer from the loss of the many roles they occupied in the wider world (Goffman, 1961; Sykes, 1958). Instead, only the role of "inmate" is available, a role that is formally powerless and dependent.

Mount Pleasant Prison: The first prison constructed for women in the United States. Built in 1839 close to the Sing Sing Prison for men in New York, it was in part administered by Sing Sing but had its own buildings, staff, and administrator.

National Probation Act of 1925: The act that initiated the legal use of probation in the United States.

Natural law: A framework whose adherents believe that what is good is that which is natural.

Needs principle: A principle that refers to an offender's prosocial needs, the lack of which puts him or her at risk for reoffending, and that suggests these needs should receive attention in program targeting.

Newgate Prison in Simsbury, Connecticut: Early colonial "prison" that started as a copper mine. During its 54 years of operation (from 1773 to 1827), some 800 inmates passed through its doors. The mine was originally worked in 1705, and one-third of the taxes it paid to the town of Simsbury at that time were used to support Yale College (Phelps, 1860/1996, p. 15).

New-generation or podular direct-supervision jails: Jails that have two key components: a rounded or "podular" architecture for living units and the "direct," as opposed to indirect or intermittent, supervision of inmates by staff; in other words, staff are to be in the living units full-time. Other important facets of these jails are the provision of more goods and services in the living unit (e.g., access to telephones, visiting booths, recreation, library books) and more enriched leadership and communication roles for staff.

New Mexico Prison riot (1980): Prison riot over the conditions of confinement and crowding, which were at epidemic levels. Despite repeated warnings that a riot was going to occur, the administration and staff failed to adequately prepare. The state eventually retook the prison; however, over 3 days, 33 inmates were killed by other inmates. Numerous other inmates, along with staff hostages, were beaten or raped, and millions of dollars in damage was done.

New York prison system (Auburn and Sing Sing): Prisons that included congregate work and eating arrangements but silent and separate housing. This mode of operation allowed prison managers to offset the cost of incarceration by allowing inmates to work together and hence produce more. When inmates were allowed out of their cells, they could also perform maintenance jobs and other tasks in the prison, such as cleaning and cooking, which also reduced the cost of incarcerating. The ball and chain, lockstep, and striped uniforms also originated in these prisons.

Noble cause: "A profound moral commitment to make the world a safer place to live. Put simply, it is getting bad guys off the street. Police believe they're on the side of angels and their purpose in life is getting rid of bad guys" (Crank & Caldero, 2000, p. 35).

Norfolk Island: An English penal colony operated 1,000 miles off the Australian coast. It was established in 1788 as a place designated for prisoners from England and Australia and was regarded as a brutal and violent island prison where inmates were poorly fed, clothed, and housed and were mistreated by staff and their fellow inmates. Alexander Maconochie, an ex-naval captain, asked to be transferred to Norfolk, usually an undesirable placement, so that he could put into practice some ideas he had about prison reform, which he successfully did, vastly improving conditions at the prison.

Offender needs: Deficiencies in offenders' lives that hinder their making a commitment to a prosocial pattern of behavior.

Offender risk: The probability that a given offender will reoffend and thus the threat that he or she poses to the community.

Official deviance: When officials act in a way that benefits their organization but violates laws or formal rules.

Overcrowding: A phenomenon that occurs when the number of inmates exceeds the physical capacity (i.e., beds and space) available.

Pains of imprisonment: Perils described as the "deprivation of liberty, the deprivation of goods and services, the deprivation of heterosexual relationships, the deprivation of autonomy, and the deprivation of security" (Sykes, 1958, pp. 63–83).

Panopticon: A rounded prison design in which multi-tiered cells are built around a hub so that correctional staff can view all inmates without being observed.

Parens patriae: A legal principle giving the state the right to intercede and act in the best interest of children or any other legally incapacitated persons such as the mentally ill.

Parole: The release of prisoners from prison before completing their full sentences.

Parole board: A panel of people presumably qualified to make judgments about the suitability of a prisoner to be released from prison after having served some specified time of his or her sentence.

Patriarchy: Involves the attitudes, beliefs, and behaviors that value men and boys over women and girls. Members of patriarchal societies tend to believe that men and boys are worth more than women and girls. They also believe that women and girls, as well as men and boys, should have certain restricted roles to play and that those of the former are less important than those of the latter. Therefore, education, work or training that helps one to make a living, and better pay are more important to secure for men and boys than for women and girls, who are best suited for more feminine and, by definition in a patriarchal society, less worthy professions.

Penal harm: A movement in corrections based on retribution in sentencing and the infliction of greater harm while inmates are under correctional supervision.

Penal help: A movement that includes the reform of state laws to liberalize marijuana use, the repeal of harsh sentences, and the reduction in the use of incarceration coupled with the increased use of rehabilitation, restorative justice, and reentry programming. Taken together, these indicate that there has been a societal shift away from penal harm as a guiding principle of corrections.

Pennsylvania prison system (Walnut Street Jail, Western and Eastern Pennsylvania prisons): Prisons that emphasized silent and separate eating and working and living arrangements that isolated inmates in their cells, restricted their contact with others, and reinforced the need for penitence. When labor was allowed at all, it was a solitary affair in one's cell.

Penology: Study of the processes adopted and the institutions involved in the punishment and prevention of crime.

Positivists: Those who believe that human actions have causes and that these causes are to be found in the thoughts and experiences that typically precede those actions.

Power: The ability to "get people to do what they otherwise wouldn't" (Dahl, 1961).

Predisposition report: A report done in juvenile courts that is analogous to a presentence investigation report in adult courts.

Presentence investigation report: Report written by the probation officer informing the judge of various aspects of the offense for which the defendant is being sentenced as well as providing information about the defendant's background (educational, family, and employment history), character, and criminal history.

Principle of utility: Positing that human action should be judged moral or immoral by its effects on the happiness of the community and that the proper function of the legislature is to make laws aimed at maximizing the pleasure and minimizing the pain of the population— "the greatest happiness for the greatest number."

Prisonization: The adopting of the inmate subculture by inmates.

Prison Rape Elimination Act of 2003: Act mandating that the Bureau of Justice Statistics collect data on sexual assaults in adult and juvenile jails and prisons and that the agency identify facilities with high levels of victimization.

Prisons: Correctional facilities that have a philosophy of penitence (hence "penitentiary") and that were created as a grand reform in that they represented, in theory at least, a major improvement over the brutality of punishment that characterized early Western, English, and American law and practice.

Prison subculture: Norms, values, beliefs, and even language of the prison.

Privatization: A phenomenon that occurs in corrections when services or whole correctional institutions are provided or operated by private businesses or corporations.

Probation: A sentence imposed on convicted offenders that allows them to remain in the community under the supervision of a probation officer instead of being sent to prison.

Problem-solving courts: Alternatives to traditional criminal courts that cannot adequately address the problems of offenders with special needs and other issues such as alcoholism and mental health problems.

Profession: Regarding the positions of corrections officers and staff, distinguished by prior educational attainment involving college, formal training on the job or just prior to the start of the job, pay and benefits that are commensurate with the work, the ability to exercise discretion, and work that is guided by a code of ethics.

Professionalization: Includes the enforcement of professional standards for their new hires in corrections such as required college-level educational background, sufficient training, pay that is commensurate with job requirements, training that sufficiently prepares people for the job, and a code of ethics that drives the work practice.

Prosecutorial discretion: Allows prosecutors to file some cases in either adult or juvenile court.

Punishment: The act of imposing some unwanted burden such as fines, probation, imprisonment, or death on convicted persons in recompense for their crimes.

Quid pro quo sexual harassment: Involves something for something, as in you give your boss sexual favors and he allows you to keep your job.

Race: The skin color and features of a group of people. It is based on biology.

Rationality: The state of having good sense and sound judgment based on the evidence before us.

Recidivism: When an ex-offender commits further crimes.

Reentry: The process of reintegrating offenders into the community after release from jail or prison. Part of that process is preparing offenders through the use of various programs targeting their risks and needs so that they will have a chance of remaining in the community.

Rehabilitation: A philosophy of punishment aimed at "curing" criminals of their antisocial behavior.

Reintegration: A philosophy of punishment that aims to use the time criminals are under correctional supervision to prepare them to reenter the free community as well equipped to do so as possible.

Religious perspective: A perspective employed by people who believe that "what is good is that which conforms to God's will" (Pollock, 1998, p. 48).

Residential substance abuse treatment (RSAT): A community that typically lasts 6 to 12 months and is composed of inmates in need of substance abuse treatment and whose parole dates are set to coincide with the end of the program. RSAT inmates are separated from the negativity and violence of the rest of the prison and are provided with extensive cognitive-behavioral counseling and attend Alcoholics Anonymous (AA) and Narcotics Anonymous (NA) meetings as well as many other kinds of rehabilitative classes.

Responsivity principle: A principle maintaining that if offenders are to respond to treatment in meaningful and lasting ways, counselors must be aware of their different developmental stages, learning styles, and need to be treated with respect and dignity.

Restitutive justice: A philosophy of punishment driven by simple deterrence and a need to repair the wrongs done.

Restorative justice: A system of justice that gives approximately equal weight to community protection, offender accountability, and the offender. It is oriented to repairing the harm caused by the crime and involves a face-to-face confrontation between the victim and perpetrator in the hope of arriving at a mutually agreeable solution.

Retribution: A philosophy of punishment demanding that criminals' punishments match the degree of harm the criminals have inflicted on their victims—that is, what they justly deserve.

Retributive justice: A philosophy of punishment driven by a passion for revenge.

Risk, needs, and responsivity (RNR) model: A treatment correctional model maintaining that offenders and the community are better served if offenders' risks for reoffending and their needs (their deficiencies such as lack of job skills) are addressed in a way that matches their developmental stage.

Risk principle: A principle that refers to an offender's probability of reoffending and maintains that those with the highest risk should be targeted for the most intense treatment.

Role: What a person does on the job every day.

Rule of law: The principle that law, not men, govern and that no one is above the law.

Section 1983 suits: A mechanism for state prison inmates to sue state officials in federal court regarding their confinement and their conditions of confinement. Section 1983 is part of the Civil Rights Act of 1871, which was initially enacted to protect southern blacks from state officials and the Ku Klux Klan.

Selective incapacitation: A punishment strategy that largely reserves prison for a distinct group of offenders composed primarily of violent repeat offenders.

Sentence: A punitive penalty ordered by the court after a defendant has been convicted of a crime either by a jury, by a judge, or in a plea bargain.

Sentencing disparity: Wide variation in sentences received by different offenders that may be legitimate or discriminatory.

Sentencing guidelines: Scales for numerically computing sentences that offenders should receive based on the crimes they committed and on their criminal records.

Shock probation: A type of sentence aimed at shocking offenders into going straight by exposing them to the reality of prison life for a short period followed by probation.

Specific deterrence: The supposed effect of punishment on the future behavior of persons who experience the punishment.

Split sentences: Sentences that require convicted persons to serve brief periods of confinement in a county jail prior to probation placement.

Stanford Prison Experiment: A 1971 experiment conducted at Stanford University that used volunteer students, divided into officers and inmates, in a makeshift "prison" (Haney et al., 1981). In the end, about a third of the "officers" engaged in the abuse of "inmates," and other "officers" stood by while it was going on. The experiment was stopped after a few days and is often referenced as an example of how correctional work, and the subcultures that develop as part of the job, can foster corrupt behavior by officers.

Stateville Prison: Built in Illinois as a panopticon in 1925 in reaction to the deplorable conditions of the old Joliet prison built in 1860 (J. Jacobs, 1977).

Status offenders: Juveniles who commit certain actions that are legal for adults but not for children such as smoking and not obeying parents.

Status offenses: Offenses that apply only to juveniles such as smoking and disobeying parents.

Statutory exclusion: Waivers in cases where state legislatures have statutorily excluded certain serious offenses from the juvenile courts for juveniles over a certain age, which varies from state to state.

Street-level bureaucrat: A public-sector worker with discretion who has too many clients with too many needs and not enough resources to meet those needs.

Subculture: A subset of a larger culture with its own norms, values, beliefs, traditions, and history of a group of people.

Supermax prisons: High-security prisons, both internally and externally, that hold those who are violent or disruptive in other prisons in the state or federal system. Inmates are confined to their windowless cells 23 hours a day except for showers three times a week (where they are restrained) and solitary exercise time a couple times a week. They eat in their cells. Visiting and programming are very limited.

Teleological ethical systems: Systems focused on the consequences of the act.

Therapeutic communities (TCs): Residential communities providing dynamic, "mutual self-help" environments and offering long-term opportunities for attitude and behavioral change and the learning of constructive, prosocial ways of coping with life.

Total institution: "A place of residence and work where a large number of like-situated individuals, cut off from the wider society for an appreciable period of time, together lead an enclosed, formally administered round of life" (Goffman, 1961, p. xiii).

Transportation: A sentence whereby the convicted person would be sent to another country via a ship whose captain owned the right to sell the convict's labor for a period of time. The captain could in turn sell the convicted person's labor to others in the new land. It was in use for roughly 350 years (from 1607 to 1953) by English and European countries.

Truth-in-sentencing laws: Laws that require there to be a truthful, realistic connection between the sentences imposed on offenders and the time they actually serve.

Unconditional release: A type of release from prison for inmates who have completed their entire sentences.

They are therefore released unconditionally—with no parole.

U.S. Sentencing Commission: A commission charged with creating mandatory sentencing guidelines to control judicial discretion.

Utilitarianism: "What is good is that which results in the greatest utility for the greatest number" (Pollock, 1998, p. 48).

Victim impact statement: A statement made by persons directly affected by a crime (or victims' survivors in the case of murder) to inform the court of the personal and emotional harm they have suffered as a result of the defendant's actions and, in some states, to make a sentencing recommendation.

Victim–offender reconciliation programs (VORPs): Programs designed to bring offenders and their victims together in an attempt to reconcile ("make right") the wrongs offenders have caused. It is an integral component of the restorative justice philosophy.

Waiver: A process by which a juvenile offender is "waived" (transferred) to an adult court because he or she has committed a particularly serious crime or is habitually delinquent.

Walnut Street Jail: Originally constructed in 1773 in Philadelphia, it operated as a typical local jail of the time—holding pretrial detainees and minor offenders; failing to separate by gender, age, or offense; using the fee system, which penalized the poor and led to the near starvation of some; and offering better accommodations, and even access to liquor and sex, to those who could pay for them.

Warehouse prisons: Large prisons of any security level, but more likely super-maximum or maximum-security prisons, where inmates' lives and movement are severely restricted and rule bound. There is no pretense of rehabilitation in warehouse prisons; punishment, incapacitation, and deterrence are the only justifications for such places. The more hardened and dangerous prisoners are supposed to be sent there, and their severe punishment is to serve as a deterrent to others in lower-security prisons.

Work release programs: Programs designed to control offenders in a secure environment while at the same time allowing them to maintain employment.

REFERENCES

CASES CITED

Arizona v. United States, 567 U.S. ___ (2012).

Atkins v. Virginia, 536 U.S. 304 (2002).

Bell v. Wolfish, 441 U.S. 520 (1979).

Bordenkircher v. Hayes, 434 U.S. 357 (1978).

Breed v. Jones, 421 U.S. 517 (1975).

Coffin v. Reichard, 143 F.2d 443 (6th Cir. 1944).

Coker v. Georgia, 433 U.S. 584 (1977).

Cooper v. Pate, 378 U.S. 546 (1964).

Eddings v. Oklahoma, 445 U.S. 104 (1982).

Estelle v. Gamble, 429 U.S. 97 (1976).

Ex parte Crouse, 4 Whart. 9 (Pa. 1838).

Ex parte Hull, 312 U.S. 546 (1941).

Ex parte United States, 242 U.S. 27 (1916).

Ford v. Wainwright, 477 U.S. 399 (1986).

Furman v. Georgia, 408 U.S. 238 (1972).

Graham v. Florida, 560 U.S. ___ (2010).

Gregg v. Georgia, 428 U.S. 153 (1976).

Holt v. Sarver, 309 F. Supp. 362 (1969).

Hudson v. McMillian, 503 U.S. 1 (1992).

Hudson v. Palmer, 468 U.S. 517 (1984).

In re Gault, 387 U.S. 1 (1967).

In re Winship, 397 U.S. 358 (1970).

Jackson v. Indiana, 406 U.S. 715 (1972).

Jones v. Bock, 549 U.S. 199 (2007).

Jones v. Cunningham, 371 U.S. 236 (1963).

Jordan v. Gardner, 986 F.2d 1521 (9th Cir. 1993).

Kansas v. Hendricks, 521 U.S. 346 (1997).

Kent v. United States, 383 U.S. 541 (1966).

McCleskey v. Kemp, 481 U.S. 279 (1987).

McKeiver v. Pennsylvania, 402 U.S. 528 (1971).

Mempa v. Rhay, 389 U.S. 128 (1967).

Miller v. Alabama, 567 U.S. 460 (2012).

Morrissey v. Brewer, 408 U.S. 471 (1972).

Panetti v. Quarterman, 551 U.S. 930 (2007).

Payne v. Tennessee, 501 U.S. 808 (1991).

Pennsylvania Board of Probation and Parole v. Scott, 524 U.S. 357 (1998).

Penry v. Lynaugh, 492 U.S. 302 (1989).

Pervear v. Massachusetts, 72 U.S. 475 (1866).

Powell v. Alabama, 287 U.S. 45 (1932).

Pulido v. State of California et al. (Marin Co. Sup. Ct. 1994).

Roper v. Simmons, 112 S.W. 3rd 397 (2005).

Ruffin v. Commonwealth, 62 Va. 790, 796 (1871).

Rummel v. Estelle, 445 U.S. 263 (1980).

Salazar et al. v. City of Espanola et al. (2004).

Sandin v. Conner, 515 U.S. 472 (1995).

Schall v. Martin, 104 U.S. 2403 (1984).

Smith v. Mosley, 532 F.3d 1270 (11th Cir. 2008).

Stanford v. Kentucky, 492 U.S. 361 (1989).

Thompson v. Oklahoma, 487 U.S. 815 (1988).

Turner v. Safley, 482 U.S. 78 (1987).

United States v. Booker, 543 U.S. 220 (2005).

United States v. Knights, 534 U.S. 112 (2001).

Washington v. Harper, 494 U.S. 210 (1990).

Wilson v. Seiter, 501 U.S 294 (1991).

Wolff v. McDonnell, 418 U.S. 539 (1974).

Woodson v. North Carolina, 428 U.S. 280 (1976).

WORKS CITED

Abadinsky, H. (1993). *Drug abuse: An introduction.* Chicago: Nelson–Hall.

Abadinsky, H. (2009). *Probation and parole: Theory and practice.* Upper Saddle River, NJ: Prentice Hall.

Alahmed, A. (2013, March 15). The execution of the Saudi seven. *Foreign Policy.* Available at http://www.foreignpolicy.com/articles/2013/03/15/The_execution_of_the_Saudi_Seven

Alarid, L. (2000). Along racial and gender lines: Jail subcultures in the midst of racial disproportionality. *Corrections Management Quarterly, 4,* 8–19.

Albers, P., Beauvais, P., Bonert, J., Bose, M., Langbroek, P., Renier, A., & Wahl, T. (2013). *Toward a common evaluation framework to assess mutual trust in the field of judicial cooperation in criminal matters.* Available at https://dspace.library.uu.nl/bitstream/handle/1874/309537/Langbroek_Towards_a_common_evaluation_framework_to_asess_mutual_trust_in_EU_transnational_judicial_cooperation_in_criminal_matters_2013.pdf?sequence=1

Alcock, J. (1998). *Animal behavior: An evolutionary approach* (6th ed.). Sunderland, MA: Sinauer Associates.

Alexander, M. (2010). *The new Jim Crow: Mass incarceration in the age of color-blindness.* New York: New Press.

Alexander, R. (2004). The United States Supreme Court and the civil commitment of sex offenders. *The Prison Journal, 84,* 361–378.

Alm, S. (2013). A new continuum for court supervision. *Oregon Law Review, 91,* 1180–1190.

Alosi, T. (Writer & Director). (2008). *Eastern State: Living behind the walls* [documentary film]. Folsom, CA: Dark Hollow Films.

Alvarado, J. (2009). Keeping jailers from keeping the keys to the courthouse: The Prison Litigation Reform Act's exhaustion requirement and Section 5 of the Fourteenth Amendment. *Seattle Journal for Social Justice, 8,* 323–365.

American Civil Liberties Union. (2012). *Frequently asked questions about the cost of California's death penalty.* Available at https://www.aclunc.org

American Civil Liberties Union. (2015). *Women in prison: An overview.* Available at https://www.aclu.org/words-prison-did-you-know

American Correctional Association. (1983). *The American prison: From* the beginning . . . A pictorial history. Lanham, MD: Author.

American Correctional Association. (2013). Declaration of principles. Available at www.aca.org

Amnesty International. (2004). Abuse of women in custody: Sexual misconduct and shackling of pregnant women. A state-by-state survey of policies and practices in the United States. New York: Author. Available at http://www.amnestyusa.org

Amnesty International (2013). Death penalty 2011: Alarming levels of executions in the few countries that kill. Available at www.amnesty.org

Andrews, D., & Bonta, J. (2007). The psychology of criminal conduct (5th ed.). Cincinnati, OH: Anderson.

Andrews, D., Bonta, J., & Wormith, J. (2006). The recent past and near future of risk and/or needs assessment. Crime & Delinquency, 52, 7–27.

Antonio, M. E., Young, J. L., & Wingeard, L. M. (2009). When actions and attitude count most: Assessing perceived level of responsibility and support for inmate treatment and rehabilitation programs among correctional employees. The Prison Journal, 89, 363–382.

Applegate, B. K., Cullen, F. T., & Fisher, B. S. (2001). Public support for correctional treatment: The continuing appeal of the rehabilitative ideal. In E. J. Latessa, A. Holsinger, J. W. Marquart, & J. R. Sorensen (Eds.), Correctional contexts: Contemporary and classical readings (2nd ed., pp. 506–519). Los Angeles: Roxbury.

Applegate, B. K., & Paoline, E. A., III. (2007). Jail officers' perceptions of the work environment in traditional versus new generation facilities. American Journal of Criminal Justice, 31, 64–80.

Applegate, B. K., & Sitren, A. H. (2008). The jail and the community: Comparing jails in rural and urban contexts. The Prison Journal, 88, 252–269.

Archibold, R. C. (2010, April 23). Arizona enacts stringent law on immigration. New York Times. Available at http://www.nytimes.com/2010/04/24/us/politics/24immig.html

Aronson, J., & Cole, S. (2009). Science and the death penalty: DNA, innocence, and the debate over capital punishment in the United States. Law & Social Inquiry, 34, 603–633.

Ashcroft, J., Daniels, D., & Herraiz, D. (1997). Defining drug courts: The key components. Washington, DC: U.S. Department of Justice.

Austin, J., & Irwin, J. (2001). It's about time: America's imprisonment binge. Belmont, CA: Wadsworth.

Awes, A. (Producer & Director), & Awes, M. (Producer). (2010). Who really discovered America? [documentary]. Minneapolis: Committee Films.

Balazs, G. (2006). The workaday world of a juvenile probation officer. In A. Walsh, Correctional assessment, casework, and counseling (4th ed., pp. 414–416). Alexandria, VA: American Correctional Association.

Bard, S. (1997, July 31). Idaho inmates tell of assault in Texas: Nurses, who prisoners say fondled them, have been arrested and fired. Idaho Statesman, p. B1.

Barker, V. (2006). The politics of punishing: Building a state governance theory of American imprisonment variation. Punishment & Society, 8, 5–32.

Barlow, L. W., Hight, S., & Hight, M. (2006). Jails and their communities: Piedmont Regional Jail as a community model. American Jails, 20, 38–45.

Bartollas, C., & Hahn, L. D. (1999). Policing in America. Needham Heights, MA: Allyn & Bacon.

Barton, A. (1999). Breaking the crime/drugs cycle: The birth of a new approach? Howard Journal of Criminal Justice, 38, 144–157.

Baumer, E., & Wolff, K. (2014). Evaluating contemporary crime drop(s) in America, New York City, and many other places. Justice Quarterly, 31, 5–38.

Baunach, P. J. (1992). Critical problems of women in prison. In I. L. Moyer (Ed.), The changing role of women in the criminal justice system (pp. 99–112). Prospect Heights, IL: Waveland.

Bazelon Center for Mental Health Law. (2008). Individuals with mental illness in jail and prison. Washington, DC: Author. Available at http://www.bazelon.org

Bazemore, G. (2000). What's "new" about the balanced approach? In P. Kratkoski (Ed.), Correctional counseling and treatment (pp. 1–22). Prospect Heights, IL: Waveland.

Beare, M. E., & Hogg, C. (2013). Listening in . . . to gang culture. Canadian Journal of Criminology & Criminal Justice, 55, 421–452.

Beaumont, G., & Tocqueville, A. de. (1964). On the penitentiary system in the United States and its application in France. Carbondale, IL: Southern Illinois University Press. (Original work published 1833)

Beccaria, C. (1963). On crimes and punishment (H. Paulucci, Trans.). Indianapolis, IN: Bobbs–Merrill. (Original work published 1764)

Beck, A. J., Berzofsky, M., Caspar, R., & Krebs, C. (2013). Sexual victimization in prisons and jails reported by inmates, 2011–2012. Washington, DC: U.S. Department of Justice, Office of Justice Programs, Bureau of Justice Statistics. Available at http://www.bjs.gov/content/pub/ascii/svpjri1112.txt

Beck, A. J., & Harrison, P. M. (2001). Prisoners in 2000. Washington, DC: Bureau of Justice Statistics. Available at http://www.bjs.gov/content/pub/pdf/p00.pdf

Beck, A. J., & Harrison, P. M. (2007). Sexual violence reported by correctional authorities, 2006. Washington, DC: U.S. Department of Justice, Bureau of Justice Statistics.

Beck, A. J., Harrison, P. M., & Adams, D. B. (2007). Sexual violence reported by correctional authorities, 2006. Washington, DC: U.S. Department of Justice, Office of Justice Programs. Available at http://www.bjs.gov/content/pub/pdf/svrca06.pdf

Beck, A. J., & Rantala, R. R. (2014). Sexual victimization reported by adult correctional authorities, 2009–11. Washington, DC: Bureau of Justice Statistics. Available at http://www.bjs.gov/content/pub/pdf/svraca0911.pdf

Beck, A. J., Rantala, R. R., & Rexroat, J. (2014). Allegations of sexual victimization in prisons and jails rose from 2009 to 2011 substantiated incidents remained stable. Washington, DC: U.S. Department of Justice, Office of Justice Programs, Bureau of Justice Statistics. Available at http://www.bjs.gov/content/pub/press/svraca0911pr.cfm

Becker, G. (1997). The economics of crime. In M. Fisch (Ed.), Criminology 97/98 (pp. 15–20). Guilford, CT: Duskin.

Beckett, K., Nyrop, K., Pfingst, L., & Bowen, M. (2005). Drug use, drug possession arrests, and the question of race: Lessons from Seattle. *Social Problems, 52,* 419–441.

Belbot, B., & Hemmens, C. (2010). *The legal rights of the convicted.* El Paso, TX: LFB Scholarly Publishing.

Belknap, J. (2001). *The invisible woman: Gender, crime, and justice* (2nd ed.). Belmont, CA: Wadsworth.

Bennett, K. (1995). Constitutional issues in cross-gender searches and visual observation of nude inmates by opposite-sex officers: A battle between and within the sexes. *The Prison Journal, 75,* 90–112.

Bentham, J. (1948). *A fragment on government and an introduction to the principles of morals and legislation* (W. Harrison, Ed.). Oxford, UK: Basil Blackwell. (Original work published 1789)

Bentham, J. (1969). *Panopticon papers: A Bentham reader* (M. P. Mack, Ed.). New York: Pegasus. (Original work published 1789)

Bentham, J. (2003). *The rationale of punishment.* London: Robert Heward. (Original work published 1811)

Bergner, D. (1998). *God of the rodeo: The quest for redemption in Louisiana's Angola Prison.* New York: Ballantine Books.

Berk, R., Li, A., & Hickman, L. (2005). Statistical difficulties in determining the role of race in capital cases: A re-analysis of data from the state of Maryland. *Journal of Quantitative Criminology, 21,* 365–390.

Binder, A., Geis, G., & Bruce, D. (2001). *Juvenile delinquency: Historical, cultural, and legal perspectives.* Cincinnati, OH: Anderson.

Bindzus, D. (2001). The practice of Naikan in Japanese prisons. In E. Fairchild & H. Dammer (Eds.), *Comparative criminal justice systems* (pp. 264–266). Belmont, CA: Wadsworth.

Bissonnette, G. (2006). "Consulting" the federal sentencing guidelines after Booker. *UCLA Law Review, 54,* 1497–1547.

Black, M., & Smith, R. (2003). *Electronic monitoring in the criminal justice system* (Trends and Issues in Crime and Criminal Justice, No. 254). Canberra: Australian Institute of Criminology.

Blackburn, A. G., Mullings, J. L., & Marquart, J. W. (2008). Sexual assault in prison and beyond: Toward an understanding of lifetime sexual assault among incarcerated women. *The Prison Journal, 88,* 351–377.

Blalock, H. M. (1967). *Toward a theory of minority group relations.* New York: John Wiley.

Bland, A. (2014, July 26). Tulsa County Drug Court a life-saver, new graduate says. *Tulsa World.* Available at http://www.tulsaworld.com/news/courts/tulsa-county-drug-court-a-life-saver-new-graduate-says/article_12fb55b9-c13f-53e8-a78e-5e654ea461f7.html

Bleckman, E., & Vryan, K. (2000). Prosocial family therapy: A manualized preventive intervention for juveniles. *Aggression and Violent Behavior, 5,* 343–378.

Blonigen, D. (2010). Explaining the relationship between age and crime: Contributions from the developmental literature on personality. *Clinical Psychology Review, 30,* 89–100.

Bloom, B., Owen, B., & Covington, S. (2003). *Gender responsive strategies: Research, practice, and guiding principles for women offenders.* Washington, DC: National Institute of Corrections.

Blue, E. (2012). *Doing time in the Depression: Everyday life in Texas and California prisons.* New York: New York University Press.

Blume, J., Eisenberg, T., & Wells, M. (2004). Explaining death row's population and racial composition. *Journal of Empirical Legal Studies, 1,* 165–207.

Bohm, R. (2003). *Deathquest: An introduction to the theory and practice of capital punishment in the United States* (2nd ed.). Cincinnati, OH: Anderson.

Bohm, R. (2012). *Deathquest: An introduction to the theory and practice of capital punishment in the United States* (4th ed.). New York: Routledge.

Bohm, R., & Haley, K. (2007). *Introduction to criminal justice.* New York: McGraw–Hill.

Bonczar, T. P. (2008). *Characteristics of state parole supervising agencies, 2006.* Washington, DC: U.S. Department of Justice, Office of Justice Programs, Bureau of Justice Statistics. Available at http://bjs.ojp.usdoj.gov

Bonczar, T. P. (2011). *State prison admissions, 2009: Sentence length, by offense and admission type.* Washington, DC: U.S. Department of Justice, Office of Justice Programs, Bureau of Justice Statistics.

Available at http://www.bjs.gov/index.cfm?ty=pbdetail&iid=2056

Bonta, J., Wallace-Capretta, S., & Rooney, J. (2000). Can electronic monitoring make a difference? *Crime & Delinquency, 46,* 61–75.

Bookman, C. R., Lightfoot, C. A., & Scott, D. L. (2005). Pathways for change: An offender reintegration collaboration. *American Jails, 19,* 9–14.

Boone, R. (2013a, October 23). Staffing issues known for years at private prison. *Spokesman-Review,* p. 3A.

Boone, R. (2013b, October 29). Justice Dept. won't prosecute Idaho prison guards. *Spokesman-Review,* p. 5A.

Boone, R. (2016, May 24). Fed. court upholds contempt ruling against prison company. *Moscow–Pullman Daily News,* p. 3A.

Bottcher, J., & Ezell, M. (2005). Examining the effectiveness of boot camps: A randomized experiment with a long-term follow up. *Journal of Research in Crime and Delinquency, 42,* 309–332.

Braswell, M. C., McCarthy, B. R., & McCarthy, B. J. (1991). *Justice, crime, and ethics.* Cincinnati, OH: Anderson.

British Foreign Office. (2013). *Information pack for British prisoners in Saudi Arabia.* Available at https://www.gov.uk

Britton, D. M. (2003). *At work in the iron cage: The prison as a gendered organization.* New York: New York University Press.

Broussard, D., Leichliter, J. S., Evans, A., Kee, R., Vallury, V., & McFarlane, M. M. (2002). Screening adolescents in a juvenile detention center for gonorrhea and chlamydia: Prevalence and reinfection rates. *The Prison Journal, 82,* 8–18.

Brown, M. (2006). Gender, ethnicity, and offending over the life course: Women's pathways to prison in the Aloha State. *Critical Criminology, 14,* 137–158.

Buonanno, P., & Raphael, S. (2013). Incarceration and incapacitation: Evidence from the 2006 Italian collective pardon. *American Economic Review, 103,* 2437–2465.

Bureau of Indian Affairs. (2014). Indian entities recognized and eligible to receive services from the United States Bureau of Indian Affairs. *Federal Register, 80,* 1942–1943.

Bureau of Justice Assistance. (2013). *What are problem-solving courts?*

Washington, DC: U.S. Department of Justice, Office of Justice Programs. Available at https://www.bja.gov/evaluation/program-adjudication/problem-solving-courts.htm

Bureau of Justice Statistics. (2000). *Correctional populations in the United States, 1997.* Washington, DC: Author. Available at http://www.bjs.gov/content/pub/pdf/cpus97.pdf

Bureau of Justice Statistics. (2001). *Probation and parole in the United States, 2000.* Washington, DC: Author. Available at http://www.bjs.gov/content/pub/pdf/ppus00.pdf

Bureau of Justice Statistics. (2006). *Prevalence of imprisonment in the United States.* Washington, DC: U.S. Department of Justice, Office of Justice Programs. Available at http://www.ojp.usdoj.gov/bjs

Bureau of Justice Statistics. (2007). *Prison and jail inmates at midyear series, 1998–2006.* Washington, DC: U.S. Department of Justice, Office of Justice Programs. Available at http://www.bjs.gov

Bureau of Justice Statistics. (2008). *Jail statistics: Summary of findings.* Washington, DC: U.S. Department of Justice, Office of Justice Programs. Available at http://www.bjs.gov

Bureau of Justice Statistics. (2011). *Justice expenditures and employment, FY 1982–2007—Statistical tables.* Washington, DC: Office of Justice Programs, U.S. Department of Justice. Available at http://www.bjs.gov

Bureau of Justice Statistics. (2014). *PREA data collection activities, 2014.* Washington, DC: U.S. Department of Justice, Office of Justice Programs, Bureau of Justice Statistics. Available at http://www.bjs.gov/content/pub/pdf/pdca14.pdf

Bureau of Justice Statistics. (2016). *Prisoners in 2015.* Washington, DC: Department of Justice, Office of Justice Programs, Bureau of Justice Statistics. Available at https://www.bjs.gov

Bureau of Labor Statistics. (2016a). *Labor force statistics from the Current Population Survey: Table 11.* Washington, DC: Author. Available at http://www.bls.gov/cps/cpsaat11.pdf

Bureau of Labor Statistics. (2016b). Occupational employment statistics. *Occupational employment and wages, May 2016: 33-3012*

correctional officers and jailers. Available at https://www.bls.gov/oes/oes333012.htm

Burnett, J. (2011). Town relies on troubled youth prison for profits. *National Public Radio.* Available at http://www.npr.org/2011/03/25/134850972/town-relies-on-troubled-youth-prison-for-profits

Burns, H. (1975). *Corrections: Organization and administration.* St. Paul, MN: West.

Burrell, W. (2006). *Caseload standards for probation and parole (September 2006).* Lexington, KY: American Probation and Parole Association. Available at https://cdpsdocs.state.co.us/ccjj/Resources/Ref/APPA_Caseload_Standards_PP_0906.pdf

Bushway, S., & Reuter, P. (2008). Economists' contribution to the study of crime and the criminal justice system. *Crime and Justice, 37,* 389–451.

Butterworth, B. (1995, May 25). *News release.* Available at http://myfloridalegal.com

Butts, J., & Mitchell, O. (2000). Brick by brick: Dismantling the border between juvenile and adult justice. In C. M. Friel (Ed.), *Criminal justice 2000, Vol. 2: Boundary changes in criminal justice organizations* (pp. 167–213). Washington, DC: U.S. Department of Justice, National Institute of Justice.

Bynum, J., & Thompson, W. (1999). *Juvenile delinquency: A sociological approach.* Boston: Allyn & Bacon.

Byrne, J. M., & Hummer, D. (2008). The nature and extent of prison violence. In J. M. Byrne, D. Hummer, & F. S. Taxman (Eds.), *The culture of prison violence* (pp. 12–26). Boston: Pearson.

Byrne, J. M., Hummer, D., & Stowell, J. (2008). Prison violence, prison culture, and offender change: New directions for research, theory, policy, and practice. In M. Byrne, D. Hummer, & F. S. Taxman (Eds.), *The culture of prison violence* (pp. 202–219). Boston: Pearson.

Cahalan, M. W. (1986). *Historical corrections statistics in the United States, 1850–1984.* Washington, DC: U.S. Department of Justice, Bureau of Justice Statistics.

Call, J. (2011). The Supreme Court and prisoners' rights. In E. Latessa & A. Holsinger (Eds.), *Correctional contexts* (pp. 155–169). New York: Oxford University Press.

Cameron, S. (1994). A review of the econometric evidence on the effects of capital punishment. *The Journal of Socio-Economics, 23,* 197–214.

Camp, S. D., & Gaes, G. G. (2002). Growth and quality of U.S. private prisons: Evidence from a national survey. *Criminology & Public Policy, 1,* 427–450.

Camp, S. D., Steiger, T. L., Wright, K. N., Saylor, W. G., & Gilman, E. (2013). Affirmative action and the "level playing field": Comparing perceptions of own and minority job advancement opportunities. In M. K. Stohr, T. Walsh, & C. Hemmens (Eds.), *Corrections: A text/reader* (2nd ed., pp. 360–373). Thousand Oaks, CA: Sage.

Carrigan, W. D., & Webb, C. (2015, February 20). When Americans lynched Mexicans. *New York Times,* p. A23.

Carroll, L. (1974). *Hacks, blacks, and cons: Race relations in a maximum security prison.* Lexington, MA: Lexington Books.

Carroll, L. (1982). Race, ethnicity and the social order of the prison. In R. Johnson & H. Toch (Eds.), *The pains of imprisonment* (pp. 181–203). Beverly Hills, CA: Sage.

Carson, E. A. (2014). *Prisoners in 2013.* Washington, DC: Bureau of Justice Statistics. Available at http://www.bjs.gov/content/pub/pdf/p13.pdf

Carson, E. A. (2015). *Prisoners in 2014.* Washington, DC: Bureau of Justice Statistics. Available at http://www.bjs.gov/content/pub/pdf/p14.pdf

Carson, E. A., & Anderson, E. (2016). *Prisoners in 2014.* Washington, DC: Bureau of Justice Statistics. Available at http://www.bjs.gov/content/pub/pdf/p15.pdf

Carson, E. A., & Golinelli, D. (2013). *Prisoners in 2012: Trends in admissions and releases, 1991–2012.* Washington, DC: U.S. Department of Justice, Office of Justice Programs, Bureau of Justice Statistics. Available at http://www.bjs.gov/index.cfm?ty=pbdetail&iid=4842

Carter, K. (2006). Restorative justice and the balanced approach. In A. Walsh, *Correctional assessment, casework, and counseling* (4th ed., pp. 8–11). Lanham, MD: American Correctional Association.

Carter, M., & Morris, L. (2002). *Managing sex offenders in the community.* Washington, DC: Center for Sex Offender Management.

The case for freeing the last hooligan. (2011, January 20). *South China Morning Post*. Available at http://www.scmp.com/article/736208/case-freeing-last-hooligan

Caspi, A., & Moffitt, T. (1995). The continuity of maladaptive behavior: From description to understanding in the study of antisocial behavior. In D. Cicchetti & D. Cohen (Eds.), *Manual of developmental psychology* (pp. 472–511). New York: John Wiley.

Center for Community Corrections. (1997). *Community corrections: A call for punishments that make sense.* Washington, DC: U.S. Department of Justice.

Champion, D. (2005). *Probation, parole, and community corrections* (5th ed.). Upper Saddle River, NJ: Prentice Hall.

Chen, X. (2010). The Chinese sentencing guideline: A primary analysis. *Federal Sentencing Reporter, 22,* 213–216.

Chesney-Lind, M., & Irwin, K. (2006). Still "the best place to conquer girls": Girls and the juvenile justice system. In A. V. Merlo & J. M. Pollock (Eds.), *Women, law, and social control* (pp. 271–291). Boston: Pearson.

Chesney-Lind, M., & Shelden, R. G. (1998). *Girls, delinquency, and juvenile justice* (2nd ed.). Belmont, CA: West/Wadsworth.

Civil War prisons and prisoners. (2002). *Civil War Potpourri.* Available at http://www.civilwarhome.com/prisonsandprisoners.html

Clark, J. (1991, September/October). Correctional health care issues in the nineties: Forecast and recommendations. *American Jails Magazine,* pp. 18–23.

Clarke, R., & Cornish, D. (2001). Rational choice. In R. Paternoster & R. Bachman (Eds.), *Explaining criminals and crime: Essays in contemporary criminological theory* (pp. 23–42). Los Angeles: Roxbury.

Clayton, S. L. (Ed.). (2003). Correctional officer education and training. *Corrections Compendium, 28,* 11–22.

Clear, T., Cole, G., & Reisig, M. D. (2011). *American corrections* (9th ed.). Belmont, CA: Wadsworth.

Clear, T., Rose, D., & Ryder, J. (2001). Incarceration and the community: The problem of removing and returning offenders. *Crime & Delinquency, 47,* 335–351.

Clemmer, D. (2001). The prison community. In E. J. Latessa, A. Holsinger, J. W. Marquart, & J. R. Sorensen (Eds.), *Correctional contexts: Contemporary and classical readings* (2nd ed., pp. 83–87). Los Angeles: Roxbury.

Coates, R. (1990). Victim–offender reconciliation programs in North America. In B. Galaway & J. Hudson (Eds.), *Criminal justice, restitution, and reconciliation* (pp. 177–182). Monsey, NY: Criminal Justice Press.

Cohen, A. (2013, June 9). One of the darkest periods in the history of American prisons. *Atlantic Monthly,* pp. 1–8.

Cohen, F. (2008). Correctional health care: A retrospective. *Correctional Law Reporter, 20,* 5–12.

Cohen, T., & Kyckelhahn, T. (2010). *Felony defendants in large urban counties, 2006.* Washington, DC: U.S. Department of Justice.

Colbert, D. (Ed.). (1997). *Eyewitness to America: 500 years of America in the words of those who saw it happen.* New York: Pantheon Books.

Collins, R. (2004). Onset and desistence in criminal careers: Neurobiology and the age–crime relationship. *Journal of Offender Rehabilitation, 39,* 1–19.

Comack, E. (2006). Coping, resisting, and surviving: Connecting women's law violations to their history of abuse. In L. F. Alarid & P. Cromwell (Eds.), *In her own words* (pp. 33–44). Los Angeles: Roxbury.

Conly, C. (1998). *The Women's Prison Association: Supporting women offenders and their families.* Washington, DC: National Institute of Justice.

Conover, T. (2001). *Newjack: Guarding Sing Sing.* New York: Vintage Books.

Cooper, A. (2011, February). Throwing away the key: Michelle Alexander on how prisons have become the new Jim Crow. *The Sun,* pp. 4–12.

Cooper, J., Walsh, A., & Ellis, L. (2010). Is criminology ripe for a paradigm shift? Evidence from a survey of American criminologists. *Journal of Criminal Justice Education, 21,* 332–347.

Corasanti, N. (2017, April 2). Rikers Island Commission unveils plan to shut down jail complex. *New York Times.* Retrieved May 11, 2017, from www.nytimes.com/2017/04/02/nyregion/rikers-island-jail-closure-plan

Cornelius, G. F. (2007). *The American jail: The cornerstone of modern corrections.* Upper Saddle River, NJ: Pearson/Prentice Hall.

Couch, R. (2015, February 5). Some states are closing prisons and turning them into homeless shelters, reentry centers. *Huffington Post.* Available at http://www.huffingtonpost.com/2015/02/05/closing-state-prisons_n_6614220.html

Council of State Governments Justice Center. (2013). *The impact of probation and parole populations on arrest in four California cities.* New York: Author. Available at http://csgjusticecenter.org

Council of State Governments Justice Center. (2014). *Mental health.* Available at http://csgjusticecenter.org/mental-health

Council of State Governments Justice Center. (2015, May 28). *Launch of national initiative offers counties research-based support to address growing mental health crisis in jails.* Available at https://csgjusticecenter.org/mental-health/posts/launch-of-national-initiative-offers-counties-research-based-support-to-address-growing-mental-health-crisis-in-jails

Cowburn, M. (1998). A man's world: Gender issues in working with male sex offenders in prison. *Howard Journal of Criminal Justice, 37,* 234–251.

Cox, N. R., & Osterhoff, W. E. (1991). Managing the crisis in local corrections: A public–private partnership approach. In J. Thompson & G. L. Mays (Eds.), *American jails: Public policy issues* (pp. 227–239). Chicago: Nelson–Hall.

Crabbe, J. (2002). Genetic contributions to addiction. *Annual Review of Psychology, 53,* 435–462.

Craig, S.C. (2009). A historical review of mother and child programs for incarcerated women. *The Prison Journal, 89,* 35S–53S.

Crank, J. P., & Caldero, M. A. (2000). *Police ethics: The corruption of noble cause.* Cincinnati, OH: Anderson.

Crank, J. P., & Caldero, M. A. (2011). *Police ethics: The corruption of noble cause* (3rd ed.). Cincinnati, OH: Anderson.

Crewe, B., Warr, J., Bennett, P., & Smith, A. (2014). The emotional geography of prison life. *Theoretical Criminology, 18,* 56–74.

Crime and Justice Institute at Community Resources for Justice. (2009). *Implementing evidence-based policy and practice in community corrections* (2nd ed.). Washington, DC: National Institute of Corrections. Available at http://static.nicic.gov/Library/024107.pdf

Crouch, B. (1993). Is incarceration really worse? Analysis of offenders' preferences for prison over probation. *Justice Quarterly, 10,* 67–88.

Cullen, F. T. (1994). Social support as an organizing concept for criminology: Presidential address to the Academy of Criminal Justice Sciences. *Justice Quarterly, 11,* 527–559.

Cullen, F. T. (2006). Assessing the penal harm movement. In E. J. Latessa & A. M. Holsinger (Eds.), *Correctional contexts: Contemporary and classical readings* (3rd ed., pp. 61–74). Los Angeles: Roxbury.

Cullen, F., & Gendreau, P. (2001). Assessing correctional rehabilitation: Policy, practice, and prospects. In *Criminal justice 2000* (Vol. 3, pp. 109–175). Washington, DC: National Institute of Justice.

Cullen, F. T., & Jonson, C. L. (2012). *Correctional theory: Context and consequences.* Thousand Oaks, CA: Sage.

Cullen, F. T., Jonson, C. L., & Stohr, M. K. (2014). *The American prison: Imagining a different future.* Thousand Oaks, CA: Sage.

Culley, R. (2012). "The judge didn't sentence me to be raped": *Tracy Neal v. Michigan Department of Corrections:* A 15-year battle against the sexual abuse of women inmates in Michigan. *Women & Criminal Justice, 22,* 206–225.

Currie, E. (1999). Reflections on crime and criminology at the millennium. *Western Criminology Review, 2*(1). Available at http://www.westerncriminology.org/documents/WCR/v02n1/currie/currie.html

Dahl, R. (1961). *Who governs? Democracy and power in an American city.* New Haven, CT: Yale University Press.

Daly, K., & Chesney-Lind, M. (1988). Feminism and criminology. *Justice Quarterly, 5,* 497–535.

Damrosch, L. (2010). *Discovery of America.* New York: Farrar, Straus and Giroux.

Davidson, J. (2015, September 1). Too many inmates, too few correctional officers: A lethal recipe in federal prisons. *Washington Post.* Available at https://www.washingtonpost.com/news/federal-eye/wp/2015/09/01/too-many-inmates-too-few-correctional-officers-a-lethal-recipe-in-federal-prisons/?utm_term=.6219f7569b08

Davis, K. C. (2008). *America's hidden history: Untold tales of the first pilgrims, fighting women, and forgotten founders who shaped a nation.* New York: HarperCollins.

Deane, E. (Producer & Director), & Bosch, A. (Producer & Director). (2000). *American Experience: The Rockefellers* [documentary]. Boston: WGBH Educational Foundation. Available at http://www.pbs.org/wgbh/americanexperience/films/rockefellers

Death Penalty Information Center (DPIC). (2012). *Financial costs.* Available at http://www.deathpenaltyinfo.org/costs-death-penalty

Death Penalty Information Center (DPIC). (2013). *Race of death row inmates executed since 1976.* Available at http://www.deathpenaltyinfo.org/race-death-row-inmates-executed-1976

Death Penalty Information Center (DPIC). (2017a). *Execution information accurate as of September 13, 2017 following an execution in Ohio.* Available at https://deathpenaltyinfo.org/race-death-row-inmates-executed-1976?scid=5&did=184

Death Penalty Information Center (DPIC). (2017b). *Number of executions since 1976: 1460.* Available at https://deathpenaltyinfo.org/executions-year

DeFina, R., & Arvanites, T. (2002). The weak effect of imprisonment on crime: 1971–1998. *Social Science Quarterly, 83,* 635–653.

DeHart, D. D. (2008). Pathways to prison: Impact of victimization in the lives of incarcerated women. *Violence Against Women, 14,* 1362–1381.

Delany, P., Fletcher, B., & Shields, J. (2003). Reorganizing care for the substance using offender—The case for collaboration. *Federal Probation, 67,* 64–69.

De La Torre, M. (2013). Buried voices: Mexican migrants' views on the question of illegality. *Contemporary Justice Review, 16,* 264–279.

Del Carmen, R., Parker, V., & Reddington, F. (1998). *Briefs of leading cases in juvenile justice.* Cincinnati, OH: Anderson.

DeLisi, M. (2005). *Career criminals in society.* Thousand Oaks, CA: Sage.

Deng, X., Zhang, L., & Cordilia, A. (1998). Social control and recidivism in China. *Journal of Contemporary Criminal Justice, 14,* 281–295.

Department of the Treasury. (2010, December 29). *Significant problems still exist with Internal Revenue Service efforts to identify prisoner tax refund fraud* [final report]. Washington, DC: Author.

de Quervain, D., Fischbacher, U., Treyer, V., Schellhammer, M., Schnyder, U., Buch, A., & Fehr, E. (2004). The neural basis of altruistic punishment. *Science, 305,* 1254–1259.

Diamond, J. (1997). *Guns, germs, and steel: The fates of human societies.* New York: Norton.

Diaz-Duran, C. (2010, December 31). The Scott sisters' life sentence for $11. *The Daily Beast.* Available at http://www.thedailybeast.com

Dickens, C. (1842). *American notes,* Chapter 7. The Literature Network. Available at http://www.online-literature.com

Dietz, E., O'Connell, D., & Scarpitti, F. (2003). Therapeutic communities and prison management: An examination of the effects of operating an in-prison therapeutic community on levels of institutional disorder. *International Journal of Offender Therapy and Comparative Criminology, 47,* 210–223.

DiIulio, J. J., & Piehl, A. (1991). Does prison pay? The stormy national debate over the cost-effectiveness of imprisonment. *The Brookings Review, 9*(4), 28–35.

Dillard, A. (2012). Madness alone punishes the madman: The search for moral dignity in the court's competency doctrine as applied to capital cases. *Tennessee Law Review, 79,* 461–514.

Dilworth, D. (1995). Prisoners' lawsuits burden federal civil courts. *Trial, 31,* 98–100.

Director addresses changes within BOP. (2006, March). *The Third Branch, 38.* Available at http://www.uscourts.gov/news/The-Third-Branch/06-03-01/Director_Addresses_Change_Within_BOP.aspx

Ditton, P., & Wilson, D. (1999). *Truth in sentencing in state prisons*. Washington, DC: Bureau of Justice Statistics.

Dix, D. (1967). *Remarks on prisons and prison discipline in the United States*. Montclair, NJ: Patterson Smith. (Original work published 1843; rev. ed. published 1845)

Dodgson, K., Goodwin, P., Howard, P., Llewellyn-Thomas, S., Mortimer, E., Russell, N., & Weiner, M. (2001). *Electronic monitoring of released prisoners: An evaluation of the home detention curfew scheme*. London: Home Office Research.

Dowden, C., & Tellier, C. (2004). Predicting work-related stress in correctional officers: A meta-analysis. *Journal of Criminal Justice, 32*, 31–47.

Dror, I., & Hampikian, G. (2011). Subjectivity and bias in forensic mixture interpretation. *Science and Justice, 51*, 204–208.

Drug Policy Alliance. (2016). *Drug war statistics*. Available at http://www.drugpolicy.org/drug-war-statistics

Dui Hua. (2013). *Criminal justice*. Available at http://duihua.org/wp/?page_id=136

Duran, J. (1996). Anne Viscountess Conway: A seventeenth-century rationalist. In L. L. McAlister (Ed.), *Hypatia's daughters: Fifteen hundred years of women philosophers* (pp. 92–108). Bloomington: Indiana University Press.

Durant, W., & Durant, A. (1967). *Rousseau and revolution*. New York: Simon & Schuster.

Durkheim, E. (1964). *The division of labor in society*. New York: Free Press. (Original work published 1893)

Durnescu, I. (2008). An exploration of the purposes and outcomes of probation in European jurisdictions. *Probation Journal, 55*, 273–281.

Durose, M., Cooper, A., & Snyder, H. (2014). *Recidivism of prisoners released in 30 states in 2005: Patterns for 2005 to 2010*. Washington, DC: Bureau of Justice Statistics.

Durose, M. R., Farole, D. J., & Rosenmerkel, S. P. (2010). *Felony sentences in state courts, 2006*. Washington, DC: Bureau of Justice Statistics.

Dworkin, A. (1993). Against the male flood: Censorship, pornography, and equality. In P. Smith (Ed.), *Feminist jurisprudence* (pp. 449–465). Oxford, UK: Oxford University Press.

Economist Intelligence Unit. (2014). *Democracy index 2013: Democracy under stress*. Available at www.eiu.com/public/topical_report.aspx?campaignid=DemocracyIndex2011

Ellis, A. (1989). The history of cognition in psychotherapy. In A. Freeman, K. Simon, L. Beutler, & H. Arkowitz (Eds.), *Comprehensive handbook of cognitive therapy* (pp. 5–19). New York: Plenum.

Ellis, L. (2003). Genes, criminality, and the evolutionary neuroandrogenic theory. In A. Walsh & L. Ellis (Eds.), *Biosocial criminology: Challenging environmentalism's supremacy* (pp. 13–34). Hauppauge, NY: Nova Science.

Ellis, L., & Walsh, A. (2000). *Criminology: A global perspective*. Boston: Allyn & Bacon.

Ellis, T., Lewis, C., & Sato, M. (2011). The Japanese probation service: A third sector template? *Probation Journal, 58*, 333–344.

Equal Justice Initiative. (2015). *Lynching in America: Confronting the legacy of racial terror*. Available at http://www.eji.org/lynchinginamerica

Eskridge, C. (1989). Correctional practices in Japan. *Journal of Offender Counseling Services & Rehabilitation, 14*, 5–23.

Espinosa, P. (Senior Producer), Komatsu, S. (Series Producer), & Martin, G. (Director). (1998). *The U.S.–Mexican War (1846–1848)*. Dallas: KERA Unlimited; Mexico City: Once TV.

Ewing, C., & Dudzik, K. (2014, March 5). Nushawn Williams to remain confined. *WGRZ.com: On Your Side*. Available at http://www.wgrz.com/story/news/local/2014/03/05/nushawn-williams-to-remain-confined/6089649

Farabee, D., Prendergast, M., & Anglin, M. (1998). The effectiveness of coerced treatment for drug-abusing offenders. *Federal Probation, 62*, 3–10.

Farkas, M. A. (1999). Inmate supervisory style: Does gender make a difference? *Women & Criminal Justice, 10*, 25–45.

Farkas, M. A. (2000). A typology of correctional officers. *International Journal of Offender Therapy and Comparative Criminology, 44*, 431–449.

Farkas, M. A. (2001). Correctional officers: What factors influence work attitudes? *Correctional Management Quarterly, 5*(2), 20–26.

Farkas, M. A., & Rand, K. R. L. (1999). Sex matters: A gender-specific standard for cross-gender searches of inmates. *Women & Criminal Justice, 10*, 31–56.

Farkas, M., & Stichman, S. (2002). Can treatment, punishment, incapacitation, and public safety be reconciled? *Criminal Justice Review, 27*, 256–283.

Farrington, D. P., Langan, P. A., & Tonry, M. (2004). *Cross-national studies in crime and justice*. Washington, DC: U.S. Department of Justice, Office of Justice Programs, Bureau of Justice Statistics.

Federal Bureau of Investigation. (2013). *Crime in the United States, 2012: Uniform crime reports*. Washington, DC: U.S. Government Printing Office.

Federal Bureau of Investigation. (2014). *Uniform crime reports: Crime in the United States 2012*. Washington, DC: U.S. Government Printing Office. Available at http://www.fbi.gov/about-us/cjis/ucr/crime-in-the-u.s/2012/crime-in-the-u.s.-2012/persons-arrested/persons-arrested

Federal Bureau of Investigation. (2016). *Crime in the United States, 2015: Uniform crime reports*. Washington, DC: U.S. Government Printing Office.

Federman, C. (2004). Who has the body? The paths to habeas corpus reform. *The Prison Journal, 84*, 317–339.

Feeley, M. M. (1991). The privatization of prisons in historical perspective. *Criminal Justice Research Bulletin, 6*(2), 1–10.

Fehr, E., & Gachter, S. (2002). Altruistic punishment in humans. *Nature, 415*, 137–140.

Ferri, E. (1917). *Criminal sociology*. Boston: Little, Brown. (Original work published 1897)

$15.5 million settlement for mentally ill jail detainee held in solitary confinement. (2014, April). *Prison Legal News*, p. 20. Available at https://www.prisonlegalnews.org

Finn, P., & Kuck, S. (2005). *Stress among probation and parole officers and what can be done about it*. Washington, DC: U.S. Department of Justice.

Finney, C., Stergiopoulos, E., Hensel, J., Bonato, S., & Dewa, C. S. (2013). Organizational stressors associated with job stress and burnout in correctional officers: A systematic review. *BMC Public Health, 13.* Available at http://www.biomedcentral.com/1471-2458/13/82

Firestone, J. M., & Harris, R. J. (1994). Sexual harassment in the military: Environmental and individual contexts. *Armed Forces and Society, 21,* 25–43.

Firestone, J. M., & Harris, R. J. (1999). Changes in patterns of sexual harassment in the U.S. military: A comparison of the 1988 and 1995 DOD surveys. *Armed Forces and Society, 25,* 613–632.

Fishbein, D. (2003). Neuropsychological and emotional regulatory processes in antisocial behavior. In A. Walsh & L. Ellis (Eds.), *Biosocial criminology: Challenging environmentalism's supremacy* (pp. 185–208). Hauppauge, NY: Nova Science.

Fisher, W., Roy-Bujnowski, K., Grudzinskas, A., Clayfield, J., Banks, S., & Wolff, N. (2006). Patterns and prevalence of arrest in a statewide cohort of mental care consumers. *Psychiatric Services, 57,* 1623–1628.

Flavin, J., & Desautels, A. (2006). Feminism and crime. In C. M. Renzetti, L. Goodstein, & S. L. Miller (Eds.), *Rethinking gender, crime, and justice* (pp. 11–28). Los Angeles: Roxbury.

Fleisher, M. S., & Krienert, J. L. (2009). *The myth of prison rape: Sexual culture in American prisons.* Lanham, MD: Rowman & Littlefield.

Flores, A. R., Herman, J. L., Gates, G. J., & Brown, T. N. T. (2016). *How many adults identify as transgender in the United States?* Available at http://williamsinstitute.law.ucla.edu/wp-content/uploads/How-Many-Adults-Identify-as-Transgender-in-the-United-States.pdf

Florida Department of Corrections. (2014). *Major prison gangs.* Available at http://www.dc.state.fl.us/pub/gangs/prison.html

Ford, M. (2017, May 12). Jeff Sessions reinvigorates the drug war. *The Atlantic.* Available at https://www.theatlantic.com/politics/archive/2017/05/sessions-sentencing-memo/526029/

Foster, B. (2006). *Corrections: The fundamentals.* Upper Saddle River, NJ: Prentice Hall.

Foucault, M. (1979). *Discipline and punish: The birth of the prison.* New York: Vintage Books.

Fox, L. (2017) *The supplemental poverty measure: 2016.* Washington, DC: U.S. Census Bureau. Available at https://www.census.gov/content/dam/Census/library/publications/2017/demo/p60-261.pdf

Frankel, L. (1996). Damaris Cudworth Masham: A seventeenth-century feminist philosopher. In L. L. McAlister (Ed.), *Hypatia's daughters: Fifteen hundred years of women philosophers* (pp. 128–138). Bloomington: Indiana University Press.

Freudenberg, N. (2006). Coming home from jail: A review of health and social problems facing U.S. jail populations and of opportunities for reentry interventions. *American Jails, 20,* 9–24.

Gainsborough, J. (2002). *Mentally ill offenders in the criminal justice system: An analysis and prescription.* Washington, DC: The Sentencing Project.

Gallup. (2013). *Death penalty.* Available at http://www.gallup.com/poll/1606/deathpenalty.aspx

Gard, R. (2007). The first probation officers in England and Wales. *British Journal of Criminology, 47,* 1–17.

Gardner, L. (1996, March 1). Lessons from abroad: Japan's parole models. *Policy Review, 75* [Online]. Available at http://www.hoover.org/research/lessons-abroad-0

Garland, B., & Frankel, M. (2006). Considering convergence: A policy dialogue about behavioral genetics, neuroscience, and law. *Law and Contemporary Problems, 69,* 101–113.

Garland, B., Hogan, N., Wodahl, E., Hass, A., Stohr, M. K., & Lambert, E. (2014). Decarceration and its possible effects on inmates, staff, and communities. *Punishment and Society, 16,* 448–473.

Garland, B., & Matz, A. K. (2017). Preparing community supervision officers through undergraduate education: A study of academic and practitioner expectations. *Journal of Criminal Justice Education, 28,* 259–284.

Garland, D. (1990). *Punishment and modern society: A study in social theory.* Chicago: University of Chicago Press.

Garofalo, R. (1968). *Criminology.* Montclair, NJ: Patterson Smith. (Original work published 1885)

Gendreau, P., & Ross, R. R. (1987). Revivification of rehabilitation: Evidence from the 1980s. *Justice Quarterly, 4,* 349–407.

General Accounting Office. (1996). *Private and public prisons: Studies comparing operational costs and/or quality of service.* Washington, DC: Author.

Gettinger, S. H. (1984). *New generation jails: An innovative approach to an age-old problem.* Washington, DC: U.S. Department of Justice, National Institute of Corrections.

Giallombardo, R. (1966). *Society of women: A study of a women's prison.* New York: John Wiley.

Gibbs, A., & King, D. (2003). The electronic ball and chain? The operation and impact of home detention with electronic monitoring in New Zealand. *Australian and New Zealand Journal of Criminology, 36,* 1–17.

Gilliard, D. K., & Beck, A. J. (1997). *Prison and inmates at midyear 1996.* Washington, DC: U.S. Department of Justice, Office of Justice Programs. Available at https://www.bjs.gov/content/pub/pdf/pjimy96.pdf

Gilligan, C. (1982). *In a different voice: Psychological theory and women's development.* Cambridge, MA: Harvard University Press.

Glaze, L. E., & Bonczar, T. P. (2011). *Probation and parole in the United States, 2010.* Washington, DC: U.S. Department of Justice, Office of Justice Programs, Bureau of Justice Statistics. Available at http://www.bjs.gov/content/pub/pdf/ppus10.pdf

Glaze, L. E., Bonczar, T. P., & Zhang, F. (2010). *Probation and parole in the United States, 2009.* Washington, DC: U.S. Department of Justice, Office of Justice Programs, Bureau of Justice Statistics. Available at http://www.bjs.gov

Glaze, L., & Herberman, E. (2013). *Correctional populations in the United States, 2012.* Washington, DC: U.S. Department of Justice. Available at www.bjs.gov/content/pub/pdf/cpus12.pdf

Glaze, L. E., & Kaeble, D. (2014). *Correctional populations in the United States, 2013.* Washington, DC: Bureau of Justice Statistics. Available at http://www.bjs.gov/content/pub/pdf/cpus13.pdf

Glaze, L., & Palla, S. (2005). *Probation and parole in the United States, 2004.* Washington, DC: U.S. Department of Justice, Bureau of Justice Statistics.

Glenn, S. (2010, October 7). Board suspends license of former McNeil Island nurse. *The News Tribune* (Tacoma, WA), p. A4.

Goff, Lord of Chieveley. (1997). The future of the common law. *International and Comparative Law Quarterly, 46,* 745–760.

Goffman, E. (1961). *Asylums: Essays on the social situation of mental patients and other inmates.* Garden City, NY: Anchor Books.

Goldfarb, R. (1975). *Jails: The ultimate ghetto.* Garden City, NY: Anchor.

Goleman, D. (1995). *Emotional intelligence.* New York: Bantam Books.

Goleman, D. (2006). *Social intelligence: The new science of human relationships.* New York: Bantam Books.

Gonnerman, J. (2001). Remembering Attica: Thirty years later, the story of America's worst prison riot continues. *The Village Voice.* Available at http://www.villagevoice.com

Goodstein, L. (2006). Introduction: Gender, crime, and criminal justice. In C. M. Renzetti, L. Goodstein, & S. L. Miller (Eds.), *Rethinking gender, crime, and justice* (pp. 1–10). Los Angeles: Roxbury.

Gordon, J., Proulx, B., & Grant, P. (2013). Trepidation among the "keepers": Gendered perceptions of fear and risk of victimization among corrections officers. *American Journal of Criminal Justice, 38,* 245–265.

Gottfredson, M., & Hirschi, T. (1990). *A general theory of crime.* Stanford, CA: Stanford University Press.

Gray, T., Mays, G. L., & Stohr, M. K. (1995). Inmate needs and programming in exclusively women's jails. *The Prison Journal, 75,* 186–202.

Greenfeld, L., & Hinners, D. (1985). *Capital punishment, 1984.* Washington, DC: U.S. Department of Justice.

Grinfeld, M. (1997, August 1). Sexual predator ruling raises ethical, moral dilemmas. *Psychiatric Times,* pp. 1–4.

Gross, S., & Mauro, R. (1989). *Death and discrimination: Racial disparities in capital sentencing.* Boston: Northeastern University Press.

Grusec, J., & Hastings, P. (2007). *Handbook of socialization: Theory and research.* New York: Guilford.

Guerino, P., Harrison, P. M., & Sabol, W. J. (2012). *Prisoners in 2010.* Washington, DC: Bureau of Justice Statistics. Available at http://www.bjs.gov/content/pub/pdf/p10.pdf

Hamada, J. N. (2015). At peace with dementia. *American Jails, 29,* 34–36.

Hamilton, Z., Kigerl, A., & Hays, Z. (2015). Removing release impediments and reducing correctional costs: Evaluation of Washington State's housing voucher program. *Justice Quarterly, 32,* 255–287.

Haney, C., Banks, C., & Zimbardo, P. (1981). Interpersonal dynamics in a simulated prison. In R. R. Ross (Ed.), *Prison guard/correctional officer* (pp. 137–168). Toronto, Ontario, Canada: Butterworth.

Hanson, K., & Bussiere, M. (1998). Predicting relapse: A meta-analysis of sexual offender recidivism studies. *Journal of Consulting and Clinical Psychology, 66,* 348–362.

Harrington, P. E. (2002). Advice to women beginning a career in policing. *Women & Criminal Justice, 9,* 1–21.

Harris, J. (1973). *Crisis in corrections: The prison problem.* New York: McGraw–Hill.

Hassine, V. (1996). *Life without parole: Living in prison today.* Los Angeles: Roxbury.

Hassine, V. (2009). *Life without parole* (4th ed.). New York: Oxford University Press.

Hatch, V., & Walsh, A. (2016). *Capital punishment: Theory and practice of the ultimate penalty.* New York: Oxford University Press.

Havercamp, R., Mayer, M., & Levy, R. (2004). Electronic monitoring in Europe. *European Journal of Crime, Criminal Law, and Criminal Justice, 12,* 36–45.

Hawkes, M. Q. (1998). Edna Mahan: Sustaining the reformatory tradition. *Women & Criminal Justice, 9,* 1–21.

Hawkins, H. C. (2005). Race and sentencing outcomes in Michigan. *Journal of Ethnicity in Criminal Justice, 3,* 91–109.

Hawthorne, N. (2003). *The scarlet letter.* New York: Barnes & Noble Classics. (Original work published 1850)

Hayes, L. M. (2010). *National study of jail suicide—20 years later.* Washington, DC: U.S. Department of Justice National Institute of Corrections. Available at http://www.nicic.gov

Haynes, S. (2011). The effects of victim-related contextual factors on the criminal justice system. *Crime & Delinquency, 57,* 298–328.

Hefferman, E. (1972). *Making it in prison: The square, the cool, and the life.* New York: John Wiley.

Hemmens, C., & Atherton, E. (1999). *Use of force: Current practice and policy.* Lanham, MD: American Correctional Association.

Hemmens, C., & Marquart, J. W. (2000). Race, age, and inmate perceptions of inmate–staff relations. *Journal of Criminal Justice, 28,* 297–312.

Hemmens, C., Steiner, B., & Mueller, D. (2003). *Significant cases in juvenile justice.* Los Angeles: Roxbury

Hemmens, C., Stohr, M. K., Schoeler, M., & Miller, B. (2002). One step up, two steps back: The progression of perceptions of women's work in prisons and jails. *Journal of Criminal Justice, 30,* 473–489.

Henriques, Z. W. (1996). Imprisoned mothers and their children: Separation–reunion syndrome dual impact. *Women & Criminal Justice, 8,* 77–95.

Henriques, Z. W., & Gilbert, E. (2003). Sexual abuse and sexual assault of women in prison. In R. Muraskin (Ed.), *It's a crime: Women and justice* (pp. 258–272). Upper Saddle River, NJ: Prentice Hall.

Herberman, E. J., & Bonczar, T. P. (2015). *Probation and parole in the United States, 2013.* Washington, DC: Bureau of Justice Statistics. Available at http://www.bjs.gov/content/pub/pdf/ppus13.pdf

Hersh, S. M. (2004, May 10). Torture at Abu Ghraib: American soldiers brutalized Iraqis. How far does the responsibility go? *New Yorker Magazine.* Available at http://www.newyorker.com

Hindman, J., & Peters, J. (2001). Polygraph testing leads to better understanding adult and juvenile sex offenders. *Federal Probation, 65,* 1–15.

Hirsch, A. J. (1992). *The rise of the penitentiary.* New Haven, CT: Yale University Press.

Hirschi, T. (1969). *The causes of delinquency.* Berkeley: University of California Press.

Hirschi, T., & Gottfredson, M. (1983). Age and the explanation of crime. *American Journal of Sociology, 89,* 552–584.

Hochstetler, A., DeLisi, M., & Pratt, T. C. (2010). Social support and feelings of hostility among released inmates. *Crime & Delinquency, 56,* 588–607.

Hockenberry, S. (2013). *Juveniles in residential placement, 2010.* Washington, DC: U.S. Department of Justice, Office of Justice Programs, Office of Juvenile Justice and Delinquency Prevention. Available at http://www.ojjdp.gov/pubs/241060.pdf

Hogan, N. L., Lambert, E. G., Hepburn, J. R., Burton, V. S., & Cullen, F. T. (2004). Is there a difference? Exploring male and female correctional officers' definition of and response to conflict situations. *Women & Criminal Justice, 15,* 143–165.

Holcomb, I. (2008). *The carrying of firearms by probation officers.* Paper presented at the annual meeting of the American Criminal Justice Society, Cincinnati, OH.

Houser, K. A., & Welsch, W. (2014). Examining the association between co-occurring disorders and seriousness of misconduct by female prison inmates. *Criminal Justice & Behavior, 41,* 650–666.

Howard, J. (2000). *The state of prisons in England and Wales, with preliminary observations, and an account of some foreign prisons.* London: Routledge/Thoemmes Press. (Original work published 1775)

Hughes, K. (2006). *Justice expenditure and employment in the United States, 2003.* Washington, DC: U.S. Department of Justice, Office of Justice Programs, Bureau of Justice Statistics.

Hughes, R. (1987). *The fatal shore.* New York: Vintage Books.

Hughes, T., Wilson, D., & Beck, A. (2001). *Trends in state parole, 1990–2000.* Washington, DC: U.S. Department of Justice, Bureau of Justice Statistics.

Hulings, N. (2010, October 5). Jail ready but still too costly. *The News Tribune* (Tacoma, WA), p. A4.

Ignatieff, M. (1978). *A just measure of pain: The penitentiary in the Industrial Revolution, 1750–1850.* New York: Columbia University Press.

Impey, E., & Parnell, G. (2011). *The Tower of London: The official illustrated history.* London: Merrell.

Inciardi, J. (2007). *Criminal justice.* New York: McGraw–Hill.

Inciardi, J., Martin, S., & Butzin, C. (2004). Five-year outcomes of therapeutic community treatment of drug-involved offenders after release from prison. *Crime & Delinquency, 50,* 88–111.

Inderbitzin, M. (2006). Guardians of the state's problem children: An ethnographic study of staff members in a juvenile correctional facility. *The Prison Journal, 86,* 431–451.

Innocence Project. (2013). *DNA exonerations nationwide.* Available at http://www.innocenceproject.org/Content/DNA_Exonerations_Nationwide.php

Ireland, C., & Berg, B. (2006). Women in parole: Gendered adaptations of female parole agents in California. *Women & Criminal Justice, 18,* 131–150.

Irwin, J. (1985). *The jail: Managing the underclass in American society.* Berkeley: University of California Press.

Irwin, J. (2005). *The warehouse prison: Disposal of the new dangerous class.* Los Angeles: Roxbury.

Jacobs, B., & Wright, R. (1999). Stick-up, street culture, and offender motivation. *Criminology, 37,* 149–173.

Jacobs, J. B. (1977). *Stateville: The penitentiary in mass society.* Chicago: University of Chicago Press.

Jaffee, S., Moffitt, T., Caspi, A., & Taylor, A. (2003). Life with (or without) father: The benefits of living with two biological parents depend on the father's antisocial behavior. *Child Development, 74,* 109–126.

James, D. J., & Glaze, L. E. (2006). *Mental health problems of prison and jail inmates.* Washington, DC: U.S. Department of Justice, Office of Justice Programs.

Jay Farbstein & Associates, with Wener, R. (1989). *A comparison of "direct" and "indirect" supervision of correctional facilities: Final report.* Washington, DC: National Institute of Corrections.

Jiang, S., Xiang, D., Chen, Q., Huang, C., Yang, S., Zhang, D., & Zhao, A. (2014). Community corrections in China: Development and challenges. *The Prison Journal, 94,* 75–96.

Johnson, R. (2002). *Hard time: Understanding and reforming the prison* (3rd ed.). Belmont, CA: Wadsworth/Thomson Learning.

Johnston, N. (2009). Evolving function: Early use of imprisonment as punishment. *The Prison Journal, 89*(1), 10S–34S.

Johnston, N. (2010). Early Philadelphia prisons: Amour, alcohol, and other forbidden pleasures. *The Prison Journal, 90,* 12–23.

Jolliffe, D., & Farrington, D. (2009). *Effectiveness of interventions with adult male violent offenders.* Stockholm: Swedish Council for Crime Prevention.

Jones, J. C. (2016, January 23–24). Early Chinese contributions to Whitman County overlooked as unfair competition. *Moscow–Pullman Daily News,* p. 3D.

Jones, J. M. (2016). *U.S. death penalty support at 60%.* Available at http://www.gallup.com/poll/196676/death-penalty-support.aspx

Jones, O., & Shen, F. (2012). Law and neuroscience in the United States. In T. Spranger (Ed.), *International neurolaw: A comparative analysis* (pp. 349–380). Berlin: Springer Verlag.

Jordan, K., & Freiburger, T. (2015). The effect of race/ethnicity on sentencing: Examining sentence type, jail length, and prison length. *Journal of Ethnicity in Criminal Justice, 13,* 179–196.

Joseph, J., & Taylor, D. (Eds.). (2003). *With justice for all: Minorities and women in criminal justice.* Upper Saddle River, NJ: Prentice Hall.

Junger-Tas, J. (1996). Delinquency similar in Western countries. *Overcrowded Times, 7,* 10–13.

Jurik, N. (1985a). Individual and organizational determinants of correctional officer attitudes toward inmates. *Criminology, 23,* 523–539.

Jurik, N. C. (1985b). An officer and a lady: Organizational barriers to women working as correctional officers in men's prisons. *Social Problems, 33,* 375–388.

Jurik, N. C. (1988). Striking a balance: Female correctional officers, gender-role stereotypes, and male prisons. *Sociological Inquiry, 58,* 291–305.

Jurik, N. C., & Halemba, G. J. (1984). Gender, working conditions, and the job satisfaction of women in a non-traditional occupation: Female correctional officers in a men's prison. *Sociological Quarterly, 25,* 551–566.

Jury awards $14 million in historic SPLC case. (2015). *SPLC Report, 45*(1), 1–8.

Kaeble, D., & Bonczar, T. P. (2017). *Probation and parole in the United States, 2015.* Washington, DC: Bureau of Justice Statistics. Available at https://www.bjs.gov/content/pub/pdf/ppus15.pdf

Kaeble, D., & Glaze, L. (2016). *Correctional populations in the United States, 2015.* Washington,

DC: U.S. Department of Justice, Office of Justice Programs, Bureau of Justice Statistics. Available at https://www.bjs.gov/content/pub/pdf/cpus15.pdf

Kaeble, D., Glaze, L., Tsoutis, A., & Minton, T. (2016). *Correctional populations in the United States, 2014.* Washington, DC: U.S. Department of Justice, Office of Justice Programs, Bureau of Justice Statistics. Available at http://www.bjs.gov/content/pub/pdf/cpus14.pdf

Kaeble, D., Maruschak, L. M., & Bonczar, T. P. (2015). *Probation and parole in the United States, 2014.* Washington, DC: Bureau of Justice Statistics. Available at http://www.bjs.gov/content/pub/pdf/ppus14.pdf

Kanazawa, Y. (2007). Psychotherapy in Japan: The case of Mrs. A. *Journal of Clinical Psychology, 63,* 755–763.

Kansal, T. (2005). *Racial disparity in sentencing.* Washington, DC: The Sentencing Project. Available at http://www.sentencingproject.org

Karberg, J., & James, J. (2005). *Substance dependence, abuse, and treatment of jail inmates, 2002.* Washington, DC: U.S. Department of Justice, Office of Justice Programs, Bureau of Justice Statistics.

Katz, J. (2005). *Warren McClesky v. Ralph Kemp:* Is the death penalty in Georgia racially biased? In E. Mandery (Ed.), *Capital punishment in America: A balanced examination* (pp. 400–407). Sudbury, MA: Jones & Bartlett. Available at http://www.ourpaws.info/cramer/death/katz.htm

Kauffman, K. (1988). *Prison officers and their world.* Cambridge, MA: Harvard University Press.

Keil, T. J., & Vito, G. F. (2009). Lynching and the death penalty in Kentucky, 1866–1934. *Journal of Ethnicity in Criminal Justice, 7,* 53–68.

Kennedy, R. (1998). *Race, crime, and the law.* New York: Vintage Books.

Kerle, K. (1991). Introduction. In J. Thompson & G. L. Mays (Eds.), *American jails: Public policy issues* (pp. 1–3). Chicago: Nelson–Hall.

Kerle, K. (2003). *Exploring jail operations.* Hagerstown, MD: American Jail Association.

Kerle, K. E. (2011). *Exploring jail operations.* Unpublished manuscript.

Kim, A-S., DeValve, M., DeValve, E. Q., & Jonson, W. W. (2003). Female wardens: Results from a national survey of state correctional executives. *The Prison Journal, 83,* 406–425.

Kim, B., Benekos, P., & Merlo, A. (2016). Sex offender recidivism revisited: Review of recent meta-analyses on the effects of sex offender treatment. *Trauma, Violence, & Abuse, 17,* 105–117.

King, K., Steiner, B., & Breach, S. R. (2008). Violence in the supermax: A self-fulfilling prophecy. *The Prison Journal, 88,* 144–168.

Kirkham, C. (2013, October 22). Private prison empire rises despite startling record of juvenile abuse. *Huffington Post,* pp. 1–11.

Kirshon, J. (2010). Attica prison riot ends in bloodshed. *Examiner.com.* Available at http://www.examiner.com

Kitano, H. H. L. (1997). *Race relations* (5th ed.). Upper Saddle River, NJ: Prentice Hall.

Kitchen supervisor gets prison time for sexually abusing two prisoners. (2014, April). *Prison Legal News,* p. 20. Available at https://www.prison-legalnews.org

Kleber, H. (2003). Pharmacological treatments for heroin and cocaine dependence. *American Journal on Addictions, 12,* S5–S18.

Kleck, G. (1981). Racial discrimination in criminal sentencing: A critical evaluation of the evidence with additional evidence on the death penalty. *American Sociological Review, 46,* 783–805.

Klein, S., Berk, R., & Hickman, L. (2006). *Race and the decision to seek the death penalty in federal cases.* Santa Monica, CA: RAND.

Klingele, C. (2013). Rethinking the use of community supervision. *Journal of Criminal Law and Criminology, 103,* 1015–1070.

Klofas, J. M. (1991). Disaggregating jail use: Variety and change in local corrections over a ten-year period. In J. Thompson & G. L. Mays (Eds.), *American jails: Public policy issues* (pp. 40–58). Chicago: Nelson–Hall.

Kluger, J. (2007, February 5). The paradox of supermax. *Time,* pp. 52–53.

Knoll, C., & Sickmund, M. (2012). *Delinquency cases in juvenile court, 2009.* Washington, DC: National Center of Juvenile Justice.

Knowles, D. (2013, April 4). Saudi judge orders man surgically paralyzed to pay for childhood stabbing. *New York Daily News.* Available at http://www.nydailynews.com/news/world/saudi-judge-orders-man-surgically-paralyzed-pay-childhood-stabbing-article-1.1307910#ixzz2pB5W9krT

Kramer, J., & Ulmer, J. (2009). *Sentencing guidelines: Lessons from Pennsylvania.* Boulder, CO: Lynne Rienner.

Kruger, D. (2014, December 1). Why Texas is closing prisons in favour of rehab. *BBC Magazine.* Available at http://www.bbc.com/news/world-us-canada-30275026

Kuhn, T. (1962). *The structure of scientific revolutions.* Chicago: University of Chicago Press.

Kyckelhahn, T. (2014). *State corrections expenditures, FY 1982–2010.* Washington, DC: U.S. Department of Justice, Office of Justice Programs, Bureau of Justice Statistics. Available at http://www.bjs.gov/content/pub/pdf/scefy8210.pdf

Kyckelhahn, T. (2015). *Justice expenditures and employment extracts, 2012—Preliminary.* Washington, DC: U.S. Department of Justice, Office of Justice Programs, Bureau of Justice Statistics. Available at https://www.bjs.gov/index.cfm?ty=pbdetail&iid=5239

Lambert, E. G., Hogan, N. L., & Tucker, K. A. (2009). Problems at work: Exploring the correlates of role stress among correctional staff. *The Prison Journal, 89,* 460–481.

Langan, P. A., & Farrington, D. (1998). *Crime and justice in the United States and England and Wales, 1981–1996.* Washington, DC: Bureau of Justice Statistics.

Langan, P. A., Greenfield, L. A., Smith, S. K., Durose, M. R., & Levin, D. J. (2001). *Contacts between police and the public: Findings from the 1999 national survey.* Washington, DC: U.S. Department of Justice.

Langan, P. A., & Levin, D. (2002). *Recidivism of prisoners released in 1994.* Washington, DC: U.S. Department of Justice, Bureau of Justice Statistics.

Langan, P. A., Schmitt, E., & Durose, M. (2003). *Recidivism of sex offenders released from prison in 1994.* Washington, DC: U.S. Department of Justice, Bureau of Justice Statistics.

Latessa, W., Cullen, F., & Gendreau, P. (2002). Beyond correctional quackery—Professionalism and the possibility of effective treatment. *Federal Probation, 66,* 43–50.

Latimer, J., Dowden, C., & Muise, D. (2005). The effectiveness of restorative justice practices. *The Prison Journal, 85,* 127–144.

Laudano, J. (2013). *The high cost of corrections in America.* Available at http://www.pewstates.org/research/data-visualizations/the-high-cost-of-corrections-in-america-85899397897

La Vigne, N. G., Debus-Sherrill, S., Brazzell, D., & Downey, P. M. (2011). *Preventing violence and sexual assault in jails: A situational crime prevention approach.* Washington, DC: Urban Institute, Justice Policy Center. Available at https://www.urban.org/sites/default/files/publication/26746/412458-Preventing-Violence-and-Sexual-Assault-in-Jail-A-situational-Crime-Prevention-Approach.PDF

Lawes, L. E. (1932). *Twenty thousand years in Sing Sing.* New York: Long & Smith.

Lawrence, R., & Mahan, S. (1998). Women corrections officers in men's prisons: Acceptance and perceived job performance. *Women & Criminal Justice, 9,* 63–86.

Lee, J. A., & Visano, L. A. (1994). Official deviance in the legal system. In S. Stojokovic, J. Klofas, & D. Kalinich (Eds.), *The administration and management of criminal justice organizations: A book of readings* (pp. 202–231). Prospect Heights, IL: Waveland.

Leigey, M., & Bachman, R. (2007). The influence of crack cocaine on the likelihood of incarceration for a violent offense: An examination of a prison sample. *Criminal Justice Policy Review, 18,* 335–352.

Leip, L. A., & Stinchcomb, J. B. (2013). Should I stay or should I go? Job satisfaction and turnover intent of jail staff throughout the United States. *Criminal Justice Review, 38,* 226–241.

Lennon, T., Angier, J., Tsui, M. L., Cheng, S., & Chin, M. (2003). *Becoming American: The Chinese experience* [film]. Princeton, NJ: Films for the Humanities and Sciences.

Leshner, A. (1998). Addiction is a brain disease—and it matters. *National Institute of Justice Journal, 237,* 2–6.

Library of Congress. (2010). *Old jail, State Route 6A and Old Jail Lane, Barnstable, Barnstable County, MA.* Washington, DC: Author. Available at http://www.loc.gov/pictures/search

Lieb, S., Fallon, S. J., Friedman, S. R., Thompson, D. R., Gates, G. J., Liberti, T. M., & Mallow, R. M. (2011). Statewide estimation of racial/ethnic populations of men who have sex with men in the U.S. *Public Health Reports, 126,* 60–72.

Light, M. T., Lopez, M. H., & Gonzalez-Barrera, A. (2014, March 18). *The rise of federal immigration crimes: Unlawful reentry drives growth.* Washington, DC: Pew Research Center. Available at http://www.pewhispanic.org/2014/03/18/the-rise-of-federal-immigration-crimes

Lightfoot, C., Zupan, L. L., & Stohr, M. K. (1991). Jails and the community: Modeling the future in local detention facilities. *American Jails, 5,* 50–52.

Lin, N. (1986). Conceptualizing social support. In N. Lin, A. Dean, & W. Edsel (Eds.), *Social support, life events, and depression* (pp. 17–30). Orlando, FL: Academic Press.

Linden, D. (2006). How psychotherapy changes the brain—The contribution of functional neuroimaging. *Molecular Psychiatry, 11,* 528–538.

Lipsey, M., & Cullen, F. (2007). The effectiveness of correctional rehabilitation: A review of systematic reviews. *Annual Review of Law and Social Science, 3,* 297–320.

Lipsky, M. (1980). *Street-level bureaucracy: Dilemmas of the individual in public services.* New York: Russell Sage.

Litt, M., & Mallon, S. (2003). The design of social support networks for offenders in outpatient drug treatment. *Federal Probation, 67,* 15–22.

Liu, J., Zhao, R., Xiong, H., & Gong, J. (2012). Chinese legal traditions: Punitiveness versus mercy. *Asian Pacific Journal of Police & Criminal Justice, 9,* 17–33.

Livsey, S. (2012). *Juvenile delinquency probation caseload, 2009.* Washington, DC: U.S. Department of Justice, Office of Justice Programs, Office of Juvenile Justice and Delinquency Prevention. Available at http://www.ojjdp.gov/pubs/239082.pdf

Logan, C., & Gaes, G. (1993). Meta-analysis and the rehabilitation of punishment. *Justice Quarterly, 10,* 245–263.

Lombardo, L. X. (1982). *Guards imprisoned.* Cincinnati, OH: Anderson.

Lombardo, L. X. (2001). Guards imprisoned: Correctional officers at work. In E. J. Latessa, A. Holsinger, J. W. Marquart, & J. R. Sorensen (Eds.), *Correctional contexts: Contemporary and classical readings* (2nd ed., pp. 153–167). Los Angeles: Roxbury.

Loper, A. B., & Tuerk, E. H. (2006). Parenting programs for incarcerated parents: Current research and future directions. *Criminal Justice Policy Review, 14,* 407–427.

Lowenkamp, C., & Latessa, E. (2002). *Evaluation of Ohio's community-based corrections facilities and halfway house programs: Final report.* Cincinnati, OH: University of Cincinnati, Center for Criminal Justice Research.

Lubitz, R., & Ross, T. (2001, June). *Sentencing guidelines: Reflections on the future* (Sentencing & Corrections: Issues for the 21st Century, No. 10). Washington, DC: U.S. Department of Justice, National Institute of Justice.

Lundman, R. J. (2010). Are police-reported driving while black data a valid indicator of the race and ethnicity of the traffic law violators police stop? A negative answer with minor qualifications. *Journal of Criminal Justice, 38,* 77–87.

Lurigio, A. (2000). Persons with serious mental illness in the criminal justice system: Background, prevalence, and principles of care. *Criminal Justice Policy Review, 11,* 312–328.

Lurigio, A., & Loose, P. (2008). The disproportionate incarceration of African Americans for drug offenses: The national and Illinois perspective. *Journal of Ethnicity in Criminal Justice, 6,* 223–247.

Lutze, F. (2014). *Professional lives of community corrections officers: The invisible side of reentry.* Thousand Oaks, CA: Sage.

Lutze, F. E., & Murphy, D. W. (1999). Ultra-masculine prison environments and inmates' adjustment: It's time to move beyond the "boys will be boys" paradigm. *Justice Quarterly, 16,* 709–734.

Lutze, F. E., Rosky, J., & Hamilton, Z. (2013). Homelessness and reentry: A multistate outcome evaluation of Washington State's reentry housing program for high risk offenders. *Criminal Justice & Behavior, 20,* 1–21.

Macher, A. M. (2007). Issues in correctional HIV care: Neurological manifestations of patients with primary HIV infection. *American Jails, 21,* 49–55.

MacKenzie, D., & Brame, R. (2001). Community supervision, prosocial activities, and recidivism. *Justice Quarterly, 18,* 429–448.

Mackin, J., Lucas, L., & Lambarth, C. (2010). *Baltimore County Juvenile Drug Court outcome and cost evaluation.* Baltimore, MD: NPC Research.

Maletzky, B., & Field, G. (2003). The biological treatment of dangerous sexual offenders: A review and preliminary report of the Oregon pilot Depo-Provera program. *Aggression and Violent Behavior, 8,* 391–412.

Mallicoat, S. L. (2011). *Women and crime: A text/reader.* Thousand Oaks, CA: Sage.

Mandery, E. (2005). *Capital punishment in America: A balanced examination.* Sudbury, MA: Jones & Bartlett.

Mann, C. C. (2006). *1491: New revelations of the Americas before Columbus.* New York: Vintage Books.

Marion, N. (2002). Effectiveness of community-based programs: A case study. *The Prison Journal, 82,* 478–497.

Marquart, J. W., Barnhill, M. B., & Balshaw-Biddle, K. (2001). Fatal attraction: An analysis of employee boundary violations in a southern prison system, 1995–1998. *Justice Quarterly, 18,* 877–910.

Marsh, R., & Walsh, A. (1995). Physiological and psychosocial assessment and treatment of sex offenders: A comprehensive victim-oriented program. *Journal of Offender Rehabilitation, 22,* 77–96.

Marshall, L. (2004). The innocence revolution and the death penalty. *Ohio State Journal of Criminal Law, 1,* 573–584.

Martin, G. (2005). *Juvenile justice: Process and systems.* Thousand Oaks, CA: Sage.

Martin, S., & Jurik, N. (1996). *Doing justice, doing gender.* Thousand Oaks, CA: Sage.

Martinez, D. J. (2004). Hispanics incarcerated in state correctional facilities: Variations in inmate characteristics across Hispanic subgroups. *Journal of Ethnicity in Criminal Justice, 2,* 119–131.

Martinson, R. (1974). What works? Questions and answers about prison reform. *The Public Interest, 35,* 22–54.

Maruschak, L. M. (2006). *Medical problems of jail inmates.* Washington, DC: U.S. Department of Justice, Office of Justice Programs.

Maruschak, L. M. (2008). *Medical problems of prisoners.* Washington, DC: U.S. Department of Justice, Office of Justice Programs, Bureau of Justice Statistics.

Maruschak, L. M. (2015). *Medical problems of state and federal prisoners and jail inmates, 2011–12.* Washington, DC: Bureau of Justice Statistics. Available at https://www.bjs.gov/content/pub/pdf/mpsfpji1112.pdf

Maruschak, L., & Bonczar, T. (2013). *Probation and parole in the United States, 2012.* Washington, DC: Bureau of Justice Statistics.

Maschke, K. J. (1996). Gender in the prison setting: The privacy–equal employment dilemma. *Women & Criminal Justice, 7,* 23–42.

Maslow, A. H. (1998). *Maslow on management.* New York: John Wiley.

Maslow, A. H. (2001). A theory of human motivation. In J. M. Shafritz & J. S. Ott (Eds.), *Classics of organization theory* (pp. 152–157). Fort Worth, TX: Harcourt College. (Original work published 1943)

Mathias, R. (1995, July/August). Correctional treatment helps offenders stay drug and arrest free. *NIDA Notes.* Available at http://archives.drugabuse.gov/NIDA_Notes/NNVol10N4/Prison.html

Mattick, H. W. (1974). The contemporary jails of the United States: An unknown and neglected area of justice. In D. Glaser (Ed.), *Handbook of criminology* (pp. 777–848). Chicago: Rand McNally.

Mauer, M. (2005). *Comparative international rates of incarceration: An examination of causes and trends.* Washington, DC: The Sentencing Project.

Mauer, M. (2014). *Fewer prisoners, less crime: A tale of three states.* Available at http://www.sentencingproject.org/template/page.cfm?id=156

Mauer, M., King, R., & Young, M. (2004). *The meaning of "life": Long prison sentences in context.* Washington, DC: The Sentencing Project.

Mawby, R. (2001). *Burglary.* Cullompton, UK: Willan.

May, D. C., Applegate, B. K., Ruddell, R., & Wood, P. B. (2014). Going to jail sucks (and it doesn't matter who you ask). *American Journal of Criminal Justice, 39,* 250–266.

May, D., Wood, P., Mooney, J., & Minor, K. (2005). Predicting offender-generated exchange rates: Implications for a theory of sentence severity. *Crime & Delinquency, 51,* 373–399.

McAdams, J. (1998). Racial disparity and the death penalty. *Law and Contemporary Problems, 61,* 153–170.

McAuliffe, K. (2010). Are we still evolving? In J. Groopman (Ed.), *The best science writing of 2010* (pp. 218–231). New York: HarperCollins.

McCollister, K., French, M., & Fang, H. (2010). The cost of crime to society: New crime-specific estimates for policy and program evaluation. *Drug and Alcohol Dependence, 108,* 98–109.

McDermott, P. A., Alterman, A. I., Cacciola, J. S., Rutherford, M. J., Newman, J. P., & Mulholland, E. M. (2000). Generality of Psychopathy Checklist–Revised factors over prisoners and substance-dependent patients. *Journal of Consulting and Clinical Psychology, 68,* 181–186.

McLean, R. L., Robarge, J., & Sherman, S. G. (2006). Release from jail: Moment of crisis or window of opportunity for female detainees? *Journal of Urban Health, 83,* 382–393.

McLeod, J. (2003). *An introduction to counseling.* Buckingham, UK: Open University Press.

McNeese, T. (2010). Inmate rights: Getting the courts to listen. In A. Walsh & M. Stohr, *Correctional assessment, casework, and counseling* (5th ed., pp. 321–323). Alexandria, VA: American Correctional Association.

McNiel, D. E., Binder, R. L., & Robinson, J. C. (2005). Incarceration associated with homelessness, mental disorder, and co-occurring substance abuse. *Psychiatric Services, 56,* 840–846.

Meade, B., & Steiner, B. (2013). The effects of exposure to violence on inmate maladjustment. *Criminal Justice and Behavior, 40,* 1228–1249.

Mears, D. P. (2008). An assessment of supermax prisons using an evaluation research framework. *The Prison Journal, 88,* 43–68.

Mears, D. P. (2013). Supermax prisons: The policy and the evidence. *Criminology & Public Policy, 12*, 681–719.

Mears, D. P., Stewart, E. A., Siennick, S. E., & Simons, R. L. (2013). The code of the street and inmate violence: Investigating the salience of imported belief systems. *Criminology, 51*, 695–728.

Mello, M. (2007). Executing the mentally ill: When is someone sane enough to die? *Criminal Justice, 22*, 30–41.

Menard, S., Mihalic, S., & Huizinga, D. (2001). Drugs and crime revisited. *Justice Quarterly, 18*, 269–299.

Menninger, K. (1968). *The crime of punishment.* New York, NY: Penguin Books.

Mercier, M. (2010). *Japanese Americans in the Columbia River Basin.* Columbia River Basin Ethnic History Project. Available at http://archive.vancouver.wsu.edu/crbeha/projteam

Meredith, C., & Paquette, C. (2001). *Summary report on victim impact statement focus groups.* Ottawa, Ontario, Canada: Policy Centre for Victim Issues, Department of Justice.

Merlo, A. V., & Benekos, P. J. (2000). *What's wrong with the criminal justice system?* Cincinnati, OH: Anderson.

Mills, C. W. (1956). *The power elite.* New York: Oxford University Press.

Minnesota Department of Corrections. (2009). *Review of guidelines for revocation of parole and supervised release.* Available at https://www.leg.state.mn.us/docs/2009/mandated/090347.pdf

Minton, T. D. (2010). *Jail inmates at midyear 2009—Statistical tables.* Washington, DC: U.S. Department of Justice, Office of Justice Programs, Bureau of Justice Statistics. Available at http://bjs.ojp.usdoj.gov/index.cfm?ty=pbdetail&iid=2195

Minton, T. D. (2014). *Jails in Indian country, 2013.* Washington, DC: Bureau of Justice Statistics. Available at http://www.bjs.gov/index.cfm?ty=pbdetail&iid=5070

Minton, T. D. (2015). *Jails in Indian Country, 2014.* Washington, DC: Bureau of Justice Statistics. Available at http://www.bjs.gov/content/pub/pdf/jic14.pdf

Minton, T. D., & Golinelli, F. (2014). *Jail inmates at midyear 2013—Statistical tables.* Washington, DC: U.S. Department of Justice, Office of Justice Programs, Bureau of Justice Statistics. Available at http://www.bjs.gov/content/pub/pdf/jim13st.pdf

Minton, T. D., & Zeng, Z. (2015). *Jail inmates at midyear 2014.* Washington, DC: U.S. Department of Justice, Office of Justice Programs, Bureau of Justice Statistics. Available at http://www.bjs.gov/index.cfm?ty=pbdetail&iid=5299

Minton, T. D., & Zeng, Z. (2016). *Jail inmates in 2015.* Washington, DC: U.S. Department of Justice, Office of Justice Programs, Bureau of Justice Statistics. Available at https://www.bjs.gov/index.cfm?ty=pbdetail&iid=5872

Mitchell, O., Wilson, D., Eggers, A., & MacKenzie, D. (2012). Assessing the effectiveness of drug courts on recidivism: A meta-analytic review of traditional and non-traditional drug courts. *Journal of Criminal Justice, 40*, 60–71.

Mitford, J. (1973). *Kind and usual punishment: The prison business.* New York: Alfred A. Knopf.

Moe, A. M., & Ferraro, K. J. (2003). Malign neglect or benign respect: Women's health care in a carceral setting. *Women & Criminal Justice, 14*, 53–80.

Moffitt, T. (1993). Adolescent-limited and life-course-persistent antisocial behavior: A developmental taxonomy. *Psychological Review, 100*, 674–701.

Moffitt, T. (2005). The new look of behavioral genetics in developmental psychopathology: Gene–environment interplay in antisocial behavior. *Psychological Bulletin, 131*, 533–554.

Moffitt, T., & Walsh, A. (2003). The adolescence-limited/life-course persistent theory of antisocial behavior: What have we learned? In A. Walsh & L. Ellis (Eds.), *Biosocial criminology: Challenging environmentalism's supremacy* (pp. 125–144). Hauppauge, NY: Nova Science.

Moore, N., May, D., & Wood, P. (2008). Offenders, judges, and officers rate the relative severity of alternative sanctions compared to prison. *Probation and Parole: Current Issues, 1*, 49–70.

Morash, M. (2006). *Understanding gender, crime, and justice.* Thousand Oaks, CA: Sage.

Morash, M., Haarr, R., & Rucker, L. (1994). A comparison of programming for women and men in U.S. prisons in the 1980s. *Crime & Delinquency, 40*, 197–221.

Morgan, K. (2013). Issues in female inmate health: Results from a southeastern state. *Women & Criminal Justice, 23*, 121–142.

Morris, N. (2002). *Maconochie's Gentlemen: The story of Norfolk Island and the roots of modern prison reform.* Oxford, UK: Oxford University Press.

Moynihan, J. M. (2002, July/August). What to do with historic jails. *American Jails*, pp. 14–16.

Mueller, C. W., De Coster, S., & Estes, S. (2001). Sexual harassment in the workplace. *Work and Occupations, 28*, 411–446.

Mulick, S. (2010, November 20). Budget ax falls on McNeil. *The News Tribune* (Tacoma, WA), p. 1.

Mumola, C. J. (2000). *Incarcerated parents and their children.* Washington, DC: Bureau of Justice Statistics.

Mumola, C. J. (2005). *Suicide and homicide in state prisons and local jails.* Washington, DC: U.S. Department of Justice, Office of Justice Programs. Available at http://www.bjs.gov/content/pub/pdf/shsplj.pdf

Mumola, C. J. (2007). *Medical causes of death in state prisons, 2001–2004* [Bureau of Justice Statistics data brief]. Washington, DC: U.S. Department of Justice.

Muraskin, R. (2003). Disparate treatment in correctional facilities. In *It's a crime: Women and justice* (3rd ed., pp. 220–231). Upper Saddle River, NJ: Prentice Hall.

Mustaine, E., & Tewksbury, R. (2004). Alcohol and violence. In S. Holmes & R. Holmes (Eds.), *Violence: A contemporary reader* (pp. 9–25). Upper Saddle River, NJ: Prentice Hall.

Naday, A., Freilich, J. D., & Mellow, J. (2008). The elusive data on supermax confinement. *The Prison Journal, 88*, 69–93.

Nagel, W. G. (1973). *The new red barn: A critical look at the modern American prison.* New York: Walker.

Nagin, D. (1998). Criminal deterrence research at the onset of the twenty-first century. In M. Tonry (Ed.), *Crime and justice: A review of research* (Vol. 23, pp. 1–42). Chicago: University of Chicago Press.

Nagin, D. S., Cullen, E. T., & Jonson, C. L. (2009). Imprisonment and reoffending. In M. Tonry (Ed.), *Crime and justice: A review of research* (Vol. 38, pp. 115–200). Chicago: University of Chicago Press.

Nagin, D., & Land, K. (1993). Age, criminal careers, and population heterogeneity: Specification and estimation of a nonparametric, mixed poison model. *Criminology, 31,* 327–362.

Nagin, D., & Pepper, J. (Eds.). (2012). *Deterrence and the death penalty.* Washington, DC: National Academies Press, Committee on Law and Justice.

National Center for State Courts. (2008). *State sentencing guidelines.* Williamsburg, VA: Author.

National Center on Addiction and Substance Abuse. (2010). *Behind bars II: Substance abuse and America's prison population.* New York: Author. Available at www.casacolumbia.org

National Conference of State Legislatures. (2012). *U.S. Supreme Court rules on Arizona's immigration enforcement law.* Available at http://www.ncsl.org/research/immigration/us-supreme-court-rules-on-arizona-immigration-laws.aspx

National Institute of Corrections. (2008). *Today's jails: Are you looking for a way to coordinate jail and community health services?* Washington, DC: Author. Available at http://nicic.org/JailsDivision

National Institute of Justice. (2011). *Electronic monitoring reduces recidivism.* Washington, DC: U.S. Department of Justice.

National Institute of Justice. (2012). *"Swift and certain" sanctions in probation are highly effective: Evaluation of the HOPE program.* Available at http://www.nij.gov

National Institute of Justice. (2015). Juvenile proportion of arrests by offense, 2014. *OJJDP statistical briefing book.* Retrieved from http://www.ojjdp.gov/ojstatbb/crime/qa05102.asp?qaDate=2014

National Institute on Drug Abuse. (2006). *Principles of drug abuse treatment for criminal justice populations: A research-based guide.* Washington, DC: U.S. Department of Health and Human Services, National Institutes of Health. Available at http://www.drugabuse.gov/PODAT_CJ/

Nellis, A. (2010). Throwing away the key: The extension of life without parole sentences in the United States. *Federal Sentencing Reporter, 23*(1), 27–32.

Nelson, W. R., & Davis, R. M. (1995). Podular direct supervision: The first twenty years. *American Jails, 9,* 11–22.

Nettler, G. (1984). *Explaining crime* (3rd ed.). New York: McGraw–Hill.

Neubauer, D. (2008). *American courts and the criminal justice system.* Belmont, CA: Wadsworth.

Ney, B. (2014, January–February). 10 facts about women in jails. *American Jails Magazine,* pp. 8–10.

Noonan, M. E., & Ginder, S. (2013). *Mortality in local jails and state prisons, 2000–2011: Statistical tables.* Washington, DC: U.S. Department of Justice, Office of Justice Programs, Bureau of Justice Statistics. Available at http://www.bjs.gov/content/pub/pdf/mljsp0011.pdf

Noonan, M., Rohloff, H., & Ginder, S. (2015). *Mortality in local jails and state prisons, 2000–2013: Statistical tables.* Washington, DC: Bureau of Justice Statistics.

Northwestern Law Center for International Human Rights. (2011). *The death penalty worldwide: China.* Available at http://www.deathpenaltyworldwide.org/country-search-post.cfm?country=China

O'Connell, D., Visher, C., Martin, S., Parker, L., & Brent, J. (2011). Decide Your Time: Testing deterrence theory's certainty and celerity effects on substance-using probationers. *Journal of Criminal Justice, 39,* 261–267.

O'Connor, M. L. (2001). Noble corruption–police perjury—What should we do? In R. Muraskin & M. Muraskin (Eds.), *Morality and the law* (pp. 91–106). Upper Saddle River, NJ: Prentice Hall.

O'Donohue, W., Downs, K., & Yeater, E. (1998). Sexual harassment: A review of the literature. *Aggression and Behavior, 3,* 111–128.

Office of National Drug Control Policy. (2014). *ADAM II 2013 annual report.* Washington, DC: Executive Office of the President. Retrieved from https://www.whitehouse.gov/sites/default/files/ondcp/policy-and-research/adam_ii_2013_annual_report.pdf

O'Keefe, M. L. (2008). Administrative segregation from within: A corrections perspective. *The Prison Journal, 88,* 123–143.

Olivero, J. M., & Roberts, J. B. (1987). Marion Federal Penitentiary and the 22-month lockdown: The crisis continues. *Crime and Social Justice, 27–28,* 234–253.

Olson, S., & Dzur, A. (2004). Revisiting informal justice: Restorative justice and democratic professionalism. *Law and Society Review, 38,* 139–176.

Orland, L. (1975). *Prisons: Houses of darkness.* New York: Free Press.

Orland, L. (1995). Prisons as punishment: An historical overview. In K. C. Haas & G. P. Alpert (Eds.), *The dilemmas of corrections: Contemporary readings* (3rd ed.). Prospect Heights, IL: Waveland.

Osher, F. C. (2007). Short-term strategies to improve reentry of jail populations: Expanding and implementing the APIC model. *American Jails, 20,* 9–18.

Oshinsky, D. M. (1996). *Worse than slavery: Parchman Farm and the ordeal of Jim Crow justice.* New York: Free Press.

O'Sullivan, S. (2006). Representations of prison in nineties Hollywood cinema: From *Con Air* to *The Shawshank Redemption.* In R. Tewksbury (Ed.), *Behind bars: Readings on prison culture* (pp. 483–498). Upper Saddle River, NJ: Pearson/Prentice Hall.

Owen, B. (1998). *In the mix: Struggle and survival in a women's prison.* Albany: State University of New York Press.

Owen, B. (2005). Afterword: The case of the women. In J. Irwin (Ed.), *The warehouse prison: Disposal of the new dangerous class* (pp. 261–289). Los Angeles: Roxbury.

Owen, B. (2006). The contexts of women's imprisonment. In A. V. Merlo & J. M. Pollock (Eds.), *Women, law, and social control* (pp. 251–270). Boston: Pearson.

Owen, B., & Bloom, B. (1995). Profiling women prisoners: Findings from national surveys and a California sample. *The Prison Journal, 75,* 165–185.

Owens, E. G. (2009). More time, less crime? Estimating the incapacitative effect of sentence enhancements. *Journal of Law and Economics, 52,* 551–579.

Packer, H. (1997). Two models of the criminal process. In S. Wasserman & C. Snyder (Eds.), *A criminal procedure anthology* (pp. 3–9). Cincinnati, OH: Anderson. (Original work published 1964)

Padfield, N. (2011). An entente cordiale in sentencing? *Criminal Law and Justice Weekly, 175,* 238–292.

Paoline, E. A., III, Lambert, E. G., & Hogan, N. L. (2006). A calm and happy keeper of the keys: The impact of ACA views, relations with coworkers, and policy views on the job stress and job satisfaction of correctional staff. *The Prison Journal, 86*, 182–205.

Paparozzi, M., & Gendreau, P. (2005). An intensive supervision program that worked: Service delivery, professional orientation, and organizational supportiveness. *The Prison Journal, 85*, 445–466.

Paparozzi, M., & Guy, R. (2009). The giant that never woke: Parole authorities as the lynchpin to evidence-based practices and prisoner reentry. *Journal of Contemporary Criminal Justice, 25*, 397–411.

Pastore, A. L., & Maguire, K. (Eds.). (2000). *Sourcebook of criminal justice statistics—1999.* Washington, DC: Bureau of Justice Statistics. Available at https://www.hsdl.org/?view&did=711188

Pastore, A. L., & Maguire, K. (Eds.). (2005). *Sourcebook of criminal justice statistics—2003.* Washington, DC: Bureau of Justice Statistics. Available at https://www.ncjrs.gov/pdffiles1/Digitization/208756NCJRS.pdf

Paternoster, R. (2010). How much do we really know about criminal deterrence? *Journal of Criminal Law and Criminology, 100*, 765–823.

Paternoster, R., & Brame, R. (2003). *An empirical analysis of Maryland's death sentence system with respect to the influence of race and legal jurisdiction: Final report.* College Park: University of Maryland, Department of Criminology.

Paternoster, R., & Deise, J. (2011). A heavy thumb on the scale: The effect of victim impact evidence on capital decision making. *Criminology, 49*, 129–161.

Payne, B., DeMichele, M., & Button, D. (2008). Understanding the electronic monitoring of sex offenders. *Corrections Compendium, 33*, 1–5.

Payne, B., & Gainey, R. (2004). The electronic monitoring of offenders released from jail or prison: Safety, control, and comparisons to the incarceration experience. *The Prison Journal, 84*, 413–435.

Pearson, F., Lipton, D., Cleland, C., & Yee, D. (2002). The effects of behavioral/cognitive behavioral programs on recidivism. *Crime & Delinquency, 48*, 438–452.

Pearson, J. (2015, April 4–5). Study: NYC health workers' ethics are compromised in jails. *Moscow-Pullman Daily News*, p. 5B.

Penn, W. (1981). *The papers of William Penn, Volume One, 1644–1679* (M. M. Dunn & R. S. Dunn, Eds.). Philadelphia: University of Pennsylvania Press. (Original work written circa 1679)

Perroncello, P. (2002). Direct supervision: A 2001 odyssey. *American Jails, 15*, 25–32.

Perry, S. W. (2004). *American Indians and crime.* Washington, DC: U.S. Department of Justice, Office of Justice Programs, Bureau of Justice Statistics. Available at http://www.bjs.gov

Perry, S. (2008). *Justice expenditure and employment statistical extracts, 2006.* Washington, DC: U.S. Department of Justice, Office of Justice Programs, Bureau of Justice Statistics. Available at http://bjs.ojp.usdoj.gov

Petersilia, J. (1998). Probation in the United States, Part 1. *Perspectives, 22*, 30–41.

Petersilia, J. (2000). Parole and prisoner reentry in the United States. *Perspectives, 24*(3), 32–46.

Petersilia, J. (2001). Prisoner reentry: Public safety and reintegration challenges. *The Prison Journal, 81*, 360–375.

Petersilia, J. (2004). What works in prison reentry? Reviewing and questioning the evidence. *Federal Probation, 68*, 1–8.

Phelps, R. (1996). *Newgate of Connecticut: Its origin and early history.* Camden, ME: Picton. (Original work published 1860)

Piggott, S. (2017). Portland stabbings: Man arrested for double murder after allegedly threatening Muslim women has racist views, praised Timothy McVeigh. *Hate Watch* (Southern Poverty Law Center). Available at https://www.splcenter.org/hatewatch

Piquero, A., & Blumstein, A. (2007). Does incapacitation reduce crime? *Journal of Quantitative Criminology, 23*, 267–285.

Pitts, L. (2010, November 21). Sisters may be guilty; State of Mississippi assuredly is. *The Tacoma News Tribune*, p. B6.

Pizarro, J. M., & Narag, R. E. (2008). Supermax prisons: What we know, what we do not know, and where we are going. *The Prison Journal, 88*, 23–42.

Plato. (2008). *Laws: Project Gutenberg.* Available at http://www.gutenberg.org

Pogrebin, M. R., & Poole, E. D. (1997). The sexualized work environment: A look at women jail officers. *The Prison Journal, 77*, 41–57.

Polcin, D. (2009). Community living settings for adults recovering from substance abuse. *Journal of Groups in Addiction and Recovery, 4*, 7–22.

Pollock, J. M. (1994). *Ethics in crime and justice: Dilemmas and decisions* (2nd ed.). Belmont, CA: Wadsworth.

Pollock, J. M. (1998). *Ethics in crime and justice: Dilemmas and decisions* (3rd ed.). Belmont, CA: West/Wadsworth.

Pollock, J. (2002a). Parenting programs in women's prisons. *Women & Criminal Justice, 14*, 131–154.

Pollock, J. (2002b). *Women, prison, & crime* (2nd ed.). Belmont, CA: Wadsworth Thomson Learning.

Pollock, J. M. (2004). *Prisons and prison life: Costs and consequences.* Los Angeles: Roxbury.

Pollock, J. M. (2010). *Ethics in crime and justice: Dilemmas and decisions* (7th ed.). Belmont, CA: Wadsworth Thomson Learning.

Pollock, J. M. (2014). *Women's crimes, criminology, and corrections.* Long Grove, IL: Waveland.

Pollock, J. M., Hogan, N. L., Lambert, E. G., Ross, J. I., & Sundt, J. L. (2012). A utopian prison: Contradiction in terms? *Journal of Contemporary Criminal Justice, 28*, 60–76.

Porter, N. D. (2011). *The state of sentencing 2010: Developments in policy and practice.* Washington, DC: The Sentencing Project. Available at http://www.sentencingproject.org

Porter, N. D. (2016). *The state of sentencing 2015: Developments in policy and practice.* Washington, DC: Sentencing Project. Available at http://sentencingproject.org/wp-content/uploads/2016/02/State-of-Sentencing-2015.pdf

Porto, P., Oliveira, L., Mari, J., Volchan, E., Figueira, I., & Ventura, P. (2009). Does cognitive behavioral therapy change the brain? A systematic review of neuroimaging in anxiety disorders. *Journal of Neuropsychiatry and Clinical Neurosciences, 21*, 114–125.

Powell, K. (2006). How does the teenage brain work? *Nature, 442,* 865–867.

Pryor, J., &. Stoller, L. M. (1994). Sexual cognition processes in men high in the likelihood to sexually harass. *Personality and Social Psychology Bulletin, 20,* 163–169.

Pugh, R. B. (1968). *Imprisonment in medieval England.* Cambridge, UK: Cambridge University Press.

Puzzanchera, C., & Kang, W. (2007). *Juvenile court statistics databook.* Pittsburgh, PA: National Center for Juvenile Justice. Available at http://www.ojjdp.gov/ojstatbb/ezajcs/asp/process.asp

Quigley, B. (2010, July 26). Fourteen examples of racism in criminal justice system. *Huffington Post.* Available at http://www.huffington post.com/bill-quigley/fourteen-examples-of-raci_b_658947.html

Quinsey, V. (2002). Evolutionary theory and criminal behavior. *Legal and Criminological Psychology, 7,* 1–14.

Radelet, M., & Lacock, T. (2009). Do executions lower homicide rates? The views of leading criminologists. *Journal of Criminal Law and Criminology, 99,* 489–508.

Radzinowicz, L., & King, J. (1979). *The growth of crime: The international experience.* Middlesex, UK: Penguin Books.

Rafter, N. H. (1985). *Partial justice: Women in state prisons, 1800–1935.* Boston: Northeastern University Press.

Rafter, N. H. (2009). "Much and unfortunately neglected": Women in early and mid-nineteenth-century prisons. In M. K. Stohr, A. Walsh, & C. Hemmens (Eds.), *Corrections: A text/reader* (pp. 50–65). Thousand Oaks, CA: Sage.

Reaves, B. A. (2009). *State and local law enforcement training academies, 2006.* Washington, DC: U.S. Department of Justice, Office of Justice Programs, Bureau of Justice Statistics. Available at http://www.bjs.gov/index.cfm?ty=pbdetail&iid=1207

Reichel, P. (2005). *Comparative justice systems.* Upper Saddle River, NJ: Prentice Hall.

Reid, S. (2006). *Criminal justice* (7th ed.). Cincinnati, OH: Atomic Dog.

Reilly, R. J. (2014, February 12). DOJ threatens to withhold grants from states that aren't protecting prisoners from rape. *Huffington Post.* Available at http://www.huffington post.com/2014/02/12/doj-prisonrape_n_4775411.html

Reisig, M. (1998). Rates of disorder in higher-custody state prisons: A comparative analysis of managerial practices. *Crime & Delinquency, 44,* 229–244.

Reisig, M. D., Holtfreter, K., & Morash, M. (2002). Social capital among women offenders: Examining the distribution of social networks and resources. *Journal of Contemporary Criminal Justice, 18,* 167–187.

Rembert, D. A., & Henderson, H. (2014). Correctional officer excessive use of force: Civil liability under Section 1983. *The Prison Journal, 94,* 198–219.

Rengert, G., & Wasilchick, J. (2001). *Suburban burglary: A tale of two suburbs.* Springfield, IL: Charles C Thomas.

Restak, R. (2001). *The secret life of the brain.* New York: Dana Press/Joseph Henry Press.

Reutter, D. M. (2007, December). Arizona jail sex results in charges for guards, prisoner. *Prison Legal News,* pp. 18, 31.

Reynolds, M. O. (1998, August). *Does punishment deter?* (National Center for Policy Analysis, Policy Backgrounders No. 148). Available at http://www.ncpa.org/pub/bg148

Reynolds, R. (2009). Equal justice under law: Post-Booker, should federal judges be able to depart from the federal sentencing guidelines to remedy disparity between codefendants' sentencing? *Columbia Law Review, 109,* 538–570.

Reza, E. (2005). Gender bias in North Carolina's death penalty. *Duke Journal of Gender Law & Policy, 12,* 179–214.

Rice, S. K., Reitzel, J. D., & Piquero, A. R. (2005). Shades of brown: Perceptions of racial profiling and the intra-ethnic differential. *Journal of Ethnicity in Criminal Justice, 3,* 47–70.

Richards, S. C. (2008). USP Marion: The first federal supermax. *The Prison Journal, 88,* 6–22.

Richmond, K. M. (2014). The impact of federal prison industries employment on the recidivism outcomes of female inmates. *Justice Quarterly, 31,* 719–745.

Rideau, W. (2010). *In the place of justice: A story of punishment and deliverance.* New York: Alfred A. Knopf.

Rigby, M. (2007, December). Dallas, Texas, jail pays $950,000 for neglecting mentally ill prisoners. *Prison Legal News,* p. 22.

Roberts, J. (2011). Sentencing guidelines and judicial discretion: Evolution of the duty of courts to comply in England and Wales. *British Journal of Criminology, 51,* 997–1013.

Roberts, J. W. (1997). *Reform and retribution: An illustrated history of American prisons.* Lanham, MD: American Correctional Association.

Robertson, J. (2010). Recent legal developments: Correctional case law, 2009. *Criminal Justice Review, 35,* 260–272.

Robertson, J. E. (2014, April/May). The one million: Reimagining the jails as the institution that says "yes" to the mentally ill. *Correctional Law Reporter,* pp. 87–89.

Robinson, G., & McNeill, F. (2010). Probation in the United Kingdom. In M. Hertzog-Evans (Ed.), *Transnational criminology* (Vol. 3, pp. 741–762). Nijmegen, The Netherlands: Wolf Legal.

Robinson, M. (2005). *Justice blind: Ideals and realities of American criminal justice.* Upper Saddle River, NJ: Prentice Hall.

Robinson, M. (2008). *Death nation: The experts explain American capital punishment.* Upper Saddle River, NJ: Prentice Hall.

Rocheleau, A. M. (2013). An empirical exploration of the "pains of imprisonment" and the level of prison misconduct and violence. *Criminal Justice Review, 38*(3), 354–374.

Rodney, E., & Mupier, R. (1999). Behavioral differences between African American male adolescents with biological fathers and those without biological fathers in the home. *Journal of Black Studies, 30,* 45–61.

Rodriguez, N. (2007). Restorative justice at work: Examining the impact of restorative justice resolutions on juvenile recidivism. *Crime & Delinquency, 53,* 355–379.

Rohr, J. A. (1989). *Ethics for bureaucrats: An essay on law and values.* New York: Marcel Dekker.

Roman, J. (2013). *Cost–benefit analysis of criminal justice reforms.* Washington, DC: National Institute of Justice. Available at https://ncjrs.gov/pdffiles1/nij/241929.pdf

Rosenfeld, R. (2000). Patterns in adult homicide. In A. Blumstein & J. Wallman (Eds.), *The crime drop in America* (pp. 130–163). Cambridge, UK: Cambridge University Press.

Ross, J. L., & Richards, S. C. (2002). *Behind bars: Surviving prison*. Indianapolis, IN: Alpha Books.

Roth, M. (2006). *Prisons and prison systems: A global encyclopedia*. Westport, CT: Greenwood.

Rothman, D. J. (1980). *Conscience and convenience: The asylum and its alternatives in progressive America*. Glenview, IL: Scott Foresman.

Routh, D., Abess, G., Lee, J., Makin, D., Hemmens, C., & Stohr, M. K. (2014). *Transgender inmates in prisons: The policies and statutes*. Unpublished manuscript.

Ruddell, R. (2004). *America behind bars: Trends in imprisonment, 1950 to 2000*. New York: LFB Scholarly Publishing.

Ruddell, R., Decker, S., & Egley, A. (2006). Gang interventions in jails: A national analysis. *Criminal Justice Review, 31*, 33–46.

Ruddell, R., & Leyton-Brown, K. (2013). All in the family: The role of the sheriff's wife in 20th-century mom and pop jails. *Women & Criminal Justice, 23*, 267–285.

Russell, B. (2014, January 4). Idaho to take over operation of prison. *Spokesman-Review*, pp. B1, B3.

Sabol, W. J., & Minton, T. D. (2008). *Jail inmates at midyear 2007*. Washington, DC: Bureau of Justice Statistics. Available at http://www.bjs.gov/content/pub/pdf/jim07.pdf

Samenow, S. (1999). *Before it's too late: Why some kids get into trouble and what parents can do about it*. New York: Times Books.

Sampson, R., & Laub, J. (1999). Crime and deviance over the life course: The salience of adult social bonds. In F. Scarpitti & A. Nielsen (Eds.), *Crime and criminals: Contemporary and classical readings in criminology* (pp. 238–246). Los Angeles: Roxbury.

Santayana, G. (1905). *The life of reason: Reason in common sense*. New York: Dover.

Saylor, W., & Iwaszko, A. (2009). *One in 31: The long reach of American corrections*. Washington, DC: PEW Center on the States, PEW Charitable Trusts.

Schaffner, L. (2014). Out of sight, out of compliance: U.S. detained girls' health justice. *Criminal Justice Review, 17*(1), 63–86.

Scheidegger, K. (2006). *Supreme Court decisions on habeas corpus*. Washington, DC: The Federalist Society. Available at http://www.fed-soc.org

Scheidegger, K. (2012). Rebutting myths about race and the death penalty. *Ohio State Journal of Criminal Law, 10*, 147–165.

Schmalleger, F. (2001). *Criminal justice today* (6th ed.). Upper Saddle River, NJ: Prentice Hall.

Schmitz, J., Stotts, A., Sayre, S., DeLaune, K., & Grabowski, J. (2004). Treatment of cocaine–alcohol dependence with naltrexone and relapse prevention therapy. *American Journal on Addictions, 13*, 333–341.

Schofield, M. (1997, August 24). Tape puts for-profit prisons back in spotlight: Video shows guards abusing inmates—and jeopardizes system. *Idaho Statesman*, pp. A1, A16.

Schwirtz, M. (2014a, March 25). U.S. charges correction officer in death of a mentally ill inmate at Rikers. *New York Times*, p. A21.

Schwirtz, M. (2014b, March 26). Complaint by fired correction officer adds details about a death at Rikers. *New York Times*, p. A19.

Scroggins, J. R., & Malley, S. (2010). Reentry and the (unmet) needs of women. *Journal of Offender Rehabilitation, 49*, 146–163.

Seabrook, N. (2014, August 24). What's really wrong with Rikers. *New York Times*. Available at https://www.nytimes.com/2014/08/25/opinion/whats-really-wrong-with-rikers.html?mcubz=0

Seiter, R. (2005). *Corrections: An introduction*. Upper Saddle River, NJ: Prentice Hall.

Seiter, R., & Kadela, K. (2003). Prisoner reentry: What works, what does not, and what is promising. *Crime & Delinquency, 49*, 360–390.

Selling, D., Solimo, A., Lee, D., Horne, K., Panove, E., & Venters, H. (2014). Surveillance of suicidal and nonsuicidal self-injury in the New York City jail system. *Journal of Correctional Health Care, 20*, 163–167.

Sentencing Project, The. (2011). *Racial disparity*. Available at http://www.sentencingproject.org

Serin, R., Gobeil, R., & Preston, D. (2009). Evaluation of the persistently violent offender program. *International Journal of Offender Therapy and Comparative Criminology, 53*, 57–73.

Serrano, R. A. (2006, November 20). 9/11 prisoner abuse suit could be landmark: Rounded up, Muslim immigrants were beaten in jail. *Los Angeles Times*. Available at http://articles.latimes.com/2006/nov/20/nation/na-jail20

Service Public Francaise. (2013). *Quelles sont les différences entre une contravention, un délit et un crime? Direction de l'information légale et administrative (Premier ministre) et Ministère en charge de la justice*. Available at http://vosdroits.service-public.fr/particuliers/ F1157.xhtml

Severson, M. (2004). Mental health needs and mental health care in jails: The past, the present, and hope for the future. *American Jails, 28*, 9–18.

Sevigny, E., Fuleihan, B. & Ferdik, F. (2013). Do drug courts reduce the use of incarceration? A meta-analysis. *Journal of Criminal Justice, 41*, 416–425.

Sewell, M. (2010). Pushing execution over the constitutional line: Forcible medication of condemned inmates and the Eighth and Fourteenth Amendments. *Boston College Law Review, 51*, 1279–1322.

Sexton, L., Jenness, V., & Sumner, J. M. (2010). Where the margins meet: A demographic assessment of transgender inmates in men's prisons. *Justice Quarterly, 27*, 835–866.

Shahani, A. (2011). What is GEO Group? *National Public Radio*. Available at http://www.npr.org/2011

Sharma, H., Scheb, J., Houston, D., & Wagers, K. (2013). Race and the death penalty: An empirical assessment of first-degree murder convictions in Tennessee after *Gregg v. Georgia*. *Tennessee Journal of Race, Gender, & Social Justice, 2*, 1–39.

Sharp, B. (2006). *Changing criminal thinking: A treatment program*. Alexandria, VA: American Correctional Association.

Sharp, P., & Hancock, B. (1995). *Juvenile delinquency: Historical, theoretical, and societal reactions to youth*. Englewood Cliffs, NJ: Prentice Hall.

Sharp, S. F., & Marcus-Mendoza, S. T. (2001). It's a family affair: Incarcerated women and their families. *Women & Criminal Justice, 12*, 21–49.

Shatz, S., & Shatz, N. (2011). *Chivalry is not dead: Murder, gender, and the death penalty*. Available at http://works.bepress.com/steven_shatz/1

Shaw, V. (2010). Corrections and punishment in China: Information and analysis. *Journal of Contemporary Criminal Justice, 26,* 53–71.

Shepherd, J. (2005). Deterrence versus brutalization: Capital punishment's differing impacts among states. *Michigan Law Review, 104,* 203–256.

Sherman, L. (2005). The use and usefulness of criminology, 1751–2005: Enlightened justice and its failures. *Annals of the American Academy of Political and Social Science, 600,* 115–135.

Shilton, M. (2003). *Increasing public safety through halfway houses.* Alexandria, VA: Center for Community Corrections. Available at http://www.communitycorrections works.org

Sickmund, M., & Wan, Y. (2003). *Census of juveniles in residential placement: 2003 databook.* Washington, DC: Office of Juvenile Justice and Delinquency Prevention.

Siegel, L. (2006). *Criminology.* Belmont, CA: Thomson/Wadsworth.

Simon, H., & Wetstein, S. (2016, March 11). *Civil rights groups call for federal investigation into solitary confinement abuse in Florida prisons.* Miami: ACLU of Florida. Available at https://www.aclufl.org/en/press-releases/civil-rights-groups-call-federal-investigation-solitary-confinement-abuse-florida

Simpson, S. S., Yahner, J. L., & Dugan, L. (2008). Understanding women's pathways to jail: Analysing the lives of incarcerated women. *Australian and New Zealand Journal of Criminology, 41,* 84–108.

Skeem, J., & Manchak, S. (2008). Back to the future: From Klockars' model of effective supervision to evidence-based practice in probation. *Journal of Offender Rehabilitation, 47,* 220–247.

Skinner, B. F. (2005). *Walden two.* Indianapolis, IN: Hackett. (Original work published 1948)

Skolnick, J. (1993). Shut the door again on sociopaths [editorial]. *Los Angeles Times.* Available at http://articles.latimes.com/1993-12-16/local/me-2264_1_richard-allen-davis

Slate, R., & Vogel, R. (1997). Participative management and correctional personnel: A study of perceived atmosphere for participation in correctional decision-making and its impact on employee stress and thoughts about quitting. *Journal of Criminal Justice, 25,* 397–408.

Slate, R., Wells, T., & Wesley Johnson, W. (2003). Opening the manager's door: State probation officer stress and perceptions of participation in workplace decision-making. *Crime & Delinquency, 49,* 519–541.

Slate, R. N., & Wesley Johnson, W. (2008). *Criminalization of mental illness.* Durham, NC: Carolina Academic Press.

Smith, P., & Smith, W. A. (2005). Experiencing community through the eyes of young female offenders. *Journal of Contemporary Criminal Justice, 21,* 364–385.

Smykla, J., & Williams, J. (1996). Co-corrections in the United States of America, 1970–1990: Two decades of disadvantages for women prisoners. *Women & Criminal Justice, 8,* 61–76.

Snell, T. (2011). *Capital punishment, 2010: Statistical tables.* Washington, DC: Bureau of Justice Statistics.

Snyder, H., Espiritu, R., Huizinga, D., Loeber, R., & Petechuck, D. (2003, March). Prevalence and development of child delinquency. *Child Delinquency Bulletin Series.* Washington, DC: U.S. Department of Justice, Office of Juvenile Justice and Delinquency Prevention. Available at http://www.ncjrs.gov/pdffiles1/ojjdp/193411.pdf

Solomon, A., Dedel Johnson, K., Travis, J., & McBride, E. (2004). *From prison to work: The employment dimensions of prisoner reentry.* Washington, DC: Urban Institute, Justice Policy Center.

Solomon, A., Kachnowski, V., & Bhati, A. (2005). *Does parole work?* Washington, DC: Urban Institute, Justice Policy Center.

Solomon, E., & Garside, R. (2009). *Ten years of Labour's youth justice reforms: An independent audit.* London: Center for Crime and Justice Studies, The Hadley Trust.

Solomon, R. C. (1996). *A handbook for ethics.* Fort Worth, TX: Harcourt Brace College.

Southern Poverty Law Center. (2017). *Hate map.* Available at https://www.splcenter.org/hate-map

Spelman, W. (2000). The limited importance of prison expansion. In A. Blumstein & J. Wallman (Eds.), *The crime drop in America* (pp. 97–129). Cambridge, UK: Cambridge University Press.

Spjeldnes, S., Jung, H., & Yamatani, H. (2014). Gender differences in jail populations: Factors to consider in re-entry strategies. *Journal of Offender Rehabilitation, 53,* 75–94.

Springer, C. (1987). *Justice for juveniles.* Washington, DC: Office of Juvenile Justice and Delinquency Prevention.

Stannard, D. E. (1992). *American holocaust: Columbus and the conquest of the New World.* New York: Oxford University Press.

Staton-Tindall, M., Garner, B. R., Morey, J. T., Leukefeld, C., Krietemeyer, J., Saum, C. A., & Oser, C. B. (2007). Gender differences in treatment engagement among a sample of incarcerated substance abusers. *Criminal Justice and Behavior, 34,* 1143–1156.

Steffensmeier, D., Feldmeyer, B., Harris, C., & Ulmer, J. (2011). Reassessing trends in black violent crime, 1980–2008: Sorting out the "Hispanic effect" in Uniform Crime Reports arrests, National Crime Victimization Survey offender estimates, and U.S. prisoner counts. *Criminology, 49,* 197–251.

Steiner, B., & Giacomazzi, A. (2007). Juvenile waiver, boot camp, and recidivism in a northwestern state. *The Prison Journal, 87,* 227–240.

Stephan, J. J. (1987). *1984 census of state adult correctional facilities.* Washington, DC: Bureau of Justice Statistics. Available at http://www.bjs.gov/content/pub/pdf/csacf84.pdf

Stephan, J. J. (1992). *Census of state and federal correctional facilities, 1990.* Washington, DC: Bureau of Justice Statistics. Available at http://www.bjs.gov/content/pub/pdf/csfcf90.pdf

Stephan, J. J. (1997). *Census of state and federal correctional facilities, 1995.* Washington, DC: Bureau of Justice Statistics. Available at http://www.bjs.gov/content/pub/pdf/Csfcf95.pdf

Stephan, J. J. (2001). *Census of state and federal correctional facilities.* Washington, DC: U.S. Department of Justice, Office of Justice Programs, Bureau of Justice Statistics. Available at http://www.bjs.ojp.usdoj.gov

Stephan, J. J. (2008). *Census of state and federal correctional facilities, 2005.* Washington, DC: U.S. Department of Justice, Office of Justice Programs, Bureau of Justice Statistics. Available at http://www.bjs.gov

Stephan, J., & Karberg, J. (2003). *The census of state and federal correctional facilities.* Washington, DC: U.S. Department of Justice.

Stohr, M. K. (2006). Yes, I've paid the price, but look how much I gained! In C. M. Renzetti, L. Goodstein, & S. L. Miller (Eds.), *Rethinking gender, crime, and justice* (pp. 262–277). Los Angeles: Roxbury.

Stohr, M. K. (2014). *The etiology and status of the war on transgender women in men's prisons.* Unpublished manuscript.

Stohr, M. K., & Collins, P. A. (2009). *Criminal justice management: Theory and practice in justice-centered organizations.* New York: Oxford University Press.

Stohr, M. K., & Collins, P. A. (2014). *Criminal justice management: Theory and practice in justice-centered organizations.* London: Routledge.

Stohr, M. K., Hemmens, C., Shapiro, B., Chambers, B., & Kelly, L. (2002). Comparing inmate perceptions of two residential substance abuse treatment programs. *International Journal of Offender Therapy and Comparative Criminology, 46,* 699–714.

Stohr, M. K., Jonson, C. L., & Cullen, F. T. (2014). Lessons learned: From penal harm to penal help. In F. T. Cullen, C. L. Jonson, & M. K. Stohr (Eds.), *The American prison: Imagining a different future* (pp. 257–268). Thousand Oaks, CA: Sage.

Stohr, M. K., Lovrich, N. P., & Mays, G. L. (1997). Service v. security focus in training assessments: Testing gender differences among women's jail correctional officers. *Women & Criminal Justice, 9,* 65–85.

Stohr, M. K., Lovrich, N. P., Menke, B. A., & Zupan, L. L. (1994). Staff management in correctional institutions: Comparing DiIulio's "control model" and "employee investment model" outcomes in five jails. *Justice Quarterly, 11,* 471–497.

Stohr, M. K., Lovrich, N. P., & Wilson, G. L. (1994). Staff stress in contemporary jails: Assessing problem severity and the payoff of progressive personnel practices. *Journal of Criminal Justice, 22,* 313–328.

Stohr, M. K., Lovrich, N. P., & Wood, M. (1996). Service v. security concerns in contemporary jails: Testing behavior differences in training topic assessments. *Journal of Criminal Justice, 24,* 437–448.

Stohr, M. K., & Mays, L. G. (1993). *Women's jails: An investigation of offenders, staff, administration and programming* (Final report for Grant 92J04GHP5 awarded by the National Institute of Corrections, Jails Division). Available at http://nicic.gov/Library/008747

Stohr, M. K., Mays, G. L., Beck, A. C., & Kelley, T. (1998). Sexual harassment in women's jails. *Journal of Contemporary Criminal Justice, 14,* 135–155.

Stohr, M. K., & Wozniak, J. (2014). The green prison. In F. T. Cullen, C. L. Jonson, & M. K. Stohr (Eds.), *The American prison: Imagining a different future* (pp. 193–212). Thousand Oaks, CA: Sage.

Streib, V. (2003a). Executing women, juveniles, and the mentally retarded: Second class citizens in capital punishment. In J. Aker, R. Bohm, & C. Lanier (Eds.), *America's experiment with capital punishment: Reflections on the past, present, and future of the ultimate penal sanction* (2nd ed., pp. 301–323). Durham, NC: Carolina Academic Press.

Streib, V. (2003b). *The juvenile death penalty today: Death sentences and executions for juvenile crimes, January 1, 1973–June 30, 2003.* Available at https://deathpenaltyinfo.org/documents/JuvDeathApril2004.pdf

Sturgess, A., & Macher, A. (2005). Issues in correctional HIV care: Progressive disseminated histoplasmosis. *American Jails, 19,* 54–56.

Sundt, J. L., Castellano, T. C., & Briggs, C. S. (2008). The sociopolitical context of violence and its control: A case study of supermax and its effect in Illinois. *The Prison Journal, 88,* 94–122.

Surratt, H. L. (2003). Parenting attitudes of drug-involved women inmates. *The Prison Journal, 83,* 206–220.

Sustainability in Prisons Project. (n.d.). *Taylor's Checkerspot Butterfly Rearing Program.* Olympia, WA: The Evergreen State College. Available at http://sustainabilityinprisons.org/what-we-do/science/taylors-checkerspot-butterfly-program-2

Sweeten, G., & Apel, R. (2007). Incapacitation: Revisiting an old question with a new method and new data. *Journal of Quantitative Criminology, 23,* 303–326.

Sykes, G. M. (1958). *The society of captives: A study of a maximum security prison.* Princeton, NJ: Princeton University Press.

Sykes, G. M., & Messinger, S. (1960). The inmate social system. In R. Cloward & D. R. Dressey (Eds.), *Theoretical studies in social organization of the prison* (pp. 5–19). New York: Social Science Research Council.

Talbot, T., Gilligan, L., Carter, M., & Matson, S. (2002). *An overview of sex offender management.* Washington, DC: Center for Sex Offender Management.

Tally, H. (2015). A constitutional level of healthcare. *American Jails, 29,* 15–19.

Tapia, M. (2014). Texas Latino gangs and large urban jails: Intergenerational conflicts and issues in management. *Journal of Crime and Justice, 37,* 256–274.

Tartaro, C. (2002). Examining implementation issues with new generation jails. *Criminal Justice Policy Review, 13,* 219–237.

Tartaro, C. (2006). Watered down: Partial implementation of the new generation jail philosophy. *The Prison Journal, 86,* 284–300.

Tartaro, C., & Ruddell, R. (2006). Trouble in Mayberry: A national analysis of suicides and attempts in small jails. *American Journal of Criminal Justice, 31,* 81–101.

Taylor, R., Fritsch, E., & Caeti, T. (2007). *Juvenile justice: Policies, programs, and practices.* New York: McGraw–Hill.

Tempest, R. (2005, March 6). Death row often means a long life: California condemns many murderers, but few are ever executed. *Los Angeles Times,* p. B1.

Terrill, R. (2003). *World justice systems.* Cincinnati, OH: Anderson.

Terrill, R. (2013). *World criminal justice systems.* Cincinnati, OH: Anderson.

Tewksbury, R., & Collins, S. C. (2006). Aggression levels among correctional officers: Reassessing sex differences. *The Prison Journal, 86,* 327–343.

Tewksbury, R., & Potter, R. H. (2005). Transgender prisoners: A forgotten group. In S. Stojkovic (Ed.), *Managing special populations in jails and prisons* (pp. 15-1–15-14). New York: Civic Research Institute.

Thompson, G. (1847). *Prison life and reflections: Or a narrative of the arrest, trial, conviction,* imprisonment, treatment, observations, reflections, and deliverance of Work, Burr and Thompson, who suffered an unjust and cruel imprisonment in Missouri Penitentiary for attempting to aid some slaves to liberty. Oberlin, OH: Oberlin Press.

Thompson, J. A., & Mays, G. L. (1991). Paying the piper but changing the tune: Policy changes and initiatives for the American jail. In J. A. Thompson & G. L. Mays (Eds.), American jails: Public policy issues (pp. 240–246). Chicago: Nelson–Hall.

Tocqueville, A. de, & Goldhammer, A. (2004). Tocqueville: Democracy in America. New York: Library of America. (Original work published 1835)

Toobin, J. (2015, May 11). The Milwaukee experiment. The New Yorker, pp. 24–32.

Torrey, E., Zdanowicz, M., Kennard, A., Lamb, R., Eslinger, D., Biasotti, M., & Fuller, D. A. (2014). The treatment of persons with mental illness in prisons and jails: A state survey. Arlington, VA: Treatment Advocacy Center. Available at http://tacreports.org/storage/documents/treatment-behind-bars/treatment-behind-bars.pdf

Traut, C., & Emmert, C. (1998). Expanding the integrated model of judicial decision making: The California justices and capital punishment. The Journal of Politics, 60, 1166–1180.

Travis, A. (2013, January 8). Probation service "revolution" means wholesale privatization. The Guardian. Available at http://www.guardian.co.uk/society/2013/jan/09/probation-service-private-firms-grayling

Travis, J. (2000, May). But they all come back: Rethinking prisoner reentry (Sentencing & Corrections: Issues for the 21st Century, No. 7). Washington, DC: U.S. Department of Justice, National Institute of Justice.

Travis, J. (2005). But they all come back: Facing the challenges of prison reentry. Washington, DC: Urban Institute, Justice Policy Center.

Travis, J., & Lawrence, S. (2002). Beyond the prison gates: The state of parole in America. Washington, DC: Urban Institute, Justice Policy Center.

Travis, J., & Petersilia, J. (2001). Reentry reconsidered: A new look at an old question. Crime & Delinquency, 47, 291–313.

Trends in U.S. corrections. (2013). The Sentencing Project. Available at http://sentencingproject.org/doc/publications/inc_Trends_in_Corrections_Fact_sheet.pdf

Truman, J. L., & Langton, L. (2015). Criminal victimization, 2014. Washington, DC: Bureau of Justice Statistics. Available at http://www.bjs.gov/index.cfm?ty=pbdetail&iid=5366

Tucker, E. (2014, April 24). Longtime inmates to get clemency. Moscow–Pullman Daily News, p. 1.

Tucker, J. (2014, March 4). 5 Keys Charter School helps S.F. inmates. San Francisco Chronicle. Available at http://www.sfgate.com/bayarea/article/5-Keys-CharterSchool-helps-S-F-inmates-4233314.php

Tursun, G. (2010). Exploration of probation in Chinese criminal law. Federal Sentencing Reporter, 22, 288–293.

Ulmer, J. (2012). Recent developments and new directions in sentencing research. Justice Quarterly, 29, 1–40.

Umbreit, M. (1994). Victim meets offender: The impact of restorative justice and mediation. Monsey, NY: Criminal Justice Press.

U.S. Census Bureau. (2001). Population estimates. Available at http://www.census.gov

U.S. Census Bureau. (2006). Statistical abstract of the United States. Available at http://www.census.gov

U.S. Census Bureau. (2010). Census of governmental employment and payroll. Available at http://www.census.gov

U.S. Census Bureau. (2014a). Facts for features: Hispanic Heritage Month 2014: Sept. 15–Oct. 15. Available at http://www.census.gov/newsroom/facts-for-features/2014/cb14-ff22.html

U.S. Census Bureau. (2014b). State and local government employment and payroll data. Available at http://www.census.gov/govs/apes

U.S. Census Bureau, Population Division. (2016, June). Annual estimates of the resident population by sex, race, and Hispanic origin for the United States, states, and counties: April 1, 2010 to July 1, 2015. Available at http://factfinder.census.gov/faces/tableservices/jsf/pages/productview.xhtml?src=bkmk

U.S. Courts. (2013). Supervision costs significantly less than incarceration in federal system. Available at http://news.uscourts.gov/supervision-costs-significantly-less-incarceration-federal-system

U.S. Department of Justice. (2001). The federal death penalty system: Supplementary data, analysis, and revised protocols for capital case review. Washington, DC: Author. Available at www.justice.gov/dag/pubdoc/deathpenaltystudy.htm

U.S. Department of Justice. (2015). Department of Justice announces 50 states and territories have committed to ending prison rape. Available at https://www.justice.gov/opa/pr/department-justice-announces-50-states-and-territories-have-committed-ending-prison-rape

U.S. Department of Labor. (2010). The National Compensation Survey: Occupational earnings in the United States, 2009. Washington, DC: U.S. Bureau of Labor Statistics. Available at http://www.bls.gov/ncs/ocs/sp/nctb1349.pdf

U.S. District Courts. (2016). U.S. District Courts—judicial business 2015. Available at http://www.uscourts.gov/statistics-reports/us-district-courts-judicial-business-2015

U.S. Marshals Service. (2012). Witness protection program. Retrieved from http://www.usmarshals.gov/duties/witsec.htm

U.S. Sentencing Commission. (1995). Annual report. Washington, DC: Author.

U.S. Sentencing Commission. (2011). January 28, 2011, memorandum. Available at http://www.ussc.gov

Useem, B. (1985). Disorganization and the New Mexico prison riot. American Sociological Review, 50, 677–688.

Useem, B., & Kimball, P. A. (1989). States of siege: U.S. prison riots 1971–1986. New York: Oxford University Press.

van den Haag, E. (2003). Justice, deterrence and the death penalty. In J. Aker, R. Bohm, & C. Lanier (Eds.), America's experiment with capital punishment (pp. 233–249). Durham, NC: Carolina Academic Press.

Vanstone, M. (2000). Cognitive-behavioural work with offenders in the UK: A history of influential endeavour. Howard Journal of Criminal Justice, 39, 171–183.

Vanstone, M. (2004). Mission control: The origins of humanitarian service. Probation Journal, 51, 34–47.

Vanstone, M. (2008). The international origins and initial development of probation. British Journal of Criminology, 48, 735–755.

Van Tongeren, D. R., & Klebe, K. J. (2010). Reconceptualizing prison adjustment: A multidimensional approach exploring female offenders' adjustment to prison life. *The Prison Journal, 90,* 48–68.

Van Voorhis, P., Braswell, M., & Lester, D. (2000). *Correctional counseling and rehabilitation.* Cincinnati, OH: Anderson.

Vaske, J., Galyean, K., & Cullen, F. (2011). Toward a biosocial theory of offender rehabilitation: Why does cognitive-behavioral therapy work? *Journal of Criminal Justice, 39,* 90–102.

Vaughn, M. (2009). Substance abuse and crime: Biosocial foundations. In A. Walsh & K. M. Beaver (Eds.), *Biosocial criminology: New directions in theory and research* (pp. 176–189). New York: Routledge.

Vaughn, M. S., & Carroll, L. (1998). Separate and unequal: Prison versus free-world medical care. *Justice Quarterly, 15,* 3–10.

Vaughn, M., & Del Carmen, R. (1995). Civil liability against prison officials for inmate-on-inmate assault: Where are we and where have we been? *The Prison Journal, 75,* 69–89.

Vaughn, M. S., & Smith, L. G. (1999). Practicing penal harm medicine in the United States: Prisoners' voices from jail. *Justice Quarterly, 16,* 175–231.

Vermont Department of Corrections. (2010). *Graduated sanctions for technical violation of probation in lieu of court referral* (DOC Policy No. 347). Available at www.doc .state.vt.us

Vito, G., Allen, H., & Farmer, G. (1981). Shock probation in Ohio: A comparison of outcomes. *International Journal of Offender Therapy and Comparative Criminology, 25,* 70–76.

Vogel, R. (2004). Silencing the cells: Mass incarceration and legal repression in U.S. prisons. *Monthly Review: An Independent Socialist Magazine, 56,* 37–43.

Volkow, N. (2010). *Important treatment advances for addiction to heroin and other opiates.* Bethesda, MD: National Institute on Drug Abuse. Available at http://www.drugabuse.gov/about-nida/directors-page/messages-director/2010/10/important-treatment-advances-addiction-to-heroin-other-opiates

Walker, E. (2002). Adolescent neuro-development and psychopathology. *Current Directions in Psychological Science, 11,* 24–28.

Walker, S. (2001). *Sense and nonsense about crime and drugs.* Belmont, CA: Wadsworth.

Walker, S., Spohn, C., & DeLone, M. (1996). *The color of justice: Race, ethnicity, and crime in America.* Belmont, CA: Wadsworth.

Walmsley, R. (2013). *World prison population list.* Available at http://www .prisonstudies.org

Walmsley, R. (2016). *World prison population list.* Available at http://www .prisonstudies.org

Walsh, A. (1986). Placebo justice: Victim recommendations and offender sentences in sexual assault cases. *Journal of Criminal Law and Criminology, 77,* 1126–1141.

Walsh, A. (2006). Evolutionary psychology and criminal behavior. In J. Barkow (Ed.), *Missing the revolution: Darwinism for social scientists* (pp. 225–268). Oxford, UK: Oxford University Press.

Walsh, A. (2011). *Feminist criminology through a biosocial lens.* Durham, NC: Carolina Academic Press.

Walsh, A. (2014). *Criminological theory: Assessing philosophical assumptions.* Waltham, MA: Anderson.

Walsh, A., & Hemmens, C. (2014). *Law, justice, and society: A sociolegal approach* (3rd ed.). New York: Oxford University Press.

Walsh, A., Johnson, H., & Bolen, J. (2012). Drugs, crime, and the epigenetics of hedonic allostasis. *Journal of Contemporary Criminal Justice, 28,* 314–328.

Walsh, A., & Stohr, M. (2010). *Correctional assessment, casework, and counseling* (5th ed.). Alexandria, VA: American Correctional Association.

Walsh, A., & Yun, I. (2013). Schizophrenia: Causes, crime, and implications for criminology and criminal justice. *International Journal of Law, Crime, and Justice, 41,* 188–202.

Wang, X., & Mears, D. (2010). A multi-level test of minority threat effects on sentencing. *Journal of Quantitative Criminology, 26,* 191–215.

Ward, D., & Kassebaum, G. (2009). *Alcatraz: The gangster years.* Berkeley: University of California Press.

Ward, T., Melser, J., & Yates, P. (2007). Reconstructing the risk–need–responsivity model: A theoretical exploration and evaluation. *Aggression and Violent Behavior, 12,* 208–228.

Wei, W. (1999). The Chinese American experience: 1857–1892. *Harper's Weekly.* Available at http://www .Harpweek.com

Welch, M. (1996). *Corrections: A critical approach.* New York: McGraw–Hill.

Welch, M. (2004). *Corrections: A critical approach* (2nd ed.). Boston: McGraw–Hill.

Welch, M. (2005). *Ironies of imprisonment.* Thousand Oaks, CA: Sage.

Welsh, W. (1995). *Counties in court: Jail overcrowding and court-ordered reform.* Philadelphia, PA: Temple University Press.

Wener, R. (2005). The invention of direct supervision. *Corrections Compendium, 30*(2), 4–37.

Wener, R. (2006). Effectiveness of the direct supervision system of correctional design and management: A review of the literature. *Criminal Justice and Behavior, 33,* 392–410.

Wennerberg, I., & Pinto, S. (2009). *Sixth European Electronic Monitoring Conference—Analysis of Questionnaires.* Available at http://www.cepprobation.org/uploaded_files/EM2009%20Questionnaire%20summary.pdf

West, H. C. (2010). *Prison inmates at midyear 2009—Statistical tables.* Washington, DC: U.S. Department of Justice, Office of Justice Programs, Bureau of Justice Statistics. Available at https://www.bjs.gov/content/pub/pdf/pim09st.pdf

West, H. C., Sabol, W. J., & Greenman, S. J. (2010). *Prisoners in 2009.* Washington, DC: U.S. Department of Justice, Office of Justice Programs, Bureau of Justice Statistics. Available at http://www.bjs.gov

Western, B. (2003). *Incarceration, employment, and public policy.* Newark: New Jersey Institute for Social Justice. Available at http://www.njisj.org

Western, B. (2006). *Punishment and inequality in America.* New York: Russell Sage.

Wheeldon, J., Chavez, R. B., & Cooke, J. (2013). *Debate and dialogue in correctional settings: Maps, models, and materials.* New York: IDEBATE Press.

White, A. (2004). *Substance use and the adolescent brain: An overview with the focus on alcohol.* Durham, NC: Duke University Medical Center.

White, M. D., Goldkamp, J. S., & Campbell, S. P. (2006). Co-occurring mental illness and substance abuse in the criminal justice system. *The Prison Journal, 86,* 301–326.

Whitehead, J., & Lab, S. (1996). *Juvenile justice: An introduction.* Cincinnati, OH: Anderson.

Whitman, J. Q. (2003). *Harsh justice: Criminal punishment and the widening divide between America and Europe.* New York: Oxford University Press.

Whittick, A. (1979). *Woman into citizen.* Santa Barbara, CA: ABC–CLIO.

Wilson, D., Bouffard, L., & Mackenzie, D. (2005). A quantitative review of structured, group-oriented, cognitive-behavior programs for offenders. *Criminal Justice and Behavior, 32,* 172–204.

Wilson, J. (1975). *Thinking about crime.* New York: Vintage.

Wilson, S., & Lipsey, M. (2000). Wilderness challenge programs for delinquent youth: A meta-analysis of outcome evaluations. *Evaluation and Program Planning, 23,* 1–12.

Winfree, L. T., & Wooldredge, J. D. (1991). Exploring suicides and deaths by natural causes in America's large jails: A panel study of institutional change, 1978 and 1983. In J. Thompson & G. L. Mays (Eds.), *American jails: Public policy issues* (pp. 63–78). Chicago: Nelson–Hall.

Winter, M. M. (2003). County jail suicides in a midwestern state: Moving beyond the use of profiles. *The Prison Journal, 83,* 130–148.

Wodahl, E. J., Boman, J. H., & Garland, B. E. (2015). Responding to probation and parole violations: Are jail sanctions more effective than community-based graduated sanctions? *Journal of Criminal Justice, 43,* 242–250.

Wolff, N., Shi, J., & Blitz, C. L. (2008). Racial and ethnic disparities in types and sources of victimization inside prison. *The Prison Journal, 88,* 451–472.

Wolfgang, M., Figlio, R., & Sellin, T. (1972). *Delinquency in a birth cohort.* Chicago: University of Chicago Press.

Woo, Y., Stohr, M. K., Hemmens, C., Lutze, F. E., Hamilton, Z., & Yoon, O. K. (2014, February). *An empirical test of the social support paradigm on prisoner reentry.* Paper presented at the annual meeting of the Academy of Criminal Justice Sciences, Philadelphia.

Wood, P. B., & May, D. C. (2003). Racial differences in perceptions of the severity of sanctions: A comparison of prison with alternatives. *Justice Quarterly, 20,* 605–632.

Wood, S., & Buttaro, A. (2013). Co-occurring severe mental illnesses and substance abuse disorders as predictors of state prison inmate assaults. *Crime & Delinquency, 59,* 510–535.

Wooldredge, J. (2010). Judges' unequal contributions to extralegal disparities in imprisonment. *Criminology, 48,* 539–567.

Wooldredge, J., & Steiner, B. (2014). A bi-level framework for understanding prisoner victimization. *Journal of Quantitative Criminology, 30,* 141–162.

Wright, E. M., Salisbury, E. J., & Van Voorhis, P. (2007). Predicting the prison misconducts of women offenders. *Journal of Contemporary Criminal Justice, 23,* 310–340.

Wright, R. (1999). The evidence in favor of prisons. In F. Scarpitti & A. Nielson (Eds.), *Crime and criminals: Contemporary and classic readings in criminology* (pp. 483–493). Los Angeles: Roxbury.

Wright, R., & Decker, S. (1994). *Burglars on the job: Streetlife and residential break-ins.* Boston: Northeastern University Press.

Wu, H., & Walsh, A. (2007). Teaching statistical interaction in ANOVA and OLS regression in the context of ideology in criminal justice processing. *Free Inquiry in Creative Sociology, 35,* 27–35.

Yates, H. M. (2002). Margaret Moore: African American feminist leader in corrections. *Women & Criminal Justice, 13,* 9–26.

Yates, J. (2012). *Popular justice: Presidential prestige and executive success in the Supreme Court.* Albany: State University of New York Press.

Yochelson, S., & Samenow, S. (1976). *The criminal personality: A profile for change.* Livingston, NJ: Jason Aronson.

Young, V. D. (1994). Race and gender in the establishment of juvenile institutions: The case of the South. *The Prison Journal, 74,* 244–265.

Young, V. D. (2001). All the women in the Maryland State Penitentiary: 1812–1869. *The Prison Journal, 81,* 113–132.

Zachariadis, P. (2013). Some European prisons are shrinking and closing—what can America learn? *Takepart.* Available at http://www.takepart.com/article/2013/11/14/some-european-prisons-are-shrinking-and-closing-what-can-america-learn

Zaitz, L. (2010, October 30). Budget crunch reaches prison. *The Oregonian,* p. 1.

Zapotosky, M. (2017). Justice Department will again use private prisons. *Washington Post.* Available at https://www.washingtonpost.com/world/national-security/justice-department-will-again-use-private-prisons/2017

Zapotosky, M., & Harlan, C. (2016, August 18). Justice Department says it will end use of private prisons. *Washington Post.* Available at https://www.washingtonpost.com/news/post-nation/wp/2016/08/18/justice-department-says-it-will-end-use-of-private-prisons/?utm_term=.268cd0d2cfdc

Zedlewski, E. (1987). *Making confinement decisions* (NCJ No. 105834). Rockville, MD: U.S. Department of Justice, National Institute of Justice.

Zimmer, L. (1986). *Women guarding men.* Chicago: University of Chicago Press.

Zimmer, L. (1989). Solving women's employment problems in corrections: Shifting the burden to administrators. *Women & Criminal Justice, 1,* 55–79.

Zupan, L. L. (1991). *Jails: Reform and the new generation philosophy.* Cincinnati, OH: Anderson.

Zupan, L. L. (1992). The progress of women correctional officers in all-male prisons. In I. L. Moyer (Ed.), *The changing roles of women in the criminal justice system: Offenders, victims, and professionals* (2nd ed., pp. 323–343). Prospect Heights, IL: Waveland.

INDEX

ABOUT THE AUTHORS

Mary K. Stohr is a Professor in the Department of Criminal Justice and Criminology at Washington State University. She received a Ph.D. (1990) in political science, with specializations in criminal justice and public administration, from Washington State University. Many moons ago, and before she earned her graduate degrees, she worked as a correctional officer and then as a counselor in an adult male prison in Washington State. She has published more than 110 academic works in the areas of correctional organizations and operation, correctional personnel, inmate needs and assessment, program evaluation, gender, and victimization, among others. Her seven books, with others, include *The American Prison* (with Cullen and Jonson); *Corrections: From Research to Policy to Practice* (with Walsh); *Correctional Assessment, Casework, and Counseling* (with Walsh); *Corrections: A Text Reader* (with Walsh and Hemmens); *Criminal Justice Management: Theory and Practice in Justice-Centered Organizations* (with Collins); and *The Prison Experience* (with Hemmens). She received the Founders Award from the Academy of Criminal Justice Sciences (ACJS) in 2009 and is a Co-founder of both the Corrections Section and the Minorities and Women Section of the ACJS.

Anthony Walsh, Professor of Criminology at Boise State University, received his Ph.D. from Bowling Green State University at the ripe old age of 43. He has field experience in law enforcement and corrections. He is the author of more than 150 journal articles or book chapters and 38 books, including *Biology and Criminology* (Routledge, 2009); *Feminist Criminology Through a Biosocial Lens* (Carolina Academic Press, 2011); *Law, Justice, and Society* (with Craig Hemmens, Oxford University Press, 2011); *Correctional Assessment, Casework, and Counseling* (with Mary K. Stohr, American Correctional Association, 2011); *The Neurobiology of Criminal Behavior: Gene–Brain–Culture Interaction* (with Jon Bolen, Ashgate, 2012); *Corrections: The Essentials* (with Mary K. Stohr, SAGE, 2012); *The Science Wars: The Politics of Gender and Race* (Transaction, 2013); *Criminological Theory: Assessing Philosophical Assumptions* (Anderson/Elsevier, 2014); *Biosociology: Bridging the Biology–Sociology Divide* (Transaction, 2014); *Criminology: The Essentials* (SAGE, 2017); and *Taboo Issues in Social Science* (Vernon, 2017). His interests include biosocial criminology, statistics, and criminal justice assessment and counseling.